THE WILEY SERIES IN
MANAGEMENT AND ADMINISTRATION

ELWOOD S. BUFFA, *Advisory Editor*
University of California, Los Angeles

PRODUCTION SYSTEMS:
Planning, Analysis, and Control

PRODUCTION SYSTEMS:
Planning, Analysis, and Control

James L. Riggs
Professor and Department Head
Department of Industrial Engineering
Oregon State University

John Wiley and Sons, Inc.
New York   London   Sydney   Toronto

Copyright © 1970 by John Wiley & Sons, Inc.

All rights reserved. No part of this book may be reproduced by any means, nor transmitted, nor translated into a machine language without the written permission of the publisher.

Library of Congress Catalog Card Number: 76–101972
SBN 471 72182 4

Printed in the United States of America.

10   9   8   7   6   5   4

PREFACE

Prefaces have been cynically compared to *apologies*—attempts to justify renewal of an old theme; to *advertisements*—plugs for acceptance inserted among acknowledgments; and to *self-insurance*—careful definitions of topic boundaries designed to avoid damaging critiques. Perhaps all of these objectives are worthwhile and lurk in the shadow of any preface construction, but the avowed aim of this preface is simply a personal chat with a perspective reader.

The subject is production—an important, dynamic, and practical topic. Under a broad but realistic interpretation, it encompasses numerous professions. Managers, salesmen, programmers, engineers, economists, supervisors, consumers, and a host of others are the beneficiaries and benefactors of production. The heterogeneous topics housed under the collective "production" title provide a unifying discipline for any endeavor that converts inputs to outputs, whatever they be—dams, dollars, data, diagrams, or dictates.

Production is also a demanding subject. Even a layman can recognize the bewildering array of interacting forces that influence all significant production decisions. Many techniques have been developed to assist production decision makers. Some tools have little more rigor than rules-of-thumb. Others rely on impressive mathematics. Although it would be impractical to hope to achieve proficiency in the use of all applicable techniques, a working familiarity is an authentic and worthwhile goal. If battles for better production management are won by knowing what weapons are available, then this book is an arsenal.

Included subjects and techniques provide a substantial introduction to production concepts. The diverse topics are integrated into a conceptual framework which, hopefully, renders the material easier to comprehend and the interrelationships more visible. A balance is sought between an exclusively descriptive coverage and a strictly analytical approach. While such a balance may dismay purists at either extreme, it allows quantitative methods to be presented in the more qualitative language appreciated by most practitioners—and most aspiring practitioners.

Depth of presentation is essentially limited to an elementary level. Mathematical rigor is sacrificed for conceptual clarity; reasons for technical procedures are substituted for punctilious proofs. A university sophomore level of mathematical maturity is sufficient for most of the material. However, if math preparation is a bit shaky from disuse or underexposure, some sections in the text can be skipped. (These optional sections are marked by stars in the margin at the beginning and end.) In particular, the statistical techniques in Chapters 3, 14, and 15 can be delayed to another session. However, those with sufficient prerequisites should find the statistical applications a comfortable review and a chance to practice what is preached.

The motivating force behind adding another book to the supply of production literature is to offer a livelier, student-oriented text. Whether the bravado of the motive is matched by skill with words and ideas is left to your judgment. Specific manifestations of the effort to build a better book include:

Margin notes—anecdotes, amplifications, and annotations pertaining to the main flow of the text. Speed-readers will not miss vital facts as they flash through a page, presuming they can understand and absorb the data at their quickened pace, because the margin notes are explanatory extensions and commentaries on the basic material.

Summaries—brief reviews of the highlights of each chapter. After struggling through new material, it is handy to have a digested version as a security check. Alien vocabulary and unfamiliar concepts are clues for further study or slower speed-reading.

Examples—practical illustrations that supplement and complement text descriptions. These minicases show the details of technique applications and cast the procedures in an industrial perspective.

Questions and problems—stimulating questions that emphasize thoughtful rather than rote answers, and challenging problems that develop confidence in applying analytical methods.

In addition to the more obvious evidence of intent, extensive references and appendices are included. And, hopefully, the informal prose style will appeal to practitioners without insulting academicians.

The text is organized into three sections as suggested by the book title: planning, analysis, and control. A prologue sets the atmosphere for ensuing topics. The *Planning Section* starts with a discussion of management concepts to give perspective to the subsequent presentation of quantitative methods for forecasting, allocating, scheduling, and financially evaluating strategic alternatives. The *Analysis Section* emphasizes the qualitative aspects of tactical alternatives and the interlocking factors affecting men, machines, materials, money, and management; system objectives are stressed over component optimization. The *Control Section* reinforces system thinking by consideration of quantity, quality, and process control. An epilogue salutes the determined reader who has trekked through the previous chapters, and it cautions him that the plot thickens when textbook principles are exposed to complications from the real world.

Organization by usage and evaluation phases rather than by technical or departmental subjects scatters the application of management tools. For instance, critical path scheduling is introduced by applying networks to project planning. Later, networks and associated time charts are utilized for line-balancing and machine-scheduling analyses. In the last section, networks are again employed as control measures through the line of balance. This fragmented presentation allows the techniques to be directed at problem areas instead of clustering problem illustrations around individual tools. An adjunct benefit is that a reader already familiar with certain fundamental concepts can skip to the application refinements.

Every book is a conglomerate synthesis of the author's attitudes, associations, and experiences. A list of all the individuals to whom I owe gratitude would exhaust your patience and intimidate my memory. A less personal but still sincere maneuver is to extend thanks to the students who endured, to the fellow profs and associates who contributed, to an environment that inspired, to the industries and authors that permitted, to the reviewers that critiqued, and to my family that waited. To these donors I dedicate whatever is worthwhile in the book; the shortcomings and vagaries are my responsibility—including the apologies, advertisements, and self-insurance policies found in this preface.

JAMES L. RIGGS

Corvallis, Oregon
March, 1970

CONTENTS

ix

CONTENTS

section two ANALYSIS 183

CONTENTS

CONTENTS

xiii

CONTENTS

PRODUCTION SYSTEMS:
Planning, Analysis, and Control

CHAPTER 1

PROLOGUE

1-1 IMPORTANCE OF PRODUCTION

The subject is production. It is a broad, fascinating, and timely subject. A narrow interpretation might limit it to the mass generation of commercial products in sprawling factories. Although this aspect is certainly important and dramatic, it represents only one piece of the complete picture. Products vary from the hardware of merchandise and machines to the nebulous properties of entertainment and information. They are produced by individuals, teams, tribes, and corporations in lofts, sheds, laboratories, and factories. Despite apparent differences in raw materials, generating processes, and ultimate output, there exist many similarities. These mutual considerations form the basis for production studies by which the resources of nature are conserved and made more useful.

1-2 SHORT HISTORY OF PRODUCTION STUDIES

No one can say when man first studied production. If we rely on written proof, the date must be set well along in recorded history, but surely some early "managers" pondered better ways to produce crude wheels, utensils, and building blocks. Maybe the Egyptians even had their own version of PERT—Pyramid ERection Technique.

For modern PERT, see Section 6-5.

Awaiting documentary evidence, we must pass by the construction marvels of the Roman Empire, the artistic masterpieces of the Dark Ages, and the craftsmanship of the Middle Age guilds. During the last period, production was characterized by individual activities and muscle power instead of mechanical power.

In the 1700's, conditions changed rapidly with the introduction of steam power to replace muscle power, machine tools to reduce hand craftsmanship, and a factory system emphasizing interchangeability of manufactured parts. These conditions heralded the industrial revolution and initiated many modern management headaches. Hereditary writings about how to cure the headaches also began to appear.

"[About managers] . . . By pursuing his own interests he frequently promotes that of society more effectually than when he really intends to promote it." Adam Smith, economist, 1776.

1

At the beginning of the nineteenth century, typical factory conditions were grim by today's standards. Children 5 to 12 years old put in 12- to 13-hour days six times a week. The workplace was dismal and unsafe. Management attitudes were to equate the sensibilities of men to that of machines and to implement cost-reduction policies by brute force. Although • there were exceptions, published production guides were output oriented with attention primarily on gross physical improvements, usually to the detriment of worker dignity. Despite the lack of social concern, production concepts inaugurated in the period included departmentalized plant layouts, division of labor for training and work study, more orderly material flow, improved • cost-recording procedures, and incentive wage plans.

Events at the start of the twentieth century shored up the foundations of production studies to make the subject more compatible with the mechanistic attitudes of the physical sciences. Significant experiments by Frederick W. Taylor characterized the new "scientific" approach. He conducted and analyzed thousands of tests to identify the relevant variables of production. From these empirical observations, he designed work methods where man and machine were one—an operating unit of a man inspired by an incentive wage to service a machine efficiently according to exact instructions. He segregated the planning of activities from their implementation and placed it in the province of professional management.

Taylor's work was in tune with the vaunted reputation of contemporary scientific investigations and therefore he lodged • his concepts under the title of "scientific management." His theories received both acclaim and abuse. Critics forecasted that his mechanistic views enforced by efficiency experts would completely dehumanize industry, but others saw them as logic applied to a promising new area. Whether people agreed with him or not, his beliefs and the fervor with which he expounded them strongly stimulated industrial management.

An associate of Taylor extended his analytical methods to series of operations. Henry L. Gantt developed methods of sequencing production activities which are still in use today. His less restrictive treatment of man-machine operations added organizational and motivational overtones to Taylor's pioneering work.

Operations-oriented thinking took new substance from the literal as well as figurative marriage of engineering and psychology in the husband-wife team of Frank and Lillian Gilbreth; the

One widely admired essay was "On the Economy of Machinery and Manufactures" by Charles Babbage, mathematician and frustrated computer designer, 1832.

" 'A fair day's wages for a fair day's work': it is as just a demand as governed men ever made of governing. It is the everlasting right of man." Thomas Carlyle (1795–1881) from *Past and Present, Book I.*

The Scientific Management movement was rebuffed by a U.S. Congressional investigation in 1911 which prohibited the use of stopwatches in government services.

2

The Gilbreths included worker fatigue monotony, emotional reactions, and other human factors within the scope of motion studies.

mechanistic attitudes of engineer Frank were mitigated by the
• humanistic attitudes of psychologist Lillian. Together they showed that basic human motion patterns are common to many different work situations. Their analysis of micromotions to improve manual operations initiated time and motion studies and the use of motion pictures in work design.

The Hawthorne studies, sponsored by Harvard University, began in 1924 at the Hawthorne Works of the Western Electric Co. In one amazing case, productivity always improved regardless of changes in illumination levels. This finding led to the belief that the improvement was due entirely to a positive worker response to the attention they received in the studies.

In the 1920's and 1930's, things became more complicated as it was realized that people did not always behave as intuitively expected and that the complexities of emerging production processes required more controls. As demonstrated by the
• famous Hawthorne studies, the carrot of better wages or working conditions did not always lead to proportional increases in output; psychological factors such as morale and attention were also influential. Walter Shewhart's work provided statistical control measures to assure the precision of interchangeable parts required for the mass production techniques initiated by Henry Ford. Perhaps even more important, when applying Shewhart's statistical controls it became apparent that all the interacting factors of product design, plant layout, worker capacity, environmental conditions, materials, and customers' attitudes had to be considered. Such considerations naturally led to the study of entire production systems rather than isolated parts.

An interdisciplinary approach to system studies appeared in the war years of the 1940's, first in the form of British operational research teams. Members of the teams were not necessarily experts in the areas studied, because they applied accepted scientific methodologies to problems never before subjected to such analyses. That the results were favorable should not be surprising because analogs are found throughout nature and the works of man; knowledge borrowed from the physical sciences and applied to management problems of similar structure offers a reservoir of decision-making techniques which is still being tapped today. From its military origin, the operations research (or closely related "management science") approach has become a fountainhead of industrial applications.

"Sometimes, experts suggest, computers are bought by companies for reasons of prestige—as status symbols. Twinkling lights, spinning tape wheels, chrome cabinets are said to have a mesmerizing effect on some managers."
U.S. News & World Rept., Feb. 24, 1964.

The 1940's also saw the birth of the electronic computer. Today its influence is apparent throughout industry. Many white-collar workers fear that it portends a second industrial revolution, this time aimed at them. Middle management observes more decisions dependent on electronic assistance and,
• perhaps more poignantly, computerized controls and automatic decisions. At the top and bottom of the organizational pyramid,

the impact has been gentle, often just the pride of having a computer.

Some emotional fog about the computer issue is removed by concentrating on what has been done and what has to be done. Many mathematical techniques which we take for granted would not be feasible without the tremendous calculating speed of computers. Of course, the problems must be "programmable"—structurally adaptable to machine calculations. Therein lies the contribution of man to the modern man-machine partnership. Man must collect the necessary data (assisted by recordkeeping machines), recognize the type of problem and its potential solution format, develop or select an appropriate program, and interpret or modify the machine's output. Equivalently, the capabilities of computers must be utilized if we expect to relate and evaluate the many variables in complex production systems. Both man the decision maker and his helping machines must continue to develop just to keep pace with the problems and challenges they have already created.

"Man is one of the best general-purpose computers available and if one designs for man as a moron, one ends up with a system that requires a genius to maintain it. Thus we are not suggesting that we take man out of the system, but we are suggesting that he be properly employed in terms of both his abilities and limitations. Some designers have required that he be a hero as well as a genius," E. L. Thomas, *Design and Planning*, Hastings House, New York, 1967.

1-3 PRODUCTION AND PRODUCTION SYSTEMS

In our kaleidoscopic journey through history, we touched many facets of production without defining the subject. And if there is one obvious lesson to be learned from history it is the difficulty of and need for lucid communications. Maybe a rose by any other name does smell the same as Shakespeare pledged, but the smell would be a lot easier to describe if everyone called the same plant a rose.

For our studies we shall say that *production is the intentional act of producing something useful.* This definition is at once liberal and restrictive. It in no way limits the method by which something is produced, but it does eliminate the accidental generation of products. The questionable property of usefulness is subject to individual opinions. Some might say anything salable is useful; others would rebut that illicit drugs are certainly marketable but of uncertain worth. Even if it is agreed that useful implies a beneficial purpose, there is still room for debate on commodities such as armaments. Sidestepping the issue of conscience, we should recognize that a wide range of production processes have similar characteristics regardless of the utility of the products.

The definition of production is modified to include the system concept by stating that *a production system is the design process by which elements are transformed into useful products.* A process

4

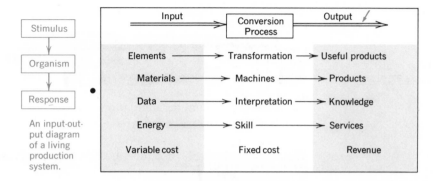

Stimulus

↓

Organism

↓

Response

An input-output diagram of a living production system.

Figure 1.1 Block diagram and examples of a production system

is an organized procedure for accomplishing the conversion of inputs into outputs, as shown in Figure 1.1.

A unit of output normally requires several types of inputs. In an industrial process the inputs account for most of the variable cost of production. Conversion facilities are associated with fixed cost, and the output produces the revenue. Elementary accounting declares that profit depends on the relationship of variable and fixed costs to revenue—the interaction of input and conversion costs to output revenue.

Another representation of production costs is given in Chapter 4.

Any system is a collection of interacting components. Each component could be a system unto itself in a descending order of simplicity. Systems are distinguished by their objectives; the objective of one system could be to produce a component which is to be assembled with other components to achieve the objective of a larger system. More sophisticated techniques are required to deal with more complex systems. It is a nip and tuck race between the development of ever more intricate systems and the development of capable management tools to control them. Perhaps man's future will be determined by the winner.

1-4 MODELS OF PRODUCTION SYSTEMS

Even the initiated find it difficult to distinguish the disciplinary boundaries staked out by management scientists, operation researchers, industrial engineers, system analysts, and others.

Early efforts in production studies now appear crude. They were crude, but so were the systems being studied. As the systems became more intricate, investigators naturally followed the proven path revealed by elaborate studies in the physical sciences —observe, hypothesize, experiment, and verify. This general approach has prospered from Taylor's introduction of "scientific management" to the presently popular "management science." It is best characterized by the construction, manipulation, and interpretation of models.

5

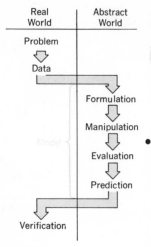

Real World	Abstract World
Problem	
⇩	
Data	
	Formulation
	⇩
	Manipulation
Model	⇩
	Evaluation
	⇩
	Prediction
Verification	

A three-dimensional plant layout could show the floor space assignments without recognizing possible vertical restrictions.

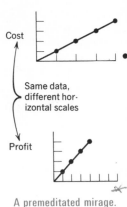

Cost

Same data, different horizontal scales

Profit

A premeditated mirage.

Types of Models

A model is a replica or abstraction of the essential characteristics of a process. It shows the relationships between cause and effect, between objectives and constraints. Problems that defy direct solutions because of size, complexity, or structure are often assessable through model simulations. The nature of the problem signals which of the following types of models is most appropriate.

Physical model. Look-alike models derive their usefulness from a change in scale. Microscopic patterns can be magnified for investigation, and huge structures can be scaled down to a manageable size. (A model of the solar system might even be confused with a model of an atom if it lacked a label.) Flow problems in a model plant are studied by easy shifts of scaled-down structures and machines which could not be duplicated with real items because of cost, confusion, or inconvenience. Some details are necessarily lost in models. In a physical replica, this loss may be an advantage where one factor, such as distance, is the key consideration, but it may render a study futile if the predominant influence is forfeited in the construction of the model.

Schematic model. Two-dimensional models are the delight of chartists. Graphs of price fluctuations, symbolic charts of activities, maps of routings, and networks of timed events all represent the real world in a digested and diagrammatic format. The pictorial aspects are useful for demonstration purposes. Some frequently encountered examples include organizational charts, flow process charts, and bar charts. Symbols on such charts can be easily rearranged to investigate the effect of re-organization. Similar experimentation with the actual workplace would be crippling.

Mathematical model. Quantitative expressions, the most abstract models, are generally the most useful. Formulas and equations have long been the servants of the physical sciences. In recent years they have been similarly recognized by the management sciences. When a mathematical model can be constructed to represent a problem situation accurately, it provides a powerful study tool; it is easy to manipulate, the effect of interacting variables is apparent, and it is precise. Whatever faults arise from the use of mathematical models usually can be traced to the underlying assumptions and premises upon which they are based.

6

In contrast to the other types of models, what to use is harder to decide than how to use it.

EXAMPLE 1.1   Construction and Evaluation of a Pricing Model

Returns from a new product have failed to meet expectations. A study is initiated with the overall objective of increasing profit. The production system that ultimately determines whether the objective is met encompasses all aspects of the product—procurement of materials, manufacturing, marketing, etc. A preliminary investigation narrows the area where action can be taken to the pricing policy. A model of the relationship between the number sold (N) and the price per unit (P) is expected to follow the equation

$$P = x - yN$$

where x and y are constants determined from market conditions.

If we assume that the general relationships in the equation are correct, we can gain some insights even without cost figures. First we observe that as the price decreases, the number of units sold increases ($N = (x - P)/y$). Letting $N = 0$, we have the limiting price (x) at which the units would sell if a shortage existed. Setting $P = 0$, we get the ratio x/y that identifies the total market potential or, more precisely, the amount that could be given away if the product was free.

Since our objective is to maximize profit, we must include the costs of producing the product. Under the belief that total cost (TC) is a function of fixed cost (F) and variable unit cost (v), we accept the formula

$$TC = F + vN$$

By reasoning similar to that applied to the price (and confirmed by common sense), we know that the total cost equals the fixed cost when no units (N) are produced (hence the name fixed cost). Now combining all the factors with respect to the output, we have

$$\text{profit} = \text{revenue} - \text{total cost}$$

$$Z = NP - TC \qquad \text{(where } Z \text{ symbolizes profit)}$$

$$Z = N(x - yN) - (F + vN) \qquad \begin{array}{l}\text{(by substitution from} \\ \text{previous equations)}\end{array}$$

$$Z = xN - yN^2 - F - vN \qquad \text{(by combining terms)}$$

Various values of x and y could be substituted in the above equation to provide a table of Z values from which the best pricing policy would be apparent. A more direct approach, using differentiation, provides an expression for the maximum value of Z. Using calculus, we get

$$\frac{dZ}{dN} = 0 = x - 2yN - v \qquad \begin{array}{l}\text{(where the differential is set equal to zero} \\ \text{to identify a maximum or minimum point)}\end{array}$$

from which

$$N = \frac{x - v}{2y}$$

Substituting the equation for the output that maximizes profit into the basic price formula, we get

$$P = x - y(N) = x - y\left(\frac{x - v}{2y}\right) = \frac{x + v}{2}$$

which is the price that provides maximum profit. Therefore, if the assumed relationships are indeed representative of the real world, the price of the product would be half the sum of the limiting amount (x) a customer would pay for the product and the variable cost (v) of producing it. The model reveals the importance of securing an accurate estimate of x and that less attention need be given to y and F. Although pricing appears to be independent of the influence of fixed cost, the actual amount of profit for a given pricing policy fluctuates with changes in F. It should also be recognized that the optimal pricing equation offers several courses of action for abiding by the preferred relationships. For instance, improved packaging would increase v and might produce disproportional increase in x. Thus a model is a tool to aid, not dictate, management thinking.

Use of Models

Example 1.1 illustrates that an evaluation of the nature of a problem does not depend on the availability of actual cost data. In fact, the arithmetic of handling data may obscure the significance of underlying assumptions. Symbols are impersonal and promote the consideration of different views rather than focusing on one "answer."

The question of the amount of detail to include in a model is implied in the example. The answer lies in a balance between accuracy and simplicity. To increase accuracy it is usually necessary to add variables and increase the complexity of relationships. Enhancing reality adds cost. An investigation can cost more than its worth. Models that are easier to solve are also usually easier to understand and apply. However, if the model is simplified to the point where it no longer represents the real world, it will indicate erroneous or misleading outcomes.

To "*satisfise*" is to strive for one level of achievement while being willing to settle for another slightly less ambitious level. Model formulation is often subject to satisfising—a sacrifice of reality for the sake of workability. The approximations may take one or more of the following forms:

1. Linear relationships are substituted in a model for actual nonlinear relationships in the system. For instance, a curve can be approximated by a number of straight-line segments that conform to the general curving pattern.
2. Variables that do not have a significant effect on the system's performance are omitted. Inventory policies are often based on the control of items that comprise the bulk of demand under the assumption that the remaining items do not warrant the cost of attention. Such compromises between the cost of evaluation and the cost of inattention should be rigorously justified.

3. Several variables are lumped together and subsequently treated as a single variable. If the variables have essentially the same characteristics, the aggregate variable will provide a good approximation. Again using inventory policy as an illustration, items that have similar demand, storage, use, and handling properties are treated identically as one variable with little loss of reality and considerably less effort.

Many schematic and mathematical models are presented in the ensuing chapters. Most of them have "satisfising" aspects. There may be a temptation in practice, often due to laziness or diffidence, to pick out a readymade model and plug custom-made data into it. The outcome could be outrageous. It also could be wholly satisfactory. The difference lies in whether the inherent assumptions of the model agree with the properties of the system to which it is applied.

Preliminary or "ballpark" estimates are legitimate candidates for "canned" models and programs.

1-5 PLANNING, ANALYSIS, AND CONTROL OF PRODUCTION SYSTEMS

C. E. Knoeppel, *Installing Efficiency Methods*, Engineering Management Co., New York, 1915.

After recognizing what is a production system and what tools are available to treat it, we face the task of execution. In 1915, C. E. Knoeppel wrote:

Given a plant and equipment with an organization to handle the work, the manufacture of all that is designed by the engineering department and sold by the sales department can be handled to best advantage only when the details, instead of being considered independently by each department, are controlled by one function which can consider each detail in connection with all the others and act as a "clearing house" for all information in any way affecting the manufacturing.

A liberal interpretation of Knoeppel's theorem could take the schematic form shown in Figure 1.2.

Problem Areas

The basic types of problems encountered in production have not changed radically since Knoeppel's era. The problem areas still tend to be confined within an organization's departmental boundaries rather than open to a "clearing house." Some of the areas well suited to a systematic evaluation are:

1. Location of plants.
2. Layout of plants and work areas.
3. Scheduling and allocation of resources.
4. Equipment selection, maintenance, and replacement.

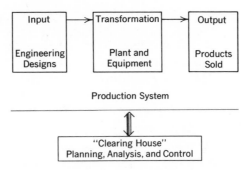

Figure 1.2 Coordination of system activities

5. Inventory policies.
6. Process design and control.
7. Work methods.
8. Quality and quantity control.

The list is by no means exhaustive. Each item could be broken down into several subheadings. What is important is the homogeneity of each problem area; common economic aspects encourage the application of mathematical models. By treating each problem area as an input-transformation-output system and subjecting it to planning, analysis, and control measures, the "clearing house" goal of coordinated production management becomes a feasible reality.

Production Decisions

The end product of planning, analysis, and control efforts is a decision. The techniques associated with each phase of an evaluation are useful only if they contribute to that end. Mathematical tools provide a degree of confidence that is lacking with intuitive judgments, but hunch aspects will always be a part of decision making. Intuition informally embraces past experiences and current events to provide a "feeling" towards a particular action. Any gambler knows that hunch players sometimes win, yet even the player cannot say why or how. Perhaps hunch explanations are just beyond the ken of our current knowledge; in the meantime it is comforting to explain the why's and how's in quantitative terms whenever possible. Therefore, while recognizing the value and need of intuitive judgment, we shall emphasize the quantitative analytical methods leading to decisions.

Planning, analysis, and control are more descriptive of the mental set of a decision maker than a rigid problem-solving procedure. Each phase is distinguished by an objective—to anticipate, to investigate, to regulate, to design. The definition of the objective points to the most suitable quantitative technique and acts as a guide to information collection. An evaluation of an existing system might have the objective of reducing costs and would likely begin with an analysis of current operating conditions and procedures. The results of the analysis phase could lead to planned improvements where the collected data would fuel planning and control efforts. Later the entire system could be subjected again to all three phases, starting with planning based on a new technological development. Objectives to update and to improve a system continually direct recurring studies in the pattern shown in Figure 1.3.

Study of Production Systems

The organization of this book follows the planning–analysis–control sequence. The content focuses primarily on mathematical models as the source and basis of production decisions, although both time-honored and recently developed schematic models receive attention.

A familiarity with the many types of models available to the modern decision maker necessarily includes contact with a wide range of mathematical techniques—statistics, probability, algebra, calculus, linear programming, arithmetic, etc. Ideally, every system analyst would have degrees in mathematics, engineering, business, and economics; be a computer expert; have 10 years of experience; and be under 30 years of age. Since very few such specimens are around, a satisfising solution is to trade depth for breadth of knowledge in the belief that familiarity with a wide but selective range of topics will allow the investigator
● to know when a more penetrating study is required and where to seek the means of conducting it. This strategy is expedited by associating evaluation methods with problem areas and with the phase of study where the methods are most likely to be productive.

The hazard of broad but shallow coverage is the creation of a self-appointed expert who knows just enough to be dangerous.

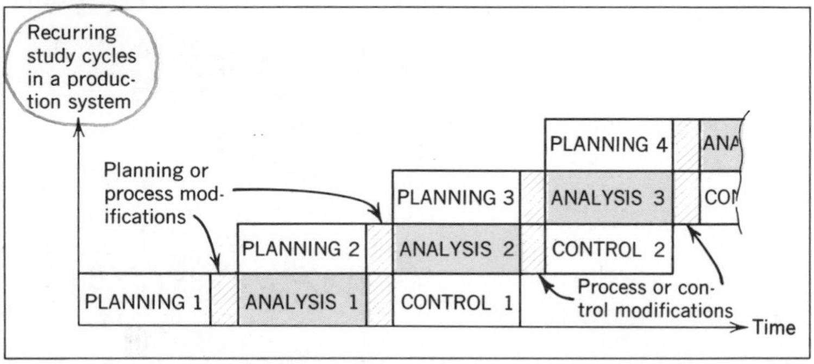

Figure 1.3 Cycles of production planning, analysis, and control

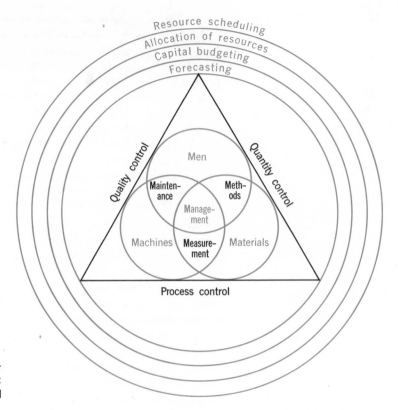

forget to add space

Figure 1.4 Text emblem symbolizing production systems: planning, analysis, and control

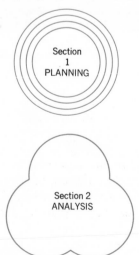

The text emblem in Figure 1.4 symbolizes the conceptual and structural framework of this book. The emblem shows the skeleton of the text—the basic organization of parts. From an inspection of the skeleton, we can anticipate what to expect from the fleshed-out whole.

The outside rings taken together represent the planning section. Each ring is a chapter treating one portion of the planning problem. The sequence of chapters follows a logical pattern of: (1) forecasting future outcomes, (2) budgeting capital to identify the most economic course of action, (3) allocating resources to the preferred action plan, and (4) committing the steps in the plan to a schedule.

The analysis section concentrates on the three basic resources represented by the inner nest of three circles—men, machines, and materials. The overlapping portions of the circles imply the coordination required to integrate effectively the application of resources. At the center, where all the circles overlap, is the core function of management.

12

Sec-
tion 3
CONTROL

The triangle enclosing the "M circles" represents the control section. Each side of the triangle denotes one area of control—quantity, quality, and process.

There is no sacrosanct sequence for the sections. As intimated in Figure 1.3, the planning-analysis-control cycle can be entered at any of the three stages; the point of entry is determined by the objective of the study. Consequently, the analysis section could be encountered before the planning section. It is more important to relate the quantitative tools and the qualitative concepts *within* the sections than to be concerned about the relationships *among* sections.

A valid reason for studying chapters in the given order is to follow the purposeful development of concepts from their introduction in the early chapters to elaboration in later pages. The validity of this approach is intuitive when you recall how difficult it was to comprehend algebra when you could barely add and subtract, or how meaningless and inane an exhibition game seems unless you know the rules and have experienced the difficulties of play. In the study of production as in learning algebra and in appreciating a game, it is unrealistic to attempt comprehension of the whole before becoming familiar with the parts. Therefore, coordination and integration are stressed in the later stages of the text, *after* the integral parts have been isolated and analyzed. An equivalent approach is applicable to real-world system studies; understanding the components precedes a system study of their integrated effects.

Precautions

While extolling the virtues of the analytical approach to system evaluations, some precautions should also be mentioned. There is obviously no single all-purpose cureall for production problems. Analytical methods are powerful tools when applied properly, and part of a proper application is a recognition of limitations. Models are only as good as the information and care put into them. Clever manipulations cannot compensate for poor data or incorrect assumptions.

Even if the data, model, and computations are commendably correct, an erroneous decision still could be forthcoming. The fault might lie in the objective of the study. A valid solution to the wrong objective leaves the original problem intact. For instance, idle time in a production line could be treated as a queuing problem with an objective to reduce the waiting time of machines; no matter how well the queuing analysis is conducted, it is largely wasted effort if the problem is actually due to product mix or sequencing troubles. Changes made to alleviate waiting lines would do little to correct the primary problem.

After obtaining a factual objective and conducting an exemplary evaluation, there is still the problem of implementation. A model offers clues to execution, but obtainment of the full effect from indicated actions depends on judgment backed by a careful appraisal of the influencing conditions in the real-world production setting. A sales forecast could be remarkably accurate and still fail to serve its intended purpose unless the information is satisfactorily converted into facility arrangements, material requisitions, manhour committments, machine schedules, and other production requirements.

Conclusion

If planning, analysis, and control of production systems appear demanding, you have the proper impression. But they can also be exciting and rewarding. Decision making always has some traumatic aspects; they are what make the action interesting. It is the confidence created by having the right evaluation tools and knowing how to use them that transforms a potentially wracking occasion into a comfortable and satisfying experience. Hopefully the material you are about to encounter will inspire this confidence. It is your decision. As Francis Bacon observed: "Some books are to be tasted, others to be swallowed, and some few to be chewed and digested."

1-6 SUMMARY

A production system is the design process by which elements are transformed into useful products. It is characterized by the input-conversion-output sequence which is applicable to a wide range of human activities.

Man's early efforts in production were exceedingly crude. As his capabilities increased after harnessing mechanical power, the new relationships of men and machines highlighted the need for improved management techniques. Pioneering efforts to meet the need borrowed their approach from methods developed in the physical sciences. Further studies included human factors and more extensive mathematical applications based on the use of computers. As production systems became more complex, modeling techniques were developed to treat the intricate relationships.

Models may take the form of physical images, schematic charts or templates, and mathematical representations of related variables. Mathematical models are the most abstract and

generally the most useful. Model formulation is often subject to "satisfising"—a sacrifice of reality for the sake of workability. Such approximations are feasible only if the essential characteristics of the system are retained in the model.

Planning, analysis, and control are phases of a system study. The study may start with any phase. Over a period of time the phases tend to be cyclically repeated. The purpose of planning, analysis, and control efforts is to provide the basis for a decision. Faulty decisions may result from applying analytical methods to the wrong objective, using unreliable data, or unsatisfactorily interpreting and implementing an indicated course of action.

Decision making can be fun if you are properly prepared.

1-7 REFERENCES

Ackoff, R. L. and M. W. Sasieni, *Fundamentals of Operations Research*, John Wiley, New York, 1968.

Beer, S., *Decision and Control*, John Wiley, New York, 1966.

Bross, I. D., *Design for Decision*, Macmillan, New York, 1957.

Chernoff, H. and L. E. Moses, *Elementary Decision Theory*, John Wiley, New York, 1959.

Hall, A. D., *A Methodology for Systems Engineering*, Van Nostrand, Princeton, N.J., 1962.

Kemeny, J. G., *A Philosopher Looks at Science*, Van Nostrand, Princeton, N.J., 1959.

Morris, W. T., *Management Science in Action*, Richard D. Irwin, Homewood, Ill., 1963.

Roll, E., *A History of Economic Thought*, Prentice-Hall, Englewood Cliffs, N.J., 1956.

Smith, A., *The Wealth of Nations*, Henry Regnery, Chicago, Ill., 1953.

Starr, K. L., *Production Management: System and Synthesis*, Prentice-Hall, Englewood Cliffs, N.J., 1964.

1-8 QUESTIONS AND PROBLEMS

1. Compare the first industrial revolution with a potential second revolution based on computer developments.

2. Look up and discuss some military applications of operations research. Do any of the military studies have counterpart industrial applications?

3. Determine several input-transformation-output production systems and describe the process by which entering elements are made more useful. Use service as an output in at least one system.

4. A widely accepted definition of engineering is: "engineering is the art of organizing men and of directing the forces and materials of nature for the benefit of the human race." Paraphrase the definition to emphasize the affinity of the engineering function to a production system.

5. Another way of classifying types of models is to categorize them as iconic, analogue, or symbolic. Give an example of a model that would fit each classification. (*Hint*: Iconic is derived from the Greek word for image.)

6. What is meant by the statement that mathematical models may not be more accurate than other types of models but are usually more precise?

7. What is meant by the statement that models can be used heuristically? Give an example.

8. Discuss "satisfising" in relation to studying several subjects in preparation for final examinations.

9. Discuss the accompanying diagram of the procedures for decision making in reference to production systems. What types of problems are likely to be encountered in each step? Could the same procedures be used for decisions in physical science studies? Where does intuition fit into the steps?

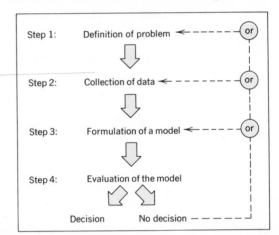

10. Consider familiar production systems such as a barber shop or gasoline station and discuss what types of models could be used for planning, analyzing, and controlling their operations. What objectives could be appropriate for each study phase?

section one   PLANNING

According to legend, before Alexander The Great began his spectacular campaign of conquest he felt the need for some assurance that his efforts would be worthwhile. The greatest seer at the time was the Oracle of Delphi. Alexander journeyed to the temple of Delphi for an audience. When he was told he would have to wait his turn for a prophesy, he broke through the guarding priests and abducted the Oracle. Because of these activities, the Oracle shrewdly proclaimed: "Alexander, thou are invincible." Taking the statement as his forecast, Alexander then assembled his armies, plotted his strategy, and launched his campaigns.

Not all forecasters will match the accuracy of the Oracle of Delphi's prediction for Alexander The Great. Equivalently, few leaders possess the managerial capabilities to live up to such a prediction. Studying the concepts of management cannot guarantee executive competence but, like the Oracle's pronouncement, it helps. Alexander studied under Aristotle. He probably was exposed to Aristotle's systematic logic and shared an interest in pioneering the science of psychology. Such studies are not far different from modern management concepts and functions (*Chapter 2*).

Even before Alexander's episode with the Oracle of Delphi, forecasting was recognized as an important accessory to planning. It is still the starting point from which strategies are formulated and campaigns are launched. Leaders demand and value predictions but often fail to understand their meanings or limitations. A system planner should know what forecasting tools are available and what assumptions influence their application (*Chapter* 3).

If forecasting can be likened to a window into the future, then resources are the keys that open the door to an anticipated course of action. Alternatives are evaluated on a comparable basis through use of the modern philosopher's stone: money; the value of different

PLANNING

17

resources are transmuted to dollar values for comparison purposes. Receipts and disbursements associated with each course of action are translated to time-equivalent amounts by interest formulas. Capital budgeting includes monetary comparison models, based on an assumption of certainty or of risk, to reveal the financial aspect for resource utilization (*Chapter 4*).

Given a course of action supported by forecasted conditions and approved by acceptable economic yardsticks, the alternative allocations for resources still must be considered. Most projects are subject to considerable resource convertibility. The application of linear programming (LP) techniques is one method of utilizing this flexibility to get the right amount of resources allocated to the right place (*Chapter 5*).

According to an old adage, "there is a time and a place for everything." If it can be assumed that the *place* is designated by the LP routines, the next step is to set the *time*. The two dimensions, time and place, are obviously related; excessive expenditures of resources may allow more accomplishments during a given time and thereby effectually "buy time." Time-cost and other resource relationships are part of network scheduling techniques such as critical path scheduling and PERT (*Chapter 6*).

Thus, *Planning* includes the identification of potential courses of action to satisfy an objective and the evaluation of means to implement the alternatives. These anticipatory efforts lead to the selection of a preferred plan. Because most significant decisions involve so many interacting elements, it is necessary to consider distinct portions of a problem independently and then integrate the partial solutions in conformance with underlying system objectives. Therefore, the decision-making process is dynamic and subject to continuous review to maintain sensitivity for ongoing conditions. Planning is just the first step (*Section One*).

CHAPTER 2

MANAGEMENT: Concepts and Organization

2-1 IMPORTANCE

''I find it disheartening that so many young businessmen today conform blindly and rigidly to patterns they believe some nebulous majority has decreed are prerequisites for approval by society and for success in business.'' J. Paul Getty, *How to Be Rich*, Playboy Press, Chicago, 1965.

It is easy to reconcile the legitimate position of *management* at the heart of the text symbol for production systems, but it is difficult to state exactly what is expected from management. First there is the question of basic management philosophy. Then there is a choice among organizational objectives which seek to recognize internal functions and integrate these with influences outside the basic production system. And, finally, there is the cornerstone consideration of how to make management decisions. All of these factors coalesce into a mixture of art and science needed for *directing the activities of others in the optimal application of all resources to accomplish planned objectives—management.*

The challenge of management is well described by J. W. Forrester:

J. W. Forrester, *Industrial Dynamics*, MIT Press, Cambridge, Mass., 1961.

The manager's task is far more difficult and challenging than the normal tasks of the mathematician, the physicist, or the engineer. In management, many more significant factors must be taken into account. The interrelationships of the factors are more complex. The systems are of greater scope. The nonlinear relationships that control the course of events are more significant. Change is more the essence of the manager's environment.

2-2 THE MANAGEMENT MAZE

Ask a man with the title of a manager what he does and you will get answers ranging from a paper shuffler to a policy maker. Better yet, ask a man immediately subordinate to this manager and you may hear him rated as an overpaid pencil pusher to the power that moves immovable objects. About all the descriptions agree upon is that management acts. How management should act to accomplish its mission is a topic with as many different answers as there are people willing to comment.

Management Theory

We can begin construction of management foundations with a 60-plus-year-old definition by Frederick Taylor, "(management

19

The lineage of management theory can be traced back at least as far as the writings of Thomas Watts in 1776 or Charles Babbage in 1832. Watts' works even have modern poignancy with their emphasis on the value of "mathematicks" to the "man of business."

● is) . . . knowing exactly what you want men to do, and then seeing that they do it in the best and cheapest way." Taylor's obvious preoccupation with efficiency is offensive to some modern advocates of permissiveness, but it is still a cornerstone of management theory. Pragmatic attention to output is justly a part of a manager's perspective, but it is not his sole concern. Workers must produce the output. The needs and wants of these workers deserve solicitude. The current tempo of social change makes worker considerations a progressively more pressing part of management's concern.

An emphasis on worker relationships is the outgrowth of a "behavioral" orientation. Contributions come from the fields of sociology, psychology, philosophy, cultural anthropology, and related disciplines. They put the spotlight on motivation, interpersonal affiliations, and social goals. Although a short-range appraisal of behavioral concerns may seem opposed to the "traditional" output orientation, a broader view reveals that they complement each other. They are both part of the body of management, a body ever growing in complexity and importance.

EXAMPLE 2.1 Development of Management Theories

Long ago management positions largely resulted from an accident of birth, intrigue, or muscle. Persons occupying exalted positions were automatically accredited with the gift of astute management. It was not until near the turn of this century that management theory began to develop as a distinct discipline. There is still no agreement on a central all-purpose theorem to govern the subject, and there may never be one because the subject has so many facets.

An overview of management trends and thinking results from tracing the developments of management movements. Although the divisions are somewhat arbitrary due to infringing concepts, five schools of management thinking are delineated in the following paragraphs.

Scientific management. The theories and practices developed in this country from the 1880's to the 1920's were christened the "scientific management movement" by Louis Brandeis. The central theme was the systematic analysis and measurement of tasks to find the "one best way." The focus was on the shop level where specialization of labor was coupled with economic incentives to increase productivity. With concentration devoted to the measured efficiency of individual jobs, little progress was made in broader organizational problems.

Management process. Early management developments in Europe centered on the problems of higher management. The writings of Henri Fayol represent the "management process school" approach. They depicted management as a collection of processes such as planning, organizing, coordinating, directing, and motivating. With the processes thus identified, it was logically argued that professional managers could be trained to skillfully apply these processes to any organization.

When the management process school crossed the Atlantic to this country, increased attention was given to coordination. Unity of command as prototyped by the military was forwarded as a means to align efforts in one direction. Vertical authority with associated responsibilities and staff—line concepts were operational additions. The more general "processes" developed earlier were enlarged upon to assume the stature of management "principles." The process school is still expanding to provide guidelines for modern management functions.

Behavioral approach. Attention to the effects of human relations on productivity has been advanced by work in the behavioral sciences. The Hawthorne experiments of the 1920's stimulated questions about the authoritarian basis of the scientific management movement. The studies suggested that interpersonal relationships had as much or more effect on productivity than work or workplace designs. Attempts to make work a more satisfying experience for employees led to several motivation theories.

Douglas McGregor depicted old-style discipline by theory *X,* a view that assumes that most people do not want to work, that some kind of club is needed to make them work, and that they would really rather be told what to do than think it out for themselves. The opposite view, theory *Y,* holds that people do not inherently dislike work, that authoritative methods are not the only way to get work done, that people do not shun responsibility, and that they will work to achieve their selected goals. A similar outlook applied to supervision makes a division between "production-centered" and "employee-centered" management. Robert Blake suggested a "managerial grid" to rate managers on a scale of 1 to 9 for each concern; a 9,1 supervisor (high concern for production (9) and low concern for people (1)) follows theory *X*.

Decision theory. A relatively recent contribution to the management movement is directed toward the power centers and communications that determine managerial action. A firm has a decision-making anatomy which may or may not conform to organizational titles and printed duty assignments. Decision theory treats both the organizational network of decision processes and the general concepts of decision making applicable to any area of management. The intent is to improve the ability of managers to evaluate a problem thoroughly and to develop the best possible solution. Thus, effort is channeled toward the intellectual processes of individuals rather than the functional processes of systems.

Quantitative analysis. Interest in quantifying management problems has escalated rapidly in the last two decades. Leading the assault have been practitioners from engineering, mathematics, economics, and computer science. The two most familiar groups representing the mathematical approach are "operations research" and "management science."

Quantitative analysis investigates the relationships in an organization that can be expressed symbolically and treated mathematically. The relationships can exist within one function of the organization or connect several functions. In this respect and others, the quantitative approach is similar to the decision-making approach; both are applicable to any organizational structure. Although both have contributed significantly to problem solving, neither has as yet offered a unifying management theory.

It appears doubtful that a consensus or universal management theory will appear in the foreseeable future. Each movement has its champions and adherents, and each has something useful to offer in particular applications. An appreciation of all the theories with perhaps special competence in one or two areas appears to be the best preparation available for effective management.

System Theory

The management maze gets more intricate when the philosophy of doing has to be converted into the act of doing. By definition and derivation, an "executive" is a doer. He has the power and function to perform. To varying extents, his power and latitude of performance are constrained by the environment within which he operates and the objectives of his function. He is part of a greater body called management, a body nominally defined by its function to direct and regulate a system judiciously.

In Section 1-3 we viewed the production system as a block diagram. The input-conversion output representation is nicely symbolistic, but it does not portray the fiercely interacting parts within the system. These day-by-day interactions are the touch-points of executive actions and the challenges to coordination.

A "system approach" to management is a password to current, fashionable thinking. Today we have "weapons systems" designed by "system engineers" and evaluated by "system analysts." The modern emphasis is not surprising in a production context because more complicated outputs logically require more intricate conversion processes. We also have the high-speed data-processing potential to integrate and control the refined processes.

A fascinating part of the system approach is that a system can be almost anything you want it to be. The formal view interprets a system as a collection of functional components interacting to achieve an objective. A man working with a machine is a system. The man-machine system is just a component in the production line system and so on, systems within systems within. . . .

If we let a triangle, as in Figure 2.1, represent the hierarchial structure of management, the system concept is illustrated by the meandering borders of the shaded areas. Within each of these areas are the parts of the organization related by a common objective, often a particular problem to solve. The purchasing function could be a system with the objective of acquiring materials economically and on time. Another system could be a division according to shared regional interests with the objective of serving markets within a defined geographical section. The boundaries of the systems probably would overlap. Then the

The governing nature and power of higher tiers of management are recognized from below by verbal abuse aimed at the "establishment" or resigned pleas that "you can't fight city hall."

"The most valuable function of system analysis is often the stimulus it gives to the invention of better systems." *Analysis for Military Decisions,* Rand Corp., Santa Monica, Calif., Nov. 1964.

"Our little systems have their day; They have their day and cease to be: They are but broken lights of Thee. And Thou, O Lord, are more than they." Lord Alfred Tennyson, *In Memoriam,* 1869.

Chapter 16 provides another example of a system demarcation: the distribution system.

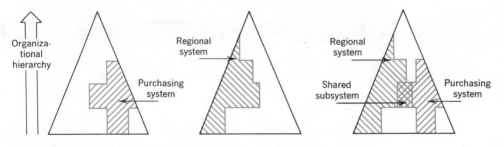

Figure 2.1 System boundaries within the organizational structure

ancient problem of serving two masters is created for the shared portion of the organization.

Some of the management confusion generated by dual system objectives can be avoided by prudent allocation of divisional lines within the organizational triangle. This approach is discussed in the following sections. Two other methods to ease the problem have already been implied. One is to think big, to put the interests of the governing system above daily operational problems. This line of reasoning is presented in detail in Section 4-2. Another method is to develop information channels and decision rules to link and control subsystems.

 ## Management of Systems

Norbert Weiner (1947) developed the term "cybernetics" from the Greek root meaning "steersman." "Plato has used the word cybernetics in his time and Ampéré has borrowed the term also as a name for the science of government; but Weiner must take the final responsibility for the currency of this ugly word, and also the credit for its aptness." S. Beer, *Cybernetics and Management.*

The study of system controls is a rapidly growing field of management research. Various labels have been pinned to the effort with the most intriguing one called *"cybernetics."* A thermostat as used to control the heating system of a building is the classic example. A furnace produces the heat. The temperature of the building it heats is measured by a thermometer. A thermostat compares the actual temperature to the desired temperature to regulate the heat. The key to operation is *feedback*; information about deviations from the system's objectives feeds back to regulate inputs and thereby control the process.

Some physical mechanisms for self-regulation are easily visible, such as the old Watt governor for steam engines. Although the basic principle is the same as shown in Figure 2.2, highly complex mechanical-electrical systems and management systems utilize more sophisticated feedback loops and regulators. Managers rely on the flow of information from above, below, and across for the feedback that connects input to output. When an executive monitors the flow to regulate input, he does so by applying his decision rules to output feedback. A kind of self-regulating system emerges when these decision rules are passed to subordinates in the form of policies and rules which allow them to control the process input without the executive's attention.

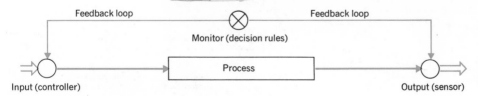

Figure 2.2 Input, output, and process control

Later we shall consider the means by which outputs are measured and how the resulting data are evaluated for process control. At this point it should be apparent that there is no straight and narrow path to follow toward successful management; it is a maze where objectives may be achieved through several apparently alternate paths—or through no apparent path.

2-3 MANAGEMENT FUNCTIONS

Slicing management by work phases leads to the planning, analysis, and control divisions described in Chapter 1. Another slicing pattern leads to work-type headings similar to the chapter titles of the text.

The management maze is reduced somewhat by partitioning it into more digestible chunks. We can slice the body that represents management into many patterns. Each pattern reveals different facets of the subject. Depending on the size, composition, and purpose of the production system, emphasis is given to some facets above others.

Several features similar to all the patterns can be noted:

1. Regardless of the division of functional areas, they overlap. Overlapping areas often require special attention and usually provide high returns for control effort.
2. Links between functional areas form a communication network by which activities of an organization are coordinated.
3. Management actions within all functional areas are basically the same. The administrative duties generally common to all subsystems include planning, organizing, staffing, directing, and controlling. Such recurring patterns give rise to the "universal truths" or "rules" of good management. They also add substance to the "generalist" role of the manager; good executives operate effectively regardless of the output or the organization of the production system.

The concept of "generalist" management conforms to the inclusive description of production systems in Section 1-3.

4. Each functional area can be divided, subdivided, and redivided again and again to reveal ever smaller operating components. As shown in Figure 2.3, one section of the purchasing function is procurement. Part of procurement is the legal division. One source of legal advice is the clerical subsection. And on and on.

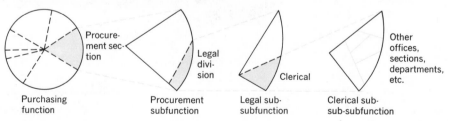

Figure 2.3 Operational subsections within basic functions

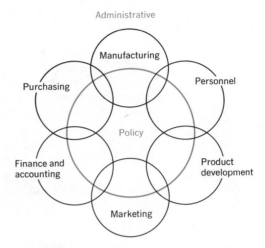

Figure 2.4 Policy and administrative functions of a large organization

Functions of an Industrial Enterprise

The major functions of a relatively large industrial firm are depicted in Figure 2.4. Similar diagrams could be developed for smaller firms, government activities, social programs, or any organization characterized by our broad definition of a production system.

The core area of the diagram represents the policy-making group within the organization. In a hierarchic triangle, this group would occupy the apex. From this lofty but core position, authority radiates outward to embrace responsibilities ranging from policy decisions for internal administrative functions to dealings with external contacts. The peripheral dealings include relations with stockholders, government agencies, competitors, and the public exclusive of customer and vendor relations handled by other sections of the firm. The commitment of an organization to social programs other than established union relations is becoming a more important policy consideration. With allegiance owed to employees, the community, and owners, policy makers have to be diplomats and statesmen as well as company managers.

The ring of functions depicted as interlocking circles in Figure 2.4 represents administrative services within an organization. Broad instructions set by the policy group are converted to overt actions by the administrative group. The overlapping portions of the circles denote the cooperation needed from the two groups in establishing overall policy and suggest the occasions where policy interpretations are necessary to achieve desired objectives.

Henry Ford II once said: "To subordinate profit to broad social goals would be totally irresponsible. On the other hand, socially responsible behavior is essential to long term growth and profitability of the corporation." *Business Week*, Nov. 2, 1968.

25

The scope of each function and its relationship to the production process are briefly discussed below.

Manufacturing. The fundamental function of a production system is output. Manufacturing includes the operations and direct support services involved with making a product. *Industrial engineering* is concerned with production scheduling, performance standards, method improvements, quality control, plant layout, and material handling. A *plant services* section typically handles shipping, receiving, storing, and transporting raw material, parts, and tools. The *plant engineering* group is usually responsible for in-plant construction and maintenance, design of tools and equipment, and other problems of a mechanical, hydraulic, or electrical nature.

Personnel. Recruitment and training of the personnel needed to operate the production system are the traditional responsibilities of the personnel function. The problem of keeping people in the organization includes health, safety, and wage administration. Labor relations and employee services and benefits are factors of increasing importance.

Product development. Some companies include research and the development of new products as a major emphasis. Nearly all companies have at least a concern for product improvement. Design efforts vary from a search for new, basic products to the development of byproducts and the economic utilization of waste products.

Marketing. Many ideas for product development come through the marketing function. Sales forecasts and estimates of the nature of future demands are developed to aid other management functions. Selling is the prime interest of marketing. Promotional work is a highly specialized activity involving advertising and customer relations. Contact with customers provides feedback about quality expected from the firm and opinions on how well the products meet quality standards.

Finance and accounting. Internal financing includes the review of budgets for operating sections, evaluation of proposed investments for production facilities, and preparation of financial statements such as balance sheets. The underlying activity is that of a scorekeeper to see how well the firm and its component departments are scoring in the business competition game.

"There is nothing more difficult to carry out nor more doubtful of success, nor more dangerous to handle, than to initiate a new order of things," said a realist named Machiavelli.

"As sort of a capsule observation, it could be said that the computer is the LSD of the business world, transforming its outlook and objectives. None of the existing goals of the twentieth-century business enterprise can survive the impact of the computer for even ten years." Marshall McLuhan and Quentin Fiore, *War and Peace in the Global Village*, Bantam Books, New York, 1968.

In this business game analogy, the accounting function could be likened to the game referee. Cost data are collected for materials, direct labor, and overhead. Special reports are prepared about scrap, parts, and finished-goods inventories; patterns of labor hours; and similar data applicable to production activities. In some firms the accounting function provides data-processing services for other divisions. In other cases, particularly where computers are utilized for problem solving instead of record-keeping, data processing is a separate function.

Purchasing. In a narrow sense, purchasing is limited to the acquisition of material from outside sources. But carrying out this basic function involves investigating the reliability of vendors, determining what materials are needed, coordinating deliveries with production schedules, and discovering new materials and processes. Since the purchasing function obviously serves the other functional areas, overlap sometimes stretches into such activities as inventory control, material inspections, shipping and receiving, subcontracting, and internal transportation.

Functions of a Production Process

Another way to group functions is according to their relative positions in a production process. The sequential arrangement in Figure 2.5 is admittedly oversimplified, even for a small firm. However it is indicative of the material and information flows that relate management functions.

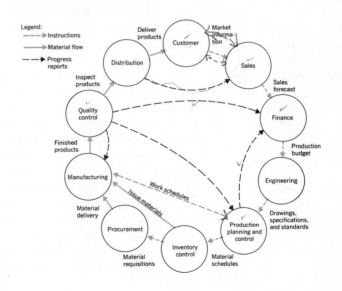

Figure 2.5 Cycle of production functions

The functions displayed in the production cycle are fairly self-descriptive. In the following chapters each will be treated in detail. Less obvious are the support functions and implied coordination of operations:

1. The indicated information and progress report paths illustrate only the formal, usually preprinted, forms of paper flow communications. If all the verbal and informal memorandum information channels were shown, the diagram would resemble a wind-blown spider web.

2. The clerical work and personnel requirements are scarcely suggested by the activity descriptions for each function. But they are very real concerns.

3. Half the cycle is completed before material begins to flow physically in the production process. The period that must be allowed (lead time) before production actually begins is a prime consideration in planning. Each function is owed its share of lead time to prepare for a new product, order, or style. The anticipation and control of lead time are among management's major responsibilities.

A popular acronym pertinent to information flow is KISS: Keep It Simple, Stupid!

2-4 ORGANIZATIONAL STRUCTURE

An organizational plan is a formal arrangement of personnel positions. It is designed to implement the basic objectives of the firm. Just as objectives vary widely, organizational structures can take innumerable patterns.

Some executives feel that a formal charting of positions of authority is deceiving because organizations do not operate according to charts. They say that the informal lines of communication are the true pipelines of information. They also cite examples where a subordinate actually issues the orders which theoretically originate from his boss. Such conditions are more aptly criticisms of a specific organization rather than a blanket condemnation of organizational patterns.

It has often been observed that the spaces between positions of authority in an organization chart are more interesting than the positions themselves.

Some plan is necessary to coordinate activities, whether or not it is followed to the letter. The diverse interests and huge size of many organizations make it impossible for all managers to know all the business objectives and operational constraints. It is doubtful if even one manager could master all of them. A hierarchic arrangement allows different levels to concern themselves with different perspectives. In theory, each step up the hierarchical ladder affords a broader sense of proportions, and the occupants view problems with better recognition of influencing factors from above and their effects on the levels immediately below. Without this integrating perspective, the welfare of individuals would suffer and performance would be less effective.

After accepting the inevitability of some sort of organization, a degree of doubt is still healthy. There can be no sacrosanct plan. As objectives change, new opportunities develop, and fresh personnel skills become available, the organization must adapt. Flexibility is akin to viability.

Line and Staff

Traditional "rags to riches" stories usually start with an ambitious young man. For illustrative purposes we shall assume that the young man begins his career by starting a company. He begins as president because he is the only employee. Being an astute working president, he soon has sufficient business to hire helpers. Now he has to manage work other than his own. As the number of workers increases, he cannot keep track of all the details so he selects leaders from the group to act as foremen. By having certain workers report to each foreman and the foremen to him, he reduces his contact obligations. He has created a line organization as shown in Figure 2.6.

Line and staff authority can be distinguished by saying line and staff personnel have, respectively, primary and secondary responsibility for the conduct of work and production.

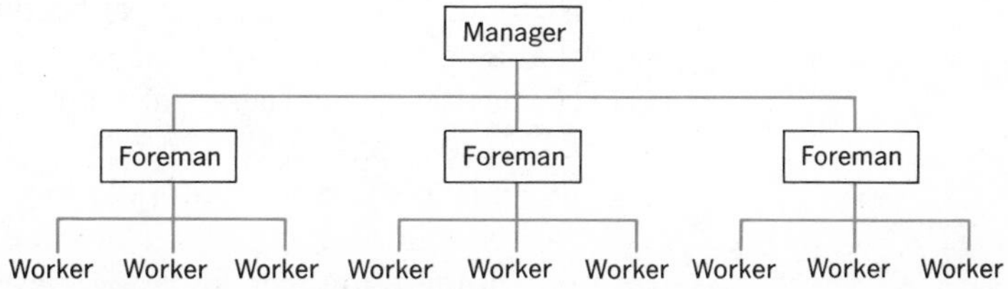

Figure 2.6 Rudimentary line organization

Line organizations are best typified by the traditional organization of military services. At every level the subordinates report to one leader: squad members to a squad leader, squad leaders to a platoon sargeant, platoon sargeants to a platoon officer, etc. This arrangement theoretically avoids conflicting assignments by limiting directives to a single source. A well-defined chain of command also speeds communications.

The simple table of organization from the foot-soldier era is far removed from the organization of today's wheel-soldiers with their multiple support units and special branches.

Let us now assume that the older but still ambitious rags-to-riches manager has had continued success. The number of foremen increased to the point where another tier of management was introduced: supervisors. But the manager could still not keep up with the increasing time demands of planning, coordinating, public relations, distribution, and other production functions. He hired special assistants. These assistants carried titles such as budget officer, industrial engineer, and design engineer. As their activities increased, additional personnel were hired. Eventually the responsibilities and authority of these groups were recognized

29

"Empire building" is a frequent fault within staff units. C. Parkinson, in his book *Parkinson's Law*, comments on the way staff size increases while the workload remains almost constant, and still everyone appears busy. Halting growth is difficult, but it is easier than cleaning out dead-wood once established.

- by a department status. Thus *staff* departments were added to supplement the line organization. The advisory nature of a staff position, as opposed to direct authority for production output, is illustrated by the organization chart in Figure 2.7.

Span of Control

The two line organizations shown in Figure 2.8 have the same number of workers. The difference is the number of subordinates supervised by one man. There is no pat answer as to which is the better arrangement. It depends on the ability of the supervisor, complexity of the task, importance of the objectives, and nature of the personnel. These factors are embodied in the concept called the *span of control.*

The high-voltage word "featherbedding" thrown at unions also applies to management ranks. Span-of-control decisions can be influential deterrents.

- A smaller span of control, fewer subordinates per management position, usually provides closer relationships and more strict control over performance. The significance of crew size may be overlooked if only the direct supervisor to worker relationships are observed. Worker to worker relationships also affect performance. A crew of one foreman (F) with two subordinates ($S1$ and $S2$) has three interpersonal links: F to $S1$, F to $S2$, and $S1$ to $S2$. The multiplier effect becomes evident when we observe that a crew of three workers ($S1$, $S2$, and $S3$) with one supervisor (F) has seven interpersonal relationships: F to $S1$, F to $S2$, F to $S3$, $S1$ to $S2$, $S1$ to $S3$, $S2$ to $S3$, and $S1$ to $S2$ to $S3$. The difficulty of achieving complete cooperation, coordination, and communication within large units is obvious. Such reasoning lies behind the limited number of upper level managers reporting to a senior manager and to the small size of research teams.

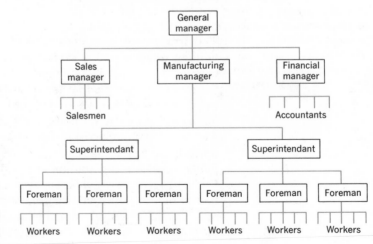

Figure 2.7 Skeletal line and staff organization

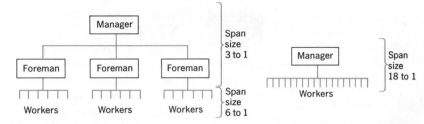

Figure 2.8 Span of control and organizational structure

Advantages gained from smaller span sizes must be weighed against economic and intangible drawbacks. Smaller crew sizes necessarily increase the number of supervisory positions and consequently raise overhead expense. The extra supervisors cause more tiers of management because each tier is affected similarly by a given span of control philosophy. The direct results of inserting more levels of management between the policy-making head and the output-producing hands are longer lines of communication and perhaps more erratic coordination. A less measurable result of multiple management tiers is the view from below to an ambitious worker: the ladder to the top has an awful lot of rungs.

Improved control techniques and better data-processing capabilities are reducing the practical difficulties of synchronizing smaller management units.

Types of Organizations

The divisions of an organization are largely determined by operating objectives. The purposes for dividing the organization into divisions are partly given by reasons for line and staff structures and the concern of span of control. An additional purpose is to provide needed service with the least confusion and the most economy. Several service-oriented patterns of departmentation are listed below.

By function performed. The personnel performing related functions are grouped together as an administrative unit. This is one of the most used organizational patterns. It has the logic of keeping specialists together where their efforts are easier to coordinate.

For example, each function shown in Figure 2.5 could be a department. An engineering department could be comprised of draftsmen, mechanical and electrical engineers, architects, craftsmen for model building, artists, technical report writers, and other personnel required to provide engineering services.

By physical location. Personnel operating in a distinct location are arranged in one administrative unit. The most common application is departmentation by geographical areas. The main

31

Transfers from one geographical location to another have become an accepted fact of life, although not always appreciated, by younger executives. In theory the transfers provide diverse training, new challenges, and a chance to become familiar with different operations. In practice, transfers provide new experiences, help spread ideas, and test the cohesiveness of families.

advantage is that local control allows the unit to respond quickly to changes in its area.

For example, sales organizations are typically divided into sales regions with a manager and staff for each region. Major executives are usually concentrated in one centrally located home office. Many manufacturing companies with nationally distributed products have warehousing or assembly plants located according to geography. A smaller scale version of divisions by physical location is found in many plants or department stores where departmental lines follow floor boundaries.

By product lines. The organization is divided into administrative units according to the type of output. In extreme cases the unit is comprised of all development, input, conversion, and output processes required to produce a certain product. In such circumstances the product divisions often are subdivided according to functions. By this means the specialization of labor is carried to extremity. The principal drawback is the duplication of functions and facilities that may lead to the underutilization of resources.

A product layout, as described in Section 8-3 for arranging plant facilities, is an extension of the product line concept.

A large corporation such as General Motors is divided into semiautonomous product divisions such as Chevrolet, Pontiac, Oldsmobile, Buick, Cadillac, GMC trucks, AC sparkplugs, etc. On a more modest scale, many manufacturers divide assembly and finishing services according to the product produced.

By customer services. Marketing and service activities are sometimes departmentalized according to the type of customer. An emphasis on customer service is the supporting thought. This form of departmentation shares most of the advantages and disadvantages recorded for product and geographic divisions.

"Whatever he [the manager] chooses to do he confronts committees, ad hoc if nothing else. If the organization of his corporation is too monolithic and he decides on decentralization, he usually winds up with a series of committees. If, on the other hand, organization is loose, the usual consequence of unification is again a series of committees."
"Management by Committee,"
Fortune, Apr. 1953.

Strongly sales-oriented organizations are most likely to have success with customer divisions. Banks, insurance companies, and retail stores are typical examples. The divisions might be by retail, wholesale, and institutional buyers; by sizes of the organizations served; or by men, women, and children.

Committees

A catalog of organizational structures is incomplete without mention of committees—formal, informal, and infamous. Much fun has been poked at the committee approach, but it can serve a purpose difficult to achieve by other means.

Committees may be permanent, such as a "standing" committee to deal with recurring problems, or they may be organized temporarily to cope with an immediate problem. A committee is usually comprised of people with diverse backgrounds related mainly by their relevance to the concern of the committee. The intents of meeting are to exchange and integrate ideas freely. The hoped-for outcomes are increased cooperation between represented groups and generation of new ideas.

Success of a committee approach is largely determined by the leader. His preparations, enthusiasm, and patience are critical. He has to make needed information and facilities available. He cannot dictate but must keep the members active. When the majority of the members oppose his views, he has the choice of going along with their decision, carrying the issue to higher authority, or exercising his right of final responsibility (assuming he has it) to reverse the majority recommendation. If an executive uses the last two alternatives too often, he soon defeats the purpose of specialized counsel.

Committee assignments can be good training schools for potential managers. They provide wide exposure to specialized activities. And any errors of the trainee will likely be corrected by more experienced group members before any harmful consequences result.

The main argument against committees is economic. Studies suggest that there may be a huge cost per action taken because committees tend to be slow acting and often outlive the purpose for which they are formed. Furthermore, actions of a committee may be controlled by vociferous minorities. Compromises are sometimes subject to political overtones, and personal conflicts started in a conference room can disrupt work on the factory floor. Some disadvantages are avoided by using committees primarily for advice and never for emergency decisions.

A disrespectful definition of a committee characterizes it as a collection of the uninterested led by the uninspired to do the unnecessary.

2-5 RELATIONSHIP OF ORGANIZATIONAL STRUCTURE AND DECISION MAKING

The most important characteristic and function of management is decision making. In this section we shall not explore the many decision-making tools available to managers; in essence that is the topic of the rest of this text. Instead, we shall establish a perspective for studying decision making within an organization.

The organization is represented by the graph shown in Figure 2.9. The decreasing ratio of authority to the number of employees is easily understood and immediately apparent in a survey of most organizations. To some extent, authority can be equated

The relationship of the organizational structure to human relations is discussed in Section 7-6.

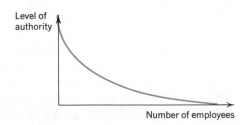

Figure 2.9 Typical distribution of authority among employees

title, pay, and responsibility. However, many impressive titles are labels for specially contrived positions which are all "window dressing" and no power. Some workers with highly cultivated, in-short-supply skills draw more salary than positions of far greater authority.

Responsibility and authority should go hand in hand. An organization is theoretically built to match responsibility with authority. Staffs share responsibility for production with their affiliated line position. Each line manager shares his authority when he assigns responsibilities to subordinates. But this assignment does not divest the manager of the basic responsibility. Just as authority is diluted from top to bottom, responsibility for an error at the lowest level can be traced, ever more faintly, all the way upward. However, actual "witch hunt" tracings are more likely to reveal a scapegoat who lacks the side-stepping nimbleness of his colleagues than the true source of error. Such is the management maze.

Hell has been defined as responsibility without authority. Checking the correspondence of authority to responsibility is a good detection device for management featherbedding.

Planning Decisions

Planning is necessary at all levels of an organization. The types of decisions the planners make can be characterized by the freedom of choice among alternatives. As displayed in Figure 2.10, the highest levels of authority have the widest choice of alternatives. At this top level, the aims and overall objectives of the organization are determined. The constraints limiting the number of possible alternatives result from the composition of the organization and its environment—state of the economy, actions of competitors, federal and state laws, resources of the firm, etc.

Each level lower in the hierarchical structure is further limited by constraints established above. Thus a goal selected at the highest level gives direction to policy makers at the next lower level. These policies are then the guidelines which the level below uses to develop procedures and directives. At a still lower level, the directives are converted to work orders and rules. At the lowest level there is only a narrow range of interpretation in deciding the exact method of performance.

The cost incurred from making an incorrect decision is similar to the freedom of choice relationship; e.g., the cost of breaking a rule is slight compared to a financial disaster resulting from a decision to develop the wrong product line.

Planning Horizons

Planning is necessarily concerned with the future. How far the planning penetrates into the future, the planning horizon, depends on the scope of the problem. Top management's concern for overall objectives is a panoramic problem. But once the long-range objectives are settled, the tactics required to implement

Difficulties encountered in extending planning frontiers further into the future are examined in Chapter 3.

34

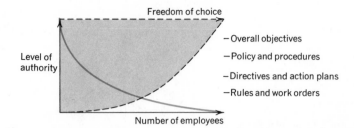

Figure 2.10 Managerial freedom in the hierarchy of authority

them are a series of short-range operations. For instance, a firm considering the introduction of a new product must first consider demand factors over a span of years. A decision to go ahead with the introduction leads to facility, supply, distribution, and similar problems over the shorter period needed to establish the product. Each problem area then explodes into detailed action plans for the next period, perhaps a few months or a year. Finally, at the operating level, scheduling decisions are in terms of weeks, days, and hours. See Figure 2.11.

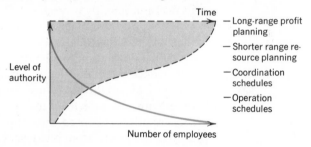

Figure 2.11 Planning horizons associated with the hierarchy of authority

Planning Intangibles

A method of comparing intangible factors while selecting a preferred alternative is suggested in Section 4-3.

Intangible considerations are factors affecting a decision which are particularly difficult to quantify. Such considerations are typically more prevalent when the scope of the problem is larger and the time span longer. For instance, site selection in a plant location problem is influenced by the "quality" of the labor force, the "beauty" of the building site, the "importance" of being located near good schools, the "reputation" of the urban area, the "desirability" of the climate, and the "value" of recreational outlets. These factors must be considered in the plant location decision although they are difficult to measure.

Some people deplore judgment for its lack of scientific bases. It is intangible. About all that is safe to surmise is that it is practical and is developed like a muscle: the more it is used the better it gets.

Many attempts have been made to insert objectivity into the consideration of intangibles, but none has had universal acceptance. Perhaps the closest chord of agreement is that intuition and judgment are vital to adequate subjective appraisals. Since we traditionally associate more skillful judgments with experience,

35

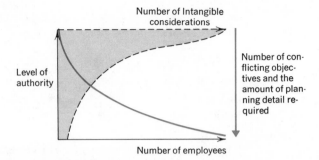

Figure 2.12 Relationship of intangible factors to the hierarchy of authority

and experience is usually a basis for higher management positions, it appears that the levels of authority exposed to the most intangibles are the levels best qualified to evaluate them. At lower levels the problems are normally easier to quantify (Figure 2.12).

Evaluation of Planning Procedures

Much can be learned about an organization from a study of its decision-making procedures. One feature of an ideal organization is the free flow of reliable information up, down, and sideways through the hierarchic levels. Each level needs complete-as-possible information for the decisions associated with that level, but it does *not* need all the details about every decision made below it. It would be absurd for a top executive to clutter his mind with minutiae from the factory floor. Such data should be sequentially condensed into appropriate feedback packages as they flow upward from one level to the next.

The amount of freedom allowed in interpreting decisions flowing downward is an indication of the organization's flexibility. The converse of condensing upward flowing data is the explosion of a policy into detailed action plans, schedules, work orders, and rules. Unless the organization is very small, top management cannot spell out the fine points required to satisfy overall objectives. Attempts to do so are evidenced by middle management "yes men." They function as postmen, passing orders from above to below. Not only are talents being wasted, but the lack of interpretation tends to make the organization inflexible.

Even a finely tuned communication network and a balanced hierarchy of authority eventually are upset by changing conditions. New external demands eventually make some positions functionally obsolete. Other positions take on new meaning and power as a reflection of the persons filling them. Whether the changes are beneficial or damaging, they should be recognized. One indicator of planning irregularities is when subordinates use a lengthier planning horizon than higher level managers.

Wherever the fault lies, it is likely to cause suboptimization. A realignment or reinstatement of authority and responsibility links will put the system back in balance.

As a fish needs water, a system manager needs a sound organizational structure before he can benefit fully from the decision-making tools and techniques we shall explore in the following chapters.

2-6 SUMMARY The practice of management is directing the activities of others in the optimal application of all resources to accomplish planned objectives.

The five management movements listed below are indicative of managerial trends and developments:

1. Scientific management—an early movement featuring the measured efficiency of shop level and individual jobs.
2. Management process—initial effort to define the processes needed to develop higher level managerial skills.
3. Behavioral approach—attention to the effects of human relations on individual and group productivity.
4. Decision theory—effort channeled toward the intellectual processes of individuals and the decision-making anatomy of an organization.
5. Quantitative analysis—investigations into the relationships within an organization that can be expressed symbolically and treated mathematically.

The management executive has the power and function to perform. His actions are constrained by the system within which he operates. Careful definition of system boundaries helps avoid contradictory controls. Cybernetics is the name given to a study of system controls emphasizing feedback. Self-regulating systems apply established decision rules to output feedback to regulate input.

System analysis is somewhat simplified by recognizing major management functions. Features common to all functional patterns include the the following:

1. Major functional areas typically overlap.
2. Links between functional areas form key communication networks.
3. Management actions within different functional areas are basically the same.
4. Many subfunctions exist within major functional areas.

One way of separating functions is by policy-making and administrative responsibilities. Another way of grouping functions is according to their positions in a production process.

Although formal organizational arrangements may not be followed rigidly, they do coordinate activities among individuals and integrate company policies. Organizational structures should mutate to meet new demands and opportunities.

In a line organization, subordinates at each level report to one superior. A staff arrangement provides specialized advisory services to the line organization.

A span of control is determined by the number of subordinates reporting to a superior. A smaller span size usually provides closer relationships and stricter control. The smaller size also increases the number of supervisory positions and lengthens lines of communication by creating more levels of management between top and bottom positions.

Service-oriented patterns of organizational structure may be by the functions performed, physical locations, product lines, or customer services provided.

Committees operate as part of an organization's structure to combine diversified skills and interests in seeking new ideas and greater cooperation. Unless committees are well directed and controlled, they tend to be costly and politically sensitive.

The most important characteristic and function of management is decision making. Higher levels of authority have greater freedom of choice among decision alternatives, longer planning horizons, and more intangibles to consider. Much can be learned about an organization from a study of its decision-making procedures.

2-7 REFERENCES   Albers, H. H., *Principles of Management* (3rd ed.), John Wiley, New York, 1969.

Beer, S., *Cybernetics and Management*, John Wiley, New York, 1959.

Bethel, L. L., F. S. Atwater, G. H. E. Smith, and H. A. Stackman, Jr., *Industrial Organization and Management* (4th ed.), McGraw-Hill, New York, 1962.

Buffa, E. S., *Modern Production Management* (3rd ed.), John Wiley, New York, 1969.

Cyert, R. M. and J. G. March, *A Behavioral Theory of the Firm*, Prentice-Hall, Englewood Cliffs, N.J., 1963.

Etzioni, A., *Modern Organizations*, Prentice-Hall, Englewood Cliffs, N.J., 1964.

Kolasa, B. J., *Introduction to Behavioral Science for Business*, John Wiley, New York, 1969.

Learned, E. P., C. R. Christensen, K. R. Andrews, and W. D. Guth, *Business Policy—Text and Cases* (2nd ed.), Richard D. Irwin, Homewood, Ill., 1969.

March, J. G. and H. A. Simon, *Organizations*, John Wiley, New York, 1958.

Moore, F. G., *Manufacturing Management* (5th ed.), Richard D. Irwin, Homewood, Ill., 1969.

Shelly, M. W. and G. L. Bryan, *Human Judgments and Optimality*, John Wiley, New York, 1964.

Shull, F. A., *Selected Readings in Management*, Richard D. Irwin, Homewood, Ill., 1962.

Timms, H. L., *Introduction to Operations Management*, Richard D. Irwin, Homewood, Ill., 1967.

Wiener, N., *Cybernetics*, John Wiley, New York, 1948.

2-8 QUESTIONS AND PROBLEMS

1. In *The Journal of Industrial Engineering* (May-June 1965), Alan J. Levy suggested that a quick view of trends in organizational theory is shown by the evolution of management thought given below.

(a) From: Efficiency as a mechanical process.
     To: Efficiency as a human process.

(b) From: Control through command.
     To: Control through communication.

(c) From: Authority from the top down.
     To: Authority from the group.

(d) From: Leadership by authority.
     To: Leadership by consent.

(e) From: Technological change by fiat.
     To: Technological change by consultation.

(f) From: A job for subsistence.
     To: A job as a satisfying experience.

(g) From: Profit from buccaneering.
     To: Profit with social responsibility.

Discuss the trends. What caused the original conditions and why were they accepted? What present-day examples can you find for the original conditions? What has led to the current trends? Why? To which one of the five management movements given in Example 2.1 could the change be attributed?

2. Why should you study management when the professionals in the discipline cannot agree on the content or even the best approach to the subject?

3. What effect on production systems can reasonably be expected from greater concern for social problems on both a local and a national level?

4. What purpose does feedback serve in a production system? What are the physical means of feedback in an industrial organization?

5. Give an example of a mechanical self-regulating system. How are decision rules implemented? What are the physical forms taken by the sensors and controllers?

6. Where will overlap in management activities likely occur among the functions displayed in Figure 2.4? How can a definition

of boundaries ease the deleterious effects of overlap? Relate the definition of boundaries to the internal lines of communication.

7. Under what conditions are staff units warranted in an organization?

8. Distinguish between authority and responsibility. How are the two related?

9. Relate the span of control concept to classroom instruction. Are the relationships similar to industrial organizations? What are the advantages and disadvantages of smaller units?

10. Describe companies that are organized according to function, location, product, and customer divisions. Give an example of each.

11. Most people have rather strong feelings about the value and function of committees in an organization. What are your opinions? Substantiate your views.

12. Why is decision making considered the most important characteristic of management?

13. What characteristics would you put on a job profile for a top-level manager to qualify him to handle decision requirements depicted in Figures 2.10, 2.11, and 2.12?

14. Comment on each view below. These views are found among many practicing managers.

   (a) An organization should be changed to fit the talents of a particularly gifted manager.

   (b) A scarcity of capable management personnel is the most common deterrent to effective expansion of a business firm.

   (c) The right to exist and make a profit is a fundamental right of a free enterprise system. Too many government controls tend to violate this privilege.

   (d) The most difficult aspect of training a managerial candidate is to get him to look at the "big picture."

   (e) The customer is always right.

   (f) Too much familiarity between workers and supervisors builds contempt for authority.

   (g) Future computerized system analyses and controls will undermine the authority and responsibility of existing managerial positions.

   (h) Economist Milton Friedman, in his 1963 book *Capitalism and Freedom*, wrote: "Few trends could so thoroughly undermine the very foundations of our free society as the acceptance by corporate officials of a social responsibility other than to make as much money for the stockholders as possible."

CHAPTER 3

FORECASTING

3-1 IMPORTANCE

"If a man takes no thought about what is distant, he will find sorrow near at hand." Confucious.

A forecast is an estimate of future activity. It can be a prediction of new product acceptance, changes in demand, or other conditions that directly influence production planning. The value of accurate forecasts is easy to see when you consider the dependent decisions. Some of the decision areas that rely on sales forecasts are shown in Figure 3.1.

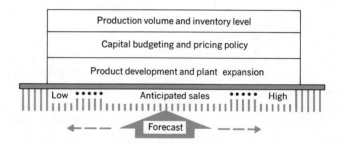

Figure 3.1 The sales forecast and production decisions

3-2 PROBLEMS

Accuracy is the measure of merit in forecasting. Where a direct cause-and-effect relationship exists, an expectation of high accuracy is legitimate. The behavior of a chemical compound or maximum stress in a new design can be accurately anticipated; but when we leave the physical sciences and enter the realm of economics, relationships become obscure.

"Economic forecasting, like weather in England, is only valid for the next six hours or so. Beyond that it is sheer guesswork." M. J. Moroney, statistician.

An exceedingly complex set of highly variable factors surrounds any significant economic question. To expect reliable answers is unrealistic. Still, some business executives expect such quality answers and some forecasters are brave (or foolish) enough to attempt them. Instead of duping each other, the executive should realize that precise business forecasts are usually impossible with currently available techniques, and the forecaster should recognize that his efforts provide an indication rather than the final word on future conditions. Such attitudes would at least reduce friction and ulcers.

41

3-3 HISTORY

Throughout history executives have felt the need for clairvoyant counselors. Kings and merchants had their crystal gazers, palm readers, and astrologers. By mixing psychological black magic with a little court intrigue, some soothsayers did very well. Others received the witch treatment. A few still have followers.

Nostradamus was a French astrologer and physician in the sixteenth century.

• The rhymed prophecies of Nostradamus have enjoyed popularity for years. Much of the clairvoyance attributed to Nostradamus and similar prognosticators is due to the open-ended, obscure wording of their forecasts. Such wording allows an interpretation of current events to conform to the predictions. This tempting format for long-range forecasts has a special appeal even today. When few specific dates or quantities are specified, ample room is left for maneuvering. Adroit interpretations might even make the general forecast appear prescient. Though such forecasts tease the imagination, they are misfits in an industrial setting.

"Carriages without horses shall go, And accidents fill the world with woe."

"Around the world thoughts shall fly in the twinkling of an eye."

"Under water men shall walk, shall ride, shall sleep, shall talk; In the air men shall be seen In white, in black and in green."

Mother Shipton's Prophecies (seventeenth century).

• Early in this century, few formal measures were made to predict future business conditions. Production levels were set by managers to correspond to their estimates of demand. Men were hired and supplies accumulated at a rate geared to the optimism of department foremen. Few companies formulated a coordinated product-demand policy.

Prior to World War II, industries started to recognize that an integrated production system was necessary. Forecasts are a coordinating link in production planning. Distinct groups were established to prepare required predictions. The age of market surveys and product questionnaires began, and frequently with it came a credibility gap that fostered subsequent disillusionment. A naive belief that sufficient expenditures could buy a reliable window into the future caused some impressive fiascos. Formal forecasting programs often became suspect.

Today the pendulum of forecasting acceptance appears to be rising again, but not at the fervent pitch previously experienced. The complicated interrelationships of today's economy make forecasts a vital step in operational planning. It is further recognized that the best forecasts will be made by people with special training, but even qualified specialists will make errors. This rational approach permits central forecasts to guide departmental planning with enough flexibility to compensate for prediction deviations.

3-4 SOURCES

Many companies cannot afford a staff of forecasting specialists. Although production planning may be under the auspices of a single man, he is still expected to provide appropriate forecasts.

To fulfill his responsibilities, he should be familiar with available statistics, be able to analyze and interpret statistical measures, and have a thorough knowledge of internal and external aspects of his operations.

A surprising amount of free information is available to aid forecasters. General data about the national economic health, pricing indexes, consumer-spending trends, etc., are offered in different magazines, newspapers, and publications from trade associations and government agencies. Even specific information about particular industries is available from various publishers.

More elaborate forecasting techniques can be employed when their expense is warranted. These methods may be used singularly, but a much better estimate results when they are used in combination with each other.

For example, Wall Street Journal, Business Week, and U.S. Department of Commerce studies.

For example, farm prices from the U.S. Department of Agriculture or construction trends from the Constructor.

Consumer Opinions

Obtained by questionnaires and interviews.

The ultimate consumer can be questioned. His opinions are objective compared to a producer's opinions, but they may change from day to day. What he intends or hopes to do and what he actually does may be two entirely different things. The relatively expensive process of determining consumer opinions can be reduced by designing the survey to glean other useful information such as the effect of promotional campaigns.

Customer Opinions

Someone who has purchased a product can be asked why he made the purchase. Answers can be solicited when the sale is completed and a questionnaire can be attached to the guarantee or to sales follow-up literature.

Distributor Surveys

Estimates of expected sales can be requested from retail outlets and the company's sales force. Retailers may be more objective than salesmen, but they are less likely to devote the time necessary for conscientious estimates. Both sources are most suitable for short-term forecasts of a year or less.

Many companies rely heavily on judgments made by their sales personnel. The sales front is where the action is. Salesmen and sales managers can spot buying trends and competitor activity. But does a good observer and a hustling agent make a good forecaster? If he is aware of influencing economic conditions and the significance of his efforts, he may be very good. By averaging many opinions, individual optimism and pessimism is somewhat cancelled. There is little doubt that the sales force is an acceptable source of estimates, and there is great doubt that it should be the sole source.

Executive Opinions

"In the field of observations, chance favors only the prepared minds." Louis Pasteur (1822–1895).

The executive-manager-supervisor level is closer to corporate policy than the sales force and, correspondingly, is further from the consumer outlook. In common with the sales force, executive opinions may be colored by personal prejudices. Opinions are secured individually or from committees and, hopefully, bias and errors are cancelled by compensating views. This divergence in viewpoints, backgrounds, and interests usually provides a good cross-section of estimates, but potentially conflicting forecasts may be difficult to reconcile to a consensus opinion.

Consensus executive forecasting is widely used. It can be obtained quickly and with little extra expense. What is usually lacking is the recognition of underlying economic factors. Opinions are extremely valuable for interpreting market data, but they are no substitute for a quantitative analysis of that data.

Marketing Trials

Development and introduction of a new product presents special problems. If the new product is a replacement or modification of an existing line, data and opinions applicable to the old product will likely be useful in anticipating the reception of the new version. When the product is radically different, new data must be generated.

Dangers include unrepresentative income levels, subject's reaction to special attention, and competition artificially obstructed.

In addition to the forecasting methods already discussed, it may be helpful to expose the new product to a very limited market trial. A trial takes on the nature of a controlled experiment where the market area and method of presentation are carefully selected and controlled. In any experiment, there is danger of selecting the wrong variables, improper handling, and lack of control. The cost of overcoming these conditions is often enormous and consequently limits the extent and scope of marketing trials.

Market Research

" . . . and I think it would be a very good thing when the manufacturers wake up—and I am not going to name names —and begin to give the things we want instead of things they think we want." President Eisenhower, 1958.

Another forecasting approach is an internal or contracted market research program. It can be used for new products or existing products for which more extensive marketing data are needed. The purpose of the research is to identify the nature of consumer consumption. After determining how general sales vary with differences in location, buyer occupation, prices, quantity, quality, consumer income, and other factors, this information is related to a specific product and a forecast is developed. The economic forces identified in a market survey are particularly valuable when combined with other forecasting methods. The means of correlating product sales with market conditions are detailed later in this chapter.

Historical Data

Basing estimates of future activity on the past performance of a product is one of the most used and reliable forecasting methods available. It has the advantage of being quantifiable and objective. Still, it is not perfect. Inaccuracies result when the economic conditions that prevailed in the past no longer operate. Judgment remains a necessary ingredient of any forecasting method.

In the following sections we shall consider different methods of analyzing collected historical data. The best method to use for a given set of data is the one that most closely approximates its pattern. In essence, we are using estimates of past performances as practice for estimating future performance; we are putting our faith in two old adages: history is a good teacher and history repeats itself. Then we must check to see if history is living up to its reputation.

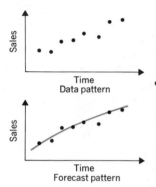

Sales / Time
Data pattern

Sales / Time
Forecast pattern

3-5 TIME-SERIES ANALYSIS

A time-series analysis defines how a certain production indicator varies with time. Total sales made each year over the last several years would be a production indicator. The manner in which the volume of sales changes on a year-to-year basis is formulated; the resulting expression establishes a sales-time relationship which is used to predict future sales levels.

A good analysis, like a good recipe, takes several steps to complete and includes several components. Paying attention to each step and each ingredient results in a better end product, a more reliable forecast. The most commonly used expression for a time-series forecast is

It takes a good cookbook plus expertise to be a master.

$$Y = TCSR$$

where:
Y = forecasted value
T = underlying trend
C = cyclic variations about the trend
S = seasonal variations within the trend
R = residual or remaining unexplained variations

Each factor in the formula helps account for the many interacting

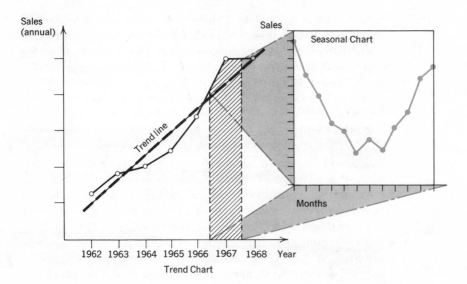

Figure 3.2 Cyclic, seasonal, and residual variations
Axes: The vertical axes in both charts represent sales volume. In the trend chart the sales per year are shown for a range of years; in the seasonal chart the amount of sales by month for a given year, 1967, is detailed.
Data: Records of past sales are indicated by circles.
Analysis: The lines connecting the circles depict the historical pattern of sales. By analyzing this known pattern, we try to anticipate where the next unknown point will occur. When this forecasted value becomes known, it in turn joins the previously known data as a foundation for the next forecast.

elements which influence the variable being forecast. The relationship of the factors is amplified in Figure 3.2

Trend

Returning now to our basic equation $Y = TCSR$, we can see that the trend (the dashed line in Figure 3.2) is a line fitted to the long-term historical pattern. The closeness of fit is measured by the aggregate distance the smooth trend line misses the data points (circles). Only in the rarest cases does the trend coincide with a line connecting all the points.

Cycles

Cyclic variations account for some of the variance between the trend line and data points. The wavelike cycles do not necessarily form a repeating pattern. They are caused by the reaction of the plotted variables to changes in general business conditions. Each industry, and probably every company within the industry, is

46

clue to the most appropriate calculation method. Further clues result from familiarity with the methods.

Some forecasting methods are very elaborate and require considerable mathematical competence. Others are of the rule-of-thumb variety and develop a prediction with simple arithmetic. Since there is no unanimous opinion as to a single "best" method, we shall investigate several of those with wide acceptance. They will be illustrated by application to the following basic data:

Generox, Inc., has been producing hand-operated, nail-driving machines for 5 years. The plant has operated at near capacity for the last 2 years. Forecasts are needed to schedule production for the coming year and to provide estimates for planning future expansion of production facilities. Sales records for the 5 years have been tabulated by quarters as shown in Table 3.1. Figure 3.5 shows a plot of total annual sales.

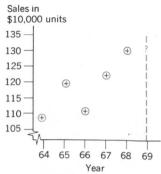

Figure 3.5 Pattern of annual sales

Table 3.1 Quarterly sales in thousands of dollars

Year	1964	1965	1966	1967	1968
Quarter 1	190	280	270	300	320
Quarter 2	370	420	360	430	440
Quarter 3	300	310	280	290	320
Quarter 4	220	180	190	200	220
Totals	1080	1190	1100	1220	1300

Least Squares

Whenever the plotted data points appear to follow a straight line, we can use the least squares method to determine the line of best fit. This line is the one that comes the closest to touching all the data points. Another way of saying the same thing is that the desired line minimizes the differences between the line and each data point. This latter explanation gives rise to the origin of the name for the least squares method; it gives the equation of the line for which the sum of the squares of the vertical distances between actual values and line values is at a minimum. A further property of the line is that the sum of the same vertical distances equals zero.

A straight line is defined by the equation $Y = a + bX$. For a time-series analysis, Y is a forecasted value at a point in time, X, measured in increments such as years from a base point. Our objective is to determine a, the value of Y at the base point, and b, the slope of the line.

$\Sigma(Y - Y_F)^2 = \text{minimum}$

where

Y = actual value

Y_F = least squares value

$\Sigma(Y - Y_F) = 0$

two equations can also be obtained by differentiating $(Y - Y_F)^2$ with respect to a then with respect to b.

affected uniquely by the causes of economic fluctuations. The situation is further complicated by inconsistent internal responses of individual firms. For instance, a signal that an areawide business cycle has bottomed out and sales are expected to rise could trigger expansion plans on one occasion, but the same indicators could lead to a "wait and see" attitude on another occasion. If expansion plans are undertaken, the same business indicators would be viewed differently the next time because of the greater capacity available.

The magnitude, timing, and pattern of cyclic fluctuations vary so widely and are due to so many causes that it is generally impractical to forecast them. Nevertheless, at least an awareness of the effect of cyclic variations should influence a forecaster. By plotting the percentage ratio between a calculated point and the actual point from a trend chart, as in Figure 3.3, some indication of cyclic irregularities is obtained. A cycle chart is based on the implied assumption that the trend line is the "normal" condition about which the cyclic variations fluctuate. This reasoning leads to curiosity about the fit of the trend line to the data and about influences accounted for in the "normal" trend.

A depressed economy would affect luxury sales differently than the sales of necessity items, and some luxury items would be affected more than others.

Seasons

Seasonal variations are fluctuations that take place in *one* year and are annually *repetitive*. Innumerable products are in demand only a portion of each year. Most of them are associated with the weather. Since weather follows a broadly predictable pattern and because production of seasonal products must be geared to demand, monthly or even weekly forecasts are common.

Errors

The last term in the basic forecasting equation, R, represents the random or chance variations which are not explained by trend, cyclic, or seasonal movements. By definition, residual variations *cannot* be forecast. They may arise from unforeseeable events such as "acts of God" or a sudden shift in politics. Such events are a bane to forecasters, but philosophically we have to admit that the variety they introduce saves us from a programmed

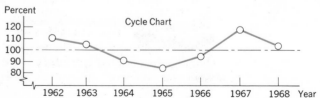

Figure 3.3 Comparison of actual values to calculated values: (actual sales/forecasted sales) × 100%

existence which would deprive life of much of its spice, interest, and alibis.

EXAMPLE 3.1 Unsophisticated Sales Forecast

An estimate is needed for the expected sales of a product during the second quarter of next year. Sales records since the product's introduction 4 years ago are available. An approximate forecast can be quickly made by plotting the sales data and visually fitting a straight line to the data. The "eyeballed" trend line in the sales chart of Figure 3.4a starts at $60,000 on the left and increases by annual increments of $10,000. The trend estimate for next year, 5, is then

$$T = \$60,000 + (\$10,000)(5) = \$110,000$$

From the cyclic variations of the sales chart, a forecaster might estimate that actual sales will be slightly greater than the trend indicates. A judgmental value of +8% or 1.08 times the trend forecast is selected.

A breakdown of annual sales by the percentage sold each quarter is shown in the quarterly sales chart of Figure 3.4b. A simple forecast by quarters could result from an arithmetic average or by a visual inspection of the quarterly data. By using the latter method, which allows more weight to be given to recent sales figures, second quarter sales are estimated to be 41% of the annual sales estimate for next year. Based on the individually developed forecast factors and the recognition that residual errors cannot be forecast, the desired estimate is calculated as

$$Y_{(2)} = TCS$$

$$\text{Sales}_{(2\text{nd quarter})} = \$110,000 \times 1.08 \times 0.41$$

$$= \$48,708$$

This example is titled "unsophisticated" because the analysis relies on inspection rather than calculation. Unsophisticated is not a synonym for worthless. The simpler "eyeball" approach may be more appropriate than refined methods. Depending on the data accessible, the time available, and the purpose intended, refinements could add cost without a corresponding increase in the value of the forecast.

3-6 TIME-SERIES CALCULATIONS

The mathematics available for analyzing data range from quick and clean arithmetic to tedious but powerful statistical techniques. Selecting the most appropriate method is no simple task. You have to seek the age-old balance between the cost of application and the value of results. A preliminary study may not warrant a detailed analysis, while a major new venture would require the most exacting methods possible. Less time and money are usually devoted to forecasts for low dollar volume products than for high ones. The more refined methods are typically employed when a company has the staff and computing capabilities to handle them, but even pros are occasionally boxed-in by a stagnant policy of "this is the way we have always done it."

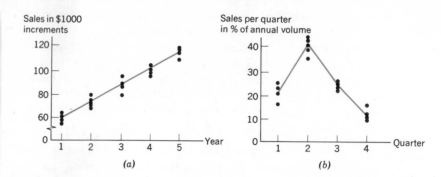

Figure 3.4 Sales data and forecasts by inspection: (a) annual sales and (b) quarterly sales

Data

For an unbiased start, the first step is to decide what type of data will be used in the forecast. Will planned production be a function of past production or will it be related to some other economic index? In this section we shall assume that time-series data are appropriate.

The next hurdle is to collect the data. This may amount to an in-house record search or generation of new information. After the information is collected, it should be questioned. Did certai events that will not reoccur affect the data? Will future ever such as new competitors or improved products make previ records inapplicable? Have population shifts or fickle cons tastes altered the applicability of earlier data? A "yes" ans these or similar questions indicates a need for caution.

Sometimes historical data can be modified to present picture of past events. For instance, a sharp decline in sal have been created by temporarily bad publicity. Afte faded and corrective measures were taken, sales return previous pattern. This period of reduced sales could b from the data used in forecasting, or records could b compensate for the atypical period. The danger in is that subjective overtones can be inserted i objective calculations.

Calculation Methods

Making the major assumption that we h data, we can proceed to the choice of a metho data to a forecast. We begin by plotting the scale. The plot does not have to be exacti to decipher is the general pattern. This p

Two equations are employed to determine a and b. The first is obtained by multiplying the straight-line equation by the coefficient of a and then summing the terms. With the coefficient of a equal to 1 and N as the number of data points, the equation becomes

$$\sum Y = Na + b\sum X$$

The second equation is developed in a similar manner. The coefficient of b is X. After multiplying each term by X and summing all the terms, we have

$$\sum XY = a\sum X + b\sum X^2$$

The two equations thus obtained are called *normal equations*.

The four sums required to solve the equations, $\sum Y, \sum X, \sum XY$, and $\sum X^2$, are obtained from a tabular approach. We can simplify the calculations by carefully selecting the base point. Because X equals the number of periods from the base point, selecting a midpoint in the time series as the base makes the $\sum X$ equal to zero. The smaller numbers resulting from a centered base point also make other required products and sums easier to handle. After the four sums are obtained, they are substituted in the normal equations and the values of a and b are calculated. Then these values are substituted into the straight-line equation to complete the forecasting formula:

$$Y_F = a + bX$$

Year	X
1964	-2
1965	-1
1966	0^*
1967	$+1$
1968	$+2$
$\sum X =$	0

*Base point

EXAMPLE 3.2 A Least Squares Line Fitted to the Trend of the Basic Problem Data

A straight, sloping line appears to be a reasonable fit for the data in Figure 3.5. To illustrate different versions of the least squares method, we shall first use 1964 as the base point and then 1966. Using a tabular format with Y as sales in \$10,000 increments to determine $\sum Y, \sum X, \sum X^2$, and $\sum XY$, we have

Year	Y	X	X^2	XY	
1964	108	0	0	0	base point
1965	119	1	1	119	
1966	110	2	4	220	
1967	122	3	9	366	
1968	130	4	16	520	
Sums	589	10	30	1225	

which yield the normal equations

$$589 = 5a + 10b$$
$$1225 = 10a + 30b$$

These equations are solved simultaneously to give

$$a = 108.4 \text{ or } \$1,084,000$$

$$b = 4.7 \text{ or } \$47,000$$

Using the same data and format but changing the base point from 1964 to 1966, we get

Year	Y	X	X^2	XY	
1964	108	-2	4	-216	
1965	119	-1	1	-119	
1966	110	0	0	0	base point
1967	122	1	1	122	
1968	130	2	4	260	
Sums	589	0	10	47	

which allow a and b to be calculated as

$$a = \frac{\sum Y}{N} = \frac{589}{5} = 117.8 \text{ or } \$1,178,000$$

$$b = \frac{\sum XY}{\sum X^2} = \frac{47}{10} = 4.7 \text{ or } \$47,000$$

A forecasting equation is developed by substituting the a and b values into the straight-line equation. The forecast for 1969 is 5 years away from the 1964 base point of the first version which provided the equation

$$Y_F = \$1,084,000 + \$47,000X$$

and the forecast

$$F_{1969} = \$1,084,000 + \$47,000\,(5) = \$1,319,000$$

Similarly, using the formula derived from a base point at 1966,

$$Y_F = \$1,178,000 + \$47,000X$$

the forecast for 1969 is 3 years from the base point and is calculated as

$$F_{1969} = \$1,178,000 + \$47,000(3) = \$1,319,000$$

A comparison of the two forecasts and the computations involved in developing the equations confirms that centering the base period shortens the arithmetic without altering forecasted values.

Exponential

Sometimes a smooth curve provides a better fit for data points than does a straight line. A smooth curve implies a uniform percentage growth or decay instead of the constant increment or or decrement exemplified by a straight line. The equation for a curve may take the exponential form, $Y = ab^x$, which indicates that Y changes at the constant rate b each period.

We can determine the values for a and b by the least squares

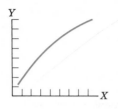

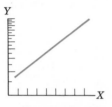

The same $Y = ab^x$ equation plotted on arithmetic scales (top) and semilogarithmic scales (bottom).

method if we convert the exponential equation to its logarithmic form:

$$\log Y = \log a + x \log b$$

The logarithmic version plots as a straight line on semilogarithmic paper; the Y scale is logarithmic and the X scale arithmetic. This property allows us to set up normal equations in the manner described in Example 3.2. Thus the normal equations

$$\sum (\log Y) = N(\log a) + \sum X(\log b)$$

$$\sum (X \log Y) = \sum X(\log a) + \sum X^2(\log b)$$

can be solved by setting up a table to obtain $\sum(\log Y)$, $\sum X$, $\sum(X \log Y)$, and $\sum X^2$. When the base point is selected to make $\sum X = 0$, the solution reduces to calculating

$$\log a = \frac{\sum (\log Y)}{N} \quad \text{and} \quad \log b = \frac{\sum (X \log Y)}{\sum X^2}$$

After solving the above equations or simultaneously solving the normal equations when $\sum X$ does not equal zero, the exponential equation is established by taking the antilogarithms of a and b.

EXAMPLE 3.3 An Exponential Line Fitted to the Trend of the Basic Problem Data

Since it is not obvious whether a straight or a curved line will fit the given data better, a smooth curve is a legitimate contender. The fitting procedure is analogous to that employed for straight lines; the variation is the use of logarithms for Y values:

Year	Y	X	X²	log Y	X log Y
1964	108	−2	4	2.0334	−4.0668
1965	119	−1	1	2.0755	−2.0755
1966	110	0	0	2.0414	0
1967	122	1	1	2.0864	2.0864
1968	130	2	4	2.1139	4.2278
Sums		0	10	10.3506	0.1719

Because $\sum X = 0$, we can solve for a and b as

$$\log a = \frac{\sum (\log Y)}{N} = \frac{10.3506}{5} = 2.0701$$

and, therefore, $a = 117.5$ or $\$1,175,000$, and

$$\log b = \frac{\sum (X \log Y)}{\sum X^2} = \frac{0.1719}{10} = 0.0172$$

53

making $b = 1.0405$ or an increase of 4.05% each period. Thus the forecasting equation is

$$\log Y = 2.0701 + 0.0172X$$

or

$$Y_F = \$1{,}175{,}000 \ (1.0405)^x$$

The values resulting from a straight line and a curve should be compared to the observed data. From Table 3.2, it appears that either equation fits the data fairly well. Differences between the fitted lines become more pronounced as the forecasts are pushed further into the future. The exponential formula continuously shows higher values beyond 1968.

Table 3.2 Comparison of fitted line predictions

Year	X	Actual Y	Straight-Line Fit $Y_F = 117.8 + 4.7x$	Curved-Line Fit $Y_F = 117.5(1.0405)^x$
1964	−2	108	108.4	108.5
1965	−1	119	113.1	112.9
1966	0	110	117.8	117.5
1967	1	122	122.5	122.3
1968	2	130	127.2	127.2
1969	3		131.9	132.3
1970	4		136.6	137.7

Five observations are too few data points to recommend definitely one fitted line over the other. At the present stage, the forecaster would have to rely on judgment. If he is optimistic, he would likely choose the exponential equation that predicts a brighter future. As historical data accumulate, the trend should become better defined and the validity of either equation will be evident by the deviations of its forecast from actual values.

Simple Average

When b in the straight-line equation $Y = a + bX$ is equal to zero, the line is level. The forecast for the next period then becomes the simple average of all the Y values to date:

$$Y_F = \frac{\sum Y}{N}$$

Calculation of a simple average for a trend forecast is then a special case of the least squares method.

Average value calculations are more often associated with seasonal variations which take place *within* an overall trend. By definition, seasonal variations are limited to fluctuations during a single year. Therefore, we must collect data for several time periods within the year to determine seasonal patterns. Monthly or quarterly records are the most common. When data covering a substantial number of years are available, the arithmetic mean of each period *within* a year tends to damp or average out cyclic effects *among* the years.

After arranging the data according to quarters, months, or whatever time increments are appropriate, the *Y* values representative of each period are totaled and the sum is divided by the number of years, *N*. The resulting mean for each period is the estimate for the next period if incremental trend effects are not pronounced. When the trend is significant, the simple average can be corrected for overall growth or decay.

A pattern of seasonal fluctuations often remains relatively constant even though the trend may rise or fall. The pattern can be easily defined by dividing the simple average of each period by the sum of the averages. The resulting figure is a percentage estimate of the amount of activity expected during each period. This seasonal index is converted to sales or other demand units by multiplying the period percentage times the annual trend forecast.

EXAMPLE 3.4   Simple Average Applied to the Seasonal Index of the Basic Problem Data

A perusal of the quarterly data from Generox, Inc., leads us to question the first year's sales. The introductory phase of a new product often exhibits a pattern all its own. After the initial advertising effort and consumer response have run their course, the seasonal variations tend to be more stable. Since the 1964 sales are not markedly different from subsequent quarterly patterns, we will include them as "clean data."

A further check on the suitability of simple averages results from plotting the periodic sales and visually fitting a trend line to each period. If the fitted lines are roughly parallel, no radical change is developing in the demand experienced each period. When the fitted lines diverge significantly, the averages for the affected periods should be corrected. In some cases a sum amounting to the approximate shift can be added and subtracted from the affected averages. In more extreme cases, it may be necessary to calculate a formula for the demand per period.

Lines sketched for the quarterly sales of Generox appear approximately parallel in Figure 3.6. Therefore, we can calculate without corrections the average sales for each quarter and the average for all quarters combined:

Year	Q1	Q2	Q3	Q4	Annual
1964	190	370	300	220	1080
1965	280	420	310	180	1190
1966	270	360	280	190	1100
1967	300	430	290	200	1220
1968	320	440	320	220	1300
Sums	1360	2020	1500	1010	5890
Averages	272	404	300	202	294.5

average of all quarters, not yearly

The accepted quarterly averages are next converted to a seasonal index. A quarterly index is

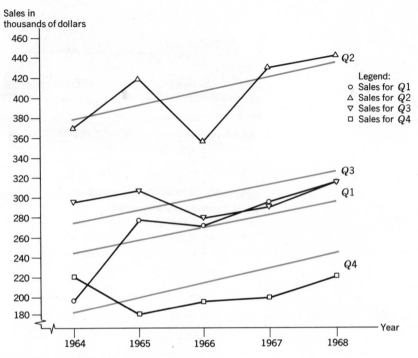

Figure 3.6 Trend of quarterly sales established by visual inspection

the quotient obtained from dividing the simple average of each quarter by the average of all quarters:

$$I_{Q1} = \frac{272}{294.5} = 0.92 \qquad I_{Q2} = \frac{404}{294.5} = 1.37$$

$$I_{Q3} = \frac{300}{294.5} = 1.02 \qquad I_{Q4} = \frac{202}{294.5} = 0.69$$

The index thus developed can be used to estimate quarterly sales for the coming year. As applied to the straight-line forecast for 1969, we have

$$F_{Q1} = \frac{\$1,319,000}{4} \times 0.92 = \$303,000$$

$$F_{Q2} = \frac{\$1,319,000}{4} \times 1.37 = \$452,000$$

$$F_{Q3} = \frac{\$1,319,000}{4} \times 1.02 = \$336,000$$

$$F_{Q4} = \frac{\$1,319,000}{4} \times 0.69 = \$228,000$$

Total $1,319,000 = trend forecast for 1969

Moving Average

A moving average forecast is obtained by summing the data points over a desired number of past periods. This number usually encompasses 1 year in order to smooth out seasonal variations. The smoothing results because high and low values during a year tend to be cancelled out. Extending the moving average to include more periods increases the smoothing effect but decreases the sensitivity of forecasts to more recent data.

A moving average is distinguished from a simple average by the requirement for consecutive calculations; each average moves forward in time to include a more recent observation while dropping the oldest point. If a given 12-month moving average is the average demand for January 1968 through December 1968, the next moving average includes the demands for February 1968 through January 1969. In the former case, the moving average represents the demand at midyear; in the latter case, it represents demand for July 30 or August 1. An average of the two values would center the demand to July.

A moving average calculated for a number of the most recent data observations is seldom a good forecast for the next period unless the data pattern is relatively constant. A seasonal index referenced to the moving average improves the forecast. An index value is calculated by dividing the actual demand by the centered moving average for that period. A more reliable index is obtained by averaging several index values for common time periods. The forecast is thereby the product of the most recent centered moving average for a period and the index value for that period.

EXAMPLE 3.5 Moving Average Applied to the Seasonal Index of the Basic Problem Data

Again we shall refer to the quarterly sales figures of Generox to develop a quarterly forecast for 1969. A four-period moving average will be used. The first moving average is one-fourth of the total sales for 1964 and represents a point in time between the end of the second quarter and the start of the third quarter. The second moving average is the sum of the last three quarters' sales in 1964 and the first quarter of 1965 divided by 4. This value is associated with the end of Q3, 1964, and the start of Q4, 1964. An average of the two numbers obtained gives a moving average centered at Q3, 1964. This procedure is repeated for all the quarters to obtain the moving averages of Table 3.3.

The last column in Table 3.3 is the seasonal index for each quarter. It is obtained by dividing the actual sales for a quarter by the centered moving average for that quarter. We can get a better estimate of a quarter's index by averaging all the values available (Table 3.4).

Table 3.3 Computation of moving averages and quarterly seasonal index values for the sales of Generox

Year	Quarter	Sales in Units of $10,000	Four-Period Moving Average	Centered Moving Average	Seasonal Index
1964	Q1	190			
	Q2	370			
	Q3	300	270	281	1.07
	Q4	220	292	298	0.74
1965	Q1	280	305	306	0.91
	Q2	420	307	302	1.39
	Q3	310	297	296	1.04
	Q4	180	295	287	0.63
1966	Q1	270	280	276	0.98
	Q2	360	273	274	1.32
	Q3	280	275	279	1.00
	Q4	190	283	286	0.66
1967	Q1	300	300	301	1.00
	Q2	430	303	304	1.42
	Q3	290	305	307	0.94
	Q4	200	310	311	0.64
1968	Q1	320	312	316	1.01
	Q2	440	320	322	1.37
	Q3	320	325		
	Q4	220			

Table 3.4 Calculation of an adjusted seasonal index

	Q1	Q2	Q3	Q4
			1.07	0.74
	0.91	1.39	1.04	0.63
	0.98	1.32	1.00	0.66
	1.00	1.42	0.94	0.64
	1.01	1.37		
Totals	3.90	5.50	4.05	2.67
Average seasonal index	0.975 +	1.375 +	1.0125 +	0.6675 = 4.03
Adjusted seasonal index	0.97 +	1.37 +	1.00 +	0.66 = 4.00

Before applying the average seasonal index, two checks should be made:

1. The average of the periodic indices should total to 1.0. In the example the average is

$$\frac{0.9750 + 1.3750 + 1.0125 + 0.6675}{4} = \frac{4.03}{4} = 1.0075$$

Therefore, the indices must be adjusted or else the sum of the quarterly forecasts will exceed the implied annual forecast by 0.75%.

2. Attention should be given to any obvious trends in a quarterly index. In Table 3.4, Q1 appears to be increasing and Q3 has a distinct downward trend.

Our adjusted seasonal index reflects the above considerations. A fraction (4.00/4.03) of each average index was taken and the results were rounded off with respect to the trend in Q3. Thus calculations provide the forecasting framework, but finishing touches are supplied by judgment.

The final step is to make a forecast. It is conducted by taking the product of the most recent centered moving average and its respective seasonal index. Forecasts for the first two quarters of 1969 are

c.m.A. s.i

$$Q1_{1969} = 316 \times 0.97 = 307 \text{ or } \$307{,}000$$

$$Q2_{1969} = 322 \times 1.37 = 441 \text{ or } \$441{,}000$$

Exponential Smoothing *Omit*

Any quantitative forecasting method serves to smooth out fluctuations in a demand pattern. In exponential smoothing, we control the smoothing characteristic by adding a factor, the smoothing constant called alpha (α), which directs more emphasis to recent demands. Although exponential smoothing can be applied to any time-series forecasting technique, we shall examine it in connection with averages.

A forecast utilizing exponential smoothing results from the equation

$$F_n = \alpha Y_{n-1} + (1 - \alpha) F_{n-1}$$

which can be rearranged as

$$F_n = F_{n-1} + \alpha(Y_{n-1} - F_{n-1})$$

where:

$$
\begin{aligned}
F_n &= \text{forecast for next period} \\
F_{n-1} &= \text{forecast for previous period} \\
\alpha &= \text{smoothing constant } (0 \le \alpha \le 1) \\
Y_{n-1} &= \text{actual value for previous period}
\end{aligned}
$$

Thus, a smoothed forecast is equal to the previous smoothed forecast plus some fraction α of the difference between the forecasted and actual values during the previous period. From this description it is apparent that we must determine a previous forecast and the value of α before a new forecast can be made.

When past data are available, the initial value, F_{n-1}, can be a simple average of the most recent N observations. Deciding on the number of data points to employ shares the same implication as considered for moving averages; when N is large the estimate is very stable but it fails to reflect more recent pattern changes. If no data are available, F_{n-1} is developed from opinions as to what the process is supposed to do.

The rationale for selecting an α value is also similar to that used for selecting the number of periods in a moving average, N. In general, α is some value between 0.1 and 0.3. The response to a changing pattern improves with higher smoothing constants just as it does with smaller values of N. This rapid response is acquired at the expense of the ability to smooth out random fluctuations. The relationship between α and N which utilizes the same average age for data is $\alpha = 2/(N + 1)$. Therefore, if we have a reason to be satisfied with a certain N value, we can easily calculate an α value that gives equivalent results.

That exponential smoothing is just a weighted average can be observed by following a series of forecasts. If we let the first forecast be F_0 and subsequent forecasts be indicated by F_1, F_2, etc., a series of predictions would appear as:

$$\text{period } 1: F_1 = \alpha Y_0 + (1 - \alpha)F_0$$
$$\text{period } 2: F_2 = \alpha Y_1 + (1 - \alpha)F_1$$
$$= \alpha Y_1 + (1 - \alpha)[\alpha Y_0 + (1 - \alpha)F_0]$$
$$\text{period } 3: F_3 = \alpha Y_2 + (1 - \alpha)F_2$$
$$= \alpha Y_2 + \alpha(1 - \alpha)Y_1 + (1 - \alpha)^2$$
$$[\alpha Y_0 + (1 - \alpha)F_0]$$

or, in general,

$$F_n = \alpha Y_{n-1} + (1 - \alpha)F_{n-1}$$
$$= \alpha Y_{n-1} + \alpha(1 - \alpha)Y_{n-2} + \alpha(1 - \alpha)^2 Y_{n-3} + \cdots$$
$$+ (1 - \alpha)^n Y_{n-n}$$

where:

$$F_n = \text{forecast for period } n$$
$$Y = \text{historical data}$$
$$Y_{n-n} = \text{starting forecast}$$
$$= F_0$$

The above function is a linear combination of all past data weighted according to the smoothing constant α. If $\alpha = 0$, no data since the original forecast are included. When $\alpha = 1$, the next forecast is the same as the most recent actual value.

EXAMPLE 3.6 Exponential Smoothing Applied to Forecasts for the Basic Problem Data

The exponential smoothing formula limits a forecast to a single period in the future. We can apply this method to the trend forecast (Table 3.1) as a weighted average of the collected data to estimate total sales for 1969. First we shall apply a smoothing constant of 0.2 to get

$$F_{1969} = (0.2)130 + (0.2)(0.8)122 + (0.2)(0.8)^2 110 + (0.2)(0.8)^3 119 + (0.8)^4 108$$

$$= (0.2)130 + (0.16)122 + (0.13)110 + (0.10)119 + (0.41)108$$

$$= 116 \text{ or } \$1{,}160{,}000$$

Next we can let $\alpha = 0.8$, which makes the formula more responsive to recent demands as shown by

$$F_{1969} = (0.8)130 + (0.8)(0.2)122 + (0.8)(0.2)^2110 + (0.8)(0.2)^3119 + (0.2)^4108$$

$$= (0.8)130 + (0.16)122 + (0.03)110 + (0.01)119 + (0.0)108$$

$$= 128 \text{ or } \$1{,}280{,}000$$

From these significantly different forecasts we can easily see the importance of a careful selection for α.

The initial forecast, F_n, for exponential smoothing can also be obtained from other averaging methods. We can forecast the sales for the first quarter of 1969 by starting from either a simple average or a moving average for Q1, 1967. We shall assume that an α value of 0.15 strikes a balance between stability and sensitivity.

Table 3.5 Exponential smoothing applied to quarterly forecasts based on simple and moving averages

Forecasting equation: $F_n = F_{n-1} + 0.15(Y_{n-1} - F_{n-1})$		
	Simple Average	Moving Average
$F_{n-1} = F_{Q1,1968}$	$\dfrac{190 + 280 + 270 + 300}{4} = 260$	316 (Unadjusted centered moving average from Table 3.3)
$Y_{n-1} = Y_{Q1,1968}$	320	320
$F_n = F_{Q1,1969}$	$260 + 0.15(320 - 260) = 269$ or $\$269{,}000$	$316 + 0.15(320 - 316)$ $= 316.6$ or $\$316{,}600$

The predictions in Table 3.5 differ greatly. This marked difference illustrates how the choice of an initial forecast can affect the subsequent forecast. Regardless of the initial prediction method, if exponential smoothing is consistently applied for several periods, the forecasts will eventually approach the same value. It is those intermediate periods that delight the second-guessers.

★ ★ ★ *Optional material.*

Comparison and Control of Time-Series Forecasts

A simple average can fit a constant trend and is considered a line-fitting method.

Two basic forecasting methods have been considered. Line-fitting equations provide a means to extrapolate forecasts several periods in the future. Iterative procedures rely on timely data to make the next forecast.

Line-fitting methods. The extent to which an equation fits a trend is evaluated by the *standard error of the estimate, S_y.* This measure of dispersion of actual data points about the line of forecasted points is calculated as

S_y is used appropriately only where $\Sigma(Y - Y_F) = 0$.

$$S_y = \sqrt{\frac{\Sigma(Y - Y_F)^2}{v}}$$

where:

Y = historical data points
Y_F = calculated fit or forecasted points
v = number of degrees of freedom

Before we attempt to utilize S_y, the assumptions included in the calculations should be explored. First, we are assuming that the forecasted value Y_F is the mean of all the Y observations associated with a certain point in time, X. Then we assume that the Y values associated with each X have the same distribution and equal variances as depicted in Figure 3.7. The significance of these conditions will be more apparent when we consider correlation analysis in this chapter.

In our examples only one Y has been given for each X, but this is not a required condition.

Our estimate of the true variance (σ^2) is $S_y{}^2$. The more observations we have, the better will be our estimate. When the number is about 30, we assume that Y values are normally distributed. Under this assumption, we expect 95% of the observations to fall between plus or minus two standard errors of the mean, $Y_F \pm 2S_y$. With fewer than 30 data points, we usually assume

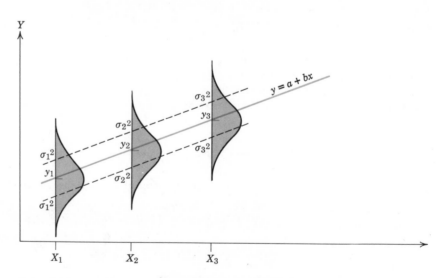

Figure 3.7 Line-fitting assumptions: Mean values fall on the predicted line; therefore, $Y_n = Y_{F_n}$. Variances are equal; therefore, $\sigma_1^2 = \sigma_2^2 = \sigma_3^2$

Student's t distribution is more representative of our data. This assumption broadens the band containing 95% of the observations. For instance, if a sloping-line prediction is based on 13 observations, 11 degrees of freedom would be used in the calculation of S_y; from the Student's t distribution table, we find that the 95% band is $Y_F \pm 2.2S_y$ units wide.

The loss of $13 - 11 = 2$ degrees of freedom is due to the two constants, a and b, in the prediction equation.

The standard error of the estimate gives a reasonable measure of the relationship of the fitted line to past data. By itself, it does not reliably measure how well the line will fit the future. Judgment must be added. To make the application of judgment easier, we can plot existing and new data on charts. The resulting pattern, interpreted with respect to standard error control limits, provides a clue to the sustained value of the predicting equation.

EXAMPLE 3.7 Calculation of Standard Errors from the Basic Problem Data

The preparation and use of charts are demonstrated by application to the simple average and least squares trend forecasting equations. The standard error of the estimate for each method is calculated as follows:

$$\text{Level line}: Y_F = \frac{\sum Y}{N} = 117.8$$

Year	Y	Y_F	$Y - Y_F$	$(Y - Y_F)^2$
1964	108	117.8	−9.8	96.04
1965	119	117.8	1.2	1.44
1966	110	117.8	−7.8	60.84
1967	122	117.8	4.2	17.64
1968	130	117.8	12.2	148.84
		Sums	0.0	224.80

$$S_y = \sqrt{\frac{\sum (Y - Y_F)^2}{N - 1}} = \sqrt{\frac{224.8}{4}} = 7.5$$

$$\text{Sloping line}: Y_F = 117.8 + 4.7X$$

Year	Y	Y_F	$Y - Y_F$	$(Y - Y_F)^2$
1964	108	108.4	−0.4	0.16
1965	119	113.1	5.9	34.81
1966	110	117.8	−7.8	60.84
1967	122	122.5	−0.5	0.25
1968	130	127.2	2.8	7.84
		Sums	0.0	103.90

$$S_y = \sqrt{\frac{\sum (Y - Y_F)^2}{N - 2}} = \sqrt{\frac{103.9}{3}} = 5.9$$

Note that the degrees of freedom for the level-line forecast number $5 - 1 = 4$, while the sloping line forecast has $5 - 2 = 3$ degrees of freedom. The difference is accounted for by the number of constants in each equation; the slope constant, b, does not occur in the level-line equation. The lower standard error for the sloping-line prediction tends to confirm the visually obvious: a sloping line fits the data better than a level one.

Two charts are illustrated in Figures 3.8 and 3.9. Both are based on limits expected to include 95% of the data. The range that accounts for a given percentage of the data is a function of the type of distribution and its standard deviation. We have calculated our estimate of the standard deviation, S_y, and have assumed that Student's t is the appropriate distribution due to the limited number of data points. While recognizing that the prediction equations have different degrees of freedom, the respective ranges from the table of Student's t values are

$$\pm 2.776 S_y = \pm 20.8 \quad \text{for the simple average forecast}$$

$$\pm 3.182 S_y = \pm 18.8 \quad \text{for the least squares forecast}$$

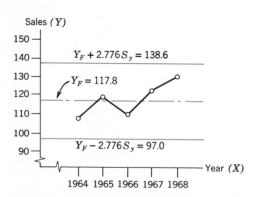

Figure 3.8 Y plot chart: control chart for the simple average forecast

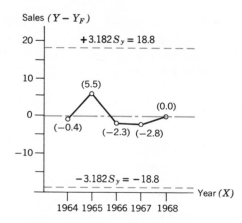

Figure 3.9 Cumulative $(Y - Y_F)$ chart: control chart for the least squares forecast

The statistical control limits based on the standard error computations can be utilized in different control chart formats. In Figure 3.8 the actual observations are plotted directly as they occur. If the fitted line is not level (sloping or curved), the control limits are set parallel to the slope or curve. The second version, shown in Figure 3.9, tracks the *cumulative* deviations $(Y - Y_F)$ of the actual values from predicted ones. In the example the last plotted point falls on the 0 line because the forecasting equation was developed by using all the data shown in the chart to make $\Sigma(Y - Y_F) = 0$. Unless the equation is absurdly revised each period, future total deviations will likely stray to either side of the 0 line.

In either chart the plotted points should randomly fall above or below the center line but within the established limits so long as the forecasting equation characterizes the data. When points accumulate on either side of the center line or if one falls beyond the control limits, the forecaster should be on the alert. Such patterns may be just chance happenings, or they may signal a change in the trend. In the shadowland of prediction, a forecaster cannot ignore any signals or clues.

Sometimes a forecast of accumulated demand for several periods is required. An approximate measure of the standard error for the cumulative demand is calculated as $S_y\sqrt{n}$ where n is the number of periods over which the forecasted demand is accumulated. As applied to the least squares forecast already developed, the standard error for a 2-year cumulative demand is calculated as follows:

Year	Period, n	Forecasted demand, F_y	Cumulative forecasted demand, ΣF_y	Standard error, $5.9\sqrt{n}$
1968	now	127.2	—	5.9
1969	+1	131.9	131.9	5.9
1970	+2	136.6	268.5	8.2

When there are enough observations, say 30 or more, a normal distribution is a legitimate assumption; the • confidence level of 95% would then be established as $1.96S_y$.

Thus, about five times in a hundred the cumulative actual demand through 1970 would fall by chance outside the range of

$$268.5 \pm 3.182(8.2) = 268.5 \pm 26.1$$
$$= 294.6 \text{ to } 242.4$$

A chart of control limits for accumulated demand would obviously show increasing divergence for extended forecasts.

In general, control charts are simple and useful tools. They primarily serve as easily maintained warning devices. Plotting historical data gives an indication of their statistical stability. Adding new data points as they become available shows whether current activities are following the historical pattern. To some extent an emerging new pattern suggests how forecasting equations can be suitably altered. A subtle but important aspect of charting is the forced continual comparison of actual and forecasted values during updating. The time to recognize change is while it is occurring.

Iterative methods. When a moving average is used directly to forecast a trend, it usually gives values that lag the actual demand.

Some trend forecasts are made by averaging the most recent N • observations.

To a large extent this condition is relieved by associating the averages with a seasonal index. However, this recourse necessarily loses the use of the most recent data; centered forecasts lag by half the number of periods used in the average.

A large N value makes the calculation of a moving average tedious. Use of a smoothing factor cuts the paperwork and computations by utilizing only the latest data observation and the previous forecast.

Control charts are also used with moving average forecasts. The limits are based on an average moving range, $M\bar{R}$, which is calculated by:

1. Obtaining the difference between actual data and values forecasted.
2. Determining the absolute value of the differences (called the moving range, MR) of the numbers from Step 1.
3. Averaging the values obtained in Step 2. Limits set at $\pm 2.66 M\bar{R}$ are based on three standard deviations and set the probability of exceeding these limits by chance at less than 0.3%. Such control charts help tell whether the past data are statistically stable and if the present data are following the past pattern.

EXAMPLE 3.8 Preparation of a Moving Range Control Chart

A competent forecaster cannot rest on his laure!s after making a good prediction; he must continually check his ongoing forecasts against actual occurrences to see if any statistically significant change is underway. A forecaster for Generox using a moving average could develop a control chart based on the calculations shown in Table 3.6.

The far-right column of the table is the moving range, MR. It denotes how close the adjusted

Table 3.6 Computation of moving ranges from the adjusted moving average sales forecast

Year	Quarter	Y	Centered Moving Average	Adjusted Seasonal Index	Y_F	$Y - Y_F$	MR
1964	Q3	300	281	1.00	281	19	
	Q4	220	298	0.66	196	24	5
1965	Q1	280	306	0.97	296	−16	40
	Q2	420	302	1.37	415	5	21
	Q3	310	296	1.00	296	16	11
	Q4	180	287	0.66	190	−10	26
1966	Q1	270	276	0.97	269	1	11
	Q2	360	274	1.37	375	−15	16
	Q3	280	279	1.00	279	1	16
	Q4	190	286	0.66	189	1	0
1967	Q1	300	301	0.97	294	6	5
	Q2	430	304	1.37	415	15-	9
	Q3	290	307	1.00	307	−17	32
	Q4	200	311	0.66	206	−6	11
1968	Q1	320	316	0.97	307	13	19
	Q2	440	322	1.37	441	3	10

Total = $\overline{232}$

moving averages came to fitting the past data. It also establishes a standard for how well future data should fit. This standard is the average moving range:

$$MR̄ = \frac{\sum MR}{N_{MR}} = \frac{232}{15} = 15.467 \text{ or } \$15,467$$

In control charting, $MR̄$ corresponds to the previously discussed S_y. To set limits equivalent to $3S_y$, we multiply the average moving range by 2.66. Therefore, control limits of a moving range chart for the basic problem data would be

$$\pm 2.66 MR̄ = \pm 2.66 \times 15.467 = \pm 41.14$$

These limits would be placed on both sides of the mean difference line, 0. The $Y - Y_F$ values developed from future observations would be plotted on the chart as they became available. The interpretation of resulting plot patterns would be the same as described in Example 3.7.

Other methods. The calculation methods we have considered are by no means all inclusive. Time-series forecasts can also be based on algebraic series such as

$$Y = a + b_1 X + b_2 X^2 + \cdots + b_n X^n$$

or trigonometric functions such as

$$Y = a + b_1 \sin \frac{2\pi X}{b_2} + b_3 \cos \frac{2\pi X}{b_4}$$

Probability and composite models are also available. An understanding of these methods demands mathematics beyond the level and intent of this text. When there is a need for such sophistication, studies can be pursued through the books listed in the references at the end of this chapter.

At the other end of the sophistication scale is a method often called "persistence predictions." The forecast is simply that there will be no change. While this method is the essence of simplicity, it also has the intuitive appeal of sticking with a winner. Any sports fan will agree that the present champ is usually favored in the next contest.

An α value of 1 makes persistence predictions from the exponential smoothing formula.

Persistence predictions are surprisingly successful whenever forecasting conditions are relatively stable as in mortality or weather data. But persistence falls flat where profit is made by forecasting a change as in the stock market.

3-7 CORRELATION A correlation analysis examines the degree of relationship between variables. Our work with the standard error of the estimate in Section 3-6 was a step in this direction. We calculated S_y to determine how well our prediction equation fitted the

67

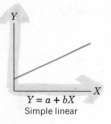

$Y = a + bX$
Simple linear

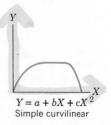

$Y = a + bX + cX^2$
Simple curvilinear

Figure 3.10 Regression lines for one independent variable

dependent variable, Y sales, to the independent variable, X years. From this beginning we can delve deeper into the correlation to obtain other useful insights.

Correlation is not limited to time-series analysis. It can be applied to the investigation of any "regression line" relating variables. Our predicting equations were regression lines relating sales to time. Sales could also be related to the gross national product, housing starts, population growth, or other economic indicators.

Simple correlation expresses the relationship between two variables and is associated with regression lines typified in Figure 3.10. Multiple correlation measures relationships among more than two variables. The surfaces shown in Figure 3.11 represent relationship between two independent variables and one dependent variable. As in previous sections, we shall focus attention on the most direct application, simple linear correlation, to understand the principles without being hobbled by excessive calculations. Many computer programs are available to relieve computational effort when it appears advisable to include a number of variables in regression equations.

Coefficient of Determination *(include this)*

The dispersion of data points about regression lines is characterized by three sums-of-squares:

$$\sum(Y - \overline{Y})^2 = \sum(Y_F - \overline{Y})^2 + \sum(Y - Y_F)^2$$

total variation   explained variation   unexplained variation

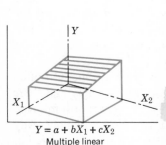

$Y = a + bX_1 + cX_2$
Multiple linear

Total variation. The deviation $(Y - \overline{Y})$, as shown in Figure 3.12, is the vertical distance between a data point and the mean of all observations, $\overline{Y} = \Sigma Y/N$. This term is a measure of the total variation of the dependent variable and is divided into two parts: the explained and the unexplained variations.

Explained variation. The variation explained by the regression line is represented by $(Y_F - \overline{Y})$. In Figure 3.12, this deviation appears as the vertical distance between the line of regression and a horizontal line at $\overline{Y}$. Thus, a b value of zero in a regression line for two variables makes $Y_F = \overline{Y}$ and the sum-of-squares of th· explained variation equals zero. This makes the total variation equal the unexplained variation as was the case for the level-line forecast, $Y_F = 117.8$, in Example 3.7. Including a slope factor b in the forecasting equation, $Y_F = 117.8 + 4.7X$, improves the prediction because the explained part of the total variation is increased.

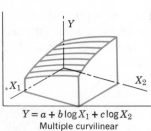

$Y = a + b\log X_1 + c\log X_2$
Multiple curvilinear

Figure 3.11 Regression lines for two independent variables

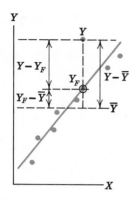

Figure 3.12 Deviation of a data point

Unexplained variation. The sum-of-squares of the unexplained variation is the familiar term used in calculating the standard error of the estimate. Because S_y measures the fit of the regression line to the data, it is logically based on the deviations unexplained by the fitted line. This term equals zero only if all the data points fall directly on the regression line. Then, of course, the regression line explicitly defines the relationship of the variables. In the more common case where the data do not coincide with the prediction equation, each deviation appears as the vertical distance from a point (Y) to the regression line.

The ratio of the sum-of-squares of the unexplained variation to the sum-of-squares of the total variation, $\Sigma(Y - Y_F)^2 / \Sigma(Y - \bar{Y})^2$, measures the proportion of the total variation that is not explained by the regression line. Therefore,

$$1 - \frac{\sum(Y - Y_F)^2}{\sum(Y - \bar{Y})^2}$$

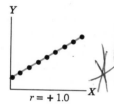

$r = +1.0$

measures the proportion of the total variation explained by the regression line. This expression is called the *coefficient of determination.*

Coefficient of Correlation

The square root of the coefficient of determination,

$$r = \sqrt{1 - \frac{\sum(Y - Y_F)^2}{\sum(Y - \bar{Y})^2}}$$

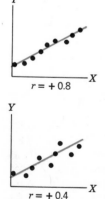

$r = +0.8$

$r = +0.4$

• is the more commonly recognized *coefficient of correlation, r.* The value under the radical can never be greater than 1 nor less than 0. However, because the radical has both positive and negative roots, the value of r is between $+1$ and -1. The plus or minus is indicative only of the slope of the regression line as depicted in the side charts. When $r = +1$, all the data points fall on an upward sloping regression line. When r is between $+1$ and 0, the regression line still slopes upward, but data points fall on either side of the line. The closer they cluster around the line, the closer r approaches 1.

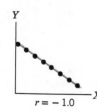

$r = -1.0$

Computation. When sufficient data are available, we can calculate r using the sums-of-squares as indicated above or, more directly, from the formula

$$r = \frac{N\sum XY - (\sum X)(\sum Y)}{\sqrt{N\sum X^2 - (\sum X)^2}\ \sqrt{N\sum Y^2 - (\sum Y)^2}}$$

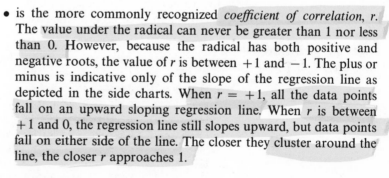

69

This equation is appropriate when the degrees of freedom do not have to be considered because there are enough data.

When data are limited, the sums-of-squares are each divided by their associated degrees of freedom. In calculating r for the sales figures in Example 3.7, we have

$$r = \sqrt{1 - \frac{\sum(Y - Y_F)^2/(N - 2)}{\sum(Y - \bar{Y})^2/(N - 1)}} = \sqrt{1 - \frac{103.1/3}{224.8/4}} = 0.617$$

The variation explained by the regression line, $Y_F = 117.8 + 4.7X$, is about $(0.617)^2 = 38\%$ of the total variance between actual sales and average sales.

Confidence. Now we have a coefficient of correlation equal to 0.617, but what can we say about our faith in the relationship it implies? We know that a greater number of observations increases our confidence in a statistic, but how many does it take to be, say, 95% confident. There are tests that allow us to make probability statements about r values obtained from a certain number of observations, N. Some critical values of r and N for 95% and 99% confidence levels are provided in Table 3.7. This table shows the value of r that must be exceeded for a sample size N to assure that the correlation coefficient is not actually zero.

The values of r in Table 3.7 were developed by a statistical test of the hypothesis that the actual value of r is zero. The hypothesis is rejected for each confidence level when r is above the values shown. Before we can be reasonably sure of some relationship, $r \neq 0$, the calculated value of r must exceed a

Table 3.7 Critical values of r for 95% and 99% confidence levels

N	95%	99%	N	95%	99%	N	95%	99%
10	0.632	0.765	30	0.361	0.463	50	0.279	0.361
12	0.576	0.708	32	0.349	0.449	60	0.254	0.330
14	0.532	0.661	34	0.339	0.436	70	0.235	0.306
16	0.497	0.623	36	0.329	0.424	80	0.220	0.287
18	0.468	0.590	38	0.320	0.413	100	0.197	0.256
20	0.444	0.561	40	0.312	0.403	150	0.161	0.210
22	0.423	0.537	42	0.304	0.393	200	0.139	0.182
24	0.404	0.515	44	0.297	0.384	400	0.098	0.128
26	0.388	0.496	46	0.291	0.376	1000	0.062	0.081
28	0.374	0.479	48	0.284	0.368			

(Source: By permission from W. J. Dixon and F. J. Massey, *Introduction to Statistical Analysis* (2nd ed.), Mc-Graw-Hill, New York, 1957.)

critical value based on the number of observations from which it is developed. Thus for a sample size of 10, $N = 10$, r must exceed ± 0.632 if we are to be 95% confident that the correlation is not just a chance occurrence. For the same sample size, r must be larger (± 0.765) to increase our confidence from 95 to 99%. As we would expect, critical r values decrease for the same confidence level as the sample size increases.

EXAMPLE 3.9 Regression and Correlation Analysis

The management of Generox, Inc., think that sales of nail drivers should logically be related to the amount spent on construction. If a relationship does exist, published government and construction industry forecasts of anticipated building levels can be used as an additional sales predictor. First a check is made to confirm that the building-level forecasts are relatively accurate. Next the national figures are broken down to conform to the Generox marketing areas. Then the records of monthly building volume and nail-driver sales for corresponding months are collected. The resulting data are tabulated as shown in Table 3.8 where the construction volume is in $100 million units and product sales are in $10,000 units. The column headings correspond to the values needed for the calculation of r and a linear regression equation.

Table 3.8 Computations required to calculate r and Y_F

Nail-driver sales $\times 10^{-4}$, Y	Construction volume $\times 10^{-8}$, X	Y^2	X^2	XY
7.1	1.8	50.51	3.24	12.78
9.9	2.3	98.01	5.29	22.78
9.0	1.9	81.00	3.61	17.10
10.4	2.6	108.16	6.76	27.04
11.1	3.1	123.21	9.61	34.41
10.9	2.8	118.81	7.84	30.52
10.5	2.9	110.25	8.41	30.45
9.8	2.4	96.04	5.76	23.52
11.1	2.8	123.21	7.84	31.08
10.2	2.5	104.04	6.25	25.50
9.7	2.3	94.09	5.29	22.31
10.9	2.8	118.81	7.84	30.52
8.8	2.1	77.44	4.41	18.48
8.6	1.9	73.96	3.61	16.34
12.3	3.2	151.29	10.24	39.36
11.4	3.0	129.96	9.00	34.20
11.2	2.8	125.44	7.84	31.36
10.2	2.6	104.04	6.76	26.52
10.7	2.7	114.49	7.29	28.89
8.6	1.9	73.96	3.61	16.34
202.4	50.4	2076.62	130.50	519.50

From this reasonably large sample, we can calculate the coefficient of correlation as

$$r = \frac{N\sum XY - (\sum X)(\sum Y)}{\sqrt{N\sum X^2 - (\sum X)^2}\sqrt{N\sum Y^2 - (\sum Y)^2}}$$

$$= \frac{20(519.5) - (50.4)(202.4)}{\sqrt{20(130.5) - (50.4)^2}\sqrt{20(2076.62) - (202.4)^2}}$$

$$r = \frac{10,390 - 10,2201}{\sqrt{2610 - 2540.16}\sqrt{41,532.4 - 40,965.7}}$$

$$= \frac{189}{(8.36)(22.82)}$$

$$= 0.991$$

Comparing the calculated $r = 0.991$ to the critical value of $r = 0.561$ in Table 3.7, we can be at least 99% confident some relationship exists between the sales of nail drivers and construction volume. The coefficient of determination

$$r^2 = (0.991)^2 = 0.982$$

specifies that about 98% of the variation in sales is explained.

Although the correlation is not exact, it is definitely worthy of consideration for prediction purposes. From the sums developed in Table 3.8, we can apply the least squares method to obtain a forecasting equation. The normal equations are

$$\sum Y = Na + b\sum X \qquad 202.4 = 20a + b(50.4)$$
$$\sum XY = a\sum X + b\sum X^2 \qquad 519.5 = a(50.4) + b(130.5)$$

which are solved for a and b to obtain

$$a = 3.37 \text{ or } \$33,700 \qquad b = 2.68 \text{ or } \$26,800$$

The forecasting equation is then

$$Y_F = 3.37 + 2.68X$$

Thus a projected construction volume of $275,000,000 for the next month would suggest a sales volume of

$$Y_F = 3.37 + 2.68(2.75) = 10.74$$

Therefore, the sales of nail drivers during the next month should be in the vicinity of $107,400.

Interpretation of Correlation Analysis

The interpretation of a regression and correlation analysis deserves respect—even suspicion. It is said that figures can lie as well as liars can figure. Recent history provides numerous examples of forecasting fiascos created by acts bordering on statistical larceny. History also records spectacular accolades earned by accurate predictions. The difference between end results is often the judgment that accompanies an analysis.

The *purpose* of forecasting is to predict the future. In doing so, we may or may not reveal a fundamental economic truth. Although it helps to know the basic foundations from which demand originates, even emanations from the source can lead to acceptable predictions. Since universal truths are seldom known, we have to inspect our estimates judiciously for shaky relationships and spurious intimations.

A value of r approaching 1 is an encouraging sign. It indicates that the relationship being investigated is potentially a useful predictor. But it is not a binding guarantee of an accurate prediction. It could be misleading because:

1. The data used to develop the regression equations are unreliable or unrepresentative.
2. An apparent correlation is a result of random chance factors.
3. A high correlation exists between two variables that are both functions of a third variable which has not been identified or included in the analysis.

The need for caution does not mean that regression and correlation analysis should be avoided. Every method of forecasting requires caution. It will be a long, long time before we can turn the crank to a collection of equations and expect foolproof answers about the future. In the meantime we must link our equations to a thorough knowledge of influencing economic elements and a careful diagnostic evaluation of each step in the forecast development.

★ ★ ★ *End optional material.*

Sales of English and math textbooks could show a high correlation, but they are both a function of an independent variable: number of students.

3-8 SUMMARY Modern production planning is heavily dependent on forecasts of demand or activity. Forecast can be developed from opinions of consumers, customers, distributors, and executives; by marketing trials and market research; or through analysis of historical data.

A time-series analysis defines how production indicators vary with time. The factors affecting a time-series forecast, $Y = TCSR$, are

T = underlying long-term trend of the indicator
C = cyclic variations about the trend
S = seasonal variations within the trend
R = residual or remaining unexplained variations

Best-fit trend lines, either straight or curved, can be developed by the least squares method. The resulting line equation is extrapolated to estimate future demand. A simple average or a moving average forecast corrected by a seasonal index damps out seasonal fluctuations to indicate future activity. Exponential smoothing places emphasis on more recent data according to the selection of α, the smoothing constant, in the forecasting equation $F_n = \alpha Y_{n-1} + (1 - \alpha)F_{n-1}$.

The choice among line-fitting and iterative forecasting methods depends on the type and quantity of data available, allowable analysis cost, and desired predicting accuracy. The standard error of the estimate, $S_y = \sqrt{\Sigma(Y - Y_F)^2/\nu}$, measures the fit obtained by line-fitting methods. It can also be incorporated in charts to evaluate forecasts with reference to current data. The iterative moving average method employs an average moving range $M\overline{R}$ in the same manner as S_y to determine if past data are statistically stable and if present data are following the past pattern.

A correlation analysis examines the degree of relationship between variables. It starts with the calculation of a regression equation which mathematically relates two or more variables. The coefficient of determination

$$r^2 = \frac{\text{explained variation}}{\text{total variation}}$$

indicates the proportion of the data dispersion explained by the regression equation. The coefficient of correlation is the square root of r^2 and measures the amount of association between variables on a scale from $+1$ to -1.

Effective use of forecasting equations requires an intimate knowledge of the economic forces affecting the prediction and a searching evaluation of the source, mechanics, and interpretation of forecasting models.

3-9 REFERENCES

Acton, F. S., *Analysis of Straight-Line Data*, John Wiley, New York, 1959.

Biegel, J. E., *Production Control: A Quantitative Approach*, Prentice-Hall, Englewood Cliffs, N.J., 1963.

Brown, R. G., *Smoothing, Forecasting, and Prediction of Discrete Time Series*, Prentice-Hall, Englewood Cliffs, N.J., 1963.

Dixon, W. J. and F. J. Massey, *Introduction to Statistical Analysis* (2nd ed.), McGraw-Hill, New York, 1957.

Ezekiel, M. and K. A. Fox, *Methods of Correlation and Regression Analysis* (3rd ed.), John Wiley, New York, 1941.

Harman, H., *Modern Factor Analysis*, Univ. of Chicago Press, Chicago, Ill., 1960.

Hummel, F. E., *Market and Sales Potentials*, Ronald Press, New York, 1961.

Thurstone, L. L., *Multiple Factor Analysis*, Univ. of Chicago Press, Chicago, Ill., 1947.

Williams, E. J., *Regression Analysis*, John Wiley, New York, 1959.

3-10 QUESTIONS AND PROBLEMS

1. Assume that you are manager of a small sawmill and logging operation. You have no formal forecasting personnel or procedures. It is now time to prepare your broad production plans for next year. An estimate of the total board feet required from the logging operation and a rough breakdown of the sizes of finished lumber are required. From what sources could estimates be obtained? Evaluate the sources.

2. Why are consumers' opinions likely to be more objective than distributors' opinions?

3. Two firms are considering market trials for new products they have developed. One firm has perfected a portable, heavy-duty, laser metal cutter; the other firm has a new educational game for preschoolers. Both plan to use the trial to determine the acceptance and potential demand for their new products. Is this plan logical for both firms? What considerations should be included in designing the market trial?

4. Why should historical data used in forecasting be questioned if you know the information is correct? Give some examples.

5. Does the sum-of-squares of $(Y - Y_F)$ for the exponential line of Example 3.3 equal zero? Why?

6. Why bother to center a moving average?

7. What limits the use of the most recently calculated moving average as a forecast for the next period? (For instance, in Example 3.5 the most recent centered moving average is 322 and might be used as the forecast for the next period, $Q1_{1969}$.)

8. Explain the statement: The response to a changing pattern improves with higher smoothing constants (α) in exponential smoothing just as it does with smaller values of N in moving average forecasts.

9. Could a standard error of the estimates, S_y, be calculated for exponential smoothing predictions? Why?

10. How is the standard error of the estimate related to the coefficient of determination?

11. How does the average moving range control chart conform to the principle of "managing by exception"?

75

12. Monthly sales in thousands of dollars for the past 2 years are shown below:

Month	2 Years ago	1 Year ago
Jan.	253	250
Feb.	236	252
Mar.	245	248
Apr.	246	241
May	260	247
June	251	244
July	249	244
Aug.	242	249
Sept.	234	251
Oct.	244	238
Nov.	246	249
Dec.	257	252

(a) Fit a line to the data and determine a forecast for the next month (January).

(b) Calculate the coefficient of correlation. Interpret your answer.

(c) Establish the cumulative demand through June of next year. What is the range within which the cumulative demand would be expected to fall 95% of the time?

(d) Establish a forecast for January of next year by use of a 6-month moving average.

(e) Select an initial forecast from part (a) and use $\alpha = 0.2$ to determine the forecast for next January by exponential smoothing.

(f) Compare the forecasts from (a), (d), and (e). Which one would you select? Why?

13. The current sales for the product depicted in Problem 12 are shown below:

Month	Sales	Month	Sales
Jan.	251	July	257
Feb.	261	Aug.	266
Mar.	258	Sept.	280
Apr.	256	Oct.	271
May	262	Nov.	293
June	258	Dec.	278

(a) Using the data of Problem 12, develop a moving range control chart and plot current sales. What conclusions can you make?

(b) Plot current sales on a chart developed from the equation used in Problem 12. Compare this chart and the information it imparts to the one in part (a) above.

(c) What forecast would you make for January of the following year? Explain your reasons.

14. Given:

Year:	1	2	3	4	5	6	7	8
Demand:	90	100	107	113	123	136	144	155

(a) Plot the data and establish a forecast for year 9.

(b) Establish the 95% confidence limits and plot them on the graph developed in part (a) above.

(c) Compare forecasts using exponential smoothing with $\alpha = 0.15$ and $F_0 = 85$ to the Y_F values obtained by the regression equation established in part (a).

15. Annual sales for a company in the steel industry closely followed the regression line $Y = 422(1.025)^X$ for a period of 12 years. During the following 5 years the sales followed $Y = 567 - 0.116X$. In the last 2 years, sales increased by 3% each year. What forecast would you make for the next year?

16. Quarterly unit demands for a product are given below:

Year	Winter	Spring	Summer	Fall	
1	81	64	73	83	30l
2	80	70	84	74	308
3	86	59	71	73	289
4	98	72	74	64	30P
5	106	68	75	60	309
	451	333	377	354	1515

(a) Using a four-period moving average, determine a seasonal adjusted index and establish a forecast for each quarter of next year.

(b) For the information in part (a), calculate the limits which would be exceeded by chance about three times in a thousand.

(c) Use line-fitting methods to determine a forecast for each period of next year.

77

CHAPTER 4

CAPITAL BUDGETING

4-1 IMPORTANCE The name of the game is money. Financing is a common challenge to both the production manager of a large corporation and the owner-manager of a small job shop. The challenge arises because there are more worthy ways to spend money than there is capital available. The capital must be budgeted or rationed to the most worthwhile projects. The problem then becomes one of making decision rules to select the most profitable expenditures. Among the questions that must be considered are:

1. Should long- or short-range objectives be optimized?
2. What is the pattern of future cash flow?
3. How should intangible considerations be included?
4. What is the risk involved?

In this chapter we shall investigate the broad aspects of the capital-budgeting problem and then concentrate on specific quantitative approaches to the solution.

4-2 TACTICS AND STRATEGIES

"Quantities derive from measurement, numbers from quantities, comparisons from numbers, and victory from comparisons." Sun Tsu, Art of War.

A popular retort by harassed managers is: "You don't understand the big picture!" Not only is the retort popular, it also is often accurate. Too much attention to the elements of production can obscure the purpose of production. At the other extreme, a • preoccupation with production is wasted if day-to-day operating problems are neglected and subsequently damage output. Profitable production depends on both efficient operations and an effective policy or, equivalently, efficient tactics and effective strategy.

There is no sharp demarcation between tactics and strategy. The military version of the terms distinguishes tactics as the art of handling troops from strategy as employment of means on a broad scale. But where does the handling of troops cease to be the employment of means? Consider a military objective to be the capture of a hill by several combat platoons. The strategic plan is for one platoon to make a diversionary frontal assault

78

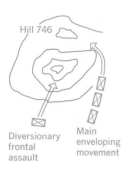

Hill 746

Diversionary
frontal
assault

Main
enveloping
movement

while the remaining platoons perform an enveloping movement. To the leader of the assault platoon, a direct attack might seem an absurd plan. He could lead his men on a gradual advance that would certainly reduce the platoon's casualties. This is a more efficient tactic from his viewpoint, but it would ruin the effectiveness of the strategic plan and would likely increase total casualties. This is an example of *suboptimization*—an attempt to optimize a tactical segment of a problem with little or no regard for the strategic effectiveness of the solution.

Suboptimization

Less bloody but similarly damaging effects of suboptimization continually plague industrial management. In a production setting, tactics could be the daily handling of men and machines. Strategy is the coordination of the entire production department with other functions of the firm. Suboptimization might develop from the commendable effort of a foreman to increase the length of production runs. This tactic would decrease the set-up costs and probably increase the efficiency of the involved men and machines. It would also increase storage costs by enlarging the inventory on hand. Perhaps the capital tied up in inventory is urgently needed elsewhere in the organization. Thus an action designed to cut costs in one area could actually decrease total profit—suboptimization.

Organizational suboptimization is logically attacked by improving communications. The approach is far easier to recognize than it is to implement. Traditionally, tables of organization are established to outline the areas of responsibility and authority of personnel. Information is ideally channeled vertically or horizontally on a "need to know" basis. Decisions are made on one level subject to review by an upper level and carried out by a lower level. Years of operation have proven that this orthogonal agreement works quite well when messages are transmitted freely and accurately. Modifications such as internal information centers are designed to take advantage of new high-speed data-processing machines.

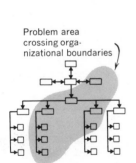

Problem area
crossing orga-
nizational boundaries

Orthogonal organization and
information flow.

The advent of computers and automated data processing has certainly increased the timeliness, quantity, and quality of information, but it has not necessarily solved the problem of suboptimization. Figure 4.1 symbolically shows an organization's flow of information and decisions concerning a tactical portion of the production system. In theory, such a flow should make each production decision compatible with the total organizational policy. The weak link in the system is people. Until all messages

79

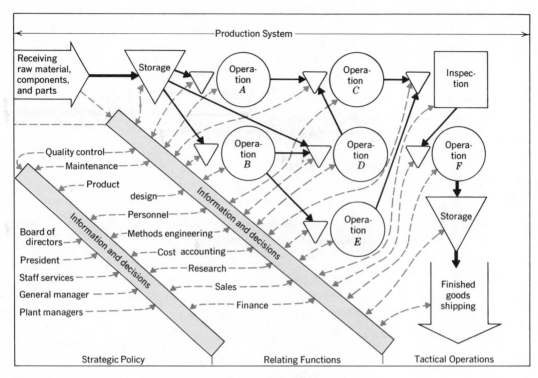

Figure 4.1 Information, decision, and product flow in a production system

are originated expeditiously, interpreted as intended, and acted upon when expected, suboptimization will remain a danger.

Sensitivity

Another aspect of tactics and strategies deals with the sensitivity of a decision, the vulnerability of an optimal solution to changes in controlling conditions. As tentative strategies are formulated, they are rated concerning effectiveness. The effectiveness scale may be in dollars, tons of production, or some nondimensional rating such as percentage points that reflect a combination of tangible and intangible factors. There are often several ways to pursue each strategy. These alternate means of executing a certain policy are then rated as to their tactical efficiency. When the tactical alternatives of a less attractive strategy rate with or above the tactics associated with the preferred strategy, we have a sensitive decision situation as shown in Figure 4.2*b*.

The degree of sensitivity in a decision situation indicates the need for additional planning. In Figure 4.2*a*, the tactics required to implement strategy *A* in both plants show a higher efficiency than any tactic available for strategy *B*. This condition confirms the superiority of strategy *A* over *B*. In the sensitive decision situation depicted in Figure 4.2*b*, the best tactic for strategy *B* rates with or above the highest tactic for strategy *A* in each plant. A slight miscalculation of efficiencies could reverse either of the top ratings. The need for more study to confirm the ratings should be apparent to the decision maker. The amount of study warranted is a function of the analysis cost and the significance of the decision. In the following sections, we shall consider several types of planning studies.

4-3 PRIMARY STUDIES Studies of an immediate nature which disregard risk and the time effect of investments are termed "primary." The assumption of certainty and the short planning horizon in no way relegate primary decisions to trivial comparisons. Many significant questions are decided by primary studies. Sometimes information is not available or the cost and time required for a complete study prohibit more extensive analysis. Particularly in a planning phase, primary studies reveal enough data to weed out unworkable alternatives.

Breakeven Analysis

An important economic figure in primary studies is the point in time or production output where a product begins to show a profit—the breakeven point. The computations or charts used

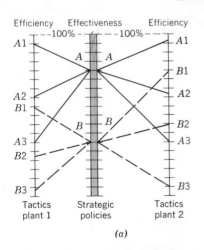

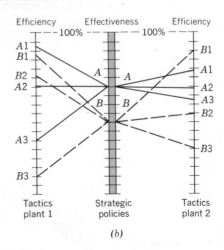

(a)   (b)

Figure 4.2 (*a*) A relatively insensitive decision situation and (*b*) a sensitive decision situation

81

to determine the breakeven point also establish a model of the relationships between revenue, fixed costs, variable costs, and output. Any variable in the model can be altered to determine its effect on the other variables. In this way, alternative courses of action may be simulated and evaluated in the planning stage.

Revenue, costs, and capacity relationships. A traditional breakeven chart shows revenue and costs as a linear function of output. As illustrated in Figure 4.3, total cost is the sum of fixed cost and total variable cost for each level of production noted on the horizontal axis. Revenue is the product of selling price and the number of units made and sold. To appreciate the diagnostic potential of the graph, we have to consider the significance of implied assumptions and the mathematical relationships of the charted variables.

Fixed costs (FC) are represented by a horizontal line. The assumption that these costs are constant over a given capacity range is feasible for two reasons. The first is that, by definition, fixed costs are expenses that continue regardless of production levels. Typical costs included in this category are rent, interest, property taxes, insurance, research, and indirect labor. The second reason is that the chart represents conditions expected over a relatively short time span. Therefore, no special capacity-induced procedures, such as layoffs or new equipment investments, are included in the limited planning range.

Unit variable costs (V) are also constant over the period and capacity range of the chart. These costs account for the direct expenses of producing a product such as spoilage, packaging, raw materials, and direct labor. Total variable cost (TVC) is the unit cost times the number of units produced (N) or $TVC = NV$.

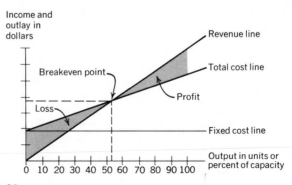

Figure 4.3 Linear breakeven chart

N = number of units
FC = fixed cost
V = unit variable cost
TVC = total variable cost
= NV
TC = total cost
= $TVC + FC$
P = unit selling price
R = revenue
= NP
Z = profit
= $R - TC$
B = breakeven volume
= $FC/(P - V)$
$P - V$ = unit contribution

A linear revenue line (R) results from the assumption that each product sells for the same price (P). When this assumption is valid, $R = NP$.

• The breakeven point (B) indicates the number of units that must be made and sold before costs equal revenue, $R = TVC + FC$. To solve for B mathematically, we simply find the value of N that equates costs and revenue; $B = N$ when $NP = NV + FC$, or

$$\text{breakeven volume} = B = \frac{\text{fixed cost}}{\text{contribution}} = \frac{FC}{P - V}$$

For production less than B, the unit contribution ($P - V$) serves to pay off the fixed cost. When N exceeds B, ($P - V$) is the *incremental profit* expected from each additional unit made and sold.

$$B.E \not= \frac{F.C}{1 - \frac{T.V.C}{T.S.V(sales)}} \qquad 200,000$$

EXAMPLE 4.1 Breakeven Alternatives

One type of appliance manufactured by a large electronics firm has consistently experienced a loss. The product must be continued in order to offer distributors a complete line. The most recent revenue and cost figures show an annual fixed cost of $90,000 and a total variable cost of $192,000 on sales of 12,000 units which account for a revenue of $240,000. Costs and revenue are directly proportional to the production rate which is 25,000 units per year at 100% capacity. What alternatives should be evaluated in an attempt to improve the product's competitive position?

At least four alternatives are immediately apparent to relieve the current loss (negative profit):

$$Z = R - (TVC + FC)$$

$$= \$240,000 - (\$192,000 + \$90,000) = -\$42,000$$

1. Fixed costs could possibly be reduced. For Z to equal zero in order to breakeven with the other variables remaining unchanged, the new fixed cost (FC') must not exceed

$$FC' = R - TVC = \$240,000 - \$192,000 = \$48,000$$

The required reduction, $90,000 - $48,000 = $42,000, equals the total current loss and would certainly be difficult to obtain by cutting only fixed costs. A check of the accounting procedures should at least be made to see if the product is bearing a disproportionate share of the total factory fixed costs such as supervisory overhead and equipment depreciation.

2. Total variable cost is a more likely candidate for a cost-reduction program. Improved methods, materials, processes, or work procedures offer potential savings. The current unit variable cost,

$$V = \frac{\$192,000}{12,000 \text{ units}} = \$16 \text{ per unit}$$

must be reduced to

$$V' = \frac{R - FC}{N} = \frac{\$240,000 - \$90,000}{12,000} = \$12.50$$

to breakeven when R, FC, and N are fixed.

83

3. Revenue can be increased by selling more units, raising the price per unit, or a combination of both actions. As opposed to internal cost control, pricing policies and sales volumes are largely restricted by factors outside the firm. Higher pricetags are easily attached to a product, but they usually make it harder to sell. Competition tends to set a limit on price boosting. (Under rather rare circumstances, a product may be immune to competitive pressure. New inventions, geographical isolation, limited supplies, or first issues may provide a temporary monopoly.) Marketing is further restricted by including the finite consumer demand along with the pressures of competition. Therefore, it appears unreasonable to rely on a new price,

$$P' = V + \frac{FC}{N} = \$16 + \frac{\$90,000}{12,000} = \$23.50$$

or an increase of $23.50 − ($240,000/12,000) = $3.50 to avoid the present deficit with other conditions fixed.

4. The question of output can be further explored by adding a new line to the traditional break-even chart—the cost of nonproduction. The new line slopes downward in Figure 4.4 as production increases. When there is no production, the loss is equal to the fixed cost of the product. At 100% capacity, the production expected when the plant is operating at its design maximum, the nonproduction costs are zero.

Each unit produced and sold reduces nonproductive costs by FC/N_{max}. For the product under consideration,

$$\text{unit nonproduction cost} = \frac{\$90,000}{25,000 \text{ units}} = \$3.60 \text{ per unit}$$

and

$$\text{total nonproduction cost} = (25,000 - 12,000) \; \$3.60 = \$46,800$$

is the penalty being paid for not using production facilities to full advantage. The only way to eliminate this cost is to produce and sell 13,000 additional units per year. The minimum incremental revenue to breakeven at full capacity is

$$P' = V + \frac{FC}{N_{max}} = \$16 + \$3.60 = \$19.60$$

which is slightly less than the present selling price, $P = \$20$. The 40-cent difference could be applied as a price reduction or allotted to the advertising budget to increase sales.

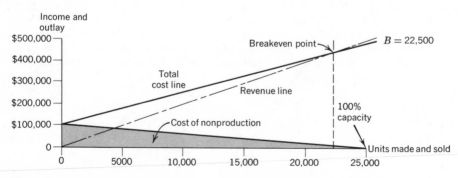

Figure 4.4 Cost of excess capacity

It is doubtful if any of the individual measures we have considered would be applied singularly. Some combination would appear more realistic. One danger in production planning is mental tunnel vision that blocks a complete survey of cost and revenue relationships.

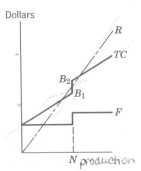

Dollars

Step increase in fixed cost with two breakeven points.

Step and slope changes in cost lines. Special pricing and cost arrangements can be incorporated in a linear breakeven analysis by allowing discontinuous lines and slopes. Occasionally fixed or variable costs rise or fall abruptly beyond a certain production level. A sharp rise in fixed costs could occur when a new machine or production line must be added to increase capacity beyond a certain point. Direct labor costs climb abruptly when overtime
• is necessary to boost output above a given level. Such variable cost changes are shown on a chart as steeper TC lines associated with affected segments of output.

if production is < N, profit up to N, loss around N, then π

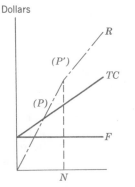

Dollars

Dumping price for sales beyond *N*.

Dumping. The practice of reducing the selling price on a distinct portion of output to utilize otherwise excess capacity is called *dumping.* It is graphically represented by a flatter slope of the revenue line over the extra output permitted through dumping. The basis for this strategy is that the main market for a product has only a limited maximum demand. In the belief that no additional units can be sold to this market, a secondary demand is developed by offering the same quality units at a lower price.
• This lower price is necessary to make the product attractive in a market area otherwise unavailable. For instance, foreign sales are a secondary market, or the same product under a different name sold through different retail outlets can be a subordinate domestic market. The obvious limitation is that the consumers must not be aware that they can get the same product at two different prices or the lower price will become the base price. When dumping works as intended, both total profit and factory utilization are improved.

EXAMPLE 4.2   Utilization of Plant Capacity

The manufacturers of "Wonderwashers" are presently operating at 75% capacity. A large retail chainstore will sell Wonderwashers under the chain's own trade name if extra accessories are added which will increase variable production cost by 4%. The tentative agreement will increase production to full capacity of the plant, but the selling price for the extra 25% output will be only 89% of the usual price for Wonderwashers. To exceed 80% capacity, the manufacturer will have to reopen an outdated assembly line where fixed costs are 25% higher and variable costs are 6% greater. The present plant operating conditions are:

1. Output: 91,500 units per year (75% plant capacity).

85

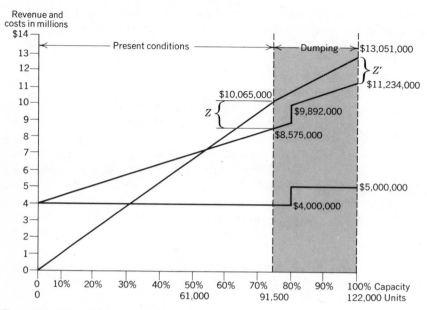

Figure 4.5 Effect of a proposed dumping agreement

2. Price: $110 per unit (wholesale price to regular distributors).
3. Variable cost: $50 per unit.
4. Fixed cost: $4,000,000.

The immediate consequences of accepting the agreement allowing 100% utilization of facilities are quite apparent in a breakeven chart as shown in Figure 4.5. At 75% capacity, incremental revenue decreases to $P' = \$110(0.89) = \$97.90$ per unit and unit variable cost increases to $V' = \$50(1.04) = \$52$. A step increase of $\$4,000,000(0.25) = \$1,000,000$ in fixed cost occurs at 80% capacity with another increase in variable cost to $55. The total profit under present conditions is

$$Z = 91{,}500(\$110) - [91{,}500(\$50) + \$4{,}000{,}000] = \$1{,}490{,}000$$

The expected profit obtained by dumping through the chain is

$$Z' = 91{,}500(\$110) + 30{,}500(\$97.90)$$
$$- [91{,}500(\$50) + 6100(\$52) + 24{,}400(\$55) + \$4{,}000{,}000(1.25)]$$
$$= \$1{,}817{,}000$$

Although the potential profit increase is inviting, the makers of Wonderwashers should look beyond the period depicted in the breakeven chart to question possible future revenue and cost changes.

1. Will the fixed cost of the old assembly line used for the 20% extra production remain as estimated? If the fixed cost increases by 35% instead of 25%, the company will lose money on the agreement.

86

2. Will selling the same product under a different brand name affect sales of Wonderwashers? A 7% drop in basic sales would make total profit less than is currently earned.
3. Can the dumping agreement be extended for several years? If so, unit variable costs on the old assembly line probably can be reduced to the level of the rest of the plant.

Nonlinear relationships. It is occasionally worthwhile to fit a curve to revenue and cost functions. Straight lines are normally close enough approximations for breakeven planning, even though real-world data seldom plot with such convenient directness. When realism or accuracy suggests nonlinear relationships, the methods discussed in Chapter 3 can be employed to develop appropriate line formulas.

Nonlinear economic models often appear quite frightening. A liberal sprinkling of differential and integral signs creates a discouraging facade. But in most cases an elementary knowledge of calculus is sufficient preparation. The graphical interpretation of curved and straight lines is similar, but calculus rather than algebra is the foundation for quantitative evaluation of nonlinear expressions.

After line-fitting procedures are applied to develop descriptive equations, the expressions can be differentiated to determine slopes for revenue, cost, or profit lines. Being curved lines, the slope changes in infinitesimal steps for different output values. The rate of change of slope is called the *marginal revenue* or *marginal cost*—difference in income or outlay caused by the next unit of output at a specified level of production. At a point where the slope is level and equal to zero, a maximum or minimum of the function is indicated. Such points are useful in deciding what level of production produces the maximum profit or minimum average unit cost. Calculations for some critical production points based on linear and nonlinear relationships are compared in Figure 4.6.

Multiple products. Some companies grow by adding new but related products to their basic line. Many factors force such diversification. As technology increases, a company has to run just to maintain its present position. Each new advance means at least a model change to remain competitive. Each model change means a wider range of products because some users stay loyal to older, familiar models. Product and production planning must organize or even govern the explosion of catalog offerings.

Decisions to add and drop products are subject to sub-optimization. One problem, which we shall term "insular

87

not responsible for *have awareness* *can be handled*

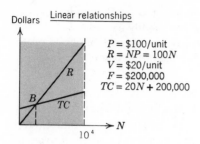

Linear relationships

Dollars

$P = \$100/\text{unit}$
$R = NP = 100N$
$V = \$20/\text{unit}$
$F = \$200,000$
$TC = 20N + 200,000$

B R TC

N

10^4

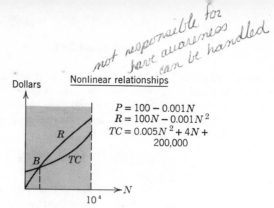

Nonlinear relationships

Dollars

$P = 100 - 0.001N$
$R = 100N - 0.001N^2$
$TC = 0.005N^2 + 4N + 200,000$

B R TC

N

10^4

To determine breakeven output, B:

Linear	Nonlinear
$Z = 0 = R - TC$	$Z = 0 = R - TC$
$\quad = 100N - 20N - 200,000$	$\quad = 100N - 0.001N^2 - 0.005N^2$
$\quad 0 = 80N - 200,000$	$\quad\quad\quad - 4N - 200,000$
$N = B = 2500$ units	$\quad 0 = -0.006N^2 + 96N - 200,000$
	$N = B = 2477$ units

To determine output for maximum profit:

Marginal profit = contribution

Contribution $= P - V = \$80/\text{unit}$

Total contribution increases as N
increases

Maximum profit $= Z_{max}$ occurs at
$N_{max} = 10,000$ for given data

Marginal profit $= dZ/dN$

$$\frac{dZ}{dN} = \frac{d(-0.006N^2 + 96N - 200,000)}{dN}$$

$$\quad = -0.012N + 96$$

Z_{max} occurs where $dZ/dN = 0$:
then $0.012N = 96$

Z_{max} occurs at $N = 96/0.012 = 8000$

To determine output for minimum average unit cost:

Average cost $= AC = \dfrac{TC}{N}$

$AC = 20 + \dfrac{200,000}{N}$

AC_{min} occurs at N_{max}

$N_{max} = 10,000$ for given data

$AC = \dfrac{TC}{N} = 0.005N + 4 + \dfrac{200,000}{N}$

AC_{min} occurs where $\dfrac{d(AC)}{dN} = 0$

$0 = 0.005 - \dfrac{200,000}{N^2}$

AC_{min} occurs at $N = \sqrt{\dfrac{200,000}{0.005}} = 6325$

Figure 4.6 Comparison of calculations for linear and nonlinear relationships

suboptimization," deals with a tendency to focus on the solution
to a particular issue at the expense of wider welfare. For instance,
one product in a family of related products could be in trouble.
To extract this product from its unfavorable position, it is
necessary to redeploy company resources such as advertising
budgets, engineering time, and capital investments. The actions
could heal the ailing product while poisoning the other family
members. A planning evaluation to avoid such problems is
described in Example 4.3.

88

EXAMPLE 4.3 Multiproduct Planning ✳

Ador, Inc., manufactures exterior and interior house doors, wooden screen doors, and overhead garage doors. House doors were the original product followed by the garage and screen doors. Increasing popularity for aluminum screen doors with consequent sagging sales for wooden screen doors inspired a study to see if the company should enter the metal door market. The study concluded that preformed metal door parts could be subcontracted and then fabricated in the plant using most of the personnel now engaged in making wooden screen doors. Very little new equipment would have to be purchased. Most of the equipment for the wooden doors could be retained because it is also used for the other products. The following cost and marketing figures presented a glowing endorsement for the proposed product.

	Wooden Screen Doors	Metal Screen Doors
Revenue	$325,000	$400,000
Variable cost	$105,000	$280,000
Fixed cost	$185,000	$60,000
Profit	$35,000	$60,000

A more comprehensive picture of product relationships is obtained by including all the economic facts in one graph. The multiproduct breakeven chart of Figure 4.7 has the total fixed cost of all Ador's products entered on the vertical scale below the zero profit point. The horizontal scale is capacity in units of production or sales. Each product is represented by a line segment sloping upward to the right. The slope of each segment is set by the product's contribution; the length is set by the number sold. The breakeven point for the chain of products occurs where the chain crosses the zero line.

Before and after information is needed for all related products to make a multiproduct chart comparison. Present and proposed data for the house and garage doors are shown below and are included in Figure 4.7.

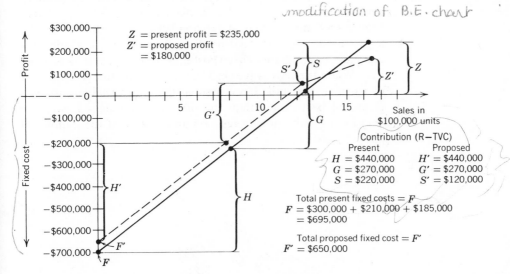

Figure 4.7 Multiproduct breakeven chart

	Present		Proposed	
	House Doors (H)	Garage Doors (G)	House Doors (H')	Garage Doors (G')
Revenue (R)	$800,000	$450,000	$800,000	$450,000
Total variable cost (TVC)	$360,000	$180,000	$360,000	$180,000
Fixed cost (F)	$300,000	$210,000	$350,000	$240,000

It is apparent from the cost estimates that the introduction of metal screen doors is not expected to boost sales of the other doors, but it will increase their burden of fixed costs. This logical but easily overlooked development results from a switch in materials. Previously, all three doors shared the fixed cost of a basically wood-oriented plant. If metal replaces one wood product without a corresponding deletion of fixed overhead, the remaining wood products must carry the load of existing plant facilities and operations. Thus we see where an "insular" study could show savings of $60,000 − $35,000 = $25,000 in the trouble area which actually create an overall loss of $235,000 − $180,000 = $55,000.

Multiple comparisons. The revenue or costs expected from several alternatives also can be displayed in a breakeven chart. Other than the visual presentation possibilities, there is little reason to commit the comparisons to a graph. A chart simply shows the result of algebraically equating each pair of alternatives. The breakeven point, B, is the output that makes two courses of action equivalent. The conditions that determine the feasibility of a production level above or below B control the decision.

Many "make or buy" decisions fit the criteria of primary comparisons which can be displayed on breakeven charts. Figure 4.8 depicts a tactical decision between building or buying a part used in a fabricated product. When a part is made by a company, some share of fixed cost must be charged to its production. When the part is purchased, there is only the variable cost of its price per unit. If we assume that the variable cost of a produced part is less than the price of a purchased part, the decision to make or buy rests on an estimate of the number of parts needed.

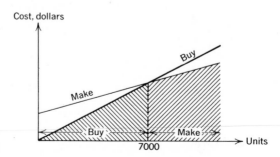

Figure 4.8 Make or buy comparison

Make or buy decisions also illustrate another type of sub-optimization. *Temporal suboptimization* is the curse of short-sighted planners; it leads to a loss of tactical efficiency through not looking far enough ahead. Assume demand for the part described in Figure 4.8 is 3000 units per year. A planning horizon of 2 years yields a preference to buy the part. This choice is obviously suboptimal if the demand for the part continues for $2\frac{1}{2}$ years or longer. With *de facto* knowledge, such errors seem foolish, but they can be avoided only by exposing the decision to the demons of uncertainty.

Intangible Comparisons

How do you measure the relative beauty of two new designs or the value of goodwill in competitive strategies? There is no general agreement as to the best or even a satisfying way to make such measurements, but everyone recognizes the need for them. These elusive considerations are called *intangibles* because they are difficult to appreciate, classify, and quantify.

Intangibles affect a decision whether or not they are formally evaluated. Sometimes they take the form of a vague feeling; at other times they create an ill-defined but urgent impression to act in a certain fashion. A step toward valid comparisons is accomplished by just recognizing that intangibles exist. Further progress is made by attempting to reduce intangibles to some rating system. And a major advance is achieved by including the ratings in a formal evaluation.

Rating. A common enigma faced by busy people is setting priorities for tackling accumulated tasks. This problem is an intangible rating puzzle because urgency has no physical dimensions that allow normal measurement comparisons. A simple listing according to the importance given each task might suffice. Such a list forms a *simple order scale*. A more elaborate method is an *interval scale* where some grade or numerical weight is attached to each task. In this approach a top level of perfection or maximum urgency is designated and all items receive a relative rating. For instance, a certain quality of workmanship would be considered the highest attainable with a rating of 100; other levels of less quality might be 90 = very good, 80 = average, 60 = barely satisfactory, 30 = unsatisfactory, and 0 = ridiculously bad. In practice, the point scoring would be tied to more complete descriptions, but the actual rating would remain more subjective than objective.

In comparing the intangible qualifications of alternatives, we

Temperature measurements are made on interval scales.

usually need two sets of ratings; one is the alternative's rank within each quality designation and the other is a measure of the relative importance among qualities. A beauty contest offers a good example. Each contestant is rated for such qualities as poise, personality, profile, and proportions. Assuming some acceptable scale for a classic profile, perfect figure, and proper composure can be agreed upon, the judges must also decide which qualities are more important. If they deem mental balance more notable than physical build, they will give higher priority or greater weight to poise than to proportions.

Exponential comparison model. Just as there are several ways to make quality ratings, there are different opinions concerning the best method for including the ratings in a comparison model. In this section we shall consider a multiplicative routine. The ratings for each quality of a pair of alternatives are raised to a power corresponding to the importance attached to the quality. The resulting numbers are multiplied together to obtain an evaluating product.

Returning to the beauty contest example, suppose two girls have the following rating:

A perfect rating is 100 points.

	Poise	Personality	Profile	Proportions
Beauty 1	80	85	85	90
Beauty 2	70	90	85	95

Also assume that the poise-personality-profile-proportions qualities have respective importance ratings of 4-3-2-2-, where higher numbers indicate more importance. By the exponential model, the evaluating product is calculated as

$$\frac{\text{Beauty 1}}{\text{Beauty 2}} = \left(\frac{80}{70}\right)^4 \left(\frac{85}{90}\right)^3 \left(\frac{85}{85}\right)^2 \left(\frac{90}{95}\right)^2$$

$$= (1.143)^4 (0.944)^3 (1)^2 (0.947)^2$$

$$= (1.69)(0.83)(1)(0.90) = 1.26$$

A product greater than 1.0 means the numerator is larger than the denominator. Since the rating routine is based on a preference for larger numbers, Beauty 1 (the numerator in the model) is the winner.

The mechanics of the comparison require all the quality ratings to show a preference for either high or low numbers.

This establishes the meaning of the evaluating product; when lower numbers are preferred, a product greater than 1.0 means that the alternative in the denominator is favored. Higher numbered importance ratings always denote the more critical qualities.

The theory supporting the exponential model starts with the concept that by making a fraction from each quality, any dimensional properties are cancelled. Then the fractions are increased exponentially to accentuate the importance weighting. Finally, these dimensionless, magnified numbers are multiplied rather than added to account for the interrelationship of the qualities. The weakness of any approach to intangible comparisons is the inherent reliance on subjective quality. However, the exponential model does allow such diverse dimensions as pounds, pecks, or pennies and such qualities as personality, profile, or proportions to be directly included in an objective appraisal routine.

EXAMPLE 4.4 A Planning Decision with Intangible Considerations

"Ipso Facto," a thriving, independent, data-processing company, is planning an image-improvement and business-expansion campaign. Three courses of action have been proposed:

1. Tell-sell—develop a staff to increase personal contacts with old and proposed clients, offer short courses and educational programs on the benefits of modern data-processing methods.
2. Soft-sell—hire a staff to put out a professional newsletter about data-processing activities, volunteer data-processing services for community and charity projects.
3. Jell-sell—hire personnel to develop new service areas and offer customized service to potential customers; donate consulting time to charitable organizations.

Only one of the three alternatives can be currently implemented owing to budgetary limitations.

The effects or returns for each alternative are rated according to desired qualities, and the importance of each quality is ranked as shown below:

	Annual Cost	Audience Reached	Immediate Effectiveness*	Long-Range Effectiveness*
Tell-sell	$120,000	80%	0.5	0.7
Soft-sell	80,000	50%	0.8	0.6
Jell-sell	95,000	40%	0.7	0.9
Importance	1	1	3	2

*Rated on an effectiveness scale with a top rating of 1.0.

Comparing Tell-sell to Soft-sell in a model showing preference for large numbers, we have

$$\frac{\text{Tell-sell}}{\text{Soft-sell}} = \left(\frac{1/120,000}{1/80,000}\right)^1 \left(\frac{80}{50}\right)^1 \left(\frac{0.5}{0.8}\right)^3 \left(\frac{0.7}{0.6}\right)^2 = 0.35$$

A definite preference is indicated for Soft-sell which is then compared to the alternative Jell-sell as

$$\frac{\text{Soft-sell}}{\text{Jell-sell}} = \left(\frac{1/80,000}{1/95,000}\right)^1 \left(\frac{50}{40}\right)^1 \left(\frac{0.8}{0.7}\right)^3 \left(\frac{0.6}{0.9}\right)^2 = 0.97$$

The narrow edge given Jell-sell in the model should suggest a need for more study or perhaps the introduction of a new alternative which combines the best features of promotional and consulting efforts.

4-4 STUDIES ASSUMING CERTAINTY

An assumption of certainty in a planning study means only one outcome is considered for each alternative. Every planner knows the unusual can occur, but in most cases it is not necessary or feasible to devote study time for an all-inclusive investigation. This practice is not as callous or incautious as it may first appear. For many outcomes there is only a very remote chance of any unexpected deviations, and such insignificant risks can be legitimately ignored. For other ventures it is almost impossible to identify all the associated risks. Even if all the risks can be identified, it is still more difficult to estimate their probability of occurrence and the magnitude of their effects. And these study efforts are expensive. Therefore, only the more sensitive and significant studies are exposed to a conscientious risk appraisal.

Primary studies are special cases under the assumption of certainty. They are limited to problems of an immediate nature not influenced by time effects. In this section we shall relax the time limit to include the longer range effect of interest on capital.

Time Value of Money

"The gain which he who lends his money upon interest acquires, without doing injury to anyone, is not to be included under the head of unlawful usury." John Calvin (1509–1564).

A dollar received a year from now is valued at less than a dollar received today. The reason is that the dollar received today can be invested and earn interest during the year. With an annual interest rate (i) of 5%, the dollar invested (principal) earns a nickel ($1 \times 0.05 = \$0.05$) in 1 year, making the future value equal to $1.05. Conversely, a future value (F) can be discounted to the present time to obtain its present worth (P) as

$$P = \frac{F}{1 + i}$$

And where $i = 0.05$:

$$\$1 = \frac{\$1.05}{(1.05)} = \$1.05(0.9525)$$

94

Equivalence. The purpose of including the time value of money in comparisons is to express each outcome in a timewise equivalent state. We observed that $1.05 1 year from now is equivalent to $1.00 received today when the annual interest rate is 5%. That is, from an investment viewpoint, we would be indifferent to $1.00 received today or $1.05 received a year later. This indifference attitude is feasible because we assume that future outcomes are certain and disregard any inflationary or immediate cash pressures.

The concept of equivalence allows us to compare alternatives realistically with different time patterns of receipts and disbursements. Knowing the amount and time of each cash transaction, we can calculate one number that is equivalent to all the transactions. Then the cash flow equivalent value for each alternative is directly contrasted for a final selection. Several equivalent time-money patterns are depicted in Figure 4.9.

Interest formulas. The task of calculating the equivalent cash flows depicted in Figure 4.9 would be very tedious if each payment was individually compounded through each time period. Fortunately tables are available to ease the reckoning. Interest tables for six discrete interest compounding formulas at various interest rates are provided in Appendix B. The six formulas comprise three future value relationships and their reciprocal present value counterparts. Mnemonic symbols for the formulas

Tables for continuous compounding can also be used. We shall limit our attention to discrete compounding because it is more widely understood, • accepted, and used by industry.

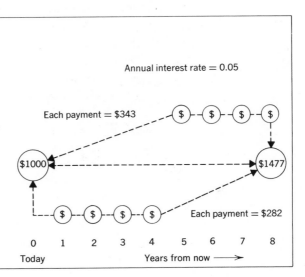

1. $1000 today are equivalent to $1477 received 8 years from now.

2. $1000 today are equivalent to $282 received at the end of each year for the next 4 years.

3. $1000 today are equivalent to $343 received at the end of years 5, 6, 7, and 8.

4. $282 received at the end of each year for the next 4 years are equivalent to $1477 received 8 years from today.

5. $343 received at the end of years 5, 6, 7, and 8 are equivalent to $1477 received at the end of year 8.

6. $282 received at the end of each year for the next 4 years are equivalent to $343 received at the end of years 5, 6, 7, and 8.

Annual interest rate = 0.05

Each payment = $343

$1000

$1477

Each payment = $282

0   1   2   3   4   5   6   7   8

Today   Years from now ⟶

Figure 4.9 Equivalent cash flows

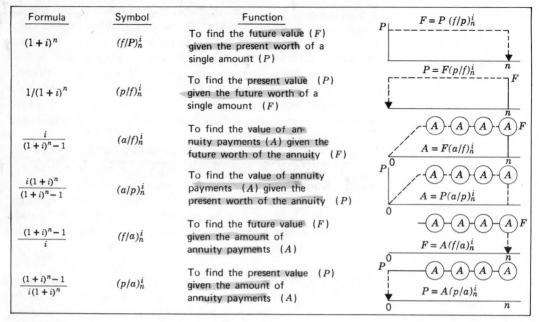

Formula	Symbol	Function	
$(1+i)^n$	$(f/P)_n^i$	To find the future value (F) given the present worth of a single amount (P)	
$1/(1+i)^n$	$(p/f)_n^i$	To find the present value (P) given the future worth of a single amount (F)	
$\dfrac{i}{(1+i)^n-1}$	$(a/f)_n^i$	To find the value of annuity payments (A) given the future worth of the annuity (F)	
$\dfrac{i(1+i)^n}{(1+i)^n-1}$	$(a/p)_n^i$	To find the value of annuity payments (A) given the present worth of the annuity (P)	
$\dfrac{(1+i)^n-1}{i}$	$(f/a)_n^i$	To find the future value (F) given the amount of annuity payments (A)	
$\dfrac{(1+i)^n-1}{i(1+i)^n}$	$(p/a)_n^i$	To find the present value (P) given the amount of annuity payments (A)	

Figure 4.10 Interest formulas, symbols, and descriptions

are used to make their application easier. The formulas, symbols, functional descriptions, and graphical cash flow representations are collected in Figure 4.10.

To use the interest formulas effectively, we must understand the mechanics of their application. The following five components are directly employed to produce equivalent quantities through interest-time conversions:

P = present worth—a lump sum value at time "now."
F = future worth—a lump sum value at a certain future point in time.
n = number of interest periods. There are often more than one interest period per year.
i = interest rate. In discrete compounding, i is the interest rate per period. Sometimes a *nominal interest rate* is quoted such as "12% compounded quarterly." This statement means that interest is compounded four times a year at a rate per period (quarter) of 3%. Therefore, to find the value of $1 invested for 1 year at 12% compounded quarterly, we have

$$F = P(1 + 0.03)^4 = \$1(1.126) = \$1.13$$

or

$$F = P(f/p)_4^3 = \$1(1.03)^4 = \$1(1.126) = \$1.13$$

96

$A =$ one annuity payment. Our interest tables are based on an annuity composed of *equal payments* occurring at *equal time intervals* with the *first payment at the end of the first period*. Annuity factors are used to convert a series of payments to an equivalent single future or present sum and to translate single sums into a series of payments occurring in the past or future.

A statement of a problem usually includes three of the P, F, i, n, and A factors and requires a solution for a fourth factor. Note that the symbol for each formula contains four of the factors. By identifying the known factors and what is unknown, we identify the appropriate formula.

EXAMPLE 4.5 Use of Interest Formulas and Symbols

The inventor of a patented production process is willing to consider a lump sum payment in place of annual royalties for the use of his process. The firm using the process believes it will be needed for 8 more years. Royalty payments will be $15,000 per year for the next 5 years and $10,000 a year for the last 3 years. Payments will be made at the beginning of each year.

If both parties agree to an annual interest of 7%, the present worth of the payments can be calculated in two steps corresponding to the two annuity patterns. The first five payments comprise an immediate outlay of $15,000 followed by an annuity of four $15,000 year-end payments. The present worth of these five payments, designated P_0 is

$$P_0 = \$15,000 + \$15,000(p/a)_4^7$$

$$= \$15,000 + \$15,000(3.387)$$

$$= \$65,805$$

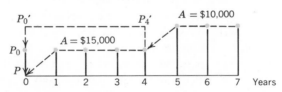

The worth of the second annuity at the end of year 4, designated P_4' is

$$P_4' = \$10,000(p/a)_3^7 = \$10,000(2.624) = \$26,240$$

It must be discounted 4 years to "now" or year 0 as

$$P_0' = P_4'(p/f)_4^7 = \$26,240(0.7629) = \$20,018$$

The present worth of all the royalty payments is then

$$P = P_0 + P_0' = \$65,805 + \$20,018 = \$85,823$$

which represents the equivalent amount that could be paid now to avoid future expenses. The single sum and the series of payments are equivalent if taxes and any changes in buying power of money are ignored.

Discounted Cash Flow Comparison Methods

Three methods are commonly applied to discounted cash flow comparisons: equivalent present worth, equivalent annual cost, and rate of return calculations. All three methods indicate the same preferred alternative from similar data when applied correctly. Why then have three methods? The answer lies in personal preferences for the way comparisons are stated (total dollars, annual dollars, or percentages) and because some methods are better suited to certain types of problems than others.

Equivalent present worth comparisons. The equivalent present worth of an alternative is determined by converting all future receipts and disbursements to a present amount and adding the immediate cash income or outlay. The resulting single value can then be compared to similarly obtained values for other alternatives. In this way, alternatives with entirely different patterns of cash flow are reduced to a standardized present worth index allowing direct evaluation of expected returns.

Present worth calculations are best suited to *coterminated projects*: comparisons where the study periods or lives of all the alternatives end at one distinct point in time. A pattern typical of coterminated projects is shown in Figure 4.11 where the solid and hollow bars represent the amount and time of costs expected from different alternatives, *J* and *K*. Costs associated with both projects terminate at the end of the 5-year study period. A large initial investment and relatively low annual costs in *J* are contrasted to larger but later expenses in *K*. The alternative with the lower present cost is preferable in terms of total discounted outlays.

The aggregate comparison figure resulting from a present worth calculation is often exceedingly large. Its magnitude may be quite frightening to the amateur unless accompanied by an explanation of its summary nature. Even to the wise, very large figures are difficult to comprehend and to put in proper perspective. One potential distortion is that the single sum may obscure

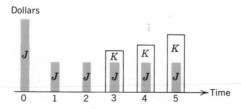

Figure 4.11 Coterminated projects *J* and *K*

financing advantages or disadvantages possible from different cash flow patterns. However, this same feature is beneficial in deciding how much can be spent in today's dollars to reap deferred savings.

EXAMPLE 4.6   Present Worth Comparison of Coterminated Projects

Special equipment to produce parts required to fulfill a contract can be developed or the work can be subcontracted. Both alternatives provide equal quality. The contract will expire in 3 years and it is doubtful if it will be renewed or a similar one obtained. A firm bid to provide the necessary 30,000 parts each year at $2 per part has been submitted by a subcontractor. If the parts are produced by the prime contractor, annual direct costs are expected to be $22,000. Indirect costs are 50% of direct costs. What is the maximum allowable developmental cost if the special equipment will have only a 10% scrap value at the termination of the contract?

Assuming an interest rate of 10% and that all transaction take place at the end of a year, we can equate the first cost of the equipment (P) less the present worth of the salvage value ($0.1P$) to the present worth of the difference between bid ($30,000 \times \$2 = \$60,000$) and production ($\$22,000 \times 1.5 = \$33,000$) costs as

$$P - 0.1P(p/f)^{10}_{3} = (\$60,000 - \$33,000)(p/a)^{10}_{3}$$

$$P[1 - 0.1(0.7513)] = \$27,000(2.487)$$

$$P = \frac{\$67,149}{0.925} = \$72,596$$

Therefore, if the special equipment can be developed for less than $72,596, its use will repay the amount invested plus 10% interest.

Equivalent annual cost comparisons. In an annual charge comparison, all receipts and disbursements occurring over a study period are converted to an equivalent yearly uniform income or outlay. Nonuniform transactions are converted to equivalent annuities through the use of appropriate interest formulas and are then added to other constant yearly transactions to provide one comparison figure. Annual costs are usually easy to collect and understand because most accounting and financial reporting periods are 1 year.

Annual cost comparisons are particularly suitable for *repeated projects:* studies involving physical assets that are renewed as necessary for continuing service over an indefinite time. Such cyclic patterns are based on the assumptions that the projects are initiated at one time, the operations do not change, and the cost figures remain constant during the foreseeable future. A common comparison is between higher priced, longer life items and lower priced, shorter life items.

EXAMPLE 4.7 Annual Cost Comparison of Repeated Projects

A material-handling problem can be solved by installing a conveyor system or by purchasing three lift trucks. The required return on invested capital is 10%. The cost pattern of each alternative is given below.

	Conveyor	Lift Trucks
First cost	$175,000	$16,000
Economic life	18 years	6 years
Salvage value	$20,000	$2400
Annual operating costs	$3000	$22,000
Annual taxes and insurance	$1000	$700

To make an annual cost comparison, we need only obtain the annuity equivalent to the capital recovery cost of the initial investment minus the discounted salvage value and add to it the other annual costs:

$$AC_{conveyor} = \$175,000(a/p)_{18}^{10} - \$20,000(a/f)_{18}^{10} + \$3000 + \$1000$$

$$= \$175,000(0.12193) - \$20,000(0.02193) + \$4000$$

$$= \$21,338 - \$438 + \$4000 = \$24,900$$

$$AC_{trucks} = \$16,000(a/p)_{6}^{10} - \$2400(a/f)_{6}^{10} + \$22,000 + \$700$$

$$= \$16,000(0.22961) - \$2400(0.12961) + \$22,700$$

$$= \$3674 - \$311 + \$22,700 = \$26,063$$

Thus the annual savings expected from installing the conveyor system rather than buying lift trucks is $26,063 - $24,900 = $1163.

The same alternative is selected by a present worth calculation for the 18-year study period, the period that coterminates both projects:

$$PW_{conveyor} = \$175,000 - \$20,000(p/f)_{18}^{10} + (\$3000 + \$1000)(p/a)_{18}^{10}$$

$$= \$175,000 - \$20,000(0.1799) + \$4000(8.201)$$

$$= \$175,000 - \$3598 + \$32,804 = \$204,206$$

$$PW_{trucks} = \$16,000 + \$13,600(p/f)_{6}^{10} + \$13,600(p/f)_{12}^{10} - \$2400(p/f)_{18}^{10}$$

$$+ (\$22,000 + \$700)(p/a)_{18}^{10}$$

$$= \$16,000 + \$13,600(0.5645) + \$13,600(0.3186)$$

$$+ \$2400(0.1799) + \$22,700(8.201)$$

$$= \$16,000 + \$7677 + \$4333 - \$432 + \$186,163 = \$213,741$$

The equivalence of the two methods is demonstrated by calculating the present worth of the annual cost as

$$PW \text{ of } AC_{conveyor} = \$24,900(p/a)_{18}^{10} = \$24,900(8.201) = \$204,205$$

$$PW \text{ of } AC_{trucks} \quad \$26,063(p/a)_{18}^{10} = \$26,063(8.201) = \$213,742$$

which differs from the first present worth calculations only by "rounding off" errors. In many problems it is necessary to combine *PW* and *AC* calculations. A frequent example is where one repeated project starts at a date different from the one with which it is compared.

Rate of return comparisons. A rate of return is the percent of an investment returned each year as gain or profit. For money invested in assets that do not depreciate in value, such as land, the rate of return is calculated as

$$\text{rate of return} = \frac{\text{net annual profit}}{\text{amount invested}} \times 100\%$$

When an asset loses value as it provides service, such as a machine producing salable products, the difference between the revenue it produces and its operation cost should meet the loss in value of the asset as well as provide a surplus or profit. This requirement is incorporated in the interest formula, $(a/p)_n^i$, which is commonly called the "capital recovery factor." In multiplying the present worth of an investment by the capital recovery factor, we determine the minimum return that will cover depreciation expense plus a certain percentage gain. As applied to a rate of return calculation for a depreciable asset, we have

$$(a/p)_n^i = \frac{\text{annual revenue} - \text{operating cost}}{\text{amount invested in asset with a service life } n}$$

where the rate of return is the value of i in the capital recovery factor.

EXAMPLE 4.8 Rate of Return for a Single Alternative

Replacing manual labor in a loading operation by automatic equipment will reduce net operating expenses by $27,200 a year. The equipment costs $100,000 and the scrap value will just cover removal cost at the end of its 5-year-life. Should the equipment be installed when the minimum acceptable rate of return on new investments is 10%?

Since the equipment is subject to physical depreciation, we calculate the rate of return as

$$\text{savings} = A \qquad \text{investment} = P$$

$$\$27{,}200 = \$100{,}000(a/p)_5^i$$

or

$$(a/p)_5^i = \frac{\$27{,}200}{\$100{,}000} = 0.27200$$

where the value of i is obtained by interpolating between the factors $(a/p)_5^{10}$ and $(a/p)_5^{12}$ as

$$i = 0.10 + 0.02 \, \frac{0.27200 - 0.26380}{0.27741 - 0.26380} = 0.112$$

The 11.2% rate of return means that the savings obtained by installing the automatic equipment will allow the initial investment of $100,000 to be repaid in 5 years plus provide annual earnings of 11.2% on the unpaid balance.

101

The rate of return is easily calculated for a single action, because the only unknown in the equation is i which is revealed by interpolation between interest rate tables for the indicated capital recovery factor. A pairwise comparison complicates the calculations because all the transactions for both alternatives must be equated to a common point in time. Several interest factors usually are included. Only one value of i will make the two alternatives equal. Therefore, the value of i that establishes the rate of return by which one alternative exceeds the other is disclosed by trial and error.

EXAMPLE 4.9 Rate of Return for a Pair of Alternatives

Another alternative for the decision situation of Example 4.8 is to replace the manual operation with semiautomatic equipment which yields a net savings of $11,000 per year on an equipment investment of $60,000. The semiautomatic equipment will last 10 years and retain a salvage value of $20,000. Which alternative offers the higher rate of return? A pairwise comparison can be made between the semiautomatic equipment and doing nothing or between the semiautomatic and automatic equipment. For the former comparison, we have

equal to or less

$$\$60{,}000(a/p)^i_{10} - \$20{,}000(a/f)^i_{10} = \$11{,}000$$

from which i is determined by trial and error to be approximately 15% as

$$\$60{,}000(a/p)^{15}_{10} - \$20{,}000(a/f)^{15}_{10} = \$60{,}000(0.19925) - \$20{,}000(0.04925)$$

$$= \$10{,}970$$

The second comparison, equating the annual cost of the two types of equipment under the repeated project assumption, appears as

$$\$60{,}000(a/p)^i_{10} - \$20{,}000(a/f)^i_{10} - \$11{,}000 = \$100{,}000(a/p)^i_5 - \$27{,}200$$

or

$$\$16{,}200 = \$100{,}000(a/p)^i_5 - \$60{,}000(a/p)^i_{10} + \$20{,}000(a/f)^i_{10}$$

and

$$(\qquad) - 11008 = (\qquad) - 27000$$

$$\$16{,}190 = \$100{,}000(a/p)^{\frac{1}{2}}_5 - \$60{,}000(a/p)^{\frac{1}{2}}_{10} + \$20{,}000(a/f)^{\frac{1}{2}}_{10}$$

Therefore the rate of return on the extra increment of investment to go from semiautomatic to automatic equipment is only 0.5%. Since this rate is well under the required return, a preference for the semiautomatic equipment is indicated.

Rate of return comparisons are very effective in evaluating the effect of additional increments of investment in a single project. For instance, we know that pumping costs go down as the diameter of a pipeline increases. Pipe comes in certain increments of size. The problem of determining the most economical diameter is solved by ascertaining the rate of return from each extra increment of investment used to lower pumping cost by increasing the diameter. Stated as a gross equation, we have

$$\text{rate of return} \doteq \frac{\text{savings resulting from increase in pipe size}}{\text{extra investment required to increase pipe diameter}}$$

Although a rate of return is a universally understood measure of economic success, there is still some danger of misinterpretation in incremental analyses. The two most common abuses are tendencies to select automatically the alternative with the greatest rate of return on *total* investment or to select the alternative offering the largest *total* investment that meets the minimum acceptable rate of return. The correct interpretation is to select the largest *incremental* investment that exceeds the minimum acceptable rate of return.

EXAMPLE 4.10 Rate of Return for Incremental Investments

Three alternative methods of accomplishing a project are shown in the table below. Each investment has the same economic life, 8 years, and no salvage value. The minimum acceptable rate of return is 10%.

	Method A		Method B		Method C
Investment	$70,000		$90,000		$100,000
Incremental investment		$20,000		$30,000*	
Net profit	$16,000		$19,100		$22,300
Incremental profit		$3100		$6300*	
Rate of return on the total investment	16%		13.5%		15%
Rate of return on incremental investment		5%		13.2%*	

*Based on the last acceptable increment of investment.

The rate of return for alternative A is calculated as

$$(a/p)_8^i = \frac{\$16,000}{\$70,000} = 0.22859$$

making $i = 16\%$. Since A is an acceptable alternative because its rate of return is greater than 10%, we next evaluate the increment of investment added to A to afford the greater profit from B:

$$(a/p)_8^i = \frac{\$3100}{\$20,000} = 0.15500$$

making $i = 5\%$. This rate of return is less than 10% for the $20,000 extra investment and makes B an *unacceptable* alternative. A comparison is always made to the *next lowest acceptable level*

103

of investment. Therefore, alternative *C* is compared to *A* in determining the rate of return for the next increment of investment:

$$(a/p)_8^i = \frac{\$22,300 - \$16,000}{\$100,000 - \$70,000} = \frac{\$6300}{\$30,000} = 0.21000$$

for which $i = 0.132$. Since this $30,000 increment shows a rate of return greater than the required minimum, *C* is the most attractive alternative. Note that *A* has a greater rate of return on the *total* investment than does *C*, but the selection of *A* instead of *C* would eliminate the opportunity to invest $30,000 at the attractive 13.2% rate.

4-5 STUDIES RECOGNIZING RISK

In capital budgeting we have no choice but to deal with the future. No one can infallibly predict what will happen in the years ahead. The best we can do is estimate. In previous sections, we made cash flow estimates for the one future state we considered most likely. This positive practice is subject to two types of errors: (1) the cash flow estimates could be inaccurate and (2) the future state upon which the flow is based could be incorrectly stated.

Every planner knows that his cash flow estimates are indeed estimates. Variability is a recognized factor in every phase of production systems; the properties of materials vary over time and with sources, the quality and quantity of worker output fluctuate widely, and even machines occasionally perform in unanticipated ways. A planner would drive himself to distraction trying to account for the infinite number of deviations which could upset his cash flow proposals. To avoid an obsession with tactical estimating details, we can adopt a strategic plan of applying a broad safety factor or other means of overdesign. In economic studies, an obvious safety factor is to require an overly high rate of return or an unrealistically short payback period from an alternative before it is deemed acceptable. The surplus return engendered by measuring alternatives against these protective standards provides security from inaccurate estimates.

In this section our main concern is with ways to reduce the second source of estimating errors: how to include more than one future state in an evaluation. The correspondence between the past, present, and future and data, alternatives, and outcomes is depicted in Figure 4.12. We draw on past data to recognize alternatives and then look to the future to evaluate their worth.

Studies recognizing risk focus attention on the top section of the decision tree. They demand inspiration, perspiration, and judgment. Inspiration helps identify possible future states. Perspiration characterizes the effort required to estimate the cash flow associated with each state for each alternative. Judgment

Convenient categories for decision models are certainty, risk, and uncertainty. Uncertainty is distinguished from risk by the inability to assign probabilities to future states.

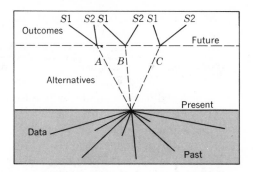

Figure 4.12 Decision tree

is used in grouping the states into workable units. For instance, the best method of carrying out a construction project could depend on the weather expected. If the work is sensitive to the amount of rainfall, the future states would be different possible precipitation levels. Assuming that the range is between 0 and 20 inches during the duration of the project, we could divide this range into any number of states corresponding to some fraction of the total. However, if we know that the same outcomes will be exhibited over ranges of 0-9, 10-14, and 15-20 inches, the effects of only three states receive attention. Then the cash outcomes are estimated for all three states for each feasible method of conducting the construction.

In addition to discerning future states and estimating their associated outcomes, the relative likelihood of each future must be assessed. For the construction project example, the probability of each level of rainfall could be estimated from past weather data. The sources of probability estimates are similar to those discussed for forecasting in Section 3-4. After numbers have been attached to all the branches ($S1$ and $S2$) of the decision tree of Figure 4.12, the final step is to select a comparison method for the risk evaluation.

Expected Value Comparison

The concept of *expectation* or *expected value* proffers a most useful and satisfying assist to risk evaluations. It is useful because it is versatile yet compels a precise statement of the problem. It is satisfying because it produces the sort of jury verdict based on an objective weighing of evidence that generates intuitive confidence.

Payoff table. All conditions for the statement of a problem recognizing risk are included in a simple format called a payoff table (Figure 4.13). All alternative courses of action available in

105

	State	
	S1 $P(1)$	S2 $P(2)$
Alternative 1	O_{11}	O_{12}
2	O_{21}	O_{22}

Figure 4.13 Payoff table

the problem situation are listed and thereby set the number of rows in the table. Each applicable future state establishes a column. Associated with each state is the probability of its occurrence. The sum of the probabilities for all the future states should equal 1.0. The cells in the table show what outcome (O) is anticipated from each alternative for each future that can occur. The outcomes can be expressed in pounds, inches, dollars, or any other units so long as the dimensions are consistent.

Evaluation. The "expectation" from each alternative is the weighted average of all its outcomes. They are weighted according to their probability of occurrence. For the alternatives in Figure 4.13, the expected values are

$$E(A1) = [O_{11} \times P(1)] + [O_{12} \times P(2)]$$
$$E(A2) = [O_{21} \times P(1)] + [O_{22} \times P(2)]$$

 If the outcomes show profit, a preference is indicated for the alternative with the largest weighted average or greater profit expectation.

EXAMPLE 4.11   Expected Value for a Study Recognizing Risk

The image-improvement campaign initiated by the "Ipso Facto" data processors was so successful that they are now considering a major expansion. The best available probability estimates of the future demand for automated data-processing services are 0.1 to decline slightly, 0.3 to remain constant, and 0.6 to increase rapidly. If Ipso Facto launches an expansion now, it feels it can capture most of the new local demand. It would also suffer a considerable loss from unused capacity if the demand declines. The conservative alternative is to try to increase facility utilization from its present 85% level to 100%. The net average annual gains or losses over 4 years for each future from the two alternatives are shown in the payoff table below.

		Decline $P(D) = 0.1$	Constant $P(C) = 0.3$	Increase $P(I) = 0.6$
Major expansion	(E)	$-\$180,000$	$-\$5000$	$\$90,000$
Increase utilization	(U)	$-\$10,000$	$\$10,000$	$\$40,000$

Using the expectation criterion, we have

$$E(E) = -\$180,000(0.1) - \$5000(0.3) + \$90,000(0.6)$$
$$= -\$18,000 - \$1500 + \$54,000 = \$34,500$$
$$E(U) = -\$10,000(0.1) + \$10,000(0.3) + \$40,000(0.6)$$
$$= -\$1000 + \$3000 + \$24,000 = \$26,000$$

which indicate a preference for major expansion.

	S1 0.1	S2 0.9	E .
A1	0	$200	$180
A2	$12.000	– $1000	$300

Figure 4.14 Expected value

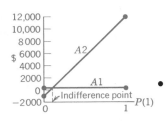

Indifference points can also be determined graphically as shown for the data from Figure 4.14.

Interpretation. The expected value of an alternative, such as $300 for A2 in Figure 4.14, is the average gain expected from repeatedly choosing A2 in the same decision situation. Actually, each time an outcome occurs, it will have a value of +$12,000 or –$1000. Since precisely identical decision situations can hardly be expected too often in an industrial setting, the expectation outcomes cannot be followed blindly. If a $1000 loss would be acutely painful, it might be wise to eliminate that alternative from the table regardless of the attractiveness of other outcomes. When a conservative approach is dictated by intangible factors, a very safe alternative is a prudent choice, even when the expectation of a riskier one is greater. Such decisions are subjective options accrued from factors not included in the payoff table. Expectation is a guide, not a dictate; but when followed over the long run, even when individual problems are not identical, it offers a sound, objective principle of choice.

Sometimes there is considerable disagreement or uncertainty about the probability of each future. One way to avoid the dilemma of pinpointing an exact probability estimate is to calculate an "indifference probability level." Letting $P(1)$ and $P(2) = 1 - P(1)$ be the probabilities for the two future states in Figure 4.14, the indifference probability is calculated as

$$E(A1) = E(A2)$$

$$\$0(P1) + \$200[1 - P(1)] = \$12,000(P1) - \$1000[1 - P(1)]$$

$$P(1) = \frac{\$1000 + \$200}{\$12,000 + \$1000 + \$200} = 0.09$$

indicating that when the probability of $S1 = 0.09$, the expected value of both alternatives is the same and a decision maker would be indifferent to either course of action. Consequently, any estimate for $P(1)$ in the range of 0.091 to 1.0 would swing the preference to A2. It is usually easier to extract a consensus from a policy-making group when they are offered a range rather than a point to agree upon.

Spending extra effort and money can usually improve the reliability of probability estimates. When it appears that research can increase estimating confidence, the question becomes how much is it feasible to spend. An indication is obtained by calculating the *value of perfect information.* Using the data from Figure 4.14, we would always choose A2 for a gain of $12,000 if we knew S1 was *sure* to occur. Similarly, if we *knew* S2 would transpire, we would always follow A1 for a gain of $200 instead of a $1000 loss from using A2. Since A1 and A2 are expected to

107

occur, respectively, 1 time and 9 times in 10, the expected return from prescient knowledge is

$$\$12,000(0.1) + \$200(0.9) = \$1380$$

The difference between the expectation with perfect information and the preferable alternative $A2$ based on blindness is the value of perfect information, $\$1380 - \$300 = \$1080$. Thus we presumably would be willing to pay $\$1080$ for perfect information each time a decision is required in the given situation. The only hitch is to find the marketplace where perfect information is sold.

★ ★ ★ *Optional material.* OMIT

Discounted Decision Tree Comparisons

The hybrid comparison technique resulting from a combination of the expectation principle with the time value of money is a discounted decision tree. Its illustrative branching format is particularly useful for planning and presentation. The evaluation based on the expectation of discounted cash flow is realistically direct; inclusion of extended time-oriented decisions adds versatility.

For additional details, see J. F. Magee, "Decision Trees for Decision Making," *Harvard Bus. Rev.*, July–Aug. 1964.

Format. The initial identification of future states and associated outcomes for each alternative is integral to any risk evaluation. The distinctive feature of a discounted decision tree evaluation is the portrayal of successive decisions. Such decisions arise when the primary or immediate decision depends on which course of action is followed at a decision point some periods in the future.

The upper branch of the decision tree in Figure 4.15 contains a successive decision based on conditional alternatives. The first decision to select a course of action at time zero is denoted by the square at the left, $D1$. Time flows from left to right. The dotted line connecting $D1$ to the circled $A1$ represents a possible course of action, alternative 1. The two solid lines from $A1$ indicate possible outcomes from the alternative; the top line $O1$ shows the expected returns over both time periods while the lower line $O2$ represents returns for only the first period. The second square $D2$ indicates that a second decision will be made, *if* the outcome $O2$ occurs. That is, the choice between $A11$ and $A12$ will be made only if the future state represented by $O2$ transpires. The conditional outcomes for the two alternatives from the second decision point are denoted as $O2a$–d.

The conditions creating the need for a second decision point

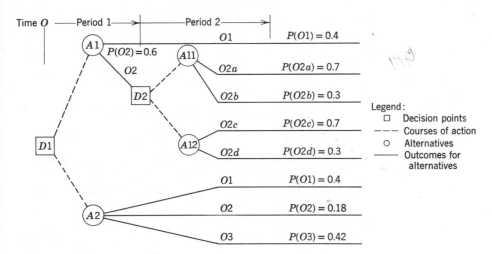

Figure 4.15 Decision tree format

originate from a desire to modify a course of action if a certain future state occurs. Let us assume the outcomes in Figure 4.15 pertain to the following three estimates of future facility utilization:

State 1. Constant throughout the two periods: $P(C_1C_2) = 0.4$.
State 2. Increase by 20% during the first period, then constant for the second: $P(I_1C_2) = 0.18$.
State 3. Continue to increase for both periods: $P(I_1I_2) = 0.42$.

From these estimates we can say that the probability of an increase during the first period is

$$P(I_1) = P(I_1C_2) + P(I_1I_2) = 0.18 + 0.42 = 0.60$$

Further, the probability of an increase during the second period, *given* that utilization increased in the first period, is

$$P(I_2|I_1) = \frac{P(I_1I_2)}{P(I_1)} = \frac{0.42}{0.60} = 0.7$$

Then the probability of constant utilization given a first period increase is $1 - P(I_2|I_1) = 1 - 0.7 = 0.3$, or

$$P(C_2|I_1) = \frac{P(I_1C_2)}{P(I_1)} = \frac{0.18}{0.60} = 0.3$$

Thus, *D2* represents a decision to modify *A1* if future I_1 occurs.

Evaluation. The outcomes for each alternative are first discounted to a common point in time. For *D2*, this point is the beginning

109

of the second time period; for $D1$ it is the beginning of the first time period or "now." After the present worth of all the receipts and disbursements is added to any initial costs, the expectation for each alternative is determined from the weighted outcomes. For the alternatives at $D2$, we have

$$E(A11) = [PW(O2a) \times P(O2a)] + [PW(O2b) \times P(O2b)]$$

$$E(A12) = [PW(O2c) \times P(O2c)] + [PW(O2d) \times P(O2d)]$$

where PW is the present worth of the outcomes at the beginning of period 2. From the two expectations the most profitable is selected to designate the preferred alternative at $D2$.

After completing the evaluation at $D2$, we proceed to $A1$ because *decisions are always made in reverse chronological order.* The preferred dependent alternative from each decision point becomes an outcome for its related alternative from an earlier decision point. If we assume that $A11$ was the preferred alternative from $D2$, the expected value of $A11$ is included in $O2$ to account for states 2 and 3 of alternative $A1$. Therefore the expectation of $A1$ is

$$E(A1) = [PW(O1) \times P(O1)] + \{PW[O2 + E(A11)] \times P(O2)\}$$

which is compared to

$$E(A2) = [PW(O1) \times P(O1)] + [PW(O2) \times P(O2)]$$
$$+ [PW(O3) \times P(O3)]$$

where PW is the present worth of the outcomes at the beginning of the first period. The more valuable expectation determines which primary alternative is preferred at $D1$.

EXAMPLE 4.12 Discounted Decision Free Comparison of Conditional Alternatives

A decision has been made about expanding the capacity of Ipso Facto. Additional data-processing equipment can be purchased or leased. A 2-year renewable lease provides high-capacity equipment at a lower initial cost than comparable equipment can be purchased. Another alternative is to purchase half the equipment now and delay the remainder for 2 years. The study period is 4 years. Only if the demand increases for the first 2 years would the rest of the equipment necessary to achieve high capacity be purchased. Similarly, if the demand is constant during the first 2 years, the lease could be dropped and half the equipment purchased for the last 2 years.

The probability of demand is estimated as:

constant for years 0–4	$P(C_1 C_2)$	$= 0.10$
constant 0–2, increase 2–4	$P(C_1 I_2)$	$= 0.30$
increase 0–2, constant 2–4	$P(I_1 C_2)$	$= 0.06$
increase for years 0–4	$P(I_1 I_2)$	$= 0.54$

The expected net receipts excluding lease or capital recovery costs for high-capacity equipment are

constant demand for years 0–4	$30,000 per year
constant 0–2, increase 2–4	$30,000 per year, $45,000 per year
increase 0–2, constant 2–4	$35,000 per year, $45,000 per year
increase for years 0–4	$60,000 per year

If only half the equipment is purchased to provide service, the net receipts will be 80% of the amount for full equipment to a maximum of $40,000 per year.

The annual cost of leasing high-capacity equipment is $25,000. The purchase price of the same equipment is $100,000, and it can be purchased in two equal parts to provide approximately half the capacity each time. The salvage values are 40% of the first cost after 2 years and 20% of the initial cost after 4 years.

The decision is to be based on the expected value of the discounted cash flow subject to a minimum acceptable rate of return of 10%.

A preliminary evaluation can begin with a skeleton decision tree layout of alternatives and outcomes as shown in Figure 4.16. The primary decision is between leasing ($L1$) full-capacity equipment and purchasing ($P\frac{1}{2}$) half-capacity equipment. Conditional decisions for each alternative are available. If demand is constant in the first 2 years, the lease can be continued ($L2$) or dropped in favor of ($P\frac{1}{2}''$). Similarly, after an increase for 2 years the rest of the equipment can be purchased ($P1$) or operations can be continued with half capacity ($P\frac{1}{2}'$). The conditional probabilities for demand in the second biennium are

$$P(C_2 | I_1) = \frac{0.06}{0.60} = 0.10$$

$$P(I_2 | I_1) = 0.90$$

$$P(C_2 | C_1) = \frac{0.10}{0.40} = 0.25$$

$$P(I_2 | C_1) = 0.75$$

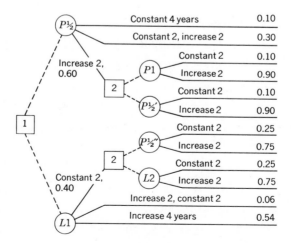

Constant 4 years	0.10
Constant 2, increase 2	0.30
Constant 2	0.10
Increase 2	0.90
Constant 2	0.10
Increase 2	0.90
Constant 2	0.25
Increase 2	0.75
Constant 2	0.25
Increase 2	0.75
Increase 2, constant 2	0.06
Increase 4 years	0.54

Figure 4.16 Future states and alternatives

111

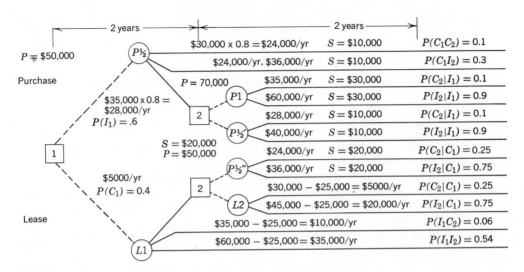

Figure 4.17 Cash flow for primary and conditional alternatives

Adding the cost data completes the problem representation shown in Figure 4.17. Purchase prices are noted at decision points and salvage values at outcome terminals. Note that the amount of salvage depends on the age of the equipment from a decision point; the used equipment has a value of $0.4P = \$20,000$ at 2 years and $0.2P = \$10,000$ at 4 years. Since no capital recovery costs are associated with leasing, outcomes are annual net receipts less yearly lease expense.

The first comparison can be of either primary alternative, but it must start with decision point 2. If we select the purchasing alternative for our initial calculations, the expected value of the receipts from buying the rest of the equipment at decision point 2-$P1$ is

$$E(P1) = \$35,000(p/a)_2^{10}(0.1) + \$60,000(p/a)_2^{10}(0.9)$$

$$= \$35,000(1.736)(0.1) + \$60,000(1.736)(0.9) = \$99,820$$

Capital costs for $P1$ include the purchase price of the new equipment ($P = \$50,000$) less the present worth of the salvage value ($S = 0.4P = \$20,000$) and the change in worth of the salvage value of the equipment at time zero (from $0.4P$ to $0.2P$):

$$\text{cost} = \$50,000 - \$20,000(p/f)_2^{10} + \$20,000 - \$10,000(p/f)_2^{10}$$

$$= \$70,000 - \$30,000(0.8264) = \$45,208$$

Subtracting the expected receipts from the equipment cost, we have the profit expectation for $P1$:

$$\text{profit }(P1) = \$99,820 - \$45,208 = \$54,612$$

Turning attention to the lower branch of decision point 2, we have equivalent calculations for the expected profit from continued use of half the equipment, $P\frac{1}{2}'$:

$$\text{profit }(P\frac{1}{2}') = E(P\frac{1}{2}') - 0.4(\$50,000) + PW(0.2 \times \$50,000)$$

$$= \$28,000(p/a)_2^{10}(0.1) + \$40,000(p/a)_2^{10}(0.9) - \$20,000$$

$$+ \$10,000(p/f)_2^{10}$$

$$= \$4851 + \$62,496 - \$20,000 + \$8264 = \$55,264$$

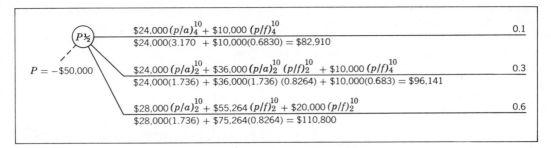

Figure 4.18

Therefore, alternative $P\frac{1}{2}'$ is chosen and serves as an outcome for the primary alternative $P\frac{1}{2}$.

The calculations required to determine the present worth of the cash flow for the outcomes of $P\frac{1}{2}$ are indicated on the revised decision tree branch shown in Figure 4.18. The expected profit for $P\frac{1}{2}$ is

$$\text{profit } (P\frac{1}{2}) = \$82,910(0.1) + \$96,141(0.3) + \$110,800(0.6) - \$50,000$$

$$= \$8291 + \$28,842 + \$66,480 - \$50,000 = \mathbf{\$50,613}$$

To evaluate the primary lease alternative, we must again start at decision point 2. The expected profit from each alternative is

$$\text{profit } (P\frac{1}{2}'') = \$24,000(p/a)_2^{10}(0.25) + \$36,000(p/a)_2^{10}(0.75) + \$20,000(p/f)_2^{10} - \$50,000$$

$$= \$10,416 + \$46,872 + \$13,660 - \$50,000 = \$20,948$$

$$\text{profit } (L2) = \$5000(p/a)_2^{10}(0.25) + \$25,000(p/a)_2^{10}(0.75) = \$28,210$$

With the apparent selection of $L2$, the lease branch of the decision tree becomes as shown in Figure 4.19. The expected profit from leasing is

$$\text{profit } (L1) = \$37,200(0.4) + \$31,700(0.06) + \$110,950(0.54)$$

$$= \$14,880 + \$1902 + \$59,913 = \mathbf{\$76,695}$$

The primary decision at point 1 is thus resolved to a comparison of the present worth of expected returns from leasing full-capacity equipment for 4 years (\$76,695) to the present worth return expectation from 4 years of using purchased equipment with half the capacity of the

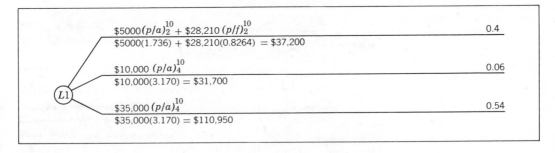

Figure 4.19

leased equipment ($50,613). The difference between the two alternatives, $26,082, suggests it would be preferable to lease the equipment unless there are overriding intangible considerations. In this regard it should be noted that an annuity equal to the present worth of the savings from leasing for the 4-year period at an interest rate of 10% is

$$A = \$26,082(a/p)_4^{10} = \$26,082(0.31547) = \$8216$$

★ ★ ★ *End optional material.*

4-6 CAPITAL RATIONING

A new investment must pass three tests before any overt action is undertaken:

1. An economic evaluation compares the cost of initiating and operating a project to the benefits expected to determine if it is worth doing.
2. An intangible evaluation investigates the worthiness of a project in terms of human values which are difficult to express quantitatively.
3. A financial evaluation compares the attractiveness of investments in different projects in relation to the quantity and quality of available investment funds.

To some extent each test is a gate to acceptance, because a project can be shut out for a decidedly subminimal showing in any one category. For the projects that survive the cutoff levels, a low rating in one test may be compensated for by a strong showing in another test.

In this chapter we have considered several comparison methods applied to the economic and intangible tests. These same methods are appropriate for financial evaluations; instead of comparing alternatives to each other, the comparisons match projects to each other and to the source or amount of financing funds. This capital-rationing precedure can be roughly classified according to the scarcity of funds.

When unlimited funds are assumed to be available from borrowing, the returns from a project are measured against the cost of capital used to implement the project.

The theoretical assumption of unlimited funds is merely an aid to analysis. There is always some actual upper limit to borrowing because the escalating interest rates charged for extended borrowing tend to set a practical bound.

When a top limit is assumed for the amount of capital available in a given period, the projects must compete against each other to secure a portion of the limited funding.

Under the assumption of unlimited funds, a rate of return comparison is particularly suitable. The profit expected from each project compared to the investment sets a project rate of return. This rate is then compared to the rate that must be paid for borrowed capital. In theory, all the projects with return percentages greater than the interest charges for loans are

Project Rate of Return	Capital Inventory
25%	6%
21%	7%
15%	10%
Cutoff	
12%	12%
9%	13%
8%	14%

acceptable. In practice, a "capital inventory" approach is useful. A *capital inventory* is a schedule of available capital sources listed in order of increasing interest rates. The sources may be internal funds such as retained earnings or external funds such as bond issues. The least expensive funds from the capital inventory are allocated to projects with the largest rates of return. The allocation is continued until the project rate of return is equal to or less than the cost of money to finance it.

When the source of capital is limited to internally generated sums or a maximum set by management policy, the problem is to determine which of several attractive projects should be funded. This problem is prevalent in tactical situations such as departmental budgets. Procedures designed to meet the problem range from elaborate to simple. The more extensive comparisons include the time it takes for returns from a project to repay the initial investment, intangible considerations such as customer impressions, relative contribution of the production area where an investment is anticipated, and required returns weighted according to forecasted growth of the operations benefiting from the investment. A simpler approach is to establish a ratio between the equivalent annual profit from an investment based on a firm's cost of capital and the amount of the investment. Capital is rationed by allocating funds to the projects with the highest ratios until the source is exhausted.

After a comparison method is selected, there may still be difficulties. Some projects are not independent. For instance, project *A* could have a very high rate of return but it is not feasible unless project *B*, with a lower rate of return, is also instigated. Similarly, full benefits from a project may not be realized without subsequent investments that depend on future budgets. The actual cost of capital can also be questionable. How much should retained earnings earn? Such questions and a multitude of funding policies guarantee that capital budgeting will remain an occasionally bewildering and always challenging subject.

4-7 SUMMARY Production decisions associated with operations involve tactical alternatives measured by their efficiency. Strategic alternatives pertain to broader or longer range decisions and are rated as to effectiveness. Suboptimization occurs when a tactical segment of a problem is optimized without regard to its strategic effectiveness. Types of suboptimization include organizational (communication problems), insular (multiple-product issues), and temporal (planning-horizon questions) suboptimization.

A decision situation is highly sensitive when a small change in the efficiency of a tactic can alter the preference of strategies. The degree of sensitivity is a clue to the amount of effort that should be devoted to the evaluation of alternative plans.

A breakeven analysis investigates the relationship of fixed and variable costs to revenue. The breakeven point identifies the production quantity where revenue exactly meets total cost. The amount of profit obtained from each product made and sold above the breakeven output is its contribution—the difference between unit selling price and variable cost. The practice of reducing the selling price on a distinct portion of output to utilize otherwise excess capacity is called dumping.

For nonlinear price and cost functions, the difference in income or outlay caused by the next unit of output at a specified production level is, respectively, marginal revenue or marginal cost. The point where marginal revenue equals marginal cost is the production level for maximum profit.

The difficult to quantify human values that often influence decisions are termed intangible considerations. One method of including them in an economic evaluation is the exponential pairwise comparison model based on ratios raised to a power corresponding to the importance of each quality.

Different patterns of receipts and disbursements are compared on an equivalent basis by calculating the time value of cash flow. Six interest formulas are employed to convert a single amount or a series of payments to an equivalent future or present sum or annuity. Three methods of discounted cash flow comparisons are: (1) equivalent present worth—for coterminated projects, (2) equivalent annual cost—for repeated projects, and (3) rate of return—for incremental investments.

Comparisons recognizing risk require that the applicable future states be identified and their probabilities estimated. Outcomes for each state from each alternative can be displayed in a payoff table. The expected value of an alternative is the weighted average of all its outcomes where the "weights" are obtained from the probability of each outcome's occurrence.

A discounted decision tree combines the expectation principle with the time value of money. Conditional alternatives are evaluated by determining the expectation of the discounted cash flow at successive decision points. Decisions are made in a reverse chronological order, making the outcome from a preferred dependent decision an input to an earlier decision point. The primary alternative with the highest expectation at time zero is the indicated course of action.

116

New investments should receive economic, intangible, and financial evaluations. When capital is unlimited, the rates of return from individual investment opportunities are compared to a capital inventory of available funding sources listed in order of increasing interest rates. The least expensive funds from the capital inventory are allocated to projects with the largest rates of return. When capital is limited, a ratio between a project's equivalent annual profit based on the firm's cost of capital and the project's investment requirement provides a preference scale. Capital is rationed by allocating funds to the projects with the highest ratios until the source is exhausted.

4-8 REFERENCES

Barish, N. N., *Economic Analysis for Engineering and Managerial Decision-Making,* McGraw-Hill, New York, 1962.

Bogen, J. I. and S. S. Shipman (eds.), *Financial Handbook* (4th ed.), Ronald Press, New York, 1964.

Bross, I. D., *Design for Decision*, Macmillan, New York, 1953.

Grant, E. I. and W. G. Ireson, *Principles of Engineering Economy* (4th ed.), Ronald Press, New York, 1962.

Hodges, H. G. and R. J. Ziegler, *Managing the Industrial Concern*, Houghton Mifflin, Boston, Mass., 1963.

Levin, R. I. and C. A. Kirkpatrick, *Quantitative Approaches to Management*, McGraw-Hill, New York, 1965.

MacDonald, D. L., *Corporate Risk Control*, Ronald Press, New York, 1966.

Moore, F. G., *Manufacturing Management*, Richard D. Irwin, Homewood, Ill., 1961.

Riggs, J. L., *Economic Decision Models for Engineers and Managers*, McGraw-Hill, New York, 1968.

Schweyer, H. E., *Analytic Models for Managerial and Engineering Economics*, Reinhold, New York, 1964.

Starr, K. L., *Product Design and Decision Theory*, Prentice-Hall, Englewood Cliffs, N.J., 1963.

Taylor, G. A., *Managerial and Engineering Economy: Economic Decision-Making*, Van Nostrand, Princeton, N.J., 1964.

4-9 QUESTIONS AND PROBLEMS

1. Assume you have invented the proverbial "better mousetrap" and plan to set up a production facility to manufacture your invention. List some of the strategic problems you face. What tactics are associated with these strategic considerations?

2. Give an example of how a strategic decision changes to a tactical decision as a function of an organization's growth.

3. A widely used term in government-industry contractual relationships is "cost effectiveness." Explain your interpretation of this term with respect to tactics and strategies.

4. Could an operation with a near-perfect rating in efficiency have a very low rating in effectiveness? Give an example.

5. A student's problems in getting a college education are similar to those in many production systems. Identify some courses of action that could result in:

(a) Organizational suboptimization.

(b) Insular suboptimization.

(c) Temporal suboptimization.

6. What value is there in knowing whether a decision situation is highly sensitive?

7. List several types of cost (insurance, research, depreciation, spoilage, interest, sales commissions, worker wages, executive salaries, advertising, etc.) and decide whether they are fixed or variable costs.

8. Where would a line representing income taxes be shown on a breakeven chart?

9. If the goal is to increase profit, discuss the relationship of total cost and volume to revenue under the options of increasing, maintaining, or decreasing the selling price.

10. What would you do if the ratings for an intangible quality among three products (A, B, and C) showed that A was preferred to B, B was preferred to C, and C was preferred to A?

11. How could a firm determine its "minimum acceptable rate of return"?

12. Why is the present worth comparison method associated with coterminated projects and the annual cost method with repeated projects?

13. An indifference point is often associated with an "aspiration level." How can such a point or level be used in bargaining?

14. Relate the black box input-transformation-output model to a decision tree.

15. How can you reconcile using the expected value criterion when you believe a particular decision situation will occur only once in your lifetime?

16. What use can be made of knowing the value of perfect information for a problem?

17. Identify several sources of funds that could be used to start new projects. What are some advantages and disadvantages of starting a new project as opposed to making an additional investment in an existing project?

18. Prices are going up. Rather than just increase the pricetag on the present product, "Dooper Cleaner," the plan is to put the same product in a new box and call it "Super Dooper Cleaner." The new container will be introduced by an extravagent publicity program. Current sales are 1,000,000 boxes a year at $1 per box. Fixed costs are $300,000 and variable costs are $0.60 per unit. It

118

is anticipated that neither sales volume nor variable costs will increase, but the publicity campaign will double fixed costs. If the new price is $1.29 per box, what is the new breakeven point? How many boxes above present sales would have to be sold under the "old product plus persuasion" plan to double the present profit?

19. Sales forecasts indicate that a minimum of 5000 units will be sold each year for the next 3 years. Two design modifications are being considered for the product. One modification will increase fixed costs by $30,000 per year, but it will reduce variable costs by $8 per unit. The other modification will reduce fixed and variable costs by $7000 and $6 per unit, respectively. Variable cost is currently $30 per unit.

(a) Which design modification should be adopted?
(b) At what point would you be indifferent to the two alternatives?
(c) What comments could be made about the planning horizon?

20. A company now has a total sales volume of $2 million on four products produced in the same mill. The sales and production cost figures for the products (A–D) are shown below:

	A	B	C	D
Percent of total sales	10	20	30	40
Contribution (Percent of P)	45	40	45	35
Fixed cost charged	$70,000	$180,000	$210,000	$220,000
Profit	$20,000	–$20,000	$60,000	$60,000

Recognizing the loss incurred with product B, the company is considering dropping the product. If it is dropped, the sales volume will decrease to $1.8 million and the sales and cost pattern will change to the following figures:

	A	C	D
Percent of total sales	15	35	50
Contribution (percent of P)	45	45	35
Fixed cost charged	$100,000	$250,000	$290,000

Should product B be dropped? How do you account for the decrease of only $40,000 instead of $180,000 in fixed costs for the revised product mix?

119

21. Another alternative for the product mix described in Problem 20 is to substitute a different product for B, called BB. If BB replaces B, total sales volume and the sales-cost figures for products A and C will remain unchanged. The new values for D are: percent of sales $= 45$, contribution (percent of $P = 35$), fixed cost charged $= \$275,000$, and profit $= \$40,000$. For an increase in total profit of $\$10,000$ and an increase in total fixed cost of $\$15,000$, what will the contribution rate be for product BB?

22. A small company manufactures rubber matting for the interiors of custom carts. During the past year a revenue of $\$202,000$ from sales was earned with the given current costs:

Current Operating Costs

Direct material	$51,000
Direct labor	42,000
Maintenance	11,000
Property taxes and depreciation	17,000
Managerial and sales expense	35,000

The forecast for the next year is a drastic drop in custom cart sales, which is expected to limit mat sales to $90,000. There is insufficient time to develop new markets before next year. With a skeleton force for the reduced production, anticipated operating costs are shown below.

Expected Operating Costs

Direct material	$28,000
Direct labor	23,000
Maintenance	7,000
Property taxes and depreciation	17,000
Managerial and sales expense	35,000

The company can operate at an apparent loss, or mats can be purchased from a large supplier and resold to the custom cart builders at a price that will just meet purchase and handling costs. Either alternative will retain the market for the company until the following year when sales are expected to be at least equal to last year.

Which of the two alternatives is the better course of action?

23. Given a nonlinear price function of

$$P = 21,000n^{-1/2} \text{ dollars per unit}$$

where $V = \$1000$ per unit and $FC = \$100,000$ per period, determine:
(a) The breakeven point.
(b) The production level for maximum profit.

24. Operating expenses and revenue for a manufacturing plant are closely approximated by the following relationships:

$$R = 100n - 0.001n^2$$

$$TC = 0.005n^2 + 4n + 200,000 \qquad \text{(both in dollars)}$$

(a) What is the output for maximum profit?
(b) What is the output at the breakeven point?
(c) What is the output for minimum average cost?

25. Ten tentative product designs are being evaluated by the exponential comparison model. Each of the proposals is to be rated on a simple order scale for three intangible qualities: $Q1$, $Q2$, and $Q3$. The first quality, $Q1$, is rated twice as important as $Q2$ and four times more important than $Q3$. The design $(D1)$ that rates first in $Q1$ is last for $Q2$. The design $(D7)$ that rates second in $Q1$ rates sixth in $Q2$. What minimum rating in $Q3$ must $D1$ receive to be the selected design when low numbers indicate preference?

26. Sites for a new research lab have been narrowed to three localities. The construction cost of the plant will be approximately the same regardless of the location chosen. However, cost of land and intangible factors largely applicable to personnel recruitment vary considerably from one location to another. Based on the following ratings, which site should be selected? Ratings show consistent preference for low numbers.

	Site 1	Site 2	Site 3	Importance
Availability of technicians	2	1	5	5
Adequacy of subcontractors	3	1	3	4
Proximity to a university	10 miles	40 miles	30 miles	4
Cost of land	$300,000	$400,000	$50,000	3
Recreation potential	4	5	1	2
Climate	3	6	1	1
Transportation	1	1	3	1

27. A proposed improvement in an assembly line will have an

initial purchase and installation cost of $67,000. Annual maintenance cost will be $3500; periodic overhauls once every 3 years, including the last year of use, will cost $6000 each. The improvement will have a useful life of 12 years at which time it will have no salvage value. What is the equivalent annual expense of the lifetime costs of the improvement when interest is 8%?

28. A company borrowed $100,000 to finance a new product. The loan was for 20 years at a nominal interest rate of 6% compounded semiannually. It was to be repaid in 40 equal payments. After half the payments were made, the company decided to pay the remaining balance in one final payment at the end of the tenth year. How much was owed?

29. Five equal annual payments starting today will be invested to allow two payments of $3000 each to be drawn out 12 and 15 years from now. The two payments will close the account. Interest is 5% compounded annually. What is the amount of the payment to be made today?

30. Additional parking space for a factory can either be rented for $6000 a year on a 10-year lease or purchased for $90,000. The rental fees are payable in advance at the beginning of each year. Taxes and maintenance fees will be paid by the lessee. The land should be worth at least $60,000 after 10 years. What rate of return will be earned from the purchase of the lot?

31. Machine A has a first cost of $9000, no salvage value at the end of its 6-year useful life, and annual operating costs of $5000. Machine B costs $16,000 new and has a resale value of $4000 at the end of its 9-year economic life. Operating costs for B are $4000 per year. Compare the two alternatives on the basis of their annual costs. Which one would you select when interest is at 10%?

32. The annual cost of a piece of equipment is to be compared with a rental cost for comparable equipment. When the interest rate is 8% compounded annually, what rental charge would make the two alternatives equally attractive?

Purchase price	$12,000
Salvage value	$3500
Economic life	7 years
Annual operating costs	$2200
Taxes	2% per year of first cost
Overhauls	$1200 each at the end of years 3 and 5
Insurance	$460 for a 7-year policy payable in advance

33. "Ipso Facto" offers to handle the data-processing requirements of a company for 3 years at a lump sum price of $19,000 payable in advance. An alternative offer is to charge $7000 per year payable in advance each year. What rate of return is earned by the subscribing company if it accepts the 3-year contract rather than successive 1-year arrangements?

34. Compare the rate of return for the following plans and select the preferable alternative. The minimum acceptable rate of return is 6%.

	Plan 1	Plan 2	Plan 3
First cost	$40,000	$32,000	$70,000
Salvage value	$10,000	$6000	$20,000
Economic life	7 years	7 years	7 years
Annual receipts	$18,000	$18,000	$24,500
Annual disbursements	$11,000	$14,500	$14,500

	S1	S2
A1	−$10,000	$60,000
A2	$35,000	$35,000
A3	$120,000	−$20,000

35. Based on the given payoff table:
(a) Determine the indifference point of the alternatives and state how the values obtained can be used to aid decision making.
(b) If the probabilities of S1 and S2 are, respectively, 0.3 and 0.7, what is the value of perfect information?

36. Which of the two alternatives displayed in the decision tree of Figure 4.20 is more attractive? There are two 3-year study periods and the annual interest rate is 7%. Assuming positive values represent costs, seek the minimum cost alternative.

37. It has already been decided that accounting and billing procedures will be computerized. The question now is how much

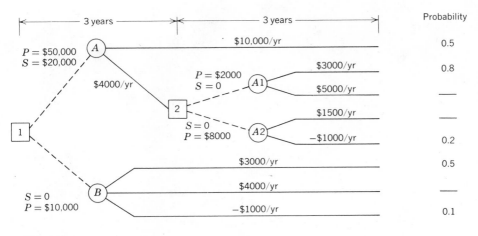

Figure 4.20

equipment should be leased. Two different capacities are being considered. The larger system (B) leases for $240,000 per year on a 4-year lease or $300,000 per year on a 2-year lease. The smaller system (S) has an annual lease cost of $110,000 and $150,000 on leases of 4 and 2 years, respectively.

A 4-year study period will be employed. The forecast is a 0.7 probability of high activity (H) for the next 2 years and 0.3 for low activity (L). If activity is high for the first 2 years, it is equally likely to be high (HH) or low (HL) for the successive 2 years. If the first 2 years produce low activity, then there is a probability of 0.8 for 2 more years of low activity (LL).

Expected savings per year from the installation of either system for the different activity patterns are shown below. These savings do not include any leasing costs but do reflect the increased accuracy, quantity, and speed expected.

	First 2 Years	Second 2 Years Given First 2
Large	$H = \$300,000$	$HH = \$350,000; HL = \$200,000$
system (B):	$L = \$200,000$	$LH = \$300,000; LL = \$100,000$
Small	$H = \$200,000$	$HH = \$250,000; HL = \$100,000$
system (S):	$L = \$100,000$	$LH = \$200,000; LL = \$50,000$

Hint: There are four primary alternatives. • Which computer system should be leased now and should it be leased for 2 or 4 years?

CHAPTER 5

ALLOCATION OF RESOURCES

5-1 IMPORTANCE In our planning steps thus far, we have attempted to peek into the future to decide which courses of action would be feasible. Then we have applied the dollar yardstick to see which one would be most worthwhile. Now we shall consider the assignment of resources to the selected plan.

Resources are allocated under the assumption of certainty. That is, for a given set of conditions deemed most realistic, the requirements of a project are analyzed to apportion available resources optimally to achieve desired objectives. Occasionally there is only one way to do things. Then allocations are anticlimactic. More commonly, there is considerable resource convertibility, and astute planning can use this flexibility to advantage.

In this chapter we shall consider formal procedures to assist resource planning. These procedures are great timesavers when appropriately applied, but they are not substitutes for creativity. They are ingenious succors in the evaluation of massed data, but they do not validate the data. Therefore, given reliable data and well-advised objectives, the described routines provide assurance that the right amounts of resources are assigned to the right places.

5-2 LINEAR PROGRAMMING

Linear means directly proportional relationships between variables. *Programming* applies to calculating procedures for solving a set of linear equations or inequations.

See for example the marginal analyses for nonlinear breakeven data in Section 4-3.

Problems of allocating scarce resources to competing activities are candidates for linear programming (LP) procedures. These procedures are appropriate whenever the variables in the problem are linearly related to each other. Applications have been extensive in industry and sometimes have produced dramatic savings. Although LP is by no means the only way to optimize returns for a given system, many fundamental relationships of quantities invite its utilization.

The development of LP is closely associated with economic theory and research. Early economic studies assumed a continuous relationship of variables which could be evaluated with calculus. While these assumptions were applicable to some

125

systems, such as agriculture, they were not satisfactory for many industrial systems. The input-output method of analysis by economist W. W. Leontiff started the trend toward LP methods. Current developments grew from the work of G. B. Dantzig who originated the simplex method of LP in 1947.

Studies of production systems present many opportunities for LP applications. LP can be employed profitably in all three evaluation stages: planning, analysis, and control. Applicable problems include planning the location of supply facilities to minimize transportation costs, analyzing operations and methods to improve profits, and controlling machine loading to achieve maximum utilization. In this section we shall first consider the graphical LP approach for determining the most profitable

Sections 7-3 and 10-5. • product mix and then the more general transportation method. In later sections, other distribution methods will be considered. The simplex method is presented in Appendix C.

5-3 GRAPHICAL METHOD

The selection of an optimal mix is an ideal introduction to LP methods. Determining the proportion of each product to produce when production resources are limited is typical of LP applications that specify how to use scarce resources to maximize profit. A two-product mix has the further advantage of simplicity which allows the key features to be easily accented.

Requirements for An LP Solution

One difficult task in evaluating production systems is to recognize the best method of attacking a problem. Often several computational techniques could be applied. Usually one of them will give better results or produce equivalent results with less effort. To identify this better method, you have to match the characteristics of the problem to the requirements of different problem-solving methods. An awareness of the following LP requirements should reveal whether a problem is amenable to this form of solution.

The objective must be stated explicitly. The objective to get the "best equipment for our purposes" is too broad to be useful. Similarly, the goal of "obtaining the best equipment for the least money" is bewilderingly indefinite. Such contradictory or nebulous aims must be reconciled before the objective function can be expressed in the necessary equation.

Alternate courses of action must be available. If there is only one

A choice without an alternative is sometimes called "Hobson's choice" in allusion to the practice of Thomas Hobson (d. 1631) who let' horses and required every customer to take the horse standing nearest the door.

way to accomplish a necessary task, the recourse is to do it the given way or to do nothing. However, when faced with Hobson's choice, at least a little doubt should be cast on the problem formulation. Perhaps a more creative effort or additional information would expose more alternatives.

Resources must be limited. Very rarely is there an unlimited supply of anything worth having, but commonly it is difficult to know how scarce a resource really is. Again it may take some imagination and considerable searching to set realistic limits on variables.

Variables must be linearly interrelated. A corollary is that the variables must be quantifiable. Relationships between variables are expressed by inequations to show that "the allocation of resource 1 plus resource 2 cannot exceed a certain quantity" or by equations to set "the number sold of product *A* plus product *B* yields a certain profit."

Product Mix—Two-Dimensional Case

Product mix problems occur when several products are produced in the same work centers. When only two products are involved, regardless of the number of work stations through which they pass, it is a two-dimensional case. That is, when the problem is displayed on a graph, the two products are shown on the *X*-*Y* axes. Data for linearly related product mix restrictions and profits are shown in Table 5.1.

Table 5.1 Production times and profit data for two products

	Hours per Unit		Hours Available
	Product *A*	Product *B*	
Machine center *J*	3	2	Up to 42
Machine center *K*	2	2	Up to 30
Machine center *L*	2	4	Up to 48
Contribution per unit	$12	$8	

Note that contribution per unit, not profit per unit, is linearly related to the number of units made and sold. See Section 5–3.

The two products, *A* and *B*, must pass through all three machine centers, *J*, *K*, and *L*, but their passage can be in any order. The contribution per unit made and sold of each product is shown at the bottom of each product's column. These figures establish a profit equation:

$$Z = \$12A + \$8B$$

127

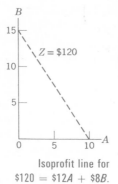

Isoprofit line for
$120 = $12A + $8B.

which states that the total profit is equal to the contribution of
A ($12) times the number produced of A plus the contribution of
B($8) times the production of B. This profit expression is the
• *objective function* which we seek to maximize. It can be depicted
graphically by a series of isoprofit lines of constant slope. A
dashed line representing all the product mixes that will yield a
total profit of $120 is shown in the margin sketch.

The colored portion of Table 5.1 shows the time relationships
of the limiting resources. At most, only 48 hours are available in
machine center L. These hours could be used to produce $\frac{48}{2} = 24$
units of A, $\frac{48}{4} = 12$ units of B, or some combination of both A
and B such as 8 units of each. This condition can be expressed by
the *inequation*

$$2A + 4B \leq 48$$

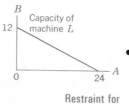

Restraint for
$2A + 4B \leq 48$.

which states that the sum of the times for both products in the
machine center must be less than or equal to ($\leq$) 48 hours. A line
representing this restraint is shown in the margin sketch. Any
• mix on or to the left of the line meets the restriction. A mix
represented by any point to the right of the line requires more
time than is available in machine center L.

Combining the three machine center restrictions:

$$3A + 2B \leq 42 \qquad \text{for machine center } J$$

$$2A + 2B \leq 30 \qquad \text{for machine center } K$$

$$2A + 4B \leq 48 \qquad \text{for machine center } L$$

The restriction $A \geq 0 \leq B$
establishes that the graph is in • with the obvious restriction that we cannot produce negative
the positive $X - Y$ quadrant. products ($A \geq 0, B \geq 0$) to save time, we have the graph shown
in Figure 5.1. The colored area is the *feasible solution* space. This
area represents all possible mixes that meet the restraints imposed

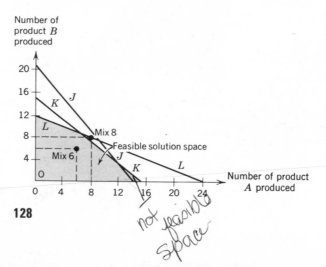

Figure 5.1 Feasible solution
space set by machine center
restraints

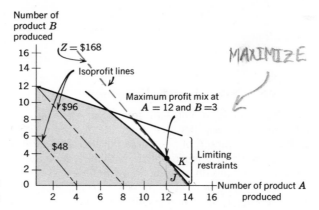

Figure 5.2 Most profitable mix identified by isoprofit lines

by the machine center time limitations. For instance, mix 6 (6 units of both A and B) is well within the time limits for all restraints, but mix 8 (8 units of A and B) exceeds the time available in machine center K ($(2 \times 8) + (2 \times 8) = 32 \nleq 30$) by two hours, making it a restraint violation.

With all feasible mix alternatives delineated, the remaining task is to select the one that meets the objective of maximizing profit. It is natural to expect that producing more products will increase profit. This is confirmed by the increasing magnitude of isoprofit lines as they depart further from the origin, O. The logical conclusion is then that the isoprofit line most distant from O but still within the feasible solution space identifies the mix that maximizes profit.

As shown in Figure 5.2, the last isoprofit line ($168) that touches the perimeter of the feasible solution polygon indicates the proportion of products for maximum profit. The mix can be read directly from the graph if the scale is large enough, or it can be determined algebraically from the restraint lines (J and K) that intersect at the indicated vertex. Because all the allowable time in each machine center is utilized at any intersection point, the coordinates can be determined from a simultaneous solution of the equations of the intersecting lines:

The problem described in Table 5.1 is also solved by the Simplex method in Appendix C. The presence of equally profitable solutions ($168) is shown to occur along constraint line J from $A = 12$ and $B = 3$ to $A = 14$ and $B = 0$.

$$-\quad\begin{array}{ll} 3A + 2B = 42 & \text{from machine center } J \\ 2A + 2B = 30 & \text{from machine center } K \end{array}$$

$$A = 12 \text{ units and } B = 3 \text{ units}$$

Thus, all the available time from machine centers J and K is utilized to produce 12 units of A and 3 units of B for a total profit of $168. Although the utilization of machine center L is 48 —

$$[(2 \times 12) + (4 \times 3)] = 12 \text{ hours short of capacity, no other}$$

combination of products will yield a greater profit.

EXAMPLE 5.1 Graphical Solution of a Mix to Minimize Cost

A concrete products company has two sources of sand and gravel aggregate. The material from one source is much coarser than the other. The cost from either source depends on pit cost, hauling, and refining. The amount of each grade of rock and sand required for the production of concrete pipe, ready-mix, and other products is fairly well known for 1 month in advance, but it changes from month to month as a function of demand. The objective of determining the proportion of material to take from each source is to *minimize* monthly procurement, handling, and storage costs. Necessary cost and quantity relationships are tabulated below.

Aggregate Size	Pounds per Ton		Tons Required
	Source 1	Source 2	
½ inch to 2 inches	600/2000	200	10,000
#4 to ½ inch	900	600	15,000
#50 to #4	400	900	20,000
Less than #50	100	300	5,000
Cost per ton	$1.51	$1.68	

The first step in solving the problem is to convert all measures to the same dimensions. Since

% of ton for each source

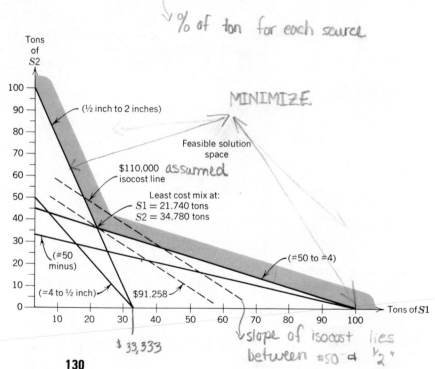

MINIMIZE

Figure 5.3

130

most units are in tons, the pounds of each aggregate size per ton can be converted to percentages of tons to establish the following restraint in equations:

$$0.30\ S1 + 0.10\ S2 \geqslant 10,000 \qquad \text{for } \tfrac{1}{2} \text{ inch to 2 inches}$$

$$0.45\ S1 + 0.30\ S2 \geqslant 15,000 \qquad \text{for } \#4 \text{ to } \tfrac{1}{2} \text{ inch}$$

$$0.20\ S1 + 0.45\ S2 \geqslant 20,000 \qquad \text{for } \#50 \text{ to } \#4$$

$$0.05\ S1 + 0.15\ S2 \geqslant \ \ 5,000 \qquad \text{for less than } \#50$$

The function to minimize is

$$\text{cost} = \$1.51 S1 + \$1.68 S2$$

These conditions can be graphically represented as in Figure 5.3.

Because the quantity of rock and sand must be greater than or equal to given monthly demands, the solution space falls to the right of the restraint lines. Two isocost lines are shown in the figure. It is apparent that cost decreases as the lines move to the left and that the lowest cost mix is defined by the intersection of the ($\tfrac{1}{2}$ inch to 2 inches) and ($\#50$ to $\#4$) aggregate size restraints. From the equations for the indicated restraints, the mix is determined to be 21,740 tons from $S1$ and 34,780 tons from $S2$. This mix exceeds the monthly 50,000-ton demand as shown in Table 5.2. But no other combination will meet the requirements at a cost less than $91,258.

Table 5.2 Quantity and cost summary of the optimal mix

Aggregate Size	Tons per Monthly Estimate Period				
	Source 1	Source 2	Total	Required	Excess
$\tfrac{1}{2}$ inch to 2 inches	6,522	3,478	10,000	10,000	0
$\#4$ to $\tfrac{1}{2}$ inch	9,783	10,433	20,216	15,000	5,216
$\#50$ to $\#4$	4,348	15,652	20,000	20,000	0
Less than $\#50$	1,087	5,217	6,304	5,000	1,304
Totals	21,740	34,780	56,520	50,000	6,520

[handwritten: limiting factors]

Cost: $1.51(21,740) + $1.68(34,780) = $91,258

Product Mix—Multidimensional Case

A graphical solution to a three-product mix depends on the utilization of planes in X-Y-Z space.

A graphical solution to a product mix problem works fine for two products, becomes difficult for three products, and is impossible for more than three products. Other solution methods are therefore required. For relatively small problems, algebraic or systematic trial-and-error solution procedures are possible, but the simplex method is usually more manageable.

Most significant applications of LP contain a formidable array of restraints and variables. In such cases, any manual approach becomes exceedingly tedious. Individual calculations are not difficult, but there are just an awful lot of them. Fortunately we can call on electronic assistance. Computer programs are widely available and extensively employed for high-capacity applications.

131

With respect to the speed and accuracy of machine-aided computations, you might question the need for a familiarity with do-it-yourself calculation methods. It is a legitimate question now, and in the future it will get more difficult to answer. Presently, we have to structure the problem to the capabilities of the computer. In the science-fiction era of tomorrow, to which our technology continually propels us, machines may qualify as analysts as well as computers. Until then, and perhaps then too, the economy of hand-versus-machine solutions is subject to a
• breakeven analysis as portrayed in the marginal sketch. It usually costs more to set up a computer solution, but it costs less to perform repeated calculations. Therefore, the more rapid hand calculation techniques should be on tap for smaller or less frequently encountered problems. And the familiarity gained from manual applications should point out when and where computer assistance is beneficial.

5-4 TRANSPORTATION METHOD OF LP

Other allocation problems include products to make or buy, plant layout, and product marketing.

The transportation method is more versatile than the graphical routine and retains the succinctness to make it a worthy tool for manual calculations. It is used to determine preferred routes for the distribution of supplies from a number of origins to different destinations. Although the name "transportation" tends to conjure images of warehouses supplying retail outlets with
• produce, the method also can be used to identify the least cost or most profitable distribution pattern for any resource.

The solution format is a matrix that defines: (1) the amount and location of both supply and demand, and (2) the cost or profit created by supplying one unit from every origin to every destination. There is no limit to the number of origins or destinations that can be included in the matrix. An optimal distribution is obtained by first developing an initial solution and then sequentially testing and revising improved solutions until no further improvements are available. There may be several equal cost-distribution patterns. These alternative routes are identified by the solution procedures.

Details of the solution procedures will be illustrated with a sample application. Assume a chain of bakeries, producing a complete line of packaged cakes, cookies, pies, and other baked desserts, plans to construct a new baking plant–distribution center. The company has two bakeries in metropolitan centers which are providing products to adjacent smaller communities. These plants operate at full capacity but cannot meet current demand. Unless unexpected competition appears, the market potential should continue to grow. To meet the anticipated demand, a new bakery will be built in one of two locations. The additional capacity will satisfy the local sales of the city in which the bakery is located and the demand of nearby cities. The problem is to decide which location will minimize the cost of distributing products.

An idea of the geographical layout and distribution pattern is available from Figure 5.4. Rectangles represent baking plant–distribution centers; circles represent the outlying cities where products are sold. The size of the symbols provides a rough indication of capacity. The arcs show possible distribution patterns. Solid lines in both the arcs and rectangles show existing routes and patterns. Dashed lines represent the alternative new plant locations and associated distribution patterns.

Only one alternative is to be selected. Thus, if B4 is the chosen bakery site, the local market M4 logically will be supplied by B4. If B3 is the selected site instead of B4, M3 will be the home market.

Packaged bakery goods are delivered by company-owned trucks to nearby cities. The product mix of the goods is customized to the market demand. The total contribution is a function of the mix, but transportation cost is a function of the volume moved. Therefore, supply, demand, and transportation costs are rated in units of truck loads. The cost per truck to supply each marketing area and the capacity relationships are given in Table 5.3. The supply at each bakery indicates the balance available for outlying markets after the local demand has been met. Thus B4 has a total capacity of 44 truck loads per day but has only 24 loads available for daily shipments to other cities after supplying M4.

All the data from Table 5.3 appropriate to the bakery site B3

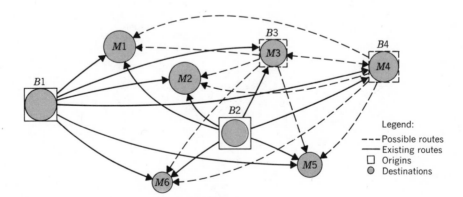

Figure 5.4 Existing and possible supply and demand pattern

Table 5.3 Data required for a transportation problem

Capacity in Truck Loads per Day				Distribution Cost per Truck Load						
Bakery	Supply	Market	Demand		M1	M2	M3	M4	M5	M6
B1	22	M1	16	B1	$14	$24	$30	$50	$44	$16
B2	18	M2	18	B2	$20	$14	$16	$32	$16	$14
B3	29	M3	15	B3	$16	$11	—	$18	$26	$45
B4	24	M4	20	B4	$35	$26	$18	—	$20	$50
		M5	10							
		M6	5							

are compactly included in a transportation matrix. As shown in Figure 5.5, the available and required quantities associated with each origin and destination are entered in the bottom row and outside right column. These entries, called *rim conditions*, correspond to the restraint lines of the graphical method. Each cell in the matrix represents a possible routing of supplies from a source to a destination. Each route has a distinct cost or profit which is shown in the left slice of the cell. The portion of the cell to the right of the slash is reserved for quantity or opportunity cost entries.

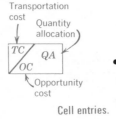

Transportation cost
Quantity allocation
TC / QA / OC
Opportunity cost

Cell entries.

Reviewing the given problem conditions with respect to the requirements for a LP solution, we have:

1. An explicit objective to minimize the total cost of distributing bakery products to the market areas.
2. Several alternative combinations of truck routes.
3. Limited supplies available from the bakery–distribution centers to satisfy the demand that is also limited.

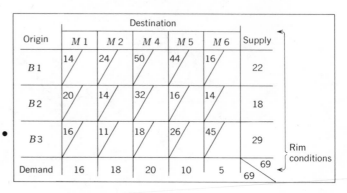

M3 is not included in the matrix because B3 automatically supplies M3.

Figure 5.5 Transportation matrix for B3 alternative

supply must = demand

134

4. Variables linearly related according to supply, demand, and distribution costs.

With the problem data and the solution method identified, we are ready to plunge into the solution procedures.

5-5 INITIAL FEASIBLE SOLUTION—VOGEL'S APPROXIMATION METHOD

An *initial* solution is a first attempt to match supply and demand along advantageous distribution routes. For it to be a *feasible* solution, it must meet the following conditions:

A cell is occupied if it contains an entry that represents a quantity transfer from an origin to a destination.

1. The rim conditions of the transportation matrix must be satisfied—the sum of the quantities in occupied cells for rows and columns must equal the corresponding rim quantities.

2. The number of occupied cells must equal one less than the sum of the number of origins (O) and destinations (D); $O + D - 1$.

3. The occupied cells must be independent positions. Dependent positions allow a round trip from an occupied cell back to itself using only horizontal and vertical movements with right angle turns at occupied cells.

Dependent positions;
X = occupied cell.

	D1	D2	D3
01	X	X	
02		X	X

Independent positions;
X = occupied cell.

Other methods of obtaining an initial solution include assignments by inspection or by the "Northwest Corner Rule" where assignments starting at the northwest corner of the matrix progressively meet rim requirements.

When two cells in the same row or column have the same minimum cost for transportation, the penalty for that row or column is zero.

The significance of the required number of occupied cells and the need for independent positions will become apparent when the initial feasible solution is checked for optimality by the stepping-stone technique (Section 5-6).

A desired but not required quality of an initial feasible solution is that it be as close as possible to the optimal solution. Iterative tests for optimality are time consuming. Spending a little extra time on the initial step often pays big dividends in time saved from subsequent steps. For this reason we shall determine the initial feasible solution through the use of Vogel's approximation method (VAM).

VAM is based on the concept of penalties charged for not making an allocation to the lowest cost route. A penalty for each row and column is calculated by subtracting the cost for transporting by the least expensive route from the next most expensive route. The cell causing the highest penalty receives the first allocation. After each cell entry, the penalties are recalculated and successive entries are made to avoid the highest penalties. When two penalties are equal, a judgment based on a mental preview of forthcoming penalties decides the issue. The process is continued until conditions for a feasible solution are met.

A detailed application of VAM to the matrix of Figure 5.5 is presented in Figure 5.6. For clarity purposes the example employs separate allocation and penalty matrices. In actual practice the shorthand form used in Section 5.7 is more convenient.

A quick check of the final allocations of the VAM solution reveals that the rim conditions are satisfied; there are $3 + 5 - 1 = 7$ allocations, and those allocations are in independent positions. Therefore, the solution is ready for the optimality check.

5-6 OPTIMAL SOLUTION—STEPPING-STONE METHOD

An optimal solution is the "best possible" course of action under the restrictions imposed by the problem. When the objective is to minimize cost, the optimal solution provides the lowest cost. A test for optimality in a transportation problem is conducted by trying to locate less expensive distribution routes. Each cell left unoccupied in the initial feasible solution is a potential new route. By calculating the cost of using each new route and comparing it with corresponding allocations from the initial solution, we can determine if any changes will provide a less expensive distribution pattern. This approach, called the *stepping-stone method*, determines if a change is advisable, where it should be made, and how much is saved by making it.

The "stepping-stone" name follows naturally from the way the method checks for optimality. A matrix can be thought of as a number of interconnected horizontal and vertical channels. Quantities can flow either way in the channels but cannot cut across them. By further assuming that right angle turns to change channel passages can be made only at occupied cells, we figuratively have the stepping-stone method; turning points (occupied cells) are stepping stones and we check the cost of using each stone as alternative distribution routes are traced.

The logic behind the stepping-stone method is apparent in its application. Starting with the initial feasible solution developed in Figure 5.6, we can select any unoccupied cell for the first check. The low transportation cost in $B2,M6$ ($14) appears to be a good candidate for a lower cost route. The check is made by calculating the cost of changing the distribution pattern to accommodate the shipment of *one* unit (truck load) from $B2$ to $M6$. Adding one unit to $B2,M6$ violates the rim conditions. To put the supply and demand relationships back in balance, we have to subtract one unit from the previous allocations to $B1,M6$ and $B2,M2$. Now the $B2$ row is in balance but column $M2$ is one unit short. By adding one unit of $B1,M2$, all the rim conditions are again

The highest cost cells in a matrix seldom provide less expensive routes and thereby deserve only a cursory check.

| Operations | Penalty Matrices | | | | | | | Allocation Matrices | | | | | | |

Stage 1

The highest penalty is circled in column $M4$. The lowest cost for $M4$ is from $B3$ where the required 20 units are allocated. $B3$ now has 9 units left.

	M1	M2	M4	M5	M6	Row Penalty
B1	14	24	50	44	16	2
B2	20	14	32	16	14	0
B3	16	11	18	26	45	5
Column Penalty	2	3	(14)	10	2	

	M1	M2	M4	M5	M6	Available
B1						22
B2						18
B3			(20)			29
Required	16	18	20	10	5	

Stage 2

$M4$ is eliminated from the penalty matrix because the demand is satisfied. Now $M5$ has the highest penalty, and 10 of the 18 units available in $B2$ are allocated to it.

	M1	M2	M5	M6	Row Penalty
B1	14	24	44	16	2
B2	20	14	16	14	0
B3	16	11	26	45	5
Column Penalty	2	3	(10)	2	

	M1	M2	M4	M5	M6	Available
B1						22
B2				(10)		18
B3			20			9
Required	16	18	0	10	5	

Stage 3

After eliminating $M5$, the penalty in row $B3$ is the highest. The lowest cost in the row is $M2$ which requires 18 units, but only 9 are still available from $B3$. Therefore, these 9 are allocated to $B2$.

	M1	M2	M6	Row Penalty
B1	14	24	16	2
B2	20	14	14	0
B3	16	11	45	(5)
Column Penalty	2	3	2	

	M1	M2	M4	M5	M6	Available
B1						22
B2				10		8
B3		(9)	20			9
Required	16	18	0	0	5	

Stage 4

With row $B3$ eliminated and the penalties recalculated, $M2$ shows the highest penalty. 9 units are required but only 8 are available in the low cost row $B2$.

	M1	M2	M6	Row Penalty
B1	14	24	16	2
B2	20	14	14	0
Column Penalty	6	(10)	2	

	M1	M2	M4	M5	M6	Available
B1						22
B2		(8)		10		8
B3		9	20			0
Required	16	9	0	0	5	

Stage 5

After the allocation of 8 units to $B2,M2$, another penalty matrix reduction serves no purpose because there is no choice for the remaining allocations. To meet the rim conditions, 16 of the 22 units available from $B1$ are rationed to $M1$, 1 to $M2$, and 5 to $M6$.

	M1	M2	M4	M5	M6	Available
B1	(16)	(1)			(5)	22
B2		8		10		0
B3		9	20			0
Required	16	1	0	0	5	

Figure 5.6 Detailed application of Vogel's approximation method

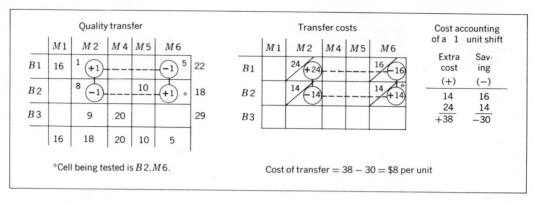

Figure 5.7 Stepping-stone transfer circuit and associated cost

satisfied. We have thus used the occupied cells as stepping stones to make a complete circuit from the cell being tested. The addition-subtraction-addition-subtraction routine of closing the quantity-transfer loop is shown in Figure 5.7.

After the transfer circuit is identified, it is a simple matter to calculate the net cost of the one-unit shift. Wherever a unit is added to a cell, that cell is charged with the transportation cost for the extra unit. Conversely, a deletion of one unit from a cell creates a savings in the amount of one unit's transportation cost. The positive and negative charges can be calculated directly from the matrix or tabulated in T-accounts as shown in Figure 5.7. By either method, the end result is one figure that tells whether it costs more or less to include the tested cell in the distribution pattern. If the extra cost exceeds the savings in the complete circuit, no changes should be made. When the negative charges (savings) are larger than the positive costs, the tested cell should be included in a revised solution.

A negative transfer cost (saving) is a positive opportunity cost because it represents a cost incurred by not selecting the best possible alternative. Similarly, an extra cost is a negative opportunity cost.

A solution is improved by transferring as many units as possible to the vacant cell that allows the greatest savings. The maximum number of units that can be transferred is limited by the smallest number in a negative cell in the transfer circuit. Using this number reduces to zero the quantity in the limiting negative cell and adds the same amount to the previously unoccupied cell. All cells in the circuit receive similar treatment, either increasing or decreasing by the limiting quantity. The total gain achieved by the shift is equal to the number of units transferred multiplied by the savings per unit.

The results from testing all unoccupied cells in the sample are given in Figure 5.8. The arbitrary order of testing unoccupied

138

cells is shown by the circled numbers in the matrix; the corresponding cells in the test circuit are given with the tested cell first in the sequence. In this example no refinements are necessary for the solution obtained by VAM. The minimum daily transportation cost expected from building the new bakery at site $B3$ is $1059.

5-7 IRREGULARITIES IN TRANSPORTATION PROBLEMS

Very few transportation problems allow such a neat, direct solution as encountered in the previous section. Sometimes the problem cannot be formulated so compactly or difficulties enter in the solution procedures. The more common irregularities and the means to overcome them are presented in this section.

Dependency

If the necessity is not clear, try to test an unoccupied cell in the margin matrix with dependent positions in Section 5.5.

After studying the stepping-stone method and the employment of closed transfer circuits, the necessity of independent locations for initial allocations should be apparent. If a dependent allocation pattern slips through a check of the initial solution, it will assuredly be discovered during revisions; a transfer circuit that includes an unoccupied cell plus an *even* number of occupied cells is telltale evidence of initial dependent locations. The cure is to rearrange the allocations by inspection and then proceed with the routine checks for unoccupied cells.

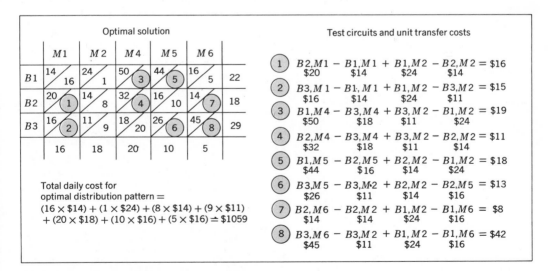

Optimal solution

	$M1$	$M2$	$M4$	$M5$	$M6$	
$B1$	14 / 16	24 / 1	50 ③	44 ⑤	16 / 5	22
$B2$	20 ①	14 / 8	32 ④	16 / 10	14 ⑦	18
$B3$	16 ②	11 / 9	18 / 20	26 ⑥	45 ⑧	29
	16	18	20	10	5	

Total daily cost for optimal distribution pattern =
$(16 \times \$14) + (1 \times \$24) + (8 \times \$14) + (9 \times \$11)$
$+ (20 \times \$18) + (10 \times \$16) + (5 \times \$16) \doteq \$1059$

Test circuits and unit transfer costs

① $B2,M1 - B1,M1 + B1,M2 - B2,M2 = \$16$
   $\$20 \quad \$14 \quad \$24 \quad \$14$

② $B3,M1 - B1,M1 + B1,M2 - B3,M2 = \$15$
   $\$16 \quad \$14 \quad \$24 \quad \$11$

③ $B1,M4 - B3,M4 + B3,M2 - B1,M2 = \$19$
   $\$50 \quad \$18 \quad \$11 \quad \$24$

④ $B2,M4 - B3,M4 + B3,M2 - B2,M2 = \$11$
   $\$32 \quad \$18 \quad \$11 \quad \$14$

⑤ $B1,M5 - B2,M5 + B2,M2 - B1,M2 = \$18$
   $\$44 \quad \$16 \quad \$14 \quad \$24$

⑥ $B3,M5 - B3,M2 + B2,M2 - B2,M5 = \$13$
   $\$26 \quad \$11 \quad \$14 \quad \$16$

⑦ $B2,M6 - B2,M2 + B1,M2 - B1,M6 = \$8$
   $\$14 \quad \$14 \quad \$24 \quad \$16$

⑧ $B3,M6 - B3,M2 + B1,M2 - B1,M6 = \$42$
   $\$45 \quad \$11 \quad \$24 \quad \$16$

Figure 5.8 Minimum distribution costs for bakery site $B3$

Degeneracy

$O + D - 1$ allocations mean the number of occupied cells is one less than the number of rows and columns.

$$1 + \varepsilon = 1$$
$$1 - \varepsilon = 1$$
$$\varepsilon - \varepsilon = 0$$

A final optimal solution can be degenerate.

When a solution has fewer than $O + D - 1$ allocations, it is *degenerate.* Both the symptoms and the cure of degeneracy are similar to those for dependency. An unsuccessful struggle to close a transfer circuit is a symptom of degeneracy; a count of occupied cells can confirm the condition. The cure is to assign an infinitesimal quantity, called epsilon (ε), to a promising unoccupied cell. Epsilon has the unusual but convenient properties of: (1) being large enough to treat the cell in which it is placed as occupied, and (2) being small enough to assume that its placement does not change rim conditions.

Degeneracy can develop in either an initial or a revised solution. In both cases it is treated the same. One or more cells receive epsilon allocations to make the total number of occupied cells equal to $O + D - 1$. The cells to receive epsilon allocations should be carefully chosen because a transfer circuit cannot have a negative epsilon stepping stone. The reason, of course, is that you cannot subtract a unit from a cell that contains only an infinitesimal part of a unit. Therefore, epsilon quantities should be introduced in cells that accommodate the solution procedures.

The second alternative available to the bakery chain described in the previous section illustrates degeneracy during the initial feasible solution. VAM is applied to a matrix including data for the alternative bakery site, B4. Instead of using reduced matrices for calculating the penalties as illustrated in Figure 5.6, the successive penalty calculations are shown outside the rim

	M1	M2	M3	M5	M6		Order of Allocations				
---	---	---	---	---	---	---	(1)	(2)	(3)	(4)	(5)
B1	14 16 24 ④4	24	30 1 44 ⑤5	44	16 5 ②2	22	2	2	16	16	—
B2	20	14 18 16 ①1	16	16	14	18	0	—	—	—	—
B4	35	26	18 14 ⑤5	20 10 ③3	50	24	2	2	2	17	17*
	16	18	15	10	5						
①	6	10*	2	4	2						
②	21	—	12	24	34*						
③	21	—	12	24*	—						
④	21*	—	12	—	—						
⑤	—	—	12	—	—						

*Indicates the highest penalty in each round of calculations.

Figure 5.9 Degenerate initial solution by VAM

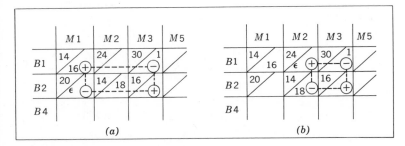

Figure 5.10 Introduction of ϵ to relieve degeneracy: (*a*) incorrect ϵ placement and (*b*) correct ϵ placement

Data for Figure 5.9 are from Table 5.3.

The maximum number that can be transferred in a circuit is the smallest allocation in a negative cell.

• requirements in Figure 5.9. The circled numbers in the matrix indicate the order in which the allocations were made. For instance, after ③ allocations, row B4 has the highest penalty (17) in round ④ of the penalty calculations. Therefore, the remaining 14 units (10 units from B4 were allocated to M5 in allocation ③) are assigned to M3 in step ⑤. After this allocation, no further penalty calculations are needed because the remaining units must be allocated according to unfilled rim requirements.

The initial solution is degenerate owing to 6 instead of $3 + 5 - 1 = 7$ occupied cells. A logical improvement is to eliminate the high cost B1,M3 route. The unoccupied cell B2,M3 makes a good starting point. In the existing degenerate condition, it is impossible to make a stepping-stone circuit around B2,M3. An epsilon quantity must be introduced. Epsilon could be added to B2,M1 to complete a transfer circuit as shown in Figure 5.10a, • but the epsilon stepping stone is negative and consequently allows only an inconsequential transfer. By placing epsilon in B1,M2, it becomes a positive transfer cell in the circuit $+B2,M3 - B1,M3 + B1,M2 - B2,M3$. A $(+16 - 30 + 24 - 14 =) -\$4$ cost or \$4 saving results from the transfer of one unit (5.10b). This transfer further increases the number of occupied cells by one and thereby eliminates the degeneracy.

After each revision it is necessary to check for possible additional improvements. With the distribution pattern altered to include the revision from Figure 5.10, one route, B2,M5, still provides further savings:

$$+ B2, M5 - B4, M5 + B4, M3 - B2, M3$$

$$+ 16 - 20 + 18 - 16 = -\$2$$

This circuit and the maximum possible one-unit shift it provides are shown in Figure 5.11.

The second and final revision reveals the optimal solution;

141

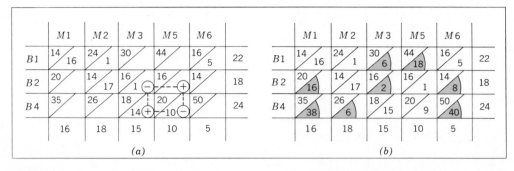

Figure 5.11 Revised and optimal solution to the bakery location problem: (*a*) distribution pattern after first revision and transfer circuit for next revision and (*b*) allocations after second revision and final, optimal distribution pattern

Note the lopsided figure • 8-shaped circuit necessary to check $B1$, $M3$ in Figure 5.11b.

	$M1$	$M2$	$M3$	$M5$
$B1$		−1	+1	
$B2$		+1		−1
$B4$			−1	+1

all remaining routes exhibit greater transfer costs as shown in the lower left corner of each unoccupied cell of the final matrix. The total transportation cost expected from locating the new bakery at site $B4$ is $1032 = (14 \times \$16) + (1 \times \$24) + (17 \times \$14) + (1 \times \$16) + (15 \times \$18) + (9 \times \$20) + (5 \times \$16)$. Selection of the $B4$ location over the $B3$ alternative provides daily distribution savings of $1059 - \$1032 = \$27$.

Alternative Optimal Solutions

Instead of a positive transfer cost in all the unoccupied cells, as was the case in Figure 5.11, one or more cells may show zero cost. A cell with a zero transfer cost denotes an alternative, equal cost routing. The inclusion of such a cell in the distribution pattern is decided by intangible factors not shown in the transportation matrix. A preference for a certain route could depend on loading convenience at the origin, reliability of the carrier, or service expected at the destination. Equivalent alternatives are valuable for the flexibility they allow.

Maximization Problems

When origins are related to destinations by a profit function instead of cost, the objective is to maximize instead of minimize. The most convenient way to deal with the maximization case is to transform the profits to *relative costs*. The transformation is conducted by subtracting the profit associated with each cell from the largest profit in the matrix. In this way the largest profit shows a zero relative cost; the objective changes to minimizing these relative costs. The solution procedures for relative costs are identical to those already described. After an optimal solution to the transformed minimization problem is determined, relative costs in occupied cells are restated in their original profit functions, and the total profit is calculated according to quantities in the optimal distribution pattern.

Unequal Supply and Demand

Actual capacity available at the origins and demand requirements of the destinations are seldom equal. There may be practical reasons other than distribution expense why certain demands should be met before others or why some supply capacity should be conserved. The reasons could evolve from strategic or tactical policy considerations and be used to balance available units politically to required units. When policy reasons are lacking, the mathematics of the solution procedures can point out where shortages or overages should exist to minimize the total distribution cost.

Excess supply capacity is accounted for in a transportation matrix by a dummy destination as shown in Figure 5.12. The demand of the dummy destination is equal to the difference between the total available and total required supplies. The cost of shipping from any origin to the dummy destination is assumed to be zero. The zero cost is rational because it represents an expense-free, fictional transfer and forces an allocation to the dummy. Excess demand is treated equivalently; a dummy origin is introduced to provide fictitious supplies, and zero transportation costs are charged to supplies from the dummy. After the origin capacities are balanced with the destination requirements, the matrix is amenable to usual solution procedures. The solution to the problem in Figure 5.12 reveals that the dummy destination is allotted 100 units from O2. The physical interpretation of the solution is that O2 ships 250 units to D1, ships 150 units to D2, and retains the last 100 units at the origin.

Reasoning similar to charging zero transportation cost to a dummy is behind the practice of charging an artificially huge • transportation cost to a cell that the route is not open or undesirable.

Figure 5.12 Supply and demand balanced by a dummy destination: (a) unbalanced rim conditions and (b) balanced rim conditions

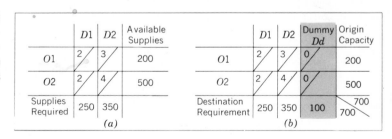

EXAMPLE 5.2 Transportation Problem Where Demand Exceeds Supply and the Objective Is to Maximize Profit

An area manager for three supermarkets (M1, M2, and M3) can obtain fresh apples from cold-storage lockers at four fruit cooperatives (C1, C2, C3, and C4). He needs 200 boxes for M1,

600 boxes for M2, and 400 boxes for M3. It is late in the apple season and supplies are limited. C1, C3, and C4 each have 400 boxes available and C2 has 300. The quality of apples, wholesale costs, and transportation costs are reflected in the following profit he expects to make per box from each source:

	C1	C2	C3	C4
M1	$8	$3	$2	$7
M2	$9	$11	$5	$2
M3	$6	$10	$6	$4

From the statement of the problem and a little preliminary arithmetic, it is apparent that the profits must be transformed to relative costs and a dummy market should be introduced to absorb the excess supply of apples. The corrective measures for the irregularities are shown below where an initial solution is developed by applying VAM.

	C1	C2	C3	C4		Penalty			
M1	3	8	9	4 200	200	1	1	1	5*
M2	2 400	0 300	6 100	9 100	600	2	2	4*	3
M3	5	1 300	5	7 100	400	4	4*	0	2
Md	0	0	0 300	0	300	0	—	—	—
	400	300	400	400	1500				

Penalty   2   0   5*   4
          1   1   1   3
          1   --- 1   3
          --- --- 1   3

*Indicates the highest penalty in each round of calculations.

A check of the unoccupied cells in the initial feasible solution reveals two transfer circuits which allow a $3 per box saving in relative cost. Either circuit (as shown on p. 145) could be used for the first revision because both lead to the same final solution. A choice of M2,C3 leads to the transfer circuit and allocations shown for the second revision in the sequential solution matrices below. The indicated transfer circuit for M3,C3 is the second revision which in turn leads to the distribution pattern for the third revision. After 200 boxes for M3 are switched from C4 to C3 in the third revision, the final solution is obtained; optimality is confirmed by the extra transfer costs associated with all unoccupied cells. Finally, relative costs are restated in profit per box to disclose the maximum expected gain. Total profit (from the optimal distribution pattern and the profit function) is:

200 boxes from C4 sold at M1 for $7/box	$1400
400 boxes from C1 sold at M2 for $9/box	$3600
200 boxes from C2 sold at M2 for $11/box	$2200
100 boxes from C2 sold at M3 for $10/box	$1000
300 boxes from C3 sold at M3 for $6/box	$1800
	$10,000

5-8 TRANSFER COSTS—MODI METHOD   MODI is the abbreviation for the modified-distribution method used to calculate transfer costs. It is generally considered faster and more convenient than the stepping-stone method for checking the optimality of a solution. Its timesaving feature is

	C1	C2	C3	C4	
M1	3/6	8/10	9/8	4/200	200
M2	2/400	0/−3	6/−100	9/−100	600
M3	5/5	1/300	5/−1	7/−100	400
Md	0/4	0/3	0/300	0/−3	300
	400	300	400	400	

First revision: $300 saving

	C1	C2	C3	C4	
M1	3/3	8/10	9/5	4/200	200
M2	2/400	0/100	6/−100	9/3	600
M3	5/2	1/200	5/−2	7/200	400
Md	0/4	0/6	0/300	0/0	300
	400	300	400	400	

Second revision: $200 saving

	C1	C2	C3	C4	
M1	3/3	8/10	9/5	4/200	200
M2	2/400	0/200	6/2	9/3	600
M3	5/2	1/100	100/−200		400
Md	0/2	0/4	0/300	/−2	300
	400	300	400	400	

Third revision: $200 saving

	C1	C2	C3	C4	
M1	3/1	8/8	9/5	4/200	200
M2	2/400	0/200	6/2	9/5	600
M3	5/2	1/100	5/300	7/2	400
Md	0/2	0/4	0/100	0/200	300
	400	300	400	400	

Optimal solution: total relative cost = $3200

that transfer costs can be calculated for all unoccupied cells without tracing any transfer circuits. After tracking disguised closed circuits through a matrix maze, a shortcut method is easy to appreciate. However, the tracking practice in the stepping-stone exercises was not wasted effort because the actual revisions, after a negative cost cell is identified, still depend on quantity shifts through a closed circuit.

The MODI method, like the stepping-stone method, enters the solution procedure after an initial feasible solution is established. The first step in applying the MODI method is to develop a key number for each row and column. The number depends on the distribution costs in the matrix and the location of initial allocations. If we let R and K stand for the rows and columns of the matrix, subscripts can designate a specific row or column key number:

$$R_i = \text{key number for row } i \ (i = 1, 2, 3, \cdots n)$$

and

$$K_j = \text{key number for column } j \ (j = 1, 2, 3, \cdots n)$$

The i for rows and j for columns are commonly encountered matrix notations.

• The same i, j notation is used to identify the transportation cost of satisfying each demand from each origin:

$$C_{ij} = \text{cost of each route (transportation cost}$$

$$\text{for cell in row } i \text{ and column } j)$$

These terms are combined to provide the equation for determining the row and column key numbers:

$$R_i + K_j = C_{ij}$$

where C_{ij} is the transportation cost of an occupied cell.

The routine for developing a set of key numbers is most easily explained by reference to a problem. In Figure 5.13, the initial feasible solution from Example 5.2 is repeated and all key number equations are listed. Many values for R and K will satisfy these equations. We are not particularly interested in the magnitude of the numbers; our concern is with the relationships between R and K. To simplify an arbitrary choice of values, we shall let the R or K number in the row or column with the most occupied cells equal zero. In Figure 5.13, row 2 ($M2$) ties for the most occupied cells so we let $R_2 = 0$. From this beginning we quickly ascertain three K values:

Note that the R and K subscripts must agree with the ● C subscripts.

$$K_1 = C_{21} - R_2 = 2 - 0 = 2$$

$$K_3 = C_{23} - R_2 = 6 - 0 = 6$$

$$K_4 = C_{24} - R_2 = 9 - 0 = 9$$

Knowing K_4, we can set up two more key row numbers:

$$R_1 = C_{14} - K_4 = 4 - 9 = -5$$

$$R_3 = C_{34} - K_4 = 7 - 9 = -2$$

which leads to

$$K_2 = C_{32} - R_3 = 1 - (-2) = 3$$

and the last key number is calculated as

$$R_4 = C_{43} - K_3 = 0 - 6 = -6$$

Initial feasible solution by VAM						MODI key number equations	
	C1	C2	C3	C4		$R_1 + K_4 = 4$	Cell M1, C4
M1	3	8	9	4 / 200	200	$R_2 + K_1 = 2$	M2, C1
M2	2 / 400	0	6 / 100	9 / 100	600	$R_2 + K_3 = 6$	M2, C3
M3	5	1 / 300	5	7 / 100	400	$R_2 + K_4 = 9$	M2, C4
Md	0	0	0 / 300	0	300	$R_3 + K_2 = 1$	M3, C2
	400	300	400	400		$R_3 + K_4 = 7$	M3, C4
						$R_4 + K_3 = 0$	Md, C3

Figure 5.13 Initial feasible solution from Example 5.2 with associated key number equations

	$K_1 = 2$	$K_2 = 3$	$K_3 = 6$	$K_4 = 9$	
$R_1 = -5$	3 / 6	8 / 10	9 / 8	4 / 200	200
$R_2 = 0$	2 / 400	0 / -3	6 / 100	9 / 100	600
$R_3 = -2$	5 / 5	1 / 300	5 / 1	7 / 100	400
$R_4 = -6$	0 / 4	0 / 3	0 / 300	0 / -3	300
	400	300	400	400	

Unoccupied cell	Equation	Transfer cost	Unoccupied cell	Equation	Transfer cost
11	$C_{11} - (R_1 + K_1)$ $3 - (-5 + 2) =$	6	33	$C_{33} - (R_3 + K_3)$ $5 - (-2 + 6) =$	1
12	$C_{12} - (R_1 + K_2)$ $8 - (-5 + 3) =$	10	41	$C_{41} - (R_4 + K_1)$ $0 - (-6 + 2) =$	4
13	$C_{13} - (R_1 + K_3)$ $9 - (-5 + 6) =$	8	42	$C_{42} - (R_4 + K_2)$ $0 - (-6 + 3) =$	3
22	$C_{22} - (R_2 + K_2)$ $0 - (0 + 3) =$	-3	44	$C_{44} - (R_4 + K_4)$ $0 - (-6 + 9) =$	-3
31	$C_{31} - (R_3 + K_1)$ $5 - (-2 + 2) =$	5			

Figure 5.14 MODI transfer cost calculations

With a little practice the key numbers can be figured out mentally without a formal statement of the equations.

The next step is to enter key numbers as the headings for appropriate rows and columns as shown in Figure 5.14. The headings serve as convenient references in the calculation of transfer costs for unoccupied cells from the basic equation:

$$\text{unit transfer cost} = C_{ij} - (R_i + K_j)$$

This equation applied to each potential new distribution route is also shown in Figure 5.14. Again, after a little practice it becomes unnecessary to write an equation for each cell to be checked; the transfer cost can be calculated mentally and entered for reference in the lower left corner of each unoccupied cell. As expected, the transfer costs are identical to those calculated by the stepping-stone method and indicate that the use of cell 22 (route $M2,C2$) or cell 44 (route $Md,C4$) will reduce the total distribution cost. The final step is also identical to the stepping-stone method; the transfer circuit closing on the cell with the largest negative transfer cost is identified and as many units as possible are allocated to the cell.

After each revision the key numbers must be recalculated. The new distribution pattern will change some or all of the R and K values. The process of establishing key numbers, calculating transfer costs for unoccupied cells, revising the solution to take advantage of negative transfer costs, and rechecking again is repeated until no additional cost-saving routes are discovered. Key number and transfer cost calculations for the optimal solution from Example 5.2 are shown in Figure 5.15.

147

	$K_1=2$	$K_2=0$	$K_3=4$	$K_4=4$	
$R_1=0$	3 /1	8 /8	9 /5	4 /200	200
$R_2=0$	2 /400	0 /200	6 /2	9 /5	600
$R_3=1$	5 /2	1 /100	5 /300	7 /2	400
$R_4=-4$	0 /2	0 /4	0 /100	0 /200	200
	400	300	400	400	

Cell	Calculations	Transfer Cost
11	$3-(0+2)=$	1
12	$8-(0+0)=$	8
13	$9-(0+4)=$	5
23	$6-(0+4)=$	2
24	$9-(0+4)=$	5
31	$5-(1+2)=$	2
34	$7-(1+4)=$	2
41	$0-(-4+2)=$	2
42	$0-(-4+0)=$	4

Figure 5.15 MODI method check of optimal solution from Example 5.2

5-9 SUMMARY

The simplex method for solving linear programming is described in Appendix C.

Linear programming is an optimizing technique appropriate for problems where the objective is explicitly stated in linear terms, alternative courses of action are available to achieve the objective, resources are limited, and variables are quantifiable and linearly related. A graphical solution is feasible for a limited class of problems such as the best mix for two or three products. The transportation routine is more versatile than the graphical method and succinct enough for hand calculations.

A transportation matrix shows the amount of supply and demand (rim conditions) and the cost to supply one unit from each origin (O) to each destination (D). A dummy origin or destination is introduced to absorb any imbalance in supply and demand. An initial feasible solution results when allocations meet the rim conditions, are in independent positions, and number $O + D - 1$. The Vogel approximation method (VAM) for determining an initial feasible solution uses row and column penalties to make initial allocations as optimal as possible.

An optimal solution to a transportation problem is developed by the stepping-stone or MODI method. In the stepping-stone method, each unoccupied cell is checked to see if its transfer cost is less than a route presently in the solution. The check is made by summing the costs of transferring one unit around a closed orthogonal circuit of occupied cells to the unoccupied cell being checked. When a new route offers a saving, as many units as possible are allocated to it. The MODI method employs row and column key numbers to discover lower cost transfer routes. After the preferred routes are known, allocations are changed by the same closed-circuit technique used in the stepping-stone method.

A degenerate allocation pattern, less than $O + D - 1$ occupied cells, is remedied by assigning an infinitesimal quantity (ϵ) to an unoccupied cell in a propitious position. This cell is considered occupied in a transfer circuit.

A maximization problem where supply and demand is related by a profit function is converted to a minimization problem by transforming profits to relative costs. The transformation is made by subtracting the profit associated with each cell from the largest profit in the matrix. After the transformation, the problem is treated by the usual minimization procedures.

5-10 REFERENCES

Ackoff, R. L. and M. W. Sasieni, *Fundamentals of Operations Research*, John Wiley, New York, 1968.

Chung, A., *Linear Programming*, Charles E. Merrill, Columbus, Ohio, 1963.

Dantzig, G. G., *Linear Programming Extensions*, Princeton Univ. Press, Princeton, N.J., 1963.

Ferguson, R. O. and L. F. Sargent, *Linear Programming: Fundamentals and Applications*, McGraw-Hill, New York, 1960.

Garvin, W. W., *Introduction to Linear Programming*, McGraw-Hill, New York, 1960.

Graves, R. L. and P. Wolfe, *Recent Advances in Mathematical Programming*, McGraw-Hill, New York, 1963.

Hadley, G., *Linear Programming*, Addison-Wesley, Reading, Mass., 1962.

Loomba, N. P., *Linear Programming: An Introductory Analysis*, McGraw-Hill, New York, 1964.

Miller, D. W. and M. K. Starr, *Executive Decisions and Operations Research*, Prentice-Hall, Englewood Cliffs, N.J., 1960.

Schuchman, A., *Scientific Decision-Making in Business*, Holt, Rinehart, and Winston, New York, 1963.

Vajda, S., *Mathematical Programming*, Addison-Wesley, Reading, Mass., 1961.

5-11 QUESTIONS AND PROBLEMS

1. Show how the product mix problem of Example 5.1 fits the requirements for a LP solution as outlined in Section 5-3.

2. With reference to a graphical solution, describe a condition where all limiting resources would be utilized to their capacity.

3. Other factors besides cost influence the use of computers versus manual solution methods described in Section 5-3. Set up and discuss the qualities to include in an exponential comparison model for deciding whether to use a computer. (Some qualities could be speed, accuracy, ease, and availability.)

4. Explain the visual checks that determine the acceptability of an initial feasible solution. Why are they necessary?

5. Discuss the way you would break a tie between two equal and highest penalties in a VAM penalty matrix.

6. Do you prefer the stepping-stone or the MODI method for determining an optimal solution? Why?

7. Why is a positive net transfer cost stated as a negative opportunity cost?

8. Describe a transfer circuit that would create a degeneracy in a revised solution.

9. Why must a cell containing ϵ in a previously degenerate solution be a positive cell in a transfer circuit?

10. Why is the smallest allocation in a negative cell of a transfer circuit the limiting quantity that can be transferred to a lower cost route (the cell being checked)?

11. Why must a complete transfer circuit contain an equal number of positive and negative cell allocations?

12. Explain the significance of a zero transfer cost for an occupied cell. How is it potentially useful?

13. Assume that a transportation matrix with a supply greater than demand shows a *profit* relationship between origins and destinations. After converting the profits to relative costs and adding a dummy destination to absorb excess supply, a zero cost is assigned to the dummy transportation routes. Is it reasonable to consider the dummy zero cost equivalent to the relative zero cost obtained from the route with the greatest profit in the original matrix?

14. A production problem is described by the following algebraic statements and is to be solved by LP methods: Maximize $3A + 3B$ subject to $4A + 7B \leq 1800$ and $3A + 11B \leq 1300$ where $A \geq 0$ and $B \geq 0$.

15. A small ceramic shop produces two products for which the market is essentially unlimited: small (S) indoor figurines and large (L) outdoor ornaments. The bottlenecks in production are the required oven time and the artistic hand glazing. The owner has no intention of increasing the capacity of the shop by additional investments in machines or by training more glazers, but he does want to use his facilities as advantageously as possible. The relevant annual data on the average availability of oven time (O) and artist time (A) and the contribution per unit produced are shown below:

	Processing Time in Hours/Unit		Hours Available per Year
	Large (L)	Small (S)	
Oven time (O)	8	5	100,000
Artist time (A)	1	2	10,000
Contribution/unit	$1.50	$2.50	

150

(a) What is the optimal product mix for the above data?

(b) Assume that a very foolish contract was signed to supply a mix of products representing 1 year's output at prices resulting in a loss to the shop; the contribution becomes $-\$0.05$ for product L and $-\$0.10$ for product S. After deciding not to renege on the contract and firing the person who signed it, how should the product mix be juggled to minimize the loss but still meet the contract?

16. A box factory currently has contracts for berry crates and pallets. Due to the closure of nearby mills, the availability of lumber is limited. The grade and size of lumber are similar for three lots on hand. The requirements to produce one crate or pallet from the material on hand are given below:

	Requirement in Board Feet		Thousands of Board Feet Available
	Berry Crate	Pallet	
Lot 1	1.2	0	21
Lot 2	0.9	4.1	24
Lot 3	0.6	6.4	60
Contribution/unit	$0.17	$0.26	

(a) How many of each product should be produced to maximize profit from the material on hand?

(b) The contribution is based on present lumber prices. How much extra could the box company pay (and still break even) for enough additional lumber with the mix of Lot 2 to keep production going until all current lumber lots are exhausted? Why might this action be considered?

17. Transportation costs in dollars per unit and the supply-demand relationships are provided below for two problems:

Problem A					
4	8	6	2	16
7	5	4	3	24
5	6	4	4	21
12	18	15	16	61
16			12	

Problem B					
94	63	71	84	56	70
59	84	65	77	68	47
85	75	60	65	70	66
70	68	86	72	62	50
33	47	49	72	32	233

(a) Determine an initial feasible solution by VAM.

(b) Obtain an optimal solution by the stepping-stone method.

(c) Obtain an optimal solution by the MODI method.

18. Assume that the supermarket manager described in Example 5.2 discovers that $M3$ needs only 300 instead of 400 crates of apples. All other conditions remain the same.

(a) Show results from applying VAM to obtain an initial feasible solution. (Show the placement of ε for the first revision.)

(b) What is the maximum possible profit? State where and what quantities are used.

19. A company has 700 out-of-style units to dispose. The units are distributed through three company-owned warehouses which supply customers in five major geographical areas. The capacity of the warehouses and market areas are listed below.

	North	South	East	West	Central	Total
Market requirements	•110	90	200	140	100	640
Warehouse capacity (units)	$W1$–240		$W2$–350		$W3$–150	

Hint: Two dummies may be introduced to balance origin and destination capacities with the supply available.

Based on the following unit transportation costs, what stock • should be assigned to the warehouses and which markets should each warehouse supply?

	North	South	East	West	Central
$W1$	7	40	10	35	14
$W2$	38	18	8	30	6
$W3$	35	16	30	9	6

20. A cost matrix where the amount available exceeds the amount required is shown below. Identify the best allocation pattern.

				Available
8	9	3	7	130
3	6	8	4	180
7	5	4	5	240
8	7	2	6	160
5	4	2	9	90
8	4	4	3	120
Required	300	100	150	200

21. A producer of exclusive jewelry products has a maximum

capacity of 600 units per year. The company can sell as many units as it can produce. An extra touch of luxury is added by packaging each jewelry set in a handmade case. Cases are hand-crafted by artists in three locations. The sets are shipped to the artists' establishments where they are individually packaged. The maximum units each artist can handle and the cost of shipping each unit to each artist are given below:

Artist	Capacity	Shipping Cost
A1	150	$2.00
A2	300	$3.00
A3	250	$1.50

The products are sent to five market areas after packaging. The current demand from each market area and the transportation cost per unit from the artist to the market area are shown below:

Market	M1	M2	M3	M4	M5
Capacity	100	200	150	100	200
A1	$1.80	$1.50	$8.00	$6.00	$5.00
A2	$2.00	$3.00	$6.00	$2.00	$3.50
A3	$2.30	$6.00	$4.00	$2.50	$2.00

Observe the same hint given in Problem 19. •

(a) How many jewelry sets should be allocated to each artist, and to which markets should the packaged units be delivered?

(b) How much extra compensation per unit should the jewelry company receive if it agrees to supply the entire demand of M3 while maintaining the same total transportation cost?

CHAPTER 6

RESOURCE SCHEDULING

6-1 IMPORTANCE

A seldom mentioned feature of network scheduling is its basis for a common language. Once learned, the standard terminology and symbols simplify planning communications between staff and line and among planners from different disciplines.

Even if we assume that the procedures in Chapter 5 gave us ways to allocate the right amounts of resources to the right places, we still face the problem of having them ready at the right time. After settling on a basic course of action, we must decide which acts to perform first. For a relatively small task, a mental list of materials coupled with another mental list of the order of accomplishment will normally suffice. For slightly larger tasks, it usually helps to commit plans to an informal "shopping list" schedule. When projects get too complex to analyze mentally or too large to "carry in your head," more formal and systematic procedures are required. In this chapter we shall investigate a network approach for integrating actions and scheduling resources.

The complexity of many of today's projects, even those of moderate size, demands not only consistent, disciplined thinking but also a method of summarizing and presenting the results of this thinking in a systematic manner. The graphical networks and associated calculation techniques assist effective thinking by sponsoring a step-by-step routine for coordinating work assignments and resource utilization with project objectives. Control criteria for the evaluation of work progress are established, and the most economical means for correcting delays are diagnosed.

Thus, network scheduling contributes to the two critical features of project planning: formulating the initial plan and monitoring progress. It operates in the delicate interface where ideas are converted to acts.

6-2 NETWORK SCHEDULING

Coordination of operations has been a concern of production planners for hundreds of years. Consider the following excerpt from the diary of a visitor to a seventeenth-century Venetian arsenal. He described the outfitting of large fighting galleys which carried crews of 171 plus 45 swordsmen. The operation

154

was obviously a cooperative effort requiring significant resource scheduling.

And as one enters the gate there is a great street on either hand with the sea in the middle, and on one side are windows opening out of the houses of the arsenal, and the same on the other side, and out came a galley towed by a boat, and from the windows they handed out to them, from one the cordage, from another the bread, from another the arms, and from another the balistas and mortars, and so from all sides everything which was required, and when the galley had reached the end of the street all the men required were on board, together with the complement of oars, and she was equipped from end to end. In this manner there came out ten galleys, fully armed, between the hours of three and nine.

Because even greater coordination is required in modern production, network scheduling has evolved.

A network depicts the sequence of activities necessary to complete a project. Segments of a project are represented by lines connected together to show the interrelationship of operations and resources. When a duration is associated with each segment, the model shows the time orientation of the total project and its internal operations. This information is used to coordinate the application of resources. The most celebrated versions of network scheduling are the **Critical Path Method** (**CPM**) and the **Program Evaluation and Review Technique** (**PERT**).

Few if any new management tools have received such wide acclaim so rapidly as CPM and PERT. The U.S. Navy developed PERT in 1958 to coordinate research and development work. It was first applied to the Polaris ballistic missile program with significant success. In the same year a similar network scheduling tool was developed by the DuPont company for industrial projects. It was called the Critical Path Method in deference to the path of critical activities that control the project's duration. Because the focal point of both PERT and CPM is a critical path of activities, both techniques will be considered under the general title "Critical Path Scheduling" (CPS). CPS is a management control tool for defining, integrating, and analyzing what must be done to complete a project economically and on time.

A network is a picture of a project, a map of requirements tracing the work from a departure point to the final completion objective. It can be a collection of all the minute details involved or only a gross outline of general functions. It can be oriented to

Venetian Ships and Shipbuilders of the Renaissance, Lane, F. C., John Hopkins Press, Baltimore, Md., 1934.

Closely related graphical techniques for operational control are presented in Section 13-4.

More elaborate networks such as signal flow graphs have not received the wide acceptance of critical path scheduling.

Other closely related techniques included in the critical path scheduling family are PEP, IMPACT, CPA, PERTCO, SCANS, GERT, NMT, and MCX.

the use of a particular physical resource or it can define broad management responsibilities. Networks have been constructed for building dams, introducing new products, organizing political campaigns, meshing new production lines with existing facilities, initiating research, coordinating charity drives, developing complex defense systems, and a multitude of other purposes. But regardless of its use, the fundamentals of network construction are the same. You have to determine a list of necessary activities, establish a restriction list that sets the order of activity accomplishment, and then combine the two lists with a set of drawing conventions to construct a graphical network.

6-3 CONSTRUCTION OF A CPS NETWORK

It is doubtful that such a small project as shown in Figure 6.1 would be subjected to CPS, but the logic is the same for more extensive applications.

An arrow diagram similar to CPS networks is shown in Figure 6.1. In very gross terms it represents the operations required to produce a custom-made machine. The project starts with the design work to satisfy the customer's specifications and culminates with the delivery of the finished product. Each arrow symbolizes a distinct activity. The chronology of the activity arrows shows the way work is expected to progress. The purpose of committing a project to a network is to allow an evaluation of different modes of operation before the work is underway. The evaluation should foretell how resources can be applied most advantageously to fulfill desired objectives such as time restrictions or budgetary limitations.

Activity List

GIGO—if you put Garbage In, you get Garbage Out.

The initial step in a CPS application is to break the project down into its component operations to form a complete list of essential activities. This task may appear easy but is usually difficult. The burden is the importance of a representative listing; without a valid list, all subsequent steps are meaningless.

An activity is a time-consuming task with a distinct beginning and end point. Some easily identified characteristic should be

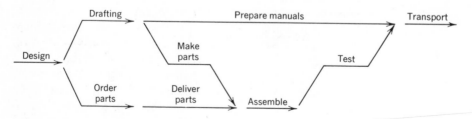

Figure 6.1 Arrow diagram of production activities

associated with each start and finish point. For instance, in Figure 6.1 the start of the first activity could be signaled by the receipt of a specification listing from the customer and could end when detailed sketches are delivered to the drafting and order departments.

The way activities are defined is influenced by planning purposes. If certain types of skilled labor or specialized machines are in short supply, activities requiring the limited resources should be separated from other operations. When certain materials are limited or difficult to procure, the physical divisions of a project that utilizes the critical materials should also be segregated. Control is usually improved by dividing activities so that each has a single responsible agency. The most common division is a production-oriented classification according to the physical elements of the product being produced. Table 6.1 illustrates how activities in a construction project can be classified to cope with anticipated trouble areas.

Table 6.1 Activity breakdowns conforming to project planning needs

Expected Difficulty	Classification of Activities	Effect
Shortage of skilled labor	According to crafts or trades	Only one type of craft is included in the performance of each activity; "finish walls" could be divided into "plaster walls" and "paint walls"
Payment received according to percentage of project completion	According to structural elements that set the completion percentages	Each activity is a component of the total project such as foundations, flooring, walls, and roof
Cooperation of subcontractors	According to responsibilities	Work done by each subcontractor is separated from other operations
Limited equipment	According to the limited resource	Portions of an activity requiring the key resource can be detached; "prepare report" is divided into "rough draft," "printouts," and "review" to show where limited computer time is required

Better activity lists are assured by using all available information. A network is a composite picture of an entire undertaking. The efforts of many people are included, and they should be consulted with regard to their expected accomplishments. Suppliers, cooperating departments, subcontractors, and other representatives should review the activity list to see if expectations pertaining to their respective interests are accurately and realistically detailed.

Restriction List

A restriction list establishes the precedence of activities. A list of operations commonly evolves from the general order of completion because it is natural to think of activities following a familiar sequence. This rough sequence forms a starting point for the restriction list. Each activity is bracketed by the answers to two questions: What must precede? What must follow? The answer to the first question identifies the *prerequisite*—the activity that immediately precedes another activity. The answer to the second question gives the *postrequisite*—the activity that immediately follows.

Accuracy and completeness are marks of a good restriction list. Accuracy stems from a careful appraisal of true priorities, not priorities set by habit. The inclination in dealing with familiar operations is to accept them as they have always been done. For instance, in sequencing the old caution "stop-look-listen," the temptation is to say you first stop, then look, and then listen. But a better restriction list would put "stop" as the prerequisite to both "look" and "listen" because the two senses can operate concurrently. Completeness is a function of the persistence with which the priority of each activity is questioned. It is easy to overlook a relationship between an activity occurring early in a project and one occurring near the end.

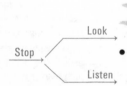

In drawing an arrow network, we are interested in the arrow that immediately follows the one just drawn—the prerequisite-postrequisite relationship. Therefore, a restriction list preferably shows only this relationship. A more extensive listing, such as all the jobs that follow each activity, is unnecessarily tedious and even contributes to errors. The activity list, prerequisite-postrequisite relationships, and a shorthand notation for the restriction list for the project depicted in Figure 6.1 are shown in Table 6.2.

Network Conventions

Each management tool seems to require special definitions and conventions; CPS is no exception. Since much of the CPS

Table 6.2 Activity and restriction lists for the project in Figure 6.1

Activity List		Activity Relationships		Restriction List*
Description	Symbol	Prerequisite	Postrequisite	
Design	A		Drafting, Order parts	$A < B,C$
Order parts	B	Design	Deliver parts	$B < D$
Drafting	C	Design	Prepare manuals, Make parts	$C < E,F$
Deliver parts	D	Order parts	Assemble	$D < G$
Prepare manuals	E	Drafting	Transport	$E < I$
Make parts	F	Drafting	Assemble	$F < G$
Assemble	G	Deliver parts, Make parts	Test	$G < H$
Test	H	Assemble	Transport	$H < I$
Transport	I	Test, Prepare manuals	—	—

*The sign $<$ is read precedes as A precedes B and C

language has been introduced already, we can now associate the language with the graphical representations.

An activity is represented by a line or arrow. This line or arrow connects two events. Each event is a specific point in time marking the beginning and/or end of an activity. A dual-purpose symbol for an event is a circle topped by a cross; the circle facilitates computer computations and the cross aids manual arithmetic. As shown in the activity chain of Figure 6.2, the first activity, "design," can be identified by the abbreviation A or by the numbered events as activity 1,2. The latter numbering system is used for computer applications. It also clarifies the definition of an event; event 2 in the chain marks the end of activity A and the beginning of activity B.

When two or more activities end with the same event, that event is referred to as a *merge*. Similarly, when two or more activities can begin at the same time, the event denoting that time is called a *burst*. A merge or a burst can be recognized in a restriction list by the occurrence of the same prerequisites or postrequisites for two or more activities. Recognition of typical

Nodal numbers of activities are a combination of the event numbers at the beginning (i node) and end (j node) of any activity; e.g., activity i,j.

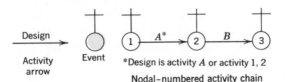

Figure 6.2 Activity and event conventions

Activity arrow · Event · *Design is activity A or activity 1, 2 · Nodal-numbered activity chain

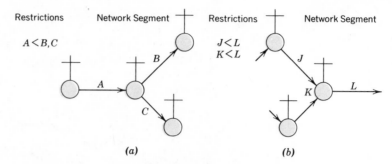

Restrictions   Network Segment   Restrictions   Network Segment

$A < B,C$ $J < L$
             $K < L$

Figure 6.3 Activity (a) burst and (b) merge patterns

(a)   (b)

recurring patterns, such as those in Figure 6.3, speeds network drawings.

A dashed-line arrow is used in a network to show the dependency of one activity on another. It is called a *dummy* activity and has all the restrictive properties of regular activities except that it requires zero time. The employment of dummies can be distinguished according to the purpose they serve; an *artificial* dummy is inserted to facilitate node numbering for computer applications and a *logic* dummy is necessary to portray graphically certain restraint relationships between nodes.

The special arrangement for graphing two activities that begin and end with the same event is shown in Figure 6.4. Both versions

Figure 6.4 Artificial dummy

The dummy could also be placed in front of *B* without changing the logic:

$A = 1,3$

dummy $= 1,2$

$B = 2,3$

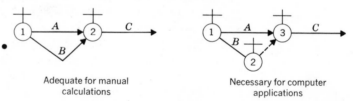

Adequate for manual calculations

Necessary for computer applications

in the figure depict the same restriction: activities A and B can start at the same time and both must be completed before activity C can begin. This relationship is visually obvious for manual manipulations, but a computer relies only on event numbers for identification and sequencing of activities. Without a dummy, both activity A and B have the same identifying event numbers 1,2 and are thereby indistinguishable in a nodal-numbering system. To avoid this duplication, an artificial dummy is introduced after either activity. The dummy forces a unique set of numbers for each activity ($A = 1,3$; $B = 1,2$; dummy $= 2,3$) without changing the logic of the network. For consistency, we shall utilize artificial dummies even when calculations are performed manually.

160

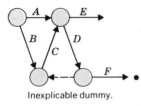

Inexplicable dummy.

Some newer computer programs do not require unique node numbers.

Careful use of logic dummies will eliminate many beginner's errors which creep into network drawings. Four of the most common mistakes are displayed in Figure 6.5. The *spillover* error illustrates how a dummy aims a restriction in one direction only; C restricts E but B does not restrict D. The *cascade* effect emphasizes that the dummy shows a zero time or simultaneous relationship between events. The incorrect version neglects the fact that all activities (and a dummy is a zero-time activity) in a merge are prerequisite to all activities in a burst from the same event. *Unnecessary* or *redundant* dummies do not spoil the logic of a network; they just create extra calculations and network complications. Every unnecessary dummy increases the computer time required to develop a schedule and introduces another chance for misinterpretation.

Network Drawing

A CPS network is merely a graphical version of the activity and restriction lists based on adopted conventions. The visual representation provides a notable communication device. The relationship of each part to the whole project is easier to comprehend when it is in network form, and mistakes of commission and omission are more apparent.

Case	Spillover	Cascade	Unnecessary	Redundant
Restriction	$A < C$ $B < E$ $C < D, E$	$A < D, E$ $B < E, F$ $C < F$	$A < C$ $B < D$ $C < D$	$A < C$ $B < C, D, E$ $C < E$
Incorrect network segment				
	B is not a prerequisite of *D*	*A* is not a prerequisite of *F*	Artificial dummy 3, 4 is unnecessary	*B* is a redundant restriction on *E*
Correct network segment				

Figure 6.5 Correct and incorrect use of network dummies

Drawing techniques vary. The initial attempt to graph a project is usually an approximate sketch. Sometimes several • activities are lumped into a single arrow to accentuate the general flow. After the overall sequence is checked, the compound activities can be subdivided into detailed operations. Very large projects are handled more conveniently by treating subdivisions independently in preliminary networks and then integrating them with dummy arrows to relate the segments. A similar • approach is suitable for portions of a project that are repeated several times. For example, in the construction of a multistory building, several floors often have essentially the same characteristics and, consequently, identical activity lists. It is necessary to make only one network for the common list; dummies are used to establish the order of cyclic repetitions of this basic network.

Networks are easier to check if all arrows flow from left to right and as many arrow crossovers as possible are eliminated. Labeling each activity with a concise description rather than a letter • symbol avoids continued reference to the activity list. Nodal numbers should be assigned after the entire network is drawn and checked, because some computational methods and computer programs require a numbering system where the node at the beginning of an activity (i node) is always smaller than the ending node (j node).

It is convenient to use a blackboard which allows easy changes for a preliminary network.

In a housing-development project, all buildings could be separate networks that are related on one master planning schedule.

Some computational methods also require the nodal numbers to be in a continuous order as 1-2-3-4-5---n.

EXAMPLE 6.1 Development of An Arrow Network for A New Product

The research department reports promising developments with a refined control unit. A laboratory model functioned reasonably well and, with minor redesign, should merit field tests. Construction of a dozen prototypes for the field tests is to be put on a critical path network. Construction can commence when the final design from the research department is submitted. As indicated in the activity list below, most operations involve securing components by inventory requisition of stock on hand, from orders to outside subcontractors, or from internal fabrication work.

Activity	Symbol	Restriction
Final design	A	$A < B,C$
Engineering analysis	B	$B < D,F,H$
Prepare layouts	C	$C < E$
Requisition material	D	$D < E$
Fabricate parts	E	$E < J$
Requisition parts	F	$F < G$
Receive parts	G	$G < J$
Place subcontracts	H	$H < I$
Receive subcontracted parts	I	$I < J$
Assemble	J	$J < K$
Inspect and test	K	

162

A network based on the activities and restrictions is constructed and questioned. An engineer notices that the amount of material needed in "fabrication" will not be known until certain layouts are completed. This condition can be shown in the network by subdividing the activity "layout" into "layout 1" and "layout 2," where the end event for "layout 1" is the completion of the layouts required for material takeoffs. Then the fabrication foreman notices that no time has been allowed for delivery of the requisitioned material. Material lead time is included by adding another activity, "receive requisitioned material." Alterations in the activity list to incorporate these revisions are shown below.

Activity	Symbol	Restriction
Final design	A	$A < B,C1$
Engineering analysis	B $-A$	$B < D1,F,H$
Prepare layout 1	$C1$ $-A$	$C1 < C2,D1$
Prepare layout 2	$C2$ $-C1$	$C2 < E$
Prepare material requisition	$D1$ $- C1, B$	$D1 < D2$
Receive requisitioned material	$D2$ $D1$	$D2 < E$

The original network, with changes required by the revised activity list shown in the inset, is given below. (Note that block numbering of the activities allows additions that do not alter the technological order of the nodal numbers.)

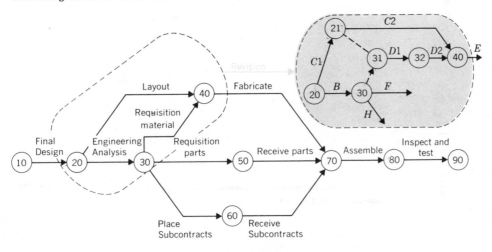

See Figure 6.6.

6-4 THE CRITICAL PATH A network composed of activities required to develop a critical path schedule would probably show the first activity labeled "investigate project" followed by a burst of three activities: "identify activities," "list restrictions," and "estimate durations." This arrangement shows that the three tasks could be performed almost concurrently or, if it is more advantageous from a resource-utilization standpoint, they could be completed in a sequence. Thus the network pictures how a project *can be done*, while a schedule establishes how it is *planned to be done*. The key to

163

network scheduling is the *critical path*, the chain of activities that determines the total project duration.

The time to conduct each activity is not required for network logic, but times are necessary to determine critical activities. Two approaches are available for estimating activity durations. A *deterministic* approach, appropriate for most industrial projects, relies on a single, most likely time estimate; a *statistical* approach uses a range of possible activity times to determine a single duration.

Most Likely Time Estimates

A single time estimate rather than a range of estimates for an activity duration is feasible for most industrial projects because the operations required are usually similar to previous experiences.

An estimate of the elapsed time required to accomplish the objectives stated in an activity's description is called the *activity duration.* All activity durations should be expressed in the same time units such as days, weeks, or months. Estimates do not reflect uncontrollable contingencies such as flash floods or unexpected legal delays, but they should account for weather conditions and other factors that at least can be anticipated.

Estimation of activity durations closely parallels the approaches discussed for forecasting. Objective sources of data for estimating include records of past performances on similar projects, historical data such as weather records or suppliers' literature, and applicable laws or regulations. Subjective estimates are obtained from persons responsible for doing the work such

A project manager's final duration estimates should be studied and accepted by subcontractors to increase confidence in the resulting schedule.

as foremen and subcontractors or from professional assistance such as consulting firms and other project managers. The reliability and applicability of the sources are bound to vary, so judgment is still the vital ingredient for converting guesstimates to estimates.

As activity durations are developed, it is often necessary to revise activity descriptions. Troublesome contradictions surface when part of the work traditionally associated with one activity is included in a different one. This condition is annoying when the sources of time estimates pertain to traditional descriptions, but it can be alleviated by either changing activity breakdowns or by breaking down traditional operations to conform to a new grouping if this arrangement better fits the management objectives. A similar problem occurs when a restriction list shows that two or more activities can theoretically be done concurrently but, in practice, some portion of one must be completed before the other can start. A timely example is a network for starting a CPS analysis. As described previously, the first burst shows that activity and restriction listing and duration estimating can occur at the same time. This is almost true for large lists, but at least a

Activity List	Symbol	Original Network Segment	Revised Network Segment that Avoids Overlap
Investigate project	A		
Identify activities	B		
List restrictions	C		
Estimate durations	D		

Figure 6.6 Network representation of overlapping activities

few activities must be identified before restricting postrequisites can be set. To portray such overlapping conditions realistically, activities are subdivided as shown in Figure 6.6.

Boundary Time Calculations

After estimated activity performance times are secured, each duration is entered beside the appropriate arrow in the network. The network is then ready for boundary time calculations. These calculations can be performed either manually or with computerized assistance to provide time relationships suitable for activity scheduling. The most useful boundary times are described below.

Earliest start (ES)—the earliest time an activity can begin when all preceding activities are completed as rapidly as possible.

Latest start (LS)—the latest time an activity can be initiated without delaying the minimum project completion time.

Earliest finish (EF)—the sum of *ES* and the activity's duration (*D*).

Latest finish (LF)—the *LS* added to the duration (*D*).

Total float (TF)—the amount of surplus time or leeway allowed in scheduling activities to avoid interference with any activity on the network critical path; the slack between the earliest and latest start times ($LS - ES = TF$).

Identification of the critical path is a byproduct of boundary time calculations. A critical activity has no leeway in scheduling and, consequently, zero total float.

165

The *ES* times are calculated manually by making a forward pass through the network, adding each activity duration in turn to the *ES* of the prerequisite activity. When a merge is encountered, the largest *ES* + *D* of the merging activities is the limiting *ES* for all activities bursting from the event. Dummies are treated exactly the same as other activities. Each limiting *ES* is recorded on the left bar of the event markers to keep track of the cumulative entries. The cross at the *i* node of an activity indicates the *ES* for that activity. Details of *ES* calculations for a small network are given in Figure 6.7.

The limiting *ES* is the latest *ES* for an event.

LS times are calculated in almost a reversed procedure from that for *ES* times. A backward pass is made through the network, subtracting activity durations from the limiting *LS* at an event. The limiting *LS*, the smallest one at a burst event, is entered on the right bar of the cross. Subsequent *LS*'s are calculated by subtracting activity durations from the *LS* on the *j*-node cross.

The main difference between *LS* and *ES* calculations is that each activity from a common event can have a different *LS* while

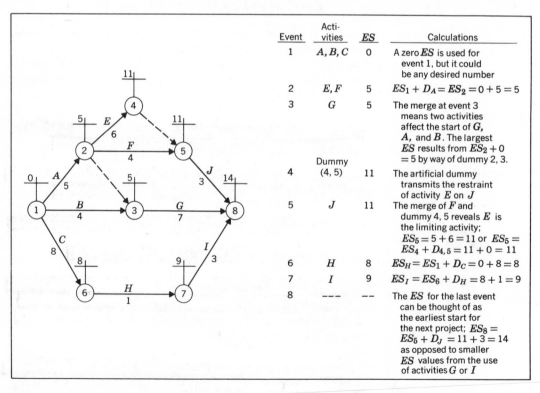

Event	Activities	*ES*	Calculations
1	*A, B, C*	0	A zero *ES* is used for event 1, but it could be any desired number
2	*E, F*	5	$ES_1 + D_A = ES_2 = 0 + 5 = 5$
3	*G*	5	The merge at event 3 means two activities affect the start of *G*, *A*, and *B*. The largest *ES* results from $ES_2 + 0 = 5$ by way of dummy 2, 3.
4	Dummy (4, 5)	11	The artificial dummy transmits the restraint of activity *E* on *J*
5	*J*	11	The merge of *F* and dummy 4, 5 reveals *E* is the limiting activity; $ES_5 = 5 + 6 = 11$ or $ES_5 = ES_4 + D_{4,5} = 11 + 0 = 11$
6	*H*	8	$ES_H = ES_1 + D_C = 0 + 8 = 8$
7	*I*	9	$ES_I = ES_6 + D_H = 8 + 1 = 9$
8	---	--	The *ES* for the last event can be thought of as the earliest start for the next project; $ES_8 = ES_5 + D_J = 11 + 3 = 14$ as opposed to smaller *ES* values from the use of activities *G* or *I*

Figure 6.7 Activity earliest start calculations

The limiting *LS* is the earliest *LS* (smallest number) in a burst.

- all activities starting from the same event have the same *ES*. To accommodate this situation, a "shelf" is connected to each activity in a burst that has a larger *LF* value than the limiting one. Thus, an individual *LS* is recorded for each activity as detailed in Figure 6.8.

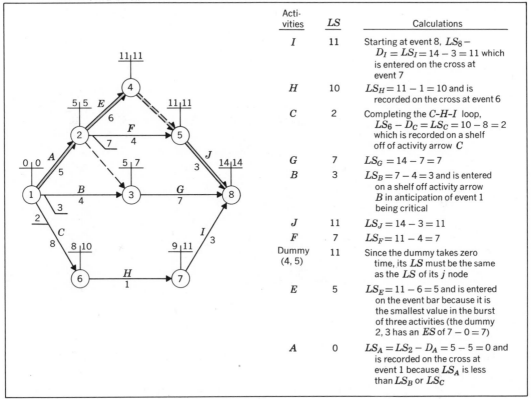

Activities	LS	Calculations
I	11	Starting at event 8, $LS_8 - D_I = LS_I = 14 - 3 = 11$ which is entered on the cross at event 7
H	10	$LS_H = 11 - 1 = 10$ and is recorded on the cross at event 6
C	2	Completing the *C-H-I* loop, $LS_6 - D_C = LS_C = 10 - 8 = 2$ which is recorded on a shelf off of activity arrow *C*
G	7	$LS_G = 14 - 7 = 7$
B	3	$LS_B = 7 - 4 = 3$ and is entered on a shelf off activity arrow *B* in anticipation of event 1 being critical
J	11	$LS_J = 14 - 3 = 11$
F	7	$LS_F = 11 - 4 = 7$
Dummy (4, 5)	11	Since the dummy takes zero time, its *LS* must be the same as the *LS* of its *j* node
E	5	$LS_E = 11 - 6 = 5$ and is entered on the event bar because it is the smallest value in the burst of three activities (the dummy 2, 3 has an *ES* of $7 - 0 = 7$)
A	0	$LS_A = LS_2 - D_A = 5 - 5 = 0$ and is recorded on the cross at event 1 because LS_A is less than LS_B or LS_C

Figure 6.8 Activity latest start calculations

Nothing is gained by calculating an *LS* for logic dummies, so no shelves should be placed on dashed-line arrows.

The initial step in *LS* calculations is to make the right bar of the last cross in the network agree with the left bar. This entry confirms the critical nature of the last event, a distinct point in time where a subsequent project relying on the resources employed in the current project can begin. Successive subtractions of activity durations from each limiting event *LS* eventually leads to a zero *LS* for the first node in the network. A nonzero *LS* for event 1 means your arithmetic needs polishing.

After the *ES* and *LS* calculations are completed, the remaining boundary times are established by routine manipulations. The

167

most direct approach is to set up a boundary timetable as shown in Table 6.3. Under the activity heading is a column of activity descriptions. (Table 6.3 lists only the activity symbols in conformance to the network of Figure 6.8.) The values for activity durations, ES's, and LS's are transferred from the network to the table. The EF column is completed by adding the activity duration to each ES. Similarly, LF times are equal to the duration plus LS. TF can be determined by the difference between the two start times or the two finish times; these differences must be the same for each activity.

Table 6.3 Boundary timetable

Activity	Duration (D)	Earliest Start (ES)	Latest Start (LS)	Earliest Finish (EF)	Latest Finish (LF)	Total Float (TF)
A	5	0	0	5	5	0
B	4	0	3	4	7	3
C	8	0	2	8	10	2
E	6	5	5	11	11	0
F	4	5	7	9	11	2
G	7	5	7	12	14	2
H	1	8	10	9	11	2
I	3	9	11	12	14	2
J	3	11	11	14	14	0

The critical path is easily identified from either the network or boundary timetable. In the network, each event with the same entries on both bars is critical. A line connecting these events along the activities responsible for the event times traces the critical path as shown by the double-lined arrows in Figure 6.8. Critical activities in the boundary timetable are indicated by zero float.

EXAMPLE 6.2 Boundary Times for the Network from Example 6.1

After an agreement on the accuracy of the revised network for field testing the new product, activity durations are secured from the different departments involved: research and development, engineering, fabrication, supply, subcontractors, etc. One person coordinates the estimating because information of an interdepartmental and intradepartmental nature is often required before realistic and practical durations can be determined. An exchange of information between the managers responsible for the activities is facilitated by routing a time-labeled network for final verification. Upon acceptance of the duration estimates, network calculations and boundary times can be developed as shown below.

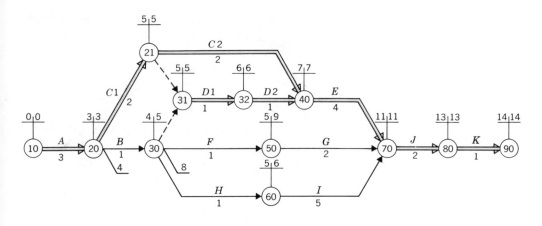

Activity	D*	ES	LS	EF	LF	TF
A	3	0	0	3	3	0
B	1	3	4	4	5	1
C1	2	3	3	5	5	0
C2	2	5	5	7	7	0
D1	1	5	5	6	6	0
D2	1	6	6	7	7	0
E	4	7	7	11	11	0
F	1	4	8	5	9	4
G	2	5	9	7	11	4
H	1	4	5	5	6	1
I	5	5	6	10	11	1
J	2	11	11	13	13	0
K	1	13	13	14	14	0

*Activity durations are in weeks.

★ ★ ★ *Optional material.*

6-5 PERT CALCULATIONS The statistical approach to activity and project durations is a characteristic of the Program Evaluation and Review Technique. This approach is appropriate for unfamiliar or experimental projects. In such projects it is difficult to agree on one, most likely time estimate for each activity because there is little or no precedence for the operations involved. In research and development work, only a very naive or adventurous manager will commit himself to a definite completion date when he is unsure of what he has to do or how to do it.

Much of the hesitancy concerning time estimations is relieved by allowing a range of estimates. Instead of a commitment to a

169

Extreme conditions such as "acts of God" are not accounted for in the range of estimates.

single duration estimate, a most likely time (m) is bracketed between an optimistic (a) and a pessimistic (b) estimate of performance time. The most likely time is the duration that would occur most often if the activity was repeated many times under the same conditions. The optimistic and pessimistic estimates are the outside limits of completion time when everything goes either all right or all wrong.

It is assumed that there is a very small probability that an actual completion time will fall outside the range a to b and that the proportion of durations within the range follows a beta distribution. If an activity was performed many times and the relative frequency of completion times was plotted, a distribution curve as shown in Figure 6.9 would result. The mean point dividing the area under the curve into two equal parts is called the expected time (t_e); it is calculated as a weighted average of the three time estimates according to the formula

The density function of the beta distribution is $K(t - a)^\alpha(b - t)^\beta$ where t = actual completion time.

$$t_e = \frac{a + 4m + b}{6} \qquad \text{where } a \leq m \leq b$$

After the expected times are computed for each activity, they are treated the same as single time estimates in determining the critical path and boundary times as illustrated in Figure 6.10.

Each activity in a PERT network also has a variance associated with its completion time. This variance measures the dispersion of possible durations and is calculated from the formula

$$\sigma_{i,j}^2 = \left(\frac{b - a}{6}\right)^2$$

where $\sigma_{i,j}^2$ = variance of an individual activity with pessimistic and optimistic performance time estimates of b and a, respectively. When $b = a$, the duration of an activity is well known and,

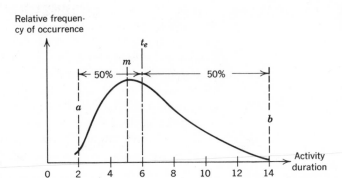

Relative frequency of occurrence

Figure 6.9 Relationship of a, b, and m to t_e

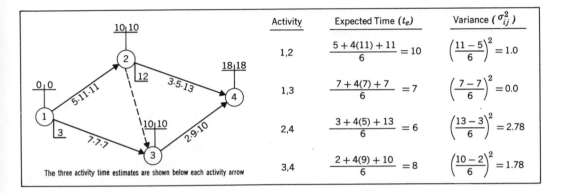

Activity	Expected Time (t_e)	Variance (σ_{ij}^2)
1,2	$\dfrac{5 + 4(11) + 11}{6} = 10$	$\left(\dfrac{11 - 5}{6}\right)^2 = 1.0$
1,3	$\dfrac{7 + 4(7) + 7}{6} = 7$	$\left(\dfrac{7 - 7}{6}\right)^2 = 0.0$
2,4	$\dfrac{3 + 4(5) + 13}{6} = 6$	$\left(\dfrac{13 - 3}{6}\right)^2 = 2.78$
3,4	$\dfrac{2 + 4(9) + 10}{6} = 8$	$\left(\dfrac{10 - 2}{6}\right)^2 = 1.78$

The three activity time estimates are shown below each activity arrow

Figure 6.10 Expected times, variances, and critical path calculations

consequently, the variance is zero. A wide variation in the outside limits of estimated times produces a large variance and indicates less confidence in estimating how long it will actually take to complete the activity. Sample calculations of activity variances are provided in Figure 6.10.

Having a variance for each activity offers the interesting potential of calculating the probability that a certain time scheduled for an event will be met. The scheduled start (SS) is called a *milestone*; it represents the planned accomplishment of an event of particular managerial importance. This significant date may originate from the need to complete a vital activity by a given date so that other portions of the project can commence, or it may result from contractual obligations outside the project.

A milestone date is compared to the *ES* of an event. The *ES* evolves from a cumulative total of activity expected durations to the milestone event. Similarly, the variance associated with that event is the sum of the variances of the activities along the path determining the milestone *ES*. The difference between the *SS* and the *ES* is the numerator in the equation

$$Z = \frac{SS - ES}{\sqrt{\Sigma \, \sigma_{ES}^2}}$$

where Z is the probability factor from which the relative likelihood is derived, and $\Sigma \, \sigma_{ES}^2$ is the sum of the individual variances of the activities used to calculate *ES*.

171

The probabilities associated with *Z* values are provided by the Normal Distribution Table in Appendix A.

The actual completion times for the milestone event are assumed to be normally distributed about *ES*. Therefore, the probability factor is a function of the normal curve areas given in Appendix A. A *Z* value of zero means that the probability of completing the event on the scheduled date is 0.50. With reference to Figure 6.10, the *Z* factor for a *SS* of 17 for event 4 is

$$Z_4 = -\frac{SS - ES}{\sqrt{\sigma_{1,2}^2 + \sigma_{3,4}^2}} = \frac{17 - 18}{\sqrt{1 + 1.78}} = \frac{-1}{1.67} = -0.6$$

As a rule-of-thumb, probabilities between 0.4 and 0.6 are considered to be a reasonable balance of risk. Above 0.6, there may be excessive resource expenditures; below 0.4 there is danger of insufficient resources causing a delay.

and indicates the *SS* (17) is 0.6 standard deviations less than the *ES* (18). This *Z* value corresponds to a probability of 0.2743. Therefore, if time "now" is zero and the time units are days, we could expect to complete the project depicted in Figure 6.10 on or before 17 days with a likelihood of 0.27. This probability is applicable without any expediting measures applied to the project. When an extra day beyond the expected 18-day project duration is allowed, the probability of meeting the milestone (19) is 0.7257:

$$Z_4 = \frac{19 - 18}{\sqrt{1 + 1.78}} = \frac{1}{1.67} = 0.6$$

A backdoor approach to milestones would set the *SS* at a date with a desired probability of completion. Thus a manager might promise a finished product on a date that is 2 standard deviations beyond the *ES* of the last event to give an 0.977 probability of meeting the date. Any probability could be incorporated in the formula $SS = ES + Z(\sqrt{\sigma_{ES}^2})$ to provide the desired safety margin.

★　★　★　*End of optional material.*

6-6 NETWORK APPLICATIONS IN PROJECT PLANNING

A network is an abstraction of a real project. The cost in time, money, and inconvenience is far less when manipulating a model project than a real project. Several network revisions may be required before the desired realism is developed or the preferred method of accomplishment is obtained. Regardless of the number of changes, paper alterations are still less expensive than a single major change in the physical project. Although most of our attention has been devoted to the coordination of activities and the perfected utilization of time, expenditures of other resources also can be incorporated into the network model.

Time-Cost Tradeoffs

An initial network often reveals that a project will take longer than anticipated. The critical path exposes the group of activities

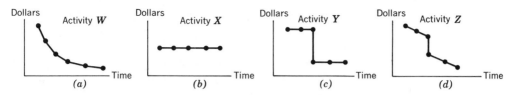

Figure 6.11 Common activity time-direct cost patterns: (*a*) increasing marginal cost function, (*b*) constant cost function, (*c*) step increase-constant cost function, and (*d*) step increase-increasing cost function

"Crash schedules" always introduce overtime, waste, confusion, and other factors • which increase an activity's cost as its duration is shortened from its normal time.

from which cuts should be made to shorten the project, but it does not indicate which cuts will be least expensive. To obtain a cost priority for reducing the project duration, more information than we used in the boundary time calculations is needed. For each activity a range of reduced completion times and associated costs are estimated as shown in Figure 6.11. Sometimes a cost is developed for each time unit cut from an activity's normal duration. More commonly, only a few (usually two) time-cost points are set, and the costs for completion points inbetween are calculated by linear interpolation.

Manual methods are available for determining not only which activities should be cut to meet a deadline but also the least expensive project duration when both direct and indirect project costs are considered. The procedure is to identify an ascending order of activity cutting costs and to make successive time reductions by using the lowest cost available. A cut always crosses the critical path; continued cutting makes more activities critical as float is reduced. The sums of direct activity cost and indirect project cost are compared for each new duration. An optimal costwise schedule is apparent when the lowest point in the total cost curve is discovered. A typical cost pattern is shown in Figure 6.12.

When a small adjustment in a project duration is required, manual methods are feasible for identifying the least expensive means. However, a manual cost analysis of a total project, even

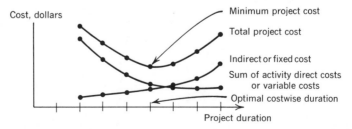

Figure 6.12 Direct, indirect, and total project cost patterns

a very small one, is a long, tedious, and error-prone process. Acceptable computer programs are widely available to relieve hand computations. These cost-evaluation programs have not been used extensively because of the difficulty in developing necessary cost data, but they will undoubtedly receive greater attention in the future.

Resource Assignments

Activity costs and durations are functions of resource expenditures. These resources—skilled and unskilled labor, supervision, equipment, materials, etc.—may be limited in quantity or quality. Activity estimates should compensate for a limited supply of a resource, and adroit scheduling should assure that the supply is applied advantageously.

In many cases the deployment of a limited resource is aided by the efficient use of float time available to noncritical activities. If only a single resource is limited, such as a one-of-a-kind machine, activities requiring that machine can be labeled and visually checked to see if the machine is scheduled to be in two places at the same time.

Another type of time chart for critical path networks is presented in Section 13-4.

Visual checks are easier if the network is converted to a time scale. One popular format is a bar chart because it can be produced as a direct computer printout. The format shown in Figure 6.13 has each activity represented by a bar of X's corresponding to its duration and beginning at the *ES*. The zeros following the X's represent the *TF* available to the activity. When activities are spaced to avoid overlapping assignments of a limited resource, float in a chain of activities must be rationed judiciously because all the activities in the chain share that float. When the float is taken by an adjustment for one activity, it is no longer available for the others. For instance, Figure 6.13 is a bar graph for the

There are many versions of Gantt or bar charts, and other formats will be used in later chapters.

I	J	D	Description	Day 1	2	3	4	5						10					15
1	2	8	A	X	X	X	X	X						I					I
1	3	4	B	X	X	X	X	0	0	0				I					I
1	6	8	C	X	X	X	X	X	X	X	X	X	0	0					I
2	4	6	E					I			X	X	X	X	X	X			I
2	5	4	F			I					I	X	X	X	X	0	0		I
3	8	7	G			I					I	X	X	X	X	X	X	X	0 0	I
6	7	1	H			I					I		X	0	0				I
7	8	3	I			I					I			X	X	X	0	0	I
5	8	3	J			I					I				I	X	X	X	I

Figure 6.13 Format of a computer generated bar chart for the network of Figure 6.8 and the boundary times of Table 6.3

174

network from Figure 6.8 where the activity chain *C-H-I* has 2 days of *TF*. If activity *C* is assigned to start on day 3 (the end of day 2), then the start times for activities *H* and *I* are also set at 11 and 12 days, respectively, because all the float in the chain is taken by the delayed start of *C*.

When no usable float remains for activities with excessive resource demands, a decision has to be made between acquiring more of the limiting resource and altering scheduled times. Methods of modifying a schedule include the following alternatives:

1. Working overtime to shorten the duration of one or more activities requiring the limited resource.
2. Shortening the duration of prerequisite or postrequisite activities to allow float for rescheduling key activities.
3. Changing resource requirements. A substitute resource may change the duration of the activity involved.
4. Extending the total project duration.

The criterion for selecting from the above alternatives will likely be cost, but less tangible factors such as goodwill and convenience may also influence the decision.

EXAMPLE 6.3   Expediting the Project Schedule for Example 6.2

A rumor that a competitor is perfecting a similar control unit has spurred the project manager to expedite the prototype field tests. A decision to reduce the project duration to 10 weeks has been made with the full realization that some confusion and considerable waste are sure to result. Through attentive network rescheduling, the disorder can be minimized.

The revised plan has "layout" preparations (*C*1 and *C*2) being done concurrently with "final design" (subdivided to *A*1 and *A*2). "Engineering analysis" (*B*) will start when "final design" is partially completed (*A*1). "Assembly" is divided into two parts to allow the "requisition parts" (*G*) to be assembled (*J*1) before the "subcontract" (*I*) and "fabricate" (*E*) parts are received. The network resulting from these modifications is shown in Figure 6.14 (see p. 176).

The changes reduce the project duration to the desired 10-week deadline, but the increased number of critical activities requires strenuous control measures. No activity times have been shortened, but the revised concurrent scheduling of some activities will certainly create challenging coordination problems. In general, the expedited project will probably cost more, be more frustrating, and come closer to meeting the 10-week milestone than the original schedule.

6-7 SUMMARY   Network scheduling is a graphical approach to the sequencing and coordination of activities necessary to complete a project economically and on time. The many versions of Critical Path Methods (CPM) and Program Evaluation and Review Techniques (PERT) are considered conglomerate subjects under the broad title of Critical Path Scheduling (CPS).

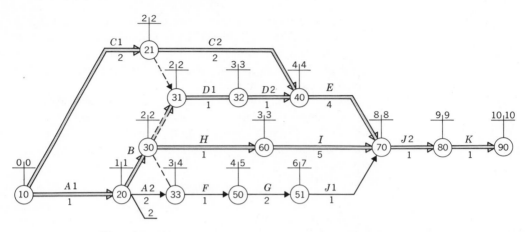

Figure 6.14

The first step in a CPS application is to break the project down into its component operations to form a complete list of essential activities. An activity is a time-consuming task with distinct beginning and end points called events. As the activity list develops, an order of completion is established by a restriction list, a statement of prerequisite-postrequisite relationships for each activity. From the two lists evolves a network drawn according to conventions, where arrows representing activities connect nodes showing the sequence of events. Dummy arrows are included to allow distinctive nodal numbering for computer applications and to show certain event restrictions.

A single activity duration is estimated in the deterministic approach; a range of time estimates is used in the statistical PERT approach. With PERT, expected times (t_e) result from the formula $t_e = (a + 4m + b)/6$ where a and b are, respectively, optimistic and pessimistic estimates and m is the most likely duration. With activity durations estimated by either method, boundary times are calculated for all network activities to determine the float available for noncritical activities and the chain of activities that sets the total project duration—the critical path.

In PERT networks the variance of activities, $\sigma^2 = [(b - a)/6]^2$ can be used to determine the probability of meeting a certain scheduled completion time called a milestone. With deterministic durations, time-cost tradeoffs can be used to identify the least cost measures to reduce the project duration.

Computer programs for CPS applications are widely available. Manual calculations are feasible for smaller problems, but electronic assistance is almost a necessity for larger ones. In network analyses, a computer can perform the boundary time calculations and generate bar charts for easier checks of resource assignments.

6-8 REFERENCES

Evarts, H. F., *Introduction to PERT*, Allyn and Bacon, Boston, Mass., 1964.

Fondahl, J. W., *A Non-Computer Approach to the Critical Path Method for the Construction Industry*, Stanford Univ. Press, Stanford, Calif., 1962.

Ford, L. R. and D. F. Fulderson, *Flows in Networks*, Princeton Univ. Press, Princeton, N.J., 1962.

Levin, R. I. and C. A. Kirkpatrick, *Planning and Control with PERT/CPM*, McGraw-Hill, New York, 1966.

Moder, J. J. and C. R. Phillips, *Project Management with CPM and PERT*, Reinhold, New York, 1964.

Muth, J. F. and G. L. Thompson, *Industrial Scheduling*, Prentice-Hall, Englewood Cliffs, N.J., 1963.

Riggs, J. L. and C. O. Heath, *Guide to Cost Reduction Through Critical Path Scheduling*, Prentice-Hall, Englewood Cliffs, N.J., 1966.

Shaffer, L. R., J. B. Ritter, and W. L. Meyer, *The Critical-Path Method*, McGraw-Hill, New York, 1965.

6-9 QUESTIONS AND PROBLEMS

1. Graphical methods have been described as applicable in the areas of survey, analysis, and presentation. Explain and give an example of how CPS techniques can be used in each of the three areas.

2. Define each of the following terms:

(a) Network.	(e) Logic dummy.	(i) Float.
(b) Merge.	(f) Critical path.	(j) Postrequisite.
(c) Earliest start.	(g) Event.	(k) Milestone.
(d) Activity.	(h) Expected time.	(l) Time-cost tradeoff.

3. What is the reason for putting the *earliest* of the *LS* times on the cross at a burst?

4. Discuss the three time estimates used in PERT networks with respect to deterministic estimates of activity durations. Which type do you think would be easier to obtain?

5. Under what conditions are m and t_e the same for an activity?

6. What is the probability of completing a project on the date set by the *LF* of the last activity in a PERT network? Why?

7. Will the probability of meeting a milestone *SS* less than the event's *ES* be greater when the variances of the activities leading to the event are smaller? Why?

8. What network convention would replace a situation where the correct logic of a restriction was shown by a two-headed dummy?

177

9. Complete the network for the project "Conduct a CPS Evaluation" begun in Figure 6.6. Use only gross activities such as "calculate boundary times" instead of detailed computation procedures for ES, LS, EF, LF, TF, etc.

10. Some computer programs print out another type of float called "free float." It is calculated by subtracting an activity's EF from the earliest start time of all postrequisite activities. Calculate the free float for the activities in the network of Figure 6.8. What value is there in knowing an activity's free float?

11. Describe the resources involved for an activity that would likely cause a time-direct cost curve similar to each of the curves shown in Figure 6.11.

12. Construct an arrow network segment to portray each of the following activity prerequisite-postrequisite relationships:

Set 1	Set 2	Set 3	Set 4	Set 5
$A < E$	$A < D,E$	$A < F$	$A < D$	$A < C,D,E$
$B < E$	$B < D,E$	$B < D,E$	$B < D,E$	$B < C,D,E$
$C < D,E$	$C < E$	$C < E$	$C < D$	$C < F$
$D < F$	$D < F$	$D < F$	$D < F$	$D < F$
$E < F$	$E < F$	$E < F$	$E < F$	$E < F$

13. Construct a CPS network to conform to the relationships given below. Note that the activities are not in alphabetical order and that there are redundant restrictions.

Activity	Must Precede
A	C
B	A,C,F
D	C,F
E	A,C

14. Construct a network based on the following restriction list.

Activity	Duration	Restriction
A	3	$A < E,F$
B	5	$B < C,D,E,F$
C	3	$C < H$
D	4	$D < G,H$
E	6	$E < G,H$
F	7	
G	4	
H	5	

From the given durations, calculate the boundary times. If the ES for the first event is 23, what is the LF of the last event?

15. The list below gives nodal-numbered activities and their durations. Each activity is described by an i and j node with its duration in parentheses. What is the minimum time by which the project can be completed?

Activity: 1,2 1,5 2,3 2,4 2,5 3,4 4,6 5,6
Duration: (5) (4) (3) (4) Dummy Dummy (2) (7)

16. A firm seeks the opinions of the local populace about adding a new process to its manufacturing facilities which will create disagreeable odors. The smell should be noticeable about 20% of the time due to prevailing winds, but the process will provide many new jobs. A survey will be made by hiring specially trained personnel to call on 5000 selected households. The interviewers will follow a questionnaire designed for this particular situation. Set up a network to show the necessary activities and estimated times for the activities, assuming you are the manager of the project and have one assistant to handle all details (questionnaire design, training, review, report, etc.). What estimate would you give for the completion time of the project for a 95% probability of meeting your milestone?

17. Given the data below for the activities required to launch the promotion of a new product:
(a) Calculate the expected time for each activity.
(b) Complete a boundary time table.
(c) Calculate the activity variances and determine the probability of completing the project in 12 weeks.
(d) Calculate the probability that the advertising will be "released" by the time of its LF.

Activity	Time Estimates			Postrequisites
	a	m	b	
A Develop training plans	2	6	10	Conduct training course D
B Select trainees	3	4	5	Conduct training course D
C Draft brochure	1	3	4	Conduct training course D Print brochure, Prepare F, G advertising
D Conduct training course	1	1	1	
E Deliver sample products	3	4	4	
F Print brochure	4	5	6	Distribute brochure I
G Prepare advertising	2	5	7	Release advertising H
H Release advertising	1	1	1	
I Distribute brochure	2	2	3	

179

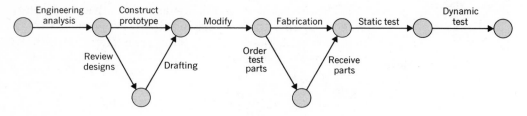

Figure 6.15

18. In what ways might the project shown in Figure 6.15 be expedited?

19. The activities in the network of Figure 6.16 that require the use of a special, one-of-a-kind machine are labeled XX. Determine the minimum project duration and show the schedule in a bar chart format.

20. Activity descriptions, durations, and node numbers (in place of a restriction list) for a construction project are given below. Complete a boundary time table for the project.

i node	*j* node	Activity Description	Duration
1	2	Move in	2
2	3	Foundation	12
3	4	Lead time for parts	4
3	6	Concrete slabs and columns	25
3	14	Filling and grading	133
4	5	Dummy	
4	14	Air conditioning and plumbing	130
5	14	Electrical	130
6	7	Lead time for framing	3
6	8	Lead time for steel	20
7	9	Framing	20
8	10	Erect structural steel	15
8	14	Other concrete work	15
9	10	Walls and insulation	25
10	11	Roof deck	14
10	14	Lath and stucco	60
11	12	Carpentry	14
11	14	Roof and sheetmetal	15
12	13	Painting	14
12	14	Hardware	45
13	14	Finishing	25
14	15	Clean up	4

180

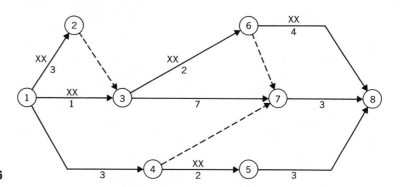

Figure 6.16

section two   ANALYSIS

To analyze means to take something apart in order to discover the nature of the whole. A simple object will yield its mysteries after quick and crude partitioning. More complex projects require planning and careful division. A production system, even a small one, has a multitude of interacting parts and considerations. An investigation based on a single dismembered part can produce a deceptive picture of the whole; it is the same as trying to visualize an entire jig-saw puzzle from a single piece. A system analysis recognizes the function of each operation with reference to the purpose of all operations. The danger of erroneous conclusions drawn from symptomatic or incomplete analyses is illustrated by the following example:

Peter Drucker, ''How to Make a Business Decision,'' *Nation's Bus.*, Apr. 1956.

A simple yet fairly common example is the scheduling problem in a manufacturing plant where, despite all efforts to plan and to schedule, production always gets into trouble, where overtime to meet delivery promises always runs up extra costs without ever quite giving satisfaction. In one such case management had practically decided to spend a substantial amount of money to increase the capacity of the plant. Then somebody pointed out that they did not know where the delay actually occurred.

When this was examined it soon became clear that the trouble was not in manufacturing at all and that no reasonable increase in plant capacity would end it. The trouble was in marketing. Salesmen promised immediate delivery for all items in the catalog including specialties that were not regularly stocked. They also gave the company's most marginal customer the same delivery promise as the company's best customer. As a result rush orders for specials or orders for small runs continuously disrupted whatever schedules manufacturing had made.

ANALYSIS

183

This integration theme is aptly depicted by the *Section Two* symbol of interlocking circles. The rings concentrate related production considerations under three headings. Overlapping segments represent subjects linked by mutual derivations. All parts coalesce to form a synergistic relationship of production factors: the whole is greater than the sum of the parts. Each part has exclusive problems, but inclusive solutions are required to optimize performance of the entire system.

Human performance is probably the most complex and unpredictable factor encountered in a production system. Nevertheless, we can identify general characteristics and a range of human abilities. Taken individually, we can only be sure that a man's performance will fluctuate from day to day as a result of a bewildering number of influencing elements. Being aware of these difficulties, we still seek to develop guidelines to understand man's abilities and to improve his performance (*Chapter 7*).

Man's basic abilities are often collected under the broad headings of data sensing, data processing, and data transmission. In categorical equivalence, work can be classified by the three functions of obtaining information, making decisions based on the information, and acting upon the decisions. Attention to man's work environment often improves the quality and quantity of the information he obtains, simplifies his decision making, and eases the implementation of the solution (*Chapter 8*).

The way men perform tasks, the time it takes to complete them, and the wages paid for their performance are all agents of the interface between men, machines, and materials. Motion principles guide the design of work operations. Method studies evaluate man-machine and man-material operations. Time studies and work sampling measure the efficiency of operations. Wage payment plans are designed to reward and encourage performance standards (*Chapter 9*).

Man designs machines and equipment to extend his basic abilities. The performance of man's creations is more predictable than his own, but reliability is still enhanced by astute scheduling, replacement policies, and maintenance programs (*Chapter 10*).

Materials are fuel for a production system. The fuel must be acquired, recorded, handled, stored, and injected into the system. Inventory policies are designed to coordinate departmental and system objectives while maintaining adequate service levels with minimal total cost (*Chapter 11*).

The heart of the analysis section is depicted by the area of maximum overlap among the circles representing the "M's" of production. This integration of men, machines, and materials was the topic of Chapter 2 from the viewpoint of management concepts and functions. In this section the same management area is treated from the outlook of what tools and techniques are available to aid the manager who has to live with and accept responsibility for all those M's (*Chapter 12*).

The thread linking analyses throughout the "M" chapters is another M, *money.* Several alternative solutions are available for most problems. Some courses of action favorably satisfy one criterion and are simultaneously unattractive when measured against a different standard. A comparison is made by rating both appealing and objectionable aspects according to their monetary effect on the system. The resulting cost outcomes are evaluated by balancing economic merits such as those below:

Cost of idleness caused by waiting	*vs*	Cost of facilities required to avoid waiting
Increased purchase price of a machine	*vs*	Decreased maintenance cost for the machine
Cost of running out of required material	*vs*	Cost of holding a safety stock of material
Higher wages paid to attract and keep skilled workers	*vs*	Cost of training and spoilage caused by employing less skilled workers

Such comparisons typify analysis (*Section Two*).

CHAPTER 7

MAN: Abilities and Performance

7-1 IMPORTANCE

Men initiate and operate production systems to serve other men. The inspiration for production is the satisfaction of human wants. The acceptance accorded a product is a measure of how well it was designed to fit the want and how well the production system functioned; not only must the design fulfill the intended purpose, the production process must deliver a product of adequate quality at an acceptable price to the market where it is wanted. Figure 7.1 characterizes how man is benefactor, component, and beneficiary of the production systems man designs, constructs, and uses.

It is easy to recognize that man is an integral part of complex systems, and it is easy to overlook that man himself is a complex system. There are many things he can do, and there are also many things he cannot do. An efficiently operating man-machine combination implies an efficient man operating an efficient machine. The muscle and blood component of the man-machine partnership deserves more attention than the metal component because man's abilities and limitations are far more difficult to comprehend than are those of his metal partners.

In the following sections we shall consider the human factor. There are few exact rules to follow, but an awareness of human abilities can sharpen our daily observations of men in action and

"Call a man a machine if you want to, but don't underestimate him when you come to do experiments on him. He's a non-linear machine; a machine that's programmed with a tape you can't find, a machine that continually changes its programming without telling you; . . . a machine that may try to outguess you in your attempts to find out what makes him tick, . . ." A. Chapanis, *Research Techniques in Human Engineering*, John Hopkins, Baltimore, 1957.

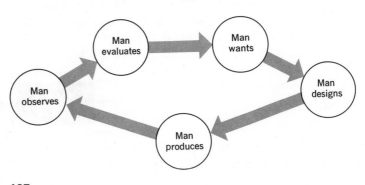

Figure 7.1 Man-oriented production cycle

help us develop guidelines for analyzing man's critical role in production.

7-2 MAN'S ABILITIES

Human factors should be the most fascinating and simple subject associated with production. After all, we are human and have daily contact with the factors that affect us. This exposure can lead to a false sense of security. Conversely, our intimate familiarity can breed contempt for the subject; continued observations of unexpected behavior might even weaken faith in human disciplines. One way to avoid the skeptical and mystical aspects which clutter the interpretation of man's behavior is to treat him as a black box.

The "black box" treatment allows us to review the inputs and outputs of the "man system" unencumbered by the intricacies of the conversion process; the conversion of inputs to outputs is blanked out by the black box (Figure 7.2). By this procedure we can concentrate on observable reactions and leave the explanation of internal linkages to medical and psychological investigators.

Data Sensing

It is estimated that man relies on his visual sense for 80% of his information about his environment.

The sources of data in any environment are tremendous in number and variety. Man can detect many forms of energy such as light waves, temperature, or internal chemical reactions. He is also blind to the extreme ranges of energy such as infrared light waves or ultrasonics. Even when the energy is of sufficient intensity, it may still be unrecognized if he is not posturally set to receive it.

One advantage of an audio over a visual warning device is that it requires no postural set to be received.

The man-stimulus interface has been intensively studied. Although sensing ability varies between individuals and with time, it is relatively easy to anticipate which cues from an environment man is physically able to detect. What are more difficult and more important to anticipate are the data that will be specifically detected and thereafter influence behavior. Several design considerations appropriate to a production environment are listed in Table 7.1.

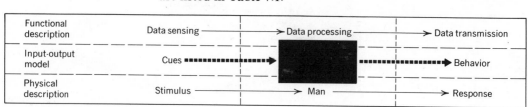

Figure 7.2 Black box input-output model of man

188

Table 7.1 Design considerations for data sensing

Data-Sensing Factors	Production Examples
Only energies of certain types can be picked up by man.	Dangerous radiation cannot be detected by man's unaided senses.
Sensory organs are more sensitive to some kinds of energies than others.	High-frequency noise is more annoying than low frequency. A bitter taste is easier to detect than a salty taste.
The capacity of sensory organs is limited; only energy of sufficient intensity will be picked up.	Verbal communication at ordinary voice level is difficult in a noisy factory because of masking background noise.
Certain energies will not register on man unless he is posturally set to receive them.	A gage displaying vital information fails its purpose unless the operator looks at it.
The same type of energy can be received differently by each individual.	A color-blind person obtains little information from color-coded controls.
Sensory organs can be damaged by overexposure to energy.	Hearing loss may result from unusually noisy plant conditions.

Data Processing

Man has a miraculous ability to process data picked up by his sense organs. He can identify the source of energies and distinguish differences in type and intensity. From these identifications and the overriding patterns of attitudes and emotions, he derives meaning that leads to judgments and decisions.

Discrimination and identification of data. The first data-processing step in the man-black box is the differentiation of stimuli contacting his body. While his greatest discriminatory skills are visual, he can make relatively fine discriminations between sounds, temperatures, pressures, odors, tastes, etc. He can also discriminate sensations arising from within his body. Chemical, electrical, and mechanical activities inside his body add to and color the discriminations made about outside stimulating energies. The aggregate discriminations are man's basic contact with his world. They are the means by which his behavior is determined and controlled.

Identification is the process of grouping differentiated sensations. In most instances, groupings rather than isolated sensations

189

are acted upon. The ability to identify rests on the ability to discriminate and is the direct result of learning shapes, scales, and models. This knowledge is stored and used when needed. Beyond learning, the ability to identify also depends on skills of recalling, organizing, manipulating, and comparing. How far man could go in storing and using experiences is difficult to determine. We do know that training can reinforce his ability and make him more adept in a particular function.

Interpretation of data. The workings of the man-black box assumes even greater complexity when we consider human social and personal abilities. Just as man's behavior is limited by his sensory and mental abilities, it is also limited by his attitudes, interests, and adjustmental abilities.

An attitude is an opinion, belief, feeling, conviction, or emotional tone which colors each and every event man encounters. The attitude is the background against which sensations and identifications are judged. Whether on a conscious level or not, man finds himself liking or disliking, approving or disapproving, wanting or not wanting, or somewhere along a scale of positive or negative feeling with regard to all he encounters. And he brings these attitudes to work with him. They may seem unreasonable or irrational, but they still influence his behavior.

What is it that interests man? He has been known to become interested in almost everything at one time or another. We hear such statements as "Joe could do a good job if he wanted to." What is really meant is that "Joe could do a good job if Joe *could* want to." The usual interpretation is that man has limitations on sensory, mental, and motor abilities but not on his interests. Interests are as necessary to success on a job as is any other ability.

Many additional adjustmental abilities vary among individuals. Some men are ambitious, striving always to get ahead. Others are willing to take things as they come. Still others do not want to get "ahead" and would refuse a promotion. There are conformists and rebels, leaders and followers, responsible men and shirkers of responsibilities. Many times these abilities or limitations are temporary; often they are basic to a person. Obviously these traits fit a person better to one job than another.

Decision making. The ability to identify and interpret data has little value alone; it is man's ability to use the data to make decisions for effective action that counts. This ability to reason, to manipulate ideas, and to judge is man's most highly developed

Table 7.2 Data input-output sequence of the "man-system"

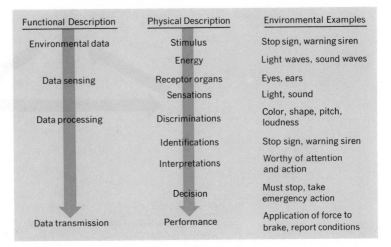

Functional Description	Physical Description	Environmental Examples
Environmental data	Stimulus	Stop sign, warning siren
	Energy	Light waves, sound waves
Data sensing	Receptor organs	Eyes, ears
	Sensations	Light, sound
Data processing	Discriminations	Color, shape, pitch, loudness
	Identifications	Stop sign, warning siren
	Interpretations	Worthy of attention and action
	Decision	Must stop, take emergency action
Data transmission	Performance	Application of force to brake, report conditions

"Any attempt to build a machine that could operate at even a moron level of intelligence would call for an expenditure of billions of dollars and parts and equipment covering hundreds of square miles." A. W. Jacobsen,

and valuable talent. In this capacity, man excels over all machines. A man-system program for given input-output could follow the sequence shown in Table 7.2.

Individuals differ considerably in their abilities to manipulate verbal symbols, numerical symbols, and figures in space and to perform problem-solving activities. Quite often the word "intelligence" is used to refer to the level of ability in such activities. While this term is highly ambiguous in some ways, it does provide a summary term for evaluating the general level of decision-making ability. But too often we regard this term with undeserved esteem. A high test score on a certain intelligence test does not guarantee a worker will do well on all jobs. An individual who makes sound judgments on a written test may make very poor judgments on social problems or panic under pressure. Some jobs of a repetitive nature may be conducted more effectively by a person with a lower intelligence score. As a tongue-twisting, summarizing conclusion, we might observe that the intelligent use of intelligence tests tests the intelligence of the intelligence tester.

Data Transmission

Overt behavior includes the exertion of force and other body movements.

In a production setting the overt behavior that follows data sensing and processing often takes the form of data transmission to other men and to machines. Such behavior is observable whereas the data processing is implied. Being easily discernible, communications between sentient beings or inanimate objects have been widely studied. In fact, we can speculate about the internal linkages and activities within the man-black box through

191

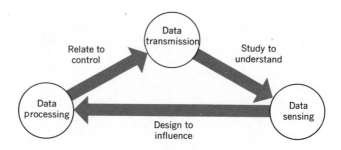

Figure 7.3 The motor performance cycle

observation of overt behavior. As depicted in Figure 7.3, to design facilities that will improve motor performance, we study motor performance.

Communication with man. Transmission of data to another person may be conducted by talking, writing, or signaling. Each device relies on symbols. This use of symbols reduces the basic sensations to classifications. Communication of these classifications attempts to reconstruct the original sensations of the sender in the mind of the receiver. Because the classifications are not identical to the sensations, structural distortions usually appear. Messages are further distorted by misinterpretation of symbols and by alterations of meaning attributable to the setting or manner in which the communications take place.

Communication with machine. Man has muscles, tendons, ligaments, bones, and joints, and he has neural connections between his sensory apparatus, his central nervous system, and his muscles. He operates and controls machines and equipment by using all or part of this makeup. Where machines or tools are not available or appropriate, he uses the same makeup to act directly on his surroundings.

Man is versatile but not infinitely so. He becomes fatigued, he can exert only so much force, and he can react only so quickly. In a production setting the environmental conditions, machines, tools, and layout can be designed to enable man to function more effectively within the constraints of his abilities and the limitations imposed by his tasks. In the final evaluation, it is man's ability to communicate and his other motor performances that pay. The payoff is maximized by attention to his individual and collective abilities.

EXAMPLE 7.1 Man Abilities Versus Machine Abilities

One characteristic which typifies the present trend of production systems is the replacement of men by machines. And machines are becoming more complex. The more ambitious automated systems tend to replace the muscle power of man and, to some extent, usurp his decision-making responsibilities. One way to allocate and justify task assignments between man and machines is to recognize where each excels. The following list offers a basis for the distribution of tasks.

A Man Is More Capable At . . .	A Machine Is More Capable At . . .
Handling unexpected events	Monitoring men and other machines
Profiting from experience	Exerting large amounts of force smoothly and precisely
Being sensitive to a wide variety of stimuli	Consistently performing routine, repetitive tasks
Using incidental intelligence with originality	Rapid computing and handling of large amounts of stored information
Improvising and adapting flexible procedures	Responding quickly to signals
Selecting own input	Reasoning deductively
Reasoning inductively	

7-3 PLACING MEN   Different workers produce different amounts regardless of wages paid, working conditions, training, motivation, or basic abilities. The poor producer is an expensive worker. Overhead and capital investment are the same for him as for the good producer. The cost of hiring a poor worker is the same as for a good worker. Tenure or seniority systems may not allow dismissal of poor workers, and often the poor worker cannot be identified until after his position has been established.

It is imperative that a procedure for picking men results in some degree of accuracy in man-job matching. Managers should never feel that they can secure perfect matchings by picking men. It may be necessary to alter certain working conditions to fit the abilities of the men available or to attract men from other locations. More specifically, a job can be tailored to the man in a reversal of the typical "man wanted" appeal.

Establishing Predictives

The objective of any employment program should be the detection of good workers *prior* to their being hired. This requires the identification of what is expected of a good worker and how a good worker differs from a poor one. These goals are easier to state than to attain.

Before answering what makes a good worker, it must be decided what success on a job means. One way to define success

193

Success Criteria

Quantity or quality of
production
Equipment damage
Training time
required
Longevity
Versatility
Promotability
Absenteeism
Accident rate
Material spoilage
Horseplay
Grievances
Company loyalty
Compatibility

• is to select the most important traits or characteristics associated with specific jobs. These criteria are largely subjective opinions of management, and they vary from plant to plant for the same job as well as from job to job. Although the judgments are subjective, they should be made on the basis of objective observations of specific situations. Another approach is to study trouble spots in production. A definition of failure is perhaps a backdoor entry to success predictives, but each trouble spot should reveal at least a strong hint of common criteria associated with deficiencies. The more serious the trouble, the more important are the criteria. Some common criteria connected with success and failure are shown in the margin notes.

Still further judgments are necessary to make the criteria meaningful. How much spoilage of material is too much spoilage? How much absenteeism is more than can be tolerated? High production is high only in that it is higher than less production. There is a point along the scale of each criterion where performance is not good enough to justify presence on the job. This is the management-determined cutoff point. Workers with performance levels above the cutoff point are acceptable and successful employees. It is simple logic that an employer should attempt to hire only those men whose performance will be above the cutoff point on the criterion scales after they go to work.

The only sure way to find the performance level of an applicant is to hire him and observe his performance. Where no criteria are available, as in a new type of job, this random selection method might be feasible; otherwise the hit-and-miss procedure could lead to an expensive game of musical chairs. A better procedure is to find the *permanent traits* of those men who are above the

Permanent Traits

Physical dimensions
Age
Sex
Appearance
Race or nationality
Acuity of senses
Attitudes, sociability,
and mental measures

• cutoff points which are different from the permanent traits of those men below the limits. For instance, it may be found that for a certain job, "tall" men (defined as over 6 feet) are "safer" workers (defined as having less than 1 lost-time accident per 5000 working hours) than are "short" workers who consistently fall in the group of "unsafe" workers. Thus height would be considered a permanent trait which could be used to predict success on that particular job. The designer of a placement program has the duty of matching such traits from a worker's historical and testing program records with his on-job performance records. The identified traits should, at a minimum, provide a predictive yardstick by which to measure candidates in the labor market.

Attracting Applicants

There is little merit in developing performance predictives if the labor supply is severely restricted. Selectivity is possible only if there is a qualified pool of applicants from which to choose. It may be economically advantageous, or sometimes a necessity, to *entice* workers to apply for work. These campaigns operate according to the age-old selling principle: if it is worth buying and buyers hear of it, it will sell. They are also subject to merchandising principles regarding false advertising and tarnished reputations.

The rule is to offer what men want. In the job market the wants may be money, prestige, location, working conditions, or many others. Again, it is management's task to determine which wants are in demand and then to weigh the cost of satisfying them against the benefits of selectivity. The task is greatly simplified by recognition given to hiring during plant planning. Locating a plant near a known labor supply cancels the need to entice qualified workers from other areas. Similarly, inviting surroundings and clean, safe, working areas attract available workers to specific plants.

When an employer cannot offer exactly what workers want, he can teach them to like what he has to offer. In ancient times men were induced to work by use of a whip. The want of freedom from the whip was taught by lashings; the means, of course, to achieve the want was work. The modern version is a Madison Avenue selling campaign that creates a want or cultivates a dissatisfaction. "Come to California where you can work and play in the sun all year." Or, conversely: "Tired of the same monotonous climate? Enjoy the change of seasons and your work in the Midwest!"

Some industries are very adept at attracting applicants. Some also suffer from unkept promises. Unless the hiring enticement is accompanied by job satisfaction, the selling effort is a waste.

Worker Attractions

Starting salary
Potential growth
Company prestige
Geographic location
Regular salary
 increases
Permanent position
Paid vacations and
 holidays
Quick advancement
Insurance and health
 plans
Company size
Educational facilities
Good climate
Retirement or
 pension plans
Housing
Challenging work

EXAMPLE 7.2 A Program to Improve Job Attractiveness

Sometime ago it became necessary to establish new research and testing facilities for nuclear investigations. The project was sponsored by the government but administered by private companies.

The first problem encountered was where to locate the establishment. The nature of the work decreed a large, nonpopulated area with abundant water resources. These conditions, though not conducive to recruiting employees, were unalterable. The best compromise location was a large government-owned, arid tract near a big river and a medium-sized town.

When the physical facilities were completed, the personnel problem arose. Highly trained, technical men were absolutely necessary. But high wages alone were not enough to attract and, particularly, to keep the caliber of men required. The factors needed for efficient operations were opposed to contented workers.

Effort was directed toward the "intangibles." Instead of trying to improve the small government housing area near the reactors, modern busses were purchased to run between the test area and the nearest established towns. These towns were encouraged and aided in developing recreational outlets. Some rental homes were built in the towns, and choice building sites were made available for individual construction. With the promise of expanded business, more retail stores moved into the area. Cosponsorship of company and civic groups provided new educational and cultural activities. The local community was well informed of the nature of the work and the type of employee at the nuclear base. Whenever possible, local people were employed for routine work. Before long the atmosphere changed from a company town to a town's company.

Screening Applicants

Sources of Predictive
Information

Test scores
Physical exams
Interviews
Job experiences
Recommendations
Mock-up trials
School records

Once there are enough applicants for a job to allow a selection, the screening phase begins. It is a two-sided process. The intents are to pick the applicant whose prediction of success for a particular job is greatest and to create a favorable impression while doing so.

Physical traits of an applicant can be determined from observations or questions. Some potential sources are listed in the margin notes. In reviewing the sources, a skeptical attitude is not unhealthy; recommendations reveal no more than what a selected recommender says, work histories tell only what someone did somewhere else, and even a carefully designed testing program reveals only what certain tests show.

Screening information should be obtained as quickly and painlessly as possible for the mutual benefit of the applicant and the hiring agency. A well-designed employment flow system gathers only the needed information through a series of progressively restrictive trials. For instance, an application received by mail could reveal the lack of desired physical traits and thereby save the applicant a wasted visit. An interview could eliminate a contender before he is subjected to an expensive battery of written tests. The number of such hurdles is largely a function of the level of employment sought, but regardless of level the applicant deserves respect. A comfortable screening experience should leave the rejected applicant feeling he has been treated fairly, and the successful applicant should believe he has found a pleasant place to work.

Man-Job Matching

When a key position is to be filled, such as a research scientist or plant manager, the predictives are very definitive and the candidate selected by the screening process is tailored to the position. Screening approval for men hired for general production does not necessarily carry with it an assignment to a particular job. Different jobs usually require special skills, attitudes, or adjustmental abilities. Some men possess several skills and the versatility to suit several openings.

The allocation of individuals to particular jobs is sometimes a matter of whim or convenience; department *A* gets the first 10 men hired today or a clerk arbitrarily sends prospects to departments. Objectivity is increased by referring only to the physical traits and predictives related to a definite job. In the case of application blanks, this objectivity is accomplished by making an overlay based on the cutoff points determined for each job. The overlay is called a *job template* and takes the physical form of a stiff, blank sheet of paper with holes cut in it. The template is placed on top of a completed application blank. Only the pertinent information for the given job shows through. The levels of traits revealed by the template windows are compared to the cutoff levels developed for the job. Since each job and possibly the same job in different departments has distinctive windows and varying cutoff scores, the template differentiates the applicants to provide at least preliminary assignment directions.

Another approach to man-job matching is the *assignment method*, a variant of linear programming. This algorithm is applicable to any matching problem where some type of rating can be given to the performance of each applicant for each position. For instance, men are matched to machines according to pieces produced per hour by each individual on each machine; teams are matched to projects by the expected cost of each team to accomplish each project. In this section we shall apply the assignment method to the allocation of men to jobs.

Let us assume that there are four candidates to fill four different jobs. In the assignment method the number of operators must equal the number of operations or, expressed another way, the format must be a square matrix. The relative ratings for each candidate for each position could be determined from test scores, trials, or subjective opinions. These ratings are then arranged in a matrix as shown in Figure 7.4. Assuming low numbers indicate a better rating for a job, we see that there is no immediately obvious solution. It is interesting to note that there are 4! = 24 possible different assignments. In a matrix with 15 candidates and 15 jobs, there would be over a trillion unique ways to match men and jobs. For such a situation, a timesaving algorithm to discover the best pattern is not a luxury—it is indispensable.

Job	1	2	3	4
Man 1	2	6	3	5
2	1	2	5	3
3	4	3	1	5
4	2	4	1	5

Figure 7.4 Matrix format

Job	1	2	3	4
Man 1	0	4	1	3
2	0	1	4	2
3	3	2	0	4
4	1	3	0	4

Figure 7.5 Row subtraction

Job	1	2	3	4
Man 1	0	3	1	1
2	0	0	4	0
3	3	1	0	2
4	1	2	0	2

Figure 7.6 Column subtraction

Job	1	2	3	4
Man 1	0	3	1	1
2	0	0	4	0
3	3	1	0	2
4	1	2	0	2

Figure 7.7 Zero-covering lines

The placement of the zero-covering lines does not affect the final solution. The only restriction is to use as few as possible.

The first step in the solution is to obtain the opportunity costs for each row and column. This step is accomplished by subtracting the smallest number in each row or column from the remaining values in the respective line. It makes no difference in the final solution whether the row or column is subtracted first. Figure 7.5 shows the row subtraction. Note that one zero occurs in each row. The other values in the row are the opportunity costs that would result from not assigning the man with the best score to his most suitable job. After each operation on the matrix, a check should be made to see if an optimum assignment has been attained. When there is a unique zero for each row and column, the best possible match is identified. In Figure 7.5 there are no zeros in the columns for jobs 2 and 4; therefore, the assignment method must be carried through at least one more step.

Column subtraction is conducted similarly to row subtraction. The lowest value in each column of the matrix resulting from the row differences is subtracted from all other values in the column. The outcome of the operation is shown in Figure 7.6. Note that columns 1 and 3 are unchanged from Figure 7.5; they already contained zeros. The zeros now reveal the opportunity costs for the man-job interactions. Again a check for an optimal solution is due. At first glance it appears that there might be a zero for each man-job match, but closer inspection shows that man 2 has three of the zero opportunity costs available. Therefore, another matrix operation is needed.

The next step is two phased and serves a dual purpose. The initial phase is to cover all the zeros in the matrix from the previous step with as few straight horizontal or vertical lines as possible. If the number of lines is equal to the number of rows (or columns), a solution has already been obtained in the previous step. As shown in Figure 7.7, the sample problem requires only three lines to cover all the zeros. Since there are 4 rows, it means that a solution has not been obtained and thereby confirms our previous conclusions reached by inspecting the zeros independently. This optimality check is the first purpose of the lines.

The second purpose and second phase is to modify the matrix in a continuing effort toward optimization. The procedure is to choose the smallest number not covered by the recently drawn lines. This number is added to all values at line intersections and subtracted from all uncovered numbers. In Figure 7.7, the smallest uncovered number is 1 in the cells for man 1,job 4 and man 3,job 2. It is added to the value of each cell at a line intersection; $0 + 1 = 1$ at man 2,job 1 and $4 + 1 = 5$ at man 2,job 3. Then

Job	1	2	3	4
Man 1	0	2	1	0
2	1	0	5	0
3	3	0	0	1
4	1	1	0	1

Figure 7.8 1 added to line intersections and subtracted from uncovered cells

Alternate assignments with the same minimum cost are often identified in the solution. This condition is signaled when there is no unique zero in a row or column.

1 is subtracted from the uncovered cells to produce the matrix shown in Figure 7.8.

For a quick check, the matrix is again subjected to zero-covering lines. In the sample problem there is no way to cover all the zeros with less than 4 orthogonal lines. Eureka, a solution! Specific assignments are identified by locating any zeros that occur uniquely in a row *or* column. The only zero in column 1 is at row 1. Therefore, man 1 is assigned to job 1. Now we have a 3×3 matrix left; row 1 and column 1 are already taken by the first assignment. In row 4 the only assignment possible is man 4 to job 3. The remaining two assignments are man 2 to job 4 and man 3 to job 2. The matchings and associated ratings are shown ● below. No other combination can provide better ratings per job. Expressed another way, this is the minimum opportunity cost schedule.

Man-job match: M1 to J1 M2 to J4 M3 to J2 M4 to J3
Man-job rating: 2   3   3   1 = 9

compare against other possible

The assignment algorithm is more flexible than it might appear from the foregoing sample. It can be used when ratings are given in profits (maximization problem) by first subtracting all the values that appear in the profit matrix from the largest number in the matrix. In effect, this process converts all values to "relative costs" and allows application of the previously described minimization algorithm. If a given man-job match is impossible or unwieldy, such an assignment can be blocked by entering a very large cost in the appropriate cell. If there is an extra operator or operation and the intent is to identify which one should be eliminated to achieve minimum cost, a dummy with zero costs in each cell is added to make the number of rows equal the number of columns. This concept was introduced in Section 5-7 to account for unequal supply and demand in the transportation method. Several of these special conditions are illustrated in Example 7.3.

assignments to try to get smaller #

EXAMPLE 7.3 Man-Job Matching by the Assignment Method

A distributor plans to penetrate a new market area. The region has been divided into four districts. Five candidates have been recommended as representatives for the new area. Because each district offers unique opportunities and each is encumbered by special difficulties, different managers are expected to perform with varying degrees of success. The anticipated annual sales by each representative in each district were estimated and are shown below (in $10,000 units).

199

ANALYSIS

District		I	II	III	IV
Sales Managers	Browne	28	19	23	12
	Greene	16	17	18	18
	Redd	24	16	22	19
	White	23	11	16	18
	Jones	21	16	21	16

The sales figures represent profit and must be converted to relative costs in order to use the minimization assignment algorithm. In the matrix below, the values in each cell have been subtracted from the maximum value in the matrix, 28, and a dummy sales district, V_d, has been added with zero costs for all assignments in its column.

	I	II	III	IV	V_d
B	0	9	5	16	0
G	12	11	10	10	0
R	4	12	6	9	0
W	5	17	12	10	0
J	7	12	7	12	0

The dummy column provides a zero for each row, making the row subtraction step redundant. Successive solution steps of column subtraction, line covering, number modification, second line-covering check, another round of number modifications, and a final line-covering check reveal the optimal assignments.

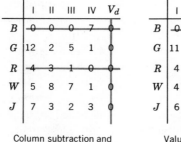

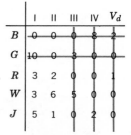

Column subtraction and first zero-covering lines

Values modified by subtracting 1 from uncovered values and adding 1 to line intersections

Values again modified according to zero-covering lines of the previous step; new zero covering lines drawn

The first assignment, the only unique zero in a row or column, is at B,I. By eliminating the B row and column I in the initial allocation, the zero at G,II is unique in column II. Now the reduced matrix appears as shown on page 201. Because there are no unique zeros in the rows or columns of the 3 × 3 reduced matrix, equally attractive alternate assignments are indicated.

The expectation of equal sales from either assignment schedule is shown on page 201. Factors other than those included in the matrix should be utilized to make the management choice between the costwise equal assignments.

	I	II	III	IV	V_d	
B	0	0	0	8	2	→ First assignment – B to I
G	10	0	3	0	0	→ Second assignment – G to II
R	3	2	0	0	1	
W	3	6	5	0	0	} Matrix reduced to 3 x 3
J	5	1	0	2	0	

Alternate schedules indicated by reduced matrix

	III	IV	V_d
R	0	0	1
W	5	0	0
J	0	2	0

	III	IV	V_d
R	0	0	1
W	5	0	0
J	0	2	0

Assignment 1:	B to I	G to II	R to III	W to IV		*J has dummy*
Expected sales:	28	17	22	18	Total:	$850,000

Assignment 2:	B to I	G to II	J to III	R to IV		
Expected sales:	28	17	21	19	Total:	$850,000

W has dummy

7-4 TRAINING MEN

From the minute an employee sets foot on plant grounds, the training program gets underway. Learning occurs whether or not production is benefited by it. By refusing to direct the learning experiences of workers, an employer does not stop learning—he merely forfeits control to chance or other factors. When a worker wants something, he will set about finding a means of achieving it. If what he finds does work, he will accept it as a means to an end. When the method does not work, he will seek more effective methods. The broad objective of a production training program is to help men discover what behavior is rewarding and how to develop skills that lead to goal satisfaction.

Orientation

The time to start training is the day employment begins. A worker who goes to work with little or no knowledge of company policies, regulations, and purpose starts with a severe handicap. He may discover these things as days pass; he may also learn what is not so and piece together a distorted picture.

Gossip is the wild card of orientation. It can work for or against and is nearly impossible to control. As E. W. Howe observed in his *Country Town Sayings:* "What people say behind your back is your standing in the community."

A knowledge of what a plant has to offer a worker and what the worker is counted on to give can be achieved by a simple orientation program. Here is where morale has its start. The layout of the plant, what goes on here and there, office rules, and plant regulations must be known to some extent before the worker can fit comfortably into the scheme of things. Many organizations give the worker a period of indoctrination at

201

company expense. Often this program includes a conducted tour, introduction to key personnel, a series of talks, a lecture, a movie, a question-and-answer session, a packet of literature, or perhaps a day to wander around and investigate the plant.

The extent and nature of orientation programs vary widely but all should be aimed at specific objectives. A review of trouble areas is fertile ground for harvesting objectives. For instance, if accidents have been a problem, safety practices should be stressed. The message may be delivered subtly by inferences and suggestions or blatantly by shocking examples and rigid directions. The best routine depends on the message, the audience, and the skills of the orientators. Worker-oriented guidelines that accent the human factor are:

1. Make him feel relaxed and part of the group.
2. Explain to him what is expected of him.
3. Be sure he knows his immediate boss.
4. Keep him occupied with meaningful activities.
5. Instruct him properly and show confidence in his ability.
6. See that he has all necessary tools and materials.
7. Give credit where it is due or criticise constructively.

Training Programs

Man cannot always do today what he might be able to do tomorrow. Through training, man learns the skills that make his intrinsic abilities valuable to a production system. All men can learn, but some are more proficient at it than others. A training program has to be planned for someone. A general indoctrination can be aimed at everyone. Special programs are directed for individuals or segments of a working group to develop certain abilities. Individuals may be selected because of promotions or recognition of special attributes. Groups, such as new employees, supervisory personnel, men on express assignments, or different levels of management, receive training that should overcome present or anticipated troubles. The extent of the training program largely depends on whether the troubles are localized or widespread.

There is no one answer to the question of what training methods to use. Many types have been developed and all have their champions. Probably the most reliable rule is to select the method that is most likely to alleviate the problem for which the training program is initiated. For instance, a program to develop specific job skills should be based on the study of errors— missing skills, steps of an operation being left out, or inefficient

Training Methods

On-the-job: task training at the workplace
Vestibule school: separate classroom area specially equipped with training aids
Apprenticeship: working with an experienced person for craft or executive training
Conference: preplanned discussion or problem solving often with outside experts
Role playing: preplanned exchange of roles
Affiliated programs: liaison with schools to teach technical skills

application of existing skills. If all workers share the same shortcomings, an inclusive demonstration and practice program is appropriate. When just a few workers make errors, a supervisor can work with them individually while they stay on the job. Several common training methods are listed in the margin notes.

While the definition of the training objective is a prominent step in the training program, it is only the first one. Unless the sessions are well organized, they will likely fail to satisfy the objectives. Selected students must understand the importance of the program. The facilities and the teachers should be fully prepared. Nearly everyone has suffered through boring, incompetent presentations held in inferior classrooms with inadequate teaching aids. The irony is that many of the former students become teachers and perpetuate the same obstacles to learning. Good teaching requires careful attention to details and plenty of preparation time. Great teaching takes even more time plus a flair that appeals to and inspires students. Since the cost of industrial training programs is due mainly to lost production and wages of the students, every effort should be made to assure that the presentations make the most profitable use of available time. Some characteristics of successful training programs are:

Too often training concentrates on "know-how" at the expense of "know-why."

1. A well-qualified instructor with positive teaching capability.
2. Carefully planned subject matter that stresses methods designed to counter specific troubles.
3. A detailed timetable of instruction that is followed.
4. Adequate physical facilities (classrooms, mock-ups, materials, etc.) that allow instruction without disturbing interruptions.
5. Motivated students that know the purpose of the training and are eager to learn. *BE HONEST*
6. A schedule long enough to include time for practice and repetition.
7. An atmosphere that allows students to make mistakes and to learn from corrections.
8. A summary that relates all parts of the training to the overall intent.
9. A follow-up routine to reinforce learning and confidence.
10. Program evaluation to detect faults that will pave the way for future improvements.

7-5 MOTIVATING MEN

Man is employed in a production system for the work he does. This work is physical, mental, or both. It takes effort. There must be reasons for man to expend the effort. His behavior in any situation, work or play, is the result of a complex pattern of

Statesmanship
⇧
Participation
⇧
Paternalism
⇧
Servitude
⇧
Slavery
⇧

The management meta-
morphosis from manipulation to
motivation.

cause-and-effect relations. It is a temptation to grab the first apparent cause, usually wages, and proclaim that its effect is work. The extension of this cause-effect formula is that the more you pay, the more work you get. Though there is some merit in the "dollars equal doing" equation, it is incomplete. The problem is to find what other elements should be included in the motivation formula.

During the World War I era the prevailing philosophy was that people worked solely to feed and shelter themselves. The way to get more out of them was to threaten in a tough, dictatorial
• voice backed by the power to fire them. From the 1930's through most of the 1950's, the feeling switched to opinions that people worked out of "loyalty" to an organization; therefore the way to increase productivity was to organize company ball teams, publish chatty house organs, pump in soft music, and pile on the fringe benefits. Today we are still searching. Money retains its influence as a motivating factor up to a certain level. Beyond that point, money and fringe benefits do not automatically lead to more productivity. Even the power to fire is a diminishing threat and motivating force owing to increased worker mobility and skill shortages. Perhaps the motivators that in the long run make better workers are psychological—feelings of responsibility and accomplishment.

An open view of motivation admits that man has many wants that affect his behavior. Each individual has his own pattern. A similar perspective applied to working conditions recognizes that different situations increase or decrease the effort required to satisfy the wants. Then the difference between the want strength of the individual and the resistance to effort resulting from a particular job yields a measure of the effective motivation for performance *that* worker has on *that* job. Although these divisions lack quantitative scales, they do provide a qualitative framework from which to observe the interaction of man and his work environment as a function of motivation.

Want Strength

"Man does not live by bread alone" is a threadbare statement because it states so clearly man's motivational needs. An employee who is paid a reasonable wage, a want no one will deny he has, usually shows up for work. How much he does on the job depends a lot on how the job provides for the whole pattern of his wants. His productivity is influenced by his personal wants such as the approval of those he respects or his version of success. It takes more than money to motivate him.

Personal wants are specific. It is not just recognition that is wanted, it is a certain kind of recognition from certain people. Promotions, attention, status, freedom, and security are all broad categories within which lodge the special wants of each individual.

A want pattern starts with the basic physiological needs for food, water, shelter, exercise, stimulation, and other factors of well-being. Less tangible wants, often referred to as psychological needs, are superimposed on the basic pattern. A man may want prestige and not actually need it in a physiological sense; but if he wants it, then he needs it psychologically to the exact extent he wants it. Man does not always want what will benefit him. His wants may seem completely irrational to an impartial observer, but what he wants is what he believes he needs. And for these wants he will work.

Wants are positive forces, forces that push man on to achievement. Man does something because he *believes* doing it will give him what he *believes* he wants. Attention to these beliefs opens the way to build want strengths in workers. Jobs should be designed to offer what is wanted, and workers should be aware of what is offered. Perhaps, as mentioned in Section 7-3, workers can even be taught to want what is offered. Whether weak or strong, sensible or irrational, simple or complex, wants cause man to act.

Resistance to Effort

In nature a state of rest is the equilibrium position. To change the state takes effort. We can view the man-black box similarly. In a state of rest, man has few of his wants satisfied. To satisfy a want takes effort. The want and the resistance to effort are opposing forces. For work to result, man's wants must be stronger than his resistance.

Contributors to Resistance

Fatigue
Discouragement
Lack of interest
Illness
Weakness
Lack of success
Laziness
Futility
Tension
Emotions
Drugs
Inferiority

Resistance to effort varies with the individual and the situation. If a man is sick, weak, or fatigued, his resistance is increased even when his wants remain strong. Noisy or unsanitary conditions, personality clashes, and autocratic supervision contribute to the resistance. Some men are more mindful of particular discouragements than others. One person can ignore distractions while another surrenders to them. Nevertheless, attention to well-established design considerations for human comfort will obviously reduce resistance for the majority. Further attention to human relations by supervisory personnel can cater to special problems of individuals and minority groups.

See Section 8-4 for design considerations to reduce resistance to effort.

Effective Motivation

The difference between want strength and the resistance to effort, as depicted in Figure 7.9, is effective motivation, the driving force to the exertion of effort on a particular task. If the task is too difficult, man will not attempt to satisfy the want.

205

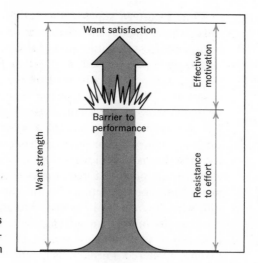

Figure 7.9 Want strength minus resistance to effort equals effective motivation

Thus, more difficult tasks require special incentives or the tasks must be redesigned to allow their accomplishment with less effective motivation. Bonus compensations are an example of the former and machine-assisted operations are an example of the latter.

Most work-for-pay situations are at a disadvantage from the start. In industrial plants the workers exert effort to earn rewards which must be converted later to want satisfaction. Thus, if someone wants a new boat, he seldom builds one; he works at a job that pays enough to buy the boat. A worker on a job which results directly in his own want satisfaction, such as building a boat, will select the most effective methods he can find and will work enthusiastically.

Profit-sharing plans are attempts at creating in employees the feeling of working for oneself. The incentive-pay and bonus schemes are designed for the same purpose. Many managers have concluded that money in routine amounts (such as an annual raise to reflect increased productivity) is largely taken for granted, anticipated before it arrives, and viewed as a justly deserved reward for past services—not as a stimulus to new effort.

Another factor affecting the reward system is the degree of immediacy. It is easier to increase effective motivation if wants are satisfied within a short time. Credit buying is a classic example of attempts to shorten the waiting period for want satisfaction. Some say it is not the employer's business how workers spend their money; but if workers waste their money and do not get their wants satisfied, job performance will suffer. An employee

206

who has to use his wages to pay off old debts soon loses his motivation to work. Company credit unions and worker counseling help combat this type of problem.

No one has been able to pin down the all-purpose, magic motivator, if it exists at all, but new theories are constantly advanced. "Participative management" is a concept proposed for seeking advice from employees in running the business and thereby encouraging them to seek want satisfaction in the firm's success. This approach leads to a less strict organization that avoids suppressing the capabilities of employees. Jobs are fitted to individual talents rather than fitting people to rigidly designed jobs.

Some theorists foresee unstructured job classifications and pay scales where employees would roam freely between related jobs, and salaries would vary widely for the same work, depending on the employee's ability. Job contents would be enlarged and the task force concept would be used to lift workers from the rut of normal routine to work on special projects. Such measures are being tested or envisioned as effective motivators to improve performance while diminishing the difference between work and leisure.

EXAMPLE 7.4 Increasing Motivation by Making Jobs More Interesting

An application of job enlargement was made at American Telephone and Telegraph Company's department of shareholder relations. The women employees, 70% of them college graduates, were unhappy in their jobs because they were continually second guessed in their handling of correspondence to AT&T's stockholders. The situation was improved by lifting supervision and allowing the women to write their own replies. This step encouraged them to become experts in the problems that interested them. Turnover dropped, productivity rose, and job satisfaction, measured on a scale of 100, soared from 33 to 90 in 6 months—all without a pay increase.

7-6 SUPERVISING MEN Supervision is necessary at all levels of a production system. At the lowest level of the organizational pyramid is the "working supervisor." Perhaps he carries no formal title, but many workers take their orders from him in his capacity as straw boss, crew chief, or gang leader. Higher on the supervisory ladder, we have managers managing managers. At any level the attitude of men to those below them can vary from mother-hen concern to dictatorial arrogance; some men fluctuate between temperaments according to time and mood. Because there are individual differences between supervisors as well as those being supervised, no strict rules fit every occasion. Therefore, two broad avenues to supervisory principles will be explored. One is to consider

207

organizational structures and procedures; the other is to give further attention to motivation resulting from human relationships.

Organizational Structure

The spinal column of any business of significant size is its organizational structure. Information flows both ways, from president to laborer and from bottom to top. The behavior of a firm internally and externally, is influenced by the speed and accuracy of the information flow. When a firm is small, say less than 30 people, the information links are short and direct; the top manager knows directly the production problems a worker is experiencing. As the firm expands, the links become tenuous and communication noise masks the information flow. Written messages replace verbal exchanges, and several layers of authority often act as barriers to the feedback of information.

Organizational charts are an overt representation of a firm's structure. They display the formal lines of authority among divisions and how the divisions are to interact. There are innumerable ways to slice and arrange divisions of authority. From
• the panoramic view, a firm can have a centralized or decentralized organization. A centralized structure takes the familiar pyramid format where each stratum has a defined responsibility that is authorized and checked by the levels above. In a decentralized structure, usually associated with large, geographically widespread companies, the divisions are treated as somewhat autonomous or self-sufficient areas of responsibility and authority. There
• are advantages with either structure. Top management's tighter control and the penetrating versatility of a master staff in the centralized organization have to be weighed against the greater motivation potential of decentralization.

The web of informal lines of communication and authority in the shadow of the formal organization plan is very significant. The published plot of organizational lines may be misleading. A centralized paper layout can be run according to decentralized philosophy by making subordinate divisions essentially self-regulating. A formal supervisor-subordinate relationship may be inverted by the social standings of the two men in the positions. Staff groups can have unstructured communications through personal friendships that do not show in the chart but lead to better coordination. The closest formal recognition given to these shadow structures is the committee. Although the com-
• mittee approach to a problem is widely criticized for its ineffectual or slow action, it does offer an opportunity to tap abilities that

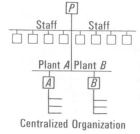

Centralized Organization

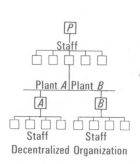

Decentralized Organization

"Consultative management" is a committee-oriented technique where top managers consult with lower levels before • making decisions.

208

are hidden or distorted by organizational titles. In this manner the proposals that evolve can reflect the opinions of those affected. The shock effect of some executive decisions are thereby cushioned, and changes are often accepted with more enthusiasm because the doers helped decide what to do.

Any chain of command has some weak links. Whenever tasks are delegated to a lower link in the chain, some authority from
• the upper position must be allotted to the lower position. Little can be accomplished without authority to use some resources, but the shift of authority does not relieve the upper position of the responsibility for the task. Most managers have personal policies to handle such situations and are also guided by written or unwritten company procedures. The "management by exception" principle allows subordinates to make routine decisions, but the more critical decisions must be shared with higher echelons. This principle encourages involvement and provides fine training unless everything unusual is treated as an exception and each exception becomes a crisis.

From a worm's view, it usually appears that all troubles run downhill and their speed depends on the gravity of the situation.

Human Relations

Person-to-person interactions occur throughout the organizational pyramid. They are important at all levels, but where are the most people? At the bottom, of course. This bit of geometry is about as far as we can go in quantifying human relations. There are few universal, timeless "truths" to rely on. Human relations is a train of episodic, variable "truths." It is a people-oriented philosophy that attempts to make the man-black box opaque. That the effort is worthwhile can be documented by many work situations where the morale of a work force has overcome obstacles flowing from poor formal organizations and physical facility handicaps.

High morale does not guarantee high production, but it does lower resistance to effort. Morale is a summation of hundreds of little things. The best directives that cascade down from top management to the operating units cannot promise high morale. It is the momentum gained from continuously healthy supervisor-worker relationships that culminates in pervasive goodwill among employees.

The working supervisor occupies a difficult, demanding, and
• important position. He spends most of his time in actual production and is the technical coordinator who keeps his group going. Although he seldom has the authority to hire and fire, he has to channel the directives from above to the workers. He has to speak the language of both management and "people." He gets

Supervisor Attributes

Not hypocritical
Confidence in higher
echelons
Effective communicator
Fair disciplinarian
Respected by superiors
and subordinates (and
both know it)

209

part of his authority from the organization and part from respect of the workers for his skill and personal characteristics.

It is easier to live up to supervisory responsibilities when they are well defined. Objectives and standards of performance should be clear and precise. Each managerial level has expectations of how subordinates should perform. For summary judgments there must be standards against which actual performance can be compared. In some cases these objectives are communicated by job descriptions, specific assignments, or statements of task criteria. In other cases the employee must ferret out the implied standards from conversations with a supervisor or fellow employees. Uncommunicated expectations can hardly guide or motivate a subordinate. Each man on each job should know the standards by which his boss judges him. He should also know the consequences of disregarding these standards.

Discipline can be a dilemma for a supervisor. He must be humane and sympathetic, yet he sometimes has to take firm action. Fewer disciplinary actions are necessary when rules are reasonable and well publicized. When punishment is deserved, it should be delivered swiftly and uniformly. For the questionable cases, Ben Franklin might have advised that "an ounce of correction is worth a pound of punishment."

> "Final accomplishments of an enterprise come from the combined work of each organizational element and from each of the people in each element. Managers assign responsibility down the line. Each responsibility for results that is assigned is simply a part of a result expected above. Managers need to make sure that all expected results are assigned and that each man at the next level down knows the result expected of him and how it is to blend in the total."
>
> *Goal Setting, Work Planning, and Review*, General Electric Co., Cincinnati, Ohio.

EXAMPLE 7.5 How Not to Supervise

Sometimes it is easier to identify the things that injure than it is to prescribe measures that improve. A postmortem analysis of social troubles usually reveals where things went wrong but seldom shows how to right the situation. Avoiding the following list of *social poisons* can save a supervisor the need to find their antidotes.

1. Start each day right. Give each worker a lecture on what he did wrong the day before.
2. Be strong and stern. Make every worker toe the line; if he doesn't, fire him. Better still, threaten him for several days.
3. Make snap judgments. If you hesitate, workers may think you don't know your business.
4. Be calm and aloof. Think first of your own welfare and the workers' problems won't seem so significant. If you continually snub the workers, they will soon reach the point where they will avoid you completely and then all your troubles will be your own.
5. Know all the details. If you find enough little matters to occupy your time, you will nearly always overlook the important problems.
6. Gain respect. Be sure the workers know how good you are. You may have to brag a little. If this doesn't work, brag a lot.
7. Be honest and blunt. If a worker looks tired, tell him so. If you tell him he is an idiot often enough, he may act like one.
8. Accept credit gracefully. If workers do a good job, take the credit for it. But don't take the blame for a wrong decision.
9. Be alert to competition. Keep your workers below you. Refuse to show them how to do anything and they will learn to do nothing.

10. Outwit your boss. Keep your workers informed of your latest exploits with the top brass. Let them know how you outwitted your own superiors and they will learn to outwit you.

7-7 SUMMARY Man is a benefactor, component, and beneficiary of the production systems he designs, constructs, and operates. He is very versatile but fragile. Although abilities and physical characteristics vary widely among individuals, many guidelines are available to help him function effectively.

Man's ability to sense, process, and transmit data is indispensable to a production system. He can discriminate between many stimuli and then use these discriminations to make identifications. The interpretation of these identifications leads to inductive decision making—man's unique and greatest ability. Decisions are transmitted to other men and machines by means of his motor abilities. Machines are more capable than man at certain tasks, but none even approaches his versatility.

Finding the best place for each man in a production system is difficult because of the differences in particular abilities between individuals. The objective of an employment program is to detect the best man-job fit; the criteria of success on a job are matched to man's permanent traits associated with the success criteria. Better matches are possible if there is a large number of applicants from which to choose. Applicants are attracted to a job if the position offers what they want. Objectivity in matching men to jobs is increased by use of job templates and the assignment algorithm. A job template allows the consideration of pertinent information only. The assignment method results in an optimal assignment of a number of men to an equal number of jobs after the value of each man on each job is known.

Man cannot always do today what he can do tomorrow. Training starts with a planned orientation to a new job. Formal training for the development of special skills can take many forms. No one format is always best, but there are guidelines to follow for any training program.

Effective motivation is the difference between man's wants and his resistance to effort. Man works for what he believes he wants even though these wants may seem irrational to an impartial observer. His resistance to effort is lessened by comfortable work conditions. When tasks are difficult, the want reward must be increased or the task made easier to maintain a level of effective motivation. Rewards are more trenchant if they are immediate. New motivational philosophies such as "participative manage-

211

ment" are being developed because modern man's wants differ from those of his immediate ancestors.

Supervision is important at all levels of an organization. The formal structure of a firm can be centralized or decentralized. The centralized structure tends to have more versatility than the decentralized format which often encourages greater motivation. However, informal operating authority and practices may be quite different from the formal structure. The working supervisor at the lower levels of the organizational pyramid is the link between plans and action. His job requires the direction and support of higher management plus the personal characteristics and experience to cultivate good human relations.

7-8 REFERENCES   Chapanis, A., W. R. Garner, and C. T. Morgan, *Applied Experimental Psychology*, John Wiley, New York, 1949.

Dale, E. and L. F. Urwick, *Staff in Organization*, McGraw-Hill, New York, 1960.

Fletcher, H., *Speech and Hearing in Communication*, Van Nostrand, Princeton, N.J., 1953.

Fogel, L. J., *Biotechnology: Concepts and Applications*, Prentice-Hall, Englewood Cliffs, N.J., 1963.

Haimann, T., *Professional Management Theory and Practice*, Houghton Mifflin, Boston, Mass., 1962.

Johnson, R. A., F. E. Kast, and J. E. Rosenzweig, *The Theory and Management of Systems*, McGraw-Hill, New York, 1963.

March, J. G. and H. A. Simon, *Organizations*, John Wiley, New York, 1958.

Sayles, L. R., *Managerial Behavior*, McGraw-Hill, New York, 1964.

Tannenbaum, R., I. R. Weschler, and F. Massarik, *Leadership and Organization*, McGraw-Hill, New York, 1961.

7-9 QUESTIONS AND PROBLEMS

1. Where does advertising fit into the man-oriented production cycle of Figure 7.1? Where would the inspiration for a new product likely occur?

2. Although assessment of man's abilities is somewhat easier by considering him a black box, what dangers are inherent in such a mechanistic approach?

3. Apply functional and physical descriptions as depicted in Table 7.2 to the following operations:

(a) Flavor-tester in a brewery.

(b) Motion picture critic.

(c) Reaction to a fire alarm.

4. From the quote "Joe could do a good job if Joe could want to," assume that Joe could be a good student. What could make Joe want to?

5. Name a machine that has a greater capability than man in each of his data-sensing, processing, and transmitting abilities. Do you think that machines will ever be built that exceed all man's abilities?

6. If the intent of a free enterprise is to make profit, why should a company consider the welfare of its employees?

7. Give an example of where each type of training method shown in the margin notes of Section 7-4 would be appropriate.

8. Relate the factors that attract applicants to a job, as described in Section 7-3, to their effectiveness as motivators. Consider their influence on want strength and resistance to effort.

9. With reference to want satisfaction, compare the employee benefits offered to build company "loyalty" with the concept of "participative management."

10. Comment by example about the historic changes in management philosophy from manipulation to motivation.

11. Why must there be the same number of rows and columns in an assignment matrix?

12. Large orders for four parts are to be assigned to four man-machine centers. Some machines are better suited to produce certain parts and their operators are more proficient at producing some parts than others. The costs to produce each part at each center are listed below:

Part	$MC1$	$MC2$	$MC3$	$MC4$
$P1$	12	9	11	13
$P2$	8	8	9	6
$P3$	14	16	21	13
$P4$	14	15	17	12

(a) Which part (P) should be assigned to each machine center (MC)?

(b) Assume a new machine has been added to the facilities above. One old machine is to be phased out. The operator on the old machine will operate the new one if it can produce one of the parts less expensively than the assignment made in part (a). The estimated cost using the new machine ($MC5$) is

Product:	$P1$	$P2$	$P3$	$P4$
Production cost at $MC5$:	11	7	15	10

Hint: Add the new machine costs and a dummy part ($P5$) to the matrix used to solve part (a). Use zero costs to produce $P5$ in each machine. ● Should the new machine be used? If so, which part should it produce?

213

ANALYSIS

13. A new office building has been constructed to allow centralization of administrative functions. Six regional managers will be moved to the new central location. All offices for the managers are on the same floor. Each office has the same room area and furnishings, but exposures and views differ. In order to please as many managers as possible, the managers were asked to rank their preferences for offices, with 6 being the most desirable and 1 the least desirable. The following rankings were submitted:

Office	201	205	209	212	216	220
Manager A	4	2	5	1	3	6
B	1	3	5	2	4	6
C	3	5	6	2	1	4
D	2	4	6	1	3	5
E	5	2	6	4	1	3
F	1	6	3	5	2	4

Determine the assignment that will provide the most overall satisfaction.

14. A year after he graduated from college and took an engineering-management post with the Konrad Construction Company, Bob Conn received his first major independent assignment. With a crew of 70 men and considerable heavy equipment, his mission was to clear 42 miles of right-of-way for a four-lane superhighway through a rugged mountain pass in the West.

He felt fortunate in having a tough but respected crew chief assigned with him. The chief had been with the company for several years and was generally regarded as a spokesman for the men, both on the job and as a representative of the union.

The crew, for the most part, had previous employment with the company and were experienced in this work. Since the right-of-way crossed uninhabited land, a company camp was set up near the work area. Wages were equal to or above union requirements and local prevailing wages.

At first the work progressed smoothly, and Bob Conn believed a positive cycle of morale was in operation. The company camp was comfortable; terrain conditions were pleasant. The few gripes he heard he dismissed as a normal condition. He had often heard that a griping worker was a contented worker. It was when the worker stopped griping and became sullen that you had to be careful.

Since the men knew their jobs, Bob left the daily directions to the crew chief. Each morning the chief would get the plans for the day from him; in the evening he would report on the progress and turn in any pertinent information. Bob occupied himself with occasional checks on the workers and worked with them if they had a particular problem. The rest of the time he spent with the surveyors or in keeping the multitude of records required by the company. The men seemed to accept him, although he had no really close friends among them. He felt they respected his work. However, he remembered the training he had received at his officers' training course in the Marines and one motto in particular: familiarity breeds contempt.

Due to weather and unexpectedly difficult terrain features, the work began to fall behind schedule. The home office sent a message to Bob urging him to make every effort to get back on schedule because the rest of the construction outfit would soon be ready to move into his section and the contract they were working on had a time-penalty clause.

Bob called in his crew chief and showed him the communication he had received. The chief said it was not the men's fault they were behind schedule. Bob agreed but emphasized that they still had to speed up. He further suggested that they move their base camp to a new location farther along the right-of-way to cut down the daily travel time on the rough access roads. The crew chief seemed reluctant to accept the plan. He mentioned the nice streamside location they currently had and that the move would put them farther away from a small town the men found popular for off-hours.

The next day the move was made. Bob instructed the chief to tell the men that it was the only possible way to recoup the schedule losses and they would work out the transportation problems so each man could go to the town at least one night a week. Other than being farther into the "wilds" and a bit less convenient, the new location seemed just as hospitable as the old one to the young manager. One and a half hours of travel time per day had been eliminated and he felt this would increase their output by a quarter of a mile a day. But it soon became apparent that the progress rate was just the same as before and a feeling of bitterness enveloped the crew.

That evening Bob planned to call in the crew chief and talk about the turn of events. He was worried and it affected his work and his temper. Late in the afternoon he received a radio call for him to return to the home office to make a personal report on work progress. The trip would require at least 8 hours of travel time each way. He told the dispatcher to get a vehicle ready for him and went to his tent for the necessary records. When he returned to find his transportation, the crew chief and three of the section leaders, each of the three carrying a suitcase, approached.

The crew chief said, "I heard you had to go back to the city and figured you wouldn't mind taking these boys with you. They have some personal problems they could get out of the way by the time you are ready to return."

Bob recognized the three as key men whose absence would certainly cut the capabilities of the whole crew. They would be gone at least 3 days. He also knew each of them was a spokesman for a segment of the crew. Bob was undecided as to what to say or do.

What would you say and do?

This problem is well suited to the "role-playing" training method. Only two "actors" are needed: the crew chief role and the manager's role. The play can start with the last quoted words of the crew chief. Either as a player or as an observer, diagnose the interaction and record your impressions.

CHAPTER 8

MAN: Work Environment and Performance

8-1 IMPORTANCE In the previous chapter we classified man's basic abilities as data sensing, processing, and transmission. In an equivalent fashion we can categorize work according to three functions: obtaining information, making decisions based on the information, and acting upon the decisions. Attention to these functions by production analysts can improve the quality and quantity of information obtained, simplify decision making, and ease implementation of decisions. Work design considerations for specific tasks will be dealt with in the next chapter. In this chapter we shall discuss the functions with respect to plant design—the physical environment consisting of location, work areas, atmospheric conditions, illumination, noise, and other variables that affect man's work performance—Figure 8.1.

8-2 PLANT LOCATION A plant location problem is not encountered every day, but the factors that can create a problem are constantly developing. Technological improvements make existing processes non-competitive. New products replace established lines. A requirement for different materials or a change in the source of materials alters supply costs. Power, water, or other resource needs are subject to production levels which in turn are a function of demand. Any or all of these factors can force a firm to question whether its plant should be altered at the present location or moved to another locality.

Whenever the plant location question does arise, it deserves careful attention because of the long-term consequences. Large manufacturing firms or big retail distributors often have staff groups that specialize in evaluating new sites. Consulting services can be utilized when a company faces an unusual relocation problem or when an objective appraisal is needed. There are
- also many sources of free advice. Communities here and abroad clamor for new industries to improve their tax base. To attract more businesses, they offer bait such as free land, free services, favorable financing, or tax benefits. Current location trends

Sources of Site Information

Chambers of commerce
Realtors
Periodicals such as *Factory* or *Modern Industry*
State and federal agencies
Transportation companies

217

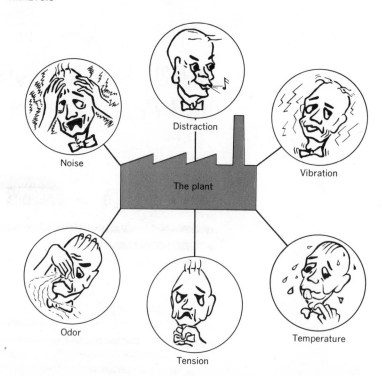

Figure 8.1 The human factor in plant and work design

Site Factors
Technical skills
Cost of labor
Raw-material sources
Highway system
Railway hub
Seaport facilities
Airport
Nearness to markets
Proximity of suppliers
In-place utilities
Community facilities
Climate
Low taxes
Available financing
Land costs

appear directed toward: (1) industrial parks in attractive suburban settings with centralized service facilities, (2) urban renewal projects "downtown," and (3) foreign sites near the export market or natural resources. Then there is the maverick owner who locates his company near where he wants to live.

At or near the top of every list of desired plant site features is labor supply. With the needed skills known, it might seem an incidental problem to locate in areas where those skills are abundant. Ideally it would be nice to have three or four times the number needed from an available labor pool to allow selectivity in hiring. On the practical side, there should be doubts when an area boasts that much available labor. Is there an unhealthy labor-management atmosphere? Are absenteeism and turnover patterns undesirable? Are labor costs and expected fringe benefits unusually high? What is the productivity expectation?

The importance of labor questions depends, of course, on the particular firm, its policies and its products. If the firm is science oriented, it should anticipate going to an area where engineers and scientists congregate because it is unlikely that many can be lured to remote sections. Some specialized skills, such as wood working or art crafts, tend to be concentrated in certain

The exponential comparison model described in Section 4-3 can be used to compare plant sites. Problem 26 in Chapter 4 is a typical application.

Other location features that attract workers were included in Section 7-3.

The transportation method of Section 5-4 dealt with the economic relationship between supply and demand locations.

regions. Semiskilled labor can often be trained from an unskilled labor pool in areas that offer compensating monetary incentives such as inexpensive land or power.

After the general geographic area has been chosen, the location still must be narrowed to a specific plot of land. The plot obviously has to be big enough for plant operations plus associated facilities such as parking and storage. Should it also allow room for expansion, landscaping, and recreational areas? Obviously the plot should have access to necessary transportation facilities and sufficient utilities. Less obvious is the cost of being distant from the homes of workers. If the labor force's bedroom area is far removed from the plant, workers must put in 9, 10, or 11 hours to earn 8-hour wages. And the nonpay hours spent fighting traffic are perhaps the toughest. Such travel restricts the number of men available and lowers job performance.

A dominant physical restriction such as proximity to harbors, markets, or natural resources often overrides people-oriented attributes of a location. Then the only question is whether the "dominating" factors are truly indispensable or is their importance a function of historical habit. We can trace the development of industrial centers by reference to changes in physical restrictions. Years ago industrial growth began in seaports because of a reliance on inexpensive ocean traffic. As the railroad network grew, the relationship of raw materials to manufacturing to markets became more flexible. Air and trucking transportation encouraged further versatility and industrial centers spread throughout the land. The distance in time between supply and demand is ever diminishing. Innovations will continue to tip the scale of physical resources versus human resources from its historical economic balance, and future fortunes will be built on these detected imbalances.

8-3 PLANT LAYOUT

Plant layout is a companion problem to plant location. A decision to relocate provides an opportunity to improve total facilities and services. A decision not to relocate is often accompanied by plans to revise the current plant arrangement. The relayout may be designed to reduce increasing production costs that gradually evolve from piecemeal expansion or to introduce an entirely new process. In either case the relayout strives to maximize production flow and labor effectiveness.

Product Flow

Symptoms of a Poor Layout

Lack of control
Congestion of men and
    materials
Excessive rehandling
Long transportation lines
Accidents
Low worker performance
Production line bottlenecks

The general layout for product flow follows a pattern set by the type of production anticipated. The three basic layouts are discussed on page 220.

219

Product layout — product moves along an "assembly line."

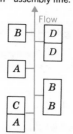

Product layout—a line or chain of facilities and auxiliary services through which a product is progressively refined. This layout is characteristic of mass or continuous production. A logical sequence of operations reduces material handling and inventories, usually lowers the production cost per unit, and is easier to control and supervise. These advantages are achieved at the expense of flexibility. The "pace" of the line is set by the slowest operation; any changes (product design, volume, etc.) in the line normally require a major investment.

Process layout — product moves to "departmental areas."

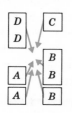

Process layout—a grouping of machines and services according to common functions for the performance of distinct operations such as welding, painting, typing, or shipping. A functional arrangement is characteristic of job and batch production. It allows good flexibility and reduces the investment in machines, but it increases handling, space requirements, production time, and the need for close supervision and planning.

Fixed layout — facilities are centered around a static product.

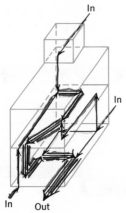

Fixed position layout—an arrangement where men and machines are brought to a product that is fixed in one position owing to its size. Ship building and heavy construction of dams, bridges, and buildings are typical examples. Such operations often enjoy high worker morale and flexibility for scheduling and design changes. However, the required movement of materials and machines may be cumbersome and costly.

Each layout has relative advantages. Sometimes the advantages characteristic of one type can be imposed on another type to produce a hybrid that lowers cost for special applications. For instance, a "job shop" in which each product is produced only after securing a customer's order could achieve the economy of an "assembly line" by mass producing basic modules which are later customized to specific orders. Similarly, the flexibility of a high volume, high investment production line is increased by planning foresight that provides space and hook-ups (power, waste disposal, material supply) for future modifications.

The initial planning of a layout is demanding, but the effort is justified by considering how difficult it is to alter facilities once they are in place. All sorts of product flow lines can be imagined— up or down, unidirectional or cross-flow, centralized or decentralized. Templates and three-dimensional models aid the visualization of flow. Merits or weaknesses of alternate arrangements within limited confines are determined by measuring the simulated steps of production. Layouts can also be evaluated by computers. The inputs to the computer include the cost and quantity of

Vertical, horizontal, and convergent production flow.

One computer layout analysis program is known as CRAFT—Computerized Relative Allocation of Facilities Technique.

• material flow, production capacities, and basic dimensions. From this information the computer is programmed to develop alternate arrangements and corresponding cost expectations.

Work Areas

Parts and materials flow from one work center to another. With the exception of highly automated production processes, men operate the work centers. Because of man's versatility, it is a temptation to subordinate his welfare to the efficient arrangement of expensive equipment and machines. A long-range outlook probably would upset this precedence.

Each type of layout has human as well as product advantages and disadvantages. For example, let us consider the economically recommended mass production assembly line. The concept is valid; it has been praised for decades. But there are still some problems. Each operator along the line has exactly the same time to accomplish his assigned task. Since human capabilities differ

See Sections 8-3 and 10-4 for details of work design and line balancing.

• between individuals and between tasks, it is a complex problem to "balance" the work at each station and to set a pace that neither wastes nor exceeds the capabilities of individuals.

It also is difficult to establish individual incentives because work is paced by the speed of an assembly line. The open, continuous arrangement of the line hinders the control of noise, odors, heat, vibrations, and other factors detrimental to human performance. Some men feel insignificant in a sprawling plant. Others tire of the repetitive tasks. And some may be perfectly happy in exactly the same environment.

The importance of careful hiring, training, and placing of men in accordance with the demands of specific situations is again evident. Special problems can usually be solved by special measures such as ear plugs for high noise levels. For each pro there is normally a con, and vice versa. The system thinker has to recognize both sides before he can weigh them.

There is no doubt that a plant should be sufficiently large to handle the operations required. This approach judges size according to technical aspects. Size may be judged also by workers' feelings. Most workers function better where they retain some singularity and gain a feeling of security. This principle is recognized by creating optimum-sized plants instead of expanding old ones to meet greater production demands. The

Plant Layout Suggestions

Keep similar activities together but avoid stringing them out
Avoid clusters of workers and structural or physical barriers
Keep buildings compact by integrating utility and service areas
Reduce congestion by having at least two sides of an area open

• same feelings are developed in big, integrated plants by organizing workers into administrative divisions to foster "family" units and, perhaps, competitive efforts. News sheets and off-work recreational teams contribute to the same effect.

221

The immediate work area, where the worker spends his time, distinctly affects his feelings and output. To some extent, space and comfort can be gained by the choice of finishing materials. Most people feel cooler in light green or blue surroundings and warmer in dark orange or red surroundings. Rooms seem larger when ceilings are light colored and cozier when walls are dark. Exposed brick, concrete, and stone seem sturdier than sheetmetal, glass, and smooth plaster.

Equipment Arrangement

Equipment and supplies used by workers should be designed and arranged for minimum effort and maximum convenience. For equipment design the key word is *flexibility*. Adjustable equipment avoids the need for individually fitted designs as well as substandard performance from workers forced to make their work fit awkward arrangements. Supplies, materials, and tools cannot always be placed within easy reach of the worker, but they should be arranged as conveniently as possible. The extra stretch to reach a cabinet or the extra steps to get material from another floor waste the energy of a worker and, equally important, disrupt ongoing activities. Even when tools are conveniently arranged, maintaining the arrangement is still a problem. Check-out clerks at tool bins, signs reminding workers to return tools, and tool shadows painted on walls are methods used to avoid misplaced equipment.

In some instances, layouts are designed to force movement. Trips to obtain supplies may provide needed exercise or a break in an otherwise monotonous routine.

More detailed analyses are warranted when a number of men and equipment must work together to perform a task. A proper arrangement should be based upon the communication and control relationships between men and machines. These relationships can be represented by *links*. Communication links include visual and auditory (usually talk links) transmissions from man to man or from equipment to man. Control links arise from the use of levers and switches or from direct contact with materials by man to control machines.

Occasionally a communication link uses the sense of touch, and a control link can go from man to equipment to equipment.

A link analysis is conducted by determining the types of links involved, assigning a value to each link, and then evaluating different arrangements of men and machines with respect to the links. The value of each links is determined from the *frequency* of its use and its *importance* when used. Usually a three-point scale for each factor is adequate: 3 (often)–2 (occasionally)–1 (seldom) for frequency and 3 (vital)–2 (useful)–1 (trivial) for importance. The composite value of each link is then the product of its frequency and importance. Different arrangements of operators and equipment are evaluated according to how well the more important links are accommodated. Trial arrangements can be made to scale on paper or, for more important operations, a three-dimensional mock-up may be warranted.

EXAMPLE 8.1 Link Analysis of Man-Machine Arrangements

A control tower is manned by three or four controllers, depending on the amount of traffic. As depicted in Figure 8.2, position number 1 is occupied by the team leader responsible for final decisions. Operators 2 and 4 are assisted by relief help from operator 3 when traffic is heavy.

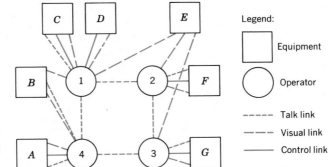

Figure 8.2 Present control tower arrangement

Each operator has control of a given traffic sector. Audio communication with the traffic is by radio. Other talk links are between controllers. Visual communications are comprised of television screens, digital readouts, and on-off lights. Most controls are switches and buttons.

The link analysis of the existing system is conducted by having "experts" agree on a consensus rating for each observable link from operator to operator and from operator to equipment. Links between equipments are not usually included in an initial evaluation. After rating the frequency and importance of use, a composite value is obtained for each link as represented below for operator 1.

Operator	Link	Equipment or Operator	Frequency Rating	×	Importance Rating	=	Composite Rating
1	――――――――	②	2	×	3	=	6
	――――――――	④	2	×	3	=	6
	――――――――	C	3	×	3	=	9
	――――――――	D	3	×	3	=	9
	――――――――	C	2	×	2	=	4
	――――――――	B	1	×	2	=	2
	――――――――	E	1	×	2	=	2
	―――――――	C	3	×	3	=	9
	―――――――	D	3	×	2	=	6

The layout is evaluated according to the way it facilitates the links. Views should not be obstructed by equipment or operators. The effect of distance and illumination on visual performance is considered. Distance is also a factor in auditory communications; shouting should never be necessary. The postural set of operators should accommodate easy visual or vocal communication. There must be sufficient room for convenient and accurate manipulation of controls.

If it is necessary to redesign the arrangement, attention is given first to the highest valued links. A mock-up may be required. Attention is given to proper ventilation, protective safety devices, noise control, and other maintenance or convenience features which will assure smoother operations by lessening physical and mental fatigue among operators.

A possible revised layout for the control tower is shown in Figure 8.3. Link values are shown in small circles for each link. The elevation of operator 1 is raised with respect to the other operators. A more thorough study would indicate the vertical placement of equipment; exact scaling would be used. Before finalizing a new design, thought should be devoted to unusual or emergency operating conditions. Care taken to assure a workable design distinguishes a craftsman from a journeyman; a design that anticipates the unexpected marks a master.

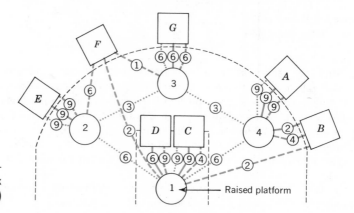

Figure 8.3 Revised control tower arrangement (composite link values are noted in small circles)

8-4 WORKING CONDITIONS

Good working conditions increase motivation by decreasing man's resistance to effort. In extreme cases the adverse effects of bad working conditions make adequate levels of performance unattainable. For example, tasks dependent on visual acuity are obviously impossible when there is insufficient light, and the expected pace of manual labor cannot be maintained without adequate ventilation and temperature control. These extreme conditions are rare in industry today because they are foolish from both social and economic viewpoints. But many subtle defects in the working environment still can be improved.

Illumination

The amount of illumination desirable for a particular job depends on the individual doing the job and the nature of the task. Some men require more light than others to make the same discriminations. Jobs that require exacting discriminations demand more illumination than less detailed work. Because of these differences, it is unrealistic to follow standard illumination levels for different areas of a plant. The more useful approach is to determine the minimum illumination needed by an average person to perform certain tasks and then alter these levels for individual preferences if necessary.

See *IES Lighting Handbook.* •

Recommended lighting levels for a multitude of situations have been published by the Illuminating Engineering Society (IES). The standard measure of light intensity used is a *footcandle* —the amount of light cast by a standard candle at a distance of

Moonlight produces about 0.5 footcandle and bright sunshine produces as much as 8000 footcandles.

• 1 foot. Some general conditions and specific minimum task recommendations are shown in Table 8.1.

The quality as well as the quantity of light affects work performance. Women appear particularly sensitive to spectral effects of lighting. A healthy individual may appear pale or sickly under certain colored lights. Blue-tinted lights cause feelings of harshness and coldness. Amber tints provide a feeling of warmth.

There has been a long-standing controversy over reactions to fluorescent versus filament lamps. Research reports have been conflicting. In general, filament lights are considered to create a "warmer" impression. •

Most workers prefer sunlight to artificial light. The preference is at least in part due to psychological reasons because there are many practical disadvantages to a reliance on sunshine for working light. To a designer it may seem that the sun operates at only two levels: too bright and too dim. Overcast days produce as little as 50 footcandles. On cloudy days the level varies according to the vagaries of passing clouds. Full sunshine is often distracting. By orienting a building to the position of the sun and by utilizing transparent and translucent materials to filter and equalize the distribution of natural light, sunshine can supplement artificial light. It can also be an expensive light source when window washing, repairs, and temperature control are considered.

Artificial Lighting

Direct—offers maximum utilization of light at the working area; often produces shadows and glare

Indirect—offers even lighting by directing light to ceiling or walls

Diffused—scatters light in all directions; causes some shadows and glare

Glare is the most harmful effect of illumination. It can cause discomfort and affect man's visual performance. There are two types of glare. The first type, *direct glare*, is caused by a light source directly in the field of vision such as the headlights of an approaching car. The other type, *reflected glare*, is caused by reflectance from a bright surface. Some ways in which glare can be limited are noted below:

• 1. Reduce direct glare by decreasing the brightness of the light source or by increasing the brightness of the area surrounding the glare source to balance the brightness ratio. A high general level of illumination also reduces the effect of reflected glare.

225

Table 8.1 Recommended levels of illumination

Task Conditions	Foot-Candles	Specific Tasks or Place
Very precise work where extreme accuracy is required	1000	Operating table for surgery, very fine assembly work
	500	Very difficult inspections
	300	Fine assembly work
Precision tasks involving small details for prolonged time periods	200	Difficult finishing and inspection work, detailed drafting, medical-dental work, fine machining
	150	Rough drafting, business machine operations
	100	Medium bench and machine work, mail sorting, filing
Prolonged tasks where speed is not essential	70	Studying, sewing, reading clear handwriting or blackboard writing, typing
	50	Sketching, wrapping and labeling, glass grinding
Normal tasks	30	Drilling, riveting, filing, paint booths and washrooms
	20	Rough machining, stairways and corridors
Casual seeing tasks that are not prolonged	10	Shipping and receiving, auditoriums
Rough seeing tasks with low contrast	5	Storage or warehouse, theater lobby during intermission

Studies have confirmed that illumination below recommended levels leads to errors and fatigue. However, increasing the intensity well beyond the recommendations does not produce proportionate reductions in errors and fatigue.

2. Place light sources so they are not in the direct field of vision and so any reflected light is not directed toward the eye.
3. Diffuse the light at the source or with baffles, window shades, etc.
4. Avoid glossy finishes for working area surfaces.
5. Use light shields, hoods, or visors if glare sources cannot otherwise be reduced.

Noise

An unwanted sound is called noise. Two aspects of noise pertain to production. One is the potential loss of hearing that can result from continued exposure to very high sound levels. The other aspect is the nuisance effect that contributes to reduced worker performance. As with illumination, there are no definitive levels that bound the regions of good to bad performance or an exact point where hearing loss develops.

The standard unit of noise measurement is the *decibel*—a logarithmic ratio of a given sound level to a standard value which is the defined threshold of audible sound (0.0002 dyne per square centimeter). Decibel ratings of some typical sound sources are listed in Table 8.2. The ratings indicate that sound energy of a quiet office is $10^4 = 10,000$ times greater than that of the threshold level, or that 40 decibels (db) is 100 times greater than 20 db.

Table 8.2 Noise levels

Decibels	Noise Source
140	City warning siren
130	Jet engine at 50 feet
120	Riveter at 4 feet
110	Circular saw
100	Pneumatic drill at 10 feet
80	Usual factory, very heavy traffic
60	Usual office, light traffic
40	Quiet office
20	Whispered conversation
0	Threshold of hearing

Sound energy becomes physically painful at about ● 140 decibels.

There is abundant evidence that a prolonged exposure to high noise levels contributes to hearing loss, but there is little agreement as to how long is long or how high is high. Most experts state that harmful effects can be expected from noise levels above 100 db; the 100 to 90-db zone is questionable. It is believed that greater hearing loss is experienced at higher frequencies (4000 cps range) than at lower frequencies (1000 to 2000 cps) and with noncontinuous impact noise than with continuous noise of the same intensity. Although the conditions conducive to hearing loss are not clearcut, production managers should heed available

The public relations aspect of factory noise on residential areas should be considered in plant location. ●

227

guidelines because occupational deafness is a potentially explosive question. Compensation claims for hearing loss could be huge.

Noise well below the level of physical harm contributes to lower worker performance. Sounds of particular kinds—infrequent, irregular, high pitched, or resounding—are distracting. A siren is useful when attached to an emergency service to attract attention, but the same sound becomes a distractor of equal potency when workers have no need to be concerned. Any increase in noise level tends to increase muscular tension and consequently increase expenditure of energy. Workers are apt to become more quickly fatigued, nervous, and irritable in a noisy environment. A degree of accommodation gradually results from continued exposure, but again we have no way of extracting the exact toll on productivity.

A steady humming sound of small variability may have an hypnotic effect which contributes to accidents.

Noise abatement and protection are the remedies for hearing loss and nuisance noise. The measures required for sound control are often complicated and costly. Acoustical engineers employ a number of techniques which fall into three main categories:

1. Control the noise at its source by replacing noisy machines and worn parts, by modifying the mounting of equipment, and by redesigning or substituting alternates that are inherently quieter.
2. Isolate the noise by creating barriers such as distance, baffles or sound absorbers between the source and the listener.
3. Provide personal protection devices such as ear plugs, ear muffs, or helmets.

The use of ear plugs can actually improve speech intelligibility by reducing levels of both speech and background noise to the point where differences can be better discriminated.

Insufficient noise is the modern counterpart to the traditional noise problem. When a room has a moderate background of sounds, nearly all workers adjust to these sounds and do not really hear any of them. When the sound background becomes too low, each little normal sound becomes a distraction. Piped-in music is often used to break the quiet so that otherwise distracting noise blends in with the background sound.

A few years ago the possibility of using musical cadence to set the work pace initiated a frenzy of research. The extensive studies are somewhat inconclusive because of the number of uncontrollable factors in a production setting. It is generally agreed that music does facilitate performance of repetitive tasks and that it may reduce accidents. The most beneficial effect is upon the morale of workers. It relieves boredom and promotes a feeling of well-being. Polls show an almost unanimous approval by workers to music at the workplace.

Atmospheric Conditions

Nearly everyone in the temperate zones of the world has experienced numbing cold and exhausting heat. In such extremes, productive work is most difficult and, fortunately, is seldom expected. In most industrial settings, it is possible and economically desirable to provide comfortable atmospheric conditions for the work area.

A healthy worker has a body temperature of approximately 98.6°. The body is equipped to keep itself close to its normal temperature by means of blood circulation and sweat glands. When body temperature begins to drop, these and other body mechanisms bring the temperature up. The resulting experience is one of feeling cold. A cold object feels cold because of the heat loss of the body; such heat transmission by direct contact with warmer or colder objects is called *conduction*. The other physical processes of body heat exchange are *convection*—transmission by the surrounding air, *radiation*—transmission by exchange of thermal energy between the body and objects, and *evaporation*— transmission of heat by the evaporation of perspiration and moisture from the lungs.

Feelings of warmth or cold are not dependent strictly on temperature. The interaction of temperature, humidity, and air circulation is largely responsible for comfort. These factors have been combined into a single rating scale called *effective temperature*—an index which combines into a single value the effect of temperature, humidity, and air movement on the sensation of warmth or cold felt by the human body. Charts of this index are published in the *ASHRAE Handbook of Fundamentals*. An approximate indication of the comfort zone is given by the curved surface in Figure 8.4.

Cold rooms at refrigeration plants and hot furnaces in steel mills are typical exceptions to ideal conditions.

Effects of Temperature

120°F—tolerable for about 1 hour
85°F—mental activities slow down
65°F–75°F—summer comfort zone
63°F–71°F—winter comfort zone
50°F—physical stiffness begins

A humidity level between 30% and 70% is comfortable for most people.

Effective temperatures above the middle 90's impair performance.

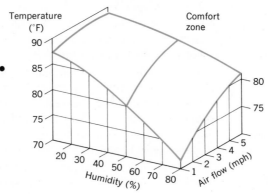

Figure 8.4 Approximate comfort region as a function of temperature, humidity, and air flow

Measures to Control Air
Impurities

Removing cause of impuri-
ties
Proper ventilation
Special exhaust measures
Personal protection such
as facemasks

Gases, such as carbon monoxide and natural gas are toxic. Workers cannot continue working in their presence, whether noticed or not. Dust and smoke, while not always toxic, are disturbing and will not be tolerated long without complaint.
• About 1 cubic foot of fresh air per minute per square foot of floor space is required for the average work area.

Fresh air is an ambiguous label. Although the air may have adequate oxygen content and be free of toxic gas, it still may stink. Many plants use processes that unavoidably produce unpleasant odors. Adaptation of workers to such odors is ordinarily fast. Most complaints come from new-hires and downwind residences. Affected communities sometimes rationalize by referring to the odors as "the smell of money."

8-5 MAN AND HIS SAFETY

Accidents are unplanned, unwanted, and improper occurrences involving the motion of a person, object, or substance which results in injury, damage, or loss.

Fail-safe is a system design concept to safeguard major functions against even freak events. Only the once-in-a-million event will trigger an accident.

Safety is an enigma. Employees do not want accidents, but they often form habits or put themselves in situations where accidents are inevitable. Employers know that accidents are expensive,
• but few recognize the true total cost.

We talk about a completely safe design, but there is no such thing. We cannot even agree on the worth of an arm, or a leg, or a life. Individually we would put an infinite value on the lives of our intimates, but how many lives must be endangered before we finally undertake expensive or inconvenient correctional
• measures? That we cannot afford to assign a lifeguard to each swimmer in a public pool or erect an automatic warning device at every intersection, crosswalk, and railroad crossing is not a sign of inhumanity; it is a realistic compromise forced on us by a lack of resources. Concern for safety has never been greater than it is today. Now the problem is to convert this concern into acts that meet our philosophical and ethical objectives within the constraints of practical economics.

Accident Costs to Employer

Direct:
  Compensation
  Medical
  Legal
Indirect:
  Machine down time
  Training and replacement
  Equipment damage
  Material waste
  Reduced production

The first safety problem is to admit that safety is a problem. Workers must not believe that accidents always happen to someone else. Management must believe that accident prevention is worth the cost. Furthermore, both workers and managers must remain impressed with their safety responsibilities for successful long-term programs. A particularly macabre incident such as a person being crushed, burned, or sliced to death can spur immediate dramatic safety measures, but continuous attention to more mundane accidents builds enduring safety patterns. Table 8.3 lists some benefits of safety practices that should have an
• obvious and prolonged appeal if those involved ponder the consequences. Each reason listed could be detailed to stress its

Table 8.3 Reasons why attention to safety is important

A conservative estimate of the ratio of hidden costs to direct costs is 4 to 1.

To Employees	To Employers
Prevents physical suffering	Prevents waste
Prevents loss of earnings	Prevents cost of retraining
Protects future earnings	Prevents unnecessary equipment replacement
Prevents mental suffering	Reduces insurance and compensation costs
Improves reputation	Improves reputation

importance. For instance, "improves reputation" could mean a wider choice of jobs and better pay to an employee; for the employer it could build public opinion and attract better employees.

Another responsibility of companies is consumer safety through the quality of its products.

When it is accepted that safety effort is emotionally satisfying and economically logical, the next step is to determine why

• accidents occur. There are two basic causes: unsafe acts by workers and unsafe working conditions. Every accident has overtones of both causes. A study by the National Safety Council indicated that when both causes are charged to the same accident, 87% involve unsafe acts and 78% involve mechanical causes. A similar study in 1955 by the State of Pennsylvania reported 82.6% and 89% of the industrial accidents involved unsafe acts

• and unsafe conditions, respectively. The reason behind identifying the cause is to categorize the effort that will prevent the accident.

Human Characteristics that Affect Safety

Recklessness
Stubbornness
Nervousness
Slowness to learn
Physical condition
Personal troubles

Unsafe Acts

Faulty work habits and careless worker behavior are classified as *unsafe acts*. An automobile driver engages in unsafe acts when he exceeds speed limits, disregards traffic rules, misjudges clearance, or fails to signal his intentions. Such behavioral patterns are learned over a period of time. As accident causes, unsafe acts are harder to detect and more difficult to control than mechanical causes. They also probably account for the most accidents and injuries.

Unsafe Acts

Ignoring rules
Operating without authority
Teasing and horseplay
Not wearing protective equipment
Unsafe lifting, pulling, and pushing
Making safety devices inoperative
Improper handling of equipment

A skilled supervisor can detect unsafe acts by observing his workforce. Too often the acts are discovered only after they cause an injury. Before the injury finally attracts corrective attention, the acts probably delay production, waste material, and cause spoilage or rejected parts. It takes a well-trained supervisor to find the acts and even more training to eradicate

• them. Anyone who has tried to overcome a long standing habit knows how difficult it is to change behavior.

Special training or retraining efforts can be directed against specific unsafe acts. A general awareness of bad habits is possible

231

from safety literature, posters, committee work, and meetings. Protective equipment such as steel-toed shoes or safety guards may allow a mistake or two without serious damage, but such safeguards do not develop better working habits. Protection from one hazard may even create a new hazard; protective gloves could make a worker clumsy or safety goggles might deprive him of needed vision.

"Accident proneness" is a convenient label to characterize some men and some jobs. The term does not really refer to the causes of accidents; rather it is a description of the number and seriousness of accidents that have already occurred. It shows a man-job misfit. A reputation for accident proneness is a justifiable excuse for investigation. A job may be particularly dangerous or a man may be a daydreamer. If so, the job can be changed to make it safer and the man can be retained, retrained, retired, or fired.

Unsafe Conditions

Accidents attributable to physical and mechanical sources within the work environment are caused by *unsafe conditions*. Disregard for design principles involved in any of the environmental factors (layout, equipment arrangement, illumination, noise, atmospheric conditions, etc.) leads to unsafe conditions. Every piece of equipment, any workspace design, and all operations must be suspects for safety improvements. Both the detective work and the corrections are easier for unsafe conditions than for unsafe acts. A checklist for accident symptoms and cures is given below.

Falling—nonslip floors, guardrails, handholds, and safety belts.

Snagging—barriers, warning signs, recessed controls, and elimination of projections that catch clothing.

Pinching—adequate room for entering and leaving, easily reached tools, correct tools, and better equipment arrangements and designs.

Bumping—increased overhead clearance, screens to catch falling objects, hard hats, warnings from moving equipment, elimination of blind corners, proper loading of material-handling equipment, and objects painted to make them more obvious.

Burning—protective clothing; emergency showers; strict maintenance of equipment involving hot metal, glass, liquids, steam, and air; color coding and proper insulation of wiring and electrical parts; warning of repairs underway; adequate fire-fighting equipment; alarm system; and first-aid training.

Blinding—goggles, shields on abrasive equipment, and attention to flash brightness causing temporary blindness that leads to other accidents.

Slipping, tripping—painted walkways that are kept clean, well-marked risers, adequate lighting, janitor work to clean up stray objects and drippings, and treads on inclines.

There are a few hazards not detectable without special equipment. Geiger counters and badges sensitive to radiation are required to detect radioactive substances. Some toxic gases give no warning to human senses. Shielding, isolation, and extra vigilance are warranted for such insidious hazards.

Many accidents are attributed to poor housekeeping. The catchall "housekeeping" term has several ramifications. Good housekeeping naturally includes litter control and janitorial cleanliness. It should also account for *consistency*. Consistent housekeeping is safer, even if it is dirty at times, because workers know where things are and can anticipate them. Work suffers when constant attention is required to react to unexpected situations, and safe habits are difficult to form. Work patterns, reliable equipment, and regularly occurring situations set the framework for safe operations.

Safety Programs

The major injury can sometimes be prevented by identifying minor accidents and eliminating causes.

From our own experiences we know that performing an unsafe act or being exposed to an unsafe condition does not result in an accident on each occasion; every jaywalker is not hit by a car and every faulty car does not get in a wreck. But exposure to these hazards eventually causes accidents, and an occasional serious injury occurs among the minor ones.

The Travelers Insurance Company has suggested the pyramidal relationship of accident seriousness shown in Figure 8.5. Work errors are the foundation of accidents. For each 300 noninjury accidents, there are 29 minor injuries and 1 major injury. The major injury may result from the first accident encountered or any one of the 330 cases represented. If these figures are correct, there are 330 opportunities to correct unsafe acts and conditions for each major injury.

Most accidents are not sudden, freakish, undetectable occurrences. Every serious injury outside the truly rare "act of God"

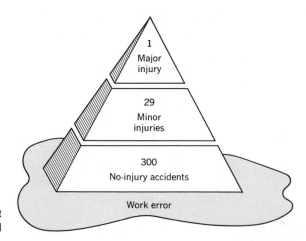

Figure 8.5 The accident pyramid

Ways to Identify Unsafe
Acts and Conditions

Observation of work
environment
Personnel surveys
Review of past records
Victim inquiries

has a history. This history involves many near misses. An
accident-prevention program should focus on the lower level of
the accident pyramid to knock out the acts and conditions that
support major injuries.

The program starts with an analysis of the cause of each
reported accident. Records of past accidents and current reports
are analyzed with respect to the nature of the injury, type of
accident, main cause, reason or underlying cause, and suggested
remedy. From this investigation a plan is formulated to counter-
act the most prevalent and serious accidents. Then the responsibility for carrying out the plan is spelled out at both the
supervisory and higher management levels. Finally, a follow-
through routine is set to control the plan and determine if
original objectives are being met. The success of the whole
program is primarily dependent on the supervisor, the key man
in determining the cause of accidents and in applying the remedy.

The supervisor's role is a lot easier if he is backed by top
management. Each plan does not have to be supported by a big
budget for flashy signs, fancy contests, and generous awards.
But top management must visibly support the program by
attending safety meetings, delegating authority to make on-the-
spot corrections of unsafe acts and conditions, and acting
immediately when accident facts become known.

If awards are used in a safety
program, they should be appropriate. Some human-interest
areas for awards are: health,
recreation, achievement,
culture, security, self-
improvement, and mystery.

Safety programs take many forms. They may include formal
classroom schooling, suggestion-box publicity, stressing maintenance or safeguarding procedures, periodic meetings and
discussions, messages calling attention to particular safety
features, and contests. All of these are designed to make work

234

safer and more productive and to try to abort "Murphy's law": "If it is possible for it to be done wrong, someone will do it sooner or later."

EXAMPLE 8.2 A Safety Program for Drivers

A complete safety program is based on all the hazards that are detrimental to the performance of the tasks for which accident prevention is intended. This total system design concept can follow the planning, analysis, and control sequence. The following outline shows the principal functions of a salesman safe-driving program.

1. **Planning**—establishing objectives and responsibilities
   A. Statement of policy—responsibility of drivers and managers, groundrules for reporting, goals
   B. Problem forecast—use of personal cars makes control of unsafe conditions difficult; majority of operators are convinced they are already good drivers; importance of prompt, accurate accident reports
   C. Appointment of program director—responsibility for direction and coordination, time and dollar budget allocations, staff selection and training plans
2. **Analysis**—evaluating the program plan and mechanics of operation
   A. Driver/salesman selection—application forms, personal interviews, written test, medical (especially eye) examination
   B. Applicant ratings—both for sales work and driving
   C. Driver testing—written and road tests
   D. Driver training—laws, equipment care, safe practices
   E. Vehicle inspection—periodic checks of salesmen's cars
   F. Accident reporting—effectiveness of existing procedures
3. **Control**—following through and checking to make the plan work
   A. Accident investigation—accident reports, victim interviews, identification of unsafe acts and practices
   B. Troublespots—locating areas where more effort should be applied, recommendations for corrective action
   C. Driver safety meetings—presentation of information from A and B to maintain awareness, extension to nonvehicular accidents
   D. Incentive program—recognition and rewards for successful cooperation, report on standings

8-6 SUMMARY This chapter about man's working environment is a companion piece to Chapter 7 about man's abilities. Physical and personal aspects of man's performance are almost indistinguishable in effect. To say performance will automatically improve with investments in better facilities is a rash generalization. It is only safe to predict that the better environment will relieve that particular deterrent to work performance. The complex interactions of man-oriented activities and the components of a production system are outlined in Figure 8.6.

A plant location should satisfy both the physical needs of

235

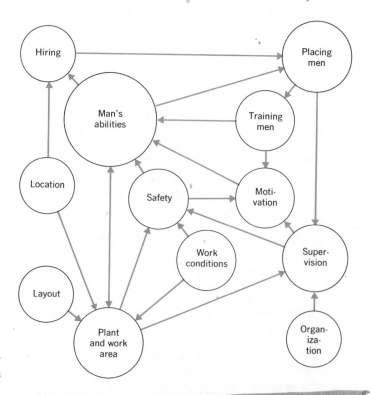

Figure 8.6 Human factor considerations

production (land, transportation and utility services, financial considerations, etc.) and employee wants (climate, community facilities, recreation, proximity to housing, etc.).

Plant layout is a companion problem to plant location. There are three basic types of product flow through a plant: (1) product layout—a line or chain of facilities and auxiliary services through which a product is progressively refined, (2) process layout—a grouping of machines and services according to common functions for the performance of distinct operations, and (3) fixed position layout—an arrangement where men and machines are brought to a stationary product. Work areas and equipment arrangements within any layout should be designed to improve man's performance. Flexibility is a prime consideration in equipment design. The arrangement of equipment can be evaluated by a link analysis based on the frequency and importance of communication and control links between men and machines.

Working conditions should maximize man's data-sensing, processing, and transmitting abilities. Good illumination is particularly important because man relies heavily on his vision.

The work area should have sufficient light intensity and quality without direct or indirect glare. Noise can cause physical damage and be detrimental to work performance. Unwanted sound can be controlled at its source, by barriers between it and workers, or by personal protective devices worn by workers. Feelings of warmth or cold are rated by effective temperature—an index which combines into a single value the effect of temperature, humidity, and air flow. Air impurities, either toxic or nontoxic, should be controlled by removal, ventilation, special exhaust, and personal protection measures.

Accidents are caused by unsafe acts and unsafe conditions. Unsafe acts are more difficult to detect and cure than unsafe mechanical conditions. Safety programs are based on investigations of accidents to determine their causes and the measures required to eliminate them. The programs may take many different forms, but success depends greatly on the supervisors involved.

8-7 REFERENCES

Apple, J. M., *Plant Layout and Materials Handling* (2nd ed.), Ronald Press, New York, 1963.

ASHRAE Handbook of Fundamentals, American Society of Heating, Refrigerating, and Air Conditioning Engineers, Inc., 345 E. 47th St., New York, 1968.

DeReamer, H. W., *Industrial Accident Prevention*, McGraw-Hill, New York, 1959.

IES Lighting Handbook (4th ed.), Illuminating Engineering Society, 1860 Broadway, New York, 1966.

McCormick, E. J., *Human Factors Engineering*, McGraw-Hill, New York, 1964.

Reed, R., Jr., *Plant Layout*, Richard D. Irwin, Homewood, Ill., 1961.

Simon, H. A., *Models of Man*, John Wiley, New York, 1957.

Van Doren, H., *Industrial Design* (2nd ed.), McGraw-Hill, New York, 1954.

Woodson, W. E., *Human Engineering Guide for Equipment Designers* (2nd ed.), Univ. of California Press, Berkeley, Calif., 1964.

8-8 QUESTIONS AND PROBLEMS

1. What reasons would lead to locating a plant in an urban renewal project, a domestic industrial park, and a foreign country? How might the workforce view each choice?

2. Some industries require two or more dominant resources that are not located in the same geographical area. For instance, in metal-reduction industries coal is seldom located beside the iron ore deposits and bauxite is far from the power sources needed to produce aluminum. What location factors should be considered in choosing a plant site for such industries? Show how the exponential comparison model (Section 4-3) could be utilized in the choice.

3. The effect of improved transportation facilities on the development of industrial centers was described in the chapter. Could the development of nuclear power have a similar effect on the future location of industries?

4. When a company needs more space to expand its operations, the usual method is to consider sites near the present location first. What are some advantages and disadvantages of this strategy?

5. If you were the sole owner of a small "brain-oriented" company that sold ideas as a product and wanted to locate the company in a resort area, what problems might you encounter? For the sake of discussion, say the staff is made up of two top dreamers, two half-time dreamers who also act as leg men, and two nondreaming, capable paperpushers who know the business thoroughly.

6. Compare the advantages and disadvantages of a process layout to a product layout with respect to material-handling cost, room required for work in process, skills of operators, machine breakdowns, utilization of machines, and need for supervision.

7. Indexes have been suggested for evaluating tentative man-machine arrangements. With reference to the link analysis technique, comment on the following suggested indexes:

   (a) Index of visibility (average visual links or average of individual display ratings).
   (b) Index of walking (walking distance of operators).
   (c) Index of talking (voice level needed to overcome distance, noise, and crosstalking speech interference).
   (d) Index of crowding (how activities of operators interfere with each other's work).
   (e) Index of accessibility (adequacy of working space and ease of exit or entry).

8. Evaluate a classroom with respect to layout and working conditions.

9. What is implied by the statement "you can buy space with a paint brush"?

10. Comment on the similarity between the measures suggested to reduce glare and those to reduce noise.

11. Compare the three forms of artificial lighting and sunlight as to the type of glare that can be expected from each. How can such glare be reduced or avoided?

12. Consider the noise situation in any industry with which you are familiar. Could hearing loss result from present noise levels? If so, what measures should be taken? If nuisance noise is present, how could it be reduced?

13. What measures can be used for environmental comfort control to facilitate each of the four physical processes of body heat exchange?

14. The effects of heat stress in exceptionally hot working conditions can be regulated to some extent by the management of personnel. Comment on the following potential actions:

(a) Selection of workers.

(b) Acclimatization.

(c) Rotation of workers.

(d) Workload reductions.

(e) Rules pertaining to water consumption, salt tablets, etc.

15. Comment on the statement "there are no accident-prone men or jobs, just accident-prone man-job matches."

16. How does the definition of an accident fit intentionally self-inflicted wounds? How do such injuries fit into a safety program?

17. Design an accident report form to go along with the program outlined in Example 8.2.

18. How can protective clothing be detrimental to the development of safe working habits?

19. What hidden costs make the ratio of indirect to direct costs of an accident so high?

20. Why are unsafe acts harder to detect and cure than unsafe mechanical conditions?

21. Discuss the human characteristic of individual differences as it applies to design considerations for:

(a) Equipment arrangements.

(b) Working conditions.

(c) Safety programs.

22. Throughout Chapters 7 and 8 there are references to economic balances between two counter-alternatives such as the psychological value of sunlight versus the practical advantages of artificial light. List and comment on 10 counterbalancing alternatives.

23 Evaluate the arrangement of the message center shown in Figure 8.7 and suggest an alternate arrangement. The links have the same meaning as given in Example 8.1.

24. The backseat driver has been a joke topic for a long time. Assuming the backseat driver can serve a useful purpose by helping the frontseat driver navigate in a strange city, use a link analysis to compare the backseat arrangement with having a map-reading helper in the front seat.

25. Suppose you are in charge of 60 typists working temporarily at wooden tables in one large room. They have complained about the noise originating in the room. New, very adequate

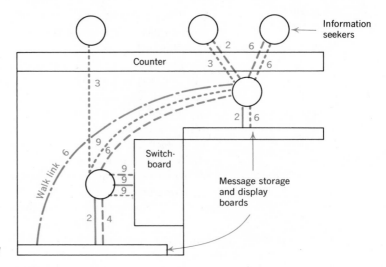

Figure 8.7

facilities will be available in 30 days. What would you do now? If you plan any noise-abatement program, comment on the cost versus expected benefits.

26. The unintentional actuation of controls has generated many accidents. They are usually caused by unsafe conditions. Several designs aimed at alleviating the cause are listed below. For each, describe where you have seen the design utilized (in automobiles, homes, kitchens, etc.) and comment on the advantages or limitations.

(a) Recessed controls (nonflush mounting).
(b) Raised barriers (surrounded by a guard).
(c) Built-in locks (special keys or combinations required).
(d) Tool actuated (screwdriver or wrench required).
(e) Mechanical or electrical interlocks (prevents operating two or more controls at the same time).
(f) Protective covers (completely enclosed by an identifying cover).

27. Originality and attention to human factors are key considerations in designing machines or operations to perform a new function. What designs can you dream up which perform the following functions?

(a) A single gage for an automobile that shows the direction and speed of movement plus the time of day.
(b) A portable roadblock which can be used day and night to warn motorists that the road is closed to through traffic.
(c) An inexpensive, self-contained, easy-to-read, and portable

240

meter which a speaker can use to warn himself when his speaking time has elapsed.

Accident descriptions typical of everyday production operations are given in Problems 28-33. Analyze each case according to the routine suggested in Section 8-5, page 234. The cases are adapted from material used in the Travelers Insurance Company's Safety Action course.

28. A utility man was attempting to lubricate a pump. It was necessary for him to stand near a large, unguarded pulley and reach in an unstable position to the lubrication point. While doing this, he was struck by the pulley and his right shoulder was lacerated and bruised. The toolpusher stated that the guard had been missing since he had been on the rig.

29. An operator was in the process of putting a caustic pump into operation after it had been repaired. Everything went as normal until a gasket on the pump let go and caustic was sprayed on the operator's face and arms. Because of the pressures involved, it is not uncommon for gaskets to fail in this way. He went to a safety shower immediately but sustained skin burns and severe burns to his eyes.

30. A deckhand on his first day of work jumped from a barge to the dockside with a line to make it fast and secure the barge. He apparently misjudged the clearance and fell against the side of the landing and into the water. His heavy clothing pulled him down and he drowned. The captain of the tow boat had instructed the deckhand. The depth of water was only 12 feet and it was generally accepted that this was not hazardous.

31. A carpenter, using a bandsaw to cut joints, was in a hurry to finish before lunch. Another employee passing behind him tickled him, causing him to strike the blade. The tip of his finger was cut off. The carpenter was known to be "jumpy," and other employees had taken advantage of this characteristic to have a little fun.

32. An employee inhaled ammonia gas when passing the leaky discharge pipe of an ammonia compressor. There was no injury from the inhalation, but he instinctively jumped aside, collided with the unguarded flywheel of a circulating pump, and bruised his shoulder.

33. An untrained operator overloads a power truck, piling material too high, and a box falls off into the aisle. Another man, who has refused to abide by instruction, comes along pulling a hand truck while walking backwards. He falls over the box and is injured against the lower frame of the cart.

34. The owner of a small machine shop is planning to relocate. He is moving the shop to a large midwestern city where land adjacent to transportation facilities demands a premium price. However, markets and suppliers are nearby. The shop will be all on one floor. Commuter service to the anticipated building area is adequate, and several lots are available on railroad spur tracks. The following list shows the minimum needed work areas and required personnel.

Rooms	Personnel	Purpose	Area (Sq. Ft.)
Office	2 secretaries, 1 clerk	Filing, communication, reproduction equipment	360
Owner's office	Owner	Reception room	200
Storage room	1 stockman	Parts and material storage, catalog service, receiving area	440
Shipping dock		Storage for shipping, packing	360
Production	8 machinists	Work and equipment area	2000
Assembly	2 welders, 2 fabricators	Fabrication equipment, overhead crane	1000
Shop office	1 foreman	Administration	72
Drafting	2 draftsmen	Drafting, filing	200
Restroom		Women	40
Washroom		Men (showers lockers)	120
Furnace room		Utilities	100

(a) Make a layout showing the product flow and work divisions. Most products are custom-made. About half the parts for fabrication are produced from raw material in the shop and the other half are catalog parts.

(b) Which rooms should have special lighting, sound proofing,

color, or heating and air conditioning considerations?
Does the work or layout present any special safety
problems?

(c) What location factors should be considered in choosing
the site for the machine shop?

35. "Four Star Wood Products" is a small, but ambitious,
woodworking company located in a middle-sized college town
on the west coast. Four college classmates pooled their resources
6 years ago to purchase a nearly bankrupt wood products
outfit. Since that time they have doubled the size of the plant and
increased production six times.

It came almost as a surprise to the four when they were notified
they were low bidders on a government contract to furnish
150,000 ammunition boxes. Their plant was capable of producing
the basic box with few modifications, but the specifications
required certain handles, locks, and labels which presented
several problems. And the due date on the contract was only
6 months away.

Each of the four owners was responsible for a phase of the
business: (1) office and accounting, (2) sales and buying, (3) plant
operations, and (4) plant engineering. The office and sales
partners handled the raw materials for the new order without
difficulty. Plant engineering anticipated only minor difficulty in
the cutting, hinging, and gluing of the boxes since the work was
similar to present orders. It was decided that the plant operations
partner would work on the remaining problems and manage the
project.

Contract specifications called for a loop-rope handle on each
end of the box, a ring-in-slot lock on the front, and different
decals on the boxes depending upon their intended use. There
was no assurance of any future contracts for the same type of
product, so it was financially impractical to buy or design
automatic equipment for this work. The only practical solution
was to set up a hand assembly and finishing line. They were
fortunate that the due date for the contract was at the end of the
summer, because they could set up a temporary working shed in
the company parking lot for the assembly and painting work.
There was not sufficient room in the existing plant.

The first thought was to hire local women for the extra
work, but the cost of additional toilet and lounge facilities
was prohibitive. The alternate solution was to stockpile the raw
boxes until school was out for the summer and then hire college
students. When a nearby vacant building was found to be
available for storage, the latter solution was chosen.

ANALYSIS

Thirty students were hired. By making the handles and locks as simple as possible, the engineer believed the boys could complete the work in 12 to 13 weeks. He allocated the jobs as follows:

> 10 workers putting on handles
> 6 workers putting on locks
> 8 workers painting
> 6 workers serving on odd jobs and
>   acting as handlers

The six handlers could aid in the plant, transport boxes from storage, fill in for absent workers, or supplement any stage that fell behind schedule. All the boys were to be paid the current local wage of $2.00 per hour for unskilled work. If they worked 6 days a week and finished 2000 boxes a day, the costs would be within contractual limits.

For the first 3 weeks the line worked at or slightly above the goal of 2000 boxes a day. The next week production averaged 1800 per day. By the middle of the following week, it was below 1700, even though the operations manager constantly checked on the line and urged them on. Two more odd-job men were hired, but production leveled at 1700 boxes a day.

The manager questioned each worker about why he thought production was falling off. In order of frequency, he noted the following excuses:

(1) We're all being paid the same but some guys are "goofing off."
(2) The outdoor shed gets too hot during the middle of the day to keep working at top efficiency.
(3) Insects in the outdoor shed are annoying and distract us from work.
(4) Working conditions are crowded and some operations are cramped.
(5) The work is boring.

The manager also noticed the morale seemed highest in the odd-job category and that most absences from work occurred on Saturday. Another point that bothered him was the number of minor but time-consuming accidents that kept occurring.

To help improve production, several measures were immediately instituted: (1) wages were changed from an hourly to a piece-rate system, (2) an addition was put on the shed, and (3) the entire structure was screened.

In the following week, production went back up to 1800, but two more accidents occurred. One boy accidentally sprayed paint into another's eyes, and another worker drove a staple into his thumb while attaching a rope handle. The crew continued to work well together and morale seemed high, but this was not reflected in increased production. At the present rate the contract could not be completed on time.

What should the manager do now?

CHAPTER 9

METHODS AND MEASUREMENT

9-1 IMPORTANCE

"Work," in its occupational sense, is the effort expended to produce something useful. • *Both manual and mental labor fall within this definition.*

Methods analysis and work measurement are the twin pillars supporting the design of work systems. The purpose of work design is to identify the most effective means of achieving necessary functions. In a production context this means the analysis of present and proposed work systems to develop an optimal transformation of inputs to output.

Historically, time study as originated by Taylor was used to establish standard times for work performance; methods study as developed by the Gilbreths was aimed at improving the manner by which work is accomplished. Through passing years the two disciplines became intertwined, the one supporting and supplementing the other. Innovations in both philosophy and techniques have provided new tools for practitioners and extended the scope of studies to even remote facets of production.

Terms associated with "methods" are: (1) operations analysis, (2) work simplification, and (3) methods engineering.

Under the heading of *methods*, we shall consider ways to improve the method of doing work. It is obviously important to know how the work is currently being done before contemplating improvements. A definitive review of the way an operation is performed results from subdividing the task into basic components. For some operations this breakdown has to provide details as fine as the movements of each finger; such microanalyses are in the province of *motion studies*. For other operations, all that is needed is the sequence of major movements such as the route of a message dispatcher; these macroevaluations are provided by a *process analysis*. Both types of studies benefit from the systematic application of well-established principles and charting techniques.

Frederick Taylor explained the main purpose of time study as the "transfer of skill from management to men."

Measurement includes both the determination of time standards for work and the application of these standards to wage payments for the work done. *Time study* is the technique of setting a time to do a specific task based on the work content of that task and allowances for fatigue and delays. Another approach to work measurement is *work sampling;* a large number of observations of a process are statistically evaluated to determine the percentage

246

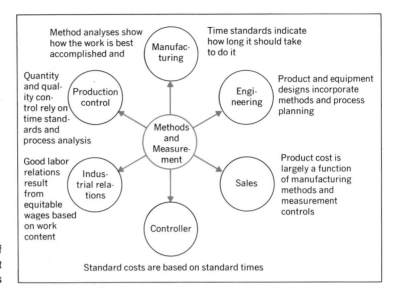

Method analyses show how the work is best accomplished and

Time standards indicate how long it should take to do it

Quantity and quality control rely on time standards and process analysis

Product and equipment designs incorporate methods and process planning

Good labor relations result from equitable wages based on work content

Product cost is largely a function of manufacturing methods and measurement controls

Standard costs are based on standard times

Figure 9.1 The influence of methods and measurement effort on other production activities

of time the process is in a given state. Results of such studies are a natural part of wage formulation. The profuse variety of *wage payment* plans all have the target of equitable payments based on the relative worth of different work assignments.

The influence of methods analysis, time measurement, and wage payment plans permeates the entire production system (Figure 9.1). The central position of methods and measurement groups makes them a fertile training ground for new management material; neophyte managers can work with the elements of production and observe the cross-flow of ideas, ideology, and occasional idiocy. It is a prime position to spot suboptimization and to apply creative countermeasures. It is the wellspring of labor peace, product competitiveness, and customer satisfaction.

9-2 PROCESS ANALYSIS

The objective of a process analysis is to improve the sequence or content of operations required to complete a task. Improvement of the operations themselves is considered in Section 9-3 as motion study. The routines for both types of investigations are similar; they rely heavily on charting techniques. Graphic representations are to movement investigations what numbers are to mathematics—a language of abbreviation that aids the statement of complex relationships and makes them easier to understand.

Charting saves writing time, directs an investigation along a logical path, and makes records more complete.

Charting finds three major areas of usage in production system

247

studies: survey, design, and presentation. *Survey charts* are used in the initial phase of an investigation to categorize present procedures. One difficult question to answer in this stage is the amount of detail to include. *Design charts* describe the proposed undertaking. They expose planned innovations to critical reviews which filter out the most promising designs. *Presentation charts* explain how something can be done. The purpose of the presentation is usually a mixture of clarification and salesmanship. Table 9.1 shows the sequence of charting and some examples. Note that the same chart format can be used in more than one charting area. For instance, breakeven charts can record the present conditions or illustrate what is expected to happen if certain changes are made.

Table 9.1 Types of charts and their purposes

Type of Chart	Purpose of Charting	Examples of Chart Formats
Survey	To consolidate data from present operations to facilitate analysis	Flow process charts to record current operating conditions
		Link charts to evaluate layouts for communication and control
		Organizational charts to show authority and responsibility
Design	To develop changes and new concepts which will improve operations	CPS networks for project planning
		Man-machine charts to optimize working cycles
Presentation	To summarize and clarify proposals in order to improve communications	Gantt and time charts for scheduling and coordination
		Breakeven charts to advertise and explain the effects of different operating alternatives

Investigation Procedures

The first step in a process analysis is to decide which process to investigate. The obvious resolution is the process whose improvement promises the greatest return, but this general

Rating factors can be used to set priorities for available study times. Rating = (potential saving/study and implementation cost) × (probability of implementation). Projects with the highest ratings receive attention first.

objective has to be narrowed to a specific process by some preinvestigation sleuthing. Operating departments usually suggest areas of investigation when methods work is a staff function. Suggestions can come from above and below or be internally generated for line operational methods work. Background information for setting priorities for studies is obtained by reviewing reports, memoranda, and directives and by discussing the subject with conversant personnel. This preinvestigation should also indicate whose help will be needed for the study and how long it will take.

The fact-finding phase of an investigation is a delicate exercise. A brute-force search is occasionally appropriate, but diplomacy is usually more productive. Outlines of the questions to be asked and the actions to be observed should be known before anyone is contacted. Department managers or supervisors should be informed of the nature and objectives of the investigation before their operating personnel are approached. More and better data result from extending similar courtesies during the investigation. Some guidelines for interviewing are:

1. Be certain the workers understand the purposes and objectives of the investigation. Try to make them feel at ease.
2. Emphasize the importance of their contribution to the success of the study. Let them do most of the talking.
3. Solicit and encourage suggestions by the workers. Do not ask questions that imply their own answers.
4. Be courteous and complimentary. Do not use trick questions.
5. Do not criticize or correct the way the workers are doing anything. The mission at this stage is to find facts, not to correct faults.

Wherever possible, verbal communications should be reinforced by the investigator's own observations; an eye witness has a better chance to get the whole story and has only himself to blame if it is incorrect.

The finished chart should neatly portray the entire operation being studied. Some common charting formats that aid completeness are described in the next section. While neatness in charting is commendable, some analysts get a reputation for being "chart happy." A proper perspective results from recognizing that good charting improves the statement of the problem, but the ultimate value of the study depends on the creative effort expended to solve the problem.

After a methods analyst is satisfied that he has enough information and has verified its quality, he then attempts to synthesize a

Distinctive chart patterns often suggest handling problems such as backtracking, uneven work distribution, and duplication of work.

Rudyard Kipling commented on 5*W* + *H* questions in "The Elephant's Child": "I keep six honest serving-men (They taught me all I knew); Their names are What and Why and When And How and Where and Who."

better way to do the work. He mentally tears the process apart with the intention of *eliminating*, *combining*, or *rearranging* operations. As a spur to his imagination, he can borrow the journalist's code of: Who? What? Where? When? How? And *why*?

Who does it—why? Could someone else do it better or cheaper? What is done—why? Does it need to be done? Where is it done—why? Can it be done less expensively someplace else? When is it done—why? Would a different sequence be better? How is it done—why? Is there a better way of doing it?

Sometimes one question leads to another and a chain reaction of suggestions develops. Two analysts can often generate more ideas working together than they can singly.

If a new method results from the mental gymnastics of analysis, it is committed to an "after" chart—a picture of the revised process. The initial draft of the "after" chart is reviewed with representatives of the staff and operating agencies concerned. With their concurrence, a test or full-scale application of the changes is inaugerated. The analyst usually provides personal supervision for the first installation of the new process. He orients the key personnel to the changes and sets up a review schedule. He should be alert to any emergencies caused by the new procedures and be prepared to make prompt revisions if the situation looks explosive.

The last step is to integrate formally the tested and reviewed process into the standard operating procedures. Minor process changes may be made by verbal agreement or insignificant adjustments. Major changes usually require modification of manuals, training programs, plant layouts, work instructions, routing slips, or other published documents. Periodic checks follow the formal installation to see that the revisions remain installed as revised.

Operation and Operator Process Charts

F. B. and L. M. Gilbreth, "Process Charts," *Transactions of ASME*, **43**, 1024–1050 (1921).

The Gilbreths' early renditions of process charts had 40 symbols for plotting activities. Since that time the number of basic symbols has decreased but the format variations for process charting are almost innumerable. And this situation is probably healthy because customized applications can make charts much more useful for particular situations such as computer procedures or forms flow analysis. The inherent weakness of mutations is that someone unaccustomed to the unique symbols or format

Standardized symbols are from "Operation and Flow Process Charts, ASME Standard 101," ASME, New York, 1947.

would have little idea of what the charts tell. We shall limit our considerations to the following standardized symbols:

○ Operation—intentional changes in one or more characteristics.

⇨ Transportation—a movement of an object or operator that is not an integral part of an operation or inspection.

□ Inspection—an examination to determine quality or quantity.

D Delay—an interruption between the immediate and next planned action.

The operation symbol is sometimes modified for paper flow analysis to:

▽ Storage—holding an object under controlled conditions.

▣ "Combined"—combining two symbols indicates simultaneous activities. The symbol shown means an inspection is conducted at the same time an operation is performed.

◎ Origin of papers

It is important to distinguish between an *operation* process chart which follows the routing and acts performed on an object and an *operator* process chart which shows the sequence of activities performed by a person. The two types should not be combined. Three typical formats for process charts designed to serve different purposes are shown in Figure 9.2. The actual

◍ Information added

○ All other

Type and Purpose	Characteristics	Illustration	
		Symbols	Description
Single column — to study the detailed steps in a relatively simple process	Charts are often drawn on printed forms; processes are shown by connecting appropriate symbols; space is provided for additional data	○□⇨D▽	Invoice in mail room
		○□⇨D▽	Determine addressee
		○□⇨D▽	To addressee's secretary
		○□⇨D▽	Placed in action tray
Multicolumn — to analyze detailed steps in the flow of work that is quite complex	Horizontal lines show operational areas; symbols are entered to show activities of the process	Operator / Activities: Mail clerk, Secretary, Manager	
Layout diagram — to improve the layout by avoiding unnecessary steps	Lines indicate the travel and symbols show the activities on a layout often drawn to scale	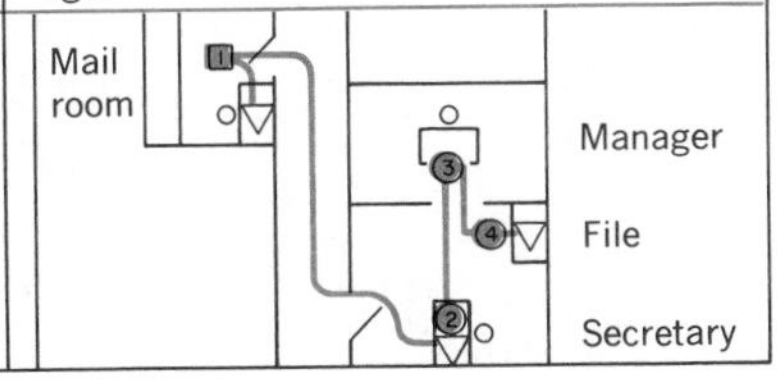 Mail room, Manager, File, Secretary	

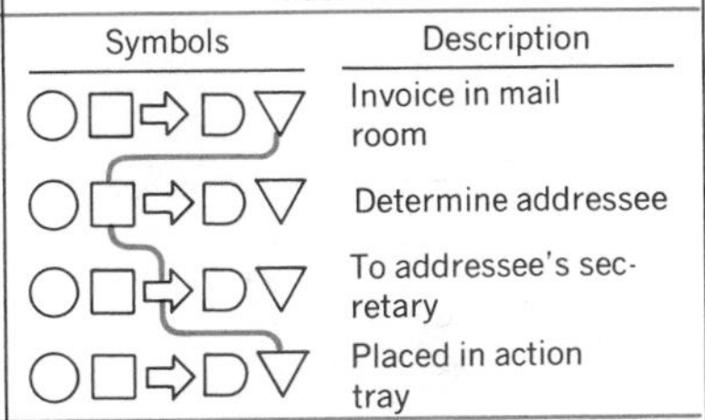

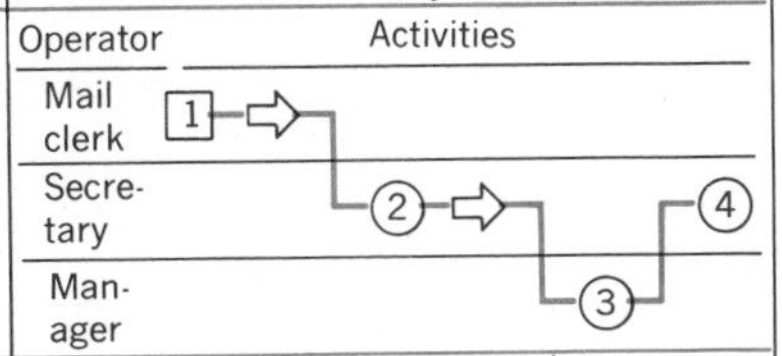

Figure 9.2 Illustrations of different process charts

251

charts represented by the illustrations would provide entries for additional details.

Subsidiary information is often neglected during the construction of charts. Sources of data should be recorded if they add validity and emphasis to the chart or if they will later help the analyst's memory. Improper titles or confusing descriptions result from skimping on words or using personal abbreviations. Legends permit a reader to understand the chart if unfamiliar conventions are used. The golden rule of charting is that everyone should get the same intended meaning from the display.

EXAMPLE 9.1   A Methods Study Using a Process Chart

One department of a material-testing lab determines the compressive strength of concrete cylinders. These cylinders (1 foot long and 6 inches in diameter) are cast at construction sites and indicate the quality of concrete being poured. They are delivered to the lab by the constructors where they are stored in a "moist room" under controlled temperature and humidity. After the curing period, usually 7 or 28 days, the cylinders are broken to see if they meet the specified strengths.

James, the supervisor of test section 1, reports the price of cylinder testing will have to be increased to meet the wage hikes given to the lab technicians. The lab manager asked the methods analyst, Irving Yu, to check the process before raising the testing price.

Yu's process chart for the present method of cylinder testing is shown in Figure 9.3. The times and distances in the chart are only approximations in the first survey. Possible corrective actions are noted in the columns on the right. From these preliminary checks, it appears the measuring might be combined with the weighing operation (measurements taken while the cylinder is on the weighing scale), the level of the cart could be raised to allow the cylinder to be rolled from the cart to the workbench, and the entire workbench could be moved closer to the hydraulic press where the cylinders are broken. The next steps are to secure additional information about the feasibility of the indicated suggestions and to estimate the implementation costs and expected savings.

Man-Machine Process Charts

Dependent relationships of men and machines are depicted on man-machine process charts. The purpose of such charts is to analyze a process to develop an economic balance of idle time for the men and machines. The related activities of men and machines are often on an intermittent basis; a sequence of worker activity is required to prepare the machine for operation, the machine has a set running time to produce a finished product, and then more activities are required to extract the product and prepare for the next run. When there are long running periods, one operator can service several machines; conversely, a low ratio of running time to preparation time indicates a "gang" of

OPERATIONS CHART

SUMMARY	UNITS	NO.	TIME	DIST.	SPACE	FLOW PROCESS CHART		Page 1 of 1	
◯		2	8a			☑ PRESENT ☐ PROPOSED	DATE 11-16-69	ANALYST	I. C. Yu
☐		4	4a			SUBJECT & QUANTITY			
⇨		6		60		1 concrete test cylinder			
D									
▽		2							

TOTALS	14	12a	60		STEPS	PERSONS & DEPT. CONTACTED	POSSIBLE ACTION

WHY? IS IT REALLY NECESSARY? a-approx.
WHAT? WHEN? WHERE? WHO? HOW?

					1	James – Test Section #1	
					2	Bob Wilson – Tech.	

STEP	SYMBOL	TIME	DIST.	SPACE	PROCESS STEPS	ELIMINATE	COMBINE	SEQUE.	PLACE	PERSON	IMPROVE
1	◯☐⇨D▽				In moist room for 28 days						
2	◯☐⇨D▽	1	4		Select cylinder from rack and place in cart (holds 12)						
3	◯☐⇨D▽		31		Cart to test bench				✓		
4	◯☐⇨D▽		6		Lift cylinder to bench (up 2 ft.)						✓
5	◯☐⇨D▽	1½			Measure diameter & length				✓		
6	◯☐⇨D▽		4		Move to scales (roll)						
7	◯☐⇨D▽	1			Weigh				✓		
8	◯☐⇨D▽		5		Move to capper						
9	◯☐⇨D▽	3	2		Cap both ends and mark						✓
10	◯☐⇨D▽				Store under wet blanket while other cylinders are capped						
11	◯☐⇨D▽		8		Move to press (by cart)						
12	◯☐⇨D▽	½			Center in press						
13	◯☐⇨D▽	2			Break						
14	◯☐⇨D▽				Observe type of break						
	◯☐⇨D▽										

Figure 9.3 Sample flow process chart

men may be required. The crew size criterion is the contribution per piece produced: the difference between the value of the piece and the sum of machine and labor cost to produce it.

A clearer picture of the man-machine relationship is obtained by showing the activities of each on a time scale. As illustrated in Figure 9.4, one man operates one machine. He has no idle time, but the machine is idle 4 minutes in each cycle. The relationship could be altered by assigning two machines to the operator or by adding a helper as shown in Figure 9.5. Assuming the following economic relationships:

$$\text{value of each piece produced} = \$4 \text{ per unit}$$
$$\text{cost of labor: operator} = \$6 \text{ per hour}$$
$$\text{helper} = \$3 \text{ per hour}$$
$$\text{burden rate of machine} = \$17 \text{ per hour}$$

the hourly contribution of each method is calculated as follows:

1 operator/1 machine			(1 operator and 1 helper)/ 1 machine		
Output: 6 pieces per hour			Output: 10 pieces per hour		
Value:	6 × $4 =	$24	Value:	10 × $4 =	$40
Cost:	Operator =	$6	Cost:	Operator =	$6
	Machine =	17		Helper =	3
				Machine =	17
	Total	23		Total	26
Contribution per hour =		$1	Contribution per hour =		$14

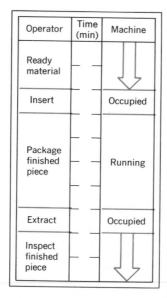

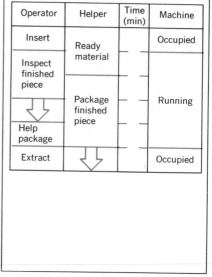

Figure 9.4 (Left) Man-machine process (⇩ indicates idle time)

Figure 9.5 (Right) Modified men-machine relationship (⇩ indicates idle time)

254

Besides the obvious monetary attractiveness, the new method allows 1 minute idle time in each cycle for unexpected delays by the operators.

EXAMPLE 9.2 Quantitative Evaluation of Man-Machine Ratios

When several machines have the same running time and identical service requirements, a quantitative approach easily identifies the optimum man-machine ratio. Assume the following times and costs are descriptive of a production process:

Operator:	Insert piece	0.60 min
	Remove finished piece	0.30 min
	Inspect piece	0.50 min
	File, burr, and set aside	0.20 min
	Walk to next machine	0.05 min
	Wage	$3.00 per hr
Machine:	Running time	3.95 min
	Burden rate	$4.80 per hr

The approximate number of machines per man is estimated by the ratio of the machine cycle time to the operator cycle time:

$$\frac{\text{machine cycle time}}{\text{operator cycle time}} = \frac{0.6 + 0.3 + 3.95}{0.6 + 0.3 + 0.5 + 0.2 + 0.05} = \frac{4.85}{1.65} = 2.9 = 3 \text{ machines/man}$$

Checking the cost for an operator servicing two and three machines, we have:

		Two machines		Three machines
Labor:	$(4.85 \text{ min}) \dfrac{\$3}{60 \text{ min}}$	$= \$0.242$	$(3)(1.65)\dfrac{3}{60}$	$= \$0.247$
Burden:	$\dfrac{4.85 \text{ min}}{\text{machine}} \dfrac{\$4.80}{60 \text{ min}}$ (2 machines) $=$	$\underline{0.776}$	$(4.95)\dfrac{\$4.80}{60}(3) =$	$\underline{1.188}$
Total cost per cycle		$= \$1.018$		$= \$1.435$
Unit cost:	$\dfrac{\$1.018}{2 \text{ pieces}}$	$= \$0.51$	$\dfrac{\$1.435}{3 \text{ pieces}}$	$= \$0.48$

In the two-machine case the limiting factor is the machine cycle time (4.85 minutes to complete one cycle); in the three-machine case the limiting condition is the man cycle time (3 × 1.65 = 4.95 minutes to service three machines). In the latter case the operator has no idle time. It is apparent from the cost figures that it is more economical to assign three machines to each operator.

9-3 MOTION STUDY The purpose of motion study is to make work performance easier and more productive by improving manual motions. The most obvious difference between process and motion analysis is the scope of the study; motion studies are oriented to the body movements of one individual. Each circle on an operator process chart is a potential area for motion economy.

The investigation routine, techniques, and attitude suitable to a motion study are similar to those befitting a process analysis. An appropriate problem is selected for study, the current method of work is observed, and creative questioning of the operation seeks a better method. The key phase is the detection of wasteful movements.

The question of what tasks man should perform cannot be accurately answered until it is determined how he can perform them. This sequence of questions seems natural for machine operation but is often transposed for man's performance.

Principles of Motion Economy ✳ Be aware of:

In chapter 7 we considered the question: "Man or machine?" When we evaluate the motor performance of man in a system, we are aided by a mechanistic set of guidelines that could just as logically be applied to a machine. The principles of motion pertain to the distribution of work over different parts of the body, preferred types of motion, and the sequence of movements; the machine design equivalent of these principles are component analysis, kinematics, and programming. The simplicity and logic of the following principles are so intrinsically satisfying that one wonders how they could possibly be overlooked:

1. Minimize the number of movements—eliminate unnecessary motions and try to combine movements.
2. Minimize the lengths of movements—keep the work area within the arc of forearm motions.
3. Balance the motion pattern—use symmetrical motions in opposite directions and avoid sharp changes in direction.
4. Move hands simultaneously—start and stop hands at the same time.
5. Minimize the number of parts of the body involved in a complex motion—if necessary, change the complex motion to a single one.
6. Minimize the muscular force required for movements—slide objects instead of lifting them.
7. Minimize the muscular effort required for control—use pre-positioned stops and mechanical guides.
8. Minimize the number of eye fixations and the distance of eye movements required—pre-position tools and materials to allow a touch system of operation.
9. Minimize the eye fixation time required for perception when this is a controlling factor—use color, shape, and size coding; provide qualitative indicators if possible.
10. Distribute actions among the members of the body in accordance with their natural capacities—relieve hands of simple repetitive jobs by using foot controls.
11. Provide holding devices—free one or both hands for more useful motions.

256

12. Provide for intermittent use of different muscles—try alternate sitting/standing or similar arrangements to relieve muscle tension by varying motion patterns.
13. Take advantage of gravity—use gravity feed for materials and dispose of objects by drop delivery.
14. Take advantage of natural rythm—arrange work to allow easy, continuous, and repeated movements that develop good work habits.

Motion Analysis

A process analysis is a macromovement study, but it also benefits from attention to the principles of motion economy.

A motion study microscopically examines an operation. The power of magnification depends on the nature and importance of the operation. Visual observations of work in progress are sufficient for gross movements such as loading trucks or felling trees. When an operation is frequently repeated and requires many small movements, a more detailed analysis may be warranted. The rapid micromovements found in some assembly operations are difficult to follow with unaided vision. Motion pictures can be used to assist such studies.

Camera studies. A *micromotion* study involves the use of a high speed (around 960 frames per minute) camera to photograph short-cycle (2 minutes or less) operations. After filming the operation, an analyst can retire to a more secluded spot and

The analysis potential of slow-motion replays is well publicized in televised sporting events.

replay the film at a slower speed to detect improper motions. This approach has advantages of thoroughness resulting from unlimited playback opportunities and instructional applications because the films document both good and bad practices. It has the disadvantage of being expensive when compared to the cost of direct observation.

A *memomotion* study makes use of a slow speed (60 frames per minute or less), automatic camera to record a long-long

Time-lapse cameras also are used as "electronic watch-dogs" in banks and for critical control records.

cycle operation or several long cycles of the same operation. The resulting films are run at higher speeds to give continuity for motion analyses. It provides a relatively inexpensive way to obtain the general operational characteristics without an on-site analyst. The recorded work patterns serve as training guides and are useful in labor disputes.

A *cyclegraph* study uses a rather exotic arrangement where flashing lights are attached to an operator's limbs and a single time exposure is taken of his work performance. The result is a picture of light smears of varying intensity that map the motion paths of the limbs, usually hands. The approach can be very effective, but it is limited to high volume work because of its expense.

257

Camera studies are often resented by workers. Even cooperative employees may become suspicious or overreact when their performance is photographed unless the analyst explains his mission. Part of the analyst's reassurance to the worker should be a caution to act naturally. Although hamming antics provide darkroom chuckles for the analysts, they defeat the fact-finding mission.

The first elements of work divisions were called "therbligs" after their originators, the Gilbreths, spelled backwards.

Motion charting. Whether the motion patterns are observed directly or recorded on film, they are often committed to paper by shorthand symbols. Some of the relatively standardized symbols are shown in Figure 9.6. Two degrees of refinement are indicated. The top set, called "get and place" elements, are appropriate for longer cycles involving arm and hand movements. The other set, for "microscopic" analyses, are associated with very short cycles detailing hand and finger movements.

The flavor of motion charting is well displayed by diagrams of concurrent hand movements. Two charts of this type are called Left-hand Right-hand and SIMO (SImultaneous MOtions). Both charts detail the simultaneous movements of an operator's right and left hands. SIMO charts are usually applied to more

Symbol	Motion	Description
	(Larger elements of an operation for "get and place" analysis)	
G	Get	Reaching and securing control of an object
P	Place	Moving an object to an intended position
U	Use	Employing a tool or instrument to accomplish a purpose
A	Assemble	Joining two objects in an intended manner
H	Hold	Supporting an object with one hand while the other hand performs work on the object
	(Smaller elements of an operation for "microscopic" analysis)	
R	Reach	Moving an unloaded hand or finger to within one inch of the intended position
G	Grasp	Securing control of an object with the fingers
H	Hold	Supporting an object with one hand while work is being performed on the object
M	Move	Moving a loaded hand or finger to within one inch of the intended target
P	Position	Aligning, orienting, or engaging one object with another
T	Turn	Rotating the forearm about its long axis
D	Delay	Hesitating while awaiting termination of an act or event
RL	Release	Relinquishing control of an object previously grasped in fingers

Figure 9.6 Work element descriptions and symbols

minute motions which are keyed to a time scale. The times are determined from a frame count or a film clock from camera studies and by stopwatch studies. Symbols such as those shown in Figure 9.6 are used to describe the movements.

The ideal area for microcharting is where a large number of workers are doing identical jobs on identical machines. Under such conditions the considerable expense needed to analyze and optimize the motion pattern of an operation is paid for by the quantity of work benefiting from the study. The area appropriate to microanalysis is the very same area where mechanical processes are most profitably applied. From a system viewpoint, a study in this area should not have the pure objective of improving manual methods; it should also be a feasibility study for new and different methods to perform the work.

An assumption that "improving the parts will improve the whole" can be misleading unless system effectiveness is considered concurrently with operation efficiency.

9-4 METHOD IMPROVEMENT PROGRAMS

Most successful method improvement programs are a hybrid of formal procedures followed by specially trained method analysts and a less formal process relying on the cooperation of operators. The main advantage of including personnel not specifically assigned to method improvement is that wider participation yields a greater concern for cost effectiveness. Suggestions from operating personnel lead to many improvements that otherwise would be overlooked. These employees have a vast reservoir of practical knowhow concerning their own jobs. Tapping this reservoir blends on-going work familiarity with the techniques of industrial engineering to produce the most pertinent work design changes and effective mechanical aids.

Work simplification is a title often given to a team approach to deliberate method change. Although approaches vary between companies, a common routine is to organize managers and workers into "methods" teams. Any expenditures with which the teams are familiar are fair game for their cost-reduction suggestions—wages, freight costs, taxes, insurance, costs of materials, yields, and work processes. Some schooling about investigation procedures, as described in Section 9-2, is provided by regular method analysts. These analysts also coordinate the program and provide follow-up service on the suggestions. The success of the teams is measured by the first-year savings resulting from the method changes they develop as compared to a previously established team goal. The contest aspect encourages competition between teams. Recognition for achieving goals is by awards, both monetary and commentary.

ANALYSIS

EXAMPLE 9.3   A Macroview of Microanalysis

In an attempt to stem an ever increasing burden of paperwork, a Methods Department investigation is requested. A preliminary survey indicates the existing equipment and staff are sufficient to handle anticipated demands if paper handling and form design are improved. Analysts interview the clerks and supervisors to get their suggestions. Attention is focused on the requisition and billing system. Procedures for certain key operations are charted. A "get and place" analysis is deemed appropriate because there are too few identical, high volume operations to warrant the application of microanalysis techniques. An example of the charted procedure for checking and endorsing one requisition form is shown by the Left-hand Right-hand chart in Figure 9.7.

The movements shown in the chart appear unnecessarily repetitive. Are three entries necessary? Does each entry have to be on a different page? Could a stamp or initial be used? Could carbon copying be incorporated? Can the In-box be designed to make the forms easier to grasp? Should several forms be piled on top of each other to allow continuous marking? Can the completed forms be removed by a drop disposal?

Answers to these questions depend on considerations beyond the immediate problem of improving one operator's motions. For instance, all entries might be consolidated on one page to improve this operation but inconvenience or misinterpretation could result in other operations. Such a solution could be a suboptimization of the system objective.

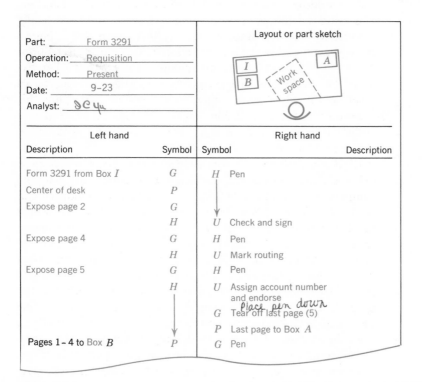

Figure 9.7

EXAMPLE 9.4 A Program for a Work Simplification Program

New gimmicks help maintain the motivation needed for successful method improvement programs. One company decided to retain the same general program as used the previous year but to modify it by awarding stamps for completed method projects—a takeoff on commercial trading stamp schemes. The stamps would be printed with method slogans such as "work smarter—not harder."

At a kickoff meeting the new plan would be presented to departmental teams. Monthly meetings of each team with a method analyst would be scheduled to present the stamps earned by individuals during the month and to allow refresher presentations of method study techniques. The status of competing teams would be publicized on bulletin boards and individual accomplishments described in a monthly methods newsletter.

At a banquet style, contest-ending celebration, the stamps could be redeemed for modest prizes or be exchanged for bingo cards in the hope of winning larger prizes. The team that surpassed its assigned goal by the greatest percentage would win individual sweepstake awards and possession of the rotating "methods improvement" trophy for next year. In this fashion, winning teams and the most successful individual efforts would be recognized by the awareness of associates and by tokens of appreciation from the company.

An inspirational problem of a different type is sometimes improved by *job enlargement*—the purposeful expansion of responsibilities and activities expected of a worker. Job specialization has evolved since the industrial revolution because of beliefs that smaller divisions of labor tend to: (1) require less supervision, (2) decrease learning time, (3) eliminate interruptions of work by closely controlled material flow and by largely automatic operations, and (4) decrease wages by employing operators with lower skill qualifications.

Job rotation is another approach to relieving monotony of repetitive tasks; workers rotate from one short-cycle task to another.

In recent years the above beliefs have been attenuated by evidence that fewer errors and faster work sometimes results from grouping several smaller work divisions into one more demanding and therefore theoretically more attention-keeping job. The decision for enlarging jobs rests on the need for extra training time, and perhaps higher personnel skills required for more complex jobs, registered against the benefits of possibly improving morale and performance from more compact operations.

9-5 TIME STUDY Time study is the handmaiden of motion study. The proof of an improved method is confirmed by a time reduction. A valid time standard for an operation depends on first identifying the best method to perform that operation. This relationship establishes the need and justification for time study; it measures the labor needed to produce a product and thereby is the basis of wage payments.

261

A "work count" is an informal method of measuring work by counting accomplishments (units produced, postings made, inspections completed, etc.) during a period of time.

• The objective of time study is to determine the *standard* time for an operation—the time required by a qualified and fully trained operator to perform the operation by a specified method while working at a normal tempo. This definition sets the routine for time studies. An operation is evaluated, and redesigned if necessary, by methods analysis. The work elements thus obtained are clocked. These clock readings are normalized by applying a rating factor to account for the operator's tempo. Then allowances are included to compensate for production interruptions. The end product is a realistic evaluation of labor accomplishment.

Study Preparation

The initial phase of a time study is to acquire sufficient familiarity and knowledge of the operation, equipment, and working conditions. An ideal situation is one where a highly skilled, cooperative operator is performing a task by approved methods under typical working conditions. When the situation is not so perfect, recorded data must be amended later to make it representative of conceived performance. It is important to

Standard data recorded for each time study include: (1) operator's name, (2) observer's name, (3) operation, (4) speed and feed of machines, (5) times the study starts and ends, and (6) date.

• record a thorough description of the actual situation at the time of the study: a sketch of the layout, tools and materials being used, unusual environmental conditions, etc.

A job is described by dividing an operator's activities into *work elements*. The elements are groupings of basic movements. Occasionally a work element may be as short as one of the micromotion elements in Figure 9.6, but more commonly the divisions are larger. The following guidelines provide a framework by which to identify distinct work elements that simplify the timing and the evaluation of observed times:

1. *Irregular* elements, those not repeated in every operation cycle, should be separated from *regular* elements. If a machine is cleaned off after every five parts produced, "cleaning" is an irregular element. Its time should be prorated over five cycles when one cycle is required to produce one part.

Since work elements are essentially microactivities, they form an activity list similar to those for CPS (Section 6-3) and share many of the same considerations.

2. *Constant* elements should be separated from *variable* elements. When the time to perform a work element depends on the size, weight, length, or shape of the piece produced, it is termed variable. "Sew edges" is a variable element if the perimeter of the piece changes from one cycle to the next.

3. *Machine*-paced elements should be separated from *operator*-controlled elements. This division helps the recognition of delays.

4. *Foreign* or accidental elements should be identified. Such

activities would be considered expected occurrences if labeled as irregular elements. Therefore, a separate list of foreign elements is kept during each timing session.

5. *End points* of each element should be easily recognized. A distinct sound or a change in contact makes readily identifiable breakoff points.

6. It is desirable to have *shorter* elements when a choice must be made, but durations less than 0.03-0.04 of a minute are difficult to time accurately.

7. *Unnecessary* movements and activities should be separated from those deemed *essential*. A skilled operator, by definition, has fewer unnecessary actions than an untrained operator. Familiarity with motion principles is a definite aid in recognizing improper movements and in designing better motion patterns.

After all the work elements in a cycle are identified and any needed motion corrections are incorporated, a complete description of each element is entered on a time study record form in the expected sequence of occurrence.

Data Collection

Element times are taken directly at the workplace by clock readings or remotely by motion picture analysis. For either course it is advisable to seek the active cooperation of the operator being observed. The timer should stand behind and out of the way of the operator. Stopwatch studies are far more numerous than camera studies owing to greater versatility and lower costs.

There are differently calibrated stopwatches. The two most commonly used are: (1) a minute decimal watch calibrated in increments of $\frac{1}{100}$ of a minute and (2) an hour decimal watch showing increments of $\frac{1}{100}$ of an hour. Both have large sweep hands that make one revolution per 100 increments, and both have smaller dials for a cumulative count of the revolutions.

There are two widely used techniques for recording elemental times:

1. *Snap-back* timing directly determines the time to complete each element. The sweep hand is at zero when each work element begins, and it turns while the work element is being performed. When the element is completed, the time consumed for its performance is read from the watch and the sweep hand is snapped back to zero, ready to begin the next element.

2. *Continuous* timing allows the stopwatch to run without

Dual and triple watch arrangements linked together on time-study boards allow direct readings while retaining features of continuous timing.

interruption through the entire duration of the study. Accumulated elemental times are recorded in sequence while the watch is running. Then each reading must be subtracted from the preceding reading to show the elapsed time of the work elements.

Both methods have their adherents. The snap-back method requires less clerical work, and delays in work procedures are

The continuous method is the most used timing technique.

• somewhat easier to handle. Errors may be introduced if snap-back reflexes are slow. Continuous timing allows better readings for very short elements but requires strict concentration to note the passing times. It forces a full accounting of all the time involved in the study.

Selected Time

The times recorded for each element will vary among observations. Variations are natural because operators do not always move at a uniform pace, motion patterns are not always identical, and tools and materials are not always replaced in exactly the same spot. A small degree of variation can even be expected from the timer as he reads his watch. However, variations traceable to unusual occurrences such as a dropped tool or a coughing fit by the operator are accounted for by deleting the affected observation. The remaining observations, now considered "representative," are averaged to determine the selected time for each element:

$$\text{Selected time to complete an element} = ST_e$$

$$ST_e = \frac{\sum(\text{elemental times of representative observations})}{\text{number of representative observations}}$$

By summing the selected elemental times, we have our best estimate of the *task selected time, ST_t*:

$$ST_t = \sum ST_e$$

where the summation includes all the work elements required to complete the task. ST_t is then the average time the operator needs to perform the task being studied. At this stage we are not prepared to say that ST_t is the standard of performance we should expect from all operators. In fact, we are not even sure that it is the true time for the observed task. What we have is a sample that should be statistically checked to determine how much confidence we can have in it.

One method of deciding upon the number of timing cycles is

Quicker methods for estimating the number of cycles required include alignment charts and tables relating the average cycle time and the range of cycle times to the number of observations. Each chart applies to only one accuracy and confidence level.

by a formula based on the standard error of the average for an element:

$$N' = \left(\frac{k/s\sqrt{N\sum X^2 - (\sum X)^2}}{\sum X}\right)^2$$

where:

N' = number of cycles needed to produce desired precision and confidence level

k/s = confidence-precision factor

X = representative element times

N = number of representative element times

Two decisions must be made in applying the formula. The first is to decide which element in the task to use for the X values. A conservative solution is assured by choosing the element with the greatest variation; the larger range of readings produces a larger variance which in turn necessitates a greater sample size for a given confidence level.

The second decision is the selection of a k/s factor—the confidence level that the desired accuracy is attained. A k/s of $2/0.05 = 40$ indicates a 95% confidence level and a $\pm5\%$ precision. The numerator, 2, is derived from the relationship that 95% of the sample observations fall within the range of ±2 standard errors of the mean. The denominator, 0.05, sets the allowable error at ±0.05 of the true element time. Similarly, the insertion of

A k/s factor of 20 is generally accepted as reasonable with respect to the overall accuracy expected in a time study.

$$k/s = 3/0.03 = 100$$

in the formula allows the calculation of the number of cycles that must be timed so that 997 times out of 1000 the ST_t will be within $\pm3\%$ of the true task time.

EXAMPLE 9.5 Stopwatch Timing

The concrete cylinder breaking operation of the material-testing lab introduced in Example 9.1 is still under investigation. The macroanalysis conducted by process charting implied further attention should be given to the capping operation. This task involves putting a hot liquid chemical compound in a mold on the end of a cylinder. The liquid quickly dries into a very hard cap. The purposes of the caps are to square off the cylinder ends and to provide a smooth surface for the uniform application of force to break the concrete. A time study will define the labor content of the capping cost for cylinder testing.

A breakdown of the capping operation reveals the nine basic work elements shown in the observation sheet (Figure 9.8). The capping operator, James Randle, is well trained and qualified to perform the task. The procedure he follows is efficient and the working conditions are favorable. A sketch of the workbench arrangement is shown at the top of the observation sheet.

The observer uses the continuous timing technique; consecutive readings from the stopwatch

Observation Sheet

Sheet __1__ of __1__ sheet

Operation __cylinder capping__

Operator __James Randle__

Conditions __experienced__

Machine. __capper model 3__

Speed _____

Material __capping compound__

Date __11-21-69__   Begin __1021__   End __1053__   Observer __I. C. Yu__

Sketches and notes

Element		1	2	3	4	5	6	7	8	9	10	STe
1. Fasten clamp on cylinder	E	08	09	09	10	08	(10)	09	08	09	09	0.09
	C	8	66	31	803	98	1580	40	11	76	70	
2. Pour hot capping compound in mold	E	25	24	31	28	30	27	33	25	31	32	0.29
	C	33	90	62	31	1228	1607	77	36	2707	3002	
3. Position cylinder in mold	E	18	19	18	17	19	19	19	18	18	19	0.18
	C	51	309	80	48	47	26	96	54	25	21	
4. Let cap cool in mold	E	51	55	55	61	60	51	54	53	57	59	0.56
	C	102	64	635	909	1307	77	2236	2507	82	80	
5. Remove cylinder to table.	E	16	15	15	16	18	17	17	16	15	17	0.16
	C	18	89	50	25	55	1721	84	48	2823	3123	
6. Pour hot capping compound in mold	E	28	29	31	29	30	27	31	25	26	26	0.28
	C	46	418	81	54	55	1721	84	48	2823	3123	
7. Position other end of cylinder in mold	E	19	18	20	19	20	21	20	20	19	20	0.20
	C	65	36	701	73	75	42	2304	6	42	43	
8. Let cap cool in mold	E	54	60	51	53	55	52	58	55	61	56	0.55
	C	219	96	752	1026	1430	94	62	2623	2903	99	
9. Remove cylinder to table and take off clamp	E	38	36	41	42	49	52	41	44	58	39	0.44
	C	57	522	93	68	79	1846	2403	67	61	3238	
11. Cap broke-repeat 6, 7 and 8	E				122		131					0.25
	C				1190		1977					
12. Refill and stir capping pot	E						154					0.10
	C						2231					
	E											
	C											

Figure 9.8

are entered in the rows marked "C." All readings are in hundredths of a minute. During the fourth and sixth cycles an irregular element ($I1$) occurs when Randle breaks a cap as he removes the cylinder from the mold. A replacement cap is formed by repeating elements 6, 7, and 8. The need to add more capping compound to the heating pot is another irregular element ($I2$) which Randle reports occurs about once every 30 caps or 15 cylinder cycles. Irregular element descriptions are added as necessary below the regular element sequence.

Ten cycles are timed in about 32 minutes. Sometime later the work elemental times are calculated as the differences between the continuous time readings. The differences are entered in the "E" rows. The average value of each row establishes the selected time for the work elements, ST_e. During the sixth observation for the first element, the operator caught his finger in the clamp while watching a girl pass by. He explained that this was the first time he had managed to pinch a finger and he doubts that it will ever happen again. Therefore, the observation is circled and discarded before calculating ST_t. The selected time for $I2$ is based on the assumption that the element will occur once every 15 cycles.

The number of cycles timed will be considered adequate if the precision is within $\pm 10\%$ at a 95% confidence level. Work element 9 has the greatest variation and is therefore used in the formula check.

$$N' = \left(\frac{2/0.10\sqrt{10 \times 19{,}542 - (440)^2}}{440} \right)^2$$

$$= \left(\frac{20\sqrt{195{,}420 - 193{,}600}}{440} \right)^2$$

where X = observation of element 9

$\sum X = 38 + 36 + \cdots + 39 \qquad = 440$

and $\sum X^2 = (38)^2 + (36)^2 + \cdots + (39)^2 = 19{,}542$

$$= \left(\frac{20\sqrt{1820}}{440} \right)^2 = \left(\frac{43}{22} \right)^2$$

$$= \text{approximately 4 cycles}$$

It thus appears that enough observations have been taken and the selected time for the capping operation is equal to

$$ST_t = 0.09 + 0.29 + 0.18 + 0.56 + 0.16 + 0.28 + 0.20 + 0.55$$

$$+ 0.44 + 0.25 + 0.10$$

$$= 3.10 \text{ minutes}$$

Normal Time

At the conclusion of a timing session, the observer faces the disagreeable prospect of assigning a leveling or *rating factor* to the operation just observed. The rating function compares the tempo of an operator's performance with the observer's conception of a "normal" pace. This comparison is difficult because there are very few solid supports upon which to base the concept of normal, and there is a shortage of aids by which to maintain a lasting conception once it is conceived. But regardless of the difficulties, some factor must be applied to *ST*'s to account for individual differences among operators before performance times can be standardized.

Rating starts with a definition of normal. A generally accepted launching point is an agreement that *a normal pace is one that can be attained and maintained by an average worker during a typical working day without undue fatigue.* Trouble comes when the adjectives in the definition are put to practice. What is an "average" worker, a "typical" work day, or "undue" fatigue? Jobs are so different that opinions are bound to vary. Thus, some time study practitioners get reputations for "tight" or "loose" ratings, the opinions of the workers about the opinions of the
• timers. Even the most skilled and experienced timing practitioners can expect disagreements over their interpretation of pace because rating factors are inherently subjective.

A measure of objectivity is introduced by recognizing certain benchmarks of normal performance. For instance, there is general agreement that the normal time to deal a deck of 52 cards into four equal piles is 0.50 minute and a normal pace for walking on a smooth, level surface is 3 miles per hour. Motion pictures of operators performing different tasks at consensus percentages of normal are available. Some films simultaneously show multiple shots of one operation as it is performed at levels above, at, and below normal tempo. Films taken for micromotion studies can be shown at different projector speeds to qualify or retrain raters.

There will probably never be a yardstick of normality that is universally applicable; different companies will use contrasting methods of measuring their versions of normal. The important aspect is the uniform maintenance of whatever level is chosen as normal.

Numerous methods of setting rating factors have been proposed. A strict reliance on speed or tempo as appraised by an observer is one of the oldest and most used methods; if the rater judges the operator to be working at a speed 90% of normal, he normalizes the selected time by multiplying it by 0.90. Another
• method, called "objective rating," considers both speed and the relative difficulty of the task being performed; both a speed factor and a difficulty factor are applied to the selected time to obtain a normal time. More elaborate methods attempt to consider skill, effort, conditions, and consistency through the use of tables or tabulated time expectations. Since there is no industrywide preference for one method; each company has an

Unions may seek timers known for their "looseness" to review standards they consider tight. Such recourse is a worthy check on rating subjectivity.

The "objective rating" system was developed by M. E. Mundel. His difficulty factors include (1) extent of body use, (2) foot pedals, (3) bimanualness, (4) eye-hand coordination, (5) handling or sensing demands, and (6) resistance encountered.

option as to technique. But once the option is exercised, it should be followed consistently if rating is to be understood and respected by the work force.

Rating factors are applied to elemental selected times (ST_e) or to the task selected time (ST_t) when the operator performs at the same level throughout the task. Ratings are formulated during the timing sessions by noting the effort and skill of the operator as well as the conditions and nature of the task in relation to the observer's image of normal. The normal time is the product of this rating and the selected time:

$$\text{normal time} = \text{selected time} \times \text{rating factor}$$

Assume the selected time for a particular task where the operator gave a consistent performance for all the elements is 0.75 minute. If the observer rated the performance at 120% of normal, then

$$\text{normal time} = 0.75 \times 1.20 = 0.90 \text{ minute}$$

The time thus stated for the task represents the time in which a qualified and well-trained operator working at normal tempo is expected to perform one cycle of the task.

Standard Time

Securing selected and normal times are intermediate steps in the development of *standard time*—the time an operation will normally require when allowances are made for interruptions. These interruptions are caused by factors external to the job itself and are therefore not accounted for by the observed elements, corrections to observations, or the rating factors.

Allowances are frequently a topic for collective bargaining where increased allowances tend to be treated as new fringe benefits.

Personal allowances are granted for the physical needs of the workers. Rest periods for light work average about 5% of the typical 8-hour work day. More exhausting work or unfavorable working conditions are reflected by allowing more personal time.

Fatigue allowances are intended to compensate for below-normal performance resulting from fatigue effects. By setting a 5% allowance, for example, the time within which a task is expected to be completed is extended by 5%, giving the worker a fair opportunity to meet normal standards. Controversy over such reasoning stems from a contention that performance deterioration does not set in until fatigue reaches serious proportions. Therefore, the normal pace should be defined in terms of the effort required to meet normal output under deleterious or strenuous work conditions. The question is further complicated

269

by: (1) the lack of any satisfactory way of measuring fatigue, and (2) modern working conditions which have almost eliminated actual muscle exhaustion. It is not surprising then to find the value of fatigue allowances subject to considerable debate and the percentages a topic of arbitration.

Delay allowances compensate for unavoidable work delays. These are inescapable interruptions to productivity caused by external forces such as power outages, defective materials, waiting lines, late deliveries, and other events over which a worker has no control. Unintentional but avoidable delays by the operators are not included. The irregularity of occurrence and duration of unavoidable delays make this allowance another ripe target for collective bargaining.

Special allowances are sometimes added to give redress for unusual and frequently temporary conditions that curtail a worker's output through no fault of his own. Exceptional maintenance requirements, temporary machine interference, and short production runs where workers are always in an initial learning period are examples. Such cases are individually treated and seldom cause much debate.

A composite total allowance is determined by adding individual allowance percentages applicable to a certain job. The standard times for tasks included in the job are calculated by adding to each normal time the product of its total allowance percentage and its duration:

standard time = normal time + (normal time) (total allowance)

or

standard time = normal time × allowance factor

where

$$\text{allowance factor} = 1 + \frac{\text{total allowance} \%}{100}$$

Sidenotes:

Delay allowances are often developed by "ratio delay" studies using techniques described in Section 9-6.

Extra allowances are often provided where a large portion of cycle time is machine controlled and operators are paid incentive wages. They may be as high as 30%.

Allowance factors go as high as 1.35 in steel plants, but the average is closer to 1.18.

EXAMPLE 9.6   Standard Time Calculation

Let us return again to the cylinder breaking process encountered in Examples 9.1 and 9.5. The evaluation of the capping operation can now be completed. Since the operator, Randle, is a competent cylinder capper, the main concern of the observer is to rate Randle's tempo with respect to a normal pace. Each capping task element is rated separately as shown on page 271; rating factors are applicable to an entire task only when all the elements in the task are subject to and performed at a uniform pace. In the cylinder capping operation the times for two elements, 4 and 8, are not controlled by the operator's pace; they depend on the time it takes the hot liquid capping compound to solidify in the mold. Such material-, product-, or machine-controlled elements are usually assigned a rating of 1.00.

	Element	ST_e (Minutes)	X	Rating Factor	=	Normal ✗ Element Time (Minutes)
1.	Clamp	0.09		1.20		0.11
2.	Pour	0.29		1.10		0.32
3.	Position	0.18		1.00		0.18
3.	Cool	0.56		1.00		0.56
5.	Remove	0.16		1.00		0.16
6.	Pour	0.28		1.10		0.31
7.	Position	0.20		1.00		0.20
8.	Cool	0.55		1.00		0.55
9.	Remove	0.44		1.00		0.44
$I1$	Repeat 6 to 8	0.25		1.30		0.32
$I2$	Refill pot	0.10		1.00		0.10

Normal task time = 3.25 minutes

It is apparent from the ratings that the observer felt Randle was working at a pace an average worker could not maintain. This is not an unusual situation when an operator is impressed because he has been selected for a time study. An observer should be sensitive to carelessness or over-exertion as was apparently indicated when Randle had to remake broken caps in element $I1$. Sometimes an uncooperative operator may play guessing games with the observer by varying his pace, a game neither can win completely.

The applicable allowance factor is more a function of the entire job, in this case the complete cylinder testing process, than of the operation of capping the cylinders:

Customary personal allowance for all lab employees	= 5%
Required handling of 30-pound cylinders and hot capping material is considered in the fatigue allowance	= 8%
Interruptions primarily owed to impromptu visits by the concrete suppliers are accounted for in the delay allowance	= 7%
Total allowance	= 20%

Adding 20% to the normal time does not mean that each cycle is expected to take $0.20 \times 3.25 = 0.65$ minute longer to complete. Instead, the 0.65-minute increments build up during normal cycles to afford time for rest breaks and other work interruptions. With an allowance factor of 1.20, the cylinder capping task has a

standard time: $3.25 \times 1.20 = 3.9$ minutes

Synthetic Times

Many operations in a plant require the same types of movements. The data collected from previous time studies are valuable for estimating times for similar work in the future. *Synthetic timing* is the name given to the use of standard data to synthesize task durations. Using already developed normal times in this fashion overcomes two prominent deficiencies of stopwatch timing: (1) time standards can be determined before a process

271

actually is in operation, and (2) after appropriate data have been developed, the time and cost of setting new time standards are significantly lowered.

The applicability of synthetic timing for an individual firm depends on the relative slopes of the two lines shown in Figure 9.9. The solid line depicts the cost of stopwatch studies as directly related to the number of time standards established. The flatter slope of the dashed line, representing synthetic timing, indicates that the variable cost per time standard set by this method is less. Where the two lines intersect depends substantially on the initial cost of developing the synthetic times. This cost is largely a function of the time study information already available and the degree of job similarity for which times must be established. Whether this extra development expenditure should be made hinges on its size and the number of time standards the organization expects to set.

The procedures and some of the techniques used to develop standard data are close to those we encountered for forecasting. In estimating sales we looked for some relationship between past sales data and independent variables such as time. For task times we hypothesize the independent variables that will significantly affect the normal time for an operation. In both cases the next steps are to collect pertinent data and test the validity of the hypothesized relationships. Line fitting and correlation techniques are useful tools for processing the data.

The most common form of standard data is based on elemental times and takes the form

$$\text{normal time for task} = NT_1 + NT_2 + \cdots + NT_n$$

where NT_n = normal time for an element characteristic of the task. The equation is merely a summation of elemental times that correspond to the characteristics of the job. For instance, if a

Synthetic timing is best suited to production involving a few basic operations on products that vary in size or material rather than in design.

Figure 9.9 is a good illustration of possible temporal sub-optimization—not looking far enough into the future to substantiate a current expenditure.

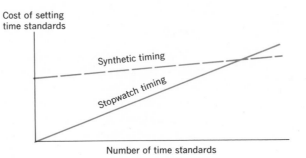

Figure 9.9 Cost relationship of setting time standards

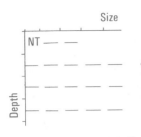

Element: "drill hole."

drilling operation is frequently encountered, a table of normal times indexed by different drill sizes versus the depth of the hole required could be developed. Whenever the element "drill hole" is obliged while synthesizing a task time, the appropriate normal time is extracted from the table according to the task characteristic of hole size and depth. This approach, using predetermined times for micromotions, is detailed in the next section.

Another method of obtaining synthetic times is to relate by formula the elemental normal times to a characteristic of the task:

$$\text{normal time for task} = fV_1 + fV_2 + \cdots + fV_n$$

where $fV_n = $ normal time expressed as a function of a characteristic task variable, V_n.

Normal times must be developed as a function of frequently encountered task characteristics before this method can be used. These times may already be available from earlier studies and need only be related to the desired variable. For instance, the element "paint" could be formulated as a function of the area to be painted. Least squares or another regression technique described in Sections 3-6 and 3-7 could be used to formulate the relationship. Supplementary time studies may be necessary if available records do not correspond to the desired range of the variable or if innovations are anticipated. Once the formulas are ready, normal times are calculated using only the magnitude of the task characteristic—pounds to lift, inches to drill, square feet to paint, number to load, miles to travel, etc.

Work elements of different classifications such as regular and irregular may bear different relationships to the same task characteristic.

Appropriate allowances are applied after the normal time computations to ascertain standard times. The synthesized times should be tested against the actual task times to confirm the hypothesized relationships. They should also be checked periodically or whenever design specifications are changed to reaffirm the validity of the parameters in the formula.

EXAMPLE 9.7 Synthetic Timing by Task Formula

Synthetic times are being developed for a warehouse facility. One operation involves transporting palleted loads from the receiving yard to the appropriate storage building. A single worker operating a lift truck is normally assigned to each shipment. A synthetic time formula is the preferred method to establish standard times for incentive pay because the number of pallets and the distance they must be moved are different for each shipment.

It is initially assumed that the time to transport a shipment will be a function of the size of the shipment and the distance from the receiving point to the storage point. The work elements composing the task are identified and classified as follows.

Element	Classification	Task Characteristic	Normal Time
1. Check-in shipment	Irregular-constant		12.30
2. Position truck	Regular-constant	Number of pallets	0.88 N
3. Pick up load	Regular-constant	Number of pallets	0.24 N
4. Transport load	Regular-variable	Travel distance	(chart)
5. Position truck	Regular-constant	Number of pallets	1.06 N
6. Deposit load	Regular-constant	Number of pallets	0.33 N
7. Return empty	Regular-variable	Travel distance	(chart)

The natural division of elements according to task characteristics takes the form

$$\text{Normal time} = f(\text{number of pallets}) + f(\text{travel distance}) + \text{constant}$$

Element 1, the storage assignment and check-in list for the shipment, occurs only once during the task and is therefore a constant in the formula: constant = 12.30 minutes. Elements 2, 3, 5, and 6 depend on the number of pallets to be moved, N: $f(\text{number}) = (0.88 + 0.24 + 1.06 + 0.33)N = 2.51N$. The relationship between normal travel time and distance is shown in Figure 9.10. Each dot represents a previous stopwatch time for a certain distance traveled. The lines are least square fits relating travel time, loaded and empty, to the distance moved, D: $f(\text{distance}) = (0.0016 + 0.0021)D$. Since this distance must be traversed for each pallet, total travel time is also a function of the number of pallets: $f(\text{total travel}) = 0.0037DN$, where D is the one-way distance and N is the number of pallet-trips. Combining the two functional relationships involving N and adding the constant term provide the complete formula:

$$\text{normal time} = (2.51 + 0.0037D)N + 12.30$$

The standard time for the job is calculated by applying an appropriate allowance to the normal time. If a 17% allowance is provided for personal time and unavoidable delays in loading and unloading, the task of transporting to storage a shipment of 10 pallets received at a dock 600 feet from the assigned warehouse has:

$$\text{standard time} = (\text{normal time})(\text{allowance factor})$$

$$= [(2.51 + 0.0037 \times 600)10 + 12.30](1.17)$$

$$\text{standard time} = 59.60 \times 1.17 = 70.73 \text{ minutes}$$

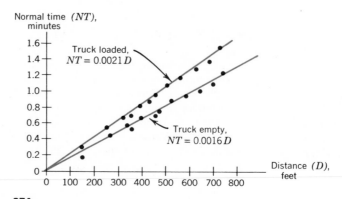

Figure 9.10

274

Predetermined Times

Predetermined times are tabulated values of normal times to complete basic motions. The tables are the outgrowth of thousands of individual motion time studies and include nearly all the movements required to synthesize any task. The concept of standardized data had been visualized since the time of Taylor and was inaugurated about 30 years ago. A large measure of its acceptance is due to the advantages previously mentioned for synthetic times: convenience and the opportunity to estimate times before an operation takes place. In addition, its use incorporates the attributes of:

Camera studies of factory operations were used extensively in developing predetermined times.

1. Eliminating the need for an observer to clock the manual movements of an operator, thereby avoiding distortions possible from observer bias.
2. Bestowing credence to task times by virtue of the very large samples from which the component times were developed.
3. Bypassing the troublesome performance rating factor by having the pace ratings already included in the tabulated values.

The application of predetermined times still requires judgment of task content and procedures, but it tends to be less obvious and thereby less objectionable to time study critics.

Groupings of predetermined time elements are useful in developing synthetic time formulas.

A decision to use predetermined times customarily entails the purchase of a packaged standard data program. The extremely high cost of developing time data has concentrated the effort to about half a dozen consulting firms that sell their system and services to practitioners. A typical program includes supplying the time data and training analysts in their use. Three of the more competitive time systems are Methods Time Measurement (MTM), Work Factor, and Basic Motion Timestudy (BMT).

Although all of the systems differ mildly in their basic motion categories, they follow rather closely the smaller work elements exhibited in Figure 9.6. Using MTM as an illustration, the nine basic tables of predetermined times are for "reach," "move," "turn and apply pressure," "grasp," "position," "release," "disengage," "eye travel and eye focus," and "body, leg, and foot motions." Each category is further refined by specific parameters. The MTM table for "reach," Table 9.2, defines three parameters:

Tables are available for grouped movements and for simplified applications where less detail is necessary.

1. Distance—the true path in inches travelled by the hand between two points.
2. Target—identification of the position and nature of five different objectives.

275

Table 9.2 Predetermined times
for the activity "reach"

Length of Reach in Inches	Time in TMU's*				Hand in Motion (TMU)		Case and Description
	Case A	Case B	Case C or D	Case E	A	B	
¾ or less	2.0	2.0	2.0	2.0	1.6	1.6	A—Reach to object in a fixed
1	2.5	2.5	3.6	2.4	2.3	2.3	location or to object in
2	4.0	4.0	5.9	3.8	3.5	2.7	other hand or on which the
3	5.3	5.3	7.3	5.3	4.5	3.6	other hand rests
4	6.1	6.4	8.4	6.8	4.9	4.3	
5	6.5	7.8	9.4	7.4	5.3	5.0	B—Reach to single object in
							location which may vary
6	7.0	8.6	10.1	8.0	5.7	5.7	slightly from cycle to cycle
7	7.4	9.3	10.8	8.7	6.1	6.5	
8	7.9	10.1	11.5	9.3	6.5	7.2	C—Reach to object jumbled
9	8.3	10.8	12.2	9.9	6.9	7.9	with other objects in a
10	8.7	11.5	12.9	10.5	7.3	8.6	group so that search and
							select occur
12	9.6	12.9	14.2	11.8	8.1	10.1	
14	10.5	14.4	15.6	13.0	8.9	11.5	D—Reach to a very small ob-
16	11.4	15.8	17.0	14.2	9.7	12.9	ject or where accurate
18	12.3	17.2	18.4	15.5	10.5	14.4	grasp is required
20	13.1	18.6	19.8	16.7	11.3	15.8	
							E—Reach to indefinite loca-
22	14.0	20.1	21.2	18.0	12.1	17.3	tion to get hand in position
24	14.9	21.5	22.5	19.2	12.9	18.8	for body balance, next mo-
26	15.8	22.9	23.9	20.4	13.7	20.2	tion, or out of way
28	16.7	24.4	25.3	21.7	14.5	21.7	
30	17.5	25.8	26.7	22.9	15.3	23.2	

*One time measurement unit (TMU) represents 0.00001 hour.

Motions are charted by symbols. An R12E symbol indicates a 12-inch hand movement from a rest position stopping at an indefinite spot.

3. Motion—the state of movement at the beginning and end of the reach.

● A task is recorded or synthesized by listing the constituent movements, extracting the appropriate table values, and summing the values to determine the normal time. Allowances are then applied as needed. At the core of this procedure there is still some question whether the basic motions are independent; if they are interdependent the sum of individual times could be misleading. Operationally it appears the time summations compare favorably with the overall validity of stopwatch studies.

Competency in application is a less academic but perhaps more practical problem. The process for determining task times may appear so simple that a beginner can get over-eager, overconfident, and overwhelmed. Blatant errors, such as failure to note that the limiting time for an operation requiring both hands is set by the hand used longest, can lead to loose standards. More subtle errors from overlooking or not recognizing the difficulty of motions produce tight standards. Quality training and thorough • familiarity with the tasks will reduce such errors of judgment and smooth the way toward the worker confidence that is vital to the acceptance of any method for setting standards.

Training tends to erode when one generation of time analysts trains the next generation. A basic MTM course consists of at least 100 hours.

9-6 WORK SAMPLING

L. H. C. Tippet pioneered the use of work sampling in the British textile industry in the 1930's.

Work sampling is a statistically based technique for analyzing work performance and machine utilization by direct observation but without a stopwatch. The analyst takes a relatively large • number of observations of a process at random intervals. Each observation is categorized as to the state of the process at the instant it is observed. In a machine utilization study, the categories could be "idle" and "working." Then the ratio of the times the machine was observed working to the total number of observations indicates the utilization of the machine.

The growing usage of work sampling stems from its advantages over conventional time study techniques for certain types of studies. It is particularly suitable for estimating unavoidable delays to establish delay allowances, for investigating the utilization of high investment assets, and for estimating the distribution of time spent by workers on different job activities. Such information is obtained by work sampling without continuous observation by an analyst. The observer arrives, determines the state of the process at a glance, checkmarks the state on a record sheet, and leaves. He does not disturb the process by long scrutiny periods, and the simple checking procedure diminishes the clerical time needed.

★ ★ ★ *Optional material.*

Sampling Theory

In a multiactivity study, each observation is in a binary state for every activity taken separately.

The whole concept of work sampling is based on the fundamental laws of probability. If we are dealing with an operation that can be in only two states (on or off, yes or no, working or idle), we know the percentage of time the two states can occur • must total to 100%. In terms of probabilities, we have the relationship expressed as

$$p + q = 1$$

277

where:

p = probability of a single observation in one state, say W for working

$q = (1 - p)$ = probability of no observation in state W

The relationship is extended to include n observations in the form

$$(p + q)^n = 1$$

where n = number of observations in the sample. This expression is expanded according to the binomial theorem to give the probability that a certain number of observations will be in state W out of a total of n observations.

The distribution of the probabilities resulting from the binomial expansion follows the binomial distribution. The mean of this distribution is equal to np and the standard deviation is equal to $\sqrt{npq}$. As n becomes large, the binominal distribution takes on the properties of the normal distribution. To use the normal approximation of the binomial distribution, we have to divide both the mean and standard deviation by the sample size:

$$\text{sample mean} = \frac{np}{n} = p$$

$$\text{sample standard deviation} = \frac{\sqrt{npq}}{n} = \sqrt{\frac{pq}{n}}$$

$$= \sqrt{\frac{p(1 - p)}{n}}$$

Relying on the normal distribution approximation, we can answer the common question plaguing time studies: How many observations should be made? The approach is identical to that employed for estimating the number of stopwatch observations needed, except we now use the sample standard deviation shown above. The selected k/s factor again sets the confidence measure that the true value of the mean falls within the range $p \pm sp$. Where N' is the number of observations taken to provide a sufficient sample for the management-defined k/s factor, we have

Shortcut methods for estimating N' include alignment charts, graphs, and tables.

$$N' = \left(\frac{k}{sp} \sqrt{p(1 - p)}\right)^2 = \left(\frac{k}{s}\right)^2 \left(\frac{1 - p}{p}\right)$$

To apply the equation for sample size, an estimate of p is required. This estimate can be derived from previous experience with the work being sampled, or a small preliminary sample, say 50 observations, can be taken for an initial indication. As a

more accurate estimation of p develops from additional observations, the equation can be solved again in terms of the new p to
reaffirm the required N'. When p measures the percentage of
time spent among several activities, the activity requiring the
• least time is utilized in the equation; using the activity with the
smallest p assures the most conservative (largest) value of N'.

Using the smallest value of p is in the same vein as using the element with the greatest range of times to calculate N'.

Work Sampling Procedures

In addition to the number of observations taken, the accuracy
of a work sampling study depends on the randomness of the
sampling and how well each state of the work is defined. Sampling
is effective only if every moment of time has an equal chance of
being selected as the occasion for an observation. An easy
• method of assuring randomness is to use a *random number table—*
a listing of numbers that follows no pattern or discernible order.
The period available for the study is divided into numbered
increments such as the number of minutes in a working day, 1
through 480. Each increment can be associated with a two-digit
random number. The range of the random numbers that indicates
a time increment in which an observation is to take place corresponds to the percentage of increments that will be utilized.
• For instance, if we wish to sample 400 out of 4000 minutes
available (10% of the 1-minute increments), the range of random
numbers is 10. Letting numbers 90 through 99 represent the
range, we look through 4000 random numbers corresponding to
4000 successive increments and schedule an observation whenever
the digits 90–99 appear.

A table of random numbers is in Appendix D.

A faster method of scheduling observations is to decide how many will be taken and then to enter a random number table, letting each three-digit sequence set an hour (first digit) and minutes (two other digits) for each observation. Impossible times are ignored.

Descriptions of each state of interest for the work must be
definitive enough to allow the observer to make a classification.
Better descriptions require less judgment. A study of whether a
machine is idle or working is relatively simple because each
state is quite apparent without judgment. However, a similar
study of whether a man is idle or working is far from simple.
Is he working if he is talking to his foreman? Is he idle when he is
leaning back in apparent thought? Such questions must be
faced and overcome by ground rules.

EXAMPLE 9.8 Work Sampling to Review Unavoidable Delay Allowances

The present delay allowance of 9% for assemblers in the capacitor plant is being reviewed.
Management feels the allowance is too high because it is based on conditions 4 years ago.
Many improvements have been made since then. The review is to be made by work sampling.
About 300 women work on capacitors. Those working on soldering and winding are paid on an
incentive plan.

The work is divided into three states : (1) idle owing to unavoidable delays, (2) idle for any reason other than unavoidable delay, and (3) working. For the study, an unavoidable delay is identified by the following conditions:

1. Conversation with a supervisor at the work station.
2. Lack of material as apparent from empty in-trays and a signal for service.
3. Equipment maintenance or repair indicated by a signal for service or the presence of repair personnel.
4. General disruption of service as evidenced by all workers being idle.

A "working" state occurs whenever an assembler is at her work station, even if she is apparently relaxing or gossiping with a coworker. Any activity not falling into the "working" or "unavoidable delay" states is classified as "unaccounted for" time. This category includes personal, fatigue, and special allowances.

A tally sheet is developed for recording observations. Then the observers have several practice rounds with a supervisor to become thoroughly familiar with the work state descriptions in relation to the postures of the workers. Observations are taken from a balcony on one side of the work area. The specific women to be observed are chosen randomly.

Management wants the study completed in 2 weeks. The standard study design has a 10% precision at a confidence level of 95%. The current allowance, 9%, is used to determine the approximate number of observations needed:

$$N' = \left(\frac{2}{0.10}\right)^2 \left(\frac{1 - 0.09}{0.09}\right) = (20)^2 \left(\frac{0.91}{0.09}\right) = 4000 + \text{observations}$$

Based on this estimate, 45 observations of 10 workers per observation are taken each day. A different schedule for the observations is made every day by reference to a random number table. The chance that workers will anticipate the observations is further reduced by randomizing the order in which individuals are checked each observation trip.

After 4500 observations, the totals for the three states show the following proportions:

States	Observations	Percentages
Unavoidable delay	354	8.8
Unaccounted for time	316	7.0
Working time	3830	84.2
Totals	4500	100.0

The number of observations is again checked for the key statistic, unavoidable delay:

$$N' = (20)^2 \left(\frac{1 - 0.088}{0.088}\right) = 4160 \text{ observations}$$

With the adequacy of the total established for the main state, it is of interest to know if the other states meet the study standards. The "working" state obviously meets the standard, but the smaller "unaccounted for" category is questionable. It is checked by rearranging the N' equation:

$$s = k \sqrt{\frac{1 - p}{p \times n}} \qquad \text{where } n = \text{actual number of observations taken of the state with percentage } p$$

$$s = 2 \sqrt{\frac{1 - 0.07}{0.07 \times 4500}} = 2 \sqrt{\frac{0.93}{315}}$$

$$s = 2 \times 0.055 = 0.11 \text{ or } 11\%$$

Thus the present unavoidable delay allowance appears about right, and management is in position to question the adequacy of other allowances.

Work Sampling Applications

Work sampling studies are highly susceptible to the "get it done yesterday" attitude. The sense of urgency that often accompanies a decision to finally undertake a study might tempt the study designer to meet the N' criterion by compressing all the observations into a single day. If enough observers were available, the study could be completed in a day; but the results would probably be misleading unless the chosen day was truly representative. The advantage of spreading observations over several days is that the effects of unusual or intermittent conditions are included without monopolizing results. A study of absenteeism would show alarming dimensions if it was conducted only on days preceding holidays; such days are only part of the overall pattern and should contribute just a proportionate influence.

It is necessary to consider the route an observer must take when his daily rounds are scheduled. A single observation is a "snap reading," but it may take considerable time to reach the point where it can be made. Time should also be allotted for the observer to judge activities, if there is a choice of several states, and to record various entries when crews are being sampled.

Control charts are useful aids when work sampling is applied to check continually an activity of particular concern. The charts portray the successive percentages obtained from sampling as a function of time. The pattern formed by the plotted points gives an indication of the trend. An "out of control" condition is conventionally indicated by values outside a three standard deviation "control limit." The limit is calculated as:

Control charting is discussed in Chapter 14.

$$\text{control limits} = \bar{p} \pm 3 \text{ standard deviations}$$

where $\bar{p} = $ average percentage obtained from periodic samples

$$\text{control limits} = \bar{p} \pm 3\sqrt{\frac{\bar{p}(1 - \bar{p})}{n}}$$

where $n = $ number of observations in each periodic sample.

A typical control chart format is shown in Figure 9.11. The value of $\bar{p}$ is based on the first 10 samples shown in Table 9.3. To set the table in perspective, assume 50 observations are taken daily of the time maintenance crews spend in Department A. The purpose of the study is to settle a dispute over the cost allocation of maintenance expense.

281

Table 9.3 p values for samples of 50 observations each

Proportion of Time Maintenance Crews Spend in Department A					
Day	p	Day	p	Day	p
1	0.16	6	0.16	11	0.15
2	0.14	7	0.18	12	0.16
3	0.13	8	0.15	13	0.18
4	0.17	9	0.15	14	0.19
5	0.17	10*	0.14	15	0.32

*0.153 = average sample for days 1–10

Based on $\bar{p} = 0.153$, the control limits are calculated as:

$$\text{upper control limit} = 0.153 + 3\sqrt{\frac{0.153(1 - 0.153)}{50}}$$

$$= 0.153 + 3 \times 0.0509$$

$$= 0.153 + 0.153 = 0.306$$

$$\text{lower control limit} = 0.153 - 0.153 = 0$$

The limits so calculated should contain 997 out of 1000 sample

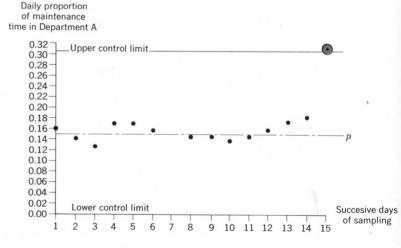

Figure 9.11 Control chart for successive samples, 50 observations each, taken of the presence of maintenance crews in Department A

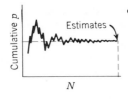

A chart of the cumulative proportions similar to Figure 9.11 can be used to estimate $\bar{p}$ and N'. The estimates are taken when the line connecting the cumulative p values stabilizes as shown above.

proportions so long as the mean of the samples remains as first computed. The first 14 samples are well within the limits. The last sample, above the upper control limit, can be attributed to one of three causes: (1) it is 1 of the 3 cases per 1000 that a point falls outside the limits by chance alone, (2) there is an assignable reason for its magnitude, or (3) it represents a new condition where $\bar{p} = 0.153$ no longer represents the mean.

The immediate consequence of a point outside the control limits is an investigation. If an assignable cause is found for the maverick point, it should be excluded from the other data, and an additional sample should be taken if necessary for the desired accuracy. The trend of the plotted points serves as a warning of potential change in $\bar{p}$.

Aside from the psychological aspects of observing and being observed, the application of work sampling for time studies is a matter of money. Observers for work sampling do not need the costly training required for a good stopwatch or predetermined time analyst. However, any rating factors applied by semitrained observers should be suspect. It is difficult and expensive to apply these other timing techniques to nonrepetitive work or where behavior over a long period is sought. The same cost and convenience factors go against using work sampling for a single worker or for micromotion studies.

Each time study technique has its own advantages and disadvantages. The choice of one over the others relies on the familiar strategy of fitting the techniques to the occasion. It is easy to become enamored with a "progressive" management tool. The temptation is to fit the occasion to the tool and hope some progressiveness rubs off on the user. Such hopes of second-hand prestige appear petty when compared to the possible system cost of myopic malfeasance.

★ ★ ★ *End optional material.*

9-7 WAGE PAYMENTS The study of work measurement inevitably leads to wage payments. In theory at least, wages paid to a worker are a measurement of the amount he does. In the relatively rare instances where pay is directly proportional to the pieces produced, money is a lineal measure of work. For most industries where wages are a function of an employment period, the relationship is obscure. Then why go to all the bother of measuring work if the wages paid for its accomplishment are so nebulously related? Although it has "cart before the horse" aspects, one reason is to find out how much is accomplished by a traditional pay scale. This information is necessary for cost accounting and provides a yardstick of job performance for wage adjustments. Another reason is the attention devoted to element and task analysis tends to define responsibilities and to make better use of workers' time.

Improving the method by which work is done increases effective motivation without changing wages. It lowers the resistance to effort by making a task easier to perform.

Wages are supposed to increase effective motivation. We observed in Section 7-5 that effective motivation is the difference between want strength and resistance to effort. Wages do not directly affect either want strength or effort resistance. They contribute to want satisfaction as the conversion factor between effort expended and want rewards. The equity of this conversion is a personal judgment by the worker. It is taken in context of the standard of living he aspires to, the overall impression of his job, and his position in relation to coworkers.

The employer also has a complicated framework by which to judge wages. His basic objectives are to produce a competitive product and to secure a reasonable return. Higher wages paid for production either detract from competitiveness or decrease return. Both reactions have serious long-range consequences. Loss of competitiveness means cutbacks with a subsequent worsening of the wage output ratio. A lower return has the chain reaction of blocking expansion, loss of investor confidence, and higher interest rates for loans. Lower wages make it difficult for the employer to secure skilled craftsmen and competent managers vital to a competitive position. Decreasing wages obviously discourages motivation, increases turnover which raises training costs, and may even increase unit labor costs.

"Labor is prior to, and independent of, capital. Capital is only the fruit of labor, and could never have existed if labor had not first existed." Abraham Lincoln, 1861.

Somewhere between the two unattractive extremes is a wage level neither too high nor too low. To discover this point once is difficult. To maintain it requires an ear sensitive to labor demands, an eye to the future, and a delicate touch on the pulse of changing economic conditions.

Wage policies are burdened by accepted wage variances between types of industries, geographical areas, and even companies within the same industry and region. Some degree of consistency is introduced by "industry averages," "geographical averages," and standard classification systems such as "grade definitions" of the U.S. Civil Service. National yardsticks such as the "cost of living" index help relate geographical wage differences to the common denominator of buying power. Internal company wage frictions are considerably reduced by carefully designed incentive wage plans and by objectivity in job evaluations.

Minimum wage laws create a floor from which all wage policies build.

Wage Incentive Plans

Incentive wages are intended to increase a worker's motivation by letting him earn proportionately higher returns from greater effort. Historically, incentive plans were part of the scientific management movement at the turn of this century. Attention was focused on questions of profit sharing, work divisions, and financial incentives for factory operations. A major accomplishment of the movement was the recognition given to the establishment of a standard rate of work for a job as a critical component of all incentive plans. The importance of realistic and acceptable standards developed by work measurement techniques becomes very apparent when the different plans are considered.

Straight piece-rate. The most direct incentive plan is a straight piece-rate scale—payment at a constant amount per unit of output. Payments are calculated from an equation based on hourly rates as

$$E = R_h\left(\frac{A}{T}\right)$$

where:

E = earnings in dollars per hour
R_h = hourly rate in dollars per hour
T = time taken per piece produced
A = time allowed or standard time per piece

or from the product of output times payment per piece as

$$E = R_p O$$

where:

R_p = piece rate in dollars per unit
O = output in pieces per hour

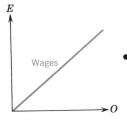

Straight piece-rate wages.

Harvest workers and many types of contract labor are paid by this method. It is easy to understand and apply. If R_h or R_p are high enough to assure the average worker an equitable wage for his normal output, it can inspire greater effort. Conversely, it can discourage a worker if he feels he can never achieve a level compatible with his wants.

Piece-rate with a guaranteed base. A piece-rate plan is made more socially and motivationally acceptable by placing a minimum level on the amount earned. The manner in which

285

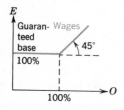

One-for-one incentive plan for output above 100%.

incentives are added to the minimum is the subject of numerous proposals.

The basic "one-for-one" plan has a set wage for production up to a level designated 100%—a normal day's work determined from production standards set by work measurement. Beyond the 100% level, a worker is paid an additional 1% of his base pay for each 1% he exceeds the normal standard. For example, if the standard rate of output is 10 (100% level) pieces per hour and an operator produces 96 pieces during an 8-hour day, his base pay for the day is increased by the fraction

$$\frac{\text{actual production} = 96 \text{ pieces}}{\text{standard production} = 10 \times 8 = 80 \text{ pieces}} = \frac{6}{5} = 120\%$$

Assuming an hourly base pay of $2.00, the result of bettering the standard by 20% increases the pay per hour to $2.00 × $\frac{6}{5}$ = $2.40. If the same operator produces only 75 pieces the following day, his hourly rate for the day would be $2.00 owing to his guaranteed minimum. That this payment plan is just a delayed action straight piece-rate scale is apparent from the equations for calculating earnings:

$$E = R_h \qquad \text{when } T \geq A$$

$$E = R_h \left(\frac{A}{T}\right) \quad \text{when } T \leq A$$

Modifications of this method vary the point at which the incentives start and vary the percentage received by the worker for production over the output corresponding to the guaranteed base. Three representative versions are described below and pictured in the margin notes.

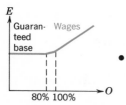

Two-stage incentive rates starting at 80%.

1. *Shortened-base incentive*—By starting incentives at less than the 100% standard, some low production workers may be encouraged to reach the output level where incentives begin. This condition is especially applicable during the installation of new pay plans and during the training or retraining periods for new workers. The incentives that apply between the shortened base and 100% are usually less than the rates for outputs above 100%.

2. *Profit-sharing incentive*—This plan is similar to the basic one-for-one plan, except the reward for output above 100% is shared with the employer. The basic equation for earnings is

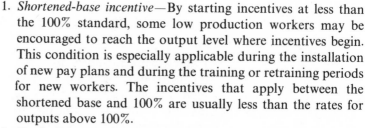

$$E = R_h \left[1 + P\left(\frac{A}{T} - 1\right)\right]$$

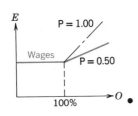

Profit sharing at $P = 0.50$
compared to a one-for-one
plan.

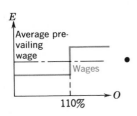

Original step incentive plan.

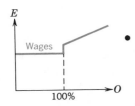

Modern step incentive plan
for meeting 100%.

where P = proportion of reward above 100% output paid to worker

A "50-50" plan ($P = 0.50$) would increase the base rate by $\frac{1}{2}\%$ for every 1% increase in output over the standard. Other versions of this basic plan vary P as a function of output increments above 100%. For instance, P could be 0.50 for output from 100% to 120% and 0.75 above 120%. Note that when $P = 1$, the one-for-one plan is in effect; when $P = 0$, the incentive reverts to a straight hourly wage.

3. *Step incentive*—The use of a single bonus for meeting an output level set at or above the 100% standard dates back to the earliest incentive proposals. Although it is not too common today, it presents an interesting concept. The guaranteed base is pegged below the prevailing average wage. When output reaches a certain level, say 110%, the rate jumps to a level well above the average wage. The net effect of this plan is to reward exceptional workers and discourage others. In line with the mechanistic thinking prevalent during the period this plan was developed, workers that did not meet the bonus criterion were supposed to be shamed into seeking employment elsewhere. Then only the "best" workers would be left. The modern version tends toward the usual guaranteed base with provisions for an immediate reward for making the 100% standard and a profit-sharing incentive beyond.

Other incentive plans. Most incentive plans are linked to individual units of output. When output is difficult to measure or is an inappropriate measure, other bases are used. Incentives can be based on the percent of rejects "saved" below a nominal standard, the amount of scrap reduction, the percentage utilization of machines, or combinations of similar factors. Attempts to include supervisors in incentive programs usually provide a percentage bonus based on improvements in crew or departmental ratings as judged by measurement of scrap, spoilage, delays, etc.

Evaluation of incentives. Most trade unions have opposed incentive plans for wage payment at some point in their history. Today, the majority opinion is still negative, but there is wider acceptance that workers can be adequately protected by collective bargaining while incentives are in effect. The hourly base rather than a per piece base and the guaranteed minimum make incentives more palatable to organized labor.

287

The following advantages and disadvantages apply generally to all incentive plans as compared to time-based wages:

1. Labor costs per unit can be estimated more accurately.
2. Less supervision is needed to keep output up to a reasonable level.
3. Work studies associated with incentives stimulate method improvements.
4. Quality and safety may suffer when workers work too fast to achieve bonus rates.
5. Payment by results may lead to opposition or restriction of output when new machines, materials, or methods are proposed.
6. Clerical work is increased.

Wages Set by Job Evaluation

Wage payments based on time are far more common than payments based on output. Time scales may be short-term hourly rates or long-term salaries. From quality, convenience, record-keeping, and labor relations viewpoints, a time-based system is preferred to an output system. The most serious drawback of a time wage is the difficulty of determining wage plans and levels that accurately reward workers for work performed. Since there are no precise standards of performance, a superior level of execution is largely a subjective judgment over which the worker has little control.

Motivationally, time wages are at a disadvantage because rewards for better performances are cumulative and delayed. The annual raise is seldom inspirational.

The purpose of job evaluation is to establish base rates for incentive plans and hourly rates for time-based wages. The general guidelines are easy to identify; more difficult and responsible jobs manned by more scarce and skillful personnel should be paid more. Getting these generalities down to dollar and cents realities is not so easy. Some evaluation methods are described in the following paragraphs.

Job ranking of occupations within a company is the simplest method of evaluation. It is based on the logical assumption that wages should be proportionate to the importance of the job to the company's welfare. An evaluation is conducted by having a committee rank jobs according to duties and responsibilities. Then rates for the key jobs are decided upon; other job rates are determined from interpolation between wages for the key jobs. The simplicity of the system is its undoing. It presupposes the rankers have unlimited familiarity with all the jobs and insert no bias in their appraisals.

Figure 9.12 illustrates key-job interpolation.

The *classification* method improves on job ranking by estab-

288

The U.S. Civil Service modifies its classification system by using points to assign grade numbers for certain occupations.

The *factor comparison* method is similar to point plans. Dollar values replace points to rate basic job requirements such as: (1) mental, (2) skill, (3) physical, (4) responsibility, and (5) working conditions.

A χ^2 test and other statistical techniques (Chapter 15) are useful for classifying personnel by the point plan.

lishing predetermined labor classifications. The widest application is found in federal classifications for civil service and military ranks. The hitch in application comes when jobs are fitted into the broad classifications. The questionable attribute of committee agreement on ranking is often utilized. On the positive side, the classification system allows a range of pay within each category to reflect merit ratings of employees. This range also provides flexibility in recruiting and reranking when a particularly fine performance or an initial placement error is recognized.

A *point plan* injects objectivity into job evaluation by assigning points to the qualifications needed to perform a job. It is the most complex and widely used of all evaluation methods. Factors common to most jobs in an organization are determined first. A typical number is from 8 to 12. Four large categories and 11 subfactors used by the National Metal Trades Association are shown in Table 9.4.

After the appropriate factors are selected and completely described, preferably with examples, the points corresponding to each degree of the factors are assigned. Then the points associated with key jobs in the company are developed by reference to appropriate degree points for each factor. A plot of the key-job totals versus the prevailing wages for the respective jobs gives a framework for pegging wages for other job point

Table 9.4 Points assigned to factor degrees for job evaluation

Factors	Degrees				
	1st	2nd	3rd	4th	5th
Skill:					
1. Education	14	28	42	56	70
2. Experience	22	44	66	88	110
3. Initiative and ingenuity	14	28	42	56	70
Effort:					
4. Physical demand	10	20	30	40	50
5. Mental and visual demand	5	10	15	20	25
Responsibility:					
6. Equipment or process	5	10	15	20	25
7. Material or product	5	10	15	20	25
8. Safety of others	5	10	15	20	25
9. Work of others	5	10	15	20	25
Job conditions:					
10. Working conditions	10	20	30	40	50
11. Hazards	5	10	15	20	25

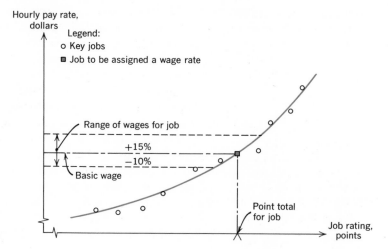

Figure 9.12 Key-job concept for assigning wage rates by inter- polation

totals. Figure 9.12 shows a line fitted to the scattergram of key-job points versus wage data and an interpolated job wage.

Details of many different wage plans and their administration are available in several references at the end of this chapter.

The administration of wage plans should be considered during the job evaluation stage. For instance, when a point plan is being initiated, there are bound to be some workers that are currently underpaid or overpaid as indexed by the point totals for their jobs. This condition is normally anticipated by allowing rates to vary in a range of perhaps 15% above the indicated wage and 10% below (Figure 9.12). But what about the workers still outside the range? Adjustments upward to the lower edge of the range present no problem. But the instigation of wage cuts, however well justified by theory, creates hostility. A compromise to avoid undermining the entire program allows exceptional wage rates to exist until their bearers leave the jobs by turnover or retraining. The need for this action should be anticipated when wage plans are developed.

Periodic, broad-scale wage hikes frequently result from negotiated labor contracts. Over a period of years these hikes can seriously distort a wage payment plan unless delicate adjustments are made. A "flat increase," the same amount given to all workers regardless of the jobs they hold, reduces the percentage differential between wages of different job classifica- tions. Then a promotion tends to take the form of a new title instead of more money. When an "across the board" percentage increase is applied, the wage differential is exaggerated in the other direction. A wage settlement that grants wage increases commensurate with point totals would be more difficult to

290

negotiate but would maintain the character of the established wage policy.

The very personal nature of any wage plan reinforces the need for objectivity in evaluation and openness in application. In the early stages of incentive plans, it was considered an attribute to have complicated formulas for wages. Still, workers found ways to decipher the confusion factors. The sociological structure today has no room for such chicanery. There is enough dissatisfaction about the fairness of individual wages, whether justified or not, without hiding the standards of evaluation. Since wages are increasingly settled in a political arena, the best advice could be President Lincoln's:

If you once forfeit the confidence of your fellow citizens, you can never regain their respect and esteem. It is true that you may fool all the people some of the time; you can even fool some of the people all the time, but you can't fool all of the people all the time.

9-8 SUMMARY The objective of a process analysis is to improve the sequence or content of the operations required to complete a task. A pre-investigation indicates which areas will benefit most from the analysis. Fact finding is done mostly by observation and interviewing. The analyst improves a process by seeking ways of eliminating, combining, and rearranging operations.

Method improvement information is often displayed on charts. Survey charting records present procedures, design charting develops innovations, and presentation charts explain proposals to help them be accepted. Process charts employ symbols for: operation (◯), transportation (⇨), inspection (☐), delay (D), and storage (▽) to portray the flow of activities concerning an operator or a product. Man-machine charts aid the visualization of dependent relationships between men and machines; an economic balance is sought for the idle time of men versus idle machines.

Motion studies attempt to make work performance easier and more productive by improving manual motions. Principles of better motions serve as reminders for evaluating an operation. Evaluations can be conducted by camera studies using high camera speeds for micromotion and slow speeds for memomotion studies. A cyclegraph study records on a single time exposure the movements of an operator as evidenced by lights attached to his limbs. Motions are charted using "get and place" elements for longer cycles or more detailed elements for "microscopic"

291

analyses of very short cycles. The elements are displayed in Left-hand Right-hand and SIMO charts.

Work simplification programs are designed to provide a team approach to deliberate method change. A job enlargement program expands the responsibilities and activities required of a worker in the belief that more comprehensive work is more interesting work.

A time study often follows a method change. The work elements identified in the preliminary methods study are categorized according to their cyclic characteristics of regular or irregular, constant or variable, machine or operator controlled, and foreign. The two most common stopwatch timing techniques are: (1) snap-back—sweep hand snaps back to zero after each element is timed, and (2) continuous—watch runs without interruption during the entire observation period.

Selected times for work elements are the averages of representative observations. The number of observations required for a given confidence-precision level (k/s factor) is determined from the equation

$$N' = \left(\frac{k/s\sqrt{N\sum X^2 - (\sum X)^2}}{\sum X}\right)^2$$

where:

X = representative element times
N = number of representative element times

A rating factor applied to a selected element time yields normal time. The purpose of applying a rating factor is to normalize the observed operator's tempo to a pace that can be attained and maintained by an average worker without undue fatigue during a typical working day. An operator working above this pace would have a rating factor greater than 1.0.

Standard times are secured by applying an allowance factor to the normal times. Personal, fatigue, delay, and special allowances are totalled to set the allowance factor. Different sequences leading to standard times are shown below:

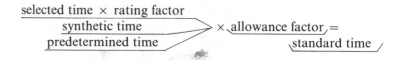

selected time × rating factor
synthetic time
predetermined time
× allowance factor =
standard time

Synthetic timing incorporates the characteristics of an operation or product in an equation to provide the normal time for a task. It is appropriate for frequently encountered tasks and allows times to be calculated before a process is actually in operation.

Predetermined times utilize tabulated values of normal times for very small motion elements. Task times are synthesized from the individual times of component micromotions. The technique can be used in place of stopwatch timing and in conjunction with synthetic timing.

Work sampling, based on the fundamental laws of probability, employs a large number of observations to determine the percentage of time a process is in a certain state. The number of samples needed to meet a selected k/s level is calculated from

$$N' = \left(\frac{k}{s}\right)^2 \left(\frac{1 - p}{p}\right)$$

where p = sample mean of the probability that the process is in a given state. A schedule of observations is developed by reference to a random number table to help assure the representativeness of a sample. Control charts based on

$$\text{control limits} = \bar{p} \pm 3\sqrt{\frac{\bar{p}(1 - \bar{p})}{n}}$$

where:

$\bar{p}$ = average probability obtained from periodic samples
n = number of observations in each sample

provide a warning for developing state changes in a process. A point outside the limits is an alarm for investigation.

Wage incentive plans are designed to increase a worker's motivation by letting him earn proportionately higher returns from greater effort. On a straight piece-rate plan, earnings are directly proportional to output. Piece-rates are often modified to provide a guaranteed minimum wage with a fractional bonus per piece added for production beyond a certain level. A step incentive introduces a one-shot bonus for reaching a specified output. Other incentive plans combine the above features or are linked to a desired function other than output. In general, time-based wage plans are preferred to incentive plans from considerations of quality, convenience, recordkeeping, and labor relations.

Job evaluation methods are required to establish base rates for both incentive plans and hourly wages of time-based plans. Job-ranking is a simple approach which relates wages to the importance of the jobs in a company. An industrywide classification method improves on job ranking through predetermined

293

labor classifications with associated wage ranges by which jobs can be categorized. A point plan is most widely used by industry. It identifies the main factors that contribute to job performance and assigns points to degrees of quality for each factor. Points for key jobs are related to wages. Then the base rates for other point totals are set by interpolation from key-job versus wage relationships.

The kinship among methods analyses, time measurement objectives and techniques, and wage payment is depicted in Figure 9.13.

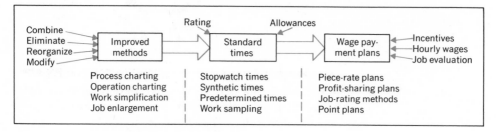

Figure 9.13 Tools and techniques of work design

9-9 REFERENCES

Backman, J., *Wage Determination: An Analysis of Wage Criteria*, Van Nostrand, Princeton, N.J., 1960.

Barnes, R. M., *Motion and Time Study* (6th ed.), John Wiley, New York, 1968.
———, *Work Sampling* (2nd ed.), John Wiley, New York, 1957.

Belcher, D. W., *Wage and Salary Administration*, Prentice-Hall, Englewood Cliffs, N.J., 1955.

Brennan, C. W., *Wage Administration*, Richard D. Irwin, Homewood, Ill., 1959.

Carroll, P., *Better Wage Incentives*, McGraw-Hill, New York, 1957.

Cartter, A., *Theory of Wages and Employment*, Richard D. Irwin, Homewood, Ill., 1959.

Eliot, J., *Equitable Payment*, John Wiley, New York, 1961.

Gantt, H. L., *Work, Wages and Profits*, Engineering Management, New York, 1913.

Gilbreth, F. B. and L. M. Gilbreth, *Fatigue Study* (2nd ed.), Macmillan, New York, 1919.

Gomberg, W., *A Trade Union Analysis of Time Study* (2nd ed.), Prentice-Hall, Englewood Cliffs, N.J., 1955.

Hansen, B. L., *Work Sampling: For Modern Management*, Prentice-Hall, Englewood Cliffs, N.J., 1960.

Johnson, F. H., *Job Evaluation*, John Wiley, New York, 1949.

Krick, E. V., *Methods Engineering*, John Wiley, New York, 1962.

Lantham, E., *Job Evaluation*, McGraw-Hill, New York, 1955.

Lovejoy, L. C., *Wage and Salary Administration*, Ronald Press, New York, 1959.

Maynard, H. B. and G. J. Stegemerten, *Guide to Methods Improvement*, McGraw-Hill, New York, 1944.

Maynard, H. B., G. J. Stegemerten, and J. L. Schwab, *Methods-Time Measurement*, McGraw-Hill, New York, 1948.

Mundel, M. E., *Motion and Time Study* (3rd ed.), Prentice-Hall, Englewood Cliffs, N.J., 1960.

Nadler, G., *Work Design*, Richard D. Irwin, Homewood, Ill., 1963.

Neibel, B. W., *Motion and Time Study*, Richard D. Irwin, Homewood, Ill., 1962.

Patton, J. A., C. L. Littlefield, and S. A. Self, *Job Evaluation, Text and Cases*, Richard D. Irwin, Homewood, Ill., 1964.

Presgrave, R. and G. B. Bailey, *Basic Motion Timestudy*, McGraw-Hill, New York, 1957.

Quick, J. H., J. H. Duncan, and J. A. Malcolm, *Work-Factor Time Standards*, McGraw-Hill, New York, 1962.

Whisler, T. L. and S. F. Harper, *Performance Appraisal*, Holt, Rinehart and Winston, New York, 1962.

9-10 QUESTIONS AND PROBLEMS

1. Why would early training in methods analysis and work measurement benefit someone interested in ultimately pursuing the following careers?

(a) Sales.
(b) Accounting.
(c) Industrial engineering.
(d) Industrial relations.
(e) Production manager.
(f) Research.
(g) Advertising.
(h) Purchasing.

2. Substantiate or refute the statement: "Methods and measurement are the wellspring of labor peace, product competitiveness, and customer satisfaction."

3. Explain how each of the following diagrams could be used to fulfill two or more of the basic purposes of charting:

(a) Architectural drawing.
(b) Pie chart.
(c) Wiring diagram.
(d) Bar chart.
(e) Histogram.
(f) Road map.

4. What factors affect a decision to make a macromotion or a micromotion analysis?

5. How does the principle of "diminishing returns" apply to motion studies?

6. What general categories of operations are appropriate for camera studies made at 1000 frames per minute and at 1 frame per minute?

7. Some unions require their permission before camera studies can be conducted in a plant. What do you think might have caused this condition? Why does it still exist?

8. How could micromotion studies be useful for training new workers?

9. Why are delays ($\square$) sometimes subdivided into avoidable

and unavoidable delays? Give an example of each as it might apply to an assembly operation.

10. When representatives of the Westinghouse Corporation approached Commodore Vanderbilt about an air brake, he stated: "I have no time to listen to fools who want to blow air on wheels to stop trains." How would this attitude at the top, middle, and lower levels of management affect a work simplification program?

11. Why is continuous timing generally preferred to snap-back timing?

12. Name and describe seven general classifications of work elements. How does recognition of the classifications aid a time analyst in breaking an operation into its component parts? Classify each work element in Example 9.5.

13. Defend or rebut the following statements:

M. K. Starr,
*Production Management:
Systems and Synthesis,* ●
Prentice Hall, Englewood Cliffs,
N.J., 1964.

(a) "We will not bandy words. Time study permits a meaningful *rough* fix to be made on the system's manpower output and costs. However, because leveling must be used, real precision can never be obtained."

E. V. Krick, *Methods
Engineering.* ●

(b) "A time study is often conducted in such a manner as to substantiate an answer that the time study man arrived at before starting to time the operator in question, as the result of experience on his part or of his taking desired take-home pay into account."

W. Gomberg, *A Trade Union
Analysis of Time Study.* ●

(c) "Other engineers may have their problems, but nothing like these. If the civil engineer wants to understand what it's like to be a time-study engineer, let him visualize a dark, eerie Halloween night on which spirits, animate and inanimate, are abroad. Along comes the bridge, which is his pride and joy, spanning a majestic river and it addresses him in these accents, 'Hey, jerk, do you know that I could have remained standing and carried just as big a load if you used one-quarter the tonnage of steel that my poor piles must hold up?' This is just an everyday experience for the time-study man."

14. Why is it so difficult for all industries to agree on a universal conception of "normal performance?"

15. How does the practice of including allowances as part of the standard time for an operation promote "effective motivation"?

16. What is the reasoning behind providing special allowances for operators paid on incentive plans when their operations are process or machine controlled?

17. What are the principal advantages and disadvantages of synthetic timing?

18. What measures can be taken to assure representative work samples?

19. Binomial theory allows only one event to either occur or not occur. Is this premise violated by the use of work sampling to determine the percentage of time a worker spends on each of several activities required in his job? Why?

20. Why should an "out of control" sample be eliminated from the circulation of $\bar{p}$ after an assignable cause for its occurrence has been found?

21. Describe the effect on: (1) wages received by the worker and (2) the direct labor cost for the units being produced when output increases above the 100% standard using each of the following wage plans:
   (a) Straight piece-rate.
   (b) One-for-one plan with a guaranteed 100% base.
   (c) Profit-sharing plan where $P = 0.40$ after 100% output.
   (d) Step incentive of 5% followed by a "50-50" plan at and above the 100% standard.
   (e) Hourly wage.

22. Some jobs defy time measurements. Tasks requiring mostly mental effort are normally paid on a time system such as a salary per month. What would be the advantages and disadvantages associated with an incentive plan for such jobs? Is there any reasonable way such jobs could be put on an incentive basis?

23. Why are time-based wages often paid weekly when it would be more economical for a company to issue paychecks only once a month?

24. A "rate buster" is an individual who works at an exceptional pace. When incentive pay is involved, this individual receives very high wages compared to other workers because his output is far above the average on which the incentives are based. He is frequently unpopular with the other workers who feel that standards will be raised by management when it is observed how much the rate buster earns.
   (a) Comment on the validity of the workers' concern about standards being raised.
   (b) Should management encourage the rate buster as a good example or should he be discouraged in order to reduce conflict among the other workers?

25. Do you think the original version of the step incentive wage plan would work today? Why?

26. Within the context of motivation, discuss the relationship of work measurement, methods analysis, incentive plans, and hourly wages.

27. Construct an operator process chart using the format shown in Example 9.1 to depict the sequence of operations required to change the front tire on an automobile. First indicate the way you would presently change a tire. Then analyze the chart to see if you can determine a better way to do it.

28. Develop a process chart to:

(a) Show how a page should be inserted in a typewriter when three carbon copies are required. Start the task by securing the paper and carbons from a desk drawer.

(b) Water a lawn when the hose and sprinkler must be removed from a garden house before being attached to a water outlet. Use a layout diagram.

29. The three projects listed below have been submitted to the methods staff as possible study areas.

Study	Estimated Annual Savings	Estimated Study and Implementation Cost	Probability of Implementation
A	$3300	$600	0.80
B	$6500	$1000	0.70
C	$9000	$1900	0.90

According to the rating factor formula of Section 9-2, which project should receive first attention? What other considerations should influence the choice?

30. Draw a man-machine chart to check the solution to the problem posed in Example 9.2.

31. A large number of semiautomatic machines produce identical products. Time studies reveal the following time in minutes for one man to service one machine:

Load machine	3.1
Remove finished product	0.6
Inspect finished product	2.4
Pack finished product	1.9
Walk to next machine	0.4

The machine takes 41.3 minutes to produce a finished product. Machine operators are paid $4.90 per hour, and the burden rate for the machine is $18.00 per hour. What is the lowest cost per unit to produce the product with the optimum ratio of men to machines?

32. Develop a Left-hand Right-hand chart for:

298

(a) Opening a pop bottle with a hand-operated bottle opener.

(b) Opening a checkbook, writing a check, and handing it to a cashier.

33. For a 95% confidence level, what value was used for the required precision in the following formula?

$$N' = \left(\frac{10\sqrt{N\sum X^2 - (\sum X)^2}}{\sum X}\right)^2$$

34. The following times were recorded for one element: 7, 8, 6, 9, 7, 7, 6, and 6. How many cycles are necessary for the time study if the error is not to exceed 5% as often as 997 times out of 1000?

35. A portion of a time study observation sheet is shown below. The continuous method of stopwatch timing was used. For this operation it is estimated that an operator has 420 minutes out of a 480-minute work day to apply to production. Determine the standard time for the task and the number of pieces produced per standard hour.

Element		1	2	3	4	5	6	7	8	9	10	ST_e	Rating Factor
1	E												0.95
	C	11	45	81	13	48	83	20	55	93	30		
2	E												1.10
	C	28	63	97	30	65	200	36	75	310	48		
3	E												1.05
	C	35	70	104	37	73	08	44	82	18	55		

36. In an 8-hour day the following conditions occur:

4 set-ups of 20 minutes each

4 10-minute coffee breaks

30 minutes for personal time

20 minutes of unavoidable delay

Standard time for an operation is 6 minutes, not including set-up time.

(a) How many complete operations can be performed in a day if an operator has a speed rating of 120%?

(b) What is the personal time percentage allowance?

37. The normal time for performing a certain task depends on the weight and surface area of the part being handled as shown in Figure 9.14. Determine the synthetic time formula for the normal time of the operation.

38. You are given the following conditions where the rating for the observed times is 1.0:

(1) A pail is in the shape of a rectangle. The bottom has a 144-square inch area. The sides are calibrated in 1-inch increments from 6 to 12. The pail weighs 6 pounds.

(2) A faucet delivers 4 cubic inches of water per second at a constant rate. Water weighs 62.4 pounds per cubic foot.

(3) An empty pail can be carried 200 feet in 1 minute. A full pail (12-inch level) can be carried 200 feet in 4 minutes. (Assume linear distribution between points.)

(a) Determine the simplest possible formula for the synthetic time to fill and transport a pail of water.

(b) What is the standard time for filling a pail to 8 inches and carrying it 100 feet when the allowance factor is 1.15?

39. Beginning with the relationship $sp = k\sqrt{(pq)/n}$, develop the equation for determining the number of work sampling observations required to conform to a given k/s factor.

40. If one state occurred 4 times in 100 observations while using the work sampling technique, determine the precision of the study using a 95% confidence level.

If the task from which the observation described above takes 20 minutes to complete, within what range in minutes should you expect the observations to fall 95 times out of 100?

41. Figure 9.15 indicates the distribution of three activity

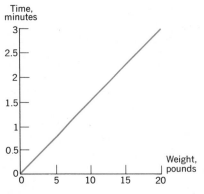

Figure 9.14

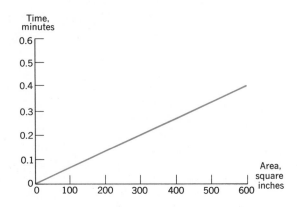

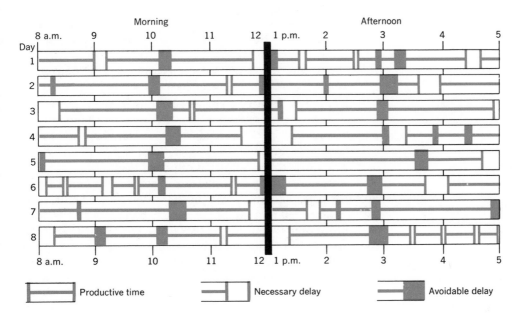

Figure 9.15

states: (1) productive time, (2) necessary delays, and (3) avoidable delays for a lift truck operator during an 8-day period.

    (a) Develop a tally sheet, determine a random observation schedule for 80 observations during the 8-day period, and make a work sampling of the lift truck operator's activities.

    (b) How many observations would be required for a k/s factor of 20 based on the limiting state?

    (c) Comment on the study with respect to the following: (1) the difficulties that might be encountered in making the study, (2) explaining to the lift truck operator what you are doing and how it is supposed to be used by management, (3) definitions of each state (both for an actual study and as the definition could apply to Figure 9.15), and the possibility that too many observations were taken in the morning or afternoon.

42. A 9-day study of work operation has been completed. During each 8-hour day, 100 random observations were made of workers engaged in the operation. The number of "operator idle" observations found for each day are given below.

Day	1	2	3	4	5	6	7	8	9
Operator idle	7	9	16	18	9	27	9	12	13

    (a) Before the above study was conducted, the total number of observations to be taken was determined by selecting a desired relative accuracy of $\pm 5\%$ at a 95% confidence level. What anticipated idle time percentage was used in the preliminary work to set $N' = 900$?

(b) What was the actual precision obtained for the above study at a 95% confidence level?

(c) From part (b) you could say you are 95% sure the idle time will be in the range from _____ to _____ minutes.

(d) If a control chart was made for this operation using a three standard deviation confidence limit, which points in the study would be considered out of control?

43. A company hopes to increase machine utilization by an incentive wage plan. Each machine has a clock on it that records running time; 330 minutes of use in an 8-hour day is considered 100% utilization. Operators receive a base pay of $4.00 per hour. The incentive plan calls for a 2% increase in base pay for each 5% machine utilization between 70% and the 100% standard; the 40-60 arrangement is linear between 231 and 330 minutes running time. A step bonus of 5% is offered for meeting the 100% standard. Above this point the incentives are 50-50 profit sharing.

(a) Graphically portray the basic relationship of machine utilization and earnings.

(b) How much will an operator earn if his machine is running 400 minutes a day?

44. Key-job points and associated wages are shown in Figure 9.16.

(a) What would an across-the-board increase of 10% do to the slope of the line from which wages for other point totals are interpolated?

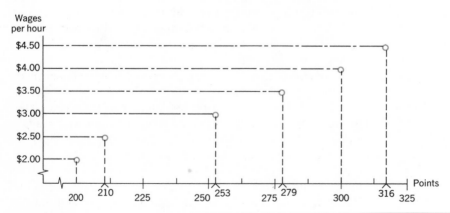

Figure 9.16

(b) What would a "flat increase" of 20 cents per hour do to the slope?

(c) Under conditions (a), (b), and the original rates, what wages should be paid to a worker performing a job with a point total of 340?

CHAPTER 10

MACHINES AND MAINTENANCE

10-1 IMPORTANCE

Machines are employed in a production sense to generate or facilitate output. They are directly involved in the process or provide auxiliary services.

"Made by hand" is a banner proclaiming an oddity that merits a higher price. Not too many years ago, similar pride was proclaimed by signs such as "machine tested." Today we live in a machine age. Some say we are in a second industrial revolution characterized by computing machines, just as the steam engine characterized the first industrial revolution. The question of "man or machine" is again raised, but a more appropriate issue is the coordination of man *and* machines.

There are no completely independent machine production systems; there is always a man-machine interface as shown in Figure 10.1. A highly automated plant with its scarcity of operating personnel gives an impression of near complete machine control, but the observation is deceptive. Men planned the facility, maintain it, feed it raw materials, and distribute its output. In the usual situation where men directly operate machines, activities at the interface are evaluated by method and measurement studies. The objective of the studies is to improve coordinated performance of men and machines.

Focusing on the machine side of the interface, we encounter two variables present in most evaluations: time and money. That duration and dollars interact was established in Chapter 4 by

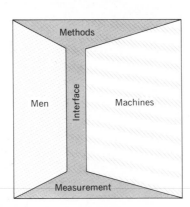

Figure 10.1 Man-machine interface

304

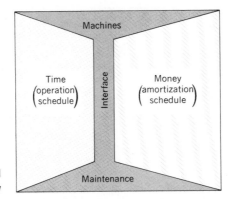

Machines

Time
(operation
schedule)

Interface

Money
(amortization
schedule)

Maintenance

Figure 10.2 Machine-oriented
interface of time and money

time value of money relationships. A machine is a capital asset.
Its loss in capital value over time is theoretically recovered from
the worth it contributes to production; the investment is
amortized. How fast it loses value is in part a function of the
maintenance program. In turn, the maintenance program is a
function of the value of the machine, the expected depreciation
pattern, and the production schedule. These relationships are
expressed in Figure 10.2 as the machine-maintenance interface of
money and time.

Amortization is the maintenance of a capital fund over a •
period of time.

In the following sections we shall first look at the money side
of the machine interface by considering the investment in
machines. Then we shall switch to the time side to investigate
machine loading and sequencing. Finally, the interface will be
evaluated in terms of maintenance–replacement policy and
waiting time analysis.

10-2 DEPRECIATION Two versions of depreciation are applicable to machines. One
version describes the loss in value over a period of time; unless
a machine has an antique value, it normally is worth less after
each year of use and ownership. The second meaning of depreciation refers to a systematic plan for recovering the capital invested
in an asset. To illustrate the two meanings, suppose a man
invested his savings in a portable sawmill. With the $20,000
mill, he went from one farm woodlot to another, felling trees and
cutting them into lumber. He made a good living for 5 years.
Then the mill started to wear out. He had to spend more and
more time on maintenance and repairs. When he tried to sell the
mill, he was offered only $1000 as its scrap value. His mill had
depreciated from the first cost of $20,000 to a salvage value of

305

$1000. If he had systematically allocated a depreciation charge, say

$$\frac{\$20,000 - \$1000}{5 \text{ years}} = \$3800 \text{ per year}$$

from the earnings of his lumber-cutting operations, he would have accumulated enough reserve to buy a new mill when the old one was worn out.

Causes of Depreciation

A typical asset becomes less valuable during its *service life*— the actual time period the asset is owned. The decrease in worth is due to a combination of the following four causes.

Physical depreciation. Normal wear and tear of operations gradually lessen the machine's ability to perform its intended function. A good maintenance program can slow decay, but only an economically questionable "rebuilding" can rejuvenate a machine to approximately its original condition. Continuously more expensive repairs are typically required to even keep an older machine operating.

"Accidental" damage is considered normal wear, but the actual amount is still a function of the care shown.

Functional depreciation. A change in demand or service expected from a machine makes it less valuable to the owner, even though it is still capable of performing its original purpose. If an original 0.01-inch tolerance requirement for parts was permanently changed to 0.0001-inch and the machine producing the parts was designed only to meet the first specification, the machine has functionally depreciated. It can still perform its intended function, but that function is no longer required.

Changes in capacity requirements, either up or down, are the main causes of functional depreciation.

Technological depreciation. The development of new and better methods of performing a function makes previous machine designs suddenly uneconomical. A "breakthrough" in technology is now such a routine happening that obsolescence is a major concern with any machine purchase. A decision to switch to new materials or improved product designs also can make existing custom equipment instantaneously obsolete.

Machine designs based on new concepts are frequently in the drawing-board stage before previous designs are in production.

Monetary depreciation. A change in the purchasing power of money causes subtle but definite depreciation. Accounting practices typically relate depreciation to the first cost of a machine, not the replacement cost. Over recent years, prices have continually increased. Therefore, the capital recovered from

Comparing replacement costs to purchase prices often leads owners to retain old machines longer than their economic life.

306

a machine's service is often insufficient to buy a replacement when the old one can no longer produce competitively. Thus, depreciation actually applies to the invested capital representing the machine rather than to the asset itself.

Under the influence of these largely unpredictable causes of depreciation, it is indeed difficult to estimate a machine's *economic life*—the number of years that minimizes the equivalent annual cost of holding an asset. Life estimates are needed to evaluate the relative attractiveness of new machine alternatives, to plan replacement schedules, and for tax purposes. The Bureau of Internal Revenue suggests life limits for different classes of machines. Past experiences aligned to reflect current practices and recent equipment designs also provide a basis for life comparisons.

Depreciation charges are deductible as operating expense when computing taxable income.

In addition to physical and legal aspects, management philosophy plays a major part in depreciation programs. On one hand is a desire to retain machines in service as long as possible to lower the per year capital recovery charge. Conversely, planning a shorter life reduces the chance of inferior quality and unexpected technological disruptions. Of course, personal opinions of managers color both views such as an attraction to a particular brand of equipment or a passion to own only the most modern machines. All views are relevant to varying extents and deserve consideration, but the evaluation should be oriented towards system merits (long-range plans of corporate objectives, utilization of personnel, product development, material control, etc.) rather than concentrated on individual machines.

Depreciation Accounting

Any asset, except land, can be treated by the depreciation methods described for machines. Land is excepted because it historically appreciates in value instead of depreciating.

Depreciation accounting serves two major purposes. It sets a pattern for recovering capital invested in an asset and it relates the cost of owning a machine to its output. In effect, a portion of the earnings derived from the operation of a machine is set aside in bookkeeping accounts toward the cost of replacement.

An ideal depreciation method is easy to use, provides a realistic pattern of cost, recovers all the capital invested, recognizes any tax advantages, and is acceptable to the Bureau of Internal Revenue. We shall consider three of the most used methods. None of the methods is exclusively better for all attributes of depreciation accounting, but all of them meet the last vital requirement.

Straight-line depreciation. This method is the simplest to apply. It allocates a constant amount to capital recovery each year.

ANALYSIS

The annual depreciation charge (ADC) is determined from the relationship

A modification of straight-line replaces the economic life by units of production during the machine's life.

$$ADC = \frac{P - S}{n}$$

where:

P = purchase price of machine
S = salvage value at the end of the machine's economic life
n = economic life in years

Sum-of-digits depreciation. This method provides larger depreciation charges during the early years of a machine's life. The annual charge is a function of the sum of the digits representing the economic life; specifically, the ratio of the digit associated with the age of the machine and the sum of all the digits. For instance, a new machine with an economic life of 5 years has a digit sum of $5 + 4 + 3 + 2 + 1 = 15$ at the time of purchase. The digit associated with the first year of ownership is 5 and the last year is 1. The ratio for the first year is then 5/15 and 1/15 for the last year. The variable annual depreciation charge is calculated from

$$ADC = \frac{\text{(digit associated with machine's age)}}{\sum\text{(digits for entire economic life)}} \times (P - S)$$

$$= \frac{2(n - N + 1)}{n(n + 1)}(P - S)$$

where N = end of year age for which depreciation is being calculated.

Double-declining-balance depreciation. This fast write-off method is based on a factor with an upper limit equal to twice the annual depreciation charge computed by the straight-line method. Since management usually wants to recover invested capital as rapidly as possible, the maximum rate is used in the following equation:

$$ADC = \left(\frac{2}{n}\right)(\text{book value})$$

where book value $= P(1 - 2/n)^N = $ purchase price minus accumulated depreciation. The $2/n$ factor sets the fraction by which the book value is reduced each year.

The choice among the three depreciation methods shown in Table 10.1 is a management decision. The greater depreciation charges in the early years provided by double-declining-balance

308

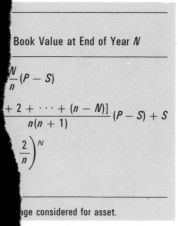

Book Value at End of Year N
$\dfrac{N}{n}(P-S)$
$\dfrac{+\,2+\cdots+(n-N)]}{n(n+1)}(P-S)+S$
$\left(\dfrac{2}{n}\right)^{N}$

...ge considered for asset.

...ttractive because they allow
...ons and generally give a more
...raight-line method is certainly the
... the constant depreciation charge
...However, when actual costs are con-
... methods may provide a more nearly
...ecause depreciation charges go down as
...r expenses increase.

...l is about to go into production. Its economic
...ave a salvage value of $5000. The depreciation
...ght-line, sum-of-digits, and double-declining-
...comparison purposes as follows.
...ual charge of

$$\dfrac{5000}{\text{s}} = \$5500 \text{ per year}$$

...uniformly from $60,000 to the $5000 salvage value

...machine $= (1 + 2 + \cdots + 10)$
$$= n\left(\dfrac{n+1}{2}\right) = 10\left(\dfrac{11}{2}\right) = 55$$

...0/55($60,000 − $5000) = $10,000; the second year's
...emaining charges continue to decrease by $1000 each
...st year the book value is $60,000 − $10,000 = $50,000
...ting rate until $S = \$5000$ at the end of the tenth year.

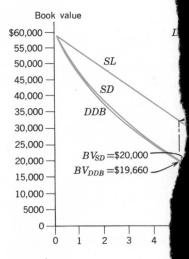

Book value

Figure 10.3

The maximum rate factor for doubl[e]
means one-fifth of the book value at th[e]
for the following year. The first year's ch[arge]
purchase price to yield the book value at th[e]

$$BV_1 = \$60,00[0]$$

Or, equivalently,

$$BV_1 = P\left(1 - \frac{2}{n}\right)^N = \$60,000[($$

Then the second year's depreciation charge is 0.[ ]

$$ADC_2 = \frac{2P}{n}\left(1 - \frac{2}{n}\right)^{N-1} = \frac{2 \times \$60,00[0]}{10}$$

The resulting book value at the end of year [ ]
$\$60,000(0.8)^2 = \$38,400$. The salvage value using [ ]
year 10:

$$S = BV_{10} = \$60,000(0.[8]$$

The results of the above calculations carried over [ ]
A comparison of the book values for the three meth[ods]
percentage of the total depreciation already accumula[ted]
73% for the sum-of-digits method, and 75% for the [ ]
last method has a different salvage value because the b[ ]
balance depreciation takes no direct account of the estim[ ]

Table 10.1 Formulas for depreciation-accounting methods*

Depreciation Method	Annual Depreciation Charge	Accumulated Depreciation	
Straight-line	$\dfrac{P - S}{n}$	$\dfrac{N}{n}(P - S)$	$P -$
Sum-of-digits	$\dfrac{2(n - N + 1)}{n(n + 1)}(P - S)$	$\dfrac{N(2n - N + 1)}{n(n + 1)}(P - S)$	$2[1$
Double-declining-balance	$\dfrac{2P}{n}\left(1 - \dfrac{2}{n}\right)^{N-1}$	$P\left[1 - \left(1 - \dfrac{2}{n}\right)^{N}\right]$	$P\left(1 -\right.$

1st. yr. $= \dfrac{2P}{n}$ only

*P = purchase price; S = salvage price; n = economic life in years; N = end-of-year

Depreciation: Guidelines and Rules, publication 456, U.S. Bureau of Internal Revenue, July 1962.

• and sum-of-digits methods are a
higher immediate tax deducti
accurate book value. The st
simplest to calculate and
makes it easy to apply.
sidered, the accelerated
constant total charge b
maintenance and repai

EXAMPLE 10.1 Comparison of Depreciation Methods

A machine has been purchased for $60,000 an
life is estimated at 10 years, at which time it will h
patterns resulting from the application of strai
balance methods are calculated and charted for

The straight-line method gives a constant ann

$$ADC = \frac{\$60,000 - \$}{10\ yea}$$

It therefore has a book value that decreases
by $5500 increments each year.

Sum of the digits for the new

The first year's depreciation charge = 1
charge = 9/55($55,000) = $9000; the r
year. Equivalently, at the end of the fir
and continues to decrease at a decelera

309

NALYSIS

Legend:
DDB = double-declining-balance
SD = sum-of-digits
SL = straight-line
BV = book value

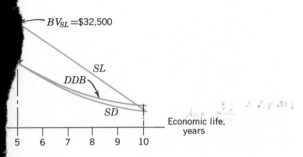

BV_{SL} =$32,500

SL

DDB

SD

Economic life, years

5 6 7 8 9 10

-declining-balance depreciation is $2/10 = 0.2$. This rate
e end of the preceding year is the depreciation charge
arge, $0.2 \times \$60,000 = \$12,000$, is subtracted from the
e end of year 1 :

$- \$12,000 = \$48,000$

$1 - 0.2)^1 = \$60,000(0.8) = \$48,000$

$2 \times \$48,000 = \$9600$, or,

$(1 - 0.2)^{2-1} = \$12,000(0.8) = \$9600$

$2 = \$48,000 - \$9600 = \$38,400$ or, $BV_2 =$
this method is the book value at the end of

$3)^{10} = \$6439$

the 10 year life are shown in Figure 10.3.
ods at half the economic life shows the
ted is 50% for the straight-line method,
double-declining-balance method. The
ook value formula for double-declining-
ated value at the end of economic life.

10-3 REPLACEMENT STUDIES

Outcomes of a decision cannot start before the moment a decision is made. Therefore, past events should not be considered unless they influence future events.

Depreciation-accounting methods relate the cost of ownership to production costs; they contribute little to replacement studies. In fact, their contribution may be misleading. A replacement study compares the operating expenses and capital costs of a machine presently owned, called a *defender*, to those of a replacement machine called a *challenger*. A study must be made on current information. The best available estimate of what a defender is worth today is the amount it can be sold for now, not what the accounting records say it is worth.

Sunk cost is the difference between the present market value and the worth shown by depreciation accounts. As depicted in Figure 10.4, straight-line depreciation yields a book value at the end of year 2 of $3000. The actual worth of the asset is set by the amount that can actually be recovered today, $2000. The sunk cost of $3000 − $2000 = $1000 appears as a loss of capital arising from life and salvage estimates made when the present defender was a challenger. The $1000 is irrelevant to the present replacement study.

Economic Evaluation of Defenders versus Challengers

Most replacement patterns are best compared by the discounted cash flow comparison models introduced in Section 4-4. The annual cost model is generally applied because cost data are normally tabulated in yearly amounts and replacements follow the "repeated projects" pattern. Part of the information needed for a comparison is the same used in depreciation accounting: purchase price, economic life, and salvage value. Operating expense and other costs associated with ownership are also needed. These factors are then discounted to equivalent bases by application of interest formulas.

Relevant replacement factors include: (1) labor costs, (2) material costs, (3) taxes, (4) insurance, (5) capital costs, (6) maintenance costs, (7) cost of waste, and (8) indirect costs.

The time value equivalence of the different methods of depreciation accounting is an interesting feature. Interest rates are not

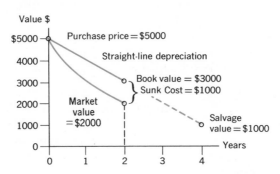

Figure 10.4 Sunk cost of an asset

Table 10.2 Equivalence of depreciation methods when interest is charged to unrecovered capital*

Year (N) (1)	Book Value at Beginning of Year N (1)	Return on Unrecovered Capital at $0.07 \times (1) = (2)$ (2)	Depreciation Charge in Year (N) (3)	Capital Recovery $(2) + (3) = (4)$ (4)	$(p/f)^7_N$ (5)	Present worth $(4) \times (5)$ (6)
			Straight-line depreciation method			
1	$4000	$280	$640	$920	0.9346	$860
2	3360	235	640	875	0.8734	764
3	2720	190	640	830	0.8163	678
4	2080	146	640	786	0.7629	600
5	1440	101	640	741	0.7130	528
				Total present worth of straight-line payments =		$3430
			Sum-of-digits depreciation method			
1	$4000	$280	$1067	$1347	0.9346	$1259
2	2933	205	853	1058	0.8734	923
3	2080	146	640	786	0.8163	642
4	1440	101	427	528	0.7629	403
5	1013	71	213	284	0.7130	203
				Total present worth of sum-of-digits payments =		$3430

*Basic data: $P = \$4000$, $S = \$800$, $n = 5$ years, and $i = 7\%$.

embodied in depreciation formulas; but if the return on invested capital is calculated, the different patterns have an identical equivalent annual cost. Table 10.2 demonstrates the equivalence by comparing the present worth of annual depreciation charges using the straight-line and sum-of-digits methods. The importance of this relationship is that it allows one basic formula to represent any depreciation method for replacement studies. The formula for capital recovery plus return is annual cost $= (P - S)(a/p)^i_n + Si$

To illustrate the equivalence, we can apply the formula to the data developed in Table 10.2 where $P = \$4000$, $S = \$800$, $n = 5$, and $i = 7\%$. By the formula for capital recovery plus return, we have:

$$\text{annual cost } (AC) = (4000 - 800)(a/p)^7_5 + 800(0.07)$$
$$= 3200(0.2439) + 56$$
$$= \$836.48$$

Then the present worth (PW) of this annuity is

$$PW = AC(p/a)_5^7 = \$836.48(4.1002)$$
$$= \$3430$$

which equals the present worth of both depreciation patterns shown in Table 10.2.

EXAMPLE 10.2 Replacement Study Based on an Annual Cost Comparison

An overhead crane conveyor system was installed in a warehouse-assembly area 15 years ago at a cost of $40,000. The economic life was estimated at 20 years with an $8000 salvage value. Depreciation accounting is by the straight-line method. Operating costs for the conveyor system, including labor and maintenance, are $18,500 per year. Because maintenance and repairs have not been excessive, the crane is now expected to last another 10 years and then have a zero salvage value. —deciding factor

✗ When the crane was installed, the products being produced were heavier and bulkier than current production. Today the same service could be provided by two lift-trucks at one-half the present operating costs. Lift trucks can be purchased for $6000 apiece with an expected life of 8 years and a salvage value equal to one-tenth their first cost. However, 2000 square feet of storage space valued at $3 per square foot per year would be lost in providing space for the trucks to maneuver. If the trucks are purchased, the crane will be dismantled at a cost of $4000 and sold at a firm bid of $9000.

Based on the company's desired rate of return of 10%, the replacement study is conducted as follows.

sold for   tear out

Capital costs. The defender, the crane, has a present value of $P = \$9000 - \$4000 = \$5000$. Latest estimates place its life at $n = 10$ years with the salvage value just equal to the cost of removal, $S = 0$. It is noted the book value, $\$40,000 - \frac{15}{20}(\$40,000 - \$8000) = \$16,000$ would show a sunk cost of $\$16,000 - \$5000 = \$11,000$. That this cost is irrelevant is apparent from the newer life and salvage figures; the sunk cost is derived from estimates now 15 years old and it plays no part in the present study.   need to look at present market value

The pair of lift trucks, the challenger, has an equivalent capital recovery plus return annual cost of

$$AC_{2\ trucks} = 2[(P - 0.1P)(a/p)_n^i + 0.1Pi]$$

$$= 2[(\$6000 - \$600)(a/p)_8^{10} + \$600(0.10)] = 2144$$

Other costs

Annual operating cost of crane conveyor system $= \$18,500$

Annual operating cost of lift trucks $= \$18,500 \times \frac{1}{2} = \$9250$

Annual cost of lost storage if trucks are used $= 2000$ sq ft $\times \$3$/sq ft

     $= \$6000$

Cost of rearranging storage:

313

Comparison Table	Defender	Challenger
Capital cost: $5000(a/p)_{10}^{10} + 0 = $5000(0.16275)$	$814	
$2[$5400(a/p)_8^{10} + $60] = $10,800(0.18744) + 120		$2144
Other costs : operating	18,500	9250
loss of storage		6000
Total cost	$19,314	$17,394

The advantage of the challenger over the defender is $19,314 − $17,394 = $1920 per year. Although the advantage is significant, it is not dramatic. The edge given to the challenger probably stems from functional causes, the products are lighter and smaller now than in the past. Is there any chance the function will change again? Should a belt conveyor also be considered? Would the operation of lift trucks create a safety hazard? Will storage space become more valuable as a result of company expansion? Such questions surround every replacement study and deserve careful attention.

Replacement Cycle Evaluation

A cyclic replacement of a machine by another machine of the same type is a special case of the general economic comparison method just discussed. It is of interest because it establishes the economic life by combined capital and operating cost considerations. The relationship is displayed in Figure 10.5 where capital costs vary inversely with time and operating costs increase with time. This pattern is typical of most production equipment.

The objective of a cycle evaluation is to find the replacement age that minimizes an asset's annual cost. The calculations follow an iterative routine where the capital cost, the decrease in salvage value to a certain age, is added to the accumulated operating cost for the same period. Each sum is divided by the respective age to give an average cost for that replacement interval. Interest can be included by determining the present worth for all the figures. For shorter intervals, say 10 periods or less, discounting seldom makes a difference in the optimal replacement age.

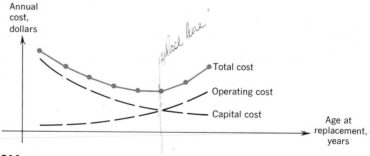

Figure 10.5 Cost pattern for increasing asset age

314

EXAMPLE 10.3 Replacement Study Based on a Life Cycle Evaluation

Small personnel vans carry work crews to remote facilities. The remote stations are expected to be manned indefinitely by the same transportation arrangement. The present replacement cycle for the vans is based on the following annual cost pattern:

Year	0	1	2	3	4	5	6	7	8
Salvage value	$4000	$2900	$2200	$1600	$1200	$900	$600	$400	$300
Operating cost	——	800	900	1100	1400	1700	2200	2700	3300

Table 10.3 indicates the optimal replacement interval is 4 years with an average total cost, (depreciation + operating cost)/number of years, of $1725 per year. The small difference in cost for years 2, 3, and 4 throws the final replacement age decision open to less tangible considerations.

(Table 10.3)

End of year	1	2	3	4	5	6	7	8
Total depreciation	$1100	$1800	$2400	$2800	$3100	$3400	$3600	$3700
Cumulative operating cost	800	1700	2800	4100	5800	8000	10700	14000
Total cost	1900	3500	5200	6900	8900	11400	14300	17700
Cost per year	$1900	$1750	$1733	$1725	$1780	$1900	$2043	$2213

good time to resell

An equipment supplier has offered to buy three 1-year old vans for $2900 each as trade-ins on two vans that have a capacity equal to the three smaller carriers. The large vans have a 3-year optimal replacement cycle with an average per year cost of $2500. The dealer points out that the switch will serve the routes just as well and the total average cost per year for the two vans is 2 × $2500 = $5000 compared to the three van average yearly cost of 3 × $1725 = $5175.

The offer is refused because the incremental cost increase for the three present vans during the next year (end of year 1 to the end of year 2) is 3($3500 − $1900) = $4800. This increment, the cost for next year, is less than the average cost of the larger vans, $5000 per year. If the dealer would accept three 2-year old vans at $2200 apiece, the deal would be advantageous because the incremental cost during year 2 is 3($5200 − $3500) = $5100. Any deviation from a cyclic replacement schedule should be evaluated from an incremental basis.

10-4 SEQUENCING

The order in which jobs pass through machines or work stations is a sequencing problem. When there are very few different types of jobs or machines, the problem is solved informally by sketching the flow mentally or on a time chart. Consider the simple 2 × 2 sequencing problem represented by the tableau in Figure 10.6; two jobs require work by two machines, M1 and M2, in that order. There are only two possible sequences, job 1 first and job 2 second or J2 < J1. The schedule resulting from each sequence is shown by the time charts. Based on a preference for the shortest total elapsed time to complete the work, the J1 < J2 sequence is selected.

Time chart drawing and application details are in ● Section 13-4.

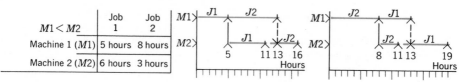

$M1 < M2$	Job 1	Job 2
Machine 1 ($M1$)	5 hours	8 hours
Machine 2 ($M2$)	6 hours	3 hours

Figure 10.6 Total elapsed time to pass two jobs through a two-machine process

Sequencing problems quickly become more tedious as the number of jobs and machines increases. With n jobs passing only from $M1$ to $M2$, there are $n!$ alternatives; it would take almost 40 million time charts to show all the sequence patterns possible for just 11 jobs. Thus, charting is not a very practical solution tool for larger exercises and, unfortunately, we have exact analytical methods for only the smaller problems. More complex problems are treated by simulation techniques, but the cost and time required to produce a satisfactory solution are still very large. Much research remains to be done in this area.

Simulation is discussed in Section 12-4.

Sequencing n Jobs Through Two Machines

A quick, simple technique provides the least elapsed time solution to the problem of sequencing any number of jobs through the same two-step process. Two-station sequences are commonly found in job-shops where the "process layout" has machines and services functionally grouped. The solution procedure utilizes the following steps:

1. List job times to pass from $M1$ to $M2$.
2. Select the shortest job time listed.
3. If the shortest time is by $M1$, that job is placed as early as possible in the job sequence. If the shortest time is by $M2$, it is placed as late as possible in the sequence. A tie between shortest job times is broken arbitrarily because it cannot affect the minimum elapsed time to complete all the jobs.
4. Delete the job selected in Step 2 from the listing in Step 1. Then repeat Steps 2, 3, and 4 until a complete sequence is obtained.

The $n \times 2$ solution technique is sometimes referred to as "Johnson's rule" after S. M. Johnson, "Optimal Two- and Three-Stage Production Schedules with Setup Times Included," Naval Research Logistics Quarterly, 1, Mar. 1954.

The technique applies to single-unit or single-type batch jobs where the jobs have no priority of completion. It is assumed there is sufficient in-process storage space and the cost of in-process inventory is the same or varies insignificantly for all units. For short processes, these assumptions are usually valid. Extended processes subject to closer inventory cost controls and expediting priorities may have an optimality criterion other than minimizing total elapsed time. Additional complicating factors include variable transportation time between machines, rework of defective units, machine breakdowns, and variable processing times caused by operator proficiencies or working conditions.

EXAMPLE 10.4 Sequencing Six Jobs Through Two Machines

The time to wash and cook batches of produce depends on their condition, type, quality, quantity, and intended end product. The time in hours to process six known batches, $J1 - J6$, through the washer and cooker is shown below:

Batches	J1	J2	J3	J4	J5	J6
Washer ($M1$)	0.4	0.7	0.3	1.2	1.1	0.9
Cooker ($M2$)	1.1	0.7	1.0	0.8	1.0	1.3

The smallest number in the listing is 0.3 for $J3$. Since it occurs for $M1$, it is placed first in the job sequence and is then deleted from the tableau:

	J1	J2	J4	J5	J6
M1	0.4	0.7	1.2	1.1	0.9
M2	1.1	0.7	0.8	1.0	1.3

Job Sequence

J3					

The next smallest job time is $J1$ by $M1$. Therefore, $J1$ is placed as near the start of the sequence as possible, the second position, and is then dropped from the tableau:

	J2	J4	J5	J6
M1	0.7	1.2	1.1	0.9
M2	0.7	0.8	1.0	1.3

Job Sequence

J3	J1				

Now a tie exists between the job times for $J2$ by $M1$ and $M2$. A decision to put $J2$ in the third or sixth position, as early or late as possible in the sequence, will not affect the total elapsed time. The choice can be resolved by other priority considerations. By letting the time in $M2$ be the deciding factor, $J2$ is placed last in the job sequence:

	J4	J5	J6
M1	1.2	1.1	0.9
M2	0.8	1.0	1.3

Job Sequence

J3	J1				J2

The remaining jobs are sequenced by the same rules. In order of attention, $J4$ is placed next to $J2$, $J6$ goes after $J1$, and $J5$ fits in the last open position. The completed sequence is

J3	J1	J6	J5	J4	J2

. An alternate sequence for $J2$ placed early instead of late is

J3	J1	J2	J6	J4	J5

. That the breaking of a tie does not affect the minimum elapsed time is demonstrated by the time charts in Figure 10.7.

Sequencing Two Jobs Through n Machines

A reverse twist to "$n \times 2$" sequencing exposes the problem of routing two jobs through n facilities, $2 \times n$. This time a graphical approach is used. The axes of the graph represent the two jobs that must be processed through the same n facilities in whatever order the facilities are needed. The areas in the chart where both

317

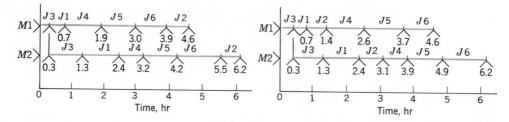

Figure 10.7

jobs could simultaneously be assigned to the same facility are blocked out. These areas must be avoided in determining the schedule of facility usage that minimizes the time to complete the jobs.

Any line drawn on the chart that avoids the blocked off areas while connecting the origin to the point representing the completion of both jobs is a feasible schedule. When a line runs horizontal, it represents exclusive work on the job scaled to the horizontal axis. Conversely, a vertical line represents work on the other job. A line 45° to the base indicates concurrent work on both jobs. Consequently, the optimal sequence is identified by the origin-to-completion-point line with the greatest amount of 45° travel.

EXAMPLE 10.5 Sequencing Two Jobs Through Six Machines

Custom products pass through six machine centers during fabrication. The time spent in each center depends on the design. For instance, one design requires a large amount of welding and very little drilling, while another design has reversed proportions. The order of work also varies for different jobs as a function of product requirements and the state of completion. The expected times obliged by two jobs in six machine centers are shown below.

	Machine Center Order and Work Times					
$J1$: Sequence	$C \to A \to E \to F \to D \to B$					
Time, hours	1	3	3	5	4	2
$J2$: Sequence	$B \to A \to E \to F \to C \to D$					
Time, hours	3	2	4	4	1	2

The above information is translated to a chart by scaling each sequence on one axis of the graph. Rectangular blocks representing simultaneous work on both jobs in one machine center are formed by overlapping projections of each machine center's time.

Two work order paths are shown on Figure 10.8. Both paths are alternate optimal solutions. The solid line indicates no work is done on $J2$ for the first 3 hours, then both jobs are in process until $J1$ is completed, and 1 more hour is spent to complete $J2$. The other path has the same amount of 45° travel, but idle times for the jobs are spaced irregularly. Time charts for the two

318

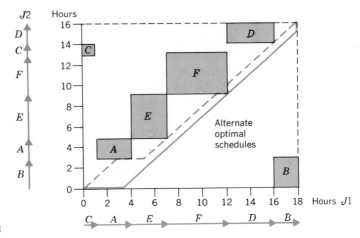

Figure 10.8

sequences, showing that the minimum total time required for both jobs is 19 hours by either path, are in Figure 10.9.

Sequencing *n* Operations for One Product

Assembly lines are most common in continuous manu- facturing industries such as automotive and electronics. • Line operations may be manual, by machines, or combinations.

Assembly line balancing is associated with a "product layout" where products are refined as they pass through a line of work centers. A designated number of work elements are performed at each center. The times to perform work elements are derived from work measurement studies. The period allowed to complete operations at each station is determined by the speed of the assembly line; all work stations share the same allowed *cycle time*. Idle or float time is created for a station when the work assigned to it takes less time than the set cycle time. The objective

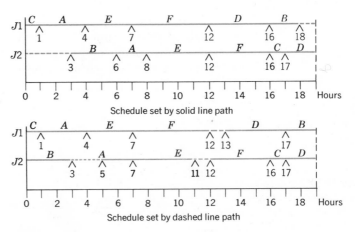

Figure 10.9

319

of line balancing is to minimize idle time while assigning operations to work stations according to a predetermined technological
sequence. A perfect balance, from a theoretical viewpoint, is
obtained when the assignments provide no idle time.

Line-balancing problems have received a great deal of attention,
perhaps more than the prevalence of assembly lines warrants.
Some techniques yield exact solutions for the given assumptions.
Others are designed to yield approximate solutions based on
practical considerations. The exclusive emphasis should not be
to get a perfect balance but to obtain the optimal layout and flow
in relation to the rest of the production operations.

An arrow network representing a product's manufacturing
sequence is shown in Figure 10.10. Each arrow denotes an
operation required on the product. The duration of each operation, a sum of the work elements for that operation, is shown
below its arrow. The complete product network maps the
metamorphic sequence from raw materials and parts to finished
work.

With the times and order of operations known, the remaining
point to decide before making the assignments is a desirable
cycle time. The sum of the durations for all 14 operations in the
network is 536 minutes. The largest individual duration establishes the minimum cycle time: 80 minutes for operation 3,7.
In turn, the minimum cycle time sets a lower limit on the number
of work stations needed, $536/80 = 6.7$; at least seven stations
are required. There may also be other commanding considerations such as a limit on machines available or workers with the
skills to perform certain operations. For example, assume
operations (1,5), (3,6), and (6,7) require time on a sophisticated
machine. If only one machine of this type is available, the limiting
cycle time is increased to $18 + 22 + 41 = 81$ minutes.

Assignment of operations to work stations is conducted in a
straightforward manner. A preliminary assignment sheet allocates
operations to the desired number of work stations in com-
formance with the sequence restrictions of the network. The

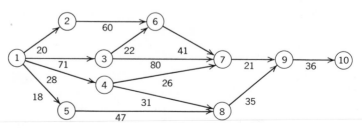

Figure 10.10 Sequence of operations required to complete a
product

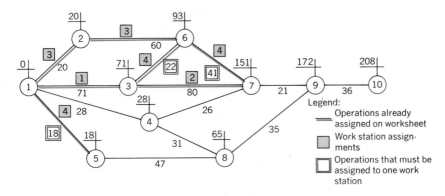

Figure 10.11 Product network showing special constraints, earliest start times, and partial work station allocations

most time-consuming operations with the earliest start times are assigned first. Special restrictions such as the assignment of certain operations to one station, noted by double squares in the network, require extra vigilance. Recordkeeping is improved by marking network operation arrows as they are entered in the assignment sheet.

Figure 10.11 shows the line-balancing network after four work stations have been allocated their operations. Number 3 work station has to finish operations 1,2 and 2,6 before the special machine station, 4, can perform operation 6,7. An initial list is completed as shown in Table 10.4 by carefully adhering to the

Table 10.4 Assignment sheet for the initial allocation of operations to work stations

Work Station	Assigned Operations			Total Time
1	1, 3			71
2	3, 7			80
3	1, 2	2, 6		20 + 60 = 80
4	1, 5	3, 6	6, 7	18 + 22 + 41 = 81
5	1, 4	4, 8	4, 7	28 + 31 + 26 = 85*
6	5, 8	8, 9		47 + 35 = 82
7	7, 9	9, 10		21 + 36 = 57

*Cycle time is 85 minutes.

Table 10.5 Improved work station assignments that decrease cycle time

Work Station	Assigned Operations			Total Time
1	1, 3			71
2	3, 7			80
3	1, 2	2, 6		20 + 60 = 80
4	1, 5	3, 6	6, 7	18 + 22 + 41 = 81*
5	1, 4	4, 7	7, 9	28 + 26 + 21 = 75
6	5, 8	4, 8		47 + 31 = 78
7	8, 9	9, 10		35 + 36 = 71

*Cycle time is 81 minutes.

321

prescribed sequence restrictions and by keeping the total time for the operations assigned to one station near the limiting cycle time, 81 minutes.

Improvements on the initial effort are initiated by noting the work station times that exceed the minimum, 81. By restructuring the assignments, an improved schedule is developed as shown in Table 10.5. A check of the assignments shows all the restriction requirements have been satisfied, and no times exceed the limiting sequence in station 4. Further juggling might be done to alter specific assignments that would benefit work performance at certain stations. For instance, quality of output might be improved by assigning a certain operation to a work station manned by an operator known to be particularly proficient at that operation.

Operation times can occasionally be adjusted to reduce idleness by redesigning equipment, changing machines, and applying motion economy principles.

The approach to line balancing just considered is mathematically unsophisticated. It relies more on resourcefulness and judgment than analysis techniques. The legitimacy of such an approach is realized when the dynamic nature of a production line is considered. The sequence of operations seldom varies, but the operation times are far from constant. Performance by human operators is continually modulated by enthusiasm, health, and social conditions. Fluctuating flow between stations means the operators must cooperate to balance internally each other's work output with the pace of the assembly line. Human behavior mocks exact formulation, but it remains a major factor in effective line balancing. Perhaps minimizing idle time is adjunct to maximizing conditions for individual and collective human effectiveness.

Impromptu line balancing occurs whenever one operator is absent and others "take up the slack."

✱ ✱ ✱   *Optional material.*

10-5 MACHINE LOADING

The sequencing measures of the previous section are applied to relatively stable or permanent assignments. Now we shall consider the case where several machines are capable of performing the same job and several job orders of relatively short duration are in process at one time. The objective is to identify the preferred facility that minimizes cost for each order. Data shown in Table 10.6 will be used to illustrate what information is needed and the solution procedure.

The information for Table 10.6 is derived from the size of orders on hand, production rates of individual machines and operators as indicated by past records, unit production costs based on work measurement studies, and available machine

322

Table 10.6 Data for machine-loading assignments *comparison Std machine*

Order Number	Order Size (pc)	Selling Price ($/pc)	Machine A		Machine B		Machine C	
			Output (pc/hr)	Cost ($/pc)	Output (pc/hr)	Cost ($/pc)	Output (pc/hr)	Cost ($/pc)
J1	532	2.00	38	1.60	50	1.00	45	0.80
J2	360	4.00	12	3.00	20	2.50	20	2.50
J3	900	1.00	90	0.50	70	0.70	55	0.80
J4	480	1.75	60	0.75	40	1.25	40	0.90
Machine time available (hr)			24		20		25	

capacity as indicated by shop schedules. The variance between machine output rates is a function of the age, type, and condition of the machine and the proficiency of the operator. Machine availability is affected by previously obligated time, maintenance schedules, and overtime arrangements. Cost per piece is determined from the operator's wage plus material costs; wages vary among operators, and waste or spoilage likely differs for each man-machine station. Two costs are not included. It is assumed the set-up costs are insignificant and fixed costs are the same for all machines. If these assumptions are false, more elaborate solution techniques such as Monte Carlo simulation can be employed.

> If the cost of doing a job is assumed to vary directly with the time to do the job, a version of the assignment method of Section 7-3 can be used. It is faster but less exacting than the transportation method.

The transportation method (Section 5-4) is utilized to assign jobs to machines. But first the data must be converted to a form suitable for the transportation matrix. The units for the rows and columns must be the same; when we previously applied the transportation method to the distribution of supplies from an origin to a destination, the units of supply and demand were numbers of identical products. In machine loading we are faced with the supply stated in hours available and the demand in pieces of output. The difficulty is overcome by converting both the supply and demand to the common unit of equivalent standard hours (ESH).

The first step in the conversion is to calculate for each machine an *index number*—an indicator of the relative production capabilities of the machines. The machine with the largest average production rate is assigned an index number of 1.0. Remaining machines are indexed in proportion to their average

323

output rate compared to the rate of the machine indexed at 1.0. For the machines in Table 10.6, we have:

	Machine A	Machine B	Machine C
Average output rate	$\dfrac{38 + 12 + 90 + 60}{4} = 50$	$\dfrac{50 + 20 + 70 + 40}{4} = 45$	$\dfrac{45 + 20 + 55 + 40}{4} = 40$
Index number	1.0	$\frac{45}{50} = 0.90$	$\frac{40}{50} = 0.80$

Knowing the index number, we can convert the machine capacity to ESH by multiplying the time available for each machine by its index number. The supply of machine time available in ESH is:

Machine	Index Number	Machine Time Available (hr)	Supply (ESH)
A	1.0	24	24
B	0.9	20	18
C	0.8	25	20

Next, the order sizes are converted to equivalent work loads by dividing each quantity by the output rate of the standard machine indexed 1.0, machine A. The demand representing each order quantity in ESH is:

Order Number	Size (pc)	Output Rate, Machine A	Demand (ESH)
J1	532	38	14
J2	360	12	30
J3	900	90	10
J4	480	60	8

The last conversion is required to relate the selling price and unit cost to ESH. The difference between the price per piece and its variable production cost is its contribution. Multiplying the contribution by the standard machine's (A's) output rate gives the contribution per ESH. The calculation steps involved for order J1 are shown below.

Order Number and Machine	Selling Price	(−)	Cost per piece	(=)	Contribution per piece	(×)	Output Rate, Machine A	(=)	Contribution per ESH
J1−A	$2.00	−	$1.60	=	$0.40	×	38	=	$15.20
J1−B	$2.00	−	$1.00	=	$1.00	×	38	=	$38.00
J1−C	$2.00	−	$0.80	=	$1.20	×	38	=	$45.60

After the contributions per ESH values are computed for every job-machine interface, all the data are dimensionally compatible and ready for transfer to the matrix format. The transportation matrix for the data developed from Table 10.6 is shown in Figure 10.12.

The solution procedure for maximization problems is treated in Section 5-7. • The remaining steps are to solve the transportation matrix and reconvert the solution to the actual machine hour assignments. The initial feasible solution using VAM is checked by the stepping-stone or MODI method and is found optimal; see matrix in Figure 10.13 on page 326. The actual machine hour assignments are calculated by dividing each allocation in the matrix by the appropriate machine index number. Thus, the assignment for Machine B to do order J2, shown as 18 in the matrix, is 18/0.9 = 20 actual hours. A tabulation of the contribution per order (actual hours x output rate x contribution rate) is totaled in Figure 10.13.

Any formal model, such as the one just considered, is always subject to interpretation. The unaccounted for set-up costs or special treatment for a valued customer could override the calculated solutions. Nevertheless, formal models provide a reference frame from which to compare other solutions. A dollar value is placed on the "valued" customer by the amount it costs above the formal optimal solution to serve him. The disclosure of costs disguised under the cloak of "goodwill" may suggest a reappraisal of preferential policies. The formal measures at least provide a quantifiable base from which the effect of intangibles can be evaluated.

Order Number	Machine			Demand, ESH (order quantity)
	A	B	C	
J1	15.2	38	45.6	14
J2	12	18	18	30
J3	45	27	18	10
J4	60	30	51	8
Supply, available time, ESH	24	18	20	62 62

Figure 10.12 Transportation matrix for machine loading

★ ★ ★ *End optional material.*

325

Order Number	Machine A	Machine B	Machine C	Demand	Contribution
J1	15.2	38	45.6 14	14	17.5 × 45 × $1.20 = $945
J2	12 6	18 18	18 6	30	(6×12×$1) + (20×20×$1.50) + (7.5×20×$1.50) = $897
J3	45 10	27	18	10	10 × 90 × $0.50 = $450
J4	60 8	30	51	8	8 × 60 × $1.00 = $225
Supply	24	18	20		Total $2517

Figure 10.13 Machine workload assignments and resulting job order contributions

10-6 MAINTENANCE

An alternative for any decision is to do nothing. Some machines are operated without servicing until they expire. Occasionally this is the least expensive maintenance policy.

Maintenance programs are intimately linked to replacement policies. All manufacturing industries follow some maintenance routine because the cost of lost production from unexpected breakdowns is significant and the capital cost of owning an asset is usually lower when the asset receives proper care. The quality of production may also be higher with better maintenance. The economic balance for a maintenance policy takes the familiar form shown in Figure 10.14.

As indicated in this figure, maintenance costs are lower when a machine is new. They increase with age because more work is needed to maintain a given level of performance. Capital costs are normally high in the first part of a machine's life and level out with age, but the cost of repairs is often more than offset by lower capital and outage costs (Figure 10.14). The better policy is the one that provides the lowest total cost.

There are many versions of maintenance programs. In our personal lives we informally practice different programs for

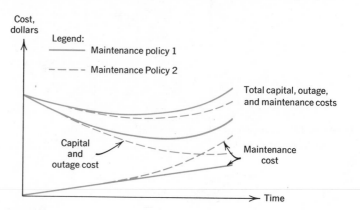

Figure 10.14 Relationship of maintenance policy to total cost

326

different items. Hand tools, small electrical appliances, and lightbulbs are normally used until they break down and are then replaced. The frequency of replacement is primarily a function of the quality purchased. When an asset serves a particularly important purpose, such as tires on an automobile, the policy is to carry a spare. The maintenance program is to check periodically the condition of the standby asset, the spare tire. Most automobile owners follow a policy of periodic maintenance (oil changes, lubrication jobs, etc.) to get less expensive and more reliable transportation. The policy is to prevent the inconvenience and high cost of a breakdown by keeping parts in a near-new condition through care and replacement.

Policies of industry are similar to personal maintenance routines, but the scale is magnified. Smaller items are often replaced before they fail. The question is how long to keep them in service. Standby machines are frequently held to reduce the impact of a breakdown of key machines. The question is how many standbys to have. Preventive maintenance is used to reduce the frequency and magnitude of major repairs. The question is whether preventive maintenance is more economical than repairs made as needed and, if it is more economical, how often should the preventive maintenance checks be made. All these questions can be treated by similar probability models as described in the following sections.

Preventive maintenance is so well accepted that the concept is simply nicknamed PM.

The size of repair facilities is another important consideration in a maintenance program. An economic balance is sought for the cost of idle repair facilities versus the cost of machines waiting to be repaired when facilities are crowded. This topic will be considered through the use of queuing theory in Section 10-7.

Group Replacement Policy

A group replacement plan is often feasible when a large number of identical low cost items are increasingly prone to fail as they age. The classical example is the replacement of streetlights at set intervals. Each lightbulb is so inexpensive that keeping individual service records is not warranted. The main cost of replacement is incurred by the truck and crew that removes a burned-out light in favor of a new one. Once the crew reaches the location where a renewal is required, little additional expense is involved.

We shall consider an individual versus group replacement model based on the following simplifying assumptions:

1. Only one type of asset with a known failure distribution is considered at a time.

327

Table 10.7 Data required to determine a group replacement policy *ignore group cost !*

			Failure Distribution					Service Cost for Replacement	
Age, n, in weeks	1	2	3	4	5	6	7	Individual	$3.00
Probability of failure by age n	0.10	0.05	0.05	0.10	0.20	0.20	0.30	Group	$0.50

2. Costs of individual and group replacements can be accurately estimated.
3. When items fail during an interval, they are replaced individually at the end of the interval. For instance, each item that fails during a week is replaced on the last day of that week.
4. When a group replacement is made, all items in the group are replaced at one time regardless of age. Thus an individual replacement made the day before a scheduled group replacement is still renewed, although it has only 1 day of service.

To illustrate the comparison method for the two replacement plans, we shall use the data in Table 10.7. It presents the failure pattern of 1000 high-intensity drying lamps used in a manufacturing process. Lamps cost $1.75 each. It is difficult to change a lamp during a working day without disrupting production. A much lower per lamp service cost results from group replacements scheduled on weekends when the production line is idle.

The comparison is made by calculating the first minimum of a curve derived from the cost of group replacements at different intervals. If this minimum, as shown in Figure 10.15, is less than the average individual replacement cost, the indicated policy is to replace all items at the interval shown by the first minimum.

According to the data in Table 10.7, each time the entire bank of lamps is replaced the cost will be $500 = 1000 lamps × $0.50/

Figure 10.15 Cost pattern of different group replacement intervals

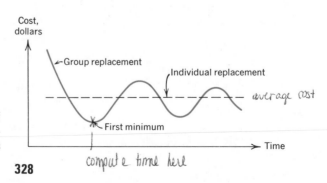

compute time here

lamp. A group replacement after 1 week would cost $500 plus the cost of individual replacements required during the week; 10% of the 1000 lamps will expire and need renewal at $3.00 per lamp. Then a one-week group replacement plan has a total cost of:

$$\text{individual replacement} + \text{group replacement} = \text{cost/week}$$
$$1000 \times \$3 \times 0.10 \quad + \quad \$500 \quad = \quad \$800$$

A 2-week plan has the same group cost of $500, but individual replacements must be made for failures during 2 weeks for the original 1000 lamps plus renewals for the burned-out lamps from the 100 replaced at the end of week 1:

$$
\begin{aligned}
&\begin{array}{l}
\text{total cost of} \\
\text{2-week group} \\
\text{replacement} \\
\text{policy}
\end{array}
=
\begin{array}{l}
\text{replacements} \\
\text{for lamps failing} \\
\text{in week 1}
\end{array}
+
\begin{array}{l}
\text{replacements} \\
\text{for lamps failing} \\
\text{in week 2}
\end{array}
+
\begin{array}{l}
\text{replacements in} \\
\text{week 2 for} \\
\text{lamps replaced} \\
\text{in week 1}
\end{array}
+
\begin{array}{l}
\text{group} \\
\text{replacement} \\
\text{cost at end} \\
\text{of week 2}
\end{array}
\end{aligned}
$$

$$= \$3000 \times 0.10 \quad + \quad \$3000 \times 0.05 + \$3000 \times 0.10 \times 0.10 + \$500$$

$$= \$300 \quad + \quad \$150 + \quad \$30 + \$500 = \$980$$

Then, cost per week = $980/2 weeks = $490

Each additional interval forms a similar but extended pattern of replacements for replacements for replacements, etc. A tabular format (Figure 10.16) simplifies the bookkeeping for the calculations. Each row corresponds to an alternative group replacement period. The entries in the body of the tableau are developed successively from the periodic expected costs; the cost for the previous period becomes the first entry for the next period. In the last columns the group replacement costs are added to the cumulative weekly costs to get the total cost for every interval. The weekly cost of each replacement period is its total cost divided by the number of weeks in the period.

The tabulated calculations from Figure 10.16 disclose a minimum expected weekly cost of $376 for a 4-week replacement

Replacement Period, Week	Individual Failure Cost During Week							Expected Cost		Group Cost	Total Cost	Weekly Cost
Week:	1	2	3	4	5	6	7	Week	Cumulative			
Probability:	0.10	0.05	0.05	0.10	0.20	0.20	0.30					
1	3000	—	—	—	—	—	—	300	300	500	800	800
2	300	3000	—	—	—	—	—	180	480	500	980	490
3	180	300	3000	—	—	—	—	183	663	500	1163	388
4	183	180	300	3000	—	—	—	342	1005	500	1505	376
5	342	183	180	300	3000	—	—	682	1687	500	2187	437
6	682	342	183	180	300	3000	—	772	2459	500	2959	493
7	772	682	342	183	180	300	3000	1142	3601	500	4101	586

[handwritten annotations: "cheaper" near row 1–2; "replace here with cost" near rows 4–5]

Figure 10.16 Expected cost of group replacement periods

329

cycle. This value is now compared to the average weekly cost of strictly individual replacements. The expected life of a lamp is the sum of the products of each weekly interval multiplied by its associated failure probability:

1 week $\times$ 0.10 + 2 weeks $\times$ 0.05 + 3 weeks $\times$ 0.05

$\qquad$ + 4 weeks $\times$ 0.10 + 5 weeks $\times$ 0.20 + 6 weeks $\times$ 0.20

$\qquad\qquad$ + 7 weeks $\times$ 0.30 = 5.05 weeks

With the cost of individual replacements at $3 per lamp, the average weekly cost is

$$\frac{1000 \text{ lamps} \times \$3/\text{lamp}}{5.05 \text{ weeks}} = \$584$$

Thus a group replacement policy for the given conditions is far superior to replacing each lamp as it expires.

Standby Machines

A provision for activating a standby machine when an online machine fails is another way to maintain service. This alternative does not take the place of routine maintenance; it serves as an insurance policy for conditions that could seriously hurt production. A regular premium must be paid for the insurance. A standby machine takes up space, must be periodically checked, and depreciates in value whether or not it is used. On the other side of the ledger, the availability of a substitute to keep a production line functioning can avert a slowdown or a shutdown of a whole series of dependent operations.

An evaluation of standby costs compared to benefits is conducted in about the same manner as a group replacement study. The failure pattern and cost of failures must be known or estimated. It is assumed that a standby machine will always operate when placed in service. An adequate inspection program for standbys is postulated to justify the assumption, and the cost of the program is included with the other expenses of keeping a spare.

A tableau similar to Figure 10.16 is used for the calculations. Each row represents the expected cost of a different number of standbys. The cost for the first alternative, no standby machine, is composed entirely of lost production expense. As the number of standbys increases, lost production costs decrease while holding costs for the standbys rise. The alternative providing the minimum total cost is preferred.

330

EXAMPLE 10.6 Selection of the Optimum Number of Standby Machines

Forty identical machines are operated at one work station. The cost in lost production and disruption to subsequent operations is estimated to be $100 per day per machine out of operation. The exact distribution of failures is not known, but it is believed to closely follow a Poisson distribution with a mean of two failures per day. Conditions get serious when six or more machines are out of operation at once. Then it is necessary to curtail activity for the rest of the line, causing an additional loss of $1000 per day. Standby machines can provide a hedge against lost production. The cost of maintaining a standby is estimated at $20 per day.

A tableau is set up for the calculations. The likelihood of machine failures is computed from the formula for Poisson probabilities:

$$P_n = \frac{e^{-\lambda}\lambda^n}{n!}$$

where:

n = number out of order

λ = mean number of failures

e = 2.7183

P_n = probability of n failures

For instance, the probability that three machines are out of order at one time is

$$P_3 = \frac{2.7183^{-2} \times 2^3}{3!} = \frac{8}{6(2.7183)^2} = 0.180$$

The entries in the body of the tableau are derived from the cost accrued by the number of machines out of order at one time. The costs increase linearly from zero for no failures to $500 for five machines concurrently out of service. Beyond five, $1000 are added to account for curtailed operations. As apparent from the completed tableau of Figure 10.17, the failure costs form a

Number of Standby Machines n:0	Cost of Lost Production for Machine Failures									Cost of Lost Production	Standby Cost	Total Cost
P_n:	1	2	3	4	5	6	7	8			
0.135	0.270	0.270	0.180	0.090	0.036	0.012	0.003	0.001			
0	0	100	200	300	400	500	1600	1700	1800	215	0	215
1	—	0	100	200	300	400	500	1600	1700	117	20	137
2	—	—	0	100	200	300	400	500	1600	55	40	95
3	—	—	—	0	100	200	300	400	500	22	60	82
4	—	—	—	—	0	100	200	300	400	7	80	87
5	—	—	—	—	—	0	100	200	300	2	100	102
6	—	—	—	—	—	—	0	100	200	1	120	121
7	—	—	—	—	—	—	—	0	100	0	140	140
8	—	—	—	—	—	—	—	—	0	0	160	160

Figure 10.17

recurring pattern. The cost expectation for each standby alternative is added to the expense of maintaining that number of standbys. The resulting total cost figures indicate that three standby machines should be used.

Preventive Maintenance

Routine maintenance is about the least glamorous job in production but one of the most important. As processes continually become more mechanized, maintenance correspondingly gets more complex while the damage potential of malfunctions soars. The backbone of a healthy preventive maintenance program is good planning and capable maintenance men backed by a supporting management policy.

All mathematical models rely on information collected on the job. The value of keeping complete, accurate, and detailed records of repairs and servicing can hardly be exaggerated.

We have already observed mathematical evaluations of maintenance alternatives involving replacement cycles and standby machines. The same tableau format can be used to • determine whether preventive maintenance (replacement of parts, overhauls, etc.) is less expensive than repairing on call. It also sets the most economical period for preventive maintenance checks by the same routine employed for replacement intervals.

There are many more elaborate models for special maintenance problems such as an inspection policy for equipment that deteriorates with age (a guided missile or a fire hose), a renewal policy for equipment that can be restored to an operating condition (recapping old tires), and replacement policies for equipment renewed after a certain length of service (replacing all tubes after they have been in service one-half their expected life). Such sophisticated analyses are appropriate when the dollar volume is large or service reliability is critical.

Typical preventive maintenance planning is more mundane than mathematical modeling. The guiding rule is that the time spent on preventive maintenance should be less than the time required for repairs, and the value imparted to machines by preventive maintenance should exceed the program cost. The logic of the rule is unassailable, but collecting the cost data to put it into effect creates a paradox: You have to try the program first to find out if it is good. The following list offers some practical • considerations which should be weighed in maintenance planning:

An adjunct but difficult part of planning is the distribution of PM costs among operating departments.

1. Machines can be "overdesigned" to improve reliability. Redundant circuits and extra bracing increase initial costs, but may produce greater than proportionate savings in maintenance costs.
2. Increasing in-process inventories can provide a buffer against the effect of machine failure. Extra stock increases carrying

332

costs, but it insulates the rest of a production line until breakdown repairs can be completed.

3. Inspections should dovetail with periods of cleaning, adjusting, and other maintenance work to reduce cost and inconvenience.

4. Training programs and disciplinary policies have a distinct effect on the amount of maintenance needed. Operators should be responsible for preventive maintenance work on their machines whenever possible. Periodic checks can be made by maintenance personnel to assure the level of care.

5. Friction, vibrations, corrosion, and erosion are physical conditions that should be detected and controlled before they develop into major problems.

Few employees receive less recognition than maintenance personnel. Their good work is taken for granted, but an occasional failure, often not their fault, may create a minor panic with hasty accusations. The ample responsibility involved in maintenance work is quite obvious; the difficulty of carrying out the work is not so apparent. Careful records of repairs and servicing are necessary, and often the data can be acquired only through the cooperation of operating departments. The coordination of an extensive maintenance program needs the backing of higher management. Besides the special skills required to diagnose failures, persistent attention to details is compulsory for inspection duties. The watchword should be a cross between the Coast Guard's motto and Murphy's law: Be prepared; if something can go wrong, it will.

10-7 WAITING LINES

The delayed effect of illwill from irate defectors is a serious penalty created by waiting lines.

Everyone has experienced the frustration of waiting in lines to obtain service. It usually seems like an unnecessary waste of time. In our private lives we have the option of seeking service elsewhere or going without the service. Such defections have direct economic consequences for the organization providing the service. When a customer leaves a waiting line, he becomes an opportunity cost; the opportunity to make a profit by providing the service is lost. An important aspect of system design is to balance this cost against the expense of additional capacity.

A machine needing repair is a customer for a service facility. When the facility is busy, the machine waits. Production capacity is lost during the waiting period. The waiting time could be reduced by cutting down the average time to repair a machine, by providing more repair areas, and by special procedures to give priority to repair work when it is seriously behind demand.

333

The net effect on waiting time from the implementation of any of these alternatives is not at all obvious. Doubling the number of service facilities does not necessarily reduce the waiting time by half because breakdowns do not occur at regular, predictable intervals and repair time varies with the extent of damage. Attempts to analyze such situations have led to the development of queuing theory.

An amazing number of waiting time situations exists in industry. At almost every stage of production, something is in temporary storage: papers wait for an executive to sign them, parts wait to be assembled, orders wait to be processed, and materials wait to be inspected or transported. In most cases such storage is justified on the grounds that the cost of waiting is less than the cost of providing service to eliminate the wait. But in a few situations, waiting lines cause significant congestion and a corresponding increase in operating costs. For example ships wait to be unloaded at docks, projects await attention by the engineering staff, aircraft wait to land at an airport, and breakdowns await repair by maintenance crews. Only conditions where substantial cost is incurred from waiting warrant analysis by queuing techniques. The cost of a thorough study may be considerable, assuming there are analysts available and capable of conducting the study.

Queuing theory rests on some formidable mathematics. It is primarily concerned with the properties of the waiting lines— the distribution of arrivals and service times, service policy, and similar considerations—not with the cost evaluations. Once a suitable queuing model is determined or developed, the cost comparisons are relatively straightforward. We shall consider some elementary applications to gain an appreciation of queuing fundamentals.

Most managerial decision makers do not have the time, inclination, nor training to develop a sophisticated queuing study. Yet they should have enough background to decide whether a study is justified and to question the reasonableness of a solution developed by specialists. It is important to recognize that theoretically correct equations will produce erroneous solutions when based on unfounded assumptions.

Queuing Concepts

The language of queuing theory is refreshingly descriptive. A *customer* is a person, machine, or object that requires *servicing*— an action performed for the customer. The customer is serviced by a *service facility*. When several customers can be serviced

The first recognized effort to analyze queues was made by a Danish engineer, A. K. Erlang, in his attempts to eliminate bottlenecks created by telephone calls on switching circuits.

To simplify the mathematical formulations it is generally assumed the population of customers is infinite.

334

at one time, the facility is said to have several *channels*. A *waiting line* or *queue* is formed whenever there are waiting customers or idle facilities.

Customers arrive at a service facility according to an *arrival distribution*—constant intervals, random rate, or other patterns. The time taken to provide the desired service follows a *service time distribution*. If every customer required exactly the same service and it was provided by automatic equipment, all service times would be constant. A more typical case is a machine breakdown service where the service time to repair it depends on the type of machine, its condition, and the seriousness of the damage; the repair time is irregular.

At first glance it might seem reasonable that a queue would never form when the average arrival rate is less than the average service rate. The reasoning is valid when both patterns are constant, but is fallacious for irregular patterns. Customers always have to wait when they arrive in groups exceeding in size the number of channels. Similarly, the occasional service time that is far larger than the average rate probably causes a waiting line to form. An ever-increasing queue is caused by the explosive condition of an average arrival rate greater than the average service rate. In general, the number of customers that have to wait increases proportionately as the arrival rate approaches the service rate.

The manner in which customers are served is called *queue discipline*. The most common assumption is first in-first out with no defectors; customers are not discouraged from joining by the length of the queue and patiently wait their turn for service. Other orders include: (1) last in-first out as encountered in some inventory policies, (2) a priority arrangement that allows a rush or emergency case to be serviced out of turn, and (3) a random selection that gives every waiting customer an equal chance of being the next to receive service.

★ ★ ★ *Optional material.*

Queuing Formulas

Four basic queue structures are illustrated in Figure 10.18. When one crew does all the work to repair a machine, we have a single-channel, single-phase case. Increasing the number of complete crews converts it to a multiple-channel, single-phase structure. By dividing the one crew into specialist teams that sequentially perform operations to repair a single machine, the structure changes to single channel, multiple phase. Adding another crew of team specialists that progressively complete

An automatic production line provides a rare example where products (customers) ride a constant speed conveyor (uniform arrival rate) and have the same cycle time at each work station (constant service rate).

"Bulk" arrivals occur when a large shipment arrives or a carrier unloads.

Unused service time, like sleep, cannot be stored for use in a busy period.

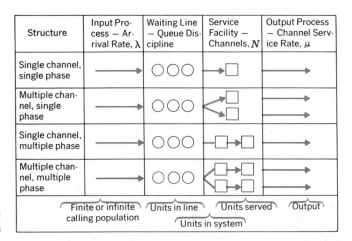

Structure	Input Process — Arrival Rate, λ	Waiting Line — Queue Discipline	Service Facility — Channels, N	Output Process — Channel Service Rate, μ
Single channel, single phase				
Multiple channel, single phase				
Single channel, multiple phase				
Multiple channel, multiple phase				

Figure 10.18 Waiting line structures

servicing one machine transforms the previous structure to multiple channel, multiple phase. A first come-first served queue discipline is diagrammed in Figure 10.18, but other disciplines could as easily apply. There are also other possible combinations such as a multiple channel, first phase followed by a single channel, second phase.

Different formulas are associated with each queue structure. The formulas also differ as a function of the applicable arrival and service time distribution. The answers usually sought through queuing formulas are:

P_n = probability of n customers being serviced or waiting to be serviced

P_0 = probability the service facility is idle (no customers in the system, $n = 0$)

L_q = mean number of customers in the waiting line

L = mean number of customers in the system (number in the queue plus number being serviced)

W_q = mean waiting time for a customer before being serviced

W = mean time in the system (customer waiting time plus servicing time)

We shall consider only single-phase cases. The applicable formulas for the desired queue characteristics are shown in Table 10.8. The Greek symbols traditionally associated with queuing theory are:

λ(lambda) = average number of arrivals per unit time

μ(mu) = average number of servicings that each channel can perform per unit time

The formulas in Table 10.8 are based on a definitive set of

336

Table 10.8 Single- and multiple channel, single-phase queing formulas

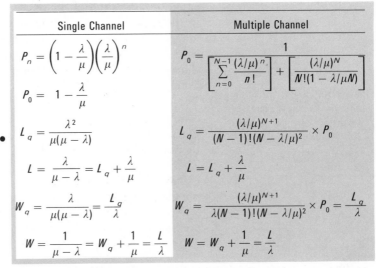

The single-channel formulas are modified for constant service times to:

$$L_q = \frac{\lambda^2}{2\mu(\mu - \lambda)}$$

and

$$W_q = \frac{\lambda}{2\mu(\mu - \lambda)}$$

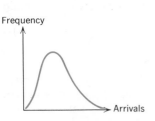

Frequency

Arrivals

Pattern of a Poisson distribution.

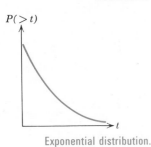

$P(>t)$

t

Exponential distribution.

assumptions. Because calculations quickly become overwhelming when different assumptions are incorporated, it is a temptation to apply the simpler expressions for all waiting line studies. The effect is similar to a quartermaster assuming all men in an army are the same size in order to simplify logistics; the policy makes the quartermaster's work easier and occasionally provides the right fit, but some results are ridiculous. The following assumptions pertain to the given formulas:

1. Arrivals follow a Poisson distribution. We previously encountered this distribution in Example 10.6 where it described the probability of machine failures. The formula given in the example would be modified to fit a queuing situation by letting n = number of customers. In general, the Poisson distribution says that on a continuous time scale there is a very small probability of an event at any particular instant and there is a very large number of times an event could occur. Translating these implications to a maintenance situation, we would say a breakdown requiring attention could occur at any instant during a day and the probability for any one instant is the same regardless of what has happened before or the length of the waiting line.

2. Servicings follow an exponential distribution. The equation for the distribution,

$$P(>t) = e^{-\mu t} \qquad \text{where } t = \text{duration of a servicing}$$

gives a reasonable approximation of many industrial servicing situations. A graph of the density function slopes downward to the right to show that the deviation from μ is greater for longer servicings than for shorter servicings. For maintenance work, this condition is interpreted as a greater probability of shorter repair times, but occasionally a task will far exceed the average repair time.

3. The average service rate is greater than the average arrival rate, $\mu > \lambda$.

4. Queue discipline is first in-first out with no defections from the waiting line.

5. The number of customers is infinite and the waiting line size is unlimited. Few real problems truly satisfy this assumption, but the theoretical effect is not seriously violated so long as the number could grow relatively large through returns to the queue after previous servicing.

The quotient of λ/μ, called the utilization factor, is expressed in units of "Erlangs" in honor of the quieuing pioneer.

EXAMPLE 10.7 Comparison of Waiting Time for Different Maintenance Facility Structures

Plans are being made for a plant enlargement. Repair facilities for machine breakdowns are barely adequate in the existing plant and will certainly not provide acceptable service when more machines are added. Records of recent repair activities show an average of four breakdowns per 8-hour shift. The pattern of breakdowns closely follows a Poisson distribution. When the new additions to the plant are completed, an average of six breakdowns per shift following the present distribution pattern is expected.

An exponentially distributed service rate of six repairs per shift is the capacity of the present repair facility. Without enlarging the capacity when the new addition is made, the utilization factor would be $\lambda/\mu = \frac{6}{6} = 1$ which looks very commendable until the impossibly large waiting time is considered:

$$W_q = \frac{\lambda}{\mu(\mu - \lambda)} = \frac{6}{6(6 - 6)} = \infty$$

Two alternatives with equivalent annual cost are available. New equipment and a larger crew for the existing station would increase the average servicing rate to 11 repairs per shift, or a second servicing station could be built in the new addition. In the latter alternative, the capacity of the two service stations would be five servicings per shift in each. Repair times would still be exponentially distributed.

The single-channel alternative would have the following characteristics when $\lambda = 6$ and $\mu = 11$:

probability of being idle $= P_0 = 1 - \frac{6}{11} = 0.45$

mean number of machines waiting for service $= L_q = \frac{6^2}{11(11 - 6)} = 0.66$

mean time before a machine is repaired (waiting time plus repair time) $= W = \frac{1}{11 - 6} = 0.2$ shift

$= 0.2 \times 8 \text{ hr/shift} = 1.6 \text{ hr}$

The values of the same characteristics for the second alternative providing two channels, $N = 2$, each with $\mu = 5$, are

$$P_0 = \cfrac{1}{\left[\sum\limits_{n=0}^{2-1} \cfrac{\left(\frac{6}{5}\right)^n}{n!}\right] + \left[\cfrac{\left(\frac{6}{5}\right)^2}{2!\left(1 - \cfrac{6}{5 \times 2}\right)}\right]} = \cfrac{1}{\left[\cfrac{\left(\frac{6}{5}\right)^0}{1} + \cfrac{\left(\frac{6}{5}\right)^1}{1}\right] + \left[\cfrac{\left(\frac{6}{5}\right)^2}{2\left(1 - \cfrac{6}{10}\right)}\right]}$$

$$= \cfrac{1}{\left[1 + \cfrac{6}{5}\right] + \left[\cfrac{36/25}{2(4/10)}\right]} = \cfrac{1}{2.2 + 1.8} = 0.25$$

$$L_q = \cfrac{\left(\frac{6}{5}\right)^{2+1}}{(2-1)!(2 - \frac{6}{5})^2} \times P_0 = \cfrac{(1.2)^3}{(1)(0.8)^2} \times 0.25 = 0.68 \text{ machine}$$

$$W = \cfrac{L_q}{\lambda} + \cfrac{1}{\mu} = \cfrac{0.68}{6} + \cfrac{1}{5} = 0.31 \text{ shift}$$

$$= 0.31 \times 8 \text{ hr/shift} = 2.5 \text{ hr}$$

By using the mean time in a repair facility (waiting time plus servicing time) as the comparison criterion, the single enlarged facility where $\mu = 11$ is preferred. Quicker return to production means less loss of output and thereby lower repair cost for the single-channel station, if the equivalent annual capital costs plus operating costs for the two alternatives are indeed the same. The single-channel alternative would be preferred with $\mu = 11$ even if the servicing time of the two-channel alternative could be increased to $\mu = 6$:

$$P_0 = \cfrac{1}{\left[\sum\limits_{n=0}^{1} \cfrac{\left(\frac{6}{6}\right)^n}{n!}\right] + \left[\cfrac{\left(\frac{6}{6}\right)^2}{2!\left(1 - \cfrac{6}{6 \times 2}\right)}\right]} = \cfrac{1}{1 + 1 + 1} = 0.33$$

$$W = \left[\cfrac{\left(\frac{6}{6}\right)^{2+1}}{6(2-1)!(2 - \frac{6}{6})^2} \times P_0\right] + \cfrac{1}{6} = \left(\cfrac{1^3}{6(1)(1)^2} \times \cfrac{1}{3}\right) + \cfrac{1}{6} = 0.22 \text{ shift}$$

$$= 1.76 \text{ hr}$$

One large facility clearly gives better theoretical service than an equivalent number of smaller facilities. A complete evaluation should check the time advantage by assigning values to hours saved. The study should also include other factors such as the logistic conveniences of a centralized location versus the greater average transportation distance between breakdowns and a repair facility when there is only one station.

★ ★ ★ *End optional material.*

Queuing Applications

Queuing theory occupies an interesting position among management tools. It is applicable to an omnipresent problem, idleness versus congestion. It is well publicized and an "in" topic for management scientists. But according to polls conducted by universities and professional journals, it is not applied as

A poll published by the *Journal of Industrial Engineering*, May 1968, showed 18% of the respondents used queuing techniques in day-to-day work. This figure can be compared to 44% for critical path scheduling and 26% for linear programming.

• widely as other, less glamorous tools. Perhaps practitioners shy away from the awesome facade created by the more sophisticated formulations. Possibly the barrier is a lack of data or the feeling that analysis effort would not provide an answer significantly better than less formal procedures. Whatever the cause, there is an unfilled potential for waiting line studies, but an effective analyst must have more than a casual familiarity with the subject.

The advantages of well-behaved theoretical functions stem from the tables and analytical solutions already developed for these distributions.

The distribution of actual arrivals and servicing times may not fit one of the theoretical distributions—Poisson, normal, • exponential, or binomial. The way to test the "goodness of fit" of an empirical to a theoretical distribution is described in Section 15-3. If formulas are available for a questionably close fit, it is a matter of judgment whether the extra effort required to develop custom formulas or to use simulation methods is compensated by improved accuracy. It should be remembered that distributions are forecasts of future patterns; it therefore makes sense to apply the precautionary measures discussed for forecasting in Chapter 3.

The cost of servicing customers is fairly easy to determine. Past performances give a good indication of operating times and material requirements. Capital costs are given by the depreciation policy. The cost of idle facilities is largely a function of depreciation expense and wages.

Predicting the cost of waiting customers is usually uncertain and always difficult. When customers arrive from internal sources, as machines in a factory sent to a maintenance facility, the expense of waiting in line is at least definable—lost production from idle machines, wages wasted for idle operators, inefficiencies in a production line caused by a vacant station, extra cost of standbys or inventory stock to take up the slack for a "down"

''Truncated'' queues are waiting lines shortened by defectors or the lack of space in which to wait. Formulas have been developed to cope with truncation.

• machine, congestion at a repair facility caused by a rash of breakdowns, and similar observable disruptions.

Estimating waiting costs for external customers is more difficult because of their uncertain behavior. Some customers may enter a queue and later defect to a competitor when they tire of waiting. Seeing a long queue may discourage potential customers from joining the waiting line. A former customer may

Customers at a restaurant can be observed leaving a line or passing by when a line exists. Whether they discover a more attractive eating place after leaving is hard to ascertain.

• permanently take his business elsewhere after enduring a long waiting period. Direct observations can indicate short-range effects of customers not joining or defecting from a queue. Long-range reactions can only be guessed at in most situations. Some form of experimentation aimed at identifying the customer population and its behavior is a guide to guessing.

340

EXAMPLE 10.8   Cost Comparison of Queuing Alternatives

A company plans to redesign its maintenance facilities. The line supervisors complain that the existing service is too slow. The cost controller claims that the five men in the facility are idle one-third of the time and the only reason repairs appear slow is they sometimes occur in bunches, causing delay. All agree that a priority system or any other queue discipline refinement would not be feasible. A compromise solution appears to be the installation of more automatic equipment to reduce the size of the maintenance crew.

A complete redesign of the present facility will cost $60,000 and allow repairs at the rate of 40 per week with two maintenance men. Adding $10,000 worth of new equipment will increase the repair rate from the present level of 15 per week to 20 per week with a crew of four. Both alternatives will have an economic life of 6 years, no salvage value, and the same repair costs. A 10% return on invested capital is required.

An average of 10 breakdowns occurs each week. The probability of a breakdown at any time is approximately uniform so an assumption of a Poisson distribution of arrivals is appropriate. The pattern and mean number of breakdowns are expected to remain about the same in the future. Wages for maintenance men average $9000 per year; the opportunity cost of having a breakdown is estimated at $30 for each day of lost production time. The variation of repair times is quite close to an exponential distribution.

The annual cost of the two equipment change alternatives are compared to determine the most favorable course of action.

Complete redesign ($\lambda = 40$).

Capital recovery cost: $60,000(a/p)_6^{10} = \$60,000(0.22961)$ $13,776

Annual operating cost: 2 men × $9000/man-yr   18,000

Annual lost production cost:

$$\frac{\text{time in a repair facility}}{\text{machine breakdown}} = W = \frac{1}{40 - 10} = 0.033 \text{ wk}$$

$$\frac{\text{total lost time}}{\text{yr}} = \frac{10 \text{ breakdowns}}{\text{wk}} \times \frac{52 \text{ wk}}{\text{yr}} \times \frac{0.033 \text{ wk}}{\text{breakdown}} = \frac{17.3 \text{ wk}}{\text{yr}}$$

$$\frac{\text{annual cost of waiting}}{\text{plus repair time}} = \frac{17.3 \text{ wk}}{\text{yr}} \times \frac{5 \text{ day}}{\text{wk}} \times \frac{\$30}{\text{day}} \qquad 2595$$

Total annual cost: $34,371

Adding equipment ($\lambda = 20$).

Capital recovery cost: $10,000(a/p)_6^{10} = \$10,000(0.22961)$ $2296

Annual operating cost: 4 men × $9000/man-yr   36,000

Annual lost production cost:

$$W = \frac{1}{20 - 10} = 0.10 \text{ wk}$$

total lost time per year = $10 \times 52 \times 0.10 = 52$ wk/yr

$$\frac{\text{annual cost of waiting}}{\text{plus repair time}} = \frac{52 \text{ wk}}{\text{yr}} \times \frac{5 \text{ day}}{\text{wk}} \times \frac{\$30}{\text{day}} \qquad 7800$$

Total annual cost: $46,096

The complete redesign of the present facility at a cost of $30,000 is clearly preferable. Now

341

this challenger is compared to the existing facility, the defender. Assuming the defender has no capital cost, a conservative assumption, we have the following.

Present facility ($\lambda = 15$).

Annual operating cost: 5 men × $9000/man-yr	$45,000
Annual lost production cost:	

$$W = \frac{1}{15 - 10} = 0.20$$

total lost time per year = $10 \times 52 \times 0.20 \times 104$ wk/yr

$$\begin{array}{ll} \text{annual cost of waiting} \\ \text{plus repair time} \end{array} = \frac{104 \text{ wk}}{\text{yr}} \times \frac{5 \text{ day}}{\text{wk}} \times \frac{\$30}{\text{day}} \qquad\qquad 15,600$$

Total annual cost: $\qquad\qquad\qquad\qquad\qquad\qquad\qquad\qquad\qquad$ $60,600

With the redesign alternative still preferred, the cost controller should be happier because the idle man hours are reduced from

$$5 \text{ men} \times 40 \text{ hr/wk}(1 - \frac{10}{15}) = 67 \text{ per week to } 2 \times 40(1 - \frac{10}{40}) = 60 \text{ man-hr/wk.}$$

The line supervisors should also be pleased that the time a machine will be lost from production should average only

$$\frac{17.3 \text{ wk/yr}}{104 \text{ wk/yr}} = 0.166$$

or about 17% of the former level.

10-8 SUMMARY

Time and money are the parameters by which machine performance and maintenance policies are measured. Time is the criterion for utilization and money is the yardstick for investment comparisons.

Depreciation refers to the loss of value of a machine over a a period of time and to a systematic plan for recovery of the capital invested. Four causes for an asset's loss of value are:

1. Physical depreciation—normal wear, tear, and damage to an asset.
2. Functional depreciation—a change in demand for services expected from an asset.
3. Technological depreciation—a new development that makes the present asset obsolete.
4. Monetary depreciation—a change in the value of money invested in an asset.

The number of years of ownership that minimizes the equivalent annual cost for an asset (the economic life) is determined by physical demands, legal requirements, and management replacement philosophy.

342

Depreciation accounting sets a pattern for recovering invested capital and relates the cost of ownership to output. Straight-line, sum-of-digits, and double-declining-balance are three widely used depreciation methods. The straight-line method is the simplest to apply because of its constant annual depreciation charge, but the other two methods allow an accelerated investment write-off. Sunk cost is the difference between the present market value and the worth shown by depreciation accounts.

A replacement study compares the asset currently in use, the defender, to a proposed replacement, the challenger. Any sunk cost for the defender is an irrelevant comparison consideration. The equivalent annual cost of capital is calculated from the formula,

$$\text{annual cost} = (P - S)(a/p)_n^i + Si$$

where P = purchase price, S = salvage value, i = interest rate, and n = remaining years of economic life. An evaluation comparing the sum of operating and capital costs for different replacement ages determines the economic life for repeated life cycles.

Sequencing procedures establish the minimum time route for processing units through work stations. Convenient methods are available for 2 (products) $\times$ n (stations) and $n \times 2$ patterns of process layouts. The sequences can be displayed on time charts. Line balancing procedures are used to sequence n operations for one product in product layouts. A network is drawn to describe the problem. A minimum cycle time and number of work stations are set by the largest operation in the line. Then operations are assigned to work stations in conformance to the sequence restrictions of the network with the objective of minimizing idle time and maximizing proficiency.

The transportation method is applicable to machine-loading situations where several machines are capable of performing the same job and several job orders of relatively short duration are in process at one time. Available hours and required output are converted to compatible units, equivalent standard hours. After the contribution of each job is related to equivalent standard hours, the data are entered in a transportation matrix. The solution reveals job to machine allocations and the expected total contribution.

Three methods of maintaining service are group replacement of worn parts, standby machines, and preventive maintenance. Cost evaluations for all of the methods utilize a tableau relating cost to failure pattern and alternatives—replacement period,

343

number of standbys, or time between preventive maintenance checks. The preferred policy is the one with the lowest cost based on the expected value of expense associated with the failure probability distribution for each alternative.

Other practical considerations for determining a maintenance policy include overdesign of machines, larger in-process inventories, coordinated inspection schedules, training programs, disciplinary measures, detection of harmful physical conditions, and recognition for maintenance personnel.

Waiting line evaluations compare the cost of congestion to the cost of providing facilities to relieve congestion. Queuing theory is concerned with the properties and behavior of waiting lines. The language associated with queuing theory includes the following terms:

1. *Customer*—a person, machine, or object requiring service.
2. *Service*—action desired by the customer.
3. *Channels*—number of servicing facilities open to customers.
4. *Queue*—the line formed when customers are idle or the channels are empty.
5. *Queue discipline*—manner in which customers are served.
6. *Arrival distribution*—pattern of customer arrivals for servicing (λ = average number of arrivals per unit time).
7. *Service time distribution*—pattern of servicing times (μ = average number of servicings each channel can perform per unit time).

The queuing formulas for the single-phase case illustrated in the chapter were based on the assumptions of a Poisson arrival distribution, exponential service time distribution, an arrival rate less than the servicing rate, first in-first out queue discipline, and an infinite calling population with no defectors or deserters from the queue. Based on these assumptions, formulas are available for the probability of a certain number of customers being serviced or waiting to be served, the mean number of customers in the system, and the mean time required by a customer in the system.

The cost of servicing customers is fairly easy to determine, but the cost of making customers wait is more complicated. When customers cannot be controlled, as opposed to a manufacturing process where products are the controllable waiting population, there are hidden costs of deserters leaving the line and defectors turning into permanently lost customers when they become disgruntled with waiting lines and seek service from a competitor.

10-9 REFERENCES

Ackoff, R. L. and M. W. Sasieni, *Fundamentals of Operations Research*, John Wiley, New York, 1968.

Barish, N. N., *Economic Analysis for Engineering and Managerial Decision-Making*, McGraw-Hill, New York, 1962.

Cox, D. R., *Renewal Theory*, Methuen, London, 1962.

Cox, D. R. and W. Smith, *Queues*, Methuen, London, John Wiley, New York, 1961.

Elmaghraby, S. E., *The Design of Production Systems*, Reinhold, New York, 1966.

Goldman, A. S. and T. B. Slattery, *Maintainability*, John Wiley, New York, 1964.

Marston, A., R. Winfrey, and J. C. Hempstead, *Engineering Evaluation and Depreciation*, McGraw-Hill, New York, 1953.

Morse, P. M., *Queues, Inventories, and Maintenance*, John Wiley, New York, 1958.

Prabhu, N. U., *Queues and Inventories*, John Wiley, New York, 1965.

Riggs, J. L., *Economic Decision Models for Engineers and Managers*, McGraw-Hill, New York, 1968.

Riordan, J., *Stochastic Service Systems*, John Wiley, New York, 1962.

Saaty, T. L., *Elements of Queuing Theory*, McGraw-Hill, New York, 1961.

Takacs, L., *Introduction to the Theory of Queues*, Oxford Univ. Press, London, 1962.

Terborgh, G., *Dynamic Equipment Policy*, McGraw-Hill, New York, 1949.

10-10 QUESTIONS AND PROBLEMS

1. A central air-conditioning unit has been installed in an office. Describe how the unit could lose value owing to each of the four causes of depreciation. Which cause would likely account for most of the decrease in value during the next:

(a) 3 years?　(b) 10 years?

2. Describe the more important causes for the retirement of:

(a) Steam locomotives.　(d) Dump trucks.

(b) Passenger cars.　(e) Automatic screw machines.

(c) Electronic computers.　(f) Wheelbarrows.

3. Make a table comparing the three depreciation methods described in Section 10-2 to the list of five desirable attributes of depreciation methods. Use the maximum rate for double-declining-balance depreciation in the comparison. Using a 1–2–3 rating system, which method do you consider most attractive?

4. Should the economic life of a machine equal the service life? Why?

5. Discuss the two major purposes of depreciation accounting with reference to assets such as a furnace, an automobile, and land. Would the purpose be better served by using replacement cost instead of purchase price?

6. Could the salvage value of an asset be negative? How?

345

7. Why do companies generally prefer accelerated depreciation methods, even though these faster write-offs cause the profit and loss statements to show lower profit during the early years of ownership?

8. A salesman agreed to purchase a building lot by making seven annual payments of $900 each. Right after the first payment was made, the salesman was transferred to a different town. Two years and two payments later the salesman returns to find he can buy an equivalent lot for $3000 because land values decreased while he was gone. A friend advises him he has a sunk cost of $600 so he should drop the contract to buy an equivalent lot. The salesman feels he will lose $2700 if he drops the contract. Assuming the salesman will suffer no penalty for reneging on his original agreement, what would you advise? How would you explain it to the salesman?

9. Comment on the following rationalization that often accompanies a decision to keep a defender with a large sunk cost when the challenger provides lower future costs: "I've had some bad luck on repairs, but it is running now, and I've got so much in it that I can't afford to sell it for what it would bring."

10. Why is it necessary to assume sufficient in-process storage space and insignificant in-process inventory costs in order to apply "Johnson's rule?"

11. Why is a perfect line balance (no idle time) theoretically ideal but less than perfect in practice? How do the human factors mentioned in Chapter 7 relate to assembly line balancing?

12. Why is it necessary to assume insignificant set-up costs and uniform fixed costs when applying the transportation method to machine loading?

13. Nearly everyone follows some variety of preventive maintenance for their personal automobiles. Comment on why the practice is so common when few owners actually know whether it saves time or money as compared to making repairs as needed. How does a preventive maintenance policy differ for a single machine versus ownership of a number of the same machines?

14. How can maintenance personnel be recognized for good work and protected from abuse when they are not at fault? Base comments on the motivational and supervisory considerations of Chapter 7. Could practical standards be developed for maintenance personnel?

15. How can a disciplinary policy affect a preventive maintenance program?

16. State a production example for each of the waiting line

structures described in Figure 10.18. For instance, a barber shop could be a multiple-channel, single-phase case.

17. Why is μ assumed to be greater than λ in queuing formulas?

18. Plan and describe a mechanical device that could simulate a single-channel, single-phase queue structure. Let marbles be the customers and their arrival and servicing rates be set by tapes with holes punched at prearranged intervals. A marble falling through a hole in the arrival tape represents a customer for the servicing station. Similarly, a marble passing through the servicing tape represents a customer served.

19. What are the practical limitations to solving waiting line problems by mathematical formulas?

20. A machine was purchased on January 1, 1970 for $6000. Installation costs were $300. It is expected to have an economic life of 7 years and a resale value of $900, but it will cost $200 to dismantle the machine and prepare it for resale. Compute the depreciation charge during the third year by each of the following depreciation methods:

(a) Straight-line depreciation.

(b) Sum-of-digits depreciation.

(c) Double-declining-balance depreciation (maximum rate).

21. If $P = \$10,000$, $S = \$1000$, and $n = 6$, what percentage of the anticipated replacement cost will have been accounted for by accumulated depreciation after half the economic life using the straight-line and sum-of-digits depreciation methods?

22. A new contract requires a special kind of machine which the contractor feels will have no use after the project is completed in 5 years. Two types of machines are suitable. The service life of machine X is 5 years and of machine Y is 3 years. From the anticipated capital cost and maintenance patterns shown below, calculate the annual cost of each machine. The minimum acceptable rate of return is 10%.

Year	Machine X	Machine Y
0	First cost = $35,000	First cost = $15,000
1	———	———
2	———	Repairs = $500
3	Overhaul = $700	Cost of new machine less trade-in = $12,000
4	———	———
5	Salvage = $1000	Salvage = $3000

23. Two years ago an office-duplicating machine was purchased for $1000. Its economic life was estimated at 5 years at which time

the salvage value would be $100. The current book value by straight-line depreciation is $640. Total material, labor, and maintenance expense is $4100 a year. A copying machine will be needed throughout the foreseeable future.

A new model produced by the manufacturers of the presently used machine sells for $1500, but its faster speed will cut annual operating costs to $3800. The manufacturer has offered $800 for the old machine as a trade-in on the new model. The expected salvage value for the new model is $200 after 10 years.

Another company leases duplicating machines at $800 a year. The lease agreement covers all maintenance and repairs which cuts the anticipated operating cost to $3500 per year. The leasing firm will buy the present machine for $500.

Using an interest rate of 8%, compare the defender to each challenger.

24. A dump truck with a first cost of $5000 has the depreciation and service cost pattern shown below.

End of year	1	2	3	4	5	6
Depreciation during year	$1800	$1200	$800	$200	$200	$200
Service cost during year	$800	$1100	$1500	$1900	$2400	$3000

(a) Assuming no interest charges are necessary for the evaluation, how many years should the truck be kept in service before replacement?

(b) Assume the truck presently owned is 2 years old. It is known that a truck will be needed for only 6 more years. When should another truck having the same cost pattern be purchased in order to minimize ownership and operating costs during the 6 years?

25. Find the sequence (or sequences) that minimizes the total elapsed time for the 10 jobs through two-machines process shown below.

Job	A	B	C	D	E	F	G	H	I	J
Time on $M1$	7	3	10	8	13	9	5	11	7	10
Time on $M2$	6	5	15	7	12	12	2	8	5	11

26. Show the optimal schedule or schedules from Problem 25 on a time chart format.

27. Use the graphical method to determine the minimum time

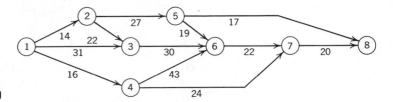

Figure 10.19

necessary to process the two jobs through the five machines with the time relationships shown below.

J1:	sequence	B	C	A	D	E
	time	3	2	4	4	2
J2:	sequence	D	C	B	A	E
	time	4	5	3	3	3

28. On a time chart, show the optimal schedule from Problem 27 that delays the start of *J*2 as long as possible without increasing the minimum total processing time.

29. A line-balancing problem is represented by the network in Figure 10.19. Determine the assignment of operations to work stations that provides the minimum possible cycle time. Arrange the assignments to prorate the idle time as evenly as possible among the work stations.

30. Assume the sequential relationships of the network in Problem 29 still apply, but operations 1, 4; 4, 7; and 5, 8 must be assigned to the same station. Complete the remaining assignments of operations to work stations to minimize the cycle time.

31. A job-shop has three orders that need immediate processing. Four machines are available. The order sizes, time available on each machine, and expected production rate for each machine are shown below.

Hourly Production Rate for Machines

Order	M1	M2	M3	M4	Pieces per Order
O1	2	8	6	3	560
O2	3	10	9	7	500
O3	15	12	10	10	1200
Available hours	90	70	60	45	

The selling price for units ordered and the unit variable cost are given in the following table.

349

	Selling	Variable Cost for Machine			
Order	Price	M1	M2	M3	M4
O1	$3.00	$2.75	$2.00	$2.25	$2.50
O1	$4.00	$3.60	$3.00	$2.90	$3.00
O3	$1.50	$0.75	$1.00	$1.00	$0.75

(a) Determine the assignment of orders to machines.

(b) What is the total contribution of the three orders?

32. A data-processing firm is considering a policy of replacing certain key electrical components on a group replacement basis instead of making repairs as needed. There are approximately 100 parts of one type that have the mortality distribution shown in the margin area. The cost of replacing the parts on an individual basis is estimated to be $1.00 per part; the cost of group replacement averages $0.30 per part. Compare the average weekly cost of the two replacement alternatives.

Week	Probability of Failure During During Week
1	0.3
2	0.1
3	0.1
4	0.2
5	0.3

33. Operators working in a "clean room" environment use magnifying equipment that has a breakdown pattern following an arithmetic progression where on 50% of the shifts no equipment fails, 25% one fails, 12.5% two fail, 6.25% three fail, etc. The 30 operators now have five standby machines. The cost of each standby is $40 per shift; the cost of lost production and servicing for a down machine averages $300 per shift. There is also a lost time cost of $30 to get the replacement machine in position when a breakdown occurs. Show the calculations that prove whether the present number of standby machines is the optimum number.

34. A plastic extrusion plant has 30 machines, each capable of producing any of the plant's product mix. An average of three machines undergo repairs with a loss in production and service amounting to $400 per machine per day. The plant has sufficient space to mount standby equipment. The cost of each standby machine is $40 per day. The number of breakdowns has a Poisson distribution. How many standbys should the plant have to minimize total cost?

35. A maintenance manager has developed the data shown on page 351 for 500 machines that exhibit similar breakdown characteristics. The present policy is to give a complete overhaul whenever a major breakdown occurs. The cost of the overhaul and repairs is $350 per machine. If the preventive maintenance work was done on a scheduled basis, the overhaul cost would be reduced to $100 per machine. Individual repairs made between

preventive maintenance periods are expected to average $150 per machine.

Number of Machines	Number of Hours Between Major Breakdowns
5	3000–4000
20	4000–5000
90	5000–6000
120	6000–7000
135	7000–8000
70	8000–9000
50	9000–10,000
10	10,000–11,000

(a) If the policy were to overhaul each machine after 8000 hours of service, how many would be expected to breakdown before the scheduled overhaul?

(b) What is the average number of hours between breakdowns? Assume all breakdowns occur at the end of each interval.

(c) What is the maintenance cost per 1000 hours of service for a machine when overhauls are made as breakdowns occur?

(d) What is the maintenance cost per 1000 hours of machine service if a preventive maintenance policy on a scheduled basis is used? What interval between preventive maintenance checks provides minimum cost?

36. Repairs in a large printing shop are handled by outside facilities. The service provided is not satisfactory so an internal repair facility is planned. Major repairs average four per week and follow a Poisson distribution. The cost in lost production is estimated at $100 per week during each repair, including waiting and servicing. Which of the following three alternatives will provide the lower total cost for repairs?

(1) One repairman paid $175 a week who can complete an average of eight repairs per week.

(2) One repairman paid $120 a week who can complete an average of five repairs per week.

(3) Two repairmen with the wages and output given in alternative (2).

Assume servicing times follow an exponential distribution.

37. Arrivals at an unloading dock follow a Poisson distribution with an average of three per hour. Trucks are unloaded at an exponential rate averaging four per hour. The cost of an idle truck is $20 per hour. The facility operates 2000 hours a year.

If improvements to the dock could increase the servicing rate to six per hour, what is the maximum investment that could be made for the improvements in order not to increase the cost of unloading? The economic life of the improvements will be 6 years with no salvage value. A rate of return of 10% is required for all investments.

38. An average of 50 calls (following a Poisson distribution) are received per hour at the dispatching office of a taxi service. There are 10 taxicabs in the fleet. The average length of a trip is 8 minutes, including travel to the customer, waiting, loading, and delivery time. Trip times follow an exponential distribution.

(a) What is the probability that a taxi is idle?
(b) It is estimated that profit from each trip is $0.20 per minute of trip time and the fixed cost of each taxi is $5.00 per hour. If the opportunity cost for a waiting customer is $0.10 per minute, would it be advisable to retire one taxi from service?

CHAPTER 11

MATERIALS

11-1 IMPORTANCE   The interrelationships and cross-flow of objectives in production are nowhere more visible than in the measures taken to procure, store, and distribute materials. The system objective is to have the right materials in the right amount at the right place at the right time. Implementation problems arise in deciding which are the proper materials, how much is needed, how to get them there, and what is the best time to act. Making such decisions for each of the multitude of items required to sustain production facilities and to provide the inputs that are transformed into product outputs is indeed a formidable undertaking.

The functions of material management are grossly represented in Figure 11.1. The first three functions may be handled within one department responsible for the entire material system. In other organizations the functions are fragmented, but the need for a comprehensive policy still remains. Guidelines are mandatory to resolve opposing dogmas such as a desire by production to replenish stock by many small orders, while purchasing claims the stock will be less expensive if purchased in larger quantities, and inventory control disagrees with both.

Purchasing has the responsibility of getting the most value from supply expenditures. To do so, as indicated by the combined operation and inspection symbol in Figure 11.1, the merits of internal purchase requests are reviewed and external trends are closely watched to determine the direction of price, service, and quality. In addition to its surveillance duties, it coordinates the administrative routines for issuing purchasing orders, following the progress of delivery, and paying for the material received.

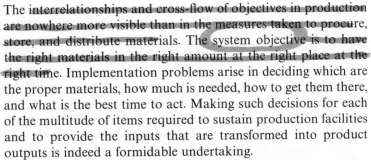

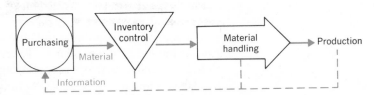

Figure 11.1 Flow and functions involved in material management

353

Stored material acts as a buffer between the demands of production activities and purchasing or between stages of production. Supplies cannot always be purchased or produced as needed; lead time is a normal delay in receiving purchased goods, and set-up times are frequently required to get facilities ready to produce a desired item. While the sense of maintaining an inventory of supplies is apparent, it is not obvious how much it will cost if the supplies are not available when needed or which procedures to follow for recording, checking, and issuing material.

Determining the most effective means of transporting raw materials, parts, subassemblies, and finished products falls within the province of material handling. Many of the topics and techniques we already have encountered are applicable to material handling: linear programming, equipment arrangement, methods and motion study, plant layout, and queuing theory. The attention devoted to material-handling problems is understandable from estimates that up to 80% of indirect labor cost in a plant or 20% to 50% of total production cost is consumed in transporting items from one place to the next.

Warehousing and finished-product distribution also could be included in the material system. Distribution is discussed in Chapter 16.

The following sections treat the three material management functions in the order shown in Figure 11.1. This separation is more pedagogical than natural. To appreciate the function of a whole system, it is first necessary to comprehend the functioning parts. Each stage of material management is irrevocably linked to the other stages and to the aggregate production process it serves.

11-2 PURCHASING

The purchasing function is the interface between a company and its suppliers. From the supplier side of the interface, the company is viewed as a customer. Accordingly, the company is catered to by the sales forces of the vendors and is susceptible to their marketing strategies. On the other side of the interface, purchasing functions as a monitor, clearing house, and pipeline to supply materials needed to maintain production. The operating units feed in their requisitions, the requests are reviewed and converted to orders, and the filled orders flow back to restock production supplies.

Purchases are roughly divided into two categories, maintenance supplies and raw materials. Spare parts, replacement tools, new machines, office supplies, and housekeeping provisions are routine but inevitable purchases. The main question is how much to keep on hand; a temporary shortage of cleaning compounds has far less impact on production than the absence of a critical replacement part for a production machine. "Raw" materials may be truly unrefined substances such as ore, oil, or plants, and they may take the form of subassemblies, manufactured components, or even complete products that are retailed by a mail-order company. For such items the buyers rely heavily on forecasts. They juggle forecasted demands for material against the expected price and delivery time for supplies.

Purchasing Function

Purchasing is a service function that supports the activities of other operations. In turn, it receives assistance from other operating units. Effective functioning requires a steady and reliable flow of information between concerned departments. The relationship of the purchasing structure to other parts of the production system is displayed in Figure 11.2. The dotted lines represent the interchange of information; the solid lines show the movement of cash and material.

Marketing information provides an indication of anticipated production output. Reliable forecasts are needed because it takes considerable time to review and process requisitions, select suppliers, issue purchase orders, and obtain delivery. Advance clues allow purchasing to shop for the best price. By watching price trends, inventories of items likely to increase in cost can be built up in advance. The speculative practice of "hedging" is possible for materials carried on an organized commodity exchange. Purchasing and marketing also work together in reciprocity agreements, arrangements made to purchase materials from a vendor who reciprocates by buying products produced by the purchaser. These "you scratch my back

"Hedging" involves buying and selling commodity "futures." Fearing a commodity price increase, a firm can buy at a given price, usually higher than the present price but lower than the anticipated future price. The quantity purchased is to be delivered at a future date.

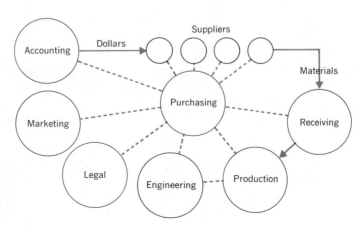

Figure 11.2 Information and material flow in the purchasing function

while I scratch yours" deals can work out nicely, but care should be given to the danger of being at the mercy of an exclusive, complacent supplier.

Production is the terminal point for most material flow and is the initiating point for most material requests. Two age-old customs color the dealings between purchasing and production. The first is a "squirrel complex" which leads production supervisors and managers to hoard supplies. This protective policy certainly limits the chance of work delays owing to a shortage of parts or materials, but it builds a big inventory which is subject to damage, loss, and obsolescence. The second custom is a "brand X complex," a preference for a particular brand that has previously provided good service. Again there are legitimate bases for such feelings because past performance is an indicator of future satisfaction. The troublesome aspect is that new products are continually being developed; a loyalty to one brand eliminates the chance to recognize equal or even higher quality at a lower price. Though it is easy to scoff at such attitudes in other people, another guilty person is visible in most mirrors.

Engineering personnel also are influenced by a brand X complex. Their preferences stem from the reputation of a supplier and are reinforced by the services rendered by the preferred vendor. When these options and actions lead to competent product design and competitive prices, they are eminently acceptable. When they represent a path of least resistance for writing specifications, they are questionable. Purchasing agents, as contacts for the firm with salesmen from prospective suppliers, often are aware of new, lower cost materials before engineering

Engineering designs utilizing nonstandard parts and stiff tolerances are enigmas to purchasing agents.

• departments. The agents usually do not have the technical knowledge to evaluate new material developments, but they should have them appraised by those who do. Distribution of appropriate literature or meetings arranged between engineers and suppliers can produce new ideas and lower procurement costs.

Legal aspects require attention whenever binding agreements are made between the company and a supplier. Standard forms, already checked for legality, are available for most routine

An old saying cautions that a man who acts as his own lawyer has a fool for a client.

• purchases. The larger, longer contracts, where special conditions are incorporated, rate a thorough legal review to assure that both sides understand their responsibilities. Company lawyers can also assist purchasing by the interpretation of new legislation or existing laws applicable to fair pricing, misrepresentation, rebates, freight rates, and similar subjects.

356

Receiving personnel report the quantity and quality of supplies received. Purchasing uses this information to appraise the service of suppliers. When shipments are late, purchasing initiates contacts with vendors to determine the state of progress. Reimbursements or allowances are negotiated for shipments damaged in transit. After a shipment is accepted by receiving, it is uncrated and moved to production facilities or to inventory storage areas.

Accounting pays for the shipments after notification of their acceptance. Prompt notification is necessary to take advantage of cash discounts awarded for quick payments. Actions taken to speed deliveries and to secure reimbursement for damaged shipments should be reported because accounting also handles the internal paperwork of inventory records, invoice checking, and other financial details for material transactions.

Purchasing functions are usually coordinated by a purchasing department under the auspices of finance or marketing. There appears to be a trend toward grouping purchasing along with other material-oriented functions within a single material management department with a top-level standing. The intricate network of information channels and the high dollar volume of activity make purchasing a prime candidate for system synthesis. By combining material procurement with control, many communication lines would be shortened and purchasing policies would likely achieve greater strategic effectiveness.

Centralized purchasing, as practiced by most companies, is a step toward systemization. Passing all orders through one office allows consolidated purchasing. Buying in greater quantities leads to cash discounts. Purchasing agents can specialize in certain accounts and negotiate more effectively with suppliers. However, centralization tends to reduce flexibility and may be less sensitive to local needs of geographically separated operations. Frequently, these disadvantages are reduced by central purchasing of high cost, high volume supplies while allowing local control of small or rush orders. Decentralization of authority for some purchases does not dilute the system principle if the wielders of authority follow system objectives. In fact, placing controlled authority at the point of responsibility can make believers out of system skeptics.

Purchasing Procedures

A purchasing cycle begins with a decision to buy material and ends when the material is accepted by the unit that instigated the order. Purchasing responsibilities extend from one end point to

"There is nothing more difficult to take in hand, more perilous to conduct, or more uncertain in its success, than to take the lead in the introduction of a new order of things." Niccolo Machiavelli (1469–1527).

357

the other and include many procedures inbetween. Some of the more important operations are described by the following sequence of purchasing activities.

1. *Receive requisitions.* Purchase requisitions are made out by personnel from all functional areas of the firm. The requisition forms include information as to what and how many items are wanted, when they should be available, and who is making the request. A column for "quantity on hand" is frequently included to force the requisitioner to check whether the items are truly needed.

    The elapsed time between placing an order and its receipt is known as "lead time." It plays a significant role in purchasing and inventory control. Most purchasing departments urge requisitioners to anticipate material demands well ahead of actual need. Early requests act as buffers for unexpected delivery delays. Allowing a long lead time also means larger inventories must be kept to carry operations over the longer wait between ordering and receiving. The practical consequence of allowing longer times for delivery seems to be that present lead times just grow to take up whatever slack is allowed. Perhaps this is due to the "squeaky wheel principle;" buyers who expect the shortest lead times complain the loudest when deliveries are late and thereby receive the most attention from suppliers. Requisitioners certainly should be aware of a minimum lead time, but an attempt should be made to correct suppliers' delivery delays instead of automatically increasing allowed lead times.

2. *Review requisitions. Value analysis* and *value engineering* are generic terms used to describe a study of the functions materials are supposed to accommodate. From a purchasing viewpoint, value analysis represents a relatively recent change from concentration on attaining the best price for a certain item to attention to the lowest cost for any item that will satisfy an intended function. The analysis answers such questions as: Could a less expensive material serve the same function? Is the function necessary? Could it be eliminated? Could other items serve the same function? Can they be simplified? Could the supplier reduce his price by a cooperative redesign or revised specifications?

    Purchasing usually does not have the authority to substitute or modify materials designated by operating units. It does have the responsibilities to question requisitions and to suggest alternatives that would lead to better prices. When the

Creative substitutes such as new alloys, synthetics, and unusual designs such as spiral nails or nylon lock fasteners have recorded huge savings.

originators know their requisitions are going to be scrutinized, more attention is normally devoted to their preparation.

A value engineering approach identifies three types of value, each having a distinct relationship to cost and function:

Use value—a monetary measure of the qualities of an item that contribute to its performance.

Esteem value—a monetary measure of the properties that contribute to its salability or desirability of ownership.

Exchange value—a monetary measure of the qualities and properties of an item that enable it to be exchanged for something else.

The equation that guides purchasing is

$$use\ value\ +\ esteem\ value\ =\ exchange\ value$$

As applied to the purchase of stationery, the equation would require assigning a dollar value first for any writing material and then placing a price on the worth of accessories such as fancy letterheads or colored paper. The exchange value is the amount that must be paid to satisfy the other functions; it is a value established by comparison and no other means.

Most attention is devoted to the use value. One way to pinpoint the use function is to force a description by two words, a verb and a noun. For instance, the primary function of a shipping container is to "protect contents." A secondary function could be to "create impression" or to "explain contents." The purpose of functional definitions of use is to focus study on frivolous or secondary functions which may unnecessarily increase cost.

The intent underlying the surface techniques of value engineering is to foster a creative questioning attitude. Purchasing has the knowledge of suppliers' offerings and competitive prices. Engineering has the know-how for technical comparisons. Operating personnel know what services they need and the practical limitations for substitutions. It takes a cooperative effort to identify new ways to do something, to evaluate them, and then to get them accepted by the users. Some practices that discourage the recognition and acceptance of change are: (1) inability or refusal to gather all the facts, (2) failure to explore all possible ways to perform a function, (3) decisions made on what is believed to be true rather than true facts, and (4) habits that were formed in the past and attitudes that keep them from changing.

Incentive clauses to promote the use of value engineering are widely included in government contracts. Savings from the value program are split at a given rate such as 90% to the government and 10% to the contractor.

"Like men with sore eyes: they find the light painful, while the darkness, which permits them to see nothing, is restful and agreeable." Dio Chryostom.

3. *Select suppliers.* Sources of supplies originate from salesmen contacts, ads in trade journals, descriptions of products in buyer's guides, correspondence, inspection tours of plants, and experience with a supplier's products. From such sources an *approved supplier list* is developed. The list results from rating vendors as to the quality of their products, prices, services, and delivery reliability. An approved list is usually developed for each class of supplies. Then a purchasing agent has only to contact a few acceptable suppliers to obtain quotes on price and delivery.

A complete, up-to-date list of suppliers is instrumental in obtaining better prices and services. New names should be continually sought, and the performance of existing suppliers should be continually monitored because poor suppliers can improve and better suppliers can get careless. Some suppliers offer exceptional technical assistance, training programs, equipment-borrowing privileges, and other inducements. When such services will be helpful, the appropriate vendor should be known. Freight rates for some purchases may swing the total cost advantage from a distant supplier with low prices to a closer supplier with slightly higher prices. Most companies distribute large orders among two or more suppliers to provide a competitive check on the major supplier (one supplier often receives 50% to 70% of the orders) and to protect against delivery defaults stemming from mismanagement, strikes, fire, or natural catastrophes.

4. *Place orders.* The normal purchasing routine of processing individual item requisitions is modified for very large, very small, and continuous purchases. Major acquisitions of unique machines and custom production facilities are *one-of-a-kind contracts.* Bids are often solicited for the entire investment—design, construction, and installation. Negotiations are conducted with several potential suppliers and usually extend over a considerable period because specifications for the asset are seldom confirmed until the supplier's resources are explored. The development of new designs is frequently a cooperative effort between the staffs of the buyer and the seller.

The purchase price of low cost, infrequently needed items may be less than the cost to process a purchase order. Processing costs are typically $8 to $20 per order or even higher. The absurdity of incurring processing costs greater than the amount of the order is obvious. Small organizations often

The possibility of a firm being its own supplier occurs in a "make or buy" decision. Purchasing represents the "buy" side of the question. The "make" side was considered in Section 4-3.

have a petty cash fund for petty purchases. More commonly, an open account is established with a supplier who inventories many minor items occasionally required. The supplier keeps track of direct orders and periodically bills the buyer. Purchasing negotiates the original *open contract* and monitors payments to keep the practice from getting out of control.

Individual purchasing orders are avoided for items in continuous demand by a *blanket purchase order*. This contract differs from an open contract in that the orders are generally predictable and for homogeneous items. A price for the items may be negotiated annually, with deliveries made on request during the year. The list price is charged for each delivery, but a discount based on total annual quantity is usually obtained at the end of the year. Both the buyer and seller receive benefits from the agreement. The buyer can negotiate at one time for a substantial portion of annual supplies and order processing cost is reduced. The seller, assured of a market for his products, can reduce his advertising and other selling expenses.

5. *Monitor orders.* Important or lengthy orders are routinely checked by purchasing to determine whether anticipated deliveries are on schedule. Production difficulties of the supplier and change orders from within his own firm can occasionally put the purchasing agent in an uncomfortable position. His production control colleagues blame late delivery on his lack of follow-up. The supplier blames order changes concocted by the agent's production control colleagues for the delays. The purchasing agent replies to both that there is not enough time to monitor every order with every supplier, especially when so many are marked "CHANGE-RUSH."

Such sensitive situations are not uncommon and merely underscore the coordination problems inherent in material management. Rescheduling is occasionally unavoidable. Disturbances are allayed by a give-and-take attitude. Internal production schedules can sometimes be altered; at times the supplier can fall behind on some deliveries to concentrate on more critical demands. The key to coordination is to keep open channels of communication, both within the firm and to the supplier. Purchasing acts as the switchboard.

6. *Receive orders.* Receipt of a contracted quantity in an acceptable condition is a signal to complete the purchase transaction. Records of the purchase are consolidated and payment is

Blanket purchasing often is applied to only a portion of annual demand, say 60%, in order to maintain a competitive bargaining position for future transactions.

Acceptance samping applicable to the inspection of shipments is discussed in Section 14-5.

361

made. The final price is possibly subject to a discount—trade, quantity, or cash.

The boast "I can get it for you wholesale" is an example of a *trade discount*, a price level determined by the classification of the buyer such as manufacturer, wholesaler, or retailer. *Quantity discounts* are a function of the number of items ordered. The justification for price reductions on larger orders results from decreased cost for selling, shipping, handling, and recordkeeping. *Cash discounts* are awarded for prompt payment of bills. A policy such as "2/10 net 30" means the purchaser can deduct 2% of the list price if he pays for the order within the first 10 days of the month following receipt of the bill. Payment is expected within 30 days, even if the discount is not utilized. Offering cash discounts is justified by time value of money considerations. Failure to take advantage of such discounts is difficult to justify; discount calculations are the pleasant aftermath of prudent purchasing.

EXAMPLE 11.1 Two Sides of the Purchaser's Supplier Rating System

The National Association of Purchasing Agents outlined a cost-ratio plan for numerically rating suppliers in their pamphlet "Evaluation of Supplier Performance" (New York, 1963). The plan attempts to attach a dollar value to each of four major procurement factors: price, quality, delivery, and service. The supplier who can consistently provide the required material at the lowest net value cost is, in theory, most frequently selected. The procedure for determining the net value cost is summarized below.

Step 1. Net delivery price = list price − discounts + freight cost + insurance, taxes, etc.

Step 2. Quality cost ratio = $\dfrac{\text{material quality costs}}{\text{total value of purchases}}$

The material quality costs are taken from past quality reports on purchases made from each supplier. These expenses include the cost for laboratory tests, incoming inspections, processing inspection reports, handling and packaging rejects, spoilage and waste, and manufacturing losses. Most of these costs are prepared by production and quality control departments. The yearly trend of the ratio indicates whether quality levels are being maintained or improved by the supplier.

Step 3. Acquisition cost ratio = $\dfrac{\text{acquisition and continuity costs}}{\text{total value of purchases}}$

The denominator of the equation is the same as in Step 2. The numerator is derived by the purchasing department from the cost of sale negotiations, communication tolls, surveys, premium transportation, monitoring, and progress reporting.

Step 4. Deliver cost ratio = acquisition cost ratio + promises-kept penalty

The cost of deliveries later than promised is expressed as a percentage of the total value of purchases delivered.

Step 5. Service cost ratio $= \dfrac{\text{maximum possible rating} - \text{supplier rating}}{\text{maximum possible rating}}$

(A supplier rating below a given level, such as 60, automatically makes the ratio = 1.0.) Service costs are determined from absolute ratings of special considerations which suppliers offer with products and services. These ratings are converted to a penalty percentage and charged against the supplier lacking the considerations. The following list illustrates how a supplier service cost ratio of $(100 - 70)/100 = 0.3$ could be obtained.

Maximum Points	Category	Supplier Rating
	Competence and Ability:	
15	Product development and advancement	11
15	Product leadership and reputation	9
10	Technical ability of staff	9
10	Capacity for volume production	8
10	Financial solvency and profitability	8
	Attitudes and Special Considerations:	
5	Labor relations record	2
10	Business approach	8
5	Field service and adaptability to changes	2
10	Warranty conditions	6
10	Communication of progress data	7
100	Total Points	70

Step 6. Net value cost = net delivery price + (net delivery price × sum of ratios from Steps 2, 4, and 5)

The comparison of suppliers is based on their present net delivery price modified by additional costs expected from the history of their past performance. For instance, a net value cost for one supplier could result in the following price and penalty pattern:

Step 1: Price quote ($114,300) − discount (10% × $114,300) + freight ($600)
= net delivery price ($103,470)

Steps 2–5: Sum of ratios = quality cost (2.2%) + delivery cost (1.2%)
+ service cost (0.3%) = 3.7%

Step 6: Net value cost = $103,470 + ($103,470 × 0.037) = $107,300

Such ratings are then compared for each order to identify the preferred supplier. (Note the similarity of this rating system to the exponential comparison model of Section 4-3. The principal difference is that all factors are given the same importance rating.)

An interesting viewpoint is developed by reviewing the rating system as it appears to the supplier. The most pertinent source of information by which a supplier can evaluate his products and services is the response of the purchaser. A purchasing policy is dedicated to maximizing returns from supply expenditures—at least that is what the supplier must believe if he is to use his sales as a criterion for improving his competitive position.

Suppliers recognize that few purchasing agents will give 100% of their orders to one vendor, but there is some maximum percentage they will give. The difference between this maximum percentage and the percentage being supplied is a measure of the opportunity cost for a supplier. Assuming a purchaser will reveal the maximum percentage, the supplier can see what potential sales are available from each buyer. The potential is an indication of how much the supplier can afford to spend to make his product and services more attractive to the purchaser. Then the problem narrows to determining what must be done to improve performance enough to obtain more orders.

The supplier rating scale pinpoints exactly where the purchaser feels the supplier is lacking. However, this information is typically considered proprietary. There are sound competitive reasons for keeping current ratings confidential. There are also sound financial reasons for revealing at least enough information to show a supplier his relative standing in each area considered important; the information can guide the supplier in his effort to improve performance and the result of the effort will provide the purchaser with more of the qualities he desires. The health of the supplier can contribute to the wealth of the user—and vice versa.

11-3 INVENTORY CONCEPTS

Hiring more men than needed for current operations in anticipation of receiving a major contract creates a manpower inventory. The shortage of some skills, such as engineering, has been blamed on stockpiling by defense industries for defense contracts.

Inventory, in a production context, is an idle resource. The resource can be animate or inanimate. Most commonly it is production material: tools, purchased parts, raw materials, office supplies, products in-process, etc. That the resource is idle does not mean it is serving no purpose. It is available when needed. It serves as an insurance policy against the unexpected breakdowns, delays, and other disturbances that could disrupt on-going production. Insurance is not free. The idle resource can be damaged or become obsolete before it serves any purpose. The task is again to secure an economic balance between the cost of loss and the cost of preventing it.

By the early 1900's, formulas were developed to analyze inventory problems, but it was not until the 1940's that the theories were widely put to practice. Inventory problems are natural candidates for formal analysis. The problem area is common to all industries, the costs involved warrant detailed attention, and few intangible considerations are embraced. These factors all lead to very neat mathematical formulations for general cases. When cases get more specific, and consequently more realistic, more sophisticated formulations are needed. We shall investigate the basic formulas and some of their more frequently encountered refinements.

Inventory Functions

It would be nice if we could completely exclude the human factor from inventory considerations. We cannot. Inventories serve many functions. The people associated with each function would prefer an inventory policy that first satisfied their pet function. The opposing nature of preferences is shown in Table 11.1.

Table 11.1 Conflicting objectives for material management

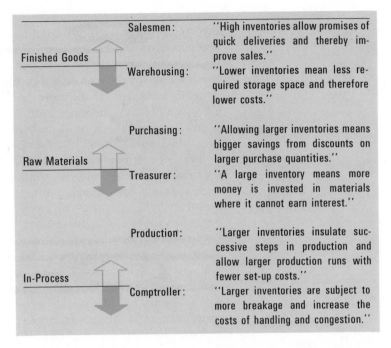

	Salesmen:	"High inventories allow promises of quick deliveries and thereby improve sales."
Finished Goods	Warehousing:	"Lower inventories mean less required storage space and therefore lower costs."
	Purchasing:	"Allowing larger inventories means bigger savings from discounts on larger purchase quantities."
Raw Materials	Treasurer:	"A large inventory means more money is invested in materials where it cannot earn interest."
	Production:	"Larger inventories insulate successive steps in production and allow larger production runs with fewer set-up costs."
In-Process	Comptroller:	"Larger inventories are subject to more breakage and increase the costs of handling and congestion."

The most important function of inventories is insulation. A reserve of material can be tapped whenever a delay in a preceding stage threatens to curtail operations in the following stage. The stages stretch the length of the production cycle, from initial inputs to delivery of final output. Material buffers are used to cushion the production process from the uncertainty of material deliveries, to decouple progressive stages of product development from disruptions in prior stages, and to provide a steady supply of finished output for the unsteady demands of customers.

The apparent functions of an inventory policy obscure many subtle ways it affects operations throughout a production system. Daily and seasonal workloads are stabilized by inventory. Stable work requirements allow workers to establish consistent work patterns; incentive wages are ineffective and supervising is more difficult when workloads fluctuate from day to day. By smoothing

The importance of reliable sales forecasting is conspicuous in deciding inventory size.

out the peaks and troughs of customer demand through inventory build-ups during slack sales periods, a relatively constant work force can be maintained. This avoids frantic hiring during rush periods and damaged worker morale or community relations during layoff periods.

The less obvious effects of finished-product inventories are

Queuing theory is directly applicable to many inventory problems. For instance, an inventory of cars in the showroom for "demonstrators" could be the number of servicing channels, and the arrivals could be potential buyers.

The model for determining the optimum number of standby machines also fits the queuing–inventory pattern.

Inventory accumulation in anticipation of a strike is an example of stockpiling. The rationale followed is that the stockpile will allow continued production during supplier's labor-management strife, and prices before negotiations will probably be lower than afterwards.

similar to the considerations for servicing facilities in queuing theory. The "idle resource" definition for inventory could easily accommodate the policy of providing extra servicing stations for emergency service. The behavior of arrivals to or in a waiting line is about the same as that of customers in a retail store. If the items they want from the store are not on hand, they may go elsewhere to make purchases instead of waiting for the retailer to order a supply. Items on display may create a surface "want" when the deeper "need" is still embryonic. This impulse buying is akin to a customer deserting a waiting line to try the service at a competing station with no waiting line. Such considerations were excluded from queuing formulas by assumption, and they are treated the same way by most inventory formulas. But the potential cost of vindicative human behavior is still very real.

Inventory policy is intimately related to purchasing policy. Most prices fluctuate above and below a general trend line. A policy of "buying down" is an attempt to make purchases whenever the price dips below the trend line. Since purchasing has no control over the general price structure, its purchases will accumulate stock at uneven intervals and in unequal quantities, depending on market conditions (Figure 11.3). When it appears that a source of supply will be temporarily shut off or prices will rise sharply, large purchases at a favorable price will markedly increase inventory levels. As shown in Figure 11.3, a speculative purchase can sometimes facilitate impressive purchasing bargains and will always create impressive purchasing stockpiles. The apparent savings from these purchasing policies must be weighed against the inventory costs of storage, handling, depreciation, and interest charges.

Inventory Costs

Costs must be assigned to the diverse inventory considerations to evaluate properly the merits of opposing functions. The more relevant costs and the symbols by which they are denoted in formulas are itemized in the following paragraphs.

Price (*P*). The value of an item is its unit purchase price if it is obtained from an outside supplier, or its unit production cost if it is produced internally. The amount invested in an item being manufactured is a function of its degree of refinement. The value of a product during its initial stage of development is little more than the aggregate cost of collecting raw materials. As it progresses through the production cycle, it accumulates a share of the fixed cost of production facilities, direct and indirect labor costs for

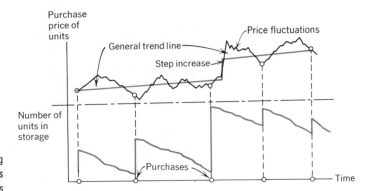

Figure 11.3 Effect of buying down and speculative purchases on inventory levels

Normal production costs can be increased by overtime labor required to meet special rush orders.

• refining operations, and direct cost of material additions. The price per piece of outside purchases also can vary as a function of quantity discounts.

Capital cost (iP). The amount invested in an item is an amount of capital not available for other purposes. If the money were invested elsewhere, a return on the investment would be expected. A charge to inventory expense is made to account for this unreceived return. The amount of the charge reflects the percentage return expected from other investments. The interest charged, i, is applied against the price, P, to support a claim for annual capital cost.

Order cost (O). Procurement costs originate from the expense of issuing an order to an outside supplier or from internal production set-up costs. Order costs include the fixed cost of maintaining an order department and the variable costs of preparing and executing purchase requisitions. Even when orders are delivered from other parts of the same company, order costs still apply. The same purchasing routine of checking inventory levels, issuing orders, follow-up, inspection, and updating inventory records pertains to internal procurement.

Set-up costs account for the physical work incurred in preparing for a production run (setting up equipment and adjusting machines) and include the clerical costs of shop orders, scheduling, and expediting. External orders, internal procurement, and set-up costs remain relatively constant regardless of the order size.

Holding cost (H). Costs originating from many sources are consolidated under the heading of holding cost. One percentage or dollar value is usually placed on the conglomerate total to account for all the sources itemized below. In general, holding costs remain fixed to a certain inventory capacity and then vary with the additional quantity stored.

1. Storage facilities: Buildings have to be owned or leased to store the inventory. The expense includes the equivalent annual cost of the investment if the facilities are owned or the rent if leased, heat, lights, and property taxes.
2. Handling: The cost of moving items to, from, and within storage includes damages, wages, and equipment expense.
3. Depreciation: The change in value of an item during storage is caused by physical deterioration, mutilation and pilferage not covered by insurance, and obsolescence.
4. Insurance: A conservative policy is to insure goods during storage. The protection is usually based on the average dollar value of the inventory.
5. Taxes: Some states levy an inventory tax periodically during a year on the amount in storage at the time. Particularly in retail outlets, such as automobile dealers, it is possible to manipulate inventory levels to have dips coincide with assessment dates.

Opportunity cost (OC). Two types of costs are associated with running out of stock when there is still a demand for the product. The first is the cost of emergency measures to expedite a rush delivery. This cost is easily identified as the difference between the usual cost of procurement and the extra cost for accelerated service. The other cost is much more difficult to divine because it involves people. When emergency procedures cannot provide a wanted item, the customer is left unsatisfied. The only apparent cost is the profit lost from the potential retail sale or the production lost. The reaction of a dissatisfied customer in terms of future business is a cost estimate of the roughest nature.

Some firms stress customer satisfaction to the point where they give greater value as a substitute for items that should have been available.

11-4 INVENTORY MODELS ASSUMING CERTAINTY

Analyses of inventory costs recognize just two patterns: costs that vary directly with the size of an order and costs that vary inversely with order quantity. All of the costs we have considered fit into these two categories. Capital and holding costs increase as the order size increases because larger orders mean higher inventory levels. These "carrying costs" are decreased by ordering smaller amounts. For a given demand, ordering smaller amounts means more orders must be placed. Placing more orders increases the total annual ordering cost. Since stock levels are allowed to dip more often when more orders are placed, there are more

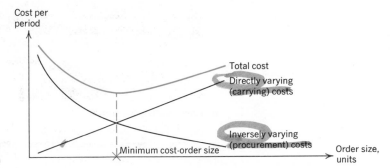

Figure 11.4 Cost–order size relationship

chances to run out of stock and opportunity costs consequently increase. The total inventory cost is then the sum of carrying and procurement costs. The relationship of directly varying, inversely varying, and total costs are shown in Figure 11.4. Inventory models quantify the relationship to identify the order size that minimizes total cost.

The inventory models considered under an assumption of certainty are based on premises that greatly simplify their structure but diminish their reality. The following assumptions and their effects are applicable to all formulas in this section.

1. The total number of units required for 1 year is known exactly:

   annual demand $= D =$ yearly usage of items

2. Demand is constant. The exact number of items needed during any time period is known when the usage rate is steady.
3. Orders are received instantaneously. This condition is not as absurd or restrictive as it first appears. It means an ordered quantity will be available when expected; the corollary is that lead time is known and constant. This assumption erases the possibility of opportunity costs being incurred; if orders can be received instantaneously, there can never be an unfilled demand.
4. Ordering costs are the same regardless of order size. Similarly, set-up costs are constant and the rate at which products are produced is known:

   manufacturing rate $= M =$ annual rate at which items can be produced

5. The purchase or production price does not fluctuate during the period considered. However, the price can vary as a function of order quantity.
6. There is sufficient space, handling capacity, and money to

369

allow the procurement of any quantity desired. The limiting maximum is to order only once a year:

procurement quantity $= Q =$ number of items ordered each replenishment period

Then, $D = Q$ when all the material required for a year's operations is secured at one time.

Economic Order Quantity

The size of an order that minimizes the total inventory cost is known as the economic order quantity, *EOQ*. The usage and replenishment pattern for the *EOQ* based on the given assumptions is shown in Figure 11.5. The vertical lines indicate instantaneous receipt of an order size Q. A constant usage rate represented by the sloping lines takes the inventory level down to zero during the interval between orders, t. The average number of items in storage is $Q/2$.

The unknowns in the triangular pattern are the peaks—amount to order, Q, and the bases—time between orders, t. Both the procurement and carrying costs graphed in Figure 11.4 are a function of Q. The annual procurement cost is the number of orders submitted per year times the cost per order:

$$\text{annual procurement cost} = O\frac{D}{Q}$$

$$= \text{cost per order} \times \frac{\text{number of units demanded per year}}{\text{number of units per order}}$$

Holding and interest costs are often combined into one percentage charge or a single monetary charge per item.

Assuming the handling cost and capital cost are based on the average inventory level, we have

• $\text{annual carrying cost} = (H + iP)\dfrac{Q}{2}$

$= \text{(holding + interest charge per unit per year)} \times \text{average inventory}$

When holding costs are based on maximum inventory, $2H$ replaces H in the carrying cost expression.

• Combining the expressions, we get the formula:

$$\text{total annual inventory cost} = O\frac{D}{Q} + (H + iP)\frac{Q}{2}$$

Recalling the shape of the total cost curve from Figure 11.4, we know the slope is zero at the minimum point. Thus, one way to determine the value of Q that minimizes total annual cost is to differentiate the expression with respect to Q and set the differential equal to zero:

$$\frac{d}{dQ}(\text{total annual cost}) = -\frac{OD}{Q^2} + \frac{H + iP}{2} = 0$$

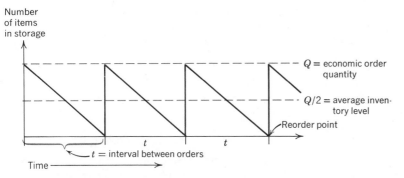

Figure 11.5 Inventory pattern of instantaneous replenishment and constant demand

The *EOQ* formula with all carrying costs collected into one term, $Q = \sqrt{2OD/H}$, was developed in 1915 by F. W. Harris.

Then solving the equation for Q, we get the *EOQ* formula

$$Q = \sqrt{\frac{2OD}{H + iP}}$$

Another method to obtain the same formula is to recall from Section 4-3 that a minimum (or maximum) occurs where the rates of change of two opposing trends in one function are equal. The marginal balance of direct and inversely varying costs for inventory occurs when procurement costs equal carrying costs. From this equality,

$$\frac{OD}{Q} = \frac{(H + iP)Q}{2}$$

we get

$$\frac{Q^2}{2} = \frac{OD}{H + iP} \quad \text{and} \quad Q = \sqrt{\frac{2OD}{H + iP}}$$

Several other statistics of interest can be calculated once Q is known. The number of orders to place in 1 year is given by the quotient of D/Q. If we assume there are 200 working days in a year, the number of working days between orders is:

$$\text{order interval} = t = \frac{200}{D/Q}$$

The complete cost of stocking an item is calculated by adding the purchase price for a year's supply to the total annual inventory cost:

$$\text{total annual stocking cost} = \frac{OD}{Q} + \frac{(H + iP)Q}{2} + PD$$

371

EXAMPLE 11.2 Calculation of An Economic Order Quantity With No Purchase Discounts

The Moore-Funn Novelty Company buys 80,000 shipping containers each year. The following costs are applicable:

$P = \$0.40$ per container

$O = \$80.00$ per order

$H = \$0.10$ per container per year

$i = 15\%$ including a charge for taxes and insurance as well as interest

One warehouse is used exclusively to hold paper products. Since the space is not utilized for other storage when inventory supplies are low, holding costs are based on the maximum rather than average inventory level. The EOQ formula thus takes the form:

$$Q = \sqrt{\frac{2OD}{2H + iP}} = \sqrt{\frac{2 \times 80 \times 80,000}{(2 \times 0.10) + (0.15 \times 0.40)}} = \sqrt{49,230,769} = 7016 \ units/order$$

The number of orders to place in 1 year is

$$\frac{D}{Q} = \frac{80,000}{7016} \doteq 11 \ times \quad approximately$$

and the time between orders based on 220 working days per year is

$$t = \frac{220}{11} = 20 \quad (every \ 4 \ wks \ )$$

The total annual stocking cost for shipping containers then becomes *including price itself*

$$\frac{OD}{Q} + \frac{(2H + iP)Q}{2} + PD = \frac{(80)(80,000)}{7016}$$

procurement + holding

$$+ \frac{(2 \times \$0.10 + 0.15 \times \$0.40)7016}{2} + \$0.40 \times 80,000$$

which is

$$\$912 + \$912 + \$32,000 = \$33,824$$

equal

Note the equality between procurement and carrying costs.

Quantity Discounts

Price discounts are often offered by suppliers to encourage larger orders. Benefits for the purchaser from bigger orders include the reduction in unit price, lower shipping and handling costs, and a reduction in ordering costs owing to fewer orders. These benefits have to be measured against the incremental increase in carrying costs. As the order size increases, more space must be provided for storage; the costs of holding the larger inventory level correspondingly increase. Another pertinent, though difficult to quantify, consideration is the risk of obsolescence or functional depreciation. Larger inventories

EOQ calculations are expedited by tables or nomographs of *Q* as a function of frequently encountered carrying and procurement costs.

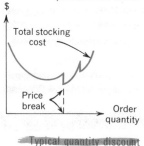

Typical quantity discount pattern.

magnify the loss that would result if design or demand changes make the stored supplies less valuable.

• Quantity discounts are evaluated by first determining the *EOQ* without a discount. When *Q* is less than the minimum quantity at which a discount is allowed, the total annual stocking cost is calculated for the minimum order quantity. This cost is then compared to the annual stocking cost when *Q* is the ordering quantity. If the discounted price produces a lower annual expense, the procedure is repeated using the minimum quantity from the

• next price break. The comparisons are continued until the quantity producing the lowest total annual stocking cost is identified. Then the savings allowed by the higher stock levels are rated against the risk of holding these levels. The risk is gaged by the stability of past demand, resale value, and suspected market trends.

EXAMPLE 11.3 Calculation of Order Size When Quantity Discounts Are Available

A supplier from which the Moore-Funn Company could obtain shipping containers has offered the following quantity discount schedule:

Price	Quantity
$P1$ = $0.40 per container	All orders up to 9999 containers
$P2$ = $0.36 per container	Orders from 10,000 to 19,999
$P3$ = $0.35 per container	Any order above 19,999 containers

From Example 11.2 the total annual stocking cost for orders of 4000 [7016] containers is known to be $33,824. Therefore, the minimum order quantity in the range of 10,000 to 19,999 will produce the least increase in carrying costs while still allowing the 10% price reduction from the $0.40 charge used to calculate Q = 7016. The annual cost for an order size of 10,000 containers is

$$\frac{(\$80)\,(80,000)}{10,000} + \frac{(2 \times \$0.10 + 0.15 \times \$0.36)10,000}{2} + \$0.36 \times 80,000$$

which is

$$\$640 + \$1270 + \$28,800 = \$30,710$$

The advantage ($33,824 − $30,710 = $3114) of increasing the order size from 7016 to 10,000 suggests the next price break should be investigated. The lowest order size for the additional discount to $P3$ = $0.35/container is 20,000:

$$\text{total annual stocking cost} = \frac{(\$80)\,(80,000)}{20,000} + \frac{(2 \times \$0.10 + 0.15 \times \$0.35)20,000}{2}$$

$$+ \$0.35 \times 80,000$$

double C_h
half C_0

$$= \$320 + \$2525 + \$28,000 = \$30,845$$

The carrying costs of this additional increment outweigh the reduction in buying price and procurement cost. The preference for an order size of 10,000 containers should receive a final

$C_h \uparrow$ more

check with marketing and production to ascertain if any changes are anticipated in container specifications, and with warehousing to be sure storage facilities can handle the larger inventory level with no increase in per unit carrying charges.

Economic Production Quantity

The conditions for instantaneous replenishment of supplies are modified slightly when the supplies are manufactured on order rather than shipped from a stockpile of already manufactured items. The difference is the supplies are shipped instantaneously *as* they are manufactured. This means items are used during the replenishment period as represented by the sloping lines rising from each reorder point in Figure 11.6.

The principal expense of procurement is the set-up cost when a firm produces its own supplies. The inventory pattern in Figure 11.6 shows production beginning the moment supplies on hand are exhausted. In practice, the reorder point would be set at some inventory level above zero to notify production that supplies soon would be needed. This lead time should allow sufficient leeway for scheduling the set-up procedures.

The replenishment period, t', is the length of time required to produce the economic production quantity, EPQ:

$$t' = \frac{Q}{M} = \frac{\text{quantity ordered}}{\text{production output per day}}$$

When D and M are stated in daily rates, the inventory level increases each day during the replenishment period by the amount $M - D$. The stock on hand reaches its peak at the end of the replenishment period where:

$$\text{maximum inventory level} = (M - D)t' = (M - D)\frac{Q}{M}$$

$$= \left(1 - \frac{D}{M}\right)Q$$

Then,

$$\text{average inventory level} = \left(1 - \frac{D}{M}\right)\frac{Q}{2}$$

which makes

$$\text{total annual } EPQ \text{ cost} = \frac{OD}{Q} + \frac{(H + iP)(1 - D/M)Q}{2}$$

where O includes set-up costs and P is the production cost, and leads to

$$Q = \sqrt{\frac{2OD}{(H + iP)(1 - D/M)}}$$

374

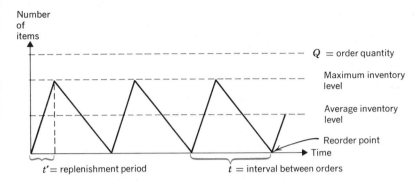

Number
of
items

Q = order quantity

Maximum inventory
level

Average inventory
level

Reorder point

Time

t' = replenishment period

t = interval between orders

Figure 11.6 Inventory pattern for usage during a replenishment period

EXAMPLE 11.4 Calculation of an Economic Production Quantity

One product produced by Moore-Funn Novelties is a voodoo doll. It has a fairly constant demand of 40,000 per year. The soft plastic body is the same for all the dolls, but the clothing is changed periodically to conform to fad hysterics. Production runs for different products require changing the molds and settings of plastic-forming machines, new patterns for the cutters and sewers, and some adjustments in the assembly area. The production rate of previous runs has averaged 2000 dolls per day. Set-up costs are estimated at $350 per production run.

A doll that sells for $2.50 at a retail outlet is valued at $0.90 when it comes off the production line. Complete carrying costs for production items are set at 20% of the production cost and are based on the average inventory level. From these cost figures, the economic production quantity is calculated as

$$Q = \sqrt{\frac{2OD}{iP(1 - D/M)}} = \sqrt{\frac{2 \times \$350 \times 40,000}{(0.20 \times \$0.90)(1 - 40,000/400,000)}}$$

$$= \sqrt{172,840,000} = 13,146$$

where

$$M = \frac{2000 \text{ dolls}}{\text{day}} \times \frac{200 \text{ days}}{\text{year}} = \frac{400,000 \text{ dolls}}{\text{year}}$$

Using the calculated Q value, production can anticipate:

$$\text{number of production runs per year} = \frac{D}{Q} = \frac{40,000}{13,146} = 3$$

$$\text{length of production run, } t' = \frac{Q}{M} = \frac{13,146}{2000} = 6.6 \text{ days}$$

and warehousing can expect:

$$\text{maximum inventory level} = \left(1 - \frac{D}{M}\right)Q = (1 - 0.1)(13,146) = 11,831$$

375

★ ★ ★ *Optional material.*

11-5 INVENTORY MODELS RECOGNIZING RISK

The *EOQ* and *EPQ* analyses represent idealized versions of material flow. The idealization contributes to quick calculations and serves as a convenient reference condition. The basic formulas clarify the sensitivity of order size to estimating errors for the interacting variables; for instance, errors in demand forecasts are less significant than might be supposed because the order quantity has a square root relationship to demand and, furthermore, the total cost is relatively unresponsive to small changes in Q.

Additional insights about material flow are gained from a familiarity with inventory models that recognize risk. Some of the restrictions imposed for conditions of certainty are relaxed to make risk models more realistic. Many different models are available to fit specific situations. We shall limit our attention to one model for treating single inventory orders and another for a continuous inventory policy. Each solution illustrates considerations common to many related inventory problems.

Single-Order Inventory Policy

A grocer stocking perishable fresh produce, a clothing buyer selecting seasonal merchandise for a ready-to-wear department, and a production planner placing parts orders for an untried product all face essentially the same risk: How large should the unique, one-of-a-kind order be when the demand is unknown? A large order protects against the opportunity costs of running out of stock; a small order minimizes the loss for products that cannot be sold.

The first step in analyzing the problem is to estimate probable demand. In a one-only situation, there are usually little data available for estimating purposes. However, the original decision to act in the unique manner must have been made on some assumptions of success. A typical recourse is to forecast the probability of discrete blocks of demand such as the increments and probabilities shown in Table 11.2.

By letting the increments of demand be the order size alternatives, the effect on inventory from following each alternative can be itemized for each possible future as shown in Table 11.3. The symmetrical tableau has a diagonal of zeros that represent the ideal order size for each demand. To the right of the zeros are negative quantities showing the amount that could have been sold if units were available—stockout quantities. To the left of the zero diagonal are quantities left over from each order size

Table 11.2 Distribution of demand

Demand, y Units	Probability of Selling Fewer Than y Units
100	0.00
200	0.20
300	0.50
400	0.90

Table 11.3 Inventory pattern for a single-period sale

	Possible Demand			
Order Size	100	200	300	400
100	0	−100	−200	−300
200	100	0	−100	−200
300	200	100	0	−100
400	300	200	100	0

when demand fails to meet expectations—depreciated quantities. The economic effect of these quantities is evaluated by assigning stockout and depreciation costs associated with shortages and oversupply.

By allotting a stockout cost of $0.50 for each unit (or $50 per 100 units) and a $1 depreciation charge for each unit purchased but not sold, the tableau of Table 11.3 is converted to the expected value format shown in Table 11.4. Thus, an oversupply of 300 units (lower left entry) is represented by a loss of $300, and a 300-unit shortage (upper right entry) is a $150 loss. The incremental probability for each demand level is taken from the cumulative totals in Table 11.2. Expected costs are calculated as the sums of the probability of each demand level multiplied by the cost resulting from that demand for each alternative order size. The alternative with the lowest expected cost is the preferred inventory policy; from Table 11.4 it is an order size of 200 with an expected cost of ($100 × 0.20) + (0 × 0.30) + ($50 × 0.40) + ($100 × 0.10) = $50.

A much shorter though less descriptive method of solving a single-order model is to employ the ratio of stockout cost to the sum of stockout plus depreciation costs to indicate the demand probability associated with the preferred order size. Specifically,

$$P(y) \leq \frac{\text{stockout cost}}{\text{stockout cost} + \text{depreciation cost}}$$

Table 11.4 Expected value of stockout and depreciation costs for order size alternatives

Order Size	Demand: Probability:	100 0.20	200 0.30	300 0.40	400 0.10	Expected cost
100		$0	$50	$100	$150	$70
200		100	0	50	100	$50
300		200	100	0	50	$75
900		300	200	100	0	$160

ANALYSIS

where $P(y)$ is the cumulative probability of demand *less than or equal* to a level that will produce the minimum cost order size. From the cumulative probabilities in Table 11.2 and the cost data used to develop Table 11.4, the order size is directed by

$$P(y) \le \frac{\$0.50}{\$1.00 + \$0.50} \le 0.33$$

to the largest demand with a cumulative probability less than or equal to 0.33: 200 units. This demand level is then equated to a preferred order size and, fortunately, agrees with the order size previously determined in Table 11.4.

A more general version of the same technique is

$$\sum^{y^*} P(y) \le \frac{P - C}{P - S}$$

where:

P = purchase price
C = wholesale or production cost
S = salvage value
y^* = demand level just below preferred order increment

EXAMPLE 11.5 Order Size for a Single Inventory Build-Up

Most single-order inventory situations are associated with perishable products. A decision as to the number of Christmas trees to stock during the short selling season could produce a situation where the salvage value would be negative. A retailer buys trees at a delivered cost of $2.00 each and sells them at an average price of $5.00. Any trees left over after the selling season cost $0.50 each for removal. The expected demand based on previous years and salted with optimistic guesswork is:

Sales of N trees	200	300	400	500	600	700	800
Probability of N sales	0.10	0.15	0.35	0.20	0.10	0.05	0.05
Probability of selling fewer than N	0.00	0.10	0.25	0.60	0.80	0.90	0.95

Then,

$$\sum^{y^*} P(y) \le \frac{P - C}{P - S} = \frac{\$5.00 - \$2.00}{\$5.00 - (-\$0.50)} \le 0.55$$

The order size is 400 trees, the largest demand level with a probability of sales less than or equal to the cost ratio $(0.10 + 0.15 = 0.25)$. If the retailer could get free disposal of unsold trees, he should raise his order size to 500 trees.

Continuing Inventory Policy

The risk of running out of supplies continuously in demand is created by variations in the usage rate and the replenishment lead

378

time. As displayed in Figure 11.7, three conditions contribute to stockouts after a replenishment order has been placed: accelerated demand, extended lead time, or a spurt in demand coupled with a delivery delay. The way to avoid running out of stock is to hold a buffer supply beyond the amount consumed by average usage during an average lead time. This *safety stock* obviously increases holding cost. The problem thus centers on determining a safety stock level that balances opportunity costs of stockouts against carrying costs for extra stock in storage.

We shall consider the case where demand is relatively stable but lead times vary. The techniques employed for the analyses are also directly applicable to the case of constant lead time but variable demand. The most practical method for evaluating the case where both demand and lead times vary is by simulation.

The approach for determining a lead time safety stock for continuing inventory is very similar to that developed for a single-order policy. The expected patterns of lead time probabilities, unit opportunity costs, and carrying costs for stored items are needed. The following data will be used to illustrate the calculations:

A continuous distribution for demand and lead times could be used as shown in Section 11-6.

$$\text{ordering cost} = O = \$60 \text{ per order}$$
$$\text{holding cost} = H = \$8 \text{ per unit per year, based on the}$$
$$\text{average inventory level}$$

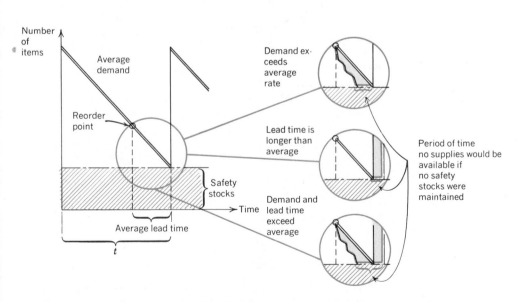

Figure 11.7 Causes of stockouts and the buffer provided by safety stock

opportunity cost $= OC =$ \$5 per day per item demanded but not available

average demand $= D =$ 10 units per day or 2000 annually

Lead Time, Days	Relative Frequency
5	0.10
6	0.15
7	0.25
8	0.20
9	0.15
10	0.10
11	0.05

The distribution of lead times shows there is a 10% chance for the shortest delivery time of 5 days, but it can take up to 11 days to receive delivery after an order is placed. The cost incurred from running out of supplies is \$5/unit $\times$ 10 units/day $=$ \$50 per day. Conversely, the cost of holding an extra day's supply in a safety stock that is not used increases the holding cost by \$8 $\times$ 10 $=$ \$80 per year. The expectation of incurring each of these costs is the basis for selecting the optimal allowed lead time. This selection in turn establishes the reorder level, which is another way of stating the safety stock level.

Shortages and overages resulting from different lead time alternatives could be shown in a tabular form analogous to Table 11.3. For each day the actual lead time exceeds the lead time provided, a shortage of 10 units is incurred, and 10 units ● accumulate for each day the lead time is shorter than anticipated. We shall bypass this tableau to enter the costs directly for each "lead time provided"–"lead time required" match in an expected value format as shown in Table 11.5.

The expected value for each lead time alternative is calculated in the usual manner as the average of costs weighted by their probability of occurrence. For instance, the 7-day lead time alternative has an expected opportunity cost of

$$E(OC) = (\$50 \times 0.20) + (\$100 \times 0.15) + (\$150 \times 0.10) + (\$200 \times 0.05) = \$50$$

and the carrying cost expectation is

$$E(CC) = (\$160 \times 0.10) + (\$80 \times 0.15) = \$28$$

The opportunity costs to the right of the zero diagonal are isolated in a separate column from the carrying costs to the left of the zeros because each affect total inventory cost in a different

Lead Time Provided	Lead Time Required							Expected Value	
	5	6	7	8	9	10	11	Carrying Cost (CC)	Opportunity Cost (OC)
	0.10	0.15	0.25	0.20	0.15	0.10	0.05		
5	0	50	100	150	200	250	300	0	$132.50
6	80	0	50	100	150	200	250	$8	87.50
7	160	80	0	50	100	150	200	28	50.00
8	240	160	80	0	50	100	150	64	25.00
9	320	240	160	80	0	50	100	124	10.00
10	400	320	240	160	80	0	50	192	2.50
11	480	400	320	240	160	80	0	268	0.00

fashion. The opportunity costs occur only at the end of an order period while carrying costs go on through the entire year. Therefore, opportunity costs are treated as an addition to order costs in the *EOQ* formula, and carrying costs are considered a safety stock expense that is added as an increment to the total annual inventory cost formula. These conditions dictate the

- procedure for determining the lowest cost, lead time policy:

Opportunity costs are difficult to estimate. Fortunately, the total inventory cost is not very sensitive to *OC* estimates. For instance, doubling *OC* estimates does not change the preferred lead time alternative from the 10-day preference shown in Table 11.6.

1. Calculate Q using the formula

$$Q_{LT} = \sqrt{\frac{2(O + OC)D}{H}}$$

where:

Q_{LT} = order size for a given lead time alternative
OC = expected value of opportunity costs for the lead time alternative

2. Calculate the total annual inventory cost for each lead time alternative from

$$\text{total inventory cost} = \frac{(O + OC)D}{Q_{LT}} + \frac{HQ_{LT}}{2} + CC$$

where CC = expected value of carrying costs for the lead time alternative.

Using the lead time alternative $LT = 7$ as an example,

$$Q_7 = \sqrt{\frac{2(60 + 50)2000}{8}} = 235 \text{ units}$$

$$\text{total inventory cost} = \frac{(60 + 50)2000}{235} + \frac{8(235)}{2} + 28$$
$$= 938 + 940 + 28 = \$1906$$

Steps 1 and 2 are repeated for all the lead time alternatives to complete the array of costs shown in Table 11.6. The minimum at the 10-day alternative means an order should be placed when the inventory level drops to 10 days × 10 units/day = 100 units. Comparison of this level to a policy of providing just enough units to meet the average lead time, 7 days, shows a safety stock of 30 units will save $1906 − $1608 = $298 a year.

Table 11.6 Total cost of lead time alternatives

Lead Time Alternative (LT)	Order Size (Q)	Total Inventory Cost
5	310	$2480
6	271	2182
7	235	1906
8	706	1710
9	194	1674
10	177	1608*
11	173	1652

*Minimum cost policy.

★ ★ ★ *End optional material.*

Expedient Inventory Policies

SAFETY STOCK FOR ↑ in usage or ↑ in lead time

Selection of a preferred single-order inventory policy involves considerable computation. The techniques illustrated for these computations are rather crude compared to more complete mathematical formulations developed for some problems. For instance, visualize the complexity that would be introduced for the lead time alternatives if we had not assumed demand was steady during lead time. Also consider how many different items may be included in one order. For example, ordering and carrying costs for the single housekeeping item "screws" could be determined without too much difficulty. But what is the individual demand for wood screws, machine screws, slot-head screws, Phillips-head screws, brass screws, steel screws, short screws, long screws, and so on? Conjugating the huge number of items that could be analyzed with the complexity of thorough analyses engenders such a formidable task that even the most ardent disciples of quantitative solutions recognize the need for abridged methods.

It is not surprising that a wide variety of expedient measures

The critical items in an inventory that deserve more attention are classified in the next section.

382

One alternative is to ignore risk and use the conditions of assumed certainty. Then the reorder point equals the product of the average demand and the average lead time.

are recommended by practitioners. Several routines are described below; many more versions are available from the references at the end of the chapter. Although the versions vary, all take cognizance of the risk imposed by usage variations during lead time.

1. *Ultraconservative method*. Take the largest daily usage ever incurred for an item and multiply it by the longest delivery time ever subjected by the supplier. The result is a huge reorder level that is as close as possible to a foolproof guarantee of never running out of stock. An item would have to be almost indispensible to operation to afford the disproportionate carrying costs. MOST EXPENSIVE

2. *Safety stock percentage method*. Carry a safety stock equal to average demand times average lead time times a percentage factor. A 25% to 40% safety factor is typically applied. If the average daily demand was 10 units, the average lead time was 9 days, and a 30% factor was used, the reorder point would be the average usage during lead time plus the safety stock:

$$\text{reorder point} = (10 \times 9) + (10 \times 9)0.30 = 117 \text{ units}$$

3. *Square root of lead time usage method*. Experience indicates lead time seldom varies from its normal length by more than the square root of that length. This relationship can be used directly to set a safety stock level when the demand is fairly constant: safety stock = square root of average usage during lead time. For the conditions introduced in method 2 ($D = 10$/day and $LT = 9$),

$$\text{reorder point} = (10 \times 9) + \sqrt{10 \times 9} = 100 \text{ units}$$

4. *Demand percentage method*. Plot past records of daily demand on a cumulative distribution graph as shown in Figure 11.8. Decide what percentage of time stockouts can be incurred without seriously damaging operations. Spot this percentage on the vertical axis, read across to the curve, and pass directly down to the horizontal axis to determine the demand associated with the acceptable stockout percentage. Then multiply this demand by the average lead time to set the reorder level. For the pattern marked in Figure 11.8, a demand of more than 12 units will occur only 10% of the time. Allowing a 10% risk of stockouts for a fairly constant lead time of 9 days will produce

$$\text{reorder point} = 12 \times 9 = 108 \text{ units}$$

383

Daily Demand (D units)	Number of Days Demand Occurred
7 or less	12
8	40
9	70
10	134
11	73
12	32
13	9
14 or more	4

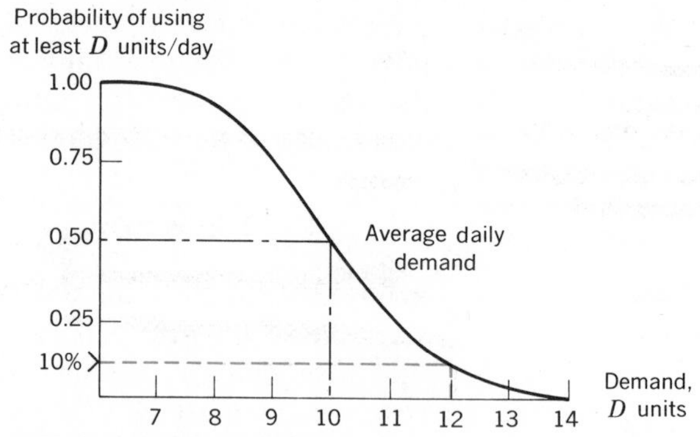

Figure 11.8 Cumulative distribution for the probability of daily demand

Since the mean of the distribution is 10 units per day, the calculated point is equivalent to a safety stock of

$$(12 \times 9) - (10 \times 9) = 18 \text{ units}$$

5. *Combination method.* Methods 2 and 3 are combined by calculating a safety stock quantity as the product of a factor giving the desired probability of being out of stock, the standard deviation of demand variation, and the square root of the average lead time. The probability factor (Z) is the standard normal deviate corresponding to the percentage of times per year a stockout is allowable. For instance, if annual demand is 2000 units and $Q = 200$, there will be 10 order periods per year. A customer service policy of only one stockout per year would allow 10% of the replenishment periods to reach a zero stock level before delivery. From the table in Appendix A of probabilities for the normal distribution, a probability of 0.10 yields a Z factor of 1.28. Then assuming the standard deviation is 1.1 units as developed from Figure 11.8 and the average lead time is 9 days,

$$\text{safety stock} = 1.28 \times 1.1 \times \sqrt{9} = 5 \text{ units}$$

and the reorder point is $(10 \times 9) + 5 = 95$ units.

Which method to use to calculate the reorder point is, of course, a management prerogative. The goal is to obtain a "reasonable" procedure for implementing an inventory policy; a reasonable method takes reasonable effort to achieve a reasonable balance between risks and the related carrying-cost burden.

The Z factor used in PERT calculations (Section 6-5) serves a purpose equivalent to its use in safety stock calculations.

The standard deviation =

$$\sqrt{\frac{\Sigma(x - \bar{x})^2}{n - 1}}$$

where:

x = daily demand

$\bar{x}$ = mean demand

n = number of days demand occurred

384

11-6 INVENTORY MANAGEMENT

Lot size and reorder point calculations are the more spectacular aspects of inventory management. Once the calculations are complete, the continuing routine commences for checking deliveries and physically keeping count of the amount on hand. It is easy to cast these problems off as paper-shuffling procedures, but a well-designed recordkeeping system can contribute as much value as can elaborate quantity specifications. More pointedly, the quantity policies are worthless exercises of logic without the physical controls to implement them.

Priorities

It is obviously uneconomical to devote the same amount of time and attention to inconsequential items and to vital supplies. This widely applicable concept has become famous as "the Pareto principle," named after the Italian economist Vilfredo Pareto. In simple terms, it says that a few activities in a group of activities, or a few items in a group of items made, purchased, sold, or stored, account for the larger part of the resources used or gained. Its application to inventory policy recognizes that a small number of production supplies account for the bulk of the total value used.

The Pareto principle translated to general management functions directs concentration on a few critical tasks which should receive the most skillful treatment because such functions produce the most good to the organization.

The division of inventory into three classes according to dollar usage is known as *ABC* analysis. The usage rating for each item is the product of its annual usage and its unit purchase or production cost. The typical pattern of dollar usage is depicted in Figure 11.9. The *A* class, upon which attention is concentrated, includes high value items whose dollar volume typically accounts for 75–80% of the material expenditures while representing only 15–20% of the quantity volume. The proportions are reversed in passing from *A* to *C* items.

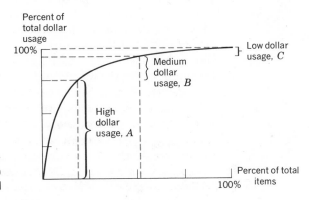

Figure 11.9 Distribution of supply expenditures with respect to quantity supplied

A selective treatment of inventory items directs formal analyses to areas where they will do the most good. The information required to develop a value-quantity distribution curve is usually easy to obtain. The plotted values guide progressive analyses; more critical items are treated first and successive evaluations are conducted as time allows. The general effect is to "buy" analysis time for the high value items by overstocking the low value items. More specific procedures are noted below.

A items. Order quantities and order points are carefully determined. Procurement costs and usage rates are reviewed each time an order is placed. Tight controls are applied to stock records and to lead time developments.

B items. EOQ and reorder level calculations are conducted and the variables are reviewed quarterly or semiannually. Normal controls and good records are expected to detect any major changes in usage.

C items. No formal calculations are made. The reorder quantity is usually a 1- or 2-year supply. Simple notations record when replenishment stocks are received, but no attempt is made to keep a running account of the stock level. A periodic review, perhaps once a year, physically checks the amount in storage.

The supply of *A* and *B* items is controlled by subjecting them to a perpetual or periodic inventory control system.

Perpetual Inventory System

A perpetual system keeps a running record of the amount in storage and replenishes the stock when it drops to a certain level by ordering a *fixed quantity.* Each time a withdrawal is made, the amount is subtracted from the previous level on a stockcard to portray accurately the quantity still on hand. In some larger, more modern establishments, stock records are kept by a *real-time* computer system; the withdrawal amount is immediately fed to a computer where the current status of *A* and *B* items is maintained. The computer signals when a reorder point is reached and may even be programmed to change the EOQ when the demand pattern appears permanently altered.

A "two-bin" system is a version of the fixed-order plan where one bin holds a quantity equal to the reorder level and the second bin holds the difference between *Q* and the reorder point. Items are used from the second bin until it is empty. This signals the

An actual second bin is not always required. Especially where the material is protected by a controlled environment, the reorder point quantity is separated from normal stock by a simple attention-getting partition such as paper.

● need for a replenishment order. During the lead time for resupply, withdrawals are made from the other bin holding the expected lead time usage quantity plus a safety stock. The cyclic procedure eliminates the need for stockcard entries, but it requires control to be sure withdrawals are not made from the reserve bin until the other is empty, and that purchasing is notified when the reserve bin is first utilized.

Periodic Inventory System

In a periodic inventory system the number of items in storage is reviewed at a fixed interval: weekly, monthly, etc. The intervals essentially follow the *ABC* concept; items with high dollar usage are checked more frequently than *C* items. After each review, an order is placed. The size of the order depends on the rate of usage during the period between checks. This variable order size is designed to bring the stock level near a maximum desired number, such as the *EOQ* plus a safety stock:

Backorders, when present, would also be subtracted in calculating the order quantity.

● order quantity = Q − present inventory + usage during lead time + safety stock

Thus the order size is larger when demand between reviews is high.

Expecting customers to mark withdrawals in a department store is, of course, absurd. It is about as bad to expect workers to record withdrawals of routinely used items such as typing paper, nails, and punch cards.

The fixed-order interval system is especially suitable for inventory situations where there are many small stock withdrawals and the order costs are low. A department store is a good ● example; visual checks of the inventory on the shelves and racks are conducted at frequent intervals. Large orders made up of many different items may be placed at one time with the warehouse. The visual checks are much more practical than recording individual withdrawals, and the periodic large orders reduce trucking charges. A combined order may also allow quantity discounts. The weaknesses of the system are due to human fallibilities of not making the periodic checks on time and not finding all the stock present because it has been mislaid or stored in more than one location.

Comparison of Perpetual and Periodic Systems

The operations of the two systems are best illustrated by example. Assume the annual demand for a class *A* item is 20,000 units. Procurement cost is $20 per order and carrying costs are $0.05 per unit per year. Then

$$Q = \sqrt{\frac{2 \times 20 \times 20,000}{0.05}} = 4000 \text{ units}$$

387

Further assuming there are 200 working days per year and the average lead time is 10 days,

$$\text{average usage during lead time} = \frac{D}{200} \times LT$$

$$= \frac{20{,}000 \text{ units}}{200 \text{ days}} \times 10 \text{ days}$$

$$= 1000 \text{ units}$$

and

$$\text{reorder interval} = \frac{200}{D/Q} = \frac{200}{5} = 40 \text{ days}$$

Based upon this information, we can follow the ups and downs of inventory levels subject to each ordering system as they react to variable demands.

The inventory patterns for both systems during a 120-day working period are shown in Figure 11.10. For the moment, we

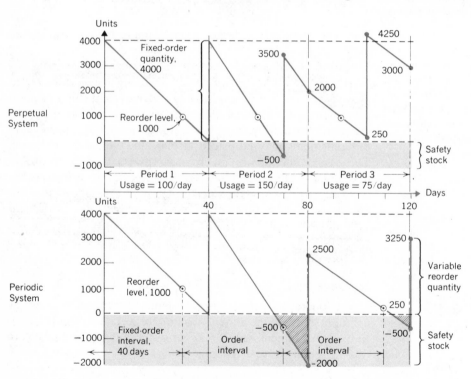

Figure 11.10 Stock level patterns for identical demands placed on perpetual and periodic inventory systems

388

shall let the safety stock, abbreviated *SS*, be some indefinite quantity that fully protects against stockouts. The span of time includes three replenishment periods of 40 days each. The effects of three different usage rates during the periods are discussed in detail below.

Replenishment period 1—usage rate of 100 units per day. Both the perpetual and periodic systems exhibit the same inventory pattern when the demand follows the expected average. The fixed-order quantity is 4000 units ordered when the stock level reaches 1000 units plus safety stock. The fixed-order interval is 40 days measured from one reorder point to the next. The desired maximum inventory level for both systems is 4000 units plus safety stock.

Replenishment period 2—usage rate of 150 units per day. The fixed-order quantity is placed after $(4000 - 1000)/150 = 20$ days. During the lead time the stock level drops to $1000 - (150 \times 10) = -500$ units or, equivalently, 500 units of safety stock are withdrawn. An order of 4000 units brings the stock level up to 3500 units plus safety stock on day 70. Then, during the last 10 days of period 2, the stock level continues to decline at the rate of 150 per day to reach 2000 units on day 80.

The first 10 days of the first fixed-order interval are not shown in Figure 11.10. • In the first 10 days of the fixed 40-day order interval (days 30 to 40 on the chart), the stock level drops to zero at the rate 100 units per day. During the remaining 30 days of the fixed interval, the stock level declines at the greater than average rate of 150 units per day to reach a -500 level when the order is placed. The order size is then $4000 - (-500) + SS = 4500 + SS$. Since the order was placed when the stock level was at -500 and usage during the lead time is $150 \times 10 = 1500$ units, the stock level for the beginning of period 3 is $(4500 + SS) - 500 - 1500 = 2500 + SS$.

Replenishment period 3—usage rate of 75 units per day. Measured from day 80 where the stock level is 2000 units, the fixed-order quantity reorder level is reached in $(2000 - 1000)/75 = 13$ days. The continuous usage of 75 units per day puts the inventory level at 250 plus safety stock when the 4000-unit order is received on day 103. Usage during the remaining days of period 3 takes the final inventory level to 3000 units at day 120.

With the stock level at 2500 units plus safety stock at day 80, 10 days into the 40-day fixed-order interval, an order is placed at day 110 when the stock level is at $(2500 + SS) - (75 \times 30) =$

389

250 + SS. The order quantity is then (4000 + SS) − (250 + SS) = 3750 units. During the lead time, withdrawals dip into the safety stock by (250 + SS) − (75 × 10) = SS − 500 units. On the final day of period 3, day 120, the stock level goes from a low of −500 to a high, just after delivery of the order, of 3750 + SS − 500 = 3250 + SS.

The patterns in Figure 11.10 reveal that stock levels tend to fluctuate more widely in the fixed-order interval system. The deeper wedges into the safety stock region indicate the reserve should be greater for the periodic than the perpetual system. The reason is that safety stock for the perpetual system protects only from usage variation during the lead time; the safety stock must protect the periodic system from usage variations during the entire fixed interval between orders. The magnitude of the added protection is implied by the changes required in some of the practical inventory methods listed in Section 11-5; formulas in methods 3 and 5, based on a fixed-order size system, must be changed to recognize the greater risk of stockouts in a fixed-interval system by changing the $\sqrt{\text{lead time}}$ in the equations to $\sqrt{\text{order interval}}$.

The greater cost of safety stock in a periodic system is usually compensated by lower clerical and data-processing costs. Loose or tight control can be enforced under either system. The management decision as to which system to use must be based on the unique characteristics of each situation. The profuse variables that could influence this decision range from a close appraisal of data-processing capabilities and cost to reliance on worn tenets such as "you can't sell what you ain't got" or "the more you carry, the faster you fall."

EXAMPLE 11.6   A "Supermarket" Inventory Policy

Establishing a semiautonomous market within a firm to supply operating departments is a recent inventory wrinkle. It has been effective for housekeeping supplies and repair work.

A quantity of expendable items such as office and janitorial supplies is traditionally issued to departments several times a year. Between issues the departments run out of some items and accumulate a surplus of others. A stockroom operates as a supermarket by displaying items on shelves with the prices marked. Departmental representatives call on the market and pick out needed supplies. The purchases are charged against the department budget. The system eliminates filling out requisitions and associated processing, reduces delivery time, lowers departmental hoarding of excess items, and still controls the dollar usage of supplies.

A similar procedure can be followed for simple maintenance and repair. Each department has a "charge-a-plate." Items requiring repair are delivered to a maintenance depot accompanied by a charge-a-plate. The time and material required to fix the item are billed on a job order to the plate address. On-the-spot comparison of repair cost versus a replacement can often be made by representatives of the department involved.

In both cases the departments are considered customers to an independent service facility. The advantages for such inventory management are: (1) the centralization of supplies and recordkeeping functions and (2) the improved sensitivity of the stocking system to current demand.

11-7 MATERIAL HANDLING AND CONTROL

Transportation of materials can be called the curse of production because it adds little value to the product but consumes a major portion of the manufacturing budget. The entire production cycle relies on material handling to link phases of product development as shown in Figure 11.11.

Material flow in a factory is analogous to a river system. Water is the material of the river. A breakdown or slowdown of a transportation link is similar to an obstruction in a river. Activities upstream from the blockade are inundated by the stagnate surplus; downstream activities are restricted to leakage or supply from other tributaries. When a number of dams are purposely built along the river, the water flow is controllable because the inventory behind each dam can be fed into the system as needed. This is the rationale for in-process inventory.

Just as a river system is influenced by the terrain and vegetation on the terrain, the material-handling system is dependent on the building design and the equipment within the buildings. The ideal way to treat material-handling problems is to anticipate them before they occur and provide facilities that overcome them. In new plant design this approach is feasible; material-handling plans using the latest model equipment are developed in conjunction with other production requirements. A more common situation is the introduction of a new production machine that makes existing material flow inadequate. The danger in ex-

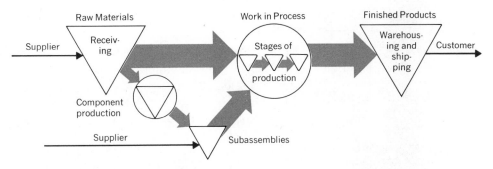

Figure 11.11 Relationship of material handling and inventory in a production process

Characteristics of Ineffective
Material Flow:

Idle machines
Build-up of unplanned in-
ventory
Damaged or lost parts
Injuries to workers
Late shipments

clusively treating one segment of the production line is that the
solution to one problem may create another one just as severe.
Again using the river system analogy, clearing one section of a
river bed to smooth flow does not improve the volume flowing
into the improved section.

Principles

The guidelines for material handling are macroextensions of
the micromovement canons presented as the principles of motion
economy in Section 9-3. The principles for material handling are
less definitive than for hand movements because material flow
is so intimately related to other production considerations such
as inventory, purchasing, scheduling, and similar product-
oriented policies. Therefore, the principles should be treated as
guidelines or thought-provokers that may lead to improved
performance. Complete obedience to the principle that "the
shortest distance between two points is a straight line" is thwarted
when an effectively immovable object sits between the two points,
but its contemplation might inspire a better route that goes up and
over instead of through.

In the transportation industry,
the loading and unloading
functions have not kept pace
with the ever-increasing travel
speed. Getting passengers on
and off airplanes is a classic
example.

1. *Eliminate*. If not, make the transportation distances as short as
   possible.
2. *Keep moving*. If not, reduce the time spent at the terminal
   points of a route as short as possible.
3. *Use simple patterns*. If not, reduce backtracking, cross-overs,
   and other congestion-producing patterns as much as facilities
   allow.
4. *Carry payloads both ways*. If not, minimize the time spent in
   "transport empty" by speed changes and route relocations.
5. *Carry full loads*. If not, consider increasing the size of unit loads,
   decreasing carrying capacity, lowering speed, or acquiring
   more versatile equipment.
6. *Use gravity*. If not, try to find another source of power that is
   as reliable and inexpensive.

Although the above principles might mask it, there are very
important aspects of material handling besides geometry and
hardware. Material considerations should include the movement
of men, machines, tools, and information. The flow system must
support the objectives of receiving, sorting, inspecting, in-
ventorying, accounting, packaging, assembling, and other production functions. And, typically, the considerations and
objectives conflict. It takes an in-depth system decision followed

392

by delicate diplomacy to establish a material-movement plan that meets service requirements without subordinating safety and economy.

Applications

Since material is a fundamental requirement of all phases of the production process, there are innumerable specific facets to concern the material-handling specialist. We shall consider briefly three broad categories common to most processes: mass transit, tool control, and information flow.

Equipment for the horizontal and vertical transportation of massed material may be classified in the following three categories.

1. *Cranes* handle material in the air above ground level to free the floor for other handling devices. Heavy, bulky, and awkward objects are logical candidates for airborne movement. Clearances, communication between floor workers and crane operators, and safety are problems associated with overhead transportation.
2. *Conveyors* may take the form of moving belts; gravity- or power-operated rollers; screws for shoveling bulk material; chains from which carriers are suspended; pipes for the pressurized flow of liquids, gases, or powdered material; and gravity chutes. The gravity-powered devices are convenient for between floor movements and are easily adaptable for layout changes.
3. *Trucks* include both hand- and power-operated vehicles. Hand-operated wagons, platforms, and leverage trucks are suited to light loads, short hauls, and cramped quarters. Lift trucks with all their multiduty attachments and tractors with or without a chain of trailers can move heavy objects and palletized or bulk containers to various locations. Safety, visibility, and maneuvering space are the main limitations.

Mechanization has had a dramatic impact on material handling in recent years. At times the technological evolution has approached a revolution. Machines were developed to move material in ways and under conditions never before possible. Sudden new developments made existing facilities noncompetitive almost overnight. In the scramble to catch up, even newer methods were developed. Now a plateau seems to have been reached where the "cream has been skimmed" from the introduction of new material-handling techniques. Certainly some industries still have to catch up to what can be done, but the bigger current problem is how to better utilize the modern equipment and to coordinate its potential more effectively with production requirements.

Tool control is a very limited but pesky material-handling problem. One of F. W. Taylor's first applications of scientific management was concerned with tool utilization. The first requirement is to procure the correct tools for the job. Once procured, the handling problem begins. Tools are usually issued to workers from centralized tool cribs. A "brass ring" control has the worker exchange his personalized brass ring for a tool, and the ring is returned when the tool is returned. A more acceptable method replaces the brass ring with a charge-a-plate or receipt slip made out by the crib attendant. The advantage of the paper record is that it indicates the amount of tool usage.

Three carbons of a tool receipt are usually made. One goes to the worker, one receipts the tool in the crib, and the last one is a permanent record.

No one denies the importance of information flow and everyone decries the amount of paper flow; the two flows can seldom be equated. Unending efforts appear to be directed at stemming the mounting flow of paper while retaining the information content —reporting by exception, tickle files, coding, etc. Campaigns often dent the flow temporarily; computerized systems cut out many reports when first initiated, but the "explanatory memo" soon filled the void. Some office innovations, such as automatic copying machines, make it easier than ever to flood operations with questionably needed data.

Reporting by exception: Reporting only the unusual; no report means no change.
Tickle file: Reminders of future events filed by the anticipated date of occurence.
Coding: Replacing word messages by symbols such as numbers for a postal zip code.

Information handling can benefit from concepts drawn from material-handling principles. The objective is to carry information from one point to another. The first question is whether the information needs to be moved. If so, how can it be done most economically? Voice communication, the oldest form of information transmission, is still effective and its use is extended by mechanical aids such as message recorders and answering services for telephones. Radios and intercom systems are being augmented by closed-circuit television systems. This greater dissemination ability proves effective only when it is combined with a policy that limits proliferation to a "need to know."

" 'The horror of that moment,' the king went on, 'I shall never, never forget!' 'You will, though,' the Queen said, 'if you don't make a memorandum of it' " Lewis Carrol, Alice's Adventures in Wonderland.

11-8 SUMMARY

The purchasing function is the interface between a company and its suppliers. A purchasing department is treated as a customer by suppliers and as a support function by other operating units. In turn, it receives assistance from both suppliers and the operating units.

Suppliers show the firm the latest developments that may reduce production costs, and they may enter into reciprocity agreements.

Marketing provides an indication of anticipated output so purchasing can speculate and take advantage of favorable price trends.

Production may hoard supplies or restrict purchases to a single supplier by requiring a specific brand name.

Engineering also may restrict purchases by narrow specifications. Purchasing should act as a go-between to acquaint engineers with new developments shown by suppliers.

Legal personnel check the legality of purchasing transactions.

Accounting pays the bills after being notified by purchasing.

A more systematic purchasing policy usually results from centralization. The flexibility of centralized purchasing is increased by local control of small or rush orders.

Purchasing activities follow the sequence below.

1. *Receive requisition.* Requisitioners should recognize the need for lead time, the elapsed time between placing an order and its receipt.
2. *Review requisition.* Value analysis is used to review the true need for requisitioned supplies. A value engineering approach evaluates the worth of an item by partitioning its cost according to

$$\text{use value} + \text{esteem value} = \text{exchange value}$$

The use value receives most attention by forcing a verb and a noun description for each primary and secondary function.

3. *Select suppliers.* An "approved suppliers list" is developed by purchasing to expedite ordering. Orders are usually spread over several suppliers to avoid complete reliance on one vendor.
4. *Place orders.* One-of-a-kind contracts are usually granted on the basis of competitive bids. Open contracts are open accounts with one supplier for direct ordering of low cost, infrequently used supplies. Items with a continuous demand are purchased under blanket purchase orders. Open and blanket contracts are designed to avoid the cost of numerous individual purchase orders.
5. *Monitor orders.* Purchasing keeps tab on the supplier's delivery schedule.
6. *Receive orders.* Purchasing or payment policies may allow trade, quantity, or cash discounts.

395

Inventory is an idle resource available when needed but subject to storage costs. Its main purpose is to insulate production from delays caused by lack of material. It also affects work stability, customer satisfaction, material-handling requirements, and purchasing policy.

Inventory costs are composed of expenses that vary directly and inversely with the size of an order. Order costs (O) and opportunity costs (OC) increase with smaller order sizes. Holding costs (H) and capital costs (iP) decrease with smaller order sizes. The order size (Q) that balances these two cost categories under assumptions of a constant demand and a known lead time is calculated by the EOQ formula:

$$Q = \sqrt{\frac{2OD}{H + iP}}$$

where D = annual demand. When the items are expended as they are produced, the EPQ formula is

$$Q = \sqrt{\frac{2OD}{(H + iP)(1 - D/M)}}$$

where M = annual manufacturing rate. The effect of quantity discounts for larger orders is evaluated by calculating the total annual cost of each level of discount by

$$\text{total annual stocking cost} = O\frac{D}{Q} + (H + iP)\frac{Q}{2} + PD$$

where the first two terms are the annual inventory cost and the last term is the purchase or production cost for a year's stock.

Two inventory models recognizing risk were considered. The optimal order quantity for a single-order policy is indicated by the formula

$$\sum^{y*} P(y) \le \frac{P - C}{P - S}$$

where:

P = purchase price
C = wholesale or production cost
S = salvage value
$y*$ = demand level just below the preferred order increment

A continuing order policy, assuming demand is relatively stable but lead time varies, uses a tableau format to aid calculation of an expected value for the carrying costs (CC) and opportunity costs (OC) of each lead time alternative. Then,

$$\text{total inventory cost} = \frac{(O + OC)D}{Q_{LT}} + \frac{HQ_{LT}}{2} + CC$$

where the *EOQ* for each lead time alternative (*LT*) is

$$Q_{LT} = \sqrt{\frac{2(O + OC)D}{H}}$$

Less formal methods of including risk in an inventory policy are given by the following expedient measures:

1. *Ultraconservative method*—based on the worst demand conditions and therefore is highly conservative.
2. *Safety stock (SS) percentage method*—

$$SS = \frac{\text{average}}{\text{demand}} \times \frac{\text{average}}{\text{lead time}} \times \frac{\text{percentage factor}}{\text{(usually 25–40\%)}}$$

3. *Square root of lead time usage method*—

$$SS = \sqrt{\text{average usage during lead time}}$$

4. *Demand percentage method*—multiplies a demand, taken from a cumulative distribution at an acceptable probability of stockouts, by the average lead time to give a reorder level.
5. *Combination method*—uses the product of a probability factor, standard deviation of demand variations, and the square root of lead time to set an acceptable safety stock level.

The inventory items that deserve the most attention are determined by an *ABC* analysis. Class *A* items, upon which attention is concentrated, typically account for 75–80% of the total dollar usage but only 15–20% of the quantity volume. The effect of following an *ABC* policy is to "buy" analysis time for the high value items by overstocking the low value items.

A perpetual inventory system replenishes stock when it drops to a certain level by ordering a fixed quantity. A two-bin version of the system simplifies recordkeeping.

A periodic inventory system has fixed review periods when a variable order quantity is placed to bring the stock level near a desired maximum. The stock levels vary more widely in a fixed-order interval than in a fixed-order quantity system. The greater safety stock required by the periodic review system is compensated by lower clerical and data-processing costs.

Material handling is a necessary evil which consumes a major portion of total production cost while contributing little value to the actual refinement of a product. Guidelines for handling are extensions of the principles of motion economy.

397

ANALYSIS

Massed materials are moved by cranes, conveyors, and trucks. In recent years, new equipment developments have provided dramatic material-handling savings. A leveling off of innovations has switched the emphasis from more mechanization to more coordination with production operations.

Tool control is a limited but pesky material-handling problem. It is best treated by multiple copy receipts by the tool crib attendant.

Information flow is linked to the paper flow problem. The extended use of voice communications and strict attention to the "need to know" principle can help stem the increase in paper flow while maintaining information flow.

11-9 REFERENCES

Ammer, D. S., *Materials Management*, Richard D. Irwin, Homewood, Ill., 1962.

Anyon, G. J., *Managing an Integrated Purchasing Process*, Holt, Rinehart and Winston, New York, 1963.

Apple, J. M., *Plant Layout and Materials Handling* (2nd ed.), Ronald Press, New York, 1963.

ASTME, *Value Engineering in Manufacturing*, Prentice-Hall, Englewood Cliffs, N.J., 1967.

Biegel, J. E., *Production Control: A Quantitative Approach*, Prentice-Hall, Englewood Cliffs, N.J., 1963.

Bolz, H. A., *Materials Handling Handbook*, Ronald Press, New York, 1958.

Buchan, J. and E. Koenigsberg, *Scientific Inventory Management*, Prentice-Hall, Englewood Cliffs, N.J., 1963.

Colton, R. R., *Industrial Purchasing Principles and Cases*, Charles E. Merrill, Columbus, Ohio, 1962.

England, W. B., *Procurement: Principles and Cases*, Richard D. Irwin, Homewood, Ill., 1962.

Hadley, G. M. and T. M. Whitlin, *Analysis of Inventory Systems*, Prentice-Hall, Englewood Cliffs, N.J., 1963.

Haynes, D. O., *Materials Handling Equipment*, Chilton, Philadelphia, Pa., 1957.

————, *Materials Handling Applications*, Chilton, Philadelphia, Pa., 1958.

Hodges, H. G., *Procurement—The Modern Science of Purchasing*, Harper and Row, New York, 1961.

Magee, J. F., *Production Planning and Inventory Control*, McGraw-Hill, New York, 1958.

Miles, L. D., *Techniques of Value Analysis and Engineering*, McGraw-Hill, New York, 1961.

Morris, W. T., *Analysis for Materials Handling Management*, Richard D. Irwin, Homewood, Ill., 1962.

Naddor, F., *Inventory Systems*, John Wiley, New York, 1966.

Olsen, R. A., *Manufacturing Management: A Quantitative Approach*, International Textbook, Scranton, Pa., 1968.

Sasieni, M. W., A. Yaspan, and L. Friedman, *Operations Research—Methods and Problems*, John Wiley, New York, 1959.

Starr, M. and D. W. Miller, *Inventory Control: Theory and Practice*, Prentice-Hall, Englewood Cliffs, N.J., 1962.

398

MATERIALS

Wagner, H. M., *Statistical Management of Inventory Systems*, John Wiley, New York, 1962.

Westing, J. H. and I. V. Fine, *Industrial Purchasing*, John Wiley, New York, 1960.

Whitin, T. M., *The Theory of Inventory Management* (2nd ed.), Princeton Univ. Press, Princeton, N.J., 1957.

11-10 QUESTIONS AND PROBLEMS

1. When a purchasing agent assumes the role of a customer, he is susceptible to many ethical questions of conduct. Comment on the following situations:

(a) A purchasing agent owns stock in a company from which the firm he represents could buy material. Should he deal with this company?

(b) Some firms provide expensive Christmas presents for purchasing agents with whom they do business. Should an agent accept all gifts offered, just modest gifts, or no gifts at all?

2. What type of requisition could be expected for the two rough divisions of purchases—maintenance supplies and raw materials?

3. Information channels between purchasing and other parts of the production system are shown in Figure 11.2. Which of these channels are more important for each of the six operations performed by purchasing (Section 11-2)?

4. How could "squirrel" and "brand X" complexes affect the need for requisition reviews? Would you say these complexes are natural reactions to past experiences? What arguments would you use as a purchasing director in rebuttal to statements defending each complex?

5. Should an engineer feel insulted when a purchasing director questions particularly tight tolerances set for a part that is to be purchased? Why?

6. Is reciprocity an ethical practice? What problems can result from its extensive use?

7. Discuss the advantages and disadvantages of centralized versus decentralized purchasing as it would apply to each of the following situations:

(a) A firm operating three "29¢ burger" shops in the same city.

(b) A firm operating three "29¢ burger" shops in three cities, each 200 miles apart.

(c) A large discount house located in one sprawling building subdivided into 18 operating departments: household supplies, drugs, hardware, sporting goods, etc.

8. A tie clasp issued to all new recruits in a branch of the Armed Forces is chrome plated, has a pivoted clasp, and contains

a replica of the insignia of the service branch. The description of the working function of the clasp could be "hold parts" where the parts are the tie and shirt. A secondary (or perhaps the basic) function is "creates impression." Show how the creation of substitute means and the evaluation depend on the functional description of the item. If the present tie clasp costs $0.93, determine a less expensive alternative based on the "holds parts" function. Does this alternative satisfy the function "creates impression?"

9. Comment on the following quotation from ASTME's publication, *Value Engineering in Manufacturing*:

It must be repeated that value engineering cannot be practiced where there are restrictions to freedom to change. If a product can only be refined superficially (and there can be many perfectly valid reasons for this), value engineering is not an appropriate cost reduction tool. For instance, it was found that wide-mouth catsup bottles could not be sold under market conditions in the late Fifties, although the wider-mouth jar was less expensive, took less storage space, and would pour at a more uniform rate. If there is substantial tooling involved for a product of doubtful sales life, it would be wiser to concentrate on substitution of materials, changes in tolerances, or methods improvements, since it is likely that these would be the types of proposals developed after an exhaustive value engineering study was completed on a project with such restrictions.

But if there is freedom to change, value engineering will bring forth the full benefits of change. Where normal cost improvement effort refines by chipping away at the subject, value engineering blasts out great chunks of cost. Many firms with a product line facing extinction have in desperation turned to value engineering when normal cost improvement has proved inadequate. But many more firms are unknowingly allowing available profit to slip by them through clinging to traditional methods of product development and refinement.

10. Should a supplier be informed of the reasons why he is not on an approved supplier list?

11. What are the advantages of splitting an order between suppliers? Can competitive pricing be maintained with an exclusive supplier?

12. Would it be wise to borrow money from a bank for 1 month at 6% simple interest in order to take advantage of a cash discount on terms "3/10 net 30"?

13. The engineering staffs of a buyer and a seller often co-operate in the development of new equipment wanted by the

buyer. Such activities are common for one-of-a-kind contracts and are not uncommon for blanket contracts. Why might purchasing encourage this cooperation and why might a vendor agree to it? Why might a vendor refuse it?

14. Give an example of the type or class of items for which each of the three ordering contracts would be appropriate.

15. If you were a purchasing director, would you follow the policy suggested in Example 11.1 of informing your suppliers about their ratings? What advantages and drawbacks should influence your decision?

16. A new, very eager scheduler has been hired to coordinate production and inventory control. It is a new position created by the need to increase the production of a relatively small firm to meet a large contract. After a work simplification study, the assembly department has a surge in output. The corresponding increase in demand for parts to assemble overtaxes the capacity of the production department. Consequently, the inventory of parts on hand falls well below the normal replenishment level. To avoid an increase in lead time, the eager scheduler raises the expected manufacturing rate. Then additional workers are hired by production to meet the greater demands.

After awhile the pace of assembly workers drifts back to a rate above the former output. But the rate is not as high as the enthusiastic surge that so often accompanies installation of a new program. Now inventory levels are above original levels and are still getting larger owing to the higher production rates made possible by the new workers. The scheduler again revises the reorder level and manufacturing rate, this time downward. This action means that no orders will go to production while the excess inventory is being used in assembly work. With no orders coming in to utilize the greater manufacturing rate, production must lay off workers.

What errors caused this overly responsive situation? How was the concept of safety stock violated? Under what conditions should reorder points be changed?

17. Using the "idle resource" definition of inventory, comment on the following physical, political, and sociological examples:
   (a) An untapped oil reserve that would lower the price of gasoline if developed.
   (b) A standing army maintained during periods of peace.
   (c) The "land bank" plan to keep land from producing crops.
   (d) Hiring extra engineers and scientists to substantiate a claim for research and development potential when bidding for major contracts.

18. Comment on the effects of inventory as it influences:
(a) Hiring and placement departments.
(b) Public relations.
(c) A customer of a wholesaler.
(d) A customer of a retailer.

19. Distinguish between "buying down" and "speculative buying." How does each practice influence an inventory policy?

20. Why are opportunity costs not included in basic EOQ formulas?

21. Give examples of production situations where $D = M$ and $D > M$.

22. Comment on the application of the Pareto principle to the following production situations:
(a) A few departments perform the bulk of production work that contributes to the profit of the firm.
(b) A small number of suppliers causes most of the delays in procuring purchased production supplies.
(c) A few operators produce most of the scrap and rejects.
(d) Most orders from purchasing come from a few vendors.

23. Would the holding costs for a two-bin inventory system more likely be based on the maximum or average inventory level? How does the two-bin method reduce clerical costs in a perpetual inventory system?

24. Would you prefer a perpetual or a periodic inventory system for class C items? Why?

25. Use the value engineering approach to describe the use function for each class in the ABC inventory divisions.

26. Which categories of equipment are more likely to be associated with a product layout and a process layout?

27. Can material handling be evaluated independently from purchasing and inventory policies?

28. What ways can you suggest for reducing terminal times between material movements?

29. What ways can you suggest for reducing "travel empty" time?

30. How does the size of unit loads affect material-handling time?

31. Is the "technological information explosion" affecting paper flow? Should it?

32. What is the advantage of knowing tool usage for a tool control plan?

33. How can a "need to know" limitation reduce paper flow? Could an overzealous application lead to legitimate accusations of favoritism and censorship?

34. A wholesaler forecasts annual sales of 200,000 units for one product. Order costs are $75 per order. Holding costs of $0.04 per unit per year and interest charges of 12% are based on the average inventory level. The cost to the wholesaler is $0.80 per unit acquired from the factory. What is the *EOQ*? What is the total annual stocking cost? What is the time between orders based on 250 working days per year?

35. Parts used in assembly work are purchased from a supplier who has a remarkable record for prompt delivery. The inventory history closely follows an instantaneous replenishment pattern. However, to be on the safe side, a policy is followed of never planning an inventory level below 500 parts. The following costs are applicable:

procurement cost = $60 per order
carrying cost = $0.20 per unit per year based on average inventory

If the demand is 40,000 parts per year used at a steady rate, what is the total annual inventory cost?

36. Determine the economic order size for the following conditions, where n refers to the number of units and holding costs are based on average inventory size:

$$O = \$10 + \$0.01n$$
$$H = \$2 + 0.01P/n^2$$
$$P = \$40 \text{ per unit}$$
$$D = 800 \text{ units per year}$$

37. The annual amount ordered from one raw material supplier is $260,000. Annual order costs are 1% of the raw material cost, and carrying costs are 18% of the average inventory level. How many weeks of supply should be ordered at one time?

38. A company currently buys 20,000 parts per year from a supplier. Each part costs $1. Ordering costs are $50 per order, and carrying costs are 20% of the purchase price based on maximum inventory. It has been suggested that the company buy a machine which can produce the parts for half the price now being paid, but set-up costs will be double the order cost. The machine can produce at an annual rate of 200,000 parts and has an economic life of 10 years at which time the salvage value will be zero. If the savings from producing this part are expected to pay half the equivalent annual cost of the machine, what is the maximum amount that can be paid for it? Capital recovery is based on an 8% interest charge.

39. Four thousand tons of raw material are used each year.

403

Order costs are $20 per order; carrying costs are $8 per ton based on the maximum storage requirement. The supplier has offered to reduce the $40 per ton price by 5% if the minimum order size is 500 tons and by another 5% if the minimum order is 1000 tons. The capacity of the present storage facility is 250 tons. Any increase in capacity will increase the carrying costs in direct ratio. Show your calculations and assumptions to prove whether the quantity discounts should be utilized.

40. A knitting mill is closing its swimming suit division to devote full production to other sportswear. It has offered its stock of 400 daring, net, see-through suits at a close-out price of $4 each. Similar models sold last year for $25 per suit, but some bathers were barred from beaches when they wore them. By spending $1600 on advertising, a retailer estimates the probability of sales this year as:

Suit sales, S	150	200	250	300	350	400
Probability of S	0.10	0.10	0.20	0.25	0.20	0.15

If the suits not sold at the regular price can be sold at special sales for $2 each, how many of the 400 suits should the retailer take?

41. A shipbuilding yard has an annual demand for 1150 bottles of acetylene. Each bottle costs $40; order and inspection costs are $55 per order. Carrying costs are 25% of the value of average inventory in storage. The yard operates 230 days per year. Interruptions to production cause opportunity costs of $40 per bottle for each day it is unavailable.

(a) What is the order interval if lead time is instantaneous?
(b) What are the total inventory cost and the optimal order size if lead time follows the pattern shown below?

Lead time	6	7	8	9	10	11	12	13	14
Relative frequency	0.00	0.04	0.08	0.38	0.24	0.12	0.09	0.03	0.02

42. All differential gears used by a manufacturer are furnished by one supplier. The inventory system operates on a fixed-order quantity basis. Procurement costs are $20 per order and the annual usage is 3200 gears. Carrying costs are $0.75 per unit per year. The average lead time is 4 days and daily demand follows the pattern shown below. (Note the Poisson distribution with a mean of 16.)

Demand	13 or less	14	15	16	17	18	19	20 or more
Occurrence	5		15	225	225	17	11	6	3

What is the order size, reorder point, and expected minimum inventory level when risk is accounted for by the:

(a) Ultraconservative method?

(b) Safety stock percentage method?

(c) Square root of lead time usage method?

(d) Demand percentage method?

(e) Combination method?

43. Throw-away filters for production machines cost $1 each and are used at an average daily rate of 25. The *EOQ* for filters is 500. Average delivery time is 4 working days. At the start of a year, the inventory level is 3000 filters. During the first 30 days, production drops and the usage of filters decreases to 15 per day. In the next 30 days, usage is at the average level, 25 per day. For the following 30 days (cumulative days 61 to 90), usage climbs to an average of 50 per day and stays at this level for the last 30 days of the 120-day span.

(a) Graph the pattern of inventory on hand when a perpetual system is used. Numerically label all the break points on the plotted line.

(b) Graph the pattern of inventory on hand when a periodic system is used. Numerically label all breaks in the plotted line.

(c) If the square root of lead time usage method is employed to calculate the safety stock, what would the safety stock be for: (1) the fixed-order quantity system, and (2) the fixed-order interval system? Compare the indicated safety stock level with need for a reserve supply in the patterns from parts (a) and (b).

CHAPTER 12

MANAGEMENT: Tools and Techniques

12-1 IMPORTANCE

In Chapter 2 we surveyed the same emblematic area and also recognized it as management, but we discussed the concepts and functions from a general approach. In this chapter we shall take a narrower view of management and treat it as a personal challenge.

Production management is well described by its core position in the emblem of this text. As shown in Figure 12.1, management is the responsibility center for planning, control, and analysis of men, machines, and materials. In viewing the functions of management, it is easy to gloss over the fact that these functions have to be performed by men, the *man* in *man*agement. In studying management, we seek the means to help men improve their performance in relation to the demands of the production system.

A dictionary defines management as: (1) "the art or manner of managing, controlling, or conducting," and (2) "the skillful use of means to accomplish a purpose." These definitions support two long-standing questions: Is management an art or a science? Is management skill or technical skill more important? Both questions assume the dichotomy that one phase of management deals with human relations, an area that has escaped most efforts toward quantification, and the other phase treats technical matters which yield to more precise formulations. This division is not unnatural, but it is difficult to imagine a managerial position exclusively devoted to only one phase. Therefore, answers to the

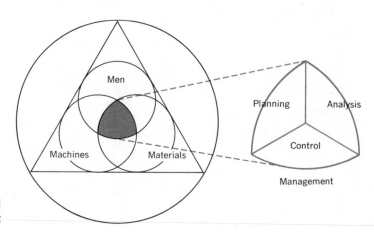

Figure 12.1 The central position of management

406

questions must be qualified by the specific position under consideration. Even then the response likely will imply a mixture of art and science skills.

In this chapter we shall view the management function from the outlook of a manager who deals with people, is aided by machines, and uses quantitative tools. The views are necessarily incomplete, because it would take many volumes to catalog all the idiosyncrasies of people, all the potentially useful machines, and all the applicable managerial techniques. We shall focus on personal skills, the use of computers, and the technique of simulation.

12-2 MANAGERIAL ACTIVITIES

Occasionally a managerial position includes work producing a direct output. For instance, a sales manager may organize the efforts of a sales staff and still do some selling himself.

A manager makes his contribution to an organization through other people. He is not a "doer" in the sense his activities can be measured directly by units of output. He may produce a report or calculations concerning certain activities, but these outputs are designed to improve the system that ultimately produces the salable product. Top level managers in an organization are far removed from actual output because they manage managers— " . . . their contribution being as it were a wheel within a wheel" (Ezekiel, 1.16).The following list includes activities common to all levels of management.

Policy making. Any operation is conducted less erratically and with greater economy of effort when objectives are clearly stated and well publicized. Policy rests on objectives. Short-range objectives should be in line with long-range plans. Subordinates should be aware of the objectives and what will constitute satisfactory performance in their attainment.

Policy evaluation. Present policies are the descendants of past policies, and future plans depend on present performances. A means of comparing actual performance to anticipated attainments must be developed. This evaluation serves as an early warning of plan failures and helps in rating subordinates.

"A good listener is not only popular everywhere, but after a while he knows something."
Wilson Mizner.

Communication. Information travels two ways in a communication channel. A great deal of attention is given to the preparation of written directives and the proper manner of delivering verbal messages. Scant attention is given to listening. A good listener grasps the message and encourages the speaker. A free flow of accurate information means the doers know what to do and the planner knows what is done.

407

Personnel relations. Since a manager, by definition, must work through other people to perform his functions, human relations is a constant and paramount consideration. Occasionally managers exhort workers to work harder on a project, but more commonly morale and motivation are outgrowths of the entire work atmosphere. Whether this atmosphere is lackadaisical, neutral, or charged largely depends on the manager. In part it is due to the way he hires, promotes, discharges, trains, compensates, and assigns workers. These activities can and should be planned ahead. The daily contacts which also contribute to the work atmosphere are spontaneous reactions. These unrehearsed episodes cannot be planned and give credence to the "art" of management.

Coordination. Certain responsibilities are associated with each management position. Theoretically, there is also sufficient authority attached to the position to carry out the responsibilities. The effective use of this authority requires considerable co-ordinating skills. Subordinates are delegated part of the authority to meet their assignments, but the final responsibility remains with the manager. When interests conflict within or between departments, the manager acts as a soothing agent cutting across organizational lines to harmonize objectives and coordinate activities. In doing so, he treads a narrow edge between dictating solutions that discourage initiative and evoking rules that stifle innovations.

Of course, a multitude of other activities devour a manager's time. He sits in on meetings, takes part in training programs, and is called on for personal appearances such as entertaining visitors or presenting awards. The impression he makes on these occasions is again part of the "art" of managing. Some principles that lead to more artful management are highlighted in Example 12.1.

EXAMPLE 12.1 Evolution of Management Responsibilities and Activities

In the off-periods each year when the forests were closed to logging, a sawyer gave vent to his artistic abilities by sculpturing wood with his chainsaw. Somewhat to his surprise the large, primitive figures were eagerly sought as decorations. He sold his works to people drawn by his local reputation. As the reputation spread, he quit his logging career to become an artist-producer.

When it appeared that demand for his product was essentially insatiable, he decided to increase production by *standardizing* his operations. From previous experimentation with designs, cutting, and finishing, he knew which designs were more popular and which techniques could be adapted to systematic production. He set up a routine of distinct operations where workers with minimum skill could do tasks that successively refined the carvings to the desired quality. These work divisions led to *specialization of labor*; workers with a limited skill or knowledge performed a task requiring only that ability.

At first the artist-producer-manager wore many hats. He acted as a salesman by contacting stores to carry his creations. He did the purchasing and kept track of inventory. After blocking out each piece produced, he supervised the finishing, inspecting, packaging, and delivery. Before long he realized he was exhausting himself and spreading his talents too thin to maintain the pace; a formal organization and additional management became necessary. Modeling his plans after the *unity of command* principle followed for centuries by military and religious organizations, he made sure every subordinate reported to only one superior. The position of each superior was carefully defined as to authority and responsibility.

Each new tier of management further separated the artist-producer-manager-president from the workers. They also changed his methods of management. He relied more on *management by exception*, receiving reports only of deviations from anticipated performance and not the "all is well" confirmations. His feedback was filtered through successive layers of staff which emphasized the need for well-trained, competent managers at each level. He still dealt with coordination problems among individuals, but these individuals represented whole departments. Although he shared authority with his staff, he retained the responsibility for the effectiveness of the system.

What was once an artist with his chainsaw evolved into a manager of managers and a production complex. The firm was born to provide an appreciated service. It survived because the service could be provided at a profit. The profit was a function of management proficiency.

12-3 MANAGEMENT AND COMPUTERS

The one activity that best characterizes management is decision making. Besides experience, the most important ingredient for competent decision making is information. In the compilation, storage, and refinement of data, modern management has acquired a powerful ally—the electronic data-processing (EDP) system. The system is built around the fantastic data-digesting and data-generating speed of a computer. We are just entering the era where the capabilities of computers are efficiently harnessed to management decisions.

History

The first computer, ENNIAC, was developed in 1946. It could make calculations at a speed equivalent to 2400 desk calculators operating at the same time. Within 5 years, speeds were increased 1000 times.

"Generation" refers to technical progress. The first generation used vacuum tubes, the second used transistors,

A century ago records of business transactions and production activities were laboriously kept by pen and paper. In the late 1800's, thought was given to machine assistance for record-keeping, and punched cards for data processing were introduced. Motor-driven, key-actuated accounting machines and calculators were widely used and consistently improved during the first half of this century. The first large-scale electronic computers came just after World War II. Succeeding generations of computers have reduced size, increased speed, and provided more versatility.

An idea of the impact of computers can be gained from reports of their usage. The first introduction of commercially produced, large-scale computers occurred in 1954. By 1957, over 450

and the third used integrated circuits. The fourth generation • of computers should provide more versatility by being hooked to associated equipment.

electronic digital computers were being used in this country. By 1961, the number swelled to about 5000 with another 6500 on order. In 1967 the number of installed computers reached 40,000. Of every $1 million U.S. businesses spent for plants and equipment in 1967, $63,000 went for computers, up from $33,000 in 1963.

One hardware (physical equipment) development which portends even further growth is *time sharing*, a design whereby many remote terminals are connected to a central computer. This system enables small businesses and even individuals to have access whenever required to a high powered machine at a reasonable cost. Computer software (the instructional material that tells computers what to do) has also developed rapidly. There are now over 80 "languages" in use and about 120,000 programmers to use them (a number estimated to be one-third less than needed). The weakest link in the chain of developments appear to be management's inability to assimilate the technological achievements as they evolve. The real power of computers is unleased only when it is integrated into the total management control system.

Applications

To appreciate electronic data processing, we should backtrack to simpler data-processing systems. Most data are subjected to six operational steps: classifying, sorting, calculating, summarizing, recording, and communicating. When men do this work, they normally complete all the work on one document before proceeding to the next. When work is departmentalized, special machines accomplish one or two steps at a time. The highest form of this latter approach is punched card equipment with the following characteristics:

1. Data are stored on punched cards. The capacity is limited on each card, but records can be extended to other cards. Both men and machines can read the cards.
2. Several machines are required because each performs only one or two processing steps. A *keypunch* enters the data on cards, a *verifier* checks the data entered, a *collator* arranges the sequence, a *sorter* sorts cards according to need, and an *accounting machine* performs calculations and prints output. Most operations for the machines are directed by control-panel wiring.
3. Considerable human participation is necessary. Human and mechanical card handling limit the speed.

410

There are two basic computer designs. *Digital* computers are emphasized because they are more widely used for EDP and industrial controls. *Analog* computers are generally more appropriate for scientific or engineering investigations. A hybrid computer combines the properties of both types.

A higher degree of mechanization is associated with a computerized system. Some characteristics of the EDP system that contribute to its greater potential are listed below.

1. Data and control instructions are stored within the machine elements. Record lengths are not limited. All six steps of processing can be performed within one machine system. No manual handling of data is required between steps.
2. Control instructions are handled automatically on command to facilitate special processing considerations.
3. Operating speeds and calculating abilities far exceed punched card systems.

A relatively unsophisticated data-processing plan for a production department is shown in Figure 12.2. The initial management decision is based largely on information about raw material and finished-product inventories, existing production commitments and potential assignments, and other data supplied or stored by the recordkeeping system. Current information allows the sales department to tell the customer what delivery schedule he can expect and helps production planning keep the promises through control of in-process materials and resource allocations.

A more elaborate plan is used by Hughes Aircraft, Fairfield Manufacturing, and other companies to simulate production schedules. Production capabilities are modeled by a computer program which includes fixed data about machines, classes of labor, number of shifts, machine-labor rates per hour, set-up times, operation times, dispatching rules, etc. Data on the status of in-process work are fed to the computer before each simulation run. The result of a simulation trial shows how the shop "should" perform with the given inputs. If it shows that high priority orders are not being completed as promised, scheduling rules can be changed *before* the orders are actually in process. Printouts

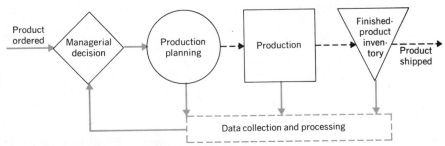

Figure 12.2 Role of EDP in production decisions

411

Control systems are either open or closed loops. An open loop displays data from the operation but does not directly exert control. A closed-loop control acts on the data automatically to make corrections on the system; components include a *sensor* to measure, a *comparer*, a *memory unit* for decision rules, and an *activator* to make the desired change.

from the computer show the expected start and stop times for successive operations for each order at each work center. Any deviations from these expectations are warnings for closer attention. Other advantages claimed for the program are reduced cycle times, increased productivity, better due date fulfillment, and less expediting.

The information flow diagrams in Figure 12.3 represent the use of computers for production planning and control. The depicted systems are considered "open loops" and are designed to reduce the amount of paperwork and human intervention for intermittent manufacturing.

Some military computer systems are still more sophisticated. The Air Defense Command's famous SAGE (Semi-Automatic

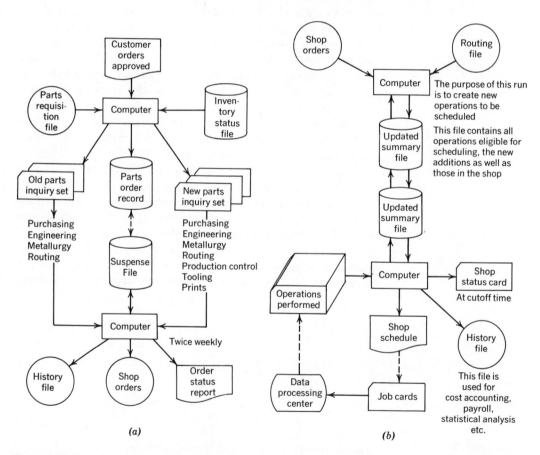

(a)   (b)

Figure 12.3 Use of computers in production planning and control: (*a*) order entry and production planning and (*b*) order status and control (From: C. L. Moodie and D. J. Novotny, "Computer Scheduling and Control Systems for Discrete Part Production," *J. Ind. Eng.* **XIX** (7), July 1968)

Ground Environment) and similar systems are said to operate on "real time"—desired data are transmitted instantaneously and without conversion to a central computer. The advantage of real-time control is the use of information as it develops; a process can react immediately to actual events rather than to a previous forecast of likely events. To facilitate the prompt response of a closed-loop system, arriving information is acted upon by the computer according to predetermined decision rules to initiate instructions to men or machines for nearly instant corrective action. Open-loop, real-time systems give access on call to the current status of operations. For instance, a scheduler can, by typing a coded request on a remote hook-up in the production area, get the latest production rates and inventory quantities needed for on-the-spot decisions.

Challenges

An attitude of "we have no problems, only challenges" is commendable for computer utilization, because the machines will surely be employed and their cost makes efficient utilization a major challenge.

One problem that is slowly disappearing from the challenge list is anxiety about what computers can or will do. Some early publicity pictured the computer as the harbinger of mass unemployment for the white-collar class. Other releases heralded EDP as a captive decision maker which could always glean the best solution. Time has proven both of these extremes wrong, but some people still fear the computers while others endow them with magical powers. Continued exposure to actual installations and familiarity with their operation will gradually subdue misapprehensions.

Another fading challenge is to secure EDP specialists. It is being met by the law of supply and demand; higher wages attract more recruits.

Acceptance of the fact that computers are here to stay makes it easier to join the EDP parade than to fight it. However, it takes more than a nod of allegiance to become an effective practitioner. You have to know how and what to ask before you can get a respectable answer. Professor Elting E. Morrison of MIT commented that most machines developed by man had inherent limits that their misuse would not tolerate:

Overloaded, abused, they stopped working, stalled, broke down, blew up; and there was the end of it. Thus they set clear limits to man's ineptitude.

Quoted in: "Is the Computer Running Wild," *U.S. News and World Rept.*, Feb. 24, 1964.

For the computers, I believe, the limits are not so obvious. Used with ignorance or stupidity, asked a foolish question, it does not collapse, it goes on to answer a fool according to his folly. And the questioner, being a fool, will go on to act upon the reply.

413

A computer is typically brought into a company to combat clerical costs. It finds a home in the controller's department where it is assigned accounting routines, little changed from the manner previously performed by less sophisticated machines. From personnel, material, and payroll accounting, its use gradually extends to production scheduling and inventory control. Eventually it may be applied to the analysis of sales, marketing, purchasing, and personnel planning. It takes time and money to develop the capabilities to treat each of these areas. It may take only a relatively small additional investment to reap far greater benefits by relating the areas through a total system analysis. David Hertz, a McKinney & Co. consultant, said:

As a superclerk, the computer has more than paid its way. Yet mounting computer expenditures are no longer matched by rising economic returns. . . . Technicians cannot take the responsibility for using the computer as a management tool, but management is not ready to accept this responsibility.

Planning computer utilization drives right to the crux of the "system" principle. The typical patchwork plan for a strict application to inventory control or another distinct area requires at least a few inputs from related areas such as purchasing or production planning. These borderline considerations leave the door ajar for more extensive interlocking considerations. The more interrelations inserted in the program, the closer the analysis comes to a system evaluation. Again, the programs do not take form overnight, and their development requires the encouragement and enforcement of top management to break through the barriers of organizational lines.

The more visionary extrapolations of EDP see the computer as the carrier for a management control system which encompasses both external and internal factors affecting production. The methodology for broad evaluations is developed under the banner of *industrial dynamics*. The actual procedures for an investigation appear rather simple in a brief description: identify a problem worthy of study, develop a verbal model of cause and effect, represent the model mathematically, and test hypotheses by disturbing the model to observe the effect of different inputs. This procedure resembles the general simulation routine described in the next section. It is the richness of the model that distinguishes the industrial dynamics approach.

A model for industrial dynamics links internal information flow concerning the organization's resources—men, machines, materials, and money—to external facets affecting the organiza-

A battle for computer time often pits engineering and operations research projects against the demands for auditing and accounting services—another area for management decisions.

Quoted in: "Computers: The Booming State of the Art," *Newsweek*, Aug. 19, 1968.

The phrase "industrial dynamics" was created by J. W. Forrester of MIT in 1957.

tion—social, economic, political, and industrial. A model including these diverse factors must be dynamically structured to achieve realism. Therefore, the closed-loop system is spliced with feedback loops connecting interrelated operations. For instance, a decision to raise prices in hope of increasing profit will influence competition and consumers. Different reactions by competitors will influence sales throughout the industry. General economic conditions and the actions of the industry will bias customers and thereby influence sales within the industry. Sales affect production of all competitors. Production costs vary and, in turn, affect profit. Profit affects policy. Policy determines price, and so on. All the influencing factors keep feeding back to change the relationships; different prices solicit different responses to change production to alter profit to . . . .

The most elaborate models cannot account for every conceivable influencing factor. But even without specific values for outputs, the models reveal trends. The changing responses from the introduction of new variables or a change in an existing variable show initial and subsequent reactions throughout the modeled system. When the responses stabilize, management has a cause-and-effect pattern by which to evaluate its alternatives for decision making.

In commenting about the future effect of industrial dynamics concepts, Professor Forrester wrote:

"Industrial Dynamics, A Major Breakthrough for Decision Makers," *Harvard Business Rev.*, July-Aug. 1958.

Just as automation requires new skills at the worker level, so will improved methods require new abilities at the management level. The executive of the future will be concerned not so much with actual operating decisions as with the basis for wise operating decisions. He will be concerned not so much with day-to-day crises as with the establishment of policies and plans that minimize emergencies.

12-4 MANAGEMENT AND SIMULATION

Simulation in a general sense means to feign or to assume the appearance of something without being the real thing. In a management sense, we use simulation to feign a real system in order to observe and learn from the behavior of the replica. This departure from reality has several advantages over observing the real system. It is usually easier and less expensive and may be more illuminating by confining attention to characteristics of particular interest.

Simulations can be done manually, but the clerical effort easily becomes exhausting.

The use of simulation techniques by management is increasing, mainly because of the wider availability of computers along with the greater sophistication of today's managers. A computer

Executives paying to play a business game offer a ready-made, economical laboratory for studies of high priced talent in operation.

An example of a manual management game designed to illustrate project control is given in Problem 18 at the end of this chapter.

simulation is one of the most effective ways for managers to learn how to treat complex business relationships without suffering the penalties of real trial-and-error experiences. Some problems managers face do not yield to the convenient solution methods encountered in previous chapters, and some managers cannot cope with the solution methods. In such cases the problems can be "run" to see the numerical effect of different alternatives rather than solved by analysis. Both the learning and problem-solving simulations rely on a model, a program that directs the responses of the simulated system.

Management Games

Simulation has extensive current use as a training technique, particularly in the form of much publicized "business games" or "simulation exercises" as they are sometimes called to avoid the connotation that goes with "games." The simulations may involve humans, singularly or in teams, as decision makers in a special environment, or they can pit human decision makers against each other or the "system" in a competitive environment.

Both the cooperative and competitive games can serve a dual purpose. One objective is to teach the participants how to react under different situations as in an "air-controller game" where controllers are exposed to simulated air traffic. A slightly different aspect of the same objective is for participants to learn from the actions of fellow players as they encounter difficult situations. A less utilized potential of the games is for psychologists and behaviorial scientists to deduce from the performance of participants how the same individuals would react to similar competitive or crisis situations in real life.

Very ambitious, computerized, management competition games have been developed. The pedagogical intent differs among games: practicing decision making, gaining analytic ability, learning from interpersonal experiences, and appreciating particular problems. Most games are programmed to emphasize a variety of problems in a relatively short time rather than a penetrating analysis.

A typical game begins with players divided into teams of five or six. They are given a brief historical resumé of a fictitious company and a report on current conditions or short-range forecasts that influence operations. Each team represents a different company, but all teams share the same information about the free or restricted market in which they compete. The companies have plants, sales regions, and several products which

The accelerated flow of time through simulation is fundamental to gaming. Quarterly decisions may take an hour to ● make. It takes only seconds for the computer to calculate and print out results of decisions.

may be supplemented or improved by research and development during the game.

For each play, a game period representing a month or a quarter of a year of real time, participants make several decisions relative to production capacity, production rates, advertising, accumulation or disposal of inventories, research budgets, dividends, etc. The computer program is constructed to simulate the reaction of the market to the combination of decisions from all the companies. The results are communicated to the teams by statements of income and expense and the balance sheet consequent to their decisions at each play.

Each new set of decisions based on the previous time period's report, and any trends that can be detected over the series of plays, are in turn digested by the computer to set the conditions for the next decision. The cycle can be repeated over any mock time span that continues to provide beneficial exercise. At least one game allows termination by bankruptcy and suicide.

★ ★ ★ *Optional material.*

Monte Carlo Technique

Monte Carlo is the colorful name given to a technique by which random numbers are generated to select events from a probability distribution of occurrences. The name is derived from possible random number generators: a flipped coin, a tossed die, a cut from a deck of cards, a draw from a hat, or even a roulette wheel. However, the most used generator is a random number table as given in Appendix D.

A heuristic solution method directs the way to a preferred solution by comparison with previous solutions, but it claims no optimality for the indicated preference. It shares with simulation and trial-and-error methods the goal of *discovering* a solution, not *deriving* it.

The Monte Carlo technique is applied to problem solving; it does not include human decision making other than possible activities represented by a known distribution of outcomes. The approach is more of a controlled experiment than a direct assault on problem variables. Instead of deriving a formula to solve or a ● heuristic process to follow, the conditions of the problem are experienced in trial runs to see what would happen as a result of different decision alternatives. The concepts of simulation by sampling are so simple that it may take restraint to keep from applying the method to every problem. It undeniably produces an answer, but there are some reservations:

1. Many rounds of simulated trials are needed to produce a solution in which confidence can be placed.
2. The trials may be more expensive in computer time or clerical effort than would be required for an analytic solution.

417

3. There is no exact measure of the precision of the solution. Since digital simulation is in numbers, more precision may be accorded the outflow of figures than is really justified by experimental conditions.
4. A slight change in conditions usually means the entire simulation process must be repeated to incorporate the revised data. A similar change in an analytically derived model can be handled by a less demanding change in a legendary "variable constant."

The routine for simulated sampling can be quickly described by a simple illustration. Suppose the arrival rate of workers calling on a supply crib to pick up equipment and expendable supplies has the pattern shown below:

Arrivals per minute, A	0	1	2	3
Probability of A	$\frac{1}{3}$	$\frac{1}{3}$	$\frac{1}{6}$	$\frac{1}{6}$

When a worker wants to check out a piece of equipment, it takes 2 minutes on the average for an attendant to serve him. Expendable supply requests average 1 minute to fulfill. There is an equal likelihood for equipment and supply requests. Service is on a first come-first served basis, and arrivals are assumed to appear at the beginning of each 1-minute increment.

The described situation obviously leads to a queuing problem where the cost of making workers wait is compared to the cost of idle crib attendants. It is also apparent that the distributions of arrivals and service times do not follow the familiar Poisson–exponential assumptions utilized in the developed queuing formulas. We, therefore, have a candidate for Monte Carlo simulation.

The general approach is represented in Figure 12.4. From the problem we draw the information to establish a model and an alternative to test by simulation. The end result is evaluated as a possible solution to the problem and may suggest the advisability of testing other alternatives.

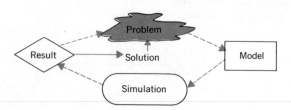

Figure 12.4 Process for Monte Carlo simulation

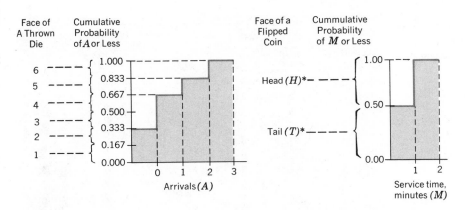

*A "head" is associated with equipment checkout time (2 minutes) and a "tail" with an expendable supply issue (1 minute).

Figure 12.5 Problem data and associated random number-generating assignments

It is easy to eliminate the alternative of one attendant because the arrival rate averages more than one per minute and the service time is 1½ minutes per arrival—an explosive queue.

It is customarily assumed that a die, deck of cards, or a coin used in simulation is "unloaded" and manipulated honestly.

For the problem under consideration, we have enough information to set up a simulation process. However, we need to know costs in order to select a sensible testing alternative. The appropriate costs are: crib attendant, $0.06 per minute or $3.60 per hour; and waiting time of workers, $0.10 per minute. Based on the costs, service times, and arrival rate, a crib operated by two attendants will be the test model.

The cumulative frequency distributions for arrivals and service times are shown in Figure 12.5. Also noted in the figure are the random number generators; one die is thrown to designate the number of arrivals in each trial and a coin is flipped to see how long it takes to serve customers after arrival. The intent of these maneuvers is to provide unbiased entries to the probability distributions. Thus a throw of a die revealing 6 spots would mean 3 arrivals during the minute represented by the throw. Similarly, since there is an equal likelihood of a 1- or 2-minute service time and a corresponding likelihood of a head or tail from the flip of a coin, one side of the coin represents each servicing.

A recordkeeping table (Table 12.1) is convenient when simulations are conducted manually; the record shows the data generated by die and coin throws. The simulation starts at cumulative time 0 with a thrown die showing a 2. This means no arrivals occur during the first minute. The second die toss is a 5 to represent 2 arrivals at the beginning of the second minute. Two coin flips, each representing one of the arrivals, are a head (H_1) and a tail (T_1). Since there are two operators available,

419

Table 12.1 Record of Monte Carlo simulation for the solution of a queuing problem

Cumulative Time	$RN_{(A)*}$	Arrivals	$RN_{(S)*}$	Servicing*	
				O_A	O_B
0	2	0			
1	5	2	$H_1 T_1$	H_1	T_1
2	3	1	H_2		H_2
3	1	0			
4	2	0			
5	6	3	$H_5 T_5 T_5$	H_5	T_5
6	1	0			T_5 1
7	5	2	$T_7 T_7$	T_7	T_7
8	1	0			
9	1	0			
10	2	0			
11	6	3	$H_{11} H_{11} T_{11}$	H_{11}	H_{11}
12	5	2	$T_{12} H_{12}$		
13	3	1	H_{13}	T_{11} 2	T_{12} 1
14	4	1	T_{14}	H_{12} 2	H_{13} 1
15	2	0			
16	1	0		T_{14} 2	
17	6	3	$T_{17} H_{17} T_{17}$	T_{17}	H_{17}
18	1	0		T_{17} 1	
19	6	3	$T_{19} H_{19} H_{19}$	T_{19}	H_{19}
20	6	3	$H_{20} T_{20} T_{20}$	H_{19} 1	
21	3	1	T_{21}		H_{20} 1
22	5	2	$H_{22} H_{22}$	T_{20} 2	
23	2	0		T_{20} 3	T_{21} 2
24	1	0		H_{22} 2	H_{22} 2
25	4	1	H_{25}		
26	2	0		H_{25} 1	
27	4	1	T_{27}		T_{27}
28	1	0			
29	5	2	$T_{29} T_{29}$	T_{29}	T_{29}
30	4	1	H_{30}	H_{30}	
31	6	3	$H_{31} H_{31} T_{31}$		H_{31}
32	1	0		H_{31} 1	
33	3	1	H_{33}		T_{31} 2
34	2	0			H_{33} 1
35	5	2	$H_{35} H_{35}$	H_{35}	
36	3	1	T_{36}		H_{35} 1
37	4	1	H_{37}	T_{36} 1	
38	5	2	$T_{38} T_{38}$	H_{37} 1	T_{38}
39	5	2	$H_{39} T_{39}$		T_{38} 1
40	4	1	T_{40}	H_{39} 1	T_{39} 1
41	5	2	$T_{41} H_{41}$		T_{40} 1
42	2	0		T_{41} 1	H_{41} 1

Table 12.1 (*continued*)

Cumulative Time	$RN_{(A)*}$	Arrivals	$RN_{(S)*}$	Servicing* O_A	Servicing* O_B
43	1	0			↓
44	5	2	$T_{44}H_{44}$	T_{44} ↓	H_{44} ↓
45	4	1	H_{45}	H_{45} ↓	
46	4	1	H_{46}		H_{46} ↓
47	1	0		↓	↓
48	2	0			
49	1	0			

*$RN_{(A)}$ = random number for arrivals; $RN_{(S)}$ = random number for servicings, O_A = operator A in tool crib, O_B = operator B in tool crib.

operator A spends his next 2 minutes satisfying the H_1 flip and operator B serves 1 minute in accordance to the T_1 flip. The next die cast, at the beginning of the third minute, is a 3 to indicate 1 arrival. Because operator A is still working to service the previous arrival, operator B performs the next 2-minute servicing in conformance to the H_2 flip for the arrival at the end of minute 2. The tabulation for 50 samples, 50 minutes, is contained in Table 12.1.

First admitting there are too few samples to obtain a definitive pattern, we at least can make some observations from the available results. The waiting time for arrivals is easily determined by comparing the time each servicing actually starts to the earliest time it could have started. The circled numbers to the right of the service-arrows show the waiting periods. The total of all the circled numbers is 37, indicating that workers were required to wait 37 minutes during the 50-minute simulation period. With a cost of $0.10 per minute for idle workers, the apparent average cost of congestion is

$$\frac{37 \text{ min} \times \$0.10/\text{min}}{\frac{50}{60} \text{ hr}} = \$4.45/\text{hr}$$

Adding a third attendant to the crib would cost $3.60 per hour and would reduce, but probably not eliminate, worker waiting time. More samples for the two-attendant model and a comparable experiment with a three-attendant model would decide the issue.

The value of a digital computer to carry out the tedious record-keeping is apparent even from a model as limited as the one just considered. It is difficult to say when enough samples have been

421

taken. Practical considerations allow more samples when the correctness of a decision is more critical. It is also logical not to stop a program when the mean of the generated data differs appreciably from the empirical mean; for instance, if the coin flipped for service times showed heads 45 out of 50 times, one would conclude the highly irregular streak should not be left as the representative pattern of service requirements.

EXAMPLE 12.2 Application of Monte Carlo Simulation to Determination of an Inventory Safety Stock Level

A new product is being stocked. Experience suggests that the daily demand rate will follow a normal distribution with a mean of 200 units and a standard deviation of 20 units. Lead times have a narrow range of from 7 to 11 days distributed as shown below:

Lead time, LT	7	8	9	10	11
Probability of LT	0.15	0.20	0.40	0.15	0.10

Monte Carlo sampling is used to investigate a safety stock level for a fixed-order inventory policy.

Two cumulative distribution patterns are developed as shown in Figure 12.6. The cumulative normal distribution comprises three standard deviations on either side of the mean. The values are adapted from the areas under a normal curve given in Appendix A. Thus a $-3\,Z$ value is associated with a demand of $200 - (3 \times 20) = 140$ and a probability of occurrence of 0.001.

A random number table is used to enter the distributions. From each block of five numbers, the first two are used to select a lead time and the last two represent the demand. A separate block could be employed for each entry, or four consecutive numbers in one block could suffice. The important concern is not to impose a pattern by repeatedly using the same set of five numbers or skipping around a table to select blocks that "seem" more random. A safe approach is to

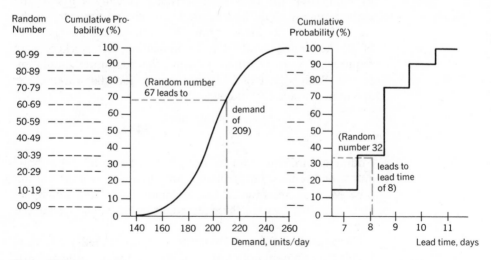

Figure 12.6

422

extract numbers in a consistent, noncyclic manner—by row or column, diagonally, up or down, etc.

Each simulated lead time and demand are multiplied together to set a demand during lead time as shown by column 3 in Table 12.2. Column 4 is the average reorder level (1800) resulting from the product of the average lead time (9 days) and the average demand rate (200 per day). The difference obtained by subtracting column 3 from column 4 is the net effect on the inventory level after each replenishment period. The cumulative effect reveals the stock on hand, column 6.

Given an initial random number block of 32867, the lead time obtained from entering the distribution at 32 is 8 days. The last two digits of the block, 67, lead to a demand of 209. These two values are shown on the cumulative distribution charts and are entered in the first row of the recordkeeping table. Then the entry for column 3 is $209 \times 8 = 1672$ which leads to the value for column 5 of $1800 - 1672 = 128$. Since the experiment starts with no units on hand, column 6 is the same as the first entry in column 5. Thereafter, column 6 is a running total of column 5.

Table 12.2 Record of Monte Carlo simulation trials

Random Number	Lead Time	Daily Demand	Demand during Lead Time	Reorder Level	(4) − (3)	Cumulative Effect of (5)
LT D	(1)	(2)	(1) × (2) = (3)	(4)	(5)	(6)
32 8 67	8	209	1672	1800	128	128
43 1 11	9	176	1584	1800	116	244
38 9 47	9	198	1782	1800	18	262
71 6 84	9	220	1980	1800	−180	82
15 6 06	7	169	1183	1800	617	699
82 2 44	10	197	1970	1800	−170	529
55 8 47	9	198	1782	1800	18	547
94 0 95	11	233	2563	1800	−763	−216
11 7 51	7	200	1400	1800	400	184
69 9 02	9	159	1431	1800	369	553

The 10 trials show inventory levels varying from +699 to −216 before replenishments are received. For this limited sample, increasing the reorder point to $1800 + 216 = 2016$ would have eliminated all stockouts at the added expense of carrying a safety stock of 216 units. A much larger sample would provide sound bases for setting a reorder level that limits stockouts to a figure deemed acceptable with respect to customer service and holding cost.

★ ★ ★ *End optional material.*

12-5 SUMMARY A competent manager artfully deals with people, utilizes machines, and possesses technical skills to effectively plan, analyze, and control the production system in which he operates. He works through other people to accomplish his aims. The activity that best characterizes his position is decision making. Other activities include:

1. *Policy making.* Formulation and clear statements of short-range objectives lead to longer range goals.
2. *Policy evaluation.* A comparison of accomplishments to objectives warns of impending difficulties and is a basis for personnel rating.
3. *Communication.* Good listening habits should accompany capable order issuing. "Management by exception" saves time by devoting attention to deviations from anticipated performance instead of to all performance reports.
4. *Personnel relations.* A work atmosphere contributing to good morale can be planned, but spontaneous contacts that also affect motivation are a function of personality, the art in management.
5. *Coordination.* Authority can and should be delegated to subordinates to perform well-defined tasks, but the responsibility for the tasks remains with the manager. He can use the authority of his position to help implement tasks by coordinating interdepartmental objectives.

The use of computers to assist management decision making is increasing. When comparing an electronic data-processing system to a punched card system, the EDP system is found to be faster, to require less human participation, and to be more versatile.

The two basic types of computers are digital and analog. Most production control facilities use the digital type. Controls can be open or closed loop. The closed-loop control acts on the data from the system according to predetermined decision rules to make corrections on the system. Open loops display the data that allow managers to initiate corrective actions when deemed necessary. A real-time system transmits desired data instantaneously and without conversion to a central computer; the advantage of real-time control is the availability of information as it develops.

Computers epitomize the system concept because their effective use requires information and action from all segments of a departmentalized organization. "Industrial dynamics" describes a methodology for broad system evaluations. It links internal information flow to the external considerations that affect the organization.

Simulation has become a practical management tool due to the data-generating and data-digesting capabilities of the computer. One use of simulation is for training. Management games provide learning experiences through simulated exercises. Most games represent the reactions of a mock company to operating decisions made by managing teams. The gaming format can also be used for research.

Monte Carlo simulation is a problem-solving technique which uses randomly generated numbers to experience the conditions of a problem. The method is particularly useful for problems that are difficult to formulate for analytic solutions. From the circumstances of the problem, a certain alternative is selected for the simulation experiment. Samples are taken from a relevant distribution by converting random numbers to influencing factors from the distribution. The samples are then inserted in the model being tested to determine their effect on the system. The process is repeated many times to increase the reality and confidence in the results.

12-6   REFERENCES

Beer, S., *Cybernetics and Management*, John Wiley, New York, 1964.

Beyer, R., *Probability Accounting for Planning and Control*, Ronald Press, New York, 1963.

Bonini, C. P., *Simulation of Information and Decisions in the Firm*, Prentice-Hall, Englewood Cliffs, N.J., 1963.

Bonini, C. P., R. K. Jaedicke, and H. M. Wagner, *Management Controls: New Directions in Basic Research*, McGraw-Hill, New York, 1964.

Bourne, C. P., *Methods of Information Handling*, John Wiley, New York, 1963.

Brooks, F. P., Jr., and K. E. Iverson, *Automatic Data Processing*, John Wiley, New York, 1963.

Buffa, E. S., *Operations Management: Problems and Models*, John Wiley, New York, 1968.

Chapin, N., *An Introduction to Automatic Computers*, Van Nostrand, Princeton, N.J., 1963.

Greenlaw, P. S., *et al.*, *Business Simulation*, Prentice-Hall, Englewood Cliffs, N.J., 1962.

Gregory, R. H. and R. L. Van Horn, *Automatic Data-Processing Systems*, Wadsworth, Belmont, Calif., 1963.

Haimann, T., *Professional Management Theory and Practice*, Houghton Mifflin, Boston, Mass., 1962.

Johnson, R. A., F. E. Kast, and J. E. Rosenzweig, *The Theory and Management of Systems*, McGraw-Hill, New York, 1963.

Ledley, R. S., *Programming and Utilizing Digital Computers*, McGraw-Hill, New York, 1962.

Madeheim, H. E., E. M. Mazze, and C. S. Stein, *Readings in Organization and Management*, Holt, Rinehart and Winston, New York, 1963.

McFarland, D. E., *Management: Principles and Practices* (2nd ed.), Macmillan, New York, 1964.

McMillan, C. and R. F. Gonzales, *Systems Analysis: A Computer Approach to Decision Models*, Richard D. Irwin, Homewood, Ill., 1965.

Schmidt, R. and W. E. Meyers, *Electronic Business Data Processing*, Holt, Rinehart and Winston, New York, 1963.

Schoderbek, P. P. (ed.), *Management Systems*, John Wiley, New York, 1967.

Sprague, R. E., *Electronic Business Systems—Management Use of On-Line-Real Time Computers*, Ronald Press, New York, 1962.

Tocher, K. D., *The Art of Simulation*, Van Nostrand, New York, 1963.

Vance, S., *Management-Decision Simulation*, McGraw-Hill, New York, 1960.

12-7 QUESTIONS AND PROBLEMS

1. Comment on the following sayings as they pertain to management:

(a) The least organization is the best organization.

(b) Too many cooks spoil the broth.

(c) Good managers, like salesmen, are born, not made.

(d) Like a turtle, you can make progress only when you stick your neck out.

(e) If you can keep your head while others are losing theirs, you just don't understand the situation.

2. Is auditing a form of feedback?

3. Why can authority, but not responsibility, be delegated?

4. What is the relationship between specialization of labor and job enlargement?

5. Explain how management by exception could be considered an extension of Pareto's principle.

6. Comment on the relationship of earned authority and position authority when:

(a) A father brings his son into the family firm at a high position.

(b) A top level manager is hired from a source outside the firm instead of promoting someone from within the firm.

7. Distinguish between computer *hardware* and *software*. With which are programmers associated? What is a computer generation?

8. What role can computers play in management by exception? Have computers contributed to the paperwork explosion? How?

9. Give an example of a closed-loop and of an open-loop control system. Identify the sensor, comparer, memory unit, and activator in the closed-loop system.

10. What are some advantages of an on-line, real-time computer system? How is the system different from a process computer and a punched card system?

11. Computers have been called "brains" and "idiots with fast reflexes." There is also the slogan GIGO—put Garbage In and you get Garbage Out. Comment on the slogan and each of the nicknames with respect to reasons for their acceptance.

12. Could computers be useful in service industries such as a

delivery service, appliance repairs, and telephone or electrical services? Is the size of the operation a major influence?

13. Under what conditions would an industrial dynamics approach to a problem be feasible? Distinguish between the simulation aspects for industrial dynamics and business games or Monte Carlo sampling.

14. Why are tables of random numbers more widely used for Monte Carlo simulation than gambling devices such as dice, cards, or coins?

15. In what manner does the number of trials in simulated sampling affect the accuracy of results?

16. What are the advantages and limitations of:

(a) Business games as a learning device?

(b) Business games as a research tool?

(c) Monte Carlo simulation to solve problems?

17. Your company daily averages $12,000 in cash receipts and $10,000 in cash disbursements. Both are normally distributed with a standard deviation of $2000 for receipts and $1000 for disbursements. How could simulation be used to help predict your average cash balance at the end of the day, maximum cash on hand, and the duration of bank loans to allow prompt payment of disbursements? Could the problem be treated as an inventory evaluation where cash is the material? Discuss.

18. The purpose of this management game is to illustrate the use of updating and time-cost tradeoffs in project planning and control. Initial plans for a project attempt to anticipate trouble areas and to provide means to overcome them if they do occur. It is almost impossible to anticipate all the chance happenings that could affect a project. The next best thing to knowing in advance what will happen is to be able to identify quickly what has happened. By updating the initial plans to reflect current conditions, operating decisions can restore the original balance between the benefits of caution and the unexpected cost arising from risk.

General procedure. You are the project manager for a construction company. The project is to build a new type ski-tow at a resort high in the mountains. Because the ski-tow relies on an untried design, and the remote, exposed position of the work site presents unusual demands, the time and cost to complete all the activities are highly uncertain.

There is also a calendar problem caused by a relatively short period of good construction weather. The resort owners want the ski-tow ready at the beginning of the snow season. Therefore, they are asking that the bids for the project state both a completion time and the cost. They also stipulate that a penalty of $30,000 per day be paid by the contractor for each day the project exceeds the contracted duration.

As the project manager, you face three decisions. The first is to determine the project duration and related bid that reflects the uncertainty involved. It is then assumed that you get the contract. Activity times will be simulated by the Monte Carlo technique to a point half-way through the project. At this point, assuming the simulated times are the actual activity durations, you may apply additional resources at extra cost if it appears the project will exceed the contracted completion time or you can save money by reducing resources if it appears you will finish early. The third decision, about two-thirds of the way through the project, is another chance to make time-cost trade offs based on the simulated activity times to that point.

Decision 1. The project activity list, restriction list, and expected range of activity times (*a*, *m*, and *b*) are shown in Table 12.3. Space is also provided in the table to enter estimated activity

Table 12.3 Activity descriptions and restrictions

| Activity | Post-requisites | Estimated Activity Times (days) | | | t_e | σ^2 |
		Optimistic	Most Likely	Pessimistic		
A	D	5	5	5	_____	_____
B	A,G,I	5	6	7	_____	_____
C	L,K	1	4	7	_____	_____
D	M	6	6	18	_____	_____
E	M	4	7	16	_____	_____
F	N,O	1	1	7	_____	_____
G	H	10	10	10	_____	_____
H	M	13	15	17	_____	_____
I	L,K	1	11	15	_____	_____
J	C,I,G	4	5	6	_____	_____
K	N,O	8	8	8	_____	_____
L	E,F	6	6	12	_____	_____
M	P,Q	5	15	25	_____	_____
N	P,Q	8	15	16	_____	_____
O	Q	5	12	43	_____	_____
P		6	8	16	_____	_____
Q	R,S	6	8	22	_____	_____
R		1	8	15	_____	_____
S		6	6	12	_____	_____

Table 12.4 Project cost and bid award as a function of duration

Duration (days)	Indirect Cost	Direct Cost	Total Cost	Bid Award
50	$1,000,000	$900,000	$1,900,000	$3,000,000
52	1,100,000	750,000	1,850,000	2,960,000
54	1,200,000	680,000	1,880,000	2,920,000
56	1,300,000	610,000	1,910,000	2,880,000
58	1,400,000	540,000	1,940,000	2,840,000
60	1,500,000	480,000	1,980,000	2,800,000
62	1,600,000	420,000	2,020,000	2,760,000
64	1,700,000	370,000	2,070,000	2,720,000
66	1,800,000	320,000	2,120,000	2,680,000
68	1,900,000	280,000	2,180,000	2,640,000
70	2,000,000	240,000	2,240,000	2,600,000
72	2,100,000	210,000	2,310,000	2,560,000
74	2,200,000	180,000	2,380,000	2,520,000
76	2,300,000	160,000	2,460,000	2,480,000
78	2,400,000	140,000	2,540,000	2,440,000

times (t_e) and the variances (σ^2) needed for network construction and evaluation.

The cost of completing the project will increase as the duration is shortened. Conversely, the amount the owners will pay for the project will increase for a shorter duration. The relationship between these costs and times is shown in Table 12.4.

The actual project completion time will be determined by a random selection from the distribution of times representing each activity. Therefore, the project duration may be more or less than the length of the critical path determined from the estimated activity times. At certain milestone events, the actual durations will be compared with those anticipated to see what time-cost tradeoffs are available. In general, about $5000 per day can be saved by extending activity durations, and it will cost about $12,500 a day to buy time. Remembering that a $30,000 penalty must be paid for each day the project extends beyond the contracted duration, determine a bid and complete lines 1 through 4 on the game score sheet (page 433).

Decision 2. You have now won the bid with the duration you determined for decision 1. Your expected profit is the difference between the total cost and the amount of the bid that is acceptable to the owners. To determine if this bid is realistic in view of the uncertainties involved, the actual activity times will be simulated.

Using a table of random numbers, determine the actual durations by sampling from the activity time distributions shown in Table 12.5. For instance, the assumed actual duration for activity C would be 5 days if the randomly selected two-digit number is in the 70's. Obtain simulated times for the durations of all activities shown in the table; complete the bottom line of the table with the sampled values.

The effect of these "actual times" on the original plans is easily observed by correcting the initial network calculations to show the sampled values; the earliest start for activity M may result from any of the three paths merging at the event. Fill in line 5 on the score sheet.

At this stage you know whether the first half of the project is on, behind, or ahead of the original schedule. Now you can "sell" time by sending one entire crew to work on another project and thereby reduce direct costs by $5000 per day for the remainder of the project. You can "buy" time by prefabricating some of the work, but this alternative will increase indirect cost by $100,000. The effect of these two alternatives is shown by the respective time distributions in Table 12.6.

Select one of the following three alternatives and enter your choice on line 6 of the score sheet.

Alternative 2.1: Sell time for $5000 per day and use the lengthened activity time distributions for the remaining portion of the project. The daily savings apply to all the days remaining in the project, but once the crew is sent away it cannot be called back.

Table 12.5 Time distributions for activities A through L

Random Numbers	Activity A	B	C	D	E	F	G	H	I	J	K	L
90–99	5	7	7	18	16	7	10	17	15	6	8	12
80–89	5	7	6	15	14	6	10	16	14	6	8	11
70–79	5	7	5	12	11	5	10	15	13	5	8	10
60–69	5	6	4	10	10	4	10	15	11	5	8	9
50–59	5	6	4	8	9	3	10	15	10	5	8	8
40–49	5	6	4	7	8	2	10	15	9	5	8	7
30–39	5	6	3	6	7	1	10	15	7	5	8	6
20–29	5	6	3	6	7	1	10	15	5	4	8	6
10–19	5	5	2	6	6	1	10	14	3	4	8	6
00–09	5	5	1	6	4	1	10	13	1	4	8	6
Actual times	—	—	—	—	—	—	—	—	—	—	—	—

Table 12.6 The effect of alternatives on activity time estimates

| | Alternative 2.1—Sell | | | | | Alternative 2.2—Buy | | | | |
| | Times | | | | | Times | | | | |
Activity	a	m	b	t_e	σ^2	a	m	b	t_e	σ^2
M	7	16	31	___	___	4	12	20	___	___
N	11	15	19	___	___	10	13	16	___	___
O	7	16	25	___	___	5	13	23	___	___
P	6	8	28	___	___	6	8	16	___	___
Q	8	10	24	___	___	4	7	16	___	___
R	2	9	16	___	___	1	6	11	___	___
S	6	8	16	___	___	6	6	6	___	___

Alternative 2.2: Buy time according to the activity time distributions in Table 12.6 by prefabricating components at company headquarters. The cost is a step increase in indirect costs of $100,000.

Alternative 2.3: Let the project continue according to the original plan using the activity time estimations made and recorded in Table 12.3.

There will be one more chance to buy or sell time after activities M, N, and O are completed.

Decision 3. Using the same procedures as before, simulate the "actual" activity completion time for activities M, N, and O from the section of Table 12.7 that corresponds to the alternative employed for decision 2.

After the actual activity durations have been simulated by entering the appropriate durations in Table 12.7, add the times to the portion of the project previously completed (correct earliest starts for M, N, and O) and enter the earliest start for activity Q on line 7 of the score sheet.

Just as work on activity Q is about to commence, it starts to snow. Heavy snow will not affect the duration of Q, but it can delay the start of activities R and S. The probability of a snow deep enough to cause delays of different magnitudes is shown by the probability distribution in Table 12.8. Considering the likelihood of snow delays and how close the project is to its contracted completion date, one of the three following alternatives may be utilized to reallocate resources to minimize the total cost:

Alternative 3.1: If the alternative 2.1 was not used, one crew

Table 12.7 Alternative time distributions for activities *M* through S

Random Numbers	Alternative 2.1							Alternative 2.2							Alternative 2.3						
	M	*N*	*O*	*P*	*Q*	*R*	*S*	*M*	*N*	*O*	*P*	*Q*	*R*	*S*	*M*	*N*	*O*	*P*	*Q*	*R*	*S*
90–99	31	19	35	28	24	16	16	20	16	33	16	16	11	6	25	16	43	16	22	15	12
80–89	27	18	30	24	21	13	14	17	15	27	14	14	9	6	22	16	30	13	18	12	11
70–79	23	17	25	21	18	11	12	15	14	22	12	12	8	6	20	15	22	11	15	10	9
60–69	20	16	19	18	15	10	11	13	14	18	11	10	7	6	18	15	18	10	12	9	8
50–59	17	15	16	16	13	9	10	12	13	15	10	9	6	6	16	15	15	9	10	8	8
40–49	16	15	15	15	12	9	9	12	13	13	9	8	6	6	14	14	14	8	9	8	7
30–39	14	14	14	13	11	8	8	11	12	12	8	7	5	6	12	13	12	7	8	7	7
20–29	12	13	12	11	10	6	8	9	12	10	8	5	4	6	10	12	10	7	8	6	7
10–19	10	12	10	8	10	4	7	7	11	8	7	3	3	6	7	10	8	6	7	4	6
00–09	7	11	7	6	8	2	6	4	10	5	6	1	1	6	5	8	5	6	6	1	6
Actual times	—	—	—	—	—	—	—	—	—	—	—	—	—	—	—	—	—	—	—	—	—

may now be deleted to save $5000 per day for the remainder of the project.

Alternative 3.2: A subcontractor can be employed to do activity *R*. The subcontractor guarantees that he will finish the activity in 7 days or he will pay any penalties that accrue from his late work. Using this alternative will add $30,000 to the indirect cost of the project.

Alternative 3.3: Make no changes from decision 2. Check line 8 on the score sheet according to which alternative is selected.

Final evaluation. Simulate the completion times for activities *P*, *Q*, *R*, and *S*. If alternative 3.1 was chosen, use the right-hand side of the activity time distribution for alternative 2.1 in Table 12.7. For the other two alternatives of decision 3, sample from the appropriate right-hand columns of Table 12-7 according to the course of action selected in decision 2. Note that activity *R* will

Table 12.8 Probability of delay

Random Numbers	Probability	Length of Delay (days)
00–39	0.40	0
40–69	0.30	1
70–89	0.20	2
90–99	0.10	3

take exactly 7 days if alternative 3.2 is used, regardless of the time distribution for that activity. Enter the simulated times to complete the bottom row for one alternative in Table 12.7.

Simulate the possible delay due to weather by using the delay distribution pattern of Table 12.8. Add any resulting delay to the completion times of activities R and S. Again note that if alternative 3.2 was selected, the subcontractor is responsible for the delay time; therefore, activity R should not include any delay charge against you.

Trace the "actual" critical path through the project (including any weather delay) and enter its duration on line 9 of the score sheet. Complete lines 10, 11, 12, and 13 on the score sheet to determine the total profit or loss from the project.

Score Sheet

CPS Management Game

Decision 1:
1. Most likely projected duration   _____
2. Contracted duration   _____
3. Probability of completing the project by the contracted duration   _____
4. Bid award (from Table 12.4 based on line 2 above)   _____

Decision 2:
5. Earliest start time for activity M _____
6a. If alternative 2.1 is used, subtract \$5000 × (line 9 − line 5)   _____
 b. If alternative 2.2 is used, add \$100,000   _____

Decision 3:
7. Earliest start time for activity Q _____
8a. If alternative 3.1 is used, subtract \$5000 × (line 9 − line 7)   _____
 b. If alternative 3.2 is used, add \$30,000   _____

Final accounting:
9. "Actual" project duration by simulation   _____
10. Total project cost (from Table 12.4 and line 9)   _____
11. Penalty charge: \$30,000 × (line 9 − line 2)   _____
12. Final cost: lines 6 + 8 + 10 + 11   _____
13. Final profit or loss: line 4 − line 12   _____

19. A service department has a constant service time of 2 minutes for all servicings. The following data on arrival rates have been observed:

Time Between Arrivals (min)	Number of Occurrences
0–0.99	150
1–1.99	250
2–2.99	550
3–3.99	300
4–4.99	150
5–5.99	50
6 or more	50

(a) Simulate 60 minutes to estimate the average length of the queue. Assume arrivals come at the beginning of each 1-minute increment.

(b) Compare the answer in part (a) to a solution obtained using a queuing formula selected from Section 10-7. How do you account for the difference?

20. Use Monte Carlo sampling to develop a solution to part (a) of Problem 38 in Chapter 10.

21. An unhealthy taxi service has eight cabs. The company tries to keep six of the dilapidated cabs operating all the time, with the other two on standby or being repaired. When a cab is started in the morning, there is 1 chance in 10 that it will not operate (if it starts it is assumed it will operate all day). If a cab does not start, two-thirds of the time it will be repaired to rejoin the fleet by the next day; there is a one-third chance that the repair will take 2 days (even after repair there is a 0.1 probability of the cab not starting). From a simulation of 100 days, what is the probability of having six, five, four, or three cabs in operating order on any day?

22. Continue the simulation begun in Example 12.2. After 50 trials, determine the size of a safety stock that allows stockouts on no more than 2 consecutive days only 5% of the time.

23. Treat Problem 17 quantitatively. Use 40 trials to determine a cash flow pattern when no money is borrowed or deposited outside the firm. Comment on the results with reference to risk and cash payment of bills.

Demand	Probability
6	0.10
5	0.20
4	0.50
3	0.20

24. A small plant uses wood chips as a raw material for one of its products. Chips are delivered in units of railway cars. The • average demand is four cars per month, but the usage varies according to the pattern shown in the margin area.

Since special unloading equipment is rented when a delivery arrives, it is desirable to have large orders. Space is available to store any size order, but stored inventory is subject to weather damage. The costs associated with wood-chip inventory are: holding cost, $60 per year per unit for maximum order; order cost, $300 per order including rental of unloading equipment; and opportunity cost, $80 per unit per week for disruption of production schedules.

Lead Time (weeks)	Probability
1	0.10
2	0.10
3	0.30
4	0.50

- The lead time varies from 1 to 4 weeks according to the distribution shown in the margin area.

Determine by simulation the preferred reorder level for wood chips.

section three CONTROL

A vague feeling of uneasiness may be associated with the word *control*. The dictionary explanations: (1) to regulate, (2) to exercise authority over, and (3) to restrain, evoke few special emotions, so the word must be chameleon-like, taking color suitable to the subject. *Control* as applied to production takes on a fairly neutral tone. It warms up a bit when applied as *worker control* and cools quickly when used as *machine control*. An interesting point is that essentially the same detection methods and regulating measures are employed for all components in a production system—people, processes, or products. Whatever the study of control may boast or lack in native appeal, it is vital to the success of production systems. The editors of *Automatic Control* go even further:

Automatic Control, Simon and Schuster, New York, 1955. •

There is going to be more and more automatic control in our lives. It is the means by which we will carry on big business and big government, production, finance, communications, trade and distribution in the complex and centrally organized civilization of our times. As citizens, we may hope to manage this revolution democratically and so to our advantage. We had better develop a clear understanding of what the term stands for and of the changes it implies in the way we make our living and conduct our affairs.

Control is the natural culmination of planning and analysis. It is the action phase, the proof, the "go" state. It is the stage where actual performance is compared to planned performance and, if found lacking, where replanning or more analysis is initiated.

Control of quantity is of universal production interest. It starts with preproduction planning, progresses through dispatching, uses expediting for corrective actions, and recycles with improvements drawn from critiques of completed control activities. Visual aids have earned time-honored respect as control devices. Newer techniques have been introduced to cope with more complex control problems (*Chapter 13*).

CONTROL

CONTROL

Control of quality concerns almost every component of a production system. Product designers establish specifications. Workers are urged to avoid mistakes. Acceptance sampling measures the quality of inputs to the production process. Control charting checks on process performance. Final inspections verify output quality. And ultimately the customer delivers the final verdict (*Chapter 14*).

Many control measures for quality and quantity utilize statistical tests. Other processes within the production system can also be evaluated by statistical methods. Variation is expected. Statistical control concepts indicate how much performance can vary before the process standards are endangered. Experiments can be designed to draw inferences about a process with only limited information (*Chapter 15*).

Under the spell of well-publicized and individually described control tools and techniques, it is easy to overlook the umbilical cord nourishing all control measures: *feedback*. As introduced in Chapter 1 and repeatedly mentioned since, it takes a prompt return flow of reliable information to make control measures work. Special attention to feedback concepts emphasizes the need to know what information to collect, when to collect it, where it is needed, and how to get it there to actuate the regulating controls (*Section Three*).

CHAPTER 13

QUANTITY CONTROL

13-1 IMPORTANCE

Quality is a contemporary consideration with quantity and will be treated in the next chapter.

Production control serves the dual purpose of directing the implementation of previously planned activities and monitoring their progress to discover and correct irregularities. Quantity control concentrates on delivering the desired output within the expected delivery date. In this respect, the control function is the action phase of production. Plans are converted into action notices which spell out exactly which men and machines will operate, what the operations will be, and when they must be done. Then the actions are compared to planned performance to provide the feedback for replanning or initiating corrective actions.

The dynamic nature of on-going control activities makes quantity control difficult to program; it benefits from well-designed procedures, good training, and pictorial management tools, but it is not adaptable to rigid formulations.

It is said "an army travels on its stomach." Equivalently, it can be said that production is carried by its inventory.

There is an interesting resemblance between production control and a military operation. Before a battle (production process), logistic planning puts the troops and supplies in a preferred strategic position (allocation and scheduling of men, machines, and materials). Tactical plans are developed for battlefield maneuvers (sequencing operations, inventory policies, machine loadings, etc.). But even the best military plans cannot fully predict the actions of the enemy (forecasting business conditions, competitors' actions, delays and breakdowns, etc.). Therefore, performance in the actual battle depends largely on individual training, equipment, supervision, and tactics. A communication net is supposed to feedback current battle reports (production operations) to the command post (production supervisors) to allow adjustments in the tactical plans. Calls for reinforcements or coordinated actions are relayed further back to headquarters (production control department). There the adjustments are evaluated and, if accepted, converted to orders. Prompt and appropriate actions are necessary at all levels, from the front lines (production line) to the General Staff (manufacturing staff), for a sensitive and reliable control system.

13-2 CONTROL DESIGNS There are many production control designs. We shall consider three basic types, but innumerable mutations have been made to fit specific situations—an eminently sound practice. A control system designed for one plant might not work in another and might not even remain effective for the original plant as production requirements change. Three divisions of production, corresponding to the plant layouts introduced in Section 8-3 and associated with the three types of control designs, are described below.

1. *Continuous production* (utilizes a product layout):
   Standardized end product and manufacturing routine.
   High volume of output produced by specialized equipment.
   Low in-process inventory and long production runs.
   Low worker skill levels.
   Limited flexibility of process.
2. *Intermittent production* (utilizes a process layout):
   Nonstandard end product requiring extensive production controls.
   Medium volume of output produced by general-purpose equipment.
   High in-process inventory and shorter production runs.
   Medium to high worker skill levels.
   More flexible process owing to versatile material-handling equipment.
3. *Special projects* (frequently utilizes fixed-position layout):
   Unique end product requiring extreme production controls.
   Low volume of output often requiring the cooperation of several subcontractors.
   High in-process inventory with a single production run.
   High worker skill levels.
   High flexibility of process.

Flow Control

Flow or serialized control applies to the control of continuous production as found in oil refineries, bottling works, cigarette-making factories, paper-making mills, and other mass manufacturing plants. The standardization of products, equipment, and work assignments allows the controls to be standardized also. The main concern is to maintain a continuous, ample supply of materials.

The high volume production means that huge quantities of raw materials must be accumulated and stored until needed.

440

The usual balance of storage cost to opportunity cost is biased by the seriousness of stockouts. Because of the inflexibility of the process, the entire operation is curtailed by a shortage of material in any part of the sequence. The volume of output requires strict attention to finished-goods inventory and a smoothly operating distribution system.

In continuous production the lines are balanced and the sequence of operations is seldom changed. Economy results from operating near maximum capacity.

Work order dispatching is largely unnecessary because of the long production runs. The workers know their repetitive work assignments without special instructions. The closest equivalent to work orders is the issuance of production releases which state the output level expected during a certain time interval. These are usually issued to production managers and supervisors who control the process flow instead of to the workers on the production line.

"Batch" or "block" control is an offshoot of flow control where the same process produces products modified as to taste, style, color, or size. Control is exercised over individual blocks or batches as they pass through the process.

Order Control

Order control, associated with intermittent production, is far more complex than flow control. The job-shop nature of the work means that production orders may come from different sources and for different quantities and designs; the time allowed for production also may vary as a result of salesmen's delivery promises. These conditions make prior planning difficult and necessitate a high degree of control over each order.

A bill of material for an order includes:

1. Name and model of product.
2. Order number and quantity.
3. Raw materials.
4. Parts by name and number.
5. Appropriate specifications, drawings, and other references.

The receipt of a "job" or "shop order" initiates action to determine what raw materials and parts are required and which production operations should be scheduled. The bill of material, routing information as to the sequence of operations, and desired delivery dates are considered in making the work schedule.

The two principle methods of scheduling are *backward scheduling* to meet a deadline and *forward scheduling* to produce as soon as possible. The former method is done by starting with the required delivery date and calculating backward to determine the release date for the order. When several subassemblies with different lead times are involved, the scheduler must work backwards along each subassembly line to set the times for component work orders (Figure 13.1).

More detailed scheduling formats are described in Section 13-4.

Forward scheduling is used most frequently for products that do not require assembly of components. In a metal mill where a certain thickness of a certain alloy is ordered, customers usually want the material as soon as they can get it or at least will take it as soon as it is available. Under these conditions the scheduler issues orders to begin production as soon as machine time is

441

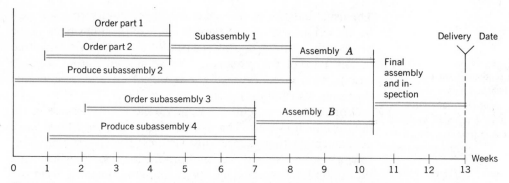

Figure 13.1 Assembly chart based on lead times required to meet a promised delivery date

available. When there is a backlog of demand, he checks requested delivery dates to set a priority; in effect, he is then combining backward and forward scheduling.

When there is a distinct limiting factor in the production flow, it receives special attention and is referred to as *load control*. For instance, if there is a very expensive or one-of-a-kind machine required for a number of different orders, all activities concerning these orders are geared to the time available on the critical machine. The purpose of load control is to ease as much as possible the effects of the bottleneck by assuring maximum utilization of the decisive asset.

Special Project Control

The special project category is reserved for distinctive or particularly important undertakings with unusual features. The most common examples are construction projects—dams, factory modifications, buildings, bridges, etc. The distinguishing characteristic is personal contact. Most orders are issued by managers and foremen directly to the workers responsible for performance. The same supervisory personnel monitor the progress and initiate corrective actions when the work falls behind expectation. These less formal and more expensive procedures are warranted by the coordination problems entailed in unifying the efforts of diverse trades to meet rigid time limitations.

Since each phase of a special project tends to rely on the completion of a previous phase, expediting measures often take the form of crash scheduling for specific segments. Big dosages of extra resources applied intermittently rapidly increase direct costs. It is difficult to control the application of added resources because the supervisory force is seldom increased during periods of accelerated activity. The use of short-range activity charting,

The "trades" involved in contracted projects include specialized skills represented by different unions and subcontracting firms.

Crash scheduling is not necessarily a reflection of poor project control. It can result from uncontrollable conditions such as weather. Extra resources applied to "buy"

442

time include overtime and employing more men and materials than originally planned.

as described in Section 13-4, by capable controllers gives protection from soaring costs arising from congested working conditions and inefficient operations.

13-3 CONTROL ACTIONS

The multitude of considerations that go into preproduction planning have filled the previous chapters; some of the more direct tactical activities are shown in Figure 13.2. The result of these activities is a master production schedule—the foundation of all production actions. It shows how many and when products will be ready for distribution. This information is used for material control and the development of man and machine assignments for individual orders.

Dispatching

Pros and cons of centralized dispatching include:

Advantages
___
Improves coordination between facilities
Allows rapid schedule changes
Relieves foremen of extra responsibilities

Disadvantages
___
Lacks flexibility
Requires a very reliable communication system

The dispatching function marks the "go" state of production. The action that triggers manufacturing is the release of job and material orders. These orders implement operations from the master schedule. When several parts are involved, production orders are broken down into job cards for successive tasks and the methods to do them. Material issues and information about the next destination of the component are also recorded.

The exact duties of dispatching and the manner of carrying out the duties varies among companies. *Centralized dispatching* has the production control department issue detailed work orders directly to the operators performing the tasks. *Decentralized dispatching* sends general work orders to department foremen who decide which machines to use, who should use

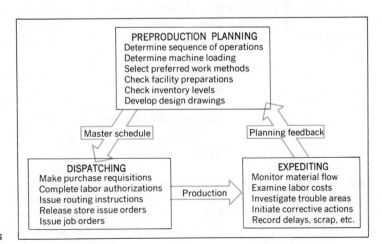

Figure 13.2 Control activities

them, and when to perform the work. After the orders are released, the dispatching function sometimes continues with the responsibility for recording actual operation times, reasons for idleness, causes of breakdowns, and similar relevant information about the schedule. At other times, these responsibilities fall under the province of expediting.

Expediting

Expediting is sometimes associated with rushing "hot" orders through production. It can serve this purpose, but it mainly combats troubles throughout the production process.

Whereas dispatching primarily consists of a flow of information, expediting is concerned with the flow of materials and components. The two functions tend to overlap both chronologically and in responsibility. The events recorded under the dispatching function are adjusted by expediting activities.

An expeditor follows the development of an order from the raw material stage to the finished product. He often is given the authority and facilities to move materials or semifinished products to relieve congestion in production flow. For instance, the failure of components to reach a certain work station is detected at the dispatching office from progress charts or data-processing output. The expeditor investigates to determine the cause of the delay. If it is caused by misinterpretation of work orders, he can clarify the points and possibly use equipment under his command to relieve a material jam. If flow circulation problems extend beyond his authority, he refers them to the production planning office for revised assignments or reallocations of resources. The resulting alterations are generally returned to the expeditor with the responsibility for implementation.

Full-time troubleshooters assigned to the production of a new product are often called "product coordinators." Their duties are similar to expediting with the added responsibility of coordinating product modifications as the need develops.

Expediting and dispatching are frequently performed under the same agency, particularly in special project control. Under a flow control design, combining the functions is also logical; dispatching is relatively straightforward due to the need for few detailed instructions, while expediting is more important owing to the seriousness of temporary flow interruptions. In order control design the two functions complement each other in the close control needed to chase orders through the plant. Whether or not the functions are combined, both must contribute to postoperation evaluations. The recommendations derived from correcting past mistakes lead to control designs that reduce repeated mistakes.

13-4 CONTROL TOOLS AND TECHNIQUES

Each company and even controllers within the same company use control devices uniquely adapted to their own requirements. The printed forms for master schedules, load analyses, factory orders, stores requisitions, stores credit memos, scrap tickets,

444

material move orders, inspection tickets, and other commonly used control records vary widely in design, size, and detail.

Visual charting is also customized. Charts vary from bar graph notes tacked to walls in a message center to massive, permanently fixed boards with chrome-plated slots for colored plastic time bars. Although the form and symbols differ, the uniform intent is to transmit information and follow the progress of actions triggered by the information. We shall consider several common management tools and techniques designed to accomplish the control mission.

Gantt Charts

Perhaps it would be more accurate to call the formats in this section "Gantt-type" charts because many modifications have been made since the original version.

When Henry L. Gantt worked at the Frankford Arsenal in 1917, he recognized the need for a formal device to cope with scheduling problems. The device he developed was a graph of output activities plotted as bars on a time scale. The same type charts are used for essentially the same purpose to this day.

The principal virtue of a Gantt chart is its simplicity. No attempt is made to recognize risk or alternative actions. Activities are committed to dates according to the preferred schedule. Deviations from the anticipated calendar are recorded to show current conditions. Through this routine, operators are given their assignments, the pattern of delays is revealed, and the changing distribution of production loads is forcefully exposed.

Three versions of Gantt charts are illustrated in Figures 13.3, 13.4, and 13.5. The charts are applied to three methods of scheduling: perpetual, periodic, and order. The different conventions and symbols illustrated could be interchanged among the types of schedules, and entirely different descriptive renditions could supplant or complement those shown. Some restraint in elaboration is advisable to retain the virtue of simplicity; cluttering a chart with too much information may destroy its data-recording and transmitting capacity.

A *perpetual loading schedule* is developed by reviewing the status of all jobs in an open order file. The amount of time required for all the jobs from each department, machine, or facility can be posted in a form similar to Figure 13.3. Postings are typically made once a week. Horizontal bars show the time "reserved" in each facility to accomplish work already on order. Relative loads of the facilities and the overall work load of the plant are clearly displayed; facilities with smaller loads may be utilized to relieve overloaded departments. The weekly updating also provides a graphic record of the changing work loads. The character of loading patterns is useful in allotting method-improvement

445

Facility	Now / Week 5	Week 6	Week 7	Week 8	Week 9	
A						
B						
C						
D						

Figure 13.3 Gantt load chart for perpetual scheduling

At the beginning of a period, the foreman of a facility is given a work list of the expected output. The list may ● contain assignments above 100% capacity on a standby basis; if all goes well, there may be time to do the extra orders.

studies, selecting capital investments, and forecasting personnel and maintenance needs.

In *periodic scheduling* the work to be accomplished within a set period, typically a week, is loaded to appropriate facilities as shown in Figure 13.4. The jobs required to complete individual orders are allotted to the facilities with no directive other than they must be completed within the period. The length of the bars in the chart represents the amount of time scheduled in each facility during the period. The line below the bar indicates the cumulative work load already scheduled ahead. Again, the backlog of work accumulated at each facility conveys to the scheduler at a glance the changing pattern of work loads and calls attention to overloads. In Figure 13.4, facility *B* has an accumulated work load of about 4 weeks which could portend trouble in meeting future commitments.

A Gantt chart is also useful for specific *order scheduling*. The simplest form uses bars whose lengths represent the time to complete work on the order. Bars are positioned in the appropriate facility row, tagged with numbers identifying the order, and located along the time scale in accordance with the completion schedule. Regard is given to facility availability and to the sequence of operations that characterizes each order; the completion schedule corresponds to the lead time considerations of an assembly chart as displayed in Figure 13.1.

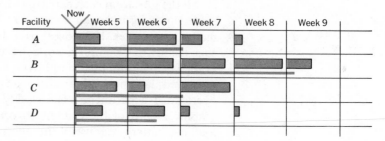

Facility	Now / Week 5	Week 6	Week 7	Week 8	Week 9	
A						
B						
C						
D						

Figure 13.4 Gantt load chart showing accumulated loads for periodic scheduling

Additional value is gained from the Gantt order chart by recording what actually occurs as work progresses. After starting with a schedule laid out by bars on a time scale, marks and symbols are imposed on the chart at each updating to show the current status of the work and the cause of deviations from planned performance. Some useful symbols for updating are given in Table 13.1.

The data-recording and transmitting capacity of Gantt charts is evident in Figure 13.5. The present date is the end of week 7, Now. Immediate work assignments for each facility are quite apparent. Facility *A* is on schedule for order 110. Facilities *B* and

Interrelationships of orders are more easily shown by the CPS time chart discussed in the next section.

• *D* are behind schedule owing to tool trouble for order 104 in facility *D* and lack of material in facility *B*. If the work on order 104 in facility *D* must be completed before work on the same order can be initiated in facility *B*, special expediting measures are indicated. Order 106 in facility *C* is the only operation ahead of schedule. The updating strongly suggests the jobs should be rescheduled; perhaps overtime, multishift operations, or additional equipment are advisable.

The given Gantt chart examples only hint at the uses that have been made of the bar chart format. The record could be of individual workers instead of facilities, and the time scale could be hours or days in place of weeks. Other notations could be used to depict information succinctly. Color coding of the bars is

Table 13.1 Typical symbols employed in updating Gantt charts

Symbol	Meaning
Y	V Marks present date on time scale
[0-101]	Bracketed line shows time allowed for completion of the designated order; in the symbol shown the order number is 101
[0-101]	Double or colored line below bracket denotes the portion of work completed by present date V
⊃⊂	X between brackets reserves time to make up for delays and to increase the schedule flexibility
R	Shows repair time for machine breakdowns or maintenance
M	Shows delay caused by missing or improper materials
T	Shows delay caused by tool trouble
P	Shows delay caused by power failure or poor operator performance (inexperience, slowness, lack of instructions, etc.)
O	Shows delay caused by operator's error

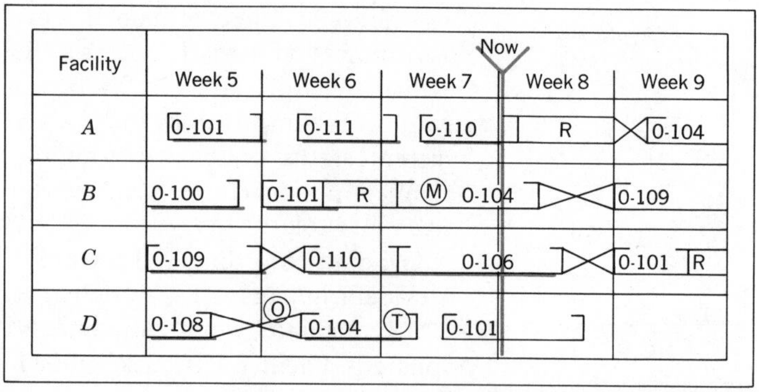

Figure 13.5 Gantt chart for order scheduling and progress reporting

often used to show distinguishing characteristics. Large and elaborate boards based on Gantt charting principles are commercially available. They use a pegboard design, revolving disks, colored strings, plastic slide inserts, and similar devices to provide a visual picture of current and planned production.

Some commercial mechanical scheduling aids are called "Productrol Boards," "Schedugraph," and "Boardmaster."

It is difficult to extend the use of bar charts to analysis. Their fine communicative attributes work against the evaluation of opposing alternatives. Adding to the bars the costs and dependency relationships required for an evaluation seriously clutters the charts. The bar format suffices for simple problems such as planning assignments for small machine centers. For more complex problems, we have CPS techniques available.

CPS Time Charts

A time chart is the end product of a CPS apalication. Previous steps were presented in Sections 6-3 and 6-4.

Critical path scheduling is most commonly applied to special projects. The graphic version used for control purposes is called a *time chart*—an arrow network drawn to a time scale. All the information available from an arrow network is incorporated in a time chart, but slightly different conventions make the time chart easier to understand and more useful for control purposes.

Converting an arrow network to a time chart amounts to making the network conform to a rectangular coordinate system. The horizontal axis indicates time; the vertical axis represents activity chains which may be associated with a division of the project or facility assignments as shown in the previously discussed bar charts. The conversion process is largely a mechanical effort, since the basic data are already tabulated in the network and the boundary time table.

Each symbol used in an arrow network has its counterpart in a time chart, as shown in Table 13.2. Solid vertical lines indicate restrictions in both directions; all activities connected to the left

448

Table 13.2 Comparison of arrow network and time chart symbols

Arrow Network	Symbol	Time Chart	Description
A / 10	Activity	A / 0 ... 10 / Caret time indicators	No arrow heads are needed in the time chart because time is known to flow from left to right.
A / 10	Critical activity	A / 0 ... 10 / ES_A EF_A	Double lines mark the critical path. Activity durations are the difference between earliest start and finish times.
B / A ② / C	Event	Event 2 — B / A C / $\widehat{ES}_{B \text{ and } C}$	Event 2 is the vertical line at the end of activity A. Separate time carets are not needed at an activity merge or burst.
A ③ C / B ② D	Dummy	A C / B D	Dummies are shown by dotted arrows drawn vertically or sloping to the right. Activities should have a word description above the line.

Event numbers can be included as part of the time carets to facilitate schedule updating by computers.

of a vertical line are prerequisite to all activities starting to the right of that line. Events are distinct points in time marked by carets—time indicators that display key moments in the left to right flow of time. Horizontal lines between carets represent activities. There is no need to mark activity durations because they are implied by the time carets; the caret at the start of an activity is the earliest start and the one at the end is the earliest finish, making the activity duration = $EF - ES$. Activity descriptions are still entered above the activity line. Other information such as the cost or resources required to complete an activity can be inserted below the activity line.

The pictorial representation of total float is one of the most revealing features of a time chart. Total float is shown as a horizontal dotted line following the last activity in a chain. All the activities in the chain share the indicated float. As shown in Figure 13.6, activities B, C, and D form a chain. The total float for each of these activities, as indicated by $TF = LS - ES$ from the arrow network, is 3 time units. Therefore, if A or B is delayed by 3 time units, no float is left for leeway in scheduling C; C thus becomes a critical activity.

449

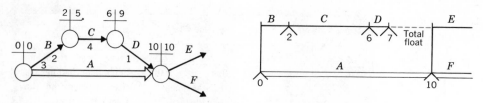

Figure 13.6 Arrow network segment and corresponding time chart segment

All the float is shown after the last activity in a chain only for convenience in the initial chart construction; it shows what leeway exists but in no way infers that it should be so assigned in the final schedule. Float lines point out areas of schedule flexibility, while the critical path sets limits to schedule juggling. Additional restrictions result from resource constraints associated with particular activities. A working schedule evolves when float time is employed to improve resource utilization.

An illustration of a resource grid is shown in Example 13.1. ● The versatility of time charts is further enhanced by adding a resource grid with the same time scale as the chart. The purpose of the grid is to record individual resource assignments. In the planning stage of a project the grid can be used to experiment with different resource assignments. In the control stage it can serve as a record for comparing actual to planned resource expenditures. For smaller projects a grid is seldom necessary, because the information can be shown by entries directly on the chart without cluttering it too badly.

When a project has fallen behind the anticipated pace, three alternatives are open to the project manager:

1. Do nothing. The duration of the project will likely be longer than planned, but the lost time might be recovered by shorter than expected completion times for remaining activities.

Applying measures that shorten one activity can place a previously noncritical activity on the critical path. ● 2. Apply additional resources. Certain activities can benefit from crash procedures, but such expense should be limited to activities with little or no float.

3. Change methods. A substitute resource, such as an automatic machine replacing a hand-operated model or subcontracting the entire job, can sometimes alter the method of accomplishing an activity to reduce its duration.

The time chart aids in the selection of the above alternatives by displaying the total effect of possible alterations.

The appropriateness of time charts versus Gantt bar charts can be judged by comparing the two formats with respect to the uses made of the charts.

450

Use	Comparison
Survey	A chronicle of information about present conditions is easier to compile with bars. If the activities have important interrelationships, a more complete representation can be made via time chart conventions.
Design	The development of a new or revised solution is usually accomplished better with a time chart because more data are displayed, especially when a resource grid is used in conjunction with the time diagram. The full effect of outcomes is easier to observe when float and dependencies are known.
Presentation	A Gantt chart is admirably suited for the presentation of summary solution and action instructions. Its simplicity eliminates most misinterpretations. When resources of several agencies interact to accomplish a project, the more complete descriptions in a time chart better reveal schedule flexibility and responsibilities for cooperative operations.

EXAMPLE 13.1 Construction and Use of a CPS Time Chart

In Examples 6.1 and 6.2, a network was developed for the construction of a prototype product. The initial arrow network was refined for better control by subdividing key activities. For the final version, repeated in Figure 13.7, a time chart is to be constructed for control purposes.

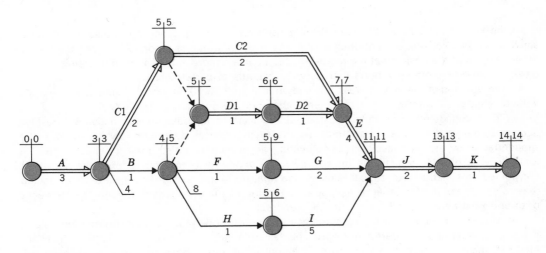

Figure 13.7

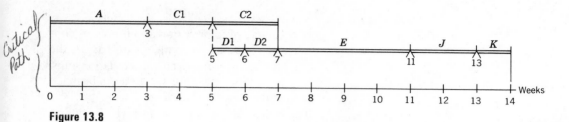

Figure 13.8

The first step in time chart construction is to set a scale large enough to present the symbols and activity descriptions clearly. In Figure 13.8, letters are used to represent activity descriptions to allow the chart to conform to the book-page size; actual applications utilize charts 60 feet or longer. It simplifies the drawing to lay out the critical activities first.

With the critical path in place, remaining activities are entered according to network restraints. Activities are shown starting at their earliest possible times in the preliminary chart. Float is inserted to complete noncritical activity chains. Float can later be distributed to schedule non-critical activities at their most economical and convenient times. See Figure 13.9.

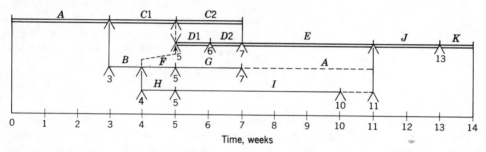

Figure 13.9

As the project progresses, the time chart is used for updating. Since the project is relatively small, an auxiliary resource accounting grid can be used for progress reporting. For larger projects, several copies of the basic chart are reproduced to facilitate more entries at each updating. Entries on these periodic progress reports then serve as records of performance.

A chart updated at the end of week 9 is shown in Figure 13.10. The critical activity E is 1 week behind schedule. As noted in the comments, the engineering analysis (activity B) took 1 week longer than scheduled. This delay postponed the start of all postrequisite activities. Besides activity B, the work on the subcontracted parts (activity I), as determined by liaison with the subcontractor by the purchasing and engineering departments, is also a week behind schedule. Since a week of float is available for activity I, the condition is not too serious; the activity is considered on schedule but critical because the float no longer exists. The main decision facing the project manager is whether to accept an extension of the total project duration to 15 weeks or to apply extra resources to make up the week delay.

Reference to the chart and the resource accounting grid below it provides information helpful in deciding what to do. Department responsibilities are noted below the activity lines in the chart. The grid shows the cumulative variance of actual manhours (above the diagonal in each cell of the grid) and costs (below the diagonal in units of $100) from the amounts budgeted. It is

452

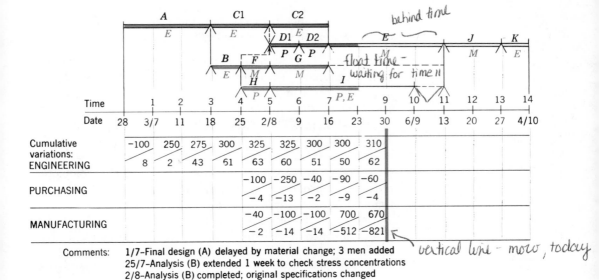

Figure 13.10

apparent that engineering expenditures considerably exceed the amount expected. The negative variance in manufacturing might be deceiving because the budgeted amounts are for an on-schedule project. Part of the low expenditures in manufacturing is owed to the late start for activity *E*. A detailed budget should be consulted to determine actual resource utilization. The grid thus serves as a warning device to signal the need for remedial action or close surveillance for current and future activities.

Line of Balance

Line of balance, like CPS, was forcefully imposed for government contracts. Many companies were initially skeptical but later recognized the value of the technique and adopted it for their own use. Again like CPS, some individuals felt it cost more to implement than it was worth for managerial control. Any management tool must be applied properly and appropriately or it becomes an expensive frill.

The line of balance method for production control combines features from a Gantt bar chart and a CPS time chart with graphs of material requirements. The method was developed by the Navy during World War II. It is most appropriate for assembly operations involving a number of distinct components. In essence, it employs the principle of management by exception through a comparison of progress on individual components to the time schedule for completed assemblies. Regular progress checks reveal the future effect of any current delays and indicate the degree of urgency for corrective action.

The application of the line of balance technique consists of four main stages, all utilizing graphic aids:

1. A graphic representation of the delivery objective.
2. A chart of the production program showing the sequence and duration of all activities required to produce a product.
3. A progress chart of the current status of component completion.

453

4. A line of balance drawn to show the relationship of component progress to the output needed to meet the delivery schedule.

Diagrams for the first three stages are displayed on one composite chart. The fourth stage relates data from all the diagrams. The complexity of the technique falls between Gantt and CPS charting. Most of the effort is demanded to develop the initial stages. Thereafter, succeeding updatings require less skill and time.

Objective chart. This chart shows the expected completion schedule of products and the actual completion rate. It is designated an *objective chart* because it shows the output objective and how well the objective is being met. As displayed in Figure 13.11, the schedule delivery curve begins at the origin and slopes upward as a function of time. The curved shape is associated with

● a new product design where learning takes place during production. In anticipation of more proficient performance during the later phases of the program, the rate of promised deliveries is greater than in the initial phase.

Learning effects are discussed in the next section.

The other curve in the objective chart is derived from the actual number of completed products delivered by a date. At each updating the number of products delivered since the last progress check is entered as an extension of the "actual deliveries" line. A dip in this line below the "scheduled deliveries" line is an obvious cause for alarm. Because an established trend towards an inadequate production pace is more difficult to reverse than an incipient trend, the main intent of the line of balance technique is to identify areas that might cause future difficulties.

Program plan. A chart of the operations required to complete one unit of the finished product is called the *program plan*. It closely resembles a time chart where all activities are scheduled at their

● latest start times. Each major row of activities is associated with one component of the final assembly. The nodes (circles) along the rows mark events that must be completed by the date in-

A convention that locates activities by latest start and finish times eliminates float. Scheduling flexibility is possible only by starting earlier than shown.

Figure 13.11 Objective chart

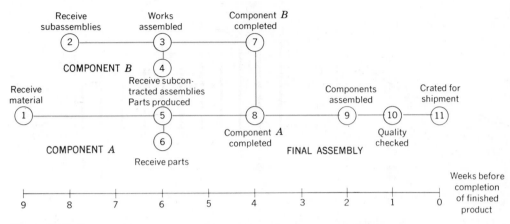

Figure 13.12 Program plan

Other symbols are sometimes
used in place of circled events •
to distinguish the source of
activities.

dicated on the time scale. Thus the chart is event oriented. In
Figure 13.12 the point in time where final assembly can begin is
marked by the completion of component *A* and component *B*.

The completed chart serves as a reference to the amount of
lead time by which each event must precede final completion. The
time scale is reversed from the normal left to right sequence to
show this lead time requirement. The raw material for component
A must be received 9 weeks before the product completion date.
The other events must also be accomplished by their respective
lead times to maintain anticipated output.

Progress chart. The *current* status of each operation designated
by an event in the program plan is shown on the *progress chart.*

Color coding of bars is often
used to define areas of •
responsibility.

Vertical bars show the physical inventory of the parts, components, and assemblies associated with the events. At each
updating, the heights of the bars are increased by the number of
units passing each event since the last progress check. The vertical
scale of the progress chart is set adjacent and equal to the vertical
axis of the objective chart as shown in Figure 13.13.

Line of balance. A line from the objective chart coursing along the
bars of the progress chart to show the *expected* number of completed items forms the *line of balance.* The line starts from the
scheduled delivery curve of the objective chart at a point associated with the time of the progress updating, *Now.* The number of
units on the vertical scale corresponds to the number of units that
should have passed the last event, represented by the last bar on
the right in the progress chart. A similar reading of what the

455

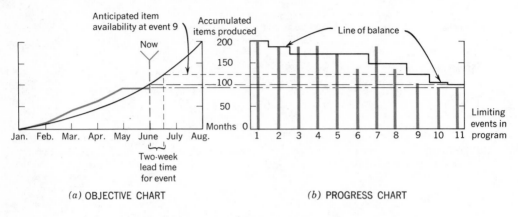

(a) OBJECTIVE CHART   (b) PROGRESS CHART

Figure 13.13 Line of balance: (a) objective chart and (b) progress chart

physical inventory should be for each event to keep the program on schedule is obtained by adding the lead time for the event under consideration to the date *Now*. The lead time thus added sets a point on the horizontal scale from which a line drawn vertically to the curve will establish the accumulated number of items expected through the event.

As illustrated in Figure 13.13, adding the 2-week lead time for event 9 (obtained from the program plan) to the *Now* date establishes a point on the curve corresponding to 130 items. This means that 130 completed assemblies (event 9) should now be available to maintain the scheduled deliveries—the number of products expected to be completed by the middle of June.

> For evaluation purposes, bars can be grouped by categories such as subcontracted components, purchased parts, and internally produced assemblies.

Starting at the right end of the progress chart, the failure to meet expected deliveries is clearly revealed by bar 11; 90 units have been delivered instead of the contracted 100 units. Passing to the left, it is also clear there is no immediate prospect for catching up because events 9 and 10 are even further below expectation. The main deficiency appears to be the subcontracted work of event 6. Until this shortage is overcome the output of component *A* will remain behind schedule.

A closer analysis of the line of balance shows the events for component *B* (3, 4, and 7) are out of balance on the positive side. This condition could result from an overapplication of resources to component *B*; a too rapid completion record can cause production problems by siphoning off resources which could be used more advantageously elsewhere and by accumulating stockpiles of components which must be handled and stored until they are needed for subsequent assemblies. From a more optimistic viewpoint, accelerated completion of some events may allow

456

resources to be diverted to lagging events. While the decision for a preferred way to remedy production difficulties awaits a thorough cause-and-effect investigation, the line of balance directs attention to likely solution alternatives.

EXAMPLE 13.2 Production Control by a Line of Balance

An order has been placed for 300 prefabricated cabins. The delivery schedule is set at 30 cabins per week. The prime contractor is a lumber dealer with subsidiary prefabricating facilities. The electrical and plumbing components will be subcontracted. Hinges, plates, metal window casings, and other hardware components will be purchased. The major portion of the work is in cutting, assembling, and packaging wood components. For this work the company has well-trained personnel and excellent facilities. The program plan is shown in Figure 13.14 where event symbols are circles for company-made assemblies, triangles for purchased parts, and squares for sub-contracted components.

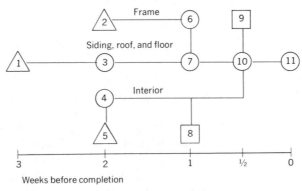

Figure 13.14

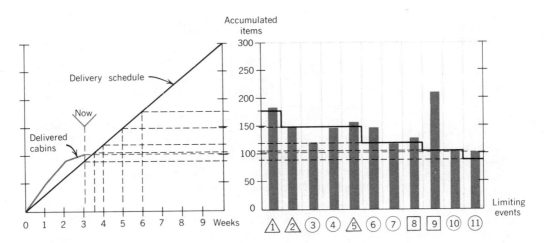

Figure 13.15

The first updating is made 2 weeks after delivery of the first 30 cabin assemblies. The result of the study is shown in Figure 13.15. From the line of balance, it appears that the present favorable delivery status will be jeopardized by difficulties being experienced in the "siding, roof, and floor" assembly, event 3. This event is almost a week behind the production schedule; the shortage will soon show in the final output count, event 11, unless remedial action is instigated. An examination of the other company-made components, circled events, does not suggest excessive resource utilization. No blame can be put on the suppliers of purchased parts because all the triangled events have bars well in balance. Therefore, the chart suggests the application of additional resources for activities preceding event 3. An investigation of these activities will indicate the most advantageous use of resources—overtime, better equipment, more supervision, more working space, improved material handling, etc.

It also appears advisable for the company to look into the delivery contract with the subcontractor responsible for event 9. By accepting early delivery, the company assumes responsibility for holding costs and possible damage before use. Prompt deliveries are nice, but too much of a good thing can be just as disruptive as a shortage.

An appraisal of the previous examples suggests the reasons why the line of balance has not been more widely utilized for control. Initially there is the usual skepticism that accompanies the introduction of any new tool, particularly one that appears to require considerable graphing time. Familiarity and computer assistance reduce these objections. A more serious demurral materializes when production is not for specified orders but rather for the general market; a market demand forecast has to be substituted for a known demand as the objective curve. A similar forecasting difficulty exists when lead time for purchased or subcontracted parts is questionable.

In progress reporting, it is normally not too difficult to obtain a physical count of inventory. But estimating a percentage completion for major items still undergoing production may be very difficult. Forecasts and estimations are limelighted because they are probabilistic inputs to an essentially deterministic control procedure. The opposing assumptions are somewhat reconciled by treating uncertainties as though they were certainties, but meaningful control then depends on the reliability of the prognostications.

A practical variant to mollify conditions of uncertainty employs a critical range in conjunction with the line of balance. The range is established from minimum and maximum allowable variations for events in the program plan. These extremes provide two entry points for each event in the objective chart. For instance, if an event has a lead time of 8 weeks with a minimum of 7 weeks and a maximum of 10 weeks, the expected accumulated item count would be read from the curve at points corresponding to entry time *Now* and 7 and 10 weeks. When these limits are transposed

An acceptable range is particularly appropriate for a computerized line of balance. The computer can be programmed to sort out items requiring special attention without committing the updating to the artwork of a progress chart.

to the line of balance, they establish a range of acceptable performance. In tune with the management by exception principle, attention is called only to items outside the acceptable range.

The similarity between line of balance and CPS methods suggests a marriage of the two techniques. The planning merits of CPS integrated with the control features of a line of balance provide a routine for project management from preliminary planning stages through final delivery. In the initial stages, critical activities of parallel critical paths are candidates for line of balance control. During the production stage, both operations and components can be followed in progress reporting. The purpose of graphically portraying the typically computerized CPS data is to provide a summary picture of the project's progress.

★ ★ ★ *Optional material.*

In research and development work, the objective chart may show budgeted funds versus actual expenditures.

Learning Curves

As stated earlier, performance today is not necessarily a guarantee of what it will be tomorrow. Individuals can learn new working skills. Groups can learn cooperative skills. The increased productivity resulting from learning can radically influence the completion time of an order. The production schedule for special projects where learning is a governing factor should take into account the change of output with experience.

An 80% learning rate has been found to be descriptive of certain operations in various industries such as aircraft instruments and frame assemblies, electronic data-processing equipment, ship construction, and automatic machine production. The meaning of an 80% learning rate is that the accumulated average time to double the number of units produced is 80% of the time required to produce the previous increment.

Assume it took 100 hours to produce the first unit and the rate of learning is 80%. The accumulated average rate to double the present output, from 1 to 2 units, is 100 hours $\times$ 0.80 = 80 hours. Since this is the *average* time per unit, the total time to produce 2 units is 80 hours $\times$ 2 = 160 hours. To again double production, from 2 to 4 units, the average per unit time decreases to 80% of the previous average, 80 hours $\times$ 0.80 = 64 hours. This makes the total time to produce 4 units is equal to 64 hours $\times$ 4 = 256 hours. Continuing this progression, we have the values tabulated in Table 13.3 where hours are generalized by converting 100 hours to 100%—the time to produce the first unit expressed as a percentage.

Figure 13.16 shows the total production hours with and

No learning takes place at a 100% learning rate; 100% is already known. The other limit approaches 50% when the second unit takes almost no time to produce. Picking up bad habits that must be "unlearned" could produce a theoretical learning rate greater than the 100% limit.

Table 13.3 Production time percentages based on an 80% rate of learning

Number of Units Produced (1)	Accumulated Average Time Percentage per Unit (2)	Total Percentage of Initial Production Time (1) × (2) = (3)
1	100.00	100.00
2	80.00	160.00
4	64.00	256.00
8	51.20	409.60
16	40.96	653.36
32	32.77	1048.64
64	26.21	1677.44
128	20.79	2684.16
256	16.78	4295.68

without learning when the first unit took 100 hours to produce. The bottom curve corresponds to the upper curve multiplied by the factor in column 2 of Table 13.3. The middle curve is based on a 90% learning rate.

It is easily recognized that column 2 in Table 13.3 is simply the learning rate raised to a power corresponding to the number of times production is doubled. This relationship is convenient for illustrative purposes but is unwieldy for practical applications. A mathematical expression of the relationship between production times and quantities is more useful.

The nonlinear relationship of column 1 to column 2 suggests an exponential function. Further, the inverse relationship of the two columns indicates a negative exponent. Letting:

$$Y = \text{accumulated average time per unit}$$
$$N = \text{number of units produced}$$
$$a = \text{time required to produce the first unit}$$
$$b = \text{exponent associated with the learning rate}$$

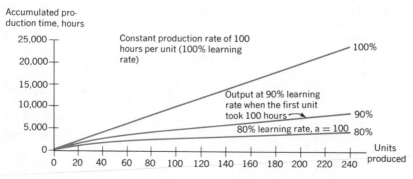

Figure 13.16 Production times at 80%, 90%, and 100% learning rates

460

The learning curve equation is
an application of exponential
line fitting discussed in
Section 3-6. • the equation takes the form

$$Y = aN^{-b} \qquad \text{or} \qquad Y = a/N^b$$

When production times are known for two levels of production bearing a binary relationship, $Y_1 = aN_1^{-b}$ and $Y_2 = aN_2^{-b}$, we can determine the exponent b that defines the proportionality. Using the data from Table 13.3 for $N = 2$ and $N = 4$ in the ratio

$$\frac{Y_1}{Y_2} = \frac{a/N_1^b}{a/N_2^b} = \frac{N_2^b}{N_1^b} = \left(\frac{2N_1}{N_1}\right)^b \qquad \text{where } N_2 = 2N_1$$

we get

$$\frac{80}{64} = \left(\frac{4}{2}\right)^b = 1.25 = 2^b$$

which yields

A table of logarithms is
provided in Appendix E. •

$$b = \frac{\log 1.25}{\log 2} = \frac{0.0969}{0.3010} = 0.322$$

By knowing that the first unit took 100% (or 100 hours as in the illustration), the expression for the accumulated average time

A learning curve plots as a
straight line on log-log paper.
Two widely separated points
suffice to set the line required to obtain readings for
other points. • becomes

$$Y = 100N^{-0.322}$$

Checking another point from Table 13.3 for corroboration, say $N = 64$, we have

$$Y = \frac{a}{N^b} = \frac{100}{64^{0.322}}$$

or

$$\log Y = \log 100 - (\log 64)(0.322)$$
$$= 2.000 - 1.8062(0.322)$$
$$= 2.000 - 0.5816 = 1.4184$$
$$Y = \text{antilog of } 1.4184 = 26.21$$

which, as advertised, agrees with the tabulated value.

EXAMPLE 13.3   Calculation of Individual Unit Times When Production Is Subject to Learning

A government contract for the construction of five prototype missile assemblies is based on an 87% learning rate. The first unit produced took 190,000 manhours. To compare actual performance with the contracted production rate, the time to complete each additional unit is calculated. The total production time is determined from the expression

$$Y_i = aN^c \qquad \text{where } c = 1 - b \text{ and}$$
$$i = \text{cumulative unit of output}$$

461

Assuming 87% is indeed the applicable learning rate, the total production time for the first two units must be $2 \times 87\% = 174\%$ of the time required for the first unit. Then, using 100% as equivalent to the 190,000 manhours taken for the first unit, the ingredients for the total production time equation are $Y_2 = 174\%$, $a = 100\%$, and $N_2 = 2$ which produce

$$174 = 100(2)^c$$

and

$$2^c = \frac{174}{100} = 1.74$$

or

$$c(\log 2) = \log 1.74$$

to yield

$$c = \frac{\log 1.74}{\log 2} = \frac{0.2406}{0.3010} = 0.799$$

The time to produce each individual unit is then calculated from

$$Y_i = a[N_i^{0.799} - (N_i - 1)^{0.799}]$$

By using this equation, the expected time to produce the third unit is

$$Y_3 = 190,000[3^{0.799} - (3 - 1)^{0.799}]$$

Then, $(3 - 1)^{0.799} = (2)^{0.799} = 1.74$ (from previous calculations) and

$$3^{0.799} = \text{antilog } 0.799(\log 3)$$

$$= \text{antilog } 0.799(0.4771) = \text{antilog } 0.3812$$

$$= 2.41$$

so

$$Y_3 = 190,000(2.41 - 1.74) = 127,300 \text{ manhours}$$

The individual unit times and total production time based on an 87% learning rate for all five units are shown below.

Units	Individual	Total
1	190,000	190,000
2	140,600	330,600
3	127,300	457,900
4	117,800	575,700
5	112,100	687,800

Learning curves for intermittent production are often well defined from previous experience with similar operations. Continuous production is seldom influenced by group learning, but individuals entering the system can be expected to pass through a learning period.

The major influence learning has on the completion time of special projects is quite apparent, but the mechanics of applying a learning factor can easily lead to deceptive results. By definition, special projects comprise unique products, often entailing untried designs and unfamiliar production techniques. For such projects it cannot be known with certainty the exact rate of learning or even to which portions of the project the learning factor should be applied. The most conspicuous learning area is in manual performance which determines direct labor cost. But correlative costs of direct materials and supervision overhead can be expected to decline with improved manual performance owing to less waste, fewer rejects, and reduced supervisory demands. During the initial phase of a project, it is generally wise to calculate learning curves from several bases to identify better where learning *actually* affects operations instead of where it is *supposed* to be influential.

An investigation of the rate of learning for individual operators may attract attention to instructional costs and hiring policies. Figure 13.17 shows a smoothed learning curve. The area of triangle 1-2-3 represents lost production during the learning period. It accounts for extra labor costs to maintain a desired level of production, higher material cost due to inefficient usage, training expense, and fixed costs of overhead. In applying a learning curve, it should be recognized that all operators do not start at the same point on the curve; the curve may follow a step pattern where improvements are made from one plateau to the next.

Operations controlled more by machine speeds and capacity than by operator skills are less subject to the learning process.

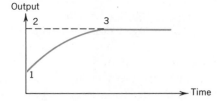

Figure 13.17 Learning curve for an individual worker

A learning curve, like other control tools, can engender a false sense of security when operations follow an anticipated pattern for awhile but then veer away because the true cause for performance deviations has not been identified. Similarly, other factors such as method changes or model redesigns can obscure an anticipated trend actually in effect. The difficult search for elusive cause-and-affect data is unending. The decision to adopt a probable relationship for production control rests with the manager—the terminal screen for operating information and the final weighing station for operational alternatives.

★ ★ ★ *End optional material.*

13-5 SUMMARY Quantity control concentrates on delivering the desired output within the expected delivery date. Production plans are converted into action notices that spell out exactly which men and machines will operate, what the operations will be, and when they must be done. Then the actions are compared to planned performance to provide feedback for replanning or initiating corrective action.

The choice of control designs and the control techniques depends on the type of production to be controlled.

The three basic types of production are continuous, intermittent, and special projects; they are nominally associated with product, process, and position layouts, respectively.

Flow control is applied to continuous production where products, equipment, and work assignments are standardized. The emphasis on continuous flow for high volume output requires high raw material inventory levels but a relatively low in-process inventory level. Supervisory control is simplified by essentially unchanging work assignments which entail relatively low skill levels.

Order control is associated with intermittent production. The work schedules must be closely controlled because shop orders are sequenced through different production patterns. The two principal methods of scheduling are: (1) *backward* to meet a deadline and (2) *forward* to produce as soon as possible. Load control is applied when there is a distinct limiting factor in the production flow, and particular attention is given to funneling orders through the bottleneck.

Special project control is characterized by personal contact. Managers and supervisors issue orders directly to workers, monitor progress, and initiate corrective action. Such procedures are expensive but warranted by difficult coordination problems and rigid time limitations.

A master production schedule consolidates information from preproduction planning activities. It shows how and when products will be ready for distribution. The dispatching function implements the operations from the master schedule. This function can be centralized by issuing orders directly to operators or decentralized by sending general work orders to department foremen who then make specific assignments.

Expediting is often combined with the dispatching function. Expediting is concerned with the flow of material and components, while dispatching pertains more to the flow of information. An expeditor follows the development of an order from the raw material stage to finished products. He has the responsibilities of avoiding production delays and of implementing corrective action when delays do occur. He also feeds back to production planning the information and recommendations that lead to control improvements.

Control tools and techniques vary widely. Printed forms are adapted to specific organization requirements, and charting aids are customized to accomplish specific control missions.

464

Gantt charts display production activities as bars on a horizontal time scale. Their principal virtue is simplicity which makes them commendable communication aids. They are used to show assignments derived from one of the three scheduling methods: perpetual, periodic, and order. Through the use of special marks, symbols, and colors, a Gantt chart format can also be used to record deviations from the time schedule and the causes of these irregularities.

CPS time charts are generally more appropriate than bar charts for analysis and design. A time chart is essentially an arrow network drawn to a time scale. Activity relationships and the amount of float time available are shown in a rectangular coordinate system. The versatility of the charts is enhanced by adding a resource grid that conforms to the chart's time scale. The grid, resource notations on the chart, and updating entries along the activity lines provide assistance in deciding what to do if the project falls behind schedule—do nothing, apply additional resources, or change methods.

Line of balance employs the principle of management by exception for production control by a comparison of progress on individual components to the time schedule for their completed assemblies. An objective chart shows the scheduled delivery of finished products and is updated to show actual deliveries. A program plan, an event-oriented chart similar to a time chart, shows the lead time by which each event must precede the final completion. The current status of each event is shown by a bar on the progress chart. The vertical scale of the progress chart is set adjacent and equal to the vertical axis of the objective chart. A line of balance relates the two charts to show the expected and actual number of completed items associated with each event. When uncertainties in demand or lead times are encountered, a practical variant is to establish an acceptable range within which the line of balance may fall and still be considered under control.

Learning curves help anticipate output levels when operating times decrease with experience. An 80% learning rate, typical of several industries, means the accumulated average time to double the number of units produced is 80% of the time required to produce the previous increment. The nonlinear relationship of accumulated average time, Y, to the number of units produced, N, is given by the expression

$$Y = aN^{-b}$$

where a = time required to produce the first unit, and b = exponent associated with the learning rate.

465

Group learning curves should be calculated for a number of production activities to identify how learning actually affects a project. Individual learning curves highlight costs incurred before an operator reaches an acceptable level of performance.

The decision as to which control designs, actions, and tools to utilize rests with the manager who screens information inputs and evaluates operating alternatives.

13-6 REFERENCES

Andress, F. J., "The Learning Curve as a Production Tool," *Harvard Bus. Rev.*, Jan.–Feb. 1954, 87–93.

Bock, R. H. and W. K. Holstein, *Production Planning and Control: Text and Readings*, Charles E. Merrill, Columbus, Ohio, 1963.

Department of the Navy, *Line of Balance Technology*, Office of Naval Material, Government Printing Office, Washington, D.C. 1962.

Eilon, S., *Elements of Production Planning and Control*, Macmillan, New York, 1962.

Greene, J. H., *Production Control*, Richard D. Irwin, Homewood, Ill., 1965.

Hoffman, T. R., *Production: Management and Manufacturing Systems*, Wadsworth, Belmont, Calif., 1967.

Jordan, R. B., "Learning How to Use the Learning Curve," *NAA. Bull.*, Sec. 2, Jan. 1958, 27–39.

MacNiece, E. H., *Production Forecasting, Planning, and Control*, John Wiley, New York, 1961.

Moder, J. J. and C. R. Phillips, *Project Management with CPM and PERT*, Reinhold, New York, 1964.

Muth, J. F. and G. L. Thompson, *Industrial Scheduling*, Prentice-Hall, Englewood Cliffs, N.J., 1963.

Rago, L. J., *Production Analysis and Control*, International Textbook, Scranton, Pa., 1963.

Riggs, J. L. and C. O. Heath, *Guide to Cost Reduction Through Critical Path Scheduling*, Prentice-Hall, Englewood Cliffs, N.J., 1966.

Stilian, G. N., *et al.*, *PERT: A New Management Planning and Control Technique*, American Management Association, New York, 1962.

13-7 QUESTIONS AND PROBLEMS

1. Select a production plant or product characterized by each of the three divisions of production discussed in Section 13-2. Compare the selections according to the characteristics listed for each division.

2. Could dispatching be considered the interface between production planning and production control? Why?

3. Compare the duties of a policeman to those of an expeditor.

4. Two methods of expediting are:

(1) Exception method—devote attention only to orders or situations known to be in trouble.

(2) Fathering method—watch over and attend to all problems for a group of orders.

Comment on both methods and suggest production situations for which each would be well suited.

5. What is the danger in trying to compensate for too little production capacity by increasing the number and authority of expeditors?

6. What relationship does the type of production (continuous, intermittent, and special) have to the type of scheduling used (perpetual, periodic, and order)?

7. Compare the advantages and disadvantages of Gantt charts and CPS time charts.

8. Why bother to update control charts? Would lists be an adequate substitute for charts?

9. The outstanding virtue of Gantt charts was said to be simplicity. What is the value of simplicity? For what uses is simplicity most important?

10. Why do dummies in a time chart never slope to the left?

11. Assume the construction plans for a small vacation home have been committed to a time chart. The owner-builder plans to use the cabin in August. At the end of May he finds he is 5 working days behind schedule with only 20 possible working days left before August. Give and discuss an example of how he could apply each of the three scheduling alternatives now open to him.

12. A time chart is based on activity descriptions while a program plan is based on event descriptions. Why? How could a time chart be converted to a program plan?

13. How does the line of balance method utilize the principle of management by exception?

14. Describe a computer printout based on an acceptable range of item inventory levels that could avoid the requirement for committing the information to a progress chart.

15. What can be learned from comparing the vertical bars in the progress chart to the line of balance at each updating? What can be learned from a succession of the same comparisons made over several updating periods?

16. How would you explain the meaning of a 90% rate of learning to a potential supplier? Make reference to the upper and lower limits for the learning rate.

17. What support activities would be affected by the discovery that production on a contract was actually following a 90% learning curve rather than the expected 80% learning rate?

18. Explain the relationship between the c and b exponents of learning rate expressions.

19. Comment on the importance of individual learning rates in deciding whether to carry larger inventories that level out the

production schedule or to carry a smaller safety stock and alter production output by laying off or hiring workers according to market demands.

20. Use a Gantt chart format to show the major activities you plan to accomplish during a day. Update the chart at noon and at 6:00 p.m. Note the causes of deviations from the schedule. Comment on the process and possible use of the record.

21. A box factory has received an order for 40,000 fancy fruit boxes to be delivered in 90 working days. The four pieces for the sides and ends are cut and grooved in saw line 1 where the capacity is 1300 units (4 pieces each) a day. The thinner slats for the identical tops and bottoms are cut in saw line 2 where the maximum daily output is enough slats to fabricate 6000 tops *or* bottoms. The slats are stapled to form the top and bottom assemblies at the rate of 3500 assemblies (top or bottom for a box) per day. The top assemblies are to be spray painted. The paint shop can spray and dry a maximum of 5000 lids each day. The last operation is to stack the side and end pieces between the top and bottom assemblies, collect parts for 50 boxes in a bundle, and band the bundle together; 300 bundles can be stacked and banded in 1 day. One week (5 working days) must be allowed for shipment from the factory to the buyer.

The policy is not to commence work on a new operation until the material has completely passed through the prerequisite operation. One day is allowed for leeway in sequencing. Because of the high work load, backward scheduling is utilized. No overtime should be included.

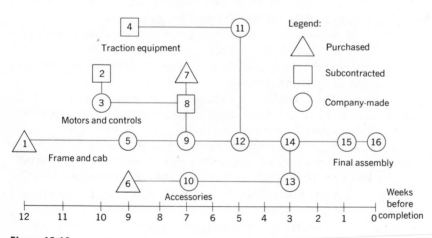

Figure 13.18

Develop a schedule for processing the order. Display the developed schedule in a Gantt chart.

22. Convert the arrow network shown in Figure 6.8 to a time chart. Show the float at the end of appropriate activity chains.

23. The project plan for reconstructing a portion of the manufacturing facilities is described below. Develop a time chart for the program where total float is shown by the conventions described in Section 13-4 and illustrated in Example 13.1.

Duration (week)	Symbol	Activities Description	Restrictions
8	A	Prepare drawings and specifications	A < B,C
4	B	Secure bids and award contract	B < D,H,I
2	C	Remove existing equipment	C < E
1	D	Reschedule production work loads	D < E
1	E	Form and pour foundations	E < F,G
2	F	Electrical modifications and renovations	F < J
1	G	Paint	G < J
1	H	Purchase and delivery of auxillary equipment	H < K
6	I	Construct new production machine	I < J
1	J	Install new production machine	J < K
2	K	Test and debug new machine and equipment	K < L
1	L	Reschedule and start production in reconstructed facility	

24. Assume you are the chairman of a committee to plan and conduct a regional convention. The date of the convention is now 20 weeks away. Most of the activities that must be accomplished are listed below.

(1) Outline plans and check with the committee.
(2) Select and secure speakers.
(3) Reserve meeting place.

CONTROL

(4) Arrange catering for banquet.
(5) Design and print programs.
(6) Distribute programs.
(7) Select and purchase awards.
(8) Reaffirm arrangements and make last-minute adjustments.
(10) Conduct banquet.
(11) Write acknowledgments.
(12) File report and statements.

Complete the list and allocate times you deem appropriate for each activity. Prepare a time chart that can be used to explain your plans to the rest of the committee.

25. Three hundred swamp buggies have been ordered by the Forest Service for timber cruising and forest development of inaccessible lands. The supplier has selected the line of balance method for production control. The program naturally divides into five divisions: securing traction subassemblies from a subcontractor, fabricating frames and cabs, obtaining motors and developing controls, building accessories, and assembling all components. The program plan is shown in Figure 13.18.
The delivery schedule calls for six buggies to be finished each week during the contract period of 50 weeks. The tenth week progress report reveals the following physical count of items associated with each event:

1–141	5–112	9–103	13–75
2–135	6–100	10–96	14–76
3–124	7–146	11–89	15–71
4–106	8–121	12–88	16–60

(a) Construct a line of balance for the current status of the program.
(b) Comment on items out of balance. Which event appears most critical? Compare the progress of purchased, sub-contracted, and company-made components.

26. A cost-plus contract has been awarded for 90 technologically new components. From similar experiences with new designs, the company has found an 85% learning rate descriptive of the process, exclusive of material costs. The first unit cost $2400 of which $600 were for material. If the contract specifies a profit of 18% on the total cost of each unit, what is the expected cost of the entire contract (total price paid for 90 units)?

27. Workers being trained to wire a complex control panel have generally followed a learning pattern where the accumulated average time is given by $Y = aN^{-0.15}$.

470

    (a) What learning rate corresponds to the given $b = 0.15$?

    (b) If a new man completed wiring on his first panel in 6 hours, how much time can he be expected to take for his second, third, and fourth panels?

    (c) How many panels will he likely complete in his first 40-hour week?

    28. Given a learning rate of 70% and that it took 20 hours to produce the first 25 units, how long should it take to produce 100 units?

    29. From the production records of a recent contract, it is found that the accumulated direct labor hours expended in producing the first 20 units were 250; 30 units later the total hours were up to 450 (time to produce 50 units). What is the learning rate?

CHAPTER 14

QUALITY CONTROL

14-1 IMPORTANCE

Within a production system, quality can take many meanings and impart different considerations. All of them are important to the managers of the system.

To a retail customer, quality is a characteristic of the product he may buy. He can accurately measure quality in only a few cases because he lacks the ability, equipment, or inclination. Instead, he relies on brand names, reputation, previous experience, and general appearance. After a product is purchased, its performance is measured against competitors and its own advertised image.

A wholesale buyer or industrial customer is better prepared to measure quality. He knows that the purchased inputs to his system ultimately affect the quality of his output and, thereby, his reputation. His large volume supports a staff and technology sufficient to verify the quality and quantity of purchases. Yet he generally cannot afford nor does he prefer to measure the quality of every item he buys. The problem is to select the important criteria of quality and then to develop a sampling plan which adequately assures conformance to the criteria with reasonable inspection costs.

Product specifications are delineated by tolerances—*permissible variations in size—and by* allowances—*differences in size between parts that fit together. For instance, a shaft with a tolerance of 1 inch* $\pm$ *0.002 inch could be designed to fit into a hole with a minimum diameter of 1.003 inches, an allowance of* $0.003 - 0.002 = 0.001$ *inch.*

Product designers stand astride the quality demands of customers and the quality capabilities of producers. Their first • responsibility is to design a product wanted by consumers. Assistance is provided by market research and other staff efforts. Then the product design specifications must be set within the production capabilities of the producer and the requisites of the buyer.

The quality theme underscoring production activities is continuous control. Its manifestations take many forms and provoke diverse attitudes. To the company statiticians, it is a challenge to develop statistical formulas compatible with the production process and quality directives. Inspectors make measurements and observations to effectuate the statistical design. Supervisors are at the interface between quality goals set by top management and the execution of programs to attain the goals, a critical position in all quality control efforts. Finally, the workers who are the basic source of quality are subjected to exhortations from quality conscious supervisors, to motivational propaganda of quality programs, and to performance ratings from inspection procedures.

All the pieces of the quality picture have to be fitted into a functional entity or it can degenerate into sporadic campaigns of hectic activity founded on a pile of inspection reports. As represented in Figure 14.1, the quality subsystem is intimately linked with the governing production system. A quality product is the result of careful design specifications, conformance to specifications, and feedback about product performance. The crucial position of the customer is evident from the design that seeks to satisfy his wants and the performance feedback that checks whether he is indeed satisfied.

In this chapter we shall emphasize the procedures and tools available to improve conformance to quality specifications. This phase of quality control has received dramatic documentary endorsements and has a well-developed body of technology associated with it. But it cannot operate in isolation. The best statistical tools and the most clever quality programs can be truly effective only if they are backed by all levels of management and are honed by feedback from the production system.

14-2 ECONOMICS OF QUALITY CONTROL

Precision describes the refinement of the product and *accuracy* pertains to conformance to design specifications.

Production quality starts with a process capable of producing to the design specifications and continues with an inspection program that ascertains if standards are being met. The initial decision concerning specifications is based on the *precision* sought by customers and the *accuracy* attainable by production facilities. Given a process capable of obtaining the required

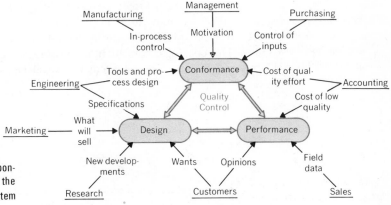

Figure 14.1 Functional responsibility for quality within the total production system

precision with desired accuracy, unacceptable variations may, and usually do, still occur. Blunt tools, misalignments caused by wear and tear on machinery, and worker carelessness contribute to inferior output from a process inherently capable of acceptable quality. The preferable means to achieve a quality output is revealed by an economic evaluation of the cost of quality assurance compared to the increase in product value financed by the cost.

Cost of Vigilance Versus Cost of Error

The interlocking nature of design decisions and continuous control is implied by the cost–value relationship shown in Figure 14.2. An initial evaluation relates the returns gained from greater product refinement to the cost of providing the refinements. The value of providing additional product refinements is determined in the marketplace, perhaps with some help from advertising. Production cost includes both capital investment to attain the necessary accuracy and the quality assurance program to sustain it.

Tactical implementation of the strategic cost–value relationships is complicated by the shades of accuracy possible for each level of refinement. Would it be more economical to accept a lower price for items that have to be held within stated tolerances 90% of the time or to ask a higher price and promise 95% meet the same specifications? Should a higher priced machine be purchased to consistently produce items within narrow tolerances or will a lower priced machine coupled with intensive sorting produce equivalent output quality? Answers to such questions are determined mainly by reference to the cost pattern shown in Figure 14.3.

In most production situations the costs of vigilance and error vary inversely. Greater vigilance may take the form of extra time taken by individual craftsmen, closer supervision, additional tests for products, and inspection of all or a portion of output. The cost of errors includes rework, rejects, and customer dissatisfaction. The tip-up at the lower end of the error cost curve

Try to think about how you write your signature as you sign your name and it will probably look like a forgery. ●

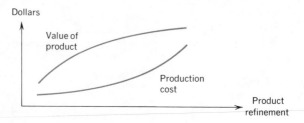

Figure 14.2 Product value and cost as a function of refinement

Dollars

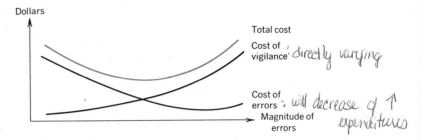

Total cost

Cost of vigilance *directly varying*

Cost of errors *will decrease of ↑ expenditures*

Magnitude of errors

Figure 14.3 Relationship of vigilance to errors

represents a condition where too much attention to errors tends to provoke mistakes; a common illustration is in typing (typical of many man-machine operations) where concentration on perfection leads to more errors than usual. Somewhere between the extremes of no vigilance and ultra-vigilance is a point where control over the magnitude of errors produces a minimum total cost.

When the cost of vigilance is primarily constituted by inspection, we may encounter a seemingly contradictory inspection cost-value relationship. Higher inspection costs, if the money is wisely spent, detect a greater proportion of defects and thereby provide a greater degree of protection from the effects of defective output. As the number of undetected defects decreases, a point is reached where further improvement is unnecessary because higher quality does not proportionately increase the value of a product. For instance, if 98% viability of grass seeds is considered acceptable, decreasing the undetected nonviable seeds below 2% would be uneconomical unless the higher quality is rewarded with a higher price. Thus it is not uncommon to find the minimum total cost obtained by an inspection plan that purposely passes some defectives.

In some processes the purpose of inspection is to examine all the output to discover any defective workmanship; for special projects such as construction work, a single item may be inspected several times during its development. In other processes, inevitably where the tests destroy the product, inspection is accomplished by examining samples from the total output. The statistical design of the sampling plan attempts to minimize the inspection cost while maintaining a desired level of confidence that the process is within established control limits.

Inspection as described in this section serves to rectify the process—bad items are sorted from the output. The rectification can upgrade output from a process otherwise not capable of meeting specifications.

Acceptance sampling examines a portion of the items being purchased to determine if the overall quality meets the standards expected from the supplier.

History of Quality Control

Formal control of quality was unnecessary when production was the province of individual craftsmen; then the personal

475

reputation of the producer was at stake with each unit of output. With mass production, division of labor, and interchangeable parts, individual pride of performance had to be buttressed by more formal controls.

Shewhart's pioneering efforts produced the book *Economic Control of Quality of Manufactured Product.*

The course of quality control was set by the work of Walter A. Shewhart of Bell Telephone Laboratories in 1924. He first applied a statistical control chart to manufactured products and later suggested statistical refinements for process control. Two other men from the Bell system, H. F. Dodge and H. C. Romig, applied statistical theory to sampling inspection to produce their widely used *Sampling Inspection Tables.*

The American Society for Quality Control, founded in 1946, publishes the monthly journal *Industrial Quality Control.*

The advent of World War II awakened an otherwise lethargic interest in statistical techniques for quality control. The armed forces adopted scientifically designed sampling inspection plans which eventually culminated in the publication of Military Standard 105 for acceptance sampling of attributes. This action put pressure on suppliers to adopt equivalent inspection procedures for their output to keep it from being rejected by the military services. The training and research that accompanied the original and subsequent governmental applications spawned an enthusiastic following and aroused interest in related statistical control techniques. Today many organizations internationally promote quality control, and numerous books and journals report new developments.

14-3 ORGANIZATION FOR QUALITY

Management for quality assurance varies from an informal arrangement where operators perform quality checks and supervisors have the final say on acceptability to an extensive organization that designs and conducts inspection checks for incoming, in-process, and outgoing material. An autonomous quality department may even have the authority to shutdown production until the source of defective output has been corrected. In most firms the authority and responsibilities of the quality group lie somewhere between the extremes. The quality staff inspects where requested and *recommends* additional controls or corrective action. When the heads of production, purchasing, or other departments disagree with quality recommendations, the disputes are pushed upstairs to a higher management level.

The interests of the company may best be served by viewing the quality organization as representatives of the customers and as consultants hired to suggest means for quality improvement. The customers represented may be consumers, distributors, or other operating division in the same company. The consulting effort may be research into new techniques, development of revised inspection plans and devices, or investigations of the source of defects. By treating the quality staff as a psuedo-independent organization, personality conflicts and pressure tactics by affected parties can be considerably reduced.

Since quality assurance enters into so many linkages within the production system (between receiving and inventory, between operations in production, between production and shipping, etc.), more support is needed from all levels of management than for most other functions. No single department or staff can assure quality by itself; it takes cooperation of on-line workers, their supervisors, and related staff organizations. Training, informational seminars, publicity, and special programs cross organizational lines. The crossovers are easier and more rewarding when they have active backing on both sides and from above.

Quality assurance is a skill. Like other skills, it takes a while to develop; and if it is not continually exercised, it will deteriorate.

Maintenance of a quality organization is justified by the return provided from expenditures for its support. Where the quality control staff has slowly increased with the growth of the company, it may be top heavy with "empire" supervisors and relegated to outmoded functions. An excess in the other direction has the quality group faddishly pursuing short-range objectives by overexploiting gimmicky quality promotions. The overall value of the quality organization should be judged by the ratio of costs incurred to costs saved, not by the glamour of its own advertisements.

It has been said that "quality is everybody's concern," but a job that belongs to everybody can easily become a job that nobody does.

EXAMPLE 14.1 Quality Improvement Through a "Zero Defect" Program

From its introduction in aerospace-defense industries in 1962, the "Zero Defect" (ZD) approach to quality improvement has spread dramatically. The reported successes have been impressive. The program aim is aptly described by its name; ZD means *no* defects. It emphasizes prevention instead of cure to get a job done correctly the first time, every time.

In essence, ZD is a motivational program sparked by a feedback routine. It recognizes that the people best prepared to eliminate errors are those who create them. It receives its impetus from enthusiastic support of all tiers of management and depends on the pride of workers to identify error-prone situations.

Two main causes for mistakes are lack of knowledge and lack of attention. The easier of the two to correct is knowledge. Errors caused by improper or insufficient training can be pointed out by more experienced workers. Revisions of training programs with subsequent follow-ups to check their adequacy would satisfy quality demands for knowledge.

Lack of attention is more serious and more difficult to combat. Sometimes the environment can be altered to compensate for a lack of attention, e.g., better communications, easier material identification, simpler movements, more complete specifications and procedures, etc. Of at least equal importance to the physical conditions is the mental indoctrination to convince workers they *can* produce zero defects. The "people are human and humans make errors" attitude must be replaced by a belief that mistakes are not normal, they do not have to happen.

477

"Error Cause Removal" is a key feature of a ZD campaign. Each worker is encouraged to identify and point attention to all causes for errors in his job. He fills out "Error Cause Identification" forms to describe his error situation and submits them to his supervisor. If he knows a solution, it too is requested. As in any suggestion plan, rapid response is vital. Potential causes for errors should be investigated and suggested solutions should be evaluated promptly. Individuals cannot be expected to apply themselves unless they are convinced the organization is serious and recognizes their efforts.

Several features typically included in the planning, initiation, and follow-through of a ZD program are noted below.

1. *Planning.* An administrator is selected and a ZD committee is organized. Representatives from all departments are included in the horizontal make-up of the committee. After planning the steps necessary to launch the program, the committee acts as a laison team.
2. *Management.* Upper and middle management are sold on the program and, even better, are personally committed to participating in and sustaining it. With active support from above, the orientation and indoctrination of supervisors are completed before the program kickoff. Communication between workers and supervisors makes or breaks the program. Support also is sought from union officials.
3. *Promotion.* Interest in the program is stirred by publicity. A "teaser" approach uses posters, bulletin board notices, and announcements in company papers or over the address system to build up enthusiasm for the climactic kickoff. The inaugural should be impressive. Mass meetings followed by individual department meetings are common. Top managers speak at the mass meeting and supervisors explain details at group get-togethers. Banners, posters, pennants, and wandering visitations remind employees throughout the kickoff day that the program is not a one-shot promotion.
4. *Continuance.* Each employee is encouraged to sign a pledge card signifying his intent to reduce mistakes. His contribution is further emphasized by the "Error Cause Removal" campaign. Individual achievements are recognized by pins, plaques, dinners, and announcements. Departments also receive recognition for meeting goals they set earlier. "Days without errors" scorecards are posted. Particularly good ideas are exchanged between departments with credit given to the originators.

Whether the ZD approach to quality improvement and maintenance is a guide or a gimmick, momentary or momentous, will be decided by experience. Its heavy reliance on motivation may make it difficult to sustain, but this same emphasis on personal pride makes the program applicable throughout the production system. Practitioners report that ZD programs contribute to safety, suggestion systems, worker-management relations, and quality control. However, a good quality assurance program must be already operating before the motivational impetus can be incorporated.

14-4 INSPECTION

In addition to maintaining quality, inspections provide information by which the performance of sorters, machines, departments, and plans can be evaluated.

The single act most closely associated with quality control is inspection. A casual acquaintance with quality inspection may provoke the image of a man in a white coat peering through a magnifying glass at passing products. Such situations do exist, but inspections predominately take other forms. For special projects the inspectors may be engineers measuring the grade of a roadbed in foul weather or technicians could test concrete samples in the comfort of a lab. Food inspectors examine the sanitation of bakeries, dairies, and restaurants. Workers producing parts use calipers and gages to determine their acceptability. Finished products such as lumber are graded for quality by inspectors. In some cases inspections can be completely mechanized. Though the means and purposes of inspections vary widely, they share the common goal of distinguishing a level of accomplishment.

When and Where to Inspect

Where to inspect depends largely on *when* the inspection is scheduled. The location of most inspection stations is at the site of production—the receiving dock for incoming shipments, the assembly area, the construction site, distribution points, etc. In a fixed position layout, inspectors must come to the product to check quality at various stages of development. In product layouts, particularly mechanized production lines, products come to the inspectors at special stations built into the line. Roving *floor inspectors* examine output from the individual work stations associated with a process layout.

Customers occasionally send inspectors to the supplier's plant to inspect quality before delivery.

Some inspections requiring special equipment and skills can only be performed in testing laboratories. On other occasions it may be more economical to transport products to a central laboratory than to take the specialists into the field or to the factory floor. It is not uncommon for products to be subjected to on-site inspection during early stages of their development and then be sent to a laboratory for special tests such as chemical composition, compressive or tensile strength, structural qualities, or length of life.

Laboratories may allow the use of less skilled inspectors through the use of standardized procedures, more automated equipment, and closer supervision. These same conditions contribute to more consistent and, thereby, more reliable tests. Where there is a choice between laboratory and onsite inspections, the listed advantages of lab examinations may be offset by the added costs of handling and congestion. On-site inspections can often be conveniently accomplished by floor operators checked occasionally by senior floor inspectors. The same roving inspectors can check machine set-ups and material inputs to avoid potential errors. Mistakes caught in a lab have to be traced back to their origin for correction.

Inspection stamps are often given to inspected items. Distinctive shapes or numbers may show the source of accepted items, the inspector, and the disposition of defectives.

Deciding when to inspect during a production process is simply a matter of common sense—when it will do the most good. Logical choices are the beginning and end of the production process. Raw material and component inputs should be inspected

479

to see whether they meet expected standards. Acceptance of substandard inputs obviously jeopardizes outgoing quality and may damage equipment or disturb process continuity. Outgoing
• products are examined to protect the producer from customer discontent or buyer rejection.

During the production process, inspections are scheduled in front of operations that are costly, irreversible, or masking. Considerable expense is avoided by eliminating defective units before they undergo a costly phase of their development or before they pass through a process that cannot be undone such as welding, pouring concrete, or mixing chemicals. Operations such as painting and encapsulating may hide defects easily detectable before the masking operation.

From the foregoing it may appear that products are continually under inspection. This view is valid in the way an artist inspects a picture he is painting; he is aware of the picture's quality as it develops, but only at the end or at critical points does he really study the quality. Similarly, workers continually check the
• quality of their own or a machine's output, but there are just a few distinct inspection stations. Constant formal surveillance would not only increase cost, it would also create an uncomfortable, "big brother is watching you" atmosphere. The timing and location of inspection points are key features in the design of any testing program.

How to Inspect

The two basic types of inspection are called "variables" and "attribute." When precise measurements are made of dimensions, weight, or other critical characteristics capable of expression on a continuous scale, the products are being subjected to *variables*
• *inspection.* The alternative to exact measurements is to set limits within which the product is judged acceptable or defective. A binary yes-no rating results from an *attribute inspection.* Since a good or bad grading normally requires less time and skill to make and uses lower cost equipment than exact measurements, attribute inspection is usually less expensive than variables inspection.

Precise measurements require closely calibrated devices—rulers, micrometers, scales, meters, etc.—capable of measuring the product's fineness standard. Devices to check attributes are
• designed to provide a quick verdict of acceptability—go-no go gages, snap gages, templates, balances, etc. Although it is preferable to have all verdicts made objectively, some attribute ratings rely on subjective judgments. A decision whether a batch of brew tastes "bad enough" or a crack is "serious enough" to cause

Reports or drawings may be inspected several times by different reviewers to detect hidden mistakes.

Even if *all* finished items are inspected, some output will still likely be defective because of inspection errors. Equivalently, good products may be rejected.

It is generally assumed that the variables measured have a normal distribution.

New devices are continually being developed to improve inspecting. Hidden flaws are revealed by magnetic, X-ray, and ultrasonic tests. Radio waves detect metal impurity. Television cameras allow vision where humans cannot venture. Computers hooked to mechanical scanning devices can inspect a rapidly moving process where humans would not have time to react.

480

rejection is certainly subject to adjudication. Training, experience, supervision, and well-defined guidelines help guard against inconsistent judgments.

Statistical sampling techniques frequently reduce inspection costs. The use of samples to replace 100% inspection is usually appropriate for machine output where units are not so likely to vary as are hand-crafted products. High production quantities and expensive inspections also suggest sampling. Then there is destructive testing (the performance test destroys the unit tested) which absolutely rules out 100% inspection. The characteristics and designs of sampling plans are the subjects of the following section.

15-4 ACCEPTANCE SAMPLING

The purpose of acceptance sampling is to recommend a specific action; it is not an attempt to estimate quality or to control quality directly. The basic action recommendation is to accept or reject the items represented by the sample. The rejection alternative can be temporized by resorting to 100% inspection to confirm the suspicion of inferior quality or by seeking a price concession to accept apparently inferior goods from a supplier.

When acceptance sampling is applied to incoming shipments, the usual practice is to accept shipments accredited by the sampling plan and return rejected shipments to the supplier for rectification or charge the cost of 100% screening to the vendor. A high rate of rejected samples may lead the buyer to seek a new supplier. The high rate is also a clear warning to the supplier; either lower quality claims or produce up to them.

When a buyer uses acceptance sampling at the supplier's plant, a rejection cancels shipment on the lot sampled.

Acceptance sampling can be utilized at inspection stations within the production process. When the inspection procedure is particularly fatiguing or monotonous, sampling may produce as good or better results than 100% inspection. More careful examinations of fewer units may actually decrease the percentage of defective items that escape detection. A lot rejected by the sampling plan is typically returned to the responsible department for 100% inspection and rework of the items found defective.

The psychological effect of 100% inspection may lead workers to rely on the inspection process to catch all their mistakes. A quantity in place of quality attitude can be costly in scrap and rework.

Of the several types of acceptance sampling plans in use, we shall pay particular attention to lot-by-lot acceptance sampling by attributes using a single sample from each lot. The sample is examined by attribute-type measuring devices. When more defective items are found in the sample than allowed by the statistical plan, the entire lot is considered of inferior quality. This version of acceptance sampling is currently the most widely used; it is easy to understand and apply.

Other versions of acceptance sampling include double, sequential, and multiple sampling plans.

481

,92 ·/ ୫୨.୨୫ .୦୧ 9୦

୨୦
.୦୧
1.୦୦ · ୨ 2

9୦.୨
9.୨ ·୦୧

·୨

★ ★ ★ *Optional material.*

Operating Characteristic Curves

As always, samples are assumed to be randomly drawn.

A sampling plan specifies the sample size (*n*) and the associated number of defectives (*c*) that cannot be exceeded without rejecting • the lot from which the sample was taken. The capability of the plan to discriminate between acceptable and unacceptable lots is revealed by its operating characteristic (*OC*) curve.

୫୦.2
/ 9.୨

An assumption that the lot is large in comparison to the sample suggests the probabilities for an *OC* curve will follow a binomial distribution. When • the sample is also large, calculations are simplified by using the Poisson or normal distribution to construct *OC* curves.

An *OC* curve for a single-sample, percentage-defective plan is shown in Figure 14.4. The horizontal axis of the graph indicates the percentage defective in the lot being sampled; the vertical axis shows the probability the lot will be accepted. A condition common to all *OC* curves is that a lot with no defective will always be accepted. As the percentage of defectives increases, the probability that it will be rejected also increases. The curve shown is based on a sample size of 50 ($n = 50$) and an acceptance number of 2 ($c = 2$). For this curve, a lot with 4% defectives has a probability of acceptance of about 0.68. Expressed another way, in a random sample of 50 items, there is about a 68% chance that two or fewer defects will be found when 4% of the lot is defective. When the lot has 8% defectives, the probability of its acceptance decreases to 0.24.

.୦2
/ ୨ ୦

1୦ ୦
19
୨ 9

1 ୦ ୦
.1 9
୫ 1

Two ways to make *OC* curves more discriminating are to increase *n* while maintaining *c* and to decrease *c* while maintaining *n*. These recourses are intuitively logical; larger samples tend to more accurately represent the lot and a decrease in the acceptance number tightens the restrictions. The shift towards the origin for these conditions is displayed in Figure 14.5.

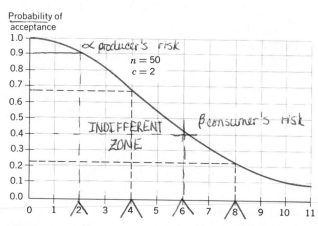

Figure 14.4 *OC* curve for sample size of 50 and acceptance number of 2

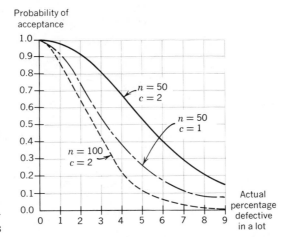

Figure 14.5 Relative discrimination of *OC* curves

The ideal *OC* curve can be obtained only by a 100% inspection of the entire lot made without inspection errors. It takes the form shown by the bold lines in Figure 14.6. If the total number of defectives in the lot is more than the indicated acceptable 4% (shaded area), the lot is rejected without question. The two curves in the figure show how increasing the sample size while maintaining the same acceptance proportion ($\frac{20}{500} = 0.04 = \frac{2}{50}$) tends to make the *OC* curve come closer to the ideal Z-shaped curve. The best sample size to apply for each set of inspecting conditions is a compromise between the value of greater precision resulting from larger samples and the inspecting cost of collecting the larger sample.

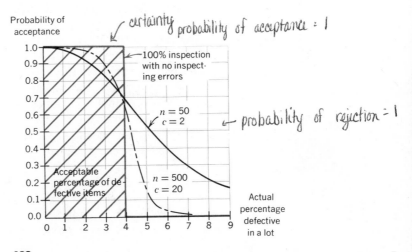

Figure 14.6 The ideal *OC* curve and approaches to it

483

Development of a Single-Sample, Percentage-Defective Plan

Sampling plans are characterized by the protection given against accepting defective lots and the assurance good lots will be accepted. A plan is designed around these two characteristics to safeguard the interests of both the receiver and supplier.

A grade of material considered adequate by the receiver is called the *acceptable quality level, AQL.* This is the level the receiver prefers to get, but he recognizes a sampling plan will accept some lots with a higher percentage of defectives. The level at which he can tolerate no further increase in defectives is called the *lot tolerance percent defectives, LTPD.* The range of quality levels between "good" lots, above *AQL,* and "bad" lots, below *LTPD,* is the "indifference" range. Ideally, lots above the *AQL* will very seldom be rejected and lots below the *LTPD* will have a low probability of acceptance.

Both the buyer and seller accept some risk that the acceptance sampling will pass lots outside the *AQL-LTPD* range. The chance that lots will be rejected while actually having fewer defectives than specified by the *AQL* is called the *producer's risk, α.* The probability of a lot being accepted with a greater percentage of defectives than set by the *LTPD* is termed *consumer's risk, β.* Typical values for the sampling risks are $\alpha = 5\%$ and $\beta = 10\%$. As an example, assume a contract calls for an *AQL* of 2% and a *LTPD* of 12%. Thus the buyer seeks only 2% defectives and will rebel if more than 12% of the items are defective. For a perfect sampling plan designed to conform to these *AQL-LTPD* values with $\alpha = 0.05$ and $\beta = 0.10$, no more than 5% of the lots rejected will have less than 2% defectives and no more than 10% of the lots accepted will have greater than 12% defectives. The *OC* curve for these theoretical relationships is shown in Figure 14.7.

As apparent from the figure, two points on the *OC* curve are established by specifying the *AQL, α,* and *LTPD, β.* The shape of the curve that passes through these points is a function of the sample size, *n,* and acceptance number, *c.* Without tabular assistance, the procedure for designing a plan to conform to given conditions is essentially trial and error. Values for *n* and *c* are arbitrarily selected, and the probabilities for accepting lots with the given *AQL* and *LTPD* are calculated. The calculated values are then compared to the desired $(1.00 - \alpha)$ and β values. Repeated trials eventually reveal a set of *n* and *c* values which produce a curve that comes very close to the $(AQL: 1.00 - \alpha)$ and $(LTPD: \beta)$ points; an exact fit is unlikely because *n* and *c* must be integers.

"Indifference" in a decision-making situation is an area where risk is so delicately balanced by return that the decision maker can claim no distinct preference.

Statistically, the rejection of good material (α) is a Type I error and acceptance of poor material (β) is a Type II. (See Section 15-2.)

484

producer risk = α
Consumer risk = β

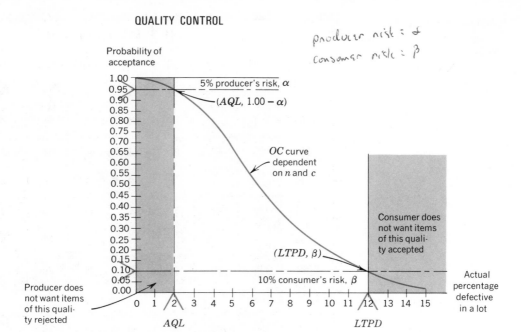

Probability of
acceptance

5% producer's risk, α

$(AQL, 1.00 - \alpha)$

OC curve
dependent
on *n* and *c*

Consumer does
not want items
of this quali-
ty accepted

$(LTPD, \beta)$

Actual
percentage
defective
in a lot

10% consumer's risk, β

Producer does
not want items
of this quali-
ty rejected

AQL

LTPD

Figure 14.7 Relationship of producer's and consumer's risks to the *OC* curve

Extensive tables for designing
sampling plans are available
in H. F. Dodge and H. G.
Romig, *Sampling Inspection.
Tables.*

Fortunately, available tables and charts relieve the tedious
search for *n* and *c* values and speed up calculations. Table 14.1
suggests *n* and *c* values under the uniform conditions of $\alpha = 0.05$
and $\beta = 0.10$. A sample size and acceptance number are indicated
by the row corresponding to the chosen *AQL* and the column
associated with the *LTPD*. For instance, a 2% *AQL* and a 12%
LTPD indicates $n = 40$ and $c = 2$. Therefore, a lot from which a
sample of 40 items is taken will be rejected when over 2 items are
found defective, and approximately 5% of the time the rejected lot
will have fewer than 2% defective. Similarly, there is a probability
of about 0.10 that fewer than 2 items in the sample of 40 are
found defective when the lot actually contains more than 12%
defective items.

EXAMPLE 14.2   Design of a Single-Sample, Percentage-Defective Sampling Plan

An acceptance sampling plan is to be designed to protect the consumer from more than 7%
defectives with a risk of 10%. The producer is expected to provide lots with about 1% defectives;
if he does so, the plan should accept such material at least 95% of the time. The two design points
for the plan are thus designated to be

$$AQL = 0.01 \qquad LTPD = 0.07$$

$$\alpha = 0.05 \qquad \beta = 0.10$$

485

Table 14.1 Suggested n and c values for single sampling plans where $\alpha = 0.05$ and $\beta = 0.10$, given *AQL* and *LTPD*

LTPD % / AQL %	4.51 to 5.60	5.61 to 7.10	7.11 to 9.00	9.01 to 11.2	11.3 to 14.0	14.1 to 18.0	18.1 to 22.4
0.451 to 0.560	80	60	60	50	15	15	10
	1	1	1	1	0	0	0
0.561 to 0.710	100	80	50	50	40	10	10
	2	1	1	1	1	0	0
0.711 to 0.900	100	80	50	40	40	30	7
	2	2	1	1	1	1	0
0.901 to 1.12	120	80	60	40	30	30	25
	3	2	2	1	1	1	1
1.13 to 1.40	150	100	60	50	30	25	25
	4	3	2	2	1	1	1
1.41 to 1.80	200	120	80	50	40	25	20
	6	4	3	2	1	1	1
1.81 to 2.24	300	150	100	60	40	30	20
	10	6	4	3	2	2	1
2.25 to 2.80	n	250	120	70	50	30	25
	c	10	6	4	3	2	2
2.81 to 3.55	n	n	200	100	60	40	25
	c	c	10	6	4	3	2
3.56 to 4.50	n	n	n	150	80	50	30
	c	c	c	10	6	4	3
4.51 to 5.60	n	n	n	n	120	60	40
	c	c	c	c	10	6	4

Each lot contains 1000 items of the same type. The sample will also be large and thus justifies the use of the Poisson distribution to calculate acceptance probabilities:

$$P_{(x)} = \frac{(np)^x}{x!} e^{-np}$$

where:

n = sample size taken from the lot

p = percentage defectives in the lot

x = number of defectives in the sample

A starting point for the calculations is available from Table 14.1. For the given AQL and $LTPD$, the apparent sample size is $n = 80$ and the acceptance number is $c = 2$. The adequacy of the indicated OC curve is determined by summing the probabilities for 0, 1, and 2 defectives occurring in a sample of 80 from lots having 1% and 7% defectives. Calculating the probability of acceptance (P_a) for lots containing 1% defectives, we have:

$$P_{(0)} = \frac{(80 \times 0.01)^0}{0!} e^{-80 \times 0.01} = \frac{(0.8)^0}{1} (0.4493) = 0.4493$$

$$P_{(1)} = \frac{(0.8)^1}{1!} e^{-0.8} = \frac{0.8}{1} (0.4493) = 0.3594$$

$$P_{(2)} = \frac{(0.8)^2}{2!} e^{-0.8} = \frac{0.64}{2} (0.4493) = \underline{0.1438}$$

$$P_a = P_{(0)} + P_{(1)} + P_{(2)} = 0.9525$$

Then the probability of rejecting a lot of 1% quality is $1.000 - 0.9525 = 0.0475$. This value compares favorably with the anticipated producer's risk of $\alpha = 5\%$.

The same calculations with p changed to 0.07 reveal the probability of accepting a lot with more than 7% defectives:

$$P_{(0)} = \frac{(80 \times 0.07)^0}{0!} e^{-80 \times 0.07} = \frac{(5.6)^0}{1} (0.0037) = 0.0037$$

$$P_{(1)} = \frac{(5.6)^1}{1!} e^{-5.6} = \frac{5.6}{1} (0.0037) = 0.0207$$

$$P_{(2)} = \frac{(5.6)^2}{2!} e^{-5.6} = \frac{31.36}{2} (0.0037) = \underline{0.0580}$$

$$P_a = P_{(0)} + P_{(1)} + P_{(2)} = 0.0824$$

For this plan there is only an 8.24% consumer's risk. Since both the producer's and consumer's risks are less than the design goals, a smaller sample size may still provide adequate protection while reducing inspection cost. Using the same acceptance number, 2, with a sample size of 75 changes the acceptance probabilities to 0.041 and 0.106 for lot defective percentages of 1 and 7, respectively.

Average Outgoing Quality

Average outgoing quality (AOQ) is a measure of the quality level resulting from an acceptance sampling plan when the rejected

487

lots are subjected to 100% rectifying inspection and defectives found in the sample are replaced by acceptable items. The quality is thus a function of the n, c, and lot fraction defective percentage, p. When a sample of size n has c or fewer defectives, the lot is passed and only the bad items in the sample are rectified by replacement with good items. When the sample contains more than c defectives, it undergoes 100% inspection where all bad items found are replaced with good ones. The rejected lots then theoretically have no defectives. Under this method of rectifying inspection, the extreme condition of perfect quality occurs only when the lot has 0 defectives or 100% defectives. In the former case, the lot is never rejected; in the latter .case, it is always rejected to force a complete rectification.

Lots between the all-good and all-bad bounds contain a certain percentage of defectives. This percentage (AOQ) is calculated from the equation

Values of P_a for different values of p are read from the ● OC curve or tables.

$$AOQ = \frac{P_a \times p(N - n)}{N} \qquad \text{where } N = \text{lot size}$$

The rationale behind the equation is that there will be no defectives in the lots rejected and in the sample taken from accepted lots. However, in the accepted lots there are $(N - n)$ items which contain the lot percentage defective, p. The product of $p(N - n)$ gives the number of defectives in the accepted lot. Multiplying this product by the probability of accepting a lot with p defectives, P_a, indicates the average number of defective items in sampled lots. This number divided by the lot size, N, is the average proportion of defectives remaining in the inspected lots, AOQ.

When N is large compared to n, a close approximation is ● $AOQ = pP_a$

A plot of AOQ values for all single-sample, rectifying sampling plans follows the pattern shown in Figure 14.8. The maximum point in the AOQ curve is known as the *average outgoing quality*

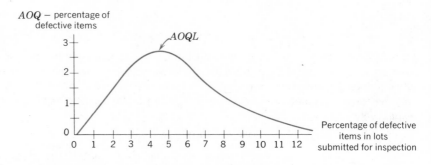

Figure 14.8 AOQ curve for a rectifying inspection process

limit, AOQL. This limiting value is the worst *AOQ* possible from the rectifying inspection process regardless of incoming quality.

EXAMPLE 14.3   Calculation of *AOQ* and *AOQL*

The consumer using the sampling plan described in Example 14.2 wants to know the *AOQ* he can expect when the plan includes rectifying inspection. If the producer is successful in his goal of providing lots with 1% (p) defective items and the preferred sampling plan uses a sample of 80 (n) from a lot of 1000 (N) with an acceptance number of 2 (c), the probability of accepting such lots (P_a) is 0.9525. Then the *AOQ* is calculated as

$$AOQ = \frac{P_a \times p(N - n)}{N} = \frac{0.9525 \times 0.01(1000 - 80)}{1000} = 0.0087$$

which means the actual quality received is expected to contain even fewer than 1% defectives. The improved quality results from replacing good for bad items discovered in the sampling and the complete rectification of lots rejected as producer's risk.

As a further check, the consumer wants to know the worst average quality he could receive from the inspection process. Since n is much smaller than N, the $AOQ = pP_a$ approximation can be used. Note that this approximation would have given $AOQ = 0.01 \times 0.9525 = 0.0095$ in place of 0.0087 in the previous calculations for $p = 0.01$. The values of P_a for each p can be calculated by the routine shown in Example 14.2, or it can be taken from *OC* curves or tables when available.

From the table below it appears the *AOQL* is about 1.68% when the incoming lot percentage defective is between 3 and 3.5:

p	n	np	P_a	$pP_a = AOQ$
0.010	80	0.8	0.95	0.0095
0.020	80	1.6	0.78	0.0156
0.030	80	2.4	0.56	0.0168 —*AOQL*
0.035	80	2.8	0.48	0.0168
0.040	80	3.2	0.34	0.0136

Since the *AOQ* for a single-sample, percentage-defective plan with rectifying inspection always follows the shape shown in Figure 14.8, there is no need to carry the calculations beyond $p = 0.04$. The curve has crested and will continue down as more lots receive 100% inspection owing to their greater rejection rate as p increases—a rare illustration of ever-worsening inputs generating ever-better output.

★ ★ ★   *End optional material.*

Other Acceptance Sampling Plans

The type of acceptance sampling plan to employ depends on the characteristics of the product and the economics of the inspection process. When exact dimensions of a product are critical, the important variables must be measured; just saying an item is defective because one variable violates a specified limit does not provide the needed information. A single sample, as discussed previously may not be the most economical plan design. The

489

In Military Standard 105-A, two sampling levels are provided: one for normal inspection and the other for tightened inspection. The tighter level is often required for new suppliers. When the supplier has proved himself, the normal inspection level is substituted.

Two tolerance limits occur when an item is rejected because its measurements fall on either side of an acceptance zone, e.g., too large or too small. The other approach is to maintain an average quality through α and β risks of extreme measurements.

When several characteristics of an item are measured, each must have its own sampling plan because means and variances of the characteristics differ.

Double sampling has the psychological appeal of providing a "second chance" for a rejected lot. Actually the reprieve is illusory and the appeal is naive because the plan can be just as discriminating as a single-sample inspection plan.

• amount of inspection is often reduced by taking two or more smaller samples and applying statistical decision rules for accepting or rejecting the lot.

Variables sampling. A single-sample, variables acceptance plan has basically the same considerations as described for attributes sampling. The main difference is the inspection process. Actual records of the measurements taken during the examination of an item are utilized. These measurements are expected to follow a normal distribution, not the binomial or Poisson distributions recognized for attributes. This change alters the relationships of

• n, c, α, β, AQL, and $LTPD$. The appropriate OC curve still shows the discriminating power of a specific plan, but it may be based on upper and lower tolerance limits instead of one tolerance grade defined by α and β.

An inspection requiring actual measurement is typically more expensive than a pass–fail evaluation. To some extent this higher cost of variables inspection is counterbalanced by the smaller sample size required to provide the same sampling discrimination as attribute inspection. The fewer items sampled per lot makes variables sampling especially attractive when the items are destroyed by the inspection process.

Another feature of variables sampling is that information about a measured characteristic, mean and variance, is more useful for

• process control than are reports of items being simply good or bad. Such cost and value considerations determine the preference when there is a choice between attribute and variables sampling.

Multiple sampling. A conclusion to employ attribute sampling is accompanied by a decision about plan design. In some cases a double sampling plan is more economical than a single sample taken from each lot. The mechanics of double sampling are pictured in Figure 14.9. The cost advantage of double sampling

• emerges when lots of very good or bad quality are accepted or rejected on the basis of the first sample, n_1. In a double sampling plan of a given discriminating power, n_1 is always smaller than n for a single sampling plan of corresponding power. Lots of mediocre quality require a second sample (n_2) in the double sampling scheme. Since $n_1 + n_2$ is greater than n of a single sample, inspection loads can be expected to increase for lots of intermediate quality.

Sequential sampling. The size of a sample can be pared even further by a sequential sampling plan. As displayed in Figure

490

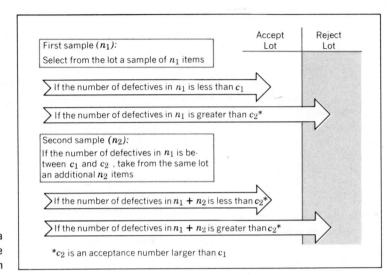

Figure 14.9 Procedure for a percentage-defective, double sampling plan

First sample (n_1):
Select from the lot a sample of n_1 items

If the number of defectives in n_1 is less than c_1

If the number of defectives in n_1 is greater than c_2*

Second sample (n_2):
If the number of defectives in n_1 is between c_1 and c_2, take from the same lot an additional n_2 items

If the number of defectives in $n_1 + n_2$ is less than c_2*

If the number of defectives in $n_1 + n_2$ is greater than c_2*

Accept Lot   Reject Lot

*c_2 is an acceptance number larger than c_1

14.10, sequential sampling is characterized by acceptance, rejection, and resampling zones. The initial sample is relatively small; in the pictured plan the minimum sample size is 10. If the first 10 items inspected all pass, the lot is accepted. Conversely, the lot is rejected if over 2 items are defective in the first 10. When the number of defectives places the sample in the intermediate zone, additional items are inspected until the sample passes into the reject or accept category. The continued inspection can be by group samples or individual items.

Sequential sampling can be based on an item-by-item inspection plan instead of • successive samples containing several items.

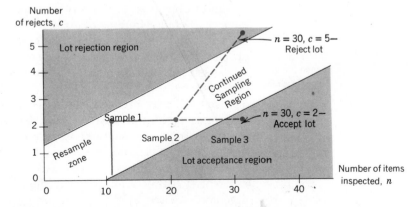

Figure 14.10 Sequential sampling plan illustrated by three samples of 10 items each

491

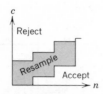

Many sequential sampling plans are truncated to force a lot rejection or acceptance decision after a specified number of items have been inspected.

Details for different sampling plan designs are well described in: A. J. Duncan, *Quality Control and Industrial Statistics.*

The sequence of samples recorded in Figure 14.10 starts with 2 defectives found in the first sample of 10. A second sample of 10 adds no more defectives, but the total sample size of 20 with 2 defectives is still inside the resampling zone. A third successive sample of 10 with no defectives would put the lot in the acceptance zone ($n = 30$, $c = 2$), or a third sample revealing 3 additional defectives would reject the lot ($n = 30$, $c = 5$). Further sampling would have been indicated if 1 or 2 defectives had been found in the third sample.

Both double and sequential sampling plans are described by OC curves with relevant α, β, AQL, and $LTPD$ characteristics. Charts and tables aid in the development of appropriate plans. In general, multiple and sequential plans require less inspection than a single-sample plan for equivalent protection, but continued sampling means inspection loads usually vary considerably between lots.

14-6 THEORY OF CONTROL CHARTS

A control chart is a graphic aid for detection of quality variations in output from a production process. As opposed to the aim of acceptance sampling (to accept or reject products already produced), control charts aid in the production of a better product. The charts have three main applications: (1) to determine the actual capability of a production process, (2) to guide modifications for improving the output quality of the process, and (3) to monitor the output. The monitoring function shows the current status of output quality and provides an early warning of deviations from quality goals.

Variations

Almost every production process is subject to some degree of *natural variability*. Innumerable small causes contribute to overall chance variations in the quality of output. The individual causes are so slight that no major portion of the variation can be traced to a single cause. These deviations are a function of the accuracy of the process, should be expected, and largely determine whether a process can deliver the precision stated for output specifications.

A record of natural variations reveals the capability of a process to meet specifications. It is generally uneconomical to attempt to improve by inspection the output quality of a process lacking inherent capabilities.

Another type of process variation is produced by *assignable causes*. As opposed to natural variations, these causes produce a relatively large variation traceable to a specific reason. Most commonly, these causes are owed to differences among machines, differences between operators, differences in materials, and differences caused by the interaction of men, materials, and/or machines.

The control problem is to distinguish between natural variations and variations due to assignable causes. A statistical knowledge of the behavior of chance variations is the foundation upon which control charting rests. A process is said to be "under control" when deviations in output are the result of chance variations. When the pattern of output deviations does not follow the distribution expected from chance causes, the process is considered "out of control" and the cause is probably assignable.

Control Limits

The frequent use of the normal distribution stems from its appropriateness for many variable sampling situations and to the central limit theorem: the means of small samples tend to be distributed according to the properties of the normal distribution regardless of the distribution from which the samples were taken.

Since the true mean (μ) and standard deviation (σ) are seldom known, control limits are based on the mean of sample means ($\bar{x}$) and the standard error of the estimate (s).

Variations produced by chance follow statistical laws. From experience with past process variations, the distributions of future variations can be anticipated. After the distribution has been identified by the mean and variance, the dispersion of samples from the described process indicates the state of the process. For instance, a sample reading far distant from the mean reading is a clue that the distribution may no longer be descriptive of the process; the process is out of control. The risk associated with a mistaken "out of control" assumption determines the control limits.

We encountered control limits as applied to forecasting in Chapter 3. Figure 14.11 shows commonly used control limits for the normal distribution. When limits are set 3 standard deviations ($\pm 3\sigma$) away from the mean, a sample from a normally distributed population has only about three chances in a thousand of appearing outside the limits when the process is under control. Stated another way, the odds of a wrong conclusion that the process is out of control when a sample reading falls outside the $\pm 3\sigma$ limit are only 26 in 10,000.

In the following discussions and examples, we shall confine our applications to control limits based on ± 3 standard deviations from the mean, the limits most used in this country.

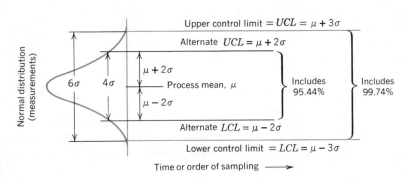

Figure 14.11 Theoretical statistical basis for control charts

14-7 TYPES OF CONTROL CHARTS Control charts have the same principal divisions as acceptance sampling: attributes and variables. Attribute control can be further divided into charts for percentage defectives and charts for the number of defects per unit. The main interest with variables is control over changes in the average and the range of measurements. Control charts for all these considerations follow the same basic format of a mean value bounded by upper and lower control limits. It is the calculation of control limits that distinguishes types of charts.

Control Charts for Variables

The best known control charts for variables record the process average, $\bar{x}$, and the range, R. The $\bar{x}$ charts show how individual measurements or the means of samples compare to the overall mean or the desired average. R charts record the variability of individual readings within a sample. These two charts complement each other because a sample must have both an acceptable average and reasonable range of measurements before the process it represents can be considered under control

As shown in Figure 14.12, output from a process could fail to

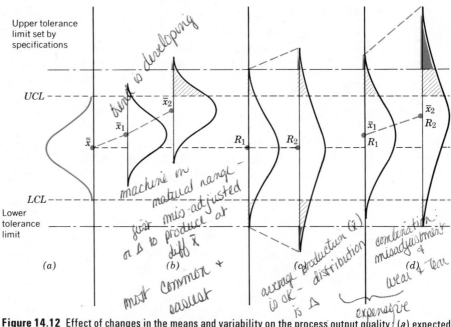

(handwritten annotations: "trend is developing", "machine in natural range first mis-adjusted at α Δ to produce diff x̄", "most common + easiest", "average (production (x̄) distribution is Δ ok", "combination misadjustment & wear expensive", "wear situation!")

Figure 14.12 Effect of changes in the means and variability on the process output quality: (a) expected distribution, (b) drift of sample means away from expected mean while range remains constant, (c) increase in range while sample mean remains constant, and (d) drift of sample mean while range increases

494

The procedure described is for control limits based on observed values. Quite often the limits are set by standard values based on what a process is expected to accomplish. In this case the center line, $\bar{X}$, and the standard deviation, σ, are given. Then the control limits are $\bar{X} \pm 3\sigma/\sqrt{n}$.

m = sample size

N = # of sample of size m
= con sample size

Control Limit Factor for for $\bar{x}$ Charts, A

n	A
2	1.880
3	1.023
4	0.729
5	0.577
6	0.483
7	0.419
8	0.373
9	0.337
10	0.308
12	0.266
14	0.235
16	0.212

× range (dispersion) for up + low control limits

Control Limit Factors for R charts, B and C

n	B	C
2	3.268	0.000
3	2.574	0.000
4	2.282	0.000
5	2.114	0.000
6	2.004	0.000
7	1.924	0.076
8	1.864	0.136
9	1.816	0.184
10	1.777	0.223
12	1.716	0.284
14	1.671	0.329
16	1.636	0.364

meet tolerance limits by a change in the mean of the process or an increase in the variation of output measurements. The condition is compounded when both the mean and variation are experiencing changes from the expected values. Information about both trends is necessary to make reasonably sound decisions about process capabilities and in-process control.

One method of setting control limits for the process mean is to use the average of the sample means for the central value and the range to estimate the variance of the process. With the sample mean calculated as

$$\bar{x} = \frac{x_1 + x_2 + \cdots + x_n}{n}$$

where x's are measurements and n = number of measurements in the sample, the estimate of the process mean is

$$\bar{\bar{x}} = \frac{\bar{x}_1 + \bar{x}_2 + \cdots + \bar{x}_N}{N}$$

where N = number of samples. The range for each sample, R, is the difference between the highest and the lowest measurements in the sample. The mean range is then

$$\bar{R} = \frac{R_1 + R_2 + \cdots + R_N}{N}$$

where R = maximum difference in measurements for each sample.

The standard deviation of the sample means is estimated from the mean range by applying a factor, A. This factor is based on the sample size. The product of $A \times \bar{R}$ sets the 3-standard deviation boundaries around the center line as:

upper control limit $= \bar{\bar{x}} + A\bar{R}$
center line $= \bar{\bar{x}}$
lower control limit $= \bar{\bar{x}} - A\bar{R}$

The associated range control chart is developed in a similar fashion. $\bar{R}$ is the center line. The upper and lower control limits utilize two factors, B and C, respectively. These factors are also a function of sample size and set 3-standard deviation bounds. The range control chart is thus defined by:

upper control limit $= B\bar{R}$
center line $= \bar{R}$
lower control limit $= C\bar{R}$

The question of sample size and frequency of sampling is usually a judgment based on the experience of the inspectors.

The considerations include facilities and inspectors available, inspection costs, sensitivity of the process for abrupt trend changes, and cost incurred from producing rejects. In general, sample sizes of four or five taken more often than larger samples are preferred. It is important to keep the samples the same size because control limits are only applicable for a distinct value of n; when n varies, different control limits are associated with each sample.

If it is necessary to control more than one quality characteristic of a product, individual $\bar{x}$ and R charts must be developed for each variable.

EXAMPLE 14.4 $\bar{x}$ and R Control Charts

A seafood processor uses his facilities to process crab, shrimp, or fish, according to the season of the year. Most operations are manual owing to the nature of the work, need for versatility, and lack of investment capital. Complaints from buyers about discrepancies in the quoted weights of packed shrimp have led the processor to initiate a control program.

The shrimp are packed in 1- and 5-pound containers. A worker scoops the small shrimp into a container and places it on a balance scale. The final weight adjustment is made by hand, adding or removing a few small shrimp from the container. It is necessary to perform the weighing quickly because microbial growth can spoil the shrimp if they are left too long without refrigeration.

The results of weighing 10 samples of five 1-pound containers are shown below. Two samples were taken each day by a random selection of containers packed during the day and stored in the cold room.

N = # of
Sample size = n = 5

Sample	Weight Measurements (pounds)					Sum	$\bar{x}$	R
1	1.04	1.01	0.98	1.02	1.00	5.05	1.010	0.06
2	1.02	0.97	0.96	1.01	1.02	4.98	0.996	0.06
3	1.01	1.07	0.99	1.03	1.00	5.10	1.020	0.08
4	0.98	0.97	1.02	0.98	0.98	4.93	0.986	0.05
5	0.99	1.03	0.98	1.02	1.02	5.03	1.006	0.04
6	1.02	0.95	1.04	1.02	0.95	4.98	0.996	0.09
7	1.00	0.99	1.01	1.02	1.01	5.03	1.006	0.03
8	0.99	1.02	1.00	1.04	1.09	5.14	1.022	0.10
9	1.03	1.04	0.99	1.02	0.94	5.02	1.004	0.10
10	1.02	0.98	1.00	0.99	1.02	5.01	1.002	0.04
						Totals:	10.048	0.65

The average weight of "1-pound" containers is

$$\bar{\bar{x}} = \frac{\sum \bar{x}}{N} = \frac{10.048}{10} = 1.0048 \text{ and } \bar{R} = \frac{\sum R}{N} = \frac{0.65}{10} = 0.065$$

These measures are the bases for the $\bar{x}$ control chart. The upper and lower control limits, which should enclose 99.73% of the measurements from the present process, are calculated as:

$$UCL = \bar{\bar{x}} + A\bar{R}$$

$$= 1.0048 + 0.577(0.065)$$

$$= 1.0048 + 0.0375 = 1.0423$$

$$LCL = \bar{\bar{x}} - A\bar{R}$$

$$= 1.0048 - 0.0375 = 0.9673$$

where A is based on the sample size of 5.
The control limits bounding the mean range, $\bar{R} = 0.065$, are determined as:

$$UCL = B\bar{R} = 2.114(0.065) = 0.137$$

$$LCL = C\bar{R} = 0.0(0.065) = 0.0$$

where B for $n = 5$ is 2.114 and C for $n = 5$ is 0.0

From this information, $\bar{x}$ and R control charts are developed. See Figures 14.13 and 14.14.

The plot of individual sample means and ranges indicates the weighing operation is under control. That is, the variation between the samples ($\bar{x}$) and within the samples (R) can be explained by random influences. Continued sampling may reveal a sample reading outside the control limits. Such a point should be investigated to confirm whether there is an assignable cause for the deviation.

The apparently satisfactory process variation should still be questioned with reference to customer complaints about "short weights." Meeting process variation limits has little worth if the limits do not satisfy output standards. Perhaps the scales should be set to produce an average weight greater than $\bar{x} = 1.0048$ to reduce the number of containers weighing less than 1 pound. Another approach to the same objective would be to mechanize the weighing operation to reduce the weight variations. Which, if either, course of action to undertake depends on the opportunity cost of dissatisfied customers in relation to the cost of the cure. Quality control

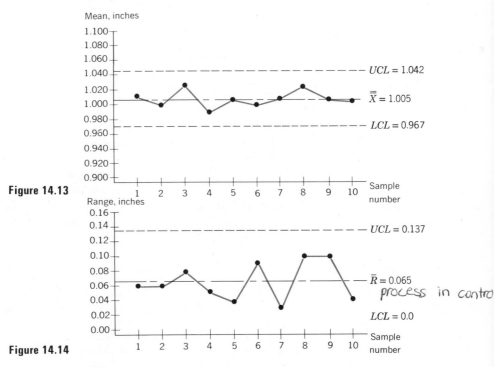

Figure 14.13

Figure 14.14

497

charts for variables contribute data for the decision and subsequently promote the process consistency needed to carry out the decision.

Control Charts for Attributes

Process quality control charts for attributes take one of two forms depending on the type of output. A *p-chart* is used when individual units are judged acceptable or defective. A *c-chart* is appropriate when the quality is best measured by the number of defects in a constant unit of output such as lineal feet of wire or square feet of cloth. Accordingly, a *p*-chart shows the variation in percentage defective and the *c*-chart shows the pattern of defects per unit of output.

p-charts. By definition, the output population classified by percentage defective is divided into two factions, acceptable or not acceptable. This two-way classification naturally leads to a binomial description of the standard error of the mean. With the central line determined by the average percentage defective during a trial period, $\bar{p}$, the typical boundaries are developed from:

$$\text{control limits} = \bar{p} \pm 3\sqrt{\frac{\bar{p}(1-\bar{p})}{n}} \qquad \text{where } \bar{p} = \frac{\sum p}{n}$$

$$n = \text{sample size}$$

when p is expressed as a decimal, or:

$$\text{control limits} = \bar{p} \pm 3\sqrt{\frac{\bar{p}(100-\bar{p})}{n}}$$

when p is expressed as a percentage.

The *p*-chart format and its interpretation are essentially the same as for control charts for variables. It is assumed that process variations due to chance are largely accounted for by the calculated control limits and points falling outside the limits are owed to extraneous factors affecting the process. Points thus isolated are invested for an assignable cause as described in Example 14.5.

EXAMPLE 14.5   Development of a *p*-Chart for Percentage Defective Control

A random sample of 50 wiring boards used in electrical assemblies is taken from the wiring assembly line each day. The boards are activated in a testing machine where a light glows if the wiring is acceptable.

Whenever a new wiring board design is required, a new control chart must be developed to measure process characteristics for that particular design. A preliminary chart is based on data

498

recorded during the initial phase of production. The number and percentage rejected during 20 consecutive days of production are shown below:

Date Sampled		Number Sampled	Number Rejected	Percentage Defective
Sept.	8	50	4	8
	9	50	3	6
	10	50	2	4
	11	50	6	12
	12	50	3	6
	15	50	1	2
	16	50	3	6
	17	50	2	4
	18	50	9	18
	19	50	5	10
	22	50	3	6
	23	50	2	4
	24	50	5	10
	25	50	2	4
	26	50	2	4
	29	50	1	2
	30	50	3	6
Oct.	1	50	2	4
	2	50	1	2
Total		1000	62	124

The preliminary estimate of the average percentage defective is

$$\bar{p} = \frac{62}{20 \times 50} (100\%) = 6.2\%$$

or, equivalently,

$$\bar{p} = \frac{124\%}{20} = 6.2\%$$

Assuming the process is already under control, $\bar{p}$ is the best available estimate of the mean and is used to estimate the standard deviation of the process as

$$\sqrt{\frac{\bar{p}(100 - \bar{p})}{n}} = \sqrt{\frac{6.2(100 - 6.2)}{50}} = 3.4\%$$

Then the control limits based on 3 standard deviations from the mean are

$UCL = 6.2\% + 3(3.4\%) = 16.4\%$

$LCL = 6.2\% - 3(3.4\%) = 0$ (because negative defectives are impossible)

Comparing the recorded data to the calculated control limits shows the sample taken on September 18 (18% rejected) is the only observation outside the control lines. An investigation of the production on this date reveals two inexperienced workers were assigned to the wiring

499

line, and some of their output was included in the sample before the floor supervisor had a chance to inspect and rectify the work. Since the occasion is not deemed typical and the assigned cause was remedied, the reading should be omitted from the data to produce the following revised chart lines:

$$\bar{p} = \frac{62 - 18}{19 \times 50} (100\%) = 4.6\%$$

$$UCL = 4.6 + 3\sqrt{\frac{4.6(100 - 4.6)}{50}} = 4.6 + 3(2.9) = 13.3\%$$

$$LCL = 4.6 - 3(2.9) = 0$$

The original and recalculated control limits are shown in Figure 14.15. The plotted points indicate the process is under control for the revised limits (dashed lines); the point with an assignable cause is still shown but is no longer considered a random fluctuation. The past data thus analyzed are adequate for immediate production control.

The next stage of process control is to see if the samples of the same size continue to fall within the designated limits. As workers gain proficiency with new wiring requirements, the average percentage of defectives may decrease. If future points on the chart randomly fluctuate around a lower center line, the improved process capability should be recognized by lower $\bar{p}$ and UCL values. The object is to set the center line as close as possible to the level at which the process actually operates. The control limits then provide a more sensitive signal to deviations outside normal variations.

c-charts. A defect is a flaw in a product. When a single defect is significant enough to cause the product's rejection, the percentage defective (*p*-chart) is the measure of control. Where the purpose of inspection is to measure the *number* of defects per unit of production, a *c*-chart is appropriate. The inspection unit may be a

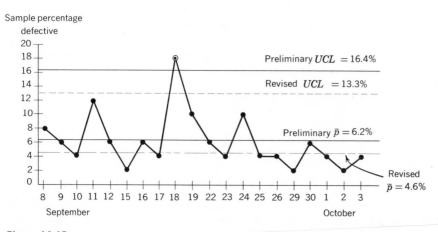

Figure 14.15

The size of the "inspection unit," like the number sampled for $\bar{p}$ or $\bar{x}$ charts, must remain constant for continued relevance of control limits.

single item like an airplane wing; a set of items such as a certain ● number of TV sets; or a block of output such as a length of belting, an area painted, or weight produced. The number of defects (c) in the unit inspected is recorded on a c-chart.

For output where there are many opportunities for defects to occur and the probability of a defect in any particular spot is small, the Poisson distribution nicely describes the sample fluctuations. With $\bar{c}$ as the average number of defects per unit, the standard deviation is $\sqrt{\bar{c}}$ and the working control limits are:

$$UCL = \bar{c} + 3\sqrt{\bar{c}}$$

$$LCL = \bar{c} - 3\sqrt{\bar{c}}$$

Again, like $\bar{p}$ and $\bar{x}$ values, $\bar{c}$ is usually estimated from past data. The given control limits will encompass practically all the values if the process is in control.

EXAMPLE 14.6 Application of a c-Chart for Control of Defects

A c-chart is used to evaluate the performance of an automated process for producing special impregnated material designed for use in extreme cold. The "inspection unit" is a continuous 10-yard roll of the cloth. Both sides of the material are inspected under high-intensity lights and magnifying screens. Defects occur from imperfections in the weave or inadequate coating. The blemishes are typically very small, 2 square centimeters or less. Checks for major imperfections due to machine malfunctions are conducted visually at the point of production.

In previous runs of the impregnated cloth, the number of defects per 10 yards has been 40, $\bar{c} = 40$. From this center line the control limits were set at:

$$UCL = 40 + 3\sqrt{40} = 40 + 3(6.3) = 59$$
$$LCL = 40 - 3\sqrt{40} = 40 - 19 = 21$$

The present production run is represented by the data shown below for the successive samples 81 through 100. The number of defects in each sample is plotted on the accompanying control chart (Figure 14.16).

Sample Number	Number of Defects per 10 Yards	Sample Number	Number of Defects per 10 Yards
81	33	91	35
82	16	92	28
83	19	93	24
84	26	94	31
85	36	95	34
86	38	96	40
87	37	97	30
88	41	98	31
89	32	99	22
90	30	100	28

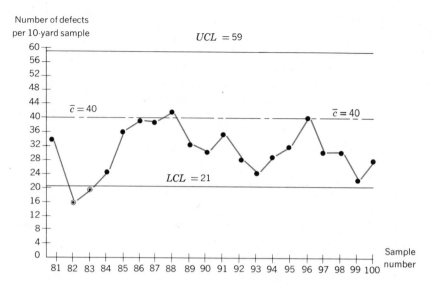

Figure 14.16

Special attention was given to the new run because a modified impregnating method was introduced. The initial samples, with only 33, 16, 19, and 26 defects, immediately raised hopes that the new method would radically improve the quality of the cloth. In conformance to control chart principles, the values outside the historical control limits were investigated for assignable causes. Some of the incipient optimism was drained by the revelation that an inspector unfamiliar with the characteristics of the special cloth had made the first inspections. He had missed blemishes that should have been counted as defects. Observations 82 and 83 were thus discounted.

The pattern of subsequent inspection reports substantiates a beneficial, but not really dramatic, decrease in defects attributable to the refined process. Most of the recent points are below the former average number of defects, $\bar{c} = 40$. Since the process average appears to have changed as a result of the new methods employed, a revision of control limits appears advisable. Samples 82 and 83 were previously eliminated for assignable causes. During the review of these samples, it was determined that the inexperience of the inspector may also have affected the results for samples 81 and 84. Therefore, the revised chart is based on the sequence of samples 85 through 100 to provide:

$$\bar{c}_r = \text{revised process average} = \frac{\sum(c_{85} + c_{86} + \cdots + c_{99})}{N} = \frac{517}{16} = 32.3$$

$$UCL_{(revised)} = \bar{c}_r + 3\sqrt{\bar{c}_r} = 32.3 + 3\sqrt{32.3} = 32.3 + 17.1 \doteq 49$$

$$LCL_{(revised)} = \bar{c}_r - 3\sqrt{\bar{c}_r} = 32.2 - 3(5.7) = 32.3 - 17.1 \doteq 15$$

All of the points recorded on the chart fall within the revised limits, indicating the process is apparently in control for the new process average. The revised limits are then applicable to future output utilizing the improved impregnating technique.

14-8 APPLICATION OF QUALITY CONTROL

" 'Manufacturers have never been more conscious of quality than they are right now. It's a problem of translating it into debugged products.' Recognizing that part of the problem is quality control rather than inherent quality, many companies now require final inspectors to sign tags attesting to the proper operation of products—the theory of these manufacturers being that to saddle specific company employees with the responsibility of finding flaws is to insure fewer faulty items." *Newsweek*, Nov. 25, 1968.

Quality control is receiving greater attention than ever before. Some critics say contemporary quality is dropping and place the blame on a lack of pride and craftsmanship in today's workers. Others place the blame for questionable quality on high-speed assembly lines where it is difficult to catch mistakes before the product is out of the factory.

Another argument states there has been no decrease at all in quality; instead, modern customers simply expect more than ever before. Elaborate and saturating advertising campaigns stress the perfection of products, and this emphasis is likely to produce expectations exceeding production capabilities. Consumer-minded marketers with their pledges and warranties set a scrambling pace for responsible production-minded managers. Few would care to argue against the worthiness of the trend, but many are wondering how to support it.

Both sampling plans and control charts are powerful allies in the pursuit of quality. They are grounded in solid mathematics and have been refined to a level where they are simple to apply. They are working evidence of the principle of management by exception. They embody more depth and facets than are immediately apparent.

We can return to control charts to illustrate some of the quality considerations recognized by experienced practitioners. The considerations evolve from a blend of theoretical knowledge and a working familiarity with the process subject to control.

A primary objective of control charting is to obtain the fastest possible warning of a deviating condition. This objective may be applied to the operation of the process itself or to the acceptance of products from the process. Sampling designs are different for the two divisions. A sample intended for process control should be selected to yield small variations *within* each sample and large variations *between* samples. When the purpose is to control outgoing quality, a sample should be *representative* of the output period, a random sample from a dated block of products.

We have observed the importance and logic of carefully examining all points falling outside the control limits. Much can also be learned from observing the pattern of points still inside the limits. The purpose is to identify a trend that can be investigated for an underlying cause before the possible cause damages production. The "theory of runs" is a probability-based routine for determining the chance occurrence of a sequence of points consistently crowding one side of the process mean. Rules-of-thumb are applied by some practitioners to serve the same purpose. The "rule of seven" indicates the process should be

Runs are often classed as "runs above" or "runs below" (sequence consistently above or below the mean) and "runs up" or "runs down" (continuous sequence of increasing or decreasing values).

investigated for nonrandom influences whenever seven consecutive points occur above or below the mean. Similar "rules" suggest close scrutiny for two consecutive points "very" close to the control limit and a run of five points successively higher or lower.

The manner in which a control chart is maintained and acted upon can influence its value. When charts are outdated or their signals disregarded, workers soon become cynical about the quality program. It would be better to hide a neglected chart because its presence advertises the lack of concern by management; the cynicism it engenders could be contagious. Conversely, a properly treated chart can encourage better performance. A prominently displayed control chart with achievable standards advances a strong psychological incentive.

Unrealistic quality goals, like any subjectively unobtainable standards, may discourage or frustrate the worker's concern for quality.

Charts are conspicuous and reputable parts of a quality control program, but they are not the whole program. Education, supervision, and training are necessary complements. In turn, a quality control program is only one area in the total production program. A concern for quality depends on other functions of the production system and, reciprocally, the concern supports the other functions. Exclusive attention to the engineering implications of quality control forfeits the quality program's potential for administrative and managerial benefits; its motivational potential could be its most significant contribution.

14-9 SUMMARY

Quality control ranges over the complete input-transformation-output sequence of a production system. Acceptance sampling measures the quality of inputs. Quality programs urge workers to avoid mistakes in the transformation process. Control charting measures the performance of a process in meeting output objectives. The total quality control effort depends on cooperation from many operating units within the organization; its success is ultimately determined by the customers it serves.

Production quality starts with a process capable of producing to design specifications. The design must meet the precision demanded by customers and be within the accuracy attainable by the process. The economics of precision versus accuracy relates the capital cost of achieving greater accuracy to the higher returns expected from supplying greater precision. Since variations creep into any production process, the cost of vigilance to reduce errors must also be related to the precision of outgoing products.

Organizations for quality assurance vary widely, but all of

them depend on active support from higher management to integrate inter- and intradepartmental efforts. By treating the quality staff as a psuedoindependent organization, personality conflicts and pressure tactics by affected parties can be considerably reduced. The overall value of the quality organization should be judged by the ratio of costs incurred to costs avoided.

Inspections are scheduled when they will do the most good. They are usually a function of the phase of product development: at the receiving point for raw materials and components; in the process before operations that are costly, irreversible, or masking; and at the end of the process before delivery. Inspectors typically follow the product in fixed position and process layouts. Formal inspections stations are associated with product layouts. Some products must be sent to central laboratories for testing. Where there is a choice between laboratory and on-site inspections, the advantages of lab standardization are compared to the added costs of handling.

The two basic types of inspections are for the control of variables—precise measurements of critical characteristics capable of expression on a continuous scale—and of attributes—an acceptable or unacceptable rating. The attribute category is further divided into percentage defectives—the percentage rejected for not meeting one product characteristic—and into defects—the number of flaws per inspection unit.

The purpose of acceptance sampling is to recommend a specific action; it is not an attempt to estimate quality or control quality directly. A lot-by-lot acceptance sampling plan for attributes specifies the sample size and the associated number of defectives that cannot be exceeded without rejecting the lot from which the sample was taken. The capability of the plan to distinguish between acceptable and unacceptable lots is revealed by its operating characteristic (OC) curve. The ideal OC curve is obtainable only from error-free, 100% inspection. The preferred plan balances the cost of taking larger samples against the greater precision obtainable from larger samples.

Sampling plans are characterized by an acceptable quality level (AQL)–the grade considered adequate by the receiver— and by the lot tolerance percent defectives ($LTPD$)–the level of defectives a receiver will just tolerate. The AQL is associated with the producer's risk, α, and the $LTPD$ with the consumer's risk, β.

Average outgoing quality (AOQ) is a measure of the quality level resulting from an acceptance plan when the rejected lots are subjected to 100% rectifying inspection and defectives in the

505

sample are replaced by acceptable items. This percentage is calculated from the equation

$$AOQ = \frac{P_a \times p(N - n)}{N}$$

There are many types of acceptance sampling plans. A single-sample, variables acceptance plan has basically the same considerations as attribute plans. Multiple sampling plans utilize a number of smaller samples to attain a desired level of discrimination. Sequential sampling is characterized by acceptance, rejection, and resampling zones; sampling is continued until the lot passes out of the resampling zone.

A control chart is a graphic aid for the detection of quality variations in a production process. It has three main uses: to determine the capability of the process, to guide modifications, and to monitor output. Control limits aid in distinguishing variations caused by chance from those due to assignable causes. An observation falls by chance outside the typical limits about 3 times in a 1000.

Control charts for variables record the average value of sample measurements ($\bar{x}$) and the range of measurements (R). Both the mean and range of a sample must be within control limits before the process represented is considered under control. One method of calculating the control limits for variables is to use pre-determined factors based upon sample size, n; the A factor is used for sample means and B and C factors are applied to sample ranges as:

$$UCL_{\bar{x}} = \bar{x} + A\bar{R} \qquad UCL_R = B\bar{R}$$
$$LCL_{\bar{x}} = \bar{x} - A\bar{R} \qquad LCL_R = C\bar{R}$$

When the sample size is not constant, different limits must be calculated for each n.

Control charts for attributes portray the percentage defective (p-chart) or the number of defects (c-chart). The p-chart control limits are based on the binomial distribution to provide.

$$\text{control limits }_{(p)} = \bar{p} \pm 3\sqrt{\frac{\bar{p}(100 - \bar{p})}{n}}$$

where $\bar{p}$ = average percentage defective. The control limits for the c-chart are derived from the Poisson distribution to give:

$$\text{control limits }_{(c)} = \bar{c} \pm 3\sqrt{\bar{c}}$$

where $\bar{c}$ = average number of defects per inspection unit. Limits

506

for both charts are often developed from process samples taken during a base period after eliminating unrepresentative observations. Control limits should be revised when the process average changes.

The administration and practiced evaluation of control charts can increase their value. Trends or runs within the control limits give advance warning of process deviations. Proper maintenance of charts can provide psychological incentives for better performance, while neglected charts or unrealistic quality standards can produce worker cynicism. Improved motivation can be a significant contribution of an integrated quality control program.

14-10 REFERENCES

Bowker, A. H. and G. L. Lieberman, *Engineering Statistics*, Prentice-Hall, Englewood Cliffs, N.J., 1959.

Burr, I. W., *Engineering Statistics and Quality Control*, Prentice-Hall, Englewood Cliffs, N.J., 1953.

Cowden, D. J., *Statistical Methods in Quality Control*, Prentice-Hall, Englewood Cliffs, N.J., 1957.

Dodge, H. F. and H. G. Romig, *Sampling Inspection Tables—Single and Double Sampling* (2nd ed.), John Wiley, New York, 1959.

Duncan, A. J., *Quality Control and Industrial Statistics* (3rd ed.), Richard D. Irwin, Homewood, Ill., 1965.

Feigenbaum, A. V., *Total Quality Control*, McGraw-Hill, New York, 1961.

Freeman, H. A., M. Friedman, F. Mosteller, and W. A. Wallis (eds.), *Sampling Inspection*, McGraw-Hill, New York, 1948.

Grant, E. L., *Statistical Quality Control* (3rd ed.), McGraw-Hill, New York, 1964.

Juran, J. M. (ed.), *Quality Control Handbook* (2nd ed.), McGraw-Hill, New York, 1962.

Landers, R. R., *Reliability and Product Assurance*, Prentice-Hall, Englewood Cliffs, N.J., 1963.

Military Standard Sampling Procedures and Tables for Inspection by Attributes, MIL-STD-105C, Government Printing Office, Washington, D.C., July 18, 1961.

Schrock, E. M., *Quality Control and Statistical Methods*, Reinhold, New York, 1957.

Shewhart, W. A., *Economic Control of Quality of Manufactured Product*, Van Nostrand, New York, 1931.

Thompson, J. E., *Inspection Organization and Methods*, McGraw-Hill, New York, 1950.

14-11 QUESTIONS AND PROBLEMS

1. If a supervisor is indeed the interface between quality control goals of management and the achievement of those goals by workers, what are his responsibilities to both sides of the interface?

2. Relate the concepts of product *precision* and production *accuracy* to the appropriate functional areas represented in Figure 14.1.

3. The value line and cost line in Figure 14.2 tend to converge at higher levels of product refinement. How could the shape of the value line be changed to parallel the cost line more closely?

4. What are some potential advantages of treating the quality assurance staff as pseudoindependent operators? What practical measures could be used to establish this relatively independent status within the organization?

5. What is the relationship between a "Zero Defect" program and the more quantitative measures of quality control such as acceptance sampling and control charts?

6. What are the advantages and disadvantages of a central laboratory inspection facility with reference to the three basic plant layouts?

7. Discuss the considerations involved in selecting the inspection points within a process.

8. Why is statistical sampling generally more suitable for machine-produced products than for hand-crafted products? Under what conditions may sampling produce better results than 100% inspection?

9. Why is acceptance sampling not considered an attempt to control the quality of a process?

10. What is an OC curve? How can an OC curve be made more discriminating? Of what value is a more discriminating curve?

11. What is the relationship between AQL and α? Between $LTPD$ and β?

12. Explain how the AOQ can decrease while the percentage of defectives increases. Refer to Figure 14.8.

13. Compare the economic and administrative considerations for single sampling, double sampling, and sequential sampling plans. What types of industrial situations could produce a preference for one of the plans?

14. Distinguish between natural variations in a process and variations due to an assignable cause. Give some examples of assignable causes.

15. What is the difference between statistical control limits and product tolerances? How do these two dimensions relate to product precision and production accuracy?

16. Why is it necessary to control both $\bar{x}$ and R variations for control of variables?

17. Why must separate charts be developed for each variable characteristic measured?

18. Distinguish between the types of inspection required for a p-chart and a c-chart.

19. Discuss why the control limits for a p-chart are based on

the binomial distribution and those for a c-chart are based on the Poisson distribution.

20. Discuss the adequacy of today's production quality and possible reasons for current conditions.

21. What is the theory of runs and how can it prove useful?

22. Comment on the administration and maintenance of control charts as they affect worker motivation.

23. In a preliminary study of a process containing five successive operations, the following data were obtained:

Operation	1	2	3	4	5
Percentage rejected	5.1	0.6	4.8	3.2	1.2
Cumulative manufacturing costs	$2.75	$3.98	$4.27	$4.85	$5.12

The standard unit of inspection is 100 products and inspectors are paid $4 per hour. Inspection times in minutes per product are in order of the operations, 1.2, 0.6, 0.5, 2.0, and 1.8.

(a) If two inspection stations are to be established, where in the sequence of operations should they be located? Why?

(b) If three inspections stations are allowed, where should they be placed? Why?

24. (a) Construct an OC curve for a single-sample, percentage-defective, lot-by-lot sampling plan where $n = 100$ and $c = 2$.

(b) On the graph developed for part (a), show by dotted lines the general shape of the curve for a 100% inspection plan and a plan where $n = 1000$ and $c = 20$.

(c) What is the $AOQL$ from part (b)? At what value of p does it occur?

(d) If $\alpha = 0.05$ and $\beta = 0.10$ for the plan in part (a), what are the AQL and the $LTPD$?

25. What size sample should be taken and how many defectives can be allowed in the sample for a consumer's risk of 5%, a producer's risk of 10%, and AQL of 1%, and an $LTPD$ of 9%? Determine the actual values of α and β for the sample plan selected.

26. Given a sampling plan defined by $n = 10$ and $c = 1$, what are the AQL and $LTPD$ for $\alpha = 0.03$ and $\beta = 0.05$? *

27. Base-period data are shown below for the development of control charts.

(a) What are the control limits and center line for the process average? Construct and discuss the $\bar{x}$ chart.

(b) What are the control limits and center line for the process variation? Construct and discuss the range chart.

509

Sample Number	x_1	x_2	x_3	x_4	x_5	x_6
1	0.498	0.492	0.510	0.505	0.504	0.487
2	0.482	0.491	0.502	0.481	0.496	0.492
3	0.501	0.512	0.503	0.499	0.498	0.511
4	0.498	0.486	0.502	0.503	0.510	0.501
5	0.500	0.507	0.509	0.498	0.512	0.518
6	0.476	0.492	0.496	0.521	0.505	0.490
7	0.483	0.487	0.495	0.488	0.502	0.486
8	0.502	0.500	0.511	0.496	0.500	0.503
9	0.492	0.504	0.472	0.515	0.498	0.487
10	0.511	0.522	0.513	0.518	0.520	0.516
11	0.488	0.512	0.501	0.498	0.492	0.498
12	0.504	0.502	0.496	0.501	0.491	0.496
13	0.501	0.413	0.499	0.496	0.508	0.502
14	0.489	0.491	0.496	0.510	0.508	0.503
15	0.511	0.499	0.508	0.503	0.496	0.505

28. One characteristic of a product, x, is inspected. From 20 samples, each of 10 measurements, the following totals are obtained:

$$\sum \bar{x} = 139.8 \qquad \sum R = 23.9$$

The specifications for the measured characteristic is 7.10 ± 0.30. Assuming the process is in control for the limits calculated from 20 samples, what conclusions can be drawn about the ability of the process to meet the specifications?

29. During the past year, an average of 32 units were found defective from 100% inspection of daily production. The output per day varied at most 2% from an average of 480 units. A review of the records revealed the number of defectives occasionally went as high as 55 and as low as 4 or 5 per day. What help might be obtained from a control chart in improving process performance?

30. Construct the appropriate control chart for the process represented by the following data collected in the past month:

Sample Number	Sample Size	Number of Defectives
1	200	3
2	200	1
3	200	0

Sample Number	Sample Size	Number of Defectives
4	200	2
5	200	4
6	200	1
7	200	2
8	200	0
9	200	3
10	200	2
11	200	1
12	200	3
13	200	6
14	200	8
15	200	5
16	200	9
17	200	3
18	200	1
19	200	0
20	200	2
21	200	3
22	200	1

What can be concluded about the behavior of the process during the past month? What limits are appropriate for controlling next month's production?

31. All the gyroscopes produced are inspected. Each is classified as acceptable or unacceptable. Those rejected are reworked until they reach an acceptable state. What can be said about the 10 days' production described below when the process has previously produced an average percentage defect of 4%? Plot the control chart.

Day	Output	Number Rejected
1	80	3
2	121	6
3	57	2
4	141	7
5	132	6
6	154	9
7	171	13
8	101	4
9	88	3
10	71	1

(*Hint:* A straightforward approach to charting nonuniform sample sizes is to use the historical average, $\bar{p} = 4$, and allow the control limits to vary according to $\pm 3\sqrt{4(100 - 4)}/\sqrt{n}$).

32. The following number of defects were obtained from the inspection of 100-foot sections of high quality, multichannel communication cable (read each line left to right to obtain the sequence of observations):

$$
\begin{array}{cccccccccccccc}
1 & 0 & 2 & 3 & 1 & 0 & 3 & 1 & 2 & 5 & 1 & 0 & 1 & 0 & 0 \\
2 & 0 & 1 & 1 & 2 & 0 & 0 & 2 & 0 & 1 & 3 & 6 & 1 & 0 & 1 \\
\end{array}
$$

Do these data come from a controlled process?

CHAPTER 15

PROCESS CONTROL: Statistical Evaluation of Operations

★ ★ ★ All sections in this chapter should be considered *optional material* and be omitted unless the reader has adequate preparation in statistics.

15-1 IMPORTANCE

"A little neglect may breed mischief: for want of a nail the shoe was lost; for want of a shoe the horse was lost; and for want of a horse the rider was lost." Benjamin Franklin.

A "process" is a method of doing something. A system is designed around a strategic process, its reason for being. Like Exekiel's vision of wheels within wheels, there are tactical processes within strategic processes and operations within tactical processes. A malfunction in a seemingly trivial operation may disrupt the continuity of the greater process and thwart the system's objectives. Thus process control extends from the fruit to the root of a production system.

Humming machines, busy people, and a steady outflow of finished products are not necessarily indicative of a healthy process. The bustling facade may hide flaws in products, cover inefficient operations, or mask violations of production standards. To detect and control deviations from expected standards, the mistakes must be exposed and their causes investigated. Neither the mistake nor the cause-and-effect relationship is often obvious until some loss is incurred. The tasks then are to test ongoing activities and to infer from incomplete data whether undesirable deviations are happening and why. The tools for the task are hypothesis tests and methods of statistical inference.

Variability must be recognized in almost all phases of production systems. In some cases the risk can be compensated for by safety factors or similar means of overdesign. In other cases, statistical measures are used to evaluate risk.

We already have observed the application of statistical techniques to forecasting, PERT, work sampling, and quality control. Many of these techniques fall under one of the hypothesis tests described in this chapter. The applications constitute a collection of statistical routines which have gained acceptance through proven worth and are now respected management tools. This chapter carries the subject of statistical inference into the

513

area of industrial experimentation. Here the methods are not so widely known nor used. The purposes of this chapter are to provide an orderly introduction to the potential of statistical tests and to highlight their areas of appropriate application.

Our coverage of the material is only a digest. Brevity increases the amount of exposure at the cost of refinement. Profuse variations are left untold, but there is still much to comprehend. Careful attention to the assumptions underlying different hypothesis tests reveals the most powerful test for each situation and helps avoid the too frequent fallacy of extracting more information than is legitimately available from the data.

Industrial uses of statistics have been likened to the utility of a street lamp for an inebriated nightwalker; he can use the lamp for support or for illumination. The support role of statistics is essentially to appraise the representativeness of collected data. Although knowing whether the data are truly descriptive of a process or just owed to chance causes adds illumination, greater enlightenment usually results from carefully designed experiments. By varying certain conditions while controlling others according to a predetermined plan, alternatives are impartially evaluated in terms of known confidence.

We might add another comparison to statistics and a street-lamp: both are available to everyone. The significant time and resource savings that accrue from the replacement of trial-and error searches by systematic tests are practical for small firms as well as industrial giants. It takes dedication and practice instead of capital investment to earn the savings, a pleasant reversal of most modern automation trends.

15-2 HYPOTHESIS TESTING

Way back in Section 1-4, we observed that model building started with a problem and data from the real world to set a framework for model formulation and evaluation in the abstract world. Hypothesis testing is a means of evaluating real-world conditions. Statistical models relied upon for hypothesis tests may not be so obviously applicable as some mathematical formulas, but the requirement of realism is just as relevant.

The problem being considered leads directly to a hypothesis such as:

1. The average amount packed in containers today is the same amount packed in each can yesterday.
2. An improved work procedure has reduced the time to produce one unit when compared to the old method.

3. The number of products produced per machine depends on the source of the raw materials used in the process.

A hypothesis can be stated more specifically in the form H_0 (hypothesis about a certain parameter) is true and $H_\emptyset$ (alternate hypothesis about the same parameter) is false. For instance, where the average amount placed in a can today is expected to equal some known amount from yesterday, then the hypothesis is $H_0 : \bar{x}_1 = \bar{x}_2$ where $\bar{x}_1$ is yesterday's average weight and $\bar{x}_2$ is today's average; the alternate hypothesis is $H_\emptyset : \bar{x}_1 \neq \bar{x}_2$. A test of these hypotheses would lead to a conclusion that the sample means are alike or unlike.

A parameter is a constant in the model such as the mean or variance.

Type I and Type II Errors

A companion step of the hypothesis statement is the selection of a level of significance, α. The value chosen for α defines the probability of rejecting the hypothesis. The most common values are 0.05 and 0.01, although each situation should be judged on its own merits with respect to the consequence of the two types of errors depicted in Table 15.1.

Table 15.1 Types of errors that affect the acceptance or rejection of a hypothesis

Decision	Accept	Reject
Hypothesis true	Correct decision	Type I error
Hypothesis false	Type II error	Correct decision

The error, designated as Type I by statisticians, that rejects a true hypothesis is controlled by the choice of α. If we believe that a true hypothesis can be allowed to be rejected only 1 time in 100, an α value of 0.01 is indicated. However, in the 99 times in 100 that the hypothesis is accepted, there is some chance that an incorrect hypothesis is also being accepted. This type of error is designated Type II, and its probability usually increases for a given sample size with smaller values of α. There is a greater risk of Type II errors in samples of smaller size.

The symbol β represents the magnitude of a Type II error.

Which type of error is more serious depends on the problem situation. In the can-packing example, the hypothesis could be that the average contents do not weigh as much as the advertised weight of the container. Then

Note that in the hypothesis $H_0 : \bar{x} \geq W$, a Type II error would be more serious.

$$H_0 : \bar{x} < W \qquad \text{where } W = \text{advertised weight}$$
$$H_\emptyset : \bar{x} \geq W \qquad \qquad \bar{x} = \text{average weight}$$

are the hypotheses and a Type I error (not recognizing that the

515

average weight was below the minimum standard) would be very serious because it could lead to customer dissatisfaction and legal penalties. In the design of a statistical test, the value of α is often specified first and the sample size is increased to limit Type II errors.

Statistical Tests

The statement of the hypothesis and the consideration of testing errors lead to the collection of data and the selection of an appropriate test. We are already familiar with the difficulties and importance of acquiring enough representative data. What we must not lose sight of is the economic balance between the cost of collecting data and opportunity costs of incorrect conclusions. It is intuitively easy to appreciate that extra costs incurred to get more information about a problem tend to increase our knowledge of the problem situation and our confidence in treating it. Such costs are relatively easy to isolate. The cost associated with making an incorrect decision is more difficult to recognize. In theory, we should be able to equate tolerable limits for α and β based on the consequences of a wrong decision with the cost of acquiring the data necessary to meet the tolerable limits. But theory is often sacrificed on the conference-table altar by expediting compromises. In industrial experimentation, it is seldom feasible to attempt exact costing of the data–error relationship, but awareness of the general proportions of the relationship provides reasonable guidelines for testing procedures.

Selection of an appropriate statistical testing formula depends on what questions are posed in the hypothesis and the distribution of sampled data. In the following sections, we shall consider several tests for standard situations and the assumptions underlying the applicability of the tests.

Data collection was treated in Chapters 3, 6, 9, and 12.

Hypothesis-testing steps are:
1. *State the hypothesis, alternate hypothesis, and assumptions.*
2. *Select a level of confidence and identify the critical region.*
3. *Calculate the test statistic.*
4. *Draw a conclusion.*

15-3 THE CHI SQUARE TEST

A rough comparison of distributions can be made by visually comparing a histogram of collected data to the shape of a distribution curve.

Tables for the χ^2 distribution are in Appendix A.

Many statistical decisions are based on the assumption that data from a real-world situation are characterized in the abstract world by a normally distributed model. Under some conditions, such as a test of population means, a decision is not particularly sensitive to the correctness of the normality assumption. More commonly it is quite important to be assured that a distribution assumed for a certain test is indeed representative of the real-world condition. A hypothesis that a set of sampled frequencies has the same distribution as the frequencies of a theoretical distribution is tested by the chi-square (χ^2) test. The decision to accept or reject the hypothesis is based on the χ^2 distribution.

Comparison of Empirical and Theoretical Distributions

The "goodness of fit" between an empirical and a theoretical distribution is based on the difference between data-generated frequencies and the tabulated frequencies for the same intervals from one of the useful distributions. The test statistic is calculated as

$$\chi^2 = \sum_{i=1}^{k} \frac{(F_i - f_i)^2}{f_i}$$

where:

F_i = observed frequencies in k classes
f_i = expected frequencies in k classes from hypothesized distribution
k = number of classes or intervals into which distribution is divided

The values for F_i are taken from the observations noted in each segment of the measurement scale appropriate to the problem. The tabulation could take the form shown in Table 15.2 where the classes might be time intervals and the observed values could be the number of times a certain characteristic appears. As a rule-of-thumb, the test is more reliable when the number of classes (k) is larger, but the number of observed frequencies in each interval should be five or more.

Table 15.2 Array of data for a χ^2 test

Classes	Observed Frequency	Theoretical Frequency
1	F_1	f_1
2	F_2	f_2
.	.	.
.	.	.
.	.	.
k	F_k	f_k

A conclusion about a statistically significant difference between two distributions is made by comparing the calculated χ^2 with a table χ^2 value indexed from the percentage points in the column headings and the degrees of freedom, $v = k - 1$. Small values of χ^2 are associated with an agreement between observed and theoretical frequencies; large values indicate a discrepancy.

EXAMPLE 15.1 Goodness of Fit Between Observed and Theoretical Values

The frequency of repair calls to a maintenance department appears to follow a Poisson distribution. Before applying queuing formulas based on this distribution, the goodness of fit is to be checked. The hypothesis is that the distribution of the arrival times has a Poisson distribution; it will be accepted at a confidence level of 0.05.

The number of arrivals per hour are tabulated for 100 arrivals and fall into the eight divisions shown below. Since the last four intervals contain only enough arrivals to conform to the rule-of-thumb limit that $F_i \geqslant 5$, they are lumped together to form a single class. The f_i values are taken from the relative frequency of each class in the theoretical Poisson distribution multiplied by the number of observations, 100.

Arrivals hour (k)	Observed Frequency (F_i)	Theoretical Frequency (f_i)	$F_i - f_i$	$(F_i - f_i)^2$	$\dfrac{(F_i - f_i)^2}{f_i}$
0	19	24.7	−5.7	32.49	1.32
1	31	34.5	−3.5	12.25	0.36
2	27	24.1	2.9	8.41	0.35
3	14	11.3	2.7	7.29	0.65
4	5 ⎫	4.0 ⎫			
5	3 ⎬ 9	1.1 ⎬ 5.4	3.6	12.96	2.40
6	0	0.2			
7	1 ⎭	0.1 ⎭			
Totals	100	100.0	0.0		5.08

The calculated $\chi^2 = 5.08$ is compared with table percentage points at $\nu = 5 - 1 = 4$ to obtain

$$\left.\begin{array}{l} \chi^2_{0.30} = 4.878 \\[4pt] \chi^2_{0.20} = 5.989 \end{array}\right\} \;<\; \chi^2_{\text{calculated}} = 5.08$$

$$\chi^2_{0.05} = 9.488$$

which means that the probability is greater than 0.20 that a χ^2 value larger than 5.08 could occur purely by chance. With the acceptable significance level at 9.488, the hypothesis that the arrival times can be represented by a Poisson distribution is accepted.

Comparisons Made by Use of Contingency Tables

The χ^2 test can also be used to indicate whether two characteristics of a process are associated. The data can be arranged in a "contingency table" format with r rows and c columns as shown in Table 15.3. One characteristic, say the age of workers, is denoted by column headings and the other characteristic, perhaps the severity of accidents during a given period, is shown by row headings. The outcomes (O_{ij}) for respective accidents per age group are entered in the cells of the table.

The hypothesis to be tested could be that the severity of accidents is independent of the age of workers or, equivalently, the seriousness of accidents is homogeneous for workers of all

Table 15.3 $r \times c$ contingency table

Characteristic II	Characteristic I				Totals
	1	2	j	c	
1	O_{11}	O_{12}	$\cdots$	O_{1c}	T_{1j}
2	O_{21}	O_{22}	$\cdots$	O_{2c}	T_{2j}
i	$\cdot$ $\cdot$ $\cdot$	$\cdot$ $\cdot$ $\cdot$	$\cdots$	$\cdot$ $\cdot$ $\cdot$	$\cdot$ $\cdot$ $\cdot$
r	O_{r1}	O_{r2}	$\cdots$	O_{rc}	T_{rj}
Totals	T_{i1}	T_{i2}	$\cdots$	T_{ic}	T_{ij}

ages. Both hypotheses are tested by the same method. An expected value, E_{ij}, is calculated for each cell based on the proportion of observations in each class. From the row and column totals, the expectation for cell_{11} (E_{11}) is calculated as

	c_1	c_2	c_3	T_i
r_1	x	x	9	20
r_2	x	3	x	12
r_3	6	x	6	17
T_i	18	15	16	49

$$E_{11} = T_{ij} \times \frac{T_{1j}}{T_{ij}} \times \frac{T_{i1}}{T_{ij}} = \frac{(T_{1j})(T_{i1})}{T_{ij}}$$

Degrees of freedom denote the numbers in an array that are free to vary. In the array above, $v = (3 - 1) \times (3 - 1) = 4$, because with the totals and any four numbers known, the rest are specified as demonstrated by solving for the x's:

After an expectation is computed for each cell, the observed frequencies (O_{ij}) are compared with the expected frequencies (E_{ij}) to obtain

$$\chi^2 = \sum_{i=1}^{r} \sum_{j=1}^{c} \frac{(O_{ij} - E_{ij})^2}{E_{ij}}$$

	c_1	c_2	c_3	T_i
r_1	4	7	9	20
r_2	8	3	1	12
r_3	6	5	6	17
T_i	18	15	16	49

which has an approximate χ^2 distribution with $(r - 1)(c - 1)$ degrees of freedom. The hypothesis is rejected when the calculated χ^2 is larger than the percentage points of the χ^2 distribution at $v = (r - 1)(c - 1)$ and the selected significance level. A rejected hypothesis leads to the conclusion that the two characteristics are dependent; for the hypothesis that accident severity is independent of age, rejection means that the data indicate the seriousness of an accident is a function of the age of the hurt worker.

EXAMPLE 15.2 χ^2 Test of Independence

In an effort to reduce the number of mistakes in a billing section, an error study is initiated. The billing clerks are divided into classes according to the number of years of experience; the errors are classified as to cause: typographical, recordkeeping, and calculation. The hypothesis

519

CONTROL

is that the type of billing error made is independent of the clerk's experience. If the hypothesis is rejected, experience will be used to assign clerks to certain types of work.

From the data displayed in the contingency table, Table 15.4, the expectation associated with each type of error and experience interval is calculated as:

Table 15.4

Experience (years)	Type of Error			Totals
	(T) c_1	(RK) c_2	(C) c_3	
.0–1 r_1	55	32	48	135
1–2 r_2	38	10	25	73
2–4 r_3	21	6	24	51
Over 4 r_4	12	2	10	24
Totals	126	50	107	283

$$E_{11} = \frac{(135)(126)}{283} = 60 \qquad E_{12} = \frac{(135)(50)}{283} = 24$$

$$E_{13} = \frac{(135)(107)}{283} = 51 \qquad E_{21} = \frac{(73)(126)}{283} = 33$$

$$E_{22} = \frac{(73)(50)}{283} = 13 \qquad E_{23} = \frac{(73)(107)}{283} = 28$$

$$E_{31} = \frac{(51)(126)}{283} = 23 \qquad E_{32} = \frac{(51)(50)}{283} = 9$$

$$E_{33} = \frac{(51)(107)}{283} = 19 \qquad E_{41} = \frac{(24)(126)}{283} = 11$$

$$E_{42} = \frac{(24)(50)}{283} = 4 \qquad E_{43} = \frac{(24)(107)}{283} = 9$$

Then:

$$\chi^2 = \frac{(55-60)^2}{60} + \frac{(32-24)^2}{24} + \frac{(48-51)^2}{51} + \frac{(38-33)^2}{33} + \frac{(10-13)^2}{13} + \frac{(25-28)^2}{28}$$

$$+ \frac{(21-23)^2}{23} + \frac{(6-9)^2}{9} + \frac{(24-19)^2}{19} + \frac{(12-11)^2}{11} + \frac{(2-4)^2}{4} + \frac{(10-9)^2}{9}$$

$$= 0.42 + 2.67 + 0.18 + 0.76 + 0.69 + 0.32 + 0.17 + 1.0 + 1.32 + 0.09 + 1.0$$

$$+ 0.11 = \textbf{8.73}$$

Since there are $(3 - 1)(4 - 1) = 6$ degrees of freedom, the critical region for an 0.05 signi-ficance level is above 12.592. Therefore, the hypothesis is accepted. The conclusion is that the error pattern of the billing clerks is about the same regardless of the number of years of ex-perience. Consequently, some other characteristic, such as education or age, will have to be investigated if the types of error are to be related to workers. If none of the characteristics pro-vides clues to the problem, other statistical tests could be made of the output and work procedures to determine if certain practices are prone to errors regardless of the worker involved.

Comparison of a Sample Variance to a Known Variance

The variability of a process is measured by its variance. A hypothesis that a sample from a normally distributed population has a variance (s^2) equal to a known value $(\sigma)^2$ is tested by the statistic

$$\chi^2 = \frac{(n - 1)s^2}{\sigma_o^2} \qquad \text{where } v = n - 1$$

The alternate hypothesis is that the variance (σ^2) of the popula-tion from which the sample is taken is not the same, greater than, or less than a given variance (σ_o^2). Any of the three alternate hypotheses are accepted if the test statistic lies within the critical regions of the χ^2 distribution depicted in Figure 15.1.

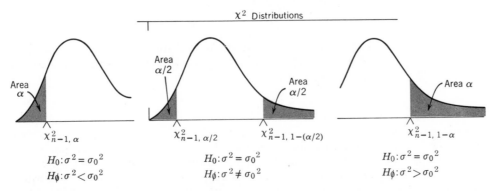

χ^2 Distributions

Area α

$\chi^2_{n-1, \alpha}$

$H_0: \sigma^2 = \sigma_0{}^2$
$H_\phi: \sigma^2 < \sigma_0{}^2$

Area $\alpha/2$

Area $\alpha/2$

$\chi^2_{n-1, \alpha/2}$ $\chi^2_{n-1, 1-(\alpha/2)}$

$H_0: \sigma^2 = \sigma_0{}^2$
$H_\phi: \sigma^2 \neq \sigma_0{}^2$

Area α

$\chi^2_{n-1, 1-\alpha}$

$H_0: \sigma^2 = \sigma_0{}^2$
$H_\phi: \sigma^2 > \sigma_0{}^2$

Figure 15.1 Critical regions at an α level of significance for the hypotheses of equal variances and associated alternate hypotheses

EXAMPLE 15.3 Limit for Acceptance that a Sample Variance Is Equal to a Known Process Variance

The standard deviation of products produced by a machine now in operation is $\sigma_0^2 = 0.082$ inch. A salesman claims that a machine he sells will produce at a much higher rate with a variation equal to or less than the machine being used. The statement of a higher production rate is accepted, but the claim about variability is to be tested.

The test will be based on 25 randomly selected products. The hypothesis is $H_0: \sigma^2 = \sigma_0^2 = 0.006724$ with the alternate hypothesis, $H_0: \sigma^2 > 0.006724$. The one-tail critical region is set

521

by $\alpha = 0.05$ and has a value of $\chi^2_{n-1,1-\alpha} = \chi^2_{24,0.95} = 36.415$. From this information, the critical value for the standard deviation of the sample is determined as

$$\chi^2_{n-1,1-\alpha} = \frac{(n-1)s^2}{\sigma_0^2} = \chi^2_{24,0.95} = \frac{(24)s^2}{0.006724} = 36.415$$

$$s = \sqrt{\frac{(36.415)(0.006724)}{24}} = \sqrt{0.010202} = 0.101 \text{ inch}$$

If s is less than 0.101 inch for the sample (assumed normally distributed), it will be accepted that both machines have the same output variation and the new machine will be preferred owing to its higher production rate.

15-4 THE Z TEST

The familiar test statistic $Z = (x - \mu)/\sigma$ is based on a normal population with a known mean, μ, and a known variance, σ^2. It can be used to test a hypothesis that a randomly selected value x came from a population characterized by μ and σ^2. More commonly, we are interested in the probability that a sample mean is equal to the mean of a known population. To test such a hypothesis, we modify the Z formula by substituting the sample mean $\bar{x}$ for x and the sample standard deviation $\sigma/\sqrt{n}$ for σ:

$$Z = \frac{\bar{x} - \mu}{\sigma/\sqrt{n}} = \frac{\bar{x} - \mu}{\sigma_{\bar{x}}}$$

The assumption that allows the substitution is that $\bar{x}$ is obtained randomly from a population that is normally distributed with a known mean and variance.

EXAMPLE 15.4 *Z Test for An "Improved" Process*

At the suggestion of an employee, a modified workbench arrangement is tried. Over several days the new arrangement is tested by timing the period to produce one standard production unit. The mean of 100 samples, 47.8 seconds, is slightly less than the average time taken by the unmodified procedure, 49.1 seconds, that has a normal distribution of performance times with a standard deviation of 5 seconds. The hypothesis H_0: $47.8 = 49.1$ is tested for a one-tail critical region at $\alpha = 0.01$ with the alternate hypothesis $H_\emptyset$: $47.8 < 49.1$:

$$Z = \frac{\bar{x} - \mu}{\sigma/\sqrt{n}} = \frac{47.8 - 49.1}{5/\sqrt{100}} = \frac{-1.3}{0.5} = -2.6$$

Because the calculated Z is greater than $Z_{0.01} = -2.326$, the hypothesis is rejected; the times do differ and the new arrangement takes significantly less time than the previous standard.

The area represented by the one-tail critical region is shown by the normal distribution curve in Figure 15.2. The zero mean of the distribution corresponds to $\mu = 49.1$; the critical region below $Z = -2.326$ is represented by observed values less than $\mu - 2.326\sigma_{\bar{x}} = 49.1 - (2.326)(0.05) = 48.98$ seconds. Thus the worker who made the suggestion deserves recognition for developing a timesaving improvement.

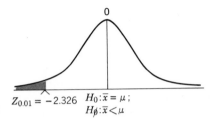

$Z_{0.01} = -2.326$ $H_0: \bar{x} = \mu$;
$H_\emptyset: \bar{x} < \mu$

Figure 15.2

Another version of the Z formula allows the comparison of two sample means. The hypothesis is that both means are equal, $H_o: \bar{x}_1 = \bar{x}_2$ (equivalently, $\bar{x}_1 - \bar{x}_2 = 0$). The normally distributed test statistic is

$$Z = \frac{\bar{x}_1 - \bar{x}_2}{\sqrt{(\sigma_1^2/n_1) + (\sigma_2^2/n_2)}}$$

where the subscripts 1 and 2 refer to two independent samples. The test compares the means of two normal distributions when both standard deviations are known. Smaller values of Z lead to an acceptance of the hypothesis that the means are equal.

EXAMPLE 15.5 Z Test of Two Sample Means

The output of two operators working on different but similar machines under the same environmental conditions reveals that operator 1 averages 8.1 minutes to produce one unit and operator 2 averages 8.9 minutes. Both averages were obtained from 25 trials. The variances of the normally distributed times for the operation of machines 1 and 2 are known to be, respectively, 3.9 and 4.0. The hypothesis is that both operators performed at the same level ($H_0: \bar{x}_1 = \bar{x}_2$; $H_\emptyset: \bar{x}_1 \neq \bar{x}_2$) and the difference between means is due to chance. Acceptance of the hypothesis rests at $\alpha = 0.05$. The critical region has two tails, each representing 0.025 of the area under the normal curve as shown in Figure 15.3.

The calculated value of Z is

$$Z = \frac{\bar{x}_1 - \bar{x}_2}{\sqrt{(\sigma_1^2/n_1) + (\sigma_2^2/n_2)}} = \frac{8.1 - 8.9}{\sqrt{(3.9/25) + (4.0/25)}}$$

$$= \frac{-0.8}{\sqrt{0.316}} = -1.43$$

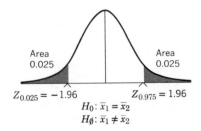

Area 0.025   Area 0.025

$Z_{0.025} = -1.96$ $Z_{0.975} = 1.96$

$H_0: \bar{x}_1 = \bar{x}_2$
$H_\emptyset: \bar{x}_1 \neq \bar{x}_2$

Figure 15.3

523

The sample means are not sufficiently different to reject the hypothesis that the workers are operating at the same level of performance.

15-5 THE t TEST

Student's t distribution is symmetrical about a vertical axis but has more area in the tails than a normal curve. As the degrees of freedom increase, the t distribution more closely resembles the normal distribution.

Each test being considered is represented by a unique distribution. For the t test, we use the symmetrical t distribution defined by the degrees of freedom, v. The test statistic is similar to the Z test with the exception that σ is replaced by s. This substitution allows a test of sample means when the standard deviation of the normally distributed population is unknown but can be estimated by the sample variance.

A sample mean is compared to a known population by the test statistic

$$t = \frac{\bar{x} - \mu}{s/\sqrt{n}}$$

For the hypothesis $H_o : \bar{x} = \mu$ and the alternate hypothesis $H_o : \bar{x} \neq \mu$ at $\alpha = 0.05$, the hypothesis is rejected for any calculated t value greater than the table value that accounts for 2.5% of the area under both ends of the distribution curve for $v = n - 1$. A hypothesis that $\bar{x} > \mu$ or $\bar{x} < \mu$ is a one-tail test, and a selection of $\alpha = 0.05$ means the critical region is the outside tail (either $+$ or $-$) at one end of the curve that accounts for 5% of the distribution.

The t test is extended to include two sample estimates from normally distributed populations where the variances are unknown but assumed equal by the test statistic

$$t = \frac{\bar{x}_1 - \bar{x}_2}{s_p\sqrt{(1/n_1) + (1/n_2)}}$$

where the pooled estimate of the standard deviation (s_p) is given by

$$s_p = \sqrt{\frac{(n_1 - 1)s_1^2 + (n_2 - 1)s_2^2}{n_1 + n_2 - 2}}$$

Because $s^2 = \Sigma(x - \bar{x})^2/(n - 1)$, the formula for s_p can be rewritten as

$$s_p = \sqrt{\frac{\Sigma(x_1 - \bar{x}_1)^2 + \Sigma(x_2 - \bar{x}_2)^2}{n_1 + n_2 - 2}}$$

The test statistic has $n_1 + n_2 - 2$ degrees of freedom and an approximate t distribution. A test of a hypothesis is conducted in the same manner as described previously, with the critical regions taken from the t distribution.

524

When there is no legitimate reason to assume equal variances for the populations from which the means are drawn, the computations become much more involved. A modification, known as the Aspin-Welch test, employs the test statistic

$$t = \frac{\bar{x}_1 - \bar{x}_2}{\sqrt{(s_1^2/n_1) + (s_2^2/n_2)}} \qquad \text{given } s^2 = \frac{\sum(x - \bar{x})^2}{n - 1}$$

where the number of degrees are calculated from

$$v = \frac{1}{\dfrac{c^2}{n_1 - 1} + \dfrac{(1 - c)^2}{n_2 - 1}} \qquad \text{given } c = \frac{s_1^2/n_1}{(s_1^2/n_1) + (s_2^2/n_2)}$$

A hypothesis is again accepted or rejected according to the value of the t distribution with v degrees of freedom at the selected confidence level.

EXAMPLE 15.6 t Test of the Difference Between Sample Means

Two makes of bandsaw blades are being considered for use in a furniture factory. Brand 1 costs more but is supposed to retain its edge longer. Blades of each type are installed and the times between filings are recorded as shown below:

Brand 1	Brand 2
23	20
26	21
23	25
29	26
25	25
$\sum = 126$	$\sum = 117$
$\bar{x}_1 = 25.2$	$\bar{x}_2 = 23.4$

It is believed that the refiling times are normally distributed and the variances are the same, although unknown. The hypothesis is $H_0: \bar{x}_1 = \bar{x}_2$ with an alternate hypothesis of $H_\emptyset: \bar{x}_1 > \bar{x}_2$. Brand 1 will be purchased if the hypothesis is rejected at $\alpha = 0.05$.

The sum-of-squares of the difference between each refiling time and the sample mean is calculated from

$$\sum(x - \bar{x})^2 = \sum x^2 - \frac{(\sum x)^2}{n}$$

to get

$$\sum(x_1 - \bar{x}_1)^2 = (23)^2 + (26)^2 + (23)^2 + (29)^2 + (25)^2 - \frac{(126)^2}{5}$$
$$= 3200 - 3175 = 25$$

and

$$\sum(x_2 - \bar{x}_2)^2 = (20)^2 + (21)^2 + (25)^2 + (26)^2 + (25)^2 - \frac{(117)^2}{5}$$

$$= 2767 - 2738 = 29$$

525

which are substituted in the s_p formula to obtain

$$s_p = \sqrt{\frac{\sum(x_1 - \bar{x}_1)^2 + \sum(x_2 - \bar{x}_2)^2}{n_1 + n_2 - 2}} = \sqrt{\frac{25 + 29}{5 + 5 - 2}} = 2.6$$

Finally, t is computed as

$$t = \frac{\bar{x}_1 - \bar{x}_2}{s_p\sqrt{(1/n_1) + (1/n_2)}} = \frac{25.2 - 23.4}{2.6\sqrt{\frac{1}{5} + \frac{1}{5}}} = \frac{1.80}{1.64} = 1.10$$

The critical region for a one-tail t test at $v = 8$ and $1 - \alpha = 0.95$ is above 1.15. Therefore, the hypothesis that the two brands do not provide significantly different refiling periods is accepted. The conclusion is to buy the less expensive brand 2.

15-6 THE F TEST In Section 15-3, we considered comparisons between sample variances and known variances. Quite often an experimenter wants to compare two variances when neither of them is known. He has two or more sets of sample data and wants to find out if they come from populations with the same standard deviation. When the populations are normally distributed and the samples are independent, the ratio of two sample variances is distributed according to the F distribution and has the test statistic

An F (after Fisher) curve for $v_1 = 9$ and $v_2 = 9$ is formed when samples of 10 are taken from two populations and the frequency of all $s_1^2\sigma_2^2/s_2^2\sigma_1^2$ ratios are recorded.

$$F = \frac{s_1^2/\sigma_1^2}{s_2^2/\sigma_2^2}$$

where s_1^2 and s_2^2 are the sample variances and σ_1^2 and σ_2^2 are the population variances from which the respective samples were taken. The hypothesis is that $\sigma_1^2 = \sigma_2^2$, and the estimates of these two parameters are represented by their unbiased (corrected for degrees of freedom, $n - 1$) estimates s_1^2 and s_2^2. Consequently, the test statistic reduces to

$$F = \frac{s_1^2}{s_2^2}$$

where the F distribution has $n_1 - 1$ and $n_2 - 1$ degrees of freedom.

The hypothesis tests follow the procedures previously described; the critical regions are akin to those depicted in Figure 15.1 with the χ^2 curve replaced by the F distribution curve. The F table values of the critical regions are indexed according to the degrees of freedom of each sample, $n_1 - 1$ and $n_2 - 1$, and the selected significance level. Because our tables provide values for one-tail tests only, the other critical region is calculated by taking the reciprocal of the appropriate value. For instance, if we select $\alpha = 0.01$ for a two-tail test with v_1 and $v_2 = 10$, the table provides $F_{v_1, v_2; \alpha/2} = F_{10,10;0.005} = 4.85$ and $F_{v_1, v_2; 1-(\alpha/2)}$ $= F_{10,10;0.995} = 1/4.85 = 0.201$. An equivalent procedure is to designate the larger variance as $s_1{}^2$ to make the $s_1{}^2/s_2{}^2$ ratio always unity or greater; then the two-tail test is always at the $F_{\alpha/2}$ end of the curve where values are available. Thus, a hypothesis that two variances are the same is supported only if the ratio of $s_1{}^2$ to $s_2{}^2$ is small.

EXAMPLE 15.7 Single and Pooled Comparisons of Sample Variances

Three companies (I, II, and III) can supply wire that supposedly meet the requirements for an electronic component. Samples of each type of wire have been subjected to tests; the means of their resistances have all met the specifications. However, the sample variances of $s_I^2 = 0.0038$, $s_{II}^2 = 0.0063$, and $s_{III}^2 = 0.0147$ differ considerably; this characteristic is important because less variation enhances reliability. The s^2 calculations were made from 25 tests of each type of wire. It appears reasonable to assume that the test results are normally distributed.

The hypothesis is that the variances are equal, and the alternate hypothesis is that they are unequal. Using the largest variance as s_1^2 in each pairwise comparison, the first ratio is formed by the variance of the sample from company II over the variance representing wire from company I:

$$F_{(II-I)} = \frac{s_{II}^2}{s_I^2} = \frac{0.0063}{0.0038} = 1.66$$

Then the other ratios are established similarly as

$$F_{(III-I)} = \frac{s_{III}^2}{s_I^2} = \frac{0.0147}{0.0038} = 3.87 \qquad F_{(III-II)} = \frac{0.0147}{0.0063} = 2.33$$

From the table at $v_1 = v_2 = 24$ and $\alpha = 0.05$, the critical region for $F_{24, 24;0.05} = 2.02$. Thus the difference between the variances of samples from companies I and II are not significant, but the variance of the sample from company III is decidedly different.

A further test can be made by pooling the variances from two samples that do not show a significant difference to obtain a new variance estimate $(s_p{}^2)$ for testing a third variance. As applied to the wire samples,

$$s_p^2 = \frac{(n_1 - 1)s_1^2 + (n_2 - 1)s_2^2}{n_1 + n_2 + 1} \qquad \text{with} \qquad v = n_1 + n_2 - 1$$

$$= \frac{(25 - 1)s_1^2 + (25 - 1)s_{II}^2}{25 + 25 - 1} = \frac{(24)(0.0038) + (24)(0.0063)}{49}$$

$$= 0.0049$$

Then the third variance, s_{III}^2, is tested as

$$F = \frac{s_{III}^2}{s_p^2} = \frac{0.0147}{0.0049} = 3.00$$

which confirms the previous indication because the calculated F value is greater than $F_{24, 49;0.05} = 1.90$ (determined by linear interpolation of table values). Therefore, the hypothesis is accepted that $s_I^2 = s_{II}^2$, and the hypotheses that $s_I^2 = s_{III}^2$ and $s_{II}^2 = s_{III}^2$ are rejected. The conclusion is that the wire supplied by either company I or II is preferable to the wire from company III.

527

15-7 ANALYSIS OF VARIANCE

The statistical technique called analysis of variance is one of the most powerful tools available for industrial experimentation. It can be used to reveal: (1) whether several means of one classification differ significantly, (2) the relationship between a variable and two or more classifications, and (3) the presence of interaction between classifications. We shall consider only a few of the potential applications of analysis of variance. In doing so it is important to recognize the types of problems that can be treated and the pertinent assumptions underlying the treatments. A wise choice of an experimental design increases the amount of inferences obtainable from a given amount of data.

One-Way Classification

Previously considered methods for testing hypotheses about sample means were limited to pairwise comparisons. In many situations it is desirable to draw inferences about several means. When the means are from samples that fit one classification, such as several ways to do a certain task or different types of material that fulfill the same purpose, the comparison is based on a "null hypothesis" that there is no difference in the means of the populations represented by the samples; $H_0: \bar{x}_1 = \bar{x}_2 = \cdots = \bar{x}_c$. The alternate hypothesis is that the means are unequal. The hypotheses are tested under the assumptions that : (1) the samples are drawn randomly, (2) the c populations are normally distributed, and (3) the c population variances are equal: $\sigma_1{}^2 = \sigma_2{}^2 = \cdots = \sigma_c{}^2$. The sensitivity of the hypothesis test to the latter two assumptions is not as great when the sample sizes are equal or nearly so.

Data for a one-way analysis of variance is arranged as shown in Table 15.5. There are c samples of n_i observations. The mean of each sample is determined by dividing the column totals by the number of observations in each column. The grand mean, $\bar{x}$, is the average of all means from c samples.

The variance of the entries in the table can be accounted for in three ways. The first is an estimate of *total variance* $s_T{}^2$, assuming all entries represent one population:

$$s_T{}^2 = \frac{\sum (x_{ij} - \bar{x})^2}{N - 1}$$

where:

$x_{ij} =$ each i value of x in column j
$\bar{x} =$ grand mean of x_{ij}
$N =$ total number of x observations

Table 15.5 Format for one-way analysis of variance

	Classification 1			
	1	2	j	c
	x_{11}	x_{12}	$\cdots$	x_{1c}
	x_{21}	x_{22}	$\cdots$	x_{2c}
	.	.	.	.
	.	.	$\cdots$	.
	.	.	.	.
	x_{n_i1}	x_{n_i2}	$\cdots$	x_{n_ic}
Totals	T_1	T_2	$\cdots$	T_c	T
Means	$\bar{x}_1$	$\bar{x}_2$	$\cdots$	$\bar{x}_c$	$\bar{\bar{x}}$

The second is the *column variance*, s_c^2, based on the assumption that the population of each column is the same:

If the sample sizes are unequal, then

$$s_c^2 = \frac{\sum_1^c \sum_1^n (\bar{x}_j - \bar{\bar{x}})^2}{c - 1}$$

$$s_c^2 = \frac{\sum n_i(\bar{x}_j - \bar{\bar{x}})^2}{c - 1}$$

where:

n_i = number of observations in each column
$\bar{x}_j$ = mean of each column
c = number of columns

And the third is the *residual variance*, s_R^2, in which the estimate of the population variance has been modified to eliminate any difference that exists between columns:

$$s_R^2 = \frac{\sum(x_{ij} - \bar{x}_j)^2}{N - c}$$

A ratio of the column variance to the residual variance, s_c^2/s_R^2, has an F distribution with $c - 1$ and $N - c$ degrees of freedom:

$$F_{c-1,N-c} = \frac{\sum n_i(\bar{x}_j - \bar{\bar{x}})^2/(c - 1)}{\sum(x_{ij} - \bar{x}_j)^2/(N - c)}$$

The F test has a one-tail critical region because the hypothesis that the means of each column are equal will be rejected only if the column variance is large in respect to the differences within the columns, s_R^2. The calculated value of F is thus compared to a

529

percentage of the F distribution defined by the degrees of freedom and a selected α; when the calculated value is larger, the null hypothesis is rejected and we conclude the sample means represent different populations.

EXAMPLE 15.8 Comparison of Means in a One-Way Classification

The Scientific Toy Company has developed a make-it-yourself robot kit. An understandable set of directions is vital because the kit contains many detailed assemblies. Three types of directions have been developed:

> Type 1   Coded instructions
> Type 2   Line drawings with explanations
> Type 3   Photographs with explanations

Each type was tested by timing the duration required to assemble a robot. The assembly time in hours using each type of instruction is shown below:

Type 1	Type 2	Type 3
4.8	5.0	5.7
4.4	4.2	4.8
5.1	4.6	5.1
4.5	3.8	4.4
$\bar{x}_1 = 4.7$	$\bar{x}_2 = 4.4$	$\bar{x}_3 = 5.0$

Recognizing that $c = 3$, $N = 12$, $n_i = 4$, and $\bar{x} = (4.7 + 4.4 + 5.0)/3 = 4.7$, the value of F is calculated as

$$F_{(3-1),(12-3)} = \frac{\sum 4(\bar{x}_j - 4.7)^2/(3-1)}{\sum (x_{ij} - \bar{x}_j)^2/(12-3)}$$

$$F_{2,9} = \frac{\frac{4}{2}[(4.7-4.7)^2 + (4.4-4.7)^2 + (5.0-4.7)^2]}{\frac{1}{9}[(4.8-4.7)^2 + (4.4-4.7)^2 + (5.1-4.7)^2 + \cdots + (4.4-5.0)^2]}$$

$$= \frac{2(0.18)}{\frac{1}{9}(2.00)} = \frac{0.36}{0.222} = 1.62$$

Based on $\alpha = 0.05$ and the F distribution defined by 2 and 9 degrees of freedom, the critical region is above $F_{2,9;0.95} = 4.26$; the null hypothesis is thereby accepted. It is concluded that the calculated value of F could have arisen from chance causes and there is no significant difference in assembly time due to the type of directions followed.

A useful identity is present in the numerators of the variance equations s_T^2, s_c^2, and s_R^2. These variance estimates are obtained from the sum-of-squares (SS) that have the relationship

$$\begin{matrix} \text{total} & & \text{column} & & \text{residual} \\ \text{sum-of-squares} & = & \text{sum-of-squares} & + & \text{sum-of-squares} \end{matrix}$$

$$\sum (x_{ij} - \bar{\bar{x}})^2 = \sum n_i(\bar{x}_j - \bar{\bar{x}})^2 + \sum (x_{ij} - \bar{x}_j)^2$$

which is abbreviated as $SS_T = SS_c + SS_R$.

The sum-of-squares identity can be demonstrated by adding and subtracting a constant $\bar{x}_j$ to the terms in SS_T to provide

$$\sum(x_{ij} - \bar{\bar{x}})^2 = \sum(x_{ij} - \bar{x}_j + \bar{x}_j - \bar{\bar{x}})^2 = \sum[(x_{ij} - \bar{x}_j) + (\bar{x}_j - \bar{\bar{x}})]^2$$

where each difference is squared to obtain

$$\sum(x_{ij} - \bar{x}_j)^2 + \sum(\bar{x}_j - \bar{\bar{x}})^2 + 2\sum(x_{ij} - \bar{x}_j)(\bar{x}_j - \bar{\bar{x}})$$

which is reduced to the original identity as

$$\sum(x_{ij} - \bar{\bar{x}})^2 = \sum n_i(\bar{x}_j - \bar{\bar{x}})^2 + \sum(x_{ij} - \bar{x}_j)^2 + 0$$

because $\Sigma(x_{ij} - \bar{x}_j) = 0$ and $(\bar{x}_j - x)^2$ taken over N items is the same as $n_i(\bar{x}_j - \bar{\bar{x}})^2$ taken over c columns when the sample sizes are equal, making $(n_i)(c) = N$.

When a sum-of-squares is divided by the degrees of freedom associated with its components, it is called a *mean square, MS*. From the formulas for the estimated variances, we know the degrees of freedom for each SS to establish the mean squares as:

$$\text{total mean square} = MS_T = \frac{SS_T}{N-1}$$

$$\text{column mean square} = MS_c = \frac{SS_c}{c-1}$$

$$\text{residual mean square} = MS_R = \frac{SS_R}{N-c}$$

Utilizing the agreement between estimated variances and mean squares results in a more convenient computational technique and a consolidated format for summarizing output. The shortcut procedure is conducted according to the following steps:

1. Square the column totals (T_j), add them $(T_1^2 + \ldots + T_c^2)$, and divide by n_i: $\Sigma(T_j)^2/n_i$.
2. Square each observation and sum them: $\Sigma(x_{ij})^2$
3. Square the sum of all the observations (T) and divide by c: T^2/c. This factor corrects the output of step 1 for any deviation of the grand mean $\bar{\bar{x}}$ from zero.
4. Calculate the column sum-of-squares:

$$SS_c = (1) - (3) = \frac{\Sigma(T_j^2)}{n_i} - \frac{T^2}{c}$$

Calculate the residual sum-of-squares:

$$SS_R = (2) - (1) = \Sigma(x_{ij})^2 - \frac{\Sigma(T_j^2)}{n_i}$$

531

Calculate the total sum-of-squares:

$$SS_T = (2) - (3) = \sum(x_{ij})^2 - \frac{T^2}{c} = SS_c + SS_R$$

The sums-of-squares are then entered in an analysis of variance table as shown in Table 15.6, they are divided by the appropriate degrees of freedom to develop the mean squares which are utilized to calculate an F value for testing the null hypothesis.

Table 15.6 One-way analysis of variance table

Source of Variation	SS	v	MS	F
Columns	SS_c	$c - 1$	MS_c	MS_c/MS_R
Residual	SS_R	$N - c$	MS_R	
Total	SS_T	$N - 1$	MS_T	

EXAMPLE 15.9   Shortcut Computations for One-Way Analysis of Variance

The calculation procedures based on sums-of-squares are illustrated by application to the assembly times from Example 15.8. Computational effort is often reduced by "coding" data. The purpose of coding is to eliminate integers that are repeated in every calculation by subtracting a convenient number such as a mean from each observation. The coded assembly times for the three types are given below:

Type 1	Type 2	Type 2
1	3	10
-3	-5	1
4	-1	4
-2	-9	-3
$T_1 = 0$	$T_2 = -12$	$T_3 = 12$

They result from subtracting the grand mean (4.7) from all the observations and raising each difference by a power of 10. (Since $\bar{x}$ for raw data is not known in advance of the coding, any convenient number is adequate for the reference code.)

After coding is accomplished, the steps in the shortcut procedure are conducted as:

1. $\sum(T_j)^2/n_j = [0 + (-12)^2 + (12)^2]/4 = 228/4 = 72$

2. $\sum(x_{ij})^2 = (1)^2 + (-3)^2 + (4)^2 + (-2)^2 + (3)^2 + \cdots + (-3)^2 = 272$

3. $T^2/c = [0 + (-12) + 12]^2/4 = 0$

4. $SS_c = (1) - (3) = 72 - 0 = 72$

   $SS_R = (2) - (1) = 272 - 72 = 200$

   $SS_T = (2) - (3) = 272 - 0 = 272$

The calculated sums-of-squares are entered in the analysis of variance table where subsequent computations reveal the same value for the F test statistic as developed in Example 15.8.

Source of Variation	SS	v	MS	F
Type of instruction (column)	72	2	36	36/22.2 = 1.62
Experimental error (residual)	200	9	22.2	
Total	272	11		

Two-Way Classification

A comparison becomes more sensitive by decreasing the experimental error; that is, the chance of committing a Type I error is decreased by reducing the residual mean square. This goal can be accomplished by carefully controlling extraneous factors which could influence the process performances. Occasionally it is impossible to lavish the desired care because of physical limitations, and always there is the need to maintain an economic balance between the cost of control and the benefits derived from extra expenditures.

Residual error can also be reduced by the experiment design. If we can recognize two factors that might account for the variation of the observations, a two-way classification is feasible. The greater sensitivity of a two-way design results from the estimate of the total variance being divided into three parts: variances due to one classification (columns), variances due to the other classification (rows), and variances due to experimental error (residual).

Observations in a two-way analysis of variance are grouped as shown in Table 15.7. There are c columns and r rows with at

Table 15.7 $r \times c$ classification table

Classification 2	Classification 1				
	1	2 $\quad j$		c	Totals
1	x_{11}	x_{12}	$\cdots$	x_{1c}	$T_{i=1}$
2	x_{21}	x_{22}	$\cdots$	x_{2c}	$T_{i=2}$
i	$\cdots$	$\cdots$	$\cdots$	$\cdots$	T_i
r	x_{r1}	x_{r2}	$\cdots$	x_{rc}	$T_{i=r}$
Totals	$T_{j=1}$	$T_{j=2}$	T_j	$T_{j=c}$	T

533

Sum-of-squares for conditions where there are more than one observation per cell are given in the next section.

least one observation in each ij cell. The total number of observations is N, and $N = (r)(c)$ when there is only one entry in each cell. The sums of all observations in each row and column are, respectively, T_i and T_j.

The significance of including the additional classification is apparent from the new sum-of-squares identity:

$$\begin{array}{cccc} \text{total} & \text{column} & \text{row} & \text{residual} \\ \text{sum-of-squares} = & \text{sum-of-squares} + & \text{sum-of-squares} + & \text{sum-of-squares} \\ \sum(x_{ij} - \bar{\bar{x}})^2 = & \sum c(\bar{x}_j - \bar{\bar{x}})^2 + & \sum r(\bar{x}_i - \bar{\bar{x}})^2 + & \sum(x_{ij} - \bar{x}_i - \bar{x}_j + \bar{\bar{x}})^2 \end{array}$$

The column sum-of-squares (SS_c) is the same as described for the one-way classification. The row sum-of-squares (SS_r) is similar in appearance and function to SS_c but it accounts for the difference between the row means and the grand mean. The residual sum-of-squares (SS_R) is developed from the deviation of each observation from the grand mean corrected for row and column variations as

$$x_{ij} - [\bar{\bar{x}} + (\bar{x}_i - \bar{\bar{x}}) + (\bar{x}_j - \bar{\bar{x}})] = x_{ij} - (\bar{x}_i + \bar{x}_j - \bar{\bar{x}})$$
$$= x_{ij} - \bar{x}_i - \bar{x}_j + \bar{\bar{x}}$$

The sum-of-squares values are converted to mean square values by dividing each by its associated degrees of freedom:

$$\text{column mean square} = MS_c = \frac{SS_c}{c - 1}$$

Degrees of freedom for MS_R are derived from the total number of observations minus the sum of rows and columns. Then one is added to show that the means of the rows and columns are the same value, $\bar{\bar{x}}$. Thus, $rc - r - c + 1$ establishes ν.

$$\text{row mean square} = MS_r = \frac{SS_r}{r - 1}$$

$$\text{residual mean square} = \frac{MS_R}{(c - 1)(r - 1)}$$

The mean squares are used to test the hypothesis that the variances due to classifications 1 and 2 and the experimental error are all estimates of the same population variance. Specifically, MS_c/MS_R and MS_r/MS_R have an F distribution with, respectively, $c - 1$, $(c - 1)(r - 1)$ and $r - 1$, $(c - 1)(r - 1)$ degrees of freedom. A calculated F value greater than an F distribution percentage at the designated significance level leads to a rejection of the hypothesis that the means of a classification are equal.

The computational technique to obtain the sums-of-squares for a two-way analysis of variance table has the following steps:

1. Square the row totals (T_i), sum them ($T_1^2 + \ldots + T_r^2$), and divide by the number of observations in each row, n_j: $\Sigma(T_i)^2/n_j$.
2. $\Sigma(T_j)^2/n_i$

534

3. $\Sigma(x_{ij})^2$
4. Sum all the observations ($\Sigma x_{ij} = T$), square (T^2), and divide by the number of observations (N): T^2/N. Again this is the "correction factor."
5. $SS_r = (1) - (4) = \Sigma(T_i)^2/n_j - T^2/N$
$SS_c = (2) - (4) = \Sigma(T_j)^2/n_i - T^2/N$
$SS_T = (3) - (4) = \Sigma(x_{ij})^2 - T^2/N$
$SS_R = SS_T - SS_r - SS_c$
$\quad = \Sigma(x_{ij})^2 - \Sigma(T_i)^2/n_j - \Sigma(T_j)^2/n_i - T^2/N$

EXAMPLE 15.10 Comparison of Means in a Two-Way Classification

The robot assembly times from Example 15.8 are cross-classified by the operators that performed each assembly. For the sake of simplicity, it is assumed that the learning effect is minimized by randomizing the types of directions and by applying them to different models. The following table shows the times coded with respect to the grand mean,

Assemblers	Instructions			Totals
	1	2	3	
1	1	3	10	14
2	-3	-5	1	-7
3	4	-1	4	7
4	-2	-9	-3	-14
Totals	0	-12	12	0

Following the shortcut procedure steps, the sums-of-squares are calculated as:

1. $\dfrac{\Sigma(T_i)^2}{n_j} = \dfrac{(14)^2 + (-7)^2 + (7)^2 + (-14)^2}{3} = \dfrac{490}{3} = 163$

2. $\dfrac{\Sigma(T_j)^2}{n_i} = \dfrac{0 + (-12)^2 + (12)^2}{4} = \dfrac{288}{4} = 72$

3. $\Sigma(x_{ij})^2 = (1)^2 + (-3)^2 + (4)^2 + \cdots + (-3)^2 = 272$

4. $\dfrac{(\Sigma x_{ij})^2}{N} = \dfrac{(1 - 3 + 4 - 2 + 3 - 5 - 1 - 9 + 10 + 1 + 4 - 3)^2}{12} = \dfrac{0}{12} = \dfrac{T^2}{N} = 0$

5. $SS_r = (1) - (4) = 163 - 0 = 163$

$SS_c = (2) - (4) = 72 - 0 = 72$

$SS_T = (3) - (4) = 272 - 0 = 272$

$SS_R = SS_T - SS_r - SS_c = 272 - 163 - 72 = 37$

With the sum-of-squares values and corresponding degrees of freedom entered in a two-way analysis of variance table, the mean squares and variance ratios are calculated. The last column in the table is the critical region determined from the appropriate degrees of freedom and a significance level of 0.05:

Source of Variation	SS	v	MS	F	Critical Region
Instructions	72	2	36	$36/6.2 = 5.907$	$F_{2,6;.95} = 5.143$
Assemblers	163	3	54.3	$54.3/6.2 = 8.788$	$F_{3,6;.95} = 4.757$
Experimental	37	6	6.2		
Totals	272	11			

Results of the F tests indicate that both null hypotheses for instructions and assemblers should be rejected. The type of instructions and the individual characteristics of the assemblers *do* affect the assembly times. However, it cannot be stated from the analysis of variance what type of instruction or what assembler characteristic leads to the most proficient assembly time; the analysis indicates only that the times differ significantly with respect to these factors.

Two-Way Classification and Interaction

Another way to reduce residual error is to identify the presence, if any, of interaction between the two classifications. A measurement of interaction attempts to define the concerted effect of class combinations on the variable. To make the interaction measurement, there must be more than one observation in each ij cell. Then the differences between the observations in each cell and the expected value for the cell are calculated to determine the variance. A large variance indicates that there is an interaction between the two classifications; for instance, in an experiment involving men and machines, the presence of interaction means that certain men work better on particular machines than on others.

The format for data is similar to that displayed in Table 15.7, except that there is an equal number of observations, k, in each cell. The row or column total is then the sum of kc or kr observations. The total sum-of-squares is partitioned into SS_r, SS_c, SS_R, and the interaction sum of squares, SS_{rc}, as shown in Table 15.8. The new term in the table is $\bar{x}_{ij}$ which indicates the average value of all k observations for each combination of classifications; it is the expected value of the combination if no interaction exists.

The computation technique for including interaction has the following procedural steps:

1. $\Sigma(T_{ik})^2/n_{jk}$
2. $\Sigma(T_{jk})^2/n_{ik}$
3. $\Sigma(x_{ijk})^2$
4. $(\Sigma x_{ijk})^2/N$
5. Sum the observations for each combination $(\overset{k}{\Sigma}x_{ij})$, square $(\overset{k}{\Sigma}x_{ij})^2$, add the squares $\overset{rc}{\Sigma}(\overset{k}{\Sigma}x_{ij})^2$, and divide by the number of observations in each cell (k): $\overset{rc}{\Sigma}(\overset{k}{\Sigma}x_{ij})^2/k$.
6. $SS_r = (1) - (4)$
   $SS_c = (2) - (4)$

536

Table 15.8 Sums-of-squares for a two-way classification with k observations in each ij combination

Source	Sum of Squares	SS	Degrees of Freedom
Column	$\sum^{r} ck(\bar{x}_j - \bar{\bar{x}})^2$	SS_c	$c - 1$
Row	$\sum^{c} rk(\bar{x}_i - \bar{\bar{x}})^2$	SS_r	$r - 1$
Interaction	$\sum^{rc} (\bar{x}_{ij} - \bar{x}_i - \bar{x}_j + \bar{\bar{x}})^2$	SS_{rc}	$(r - 1)(c - 1)$
Residual	$\sum^{rck} (x_{ijk} - \bar{x}_{ij})^2$	SS_R	$rc(k - 1)$
Totals	$\sum^{rck} (x_{ijk} - \bar{\bar{x}})^2$	SS_T	$rck - 1$

where

n = number of k observations per ij cell
$\bar{x}_{ij}$ = mean of the observations in each cell
$\bar{x}_j$ = mean of each column of ki observations
$\bar{x}_i$ = mean of each row of kj observations
$\bar{\bar{x}}$ = mean of all x_{ijk} observations

$$SS_{rc} = (5) - (4) - (SS_r + SS_c)$$
$$SS_R = (3) - (5)$$
$$SS_T = (3) - (4)$$

A random-effect model assumes the classes are random representations from one population. The F tests are then different for models of this type and for mixed random and fixed models.

The sums-of-squares are converted to mean squares in an analysis of variance table by dividing each SS by its associated degrees of freedom noted in Table 15.8.

We shall assume that the classifications represent *fixed effects*; the classes or levels of each classification are the only ones of interest. The initial step in a hypothesis test is to check for interaction by calculating

$$F_{(r-1)(c-1),\, rc(k-1)} = \frac{SS_{rc}/(r-1)(c-1)}{SS_R/rc(k-1)} = \frac{MS_{rc}}{MS_R}$$

If the test for interaction is not significant, then SS_{rc} could be pooled with SS_R for F tests of the other hypotheses. The effect would then be the same as not checking for interaction by just calculating SS_r and SS_c based on the k observations in each cell and determining SS_R by the difference between SS_T and $SS_r + SS_c$. The F test is usually more sensitive without pooling SS_{rc} and SS_R.

Care must be given to the conclusions drawn from the classification tests when interaction is significant, because a difference between class means could be a result of a particular bias of one

537

combination on the cross-classification. An interpretation of the physical reasons causing the interaction helps the formulation of logical conclusions.

EXAMPLE 15.11 A Test for Interaction

In an effort to learn more about the directions developed by the Scientific Toy Company, the same assemblers repeated the robot construction three times using each type of instructions. They worked with different robot models in random combination with types of directions. They did not know which of their performances were being timed. The results of the trials are given below.

Classification 2	Type 1	Type 2	Type 3
	Classification 1 — Directions		
Assembler 1	4.8	5.0	5.7
	5.0	4.2	4.6
	4.7	5.0	4.6
Assembler 2	4.4	4.2	4.8
	5.2	3.9	4.8
	4.2	3.8	5.0
Assembler 3	5.1	4.6	5.1
	5.6	4.0	5.0
	5.9	4.2	4.6
Assembler 4	4.5	3.8	4.4
	3.7	3.9	4.0
	4.0	4.0	3.8

The first step in the analysis is to code the data. A base of 4.7 is again used (the base is no longer the grand mean but just an arbitrary point) with the differences multiplied by 10. The row and column totals are determined and the sum of the three observations is noted in each ij cell. See Table 15.9. From this information the computation steps for the sums-of-squares are conducted as:

(1)
$$\frac{\sum(T_{ik})^2}{n_{jk}} = \frac{(13)^2 + (-20)^2 + (18)^2 + (-62)^2}{9}$$

$$= \frac{4737}{9} = 526.33$$

(2)
$$\frac{\sum(T_{jk})^2}{n_{ik}} = \frac{(7)^2 + (-58)^2 + 0}{12} = \frac{3413}{12}$$

$$= 284.42$$

(3) $\quad \sum(x_{ijk})^2 = (1)^2 + (3)^2 + (0)^2 + (5)^2 + \cdots + (-3)^2 + (-7)^2 + (-9)^2 = 1223$

(4) $\quad \dfrac{(\sum x_{ijk})^2}{N} = \dfrac{(-51)^2}{36} = 72.25$

(5)
$$\frac{\sum(\sum x_{ij})^2}{k} = \frac{\begin{matrix}[(4)^2 + (-3)^2 + (25)^2 + (-19)^2 + (1)^2 + (-22)^2 \\ + (-13)^2 + (-24)^2 + (8)^2 + (5)^2 + (6)^2 + (-19)^2]\end{matrix}}{3} = \frac{2727}{3} = 909$$

Table 15.9

	Type 1		Type 2		Type 3		Total
Assembler 1	1 3 0	4	3 −5 3	1	10 −1 −1	8	13
Assembler 2	−3 5 −5	−3	−5 −8 −9	−22	1 1 3	5	−20
Assembler 3	4 9 12	25	−1 −7 −5	−13	4 3 −1	6	18
Assembler 4	−2 −10 −7	−19	−9 −8 −7	−24	−3 −7 −9	−19	−62
Total		7		−58		0	−51

(6)

$$SS_r = (1) - (4) = 526.33 - 72.25 = 454.08$$

$$SS_c = (2) - (4) = 284.42 - 72.25 = 212.17$$

$$SS_{rc} = (5) - (4) - (SS_r + SS_c) = 909 - 72.25 - (454.08 + 212.17)$$
$$= 909 - 738.50 = 170.50$$

$$SS_R = (3) - (5) = 1223 - 909 = 314$$

$$SS_T = (3) - (4) = 1223 - 72.25 = 1150.75$$

The null hypotheses of interest concern the differences between types of directions and the presence of interaction. It is hoped that the additional data will reveal whether the performance of a particular assembler has masked the difference in performance times that should be attributed to the type of instruction utilized. A significance level of 0.01 is considered reasonable for the test.

Then the analysis of variance table is developed as:

Source of Variation	SS	v	MS	F	Critical Region
Assemblers	454.58	3	151.36	11.57	$F_{3,24,.99} = 4.72$
Instructions	212.17	2	106.08	8.11	$F_{2,24,.99} = 5.61$
Interaction	170.50	6	28.42	2.17	$F_{6,24,.99} = 3.67$
Experimental	314.00	24	13.08		
Totals	1150.75	35			

From the ratios of MS_r, MS_c, and MS_{rc} to MS_R, it appears that the null hypothesis for interaction can be accepted and the null hypotheses that the type of instructions and assemblies

539

do not affect assembly time are rejected. The rejection of the null hypothesis about the column means indicates only that they are significantly different; it does not specify which type of instruction is best. It indicates to the toy company that the type of directions included with the robot model kits does influence the assembly time. Further effort should reveal the amount and perhaps the reasons for the difference.

Extensions and Precautions

An analysis of variance is probably the most useful technique available to industrial experimenters. It is applicable to a wide variety of experiments and provides unique inferences. It is also open to misinterpretation. Any technique can be abused, but few possess so many facets to lead practitioners astray. The tests we have considered represent only a few potential applications of the method, yet even these hold plenty of pitfalls for the unwary.

Fixed, mixed, and random models. The manner in which classifications are set at the beginning of an experiment affect the conclusions made at the end. When classes are distinct groupings that represent characteristics of special interest, they are called *fixed effects*. Conclusions drawn from a test of fixed effects apply only to those effects, not to the general population from which the classes were partitioned. If the classes are casual or random representations of a total population, test results could be extended to the entire range of classes in the population. Such divisions are labeled *random effects*. A *mixed-effect* model includes fixed effects for one classification and random effects for another classification.

In a fixed model, a repeat experiment requires the use of the same four companies. A repeat of a random model experiment might include completely different companies.

As an example of the different models, samples of a product could be taken from four specific companies or from any four companies that produce the product; the former case is a fixed-effect model and the latter case is a random model. Accepting the hypothesis of equal means in both cases leads to a conclusion that product quality from the four specific companies (fixed effect) does not differ significantly or, in the random-effect case, that all companies producing the product provide comparable quality.

Besides the difference in interpretation between the model types, there is also a difference in the variance ratios used for the F tests. Fixed models have S_R^2 in the denominator for the F test of each component of variance, but the other models are not so consistent. Therefore, when mixed and random effects are encountered, special attention should be given to the appropriate ratio of variances for each component.

Pooled variances. We have noted that variances with no significant

The effect of pooling is
apparent in the comparison of
$S_R{}^2$ from Examples 15.8 and
15.10.

● differences can be pooled to obtain better estimates of the residual variance. Pooling works well when the combined variances are indeed nonsignificant, but a bias is introduced whenever a Type II error is committed. To pool or not to pool is a question the experimenter has to decide on the merits of each case. Sometimes a pooled variance is more efficient in detecting differences. If the gain from pooling is not worth the risk of introducing bias, the safer and always statistically correct course is not to pool.

Conclusions. It is tempting to review data after rejecting a null hypothesis to select the class of observations that caused the rejection. An extremely large total in a column or row is usually a valid indicator of at least part of the cause, but a truly confident conclusion must rely on a test of contrasts such as the method suggested by Scheffe (see reference at end of this chapter). Such information is a bonus for an analysis of variance because no additional assumptions are necessary and few additional calculations are required.

Rejection of the interaction null hypothesis poses special problems. Further hypothesis tests of two-way classifications are meaningless when interaction is present, because significant differences could be veiled or falsely magnified by a preferential reaction of a single cross-classification. Thus a significant interaction relegates the tests of row or column differences to a one-way analysis of variance. For instance, in an experiment where the output of several machines was originally recorded for several operators and interaction was subsequently indicated, further tests of the machine outputs could be made by separate one-way analysis of variance of the machine classes for the output of each operator.

The similarity between analysis
of variance and control charts
is apparent when compared
with material in Chapter 11.

Variations and extensions. Many techniques have been worked out for the analysis of variance of specially designed experiments.
● Most designs are variations or extensions of the fundamental approaches described in the preceding pages: two-way classifications extended to three-way classifications or the variation of "nested" categories repeated in each classification level. Because these designs can develop better insights from given data, they should be investigated when complex testing plans are being developed.

Perhaps the most important concept is simply to recognize that many statistical tools are available for hypothesis testing and their proper application supports confidence in the measurement of process control.

541

15-8 SUMMARY A statistical experiment to determine the condition of a process begins with a statement of the hypothesis (H_0) and the alternate hypothesis (H_ϕ). A level of significance (α) is selected to control the chance of making a Type I error, the rejection of a true hypothesis. A Type II error, accepting a false hypothesis, is limited by increasing the sample size and by the test design.

The χ^2, normal, t, and F distributions are employed for different statistical tests. Hypotheses, associated test statistics, and critical regions are summarized in Table 15.10.

The analysis of variance technique is one of the most powerful statistical tools available to the industrial experimenter, but it must be used carefully to avoid incorrect conclusions. The model should be categorized as fixed, random, or mixed to determine the variance ratios and extent of conclusions. When interaction is present, conclusions about row and column differences should be tested at each level of one classification. A review of established experimental designs should be made before an extensive analysis is initiated in order to obtain as much information as possible from the data.

Table 15.10 Summary of hypothesis-testing procedures

Hypothesis	Alternate Hypothesis	Statistic	Terms	Critical Region
H_0: Observed = theoretical frequencies	H_ϕ: Frequencies are not equal	$\chi^2 = \dfrac{\sum\limits^{k}(F_i - f_i)^2}{f_i}$	F_i = empirical frequency f_i = theoretical frequency k = classes of frequencies	$> \chi^2_{k-1;1-\alpha}$
H_0: Two characteristics are independent	H_ϕ: Two characteristics are dependent	$\chi^2 = \dfrac{\sum\limits^{r}\sum\limits^{c}(0_{ij} - E_{ij})^2}{E_{ij}}$	0_{ij} = observations E_{ij} = expectation r = rows c = columns $v = (r-1)(c-1)$	$> \chi^2_{v;1-\alpha}$
H_0: $\sigma^2 = \sigma_0^2$ (for σ_0 known)	H_ϕ: $\sigma^2 < \sigma_0^2$ H_ϕ: $\sigma^2 \neq \sigma_0^2$ H_ϕ: $\sigma^2 > \sigma_0^2$	$\chi^2 = \dfrac{(n-1)s^2}{\sigma_0^2}$	σ_0 = known population variance s^2 = estimated population variance n = sample size	$< \chi^2_{n-1;\alpha/2}$ $\begin{cases}< \chi^2_{n-1;\alpha}\\ \text{or}\\ > \chi^2_{n-1;1-(\alpha/2)}\end{cases}$ $> \chi^2_{n-1;1-\alpha}$
H_0: $\bar{x} = \mu$ (for μ and σ known)	H_ϕ: $\bar{x} < \mu$ H_ϕ: $\bar{x} \neq \mu$ H_ϕ: $\bar{x} > \mu$	$Z = \dfrac{\bar{x} - \mu}{\sigma/\sqrt{n}}$	$\bar{x}$ = sample mean $\sigma/\sqrt{n}$ = sample standard deviation n = sample size	$< Z_\alpha$ $\begin{cases}< Z_{\alpha/2}\\ \text{or}\\ > Z_{1-(\alpha/2)}\end{cases}$ $> Z_{1-\alpha}$

Table 15.10 (Continued)

Hypothesis	Alternate Hypothesis	Statistic	Terms	Critical Region
$H_0: \bar{x}_1 = \bar{x}_2$ (for σ known)	$H_\phi: \bar{x}_1 < \bar{x}_2$ $H_\phi: \bar{x}_1 \neq \bar{x}_2$ $H_\phi: \bar{x}_1 > \bar{x}_2$	$Z = \dfrac{\bar{x}_1 - \bar{x}_2}{\sqrt{(\sigma_1^2/n_1) + (\sigma_2^2/n_2)}}$	Subscripts refer to samples 1 and 2	Same as above
$H_0: \bar{x} = \mu$ (for μ known)	$H_\phi: \bar{x} < \mu$ $H_\phi: \bar{x} \neq \mu$ $H_\phi: \bar{x} > \mu$	$t = \dfrac{\bar{x} - \mu}{s/\sqrt{n}}$	$v = $ degrees of freedom $v = n - 1$	$< t_{v;\alpha}$ $\begin{cases} < t_{v;\alpha/2} \\ \text{or} \\ > t_{v;1-(\alpha/2)} \end{cases}$ $> t_{v;1-\alpha}$
$H_0: \bar{x}_1 = \bar{x}_2$ (variances assumed equal)	$H_\phi: \bar{x}_1 < \bar{x}_2$ $H_\phi: \bar{x}_1 \neq \bar{x}_2$ $H_\phi: \bar{x}_1 > \bar{x}_2$	$t = \dfrac{\bar{x}_1 - \bar{x}_2}{s_p\sqrt{(1/n_1) + (1/n_2)}}$	$s_p = \sqrt{\dfrac{(n_1 - 1)s_1^2 + (n_2 - 1)s_2^2}{n_1 + n_2 - 2}}$	Same as above but $v = n_1 + n_2 - 2$
$H_0: \sigma_1^2 = \sigma_2^2$ (neither variance known)	$H_\phi: \sigma_1^2 < \sigma_2^2$ $H_\phi: \sigma_1^2 \neq \sigma_2^2$ $H_\phi: \sigma_2^2 > \sigma_2^2$	$F = \dfrac{s_1^2}{s_2^2}$	For s_1^2, $v_1 = n_1 - 1$ For s_2^2, $v_2 = n_2 - 1$	$< F_{v_1,v_2;\alpha}$ $\begin{cases} < F_{v_1,v_2;\alpha/2} \\ \text{or} \\ > F_{v_1,v_2;1-(\alpha/2)} \end{cases}$ $> F_{v_1,v_2;1-\alpha}$
H_0: Means of several samples are equal (one-way classification)	H_ϕ: Means are unequal	$F = \dfrac{SS_c/(c - 1)}{SS_R/(N - c)}$	$SS_c = \sum r(\bar{x}_j - \bar{\bar{x}})^2$ $SS_R = \sum (x_{ij} - \bar{\bar{x}})^2$ $r = $ sample size $c = $ number of samples $N = cr$	$> F_{c-1,N-c;1-\alpha}$
H_0: Means of c classes are equal H_0: Means of r classes are equal	H_ϕ: Means are unequal	$F = \dfrac{SS_c/(c - 1)}{SS_R/rc(k - 1)}$ $F = \dfrac{SS_r/(r - 1)}{SS_R/rc(k - 1)}$	$SS_c = \sum^r ck(\bar{x}_j - \bar{\bar{x}})^2$ $SS_r = \sum^c rk(\bar{x}_i - \bar{\bar{x}})^2$ $SS_R = SS_{\text{residual}}$ $= \sum^{rck} (\bar{x}_{ijk} - \bar{x}_{ij})^2$	$> F_{c-1,rc(k-1);1-\alpha}$ $> F_{r-1,rc(k-1);1-\alpha}$
H_0: No interaction between classes	H_ϕ: Interaction between classes	$F = \dfrac{SS_{rc}/(r - 1)(c - 1)}{SS_R/rc(k - 1)}$	$SS_{rc} = SS_{\text{interaction}}$ $= \sum^{rc} (\bar{x}_{ij} - \bar{x}_i - \bar{x}_j + \bar{\bar{x}})^2$ $k = $ observations in each i, j cell	$> F_{(r-1)(c-1),rc(k-1);1-\alpha}$

15-9 REFERENCES
Bowker, A. H. and G. L. Lieberman, *Engineering Statistics*, Prentice-Hall, Englewood Cliffs, N.J., 1959.
Cochran, W. G. and G. M. Cox, *Experimental Designs* (2nd ed.), John Wiley, New York, 1957.

543

Fisher, R. A., *The Design of Experiments* (3rd ed.), Oliver & Boyd, London, 1942.
————, *Statistical Methods for Research Workers* (13th rev. ed.), Oliver & Boyd, London, 1958.
Guenther, W. C., *Concepts of Statistical Inference*, McGraw-Hill, New York, 1965.
Keeping, E. S., *Introduction to Statistical Inference*, Van Nostrand, Princeton, N.J., 1962.
Mood, A. M. and F. A. Graybill, *Introduction to the Theory of Statistics* (2nd ed.), McGraw-Hill, New York, 1963.
Scheffe, Henry, *The Analysis of Variance*, John Wiley, New York, 1959.

15-10 QUESTIONS AND PROBLEMS

1. Draw two overlapping, bell-shaped distribution curves on a horizontal line. Shade the portions of the area under each curve that represent a Type I and a Type II error. Redraw the curves so there is less overlap. Judging from the shaded area that corresponds to a Type II error in the curves with less overlap, what intuitive statement can be made about the probability of committing a Type II error and the proximity of the means of the two distributions?

2. Define the following terms:

(a) Hypothesis. (e) Significance level.
(b) Alternate hypothesis. (f) Critical region.
(c) Type I error. (g) Interaction.
(d) Type II error.

3. If a hypothesis is rejected when a sample of size 10 is collected, is it more likely to be accepted when a sample of 100 is collected from the same source as the original 10? Why?

4. What is the consequence of designating $\alpha = 0$ for a hypothesis text?

5. What is the consequence of reducing the significance level from 5% to 1% if the sample size remains unchanged?

6. Under what two conditions would it be unnecessary to use a statistical hypothesis test to determine if two population means are equal?

7. How do you find theoretical frequencies for a test of independence? What is meant by independence?

8. What test statistic for variances would be associated with a χ^2/v distribution?

9. From the answer for Question 8, approximately what value should χ^2 be to accept a hypothesis that the population mean is equal to a given value?

10. If a population variance is known, either a t or a Z test could be used to test the hypothesis that the mean is equal to a certain value. Why is the Z test preferred for the stated conditions?

11. Why does the pooled variance in the t test have $n_1 + n_2 - 2$

degrees of freedom while the pooled variance in the F test has $n_1 + n_2 - 1$ degrees of freedom?

12. Both the χ^2 and F tests can be used to test a hypothesis that a variance is equal to a given value. Will the results always be the same? How are the χ^2 and F distributions related?

13. What is the advantage of decreasing the residual error for an F test?

14. It is intuitively reasonable that a t test for the equality of two sample means should produce the same verdict as an F test for the same experiment. Show that the formulas for a t test of two sample means and a one-way analysis of variance with two classes are alike. Compare the critical regions to show that

$$F_{1,(N-2);\alpha} = t^2_{(n_1+n_2-2);\alpha}$$

15. A company has a plant in New England and one in the Southwest. The general profile of the workers in both plants is very similar, and each plant has about the same size workforce. In a compilation of absences due to sickness, the New England plant had 64% of the sick leaves taken for a single day and the remaining percentage averaged $3\frac{1}{2}$ days off the job. In the Southwest plant, 81% of the sick leaves were for 1 day but the remaining portion averaged 6 days away from work. Select a hypothesis to test and state your conclusions.

16. A χ^2 test can be used to test the homogeneity of a set of percentages. When used in this fashion, the test determines whether a process is "in control." The test is conducted by considering the data as a contingency table with r rows and 2 columns. The two f_i values for the given data are 13.6 and 86.4. State the hypothesis and determine whether the process represented by the listing below is in control. Use a critical region from $\alpha = 0.05$.

Sample	Defective	Acceptable
1	12	88
2	19	81
3	26	74
4	11	89
5	4	96
6	3	97
7	18	82
8	14	86
9	17	83
10	12	88
Totals	136	864

17. Over several years a public utility company received hundreds of complaints about its service personnel. An annual survey was conducted to determine the main reasons for the complaints. The survey included a rating for the service personnel, and the results changed little from year to year. To improve the image, attendance at a special "charm" school was required for all personnel who had direct contact with customers. The old and new ratings based on 500 questionnaires are shown below. Was the charm school a success?

Rating	Before Charm School	After Charm School
Good	212	220
Fair	182	218
Poor	106	62

18. A test designed to detect better salesmen was given to an entire sales force. Annual sales commissions versus test grades were tabulated. What conclusions can be drawn from the data?

	Test Scores		
Sales Commissions	100–91	90–81	80–71
Under $8000	21	16	32
$8001–$12,000	32	27	43
Over $12,000	10	22	18

19. Data collected from a process have the following pattern for intervals of one standard deviation: 9, 25, 49, 86, 102, 40, 24, 3. Are the data normally distributed?

20. Around-the-clock production has revealed some differences in the quality of output for three shifts. The workers periodically change from one shift to the next. Based on the data below, would you conclude that the timing of a shift affects the quality of output?

	Units Produced	
Shift	Defective	Acceptable
7:00 a.m. to 3:00 p.m.	31	484
3:00 p.m. to 11:00 p.m.	40	469
11:00 p.m. to 7:00 a.m.	53	408

21. Minature lightbulbs will be used for signal lights in a

complex electronic testing machine that is being designed. Two types of bulbs are available. Twenty bulbs of each type were tested to determine $\bar{x}_1 = 340$ hours with $s_1 = 35$ hours, and $\bar{x}_2 = 372$ hours with $s_2 = 26$ hours. The bulbs were randomly sampled; it is believed that the lengths of service are normally distributed and the variances are equal. $\alpha = 0.01$ is considered an appropriate test.

(a) Test $H_0: \bar{x}_1 = \bar{x}_2$ and $H_0: x_1 \neq \bar{x}_2$.

(b) Test $H_0: \bar{x} = \bar{x}_2$ and $H_0: \bar{x}_1 < x_2$.

22. Each year a garment manufacturer has two major hiring seasons, one for swimming suits and one for ski clothes. Many women are hired each time for a 2-month sewing period. Between 10% and 20% are "new hires" on each occasion.

Previously the untrained workers have been run through a quick familiarity course and put on a machine to learn as they produce. The reject rate and material waste were very high during the learning period. To remedy this situation, two new types of training programs were initiated.

Output of workers trained by both of the new methods was randomly sampled to obtain the average production rate per hour during the first and second weeks of employment. The results are shown below.

Training Type I		Training Type II	
Week 1	Week 2	Week 1	Week 2
4	10	5	11
3	12	6	10
5	10	6	10
4	11	9	13
7	12	8	12
9	15	5	10
8	14	8	14
4	10	7	13
6	12	8	11
8	13	6	10
58	119	68	114

Higher hourly production is preferred even though pay is on a piece-rate basis. After 2 weeks, most workers reach their maximum level of production and thereafter produce at a relatively constant rate. Based on records from several hundred workers trained by the old method, the average production after 2 weeks is 10.2

547

pieces per hour. The rates are normally distributed with a standard deviation of 1.3 pieces.

The critical region for statistical tests is at $\alpha = 0.05$.

(a) Compare the new training methods to the old one by assuming the sampled rates have the same variance as that known for the old rate.

(b) Compare the two new methods at both the 1- and 2-week production levels assuming the variances are equal.

(c) Compare the first-week rates of the new methods when it is believed that there is insufficient reason to assume both variances are equal.

(d) Compare the variances of the production rates for each weekly period.

(e) What conclusions can be drawn from the above tests? What recommendations would you make if both the new training routines cost the same but are more expensive than the old method?

23. A sawmill is experimenting with the production of garden mulch as a byproduct of debarking logs. Plastic bags to hold the powdered mulch are purchased for a market trial. Because production will be in limited quantities until it is determined whether there is a market for the product, the bags are filled by hand and weighed individually. Each bag is supposed to weigh 5 pounds. In an attempt to speed up the filling and weighing operation, solid containers that hold 5 pounds of mulch are filled and then emptied into the bags. A random sample of 25 bags filled from the container averages 5.2 pounds and has a standard deviation of 4 ounces.

(a) For $\alpha = 0.05$, is the container-filling idea successful?

(b) What is the interval into which $\bar{x}$ may fall for 95% confidence that the 5-pound standard is being met? How might the interval be represented physically in the container-filling operation?

(c) How large would n have to be to accept the hypothesis $H_0 : \bar{x} = \mu$ at $\alpha = 0.01$ when the other conditions are the same?

25. A machine used to fill bags to a design weight has a known standard deviation of 0.019 pound for 5-pound bags when used with a different filler material. Fifty samples are randomly taken when it is used for the mulching material described in Problem 23. The standard deviation of the samples is 0.029 pound. Test the hypothesis at $\alpha = 0.05$ that the machine has the same variation when it is used for mulch as when it is used for the other filler material.

25. A cutting machine has consistently maintained a standard deviation of 0.020 inch on 3-inch cuts. A sample taken from recent production is shown below:

Measurements of 3-inch parts

3.01	2.98	3.00	3.00	2.97
3.01	2.99	2.99	2.98	3.00
3.00	2.99	3.01	3.01	3.01
2.99	3.00	3.02	2.99	3.00
3.00	3.00	3.02	3.00	3.00

Based on a critical region of $\alpha = 0.05$, does the machine need adjustment? Test both one- and two-tail critical regions. What hypotheses and conclusions account for the differences in the tests.

26. A producer of training films developed two versions of a film to teach the rudiments of an operator's maintenance program. The films were shown in two plants that use such a program, version 1 to plant A and version 2 to plant B. The same examination was given to the viewers at both plants to determine the effectiveness of the films. The average scores at both plants were about the same, but the standard deviation was 9 points at plant A and 14 points at plant B. If the numbers of employees that took the test at plants A and B were 31 and 64, respectively, what conclusion can be drawn about the effectiveness of the two versions of the film? Let $\alpha = 0.05$.

27. A salesman has challenged the quality and price of raw materials now being supplied by another firm and has agreed to pay for a comparison. If the material from the other company has a variance greater than the proposed source, the order will be changed to the salesman's firm. One hundred samples from each source are randomly chosen and tested. The results are:

$s_1^2 = 0.00468$ for material from the salesman's firm
$s_2^2 = 0.00496$ for material from the other source

The critical region is defined by $\alpha = 0.05$. Determine the appropriate hypothesis, perform the calculations, and state the indicated conclusion.

28. Part of a strike settlement was an agreement to investigate certain production standards. One time-study man from the union, one from the company, and a mutually agreed upon consultant timed the same operation as performed by three different operators. The trials were conducted under similar

environmental conditions using identical equipment and materials. The time analysts did not know the results of each other's times. The data from the trials were coded in hundredths of minutes over 3 minutes:

	Time Analysts		
	Union	Consultant	Company
Operator 1	12	28	35
	18	20	42
Operator 2	44	40	86
	14	42	44
Operator 3	36	51	60
	40	38	75

What conclusions can be drawn from an analysis of the data? What interpretation could be made of the indicated results and what actions might be taken?

29. Parts produced by three machines are automatically fed to adjacent test units to check on the variability of the process. Recent test readings have shown unusual variation. The uniformity of the material for the products has been checked and found satisfactory. The next question is whether the variation is owed to the production machines or the testing facilities. The data collected randomly from the machines and test units show how the products vary from a desired standard:

	Test Units		
	A	B	C
Machine 1	+3	-10	0
	-2	+8	-4
	+5	+4	-2
Machine 2	+6	-3	-4
	-1	+12	+1
	-2	-2	-3
Machine 3	-4	-5	+1
	-1	-5	0
	-5	+4	-6

(a) Is there homogeneity among the machines and test units at $\alpha = 0.05$?

(b) Is there interaction between the machines and individual test units? If so, what is a possible interpretation of the physical cause of the interaction?

550

CHAPTER 16

EPILOGUE

16-1   A REVIEW   Systems!

The gambling addict has his pet system. An automobile has a cooling system. Animals have circulatory systems. Salesmen no longer sell computers; they sell complete information systems. There are military systems, judicial systems, educational systems, and production systems.

There have always been systems, but the modern ones are more impressive. They are bigger, tighter, and more complex because civilization has need for them and technology is available to support them. Standards of quality and reliability taken for granted today were inconceivable just a few decades ago. To raise or just maintain these standards while increasing the quantity and diversification of products is a continuous challenge. Old techniques merge with the new as managers race to meet the demands of the systems they manage.

One significant trend has been in the way management thinks about production problems. It is easy to say effectiveness of the whole is more important than efficiency of the parts, or that profit optimization should take the place of cost reduction. But only a skillful manager can put into practice what he knows is theoretically correct. He has to be familiar with the idiosyncrasies of the system to recognize the interplay of modifications, and he must possess the knowledge to evaluate the effects. If either the familiarity or the knowledge is lacking, system thinking suffers.

It has taken several hundred pages just to set the framework for system thinking. We have covered but a fraction of the useful tools and only intimated the coordination requirements. To appreciate the whole, we had to consider the parts first. The frequent "buts" and "ifs" attached to each tool and subject area were perspective building stipulations. These qualifiers attempted to integrate individual planks into a scaffolding for system analysis and synthesis.

Let us explore one last example to reaffirm system concepts. We could make an example out of an "ice cream man" selling his products from a pedal-operated cart. He has to consider how much to order, his best route, competition, and other business factors. Or we could discuss a huge "general" system—General Motors, General Foods, General Electric, etc. Certainly these multiproduct, multiservice giants are guided by a set of objectives that directs continuity of purpose to their diverse activities. Instead of either extreme, we shall survey a system within a system.

Again there are many choices. Advertising, packaging, or research and development are broad but distinct areas that require coordination of effort between many operating units. A good selling job, new container design, or a successful research program does not spring from the isolated efforts of one department. They are a composite of ideas, demands, reservations, and enterprise from many directions. The objective, also a function of cooperative effort, is accomplished by coordinated action of components from other systems. The descriptive nouns that commonly designate operating departments, such as marketing, sales, and purchasing, are functional adjectives for subsystem objectives. The verb that unites systems within a system to implement strategic objectives is "coordinate."

Our example is a distribution system. It is a subsystem within the confines of the larger corporate system. Although a separate department may not be devoted strictly to distribution problems, every industry gives attention to the delivery of products and services to consumers. The ratio of physical distribution costs to sales is very prominent in some industries: about 25% for the food industry and 22% for chemical, rubber, petroleum, and primary metal industries.

The objective of the distribution system, as depicted in Figure 16.1, is to serve the customer; it starts with a sale secured from the customer and ends with the delivery of the ordered product. The top halves of the circles read like an organizational chart. The lower half of each circle relates representative functions to physical distribution. A change in function originating in any organizational division will subsequently affect the overall distribution policy.

Consider a successful new marketing development. A greater customer demand increases sales and requires new production schedules to meet expected deliveries. Purchasing works with production planners to develop a procurement program. The new production schedules are converted to increased capacity at the manufacturing plant by higher machine utilization, overtime, altered material-handling routines, more workers, or other measures requiring assistance from operating divisions such as payroll, recruiting, training, engineering, and mainte-

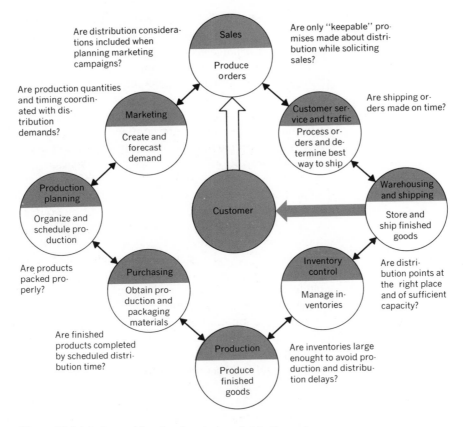

Figure 16.1 Interfaces of functional areas in a distribution system

nance. Meanwhile, customers' orders are being processed. The orders form the basis for inventory planning to facilitate storage and for traffic planning to determine shipping. Warehousing and shipping personnel arrange the physical facilities and administrative details to distribute the increased flow of products.

Each interface of specialty interests is an area of potential conflict and compromise. *Marketing* may disagree with *sales* as to the timing of campaigns. *Purchasing* could press for larger ordering quantities to take advantage of quantity discounts while *inventory management* warns against the increase in holding costs. Longer production runs with fewer set-ups are opposed by the need to find storage space for the larger output before distribution. The greater stock in warehouses pleases *customer service* because the lead time before shipment is lower. *Sales* pushes for a greater range of styles against the caution of *manufacturing* that diversification complicates production. A new

553

packaging design could be favored by *marketing, sales,* and *purchasing* while being opposed by *production planning, warehousing,* and *inventory management.*

These opposing views arise from honest and legitimate opinions about optimal tactics for *each operational area.* The disappointing aspect is that a strong conviction, even though based on valid facts and a conscientious evaluation, can be detrimental to overall performance if the tactics are confined to local considerations. Leaders are expected to be resolute, but stubborn concern coupled with a myopic outlook destroys their effectiveness.

One way to resolve differences of opinion is by executive decree. The top man can dictate policy. If he is unusually astute and diplomatically gifted, he will select the best course of action and convince participants to cooperate. But a dictatorial regime often attains its efficiency at the expense of destroyed initiative.

Another way to achieve unity is through management orientation and an environment for system thinking. The orientation includes formal training for evaluating interrelated functions and familiarity with strategic objectives. The environment includes a fast, accurate, communication network and a spirit of cooperation. Most managers are naturally inclined to devote their attention to activities immediately surrounding them; they protect subordinates and promote policies with proprietary interest. These practices are commendable so long as they do not interfere with the welfare of strategic objectives. Interference is recognized through information feedback and the ability to understand the message.

16-2 AN OVERVIEW

In the foregoing pages we dealt with many concepts that contribute to understanding and decision making. It is not unusual to get so close to a subject that familiarity distorts its position in the total scheme of activities. Perhaps we can take a step back from intimate contact to regain perspective and identify some idiosyncrasies of human nature that tangentially affect our acquired concepts.

A fascination with a particular concept or technique can be damaging if others are ignored. For instance, some analysts became so enamored with critical path scheduling that they forced its application on projects where the cost of application exceed the benefits. Some guiding principles for production decisions are listed below.

1. Intangible costs should receive as much attention as more easily perceived costs. Factors such as customer satisfaction

are admittedly difficult to quantify, but a decision excluding intangibles is a judgment rendered with incomplete evidence.

2. The more sensitive factors in a decision situation should be identified and observed closely. Since information is expensive to accumulate and analyze, focusing attention on pivotal factors produces more dependable answers with less expense.

3. Suboptimal decisions may result from adherence to tactical efficiency instead of strategic effectiveness. Minimum system costs do not necessarily accrue from the lowest costs for each segment taken individually; increasing the expense of one operation can produce larger savings in a related operation.

4. Timing is a key parameter in most production decisions. Taking account of seasonal forecasts and devoting assiduous attention to day-by-day scheduling can provide the narrow edge of competitive advantage. Time measurements also provide a yardstick by which to compute performances and the time value of money as bases for investment comparisons.

5. Human factors permeate all levels of decision making and deserve due vigilance. Although human behavior is never completely predictable, work and facility design can create an an environment conducive to better performance. Personal foibles of the decision maker also rate study; even if the scrutiny is temporarily embarrassing and ego deflating, it may lead to more satisfying performance.

6. Real-life problems seldom fit the "ready-to-wear" formulas. To tailor applications to specific situations, the assumptions upon which theoretical solution procedures are based should be known.

7. Quantitative methods cannot solve all production problems, but they define alternatives and expose costs for economic comparisons. By limelighting the numerical effect of potential actions, opportunity costs are implied for intangible factors. The use of quantitative methods substitutes the language of numbers for the more confusion-producing language of verbal diplomacy.

Of course it is easier to state guiding principles than to apply them. The concepts of system analysis and many associated techniques are far from new. Most practicing managers have at least some familiarity with them and readily give lip service to their usefulness. Yet the praise is often issued without supporting action. Rather than condemning such inaction, it is more profitable to search for the causes and thereby discover ways to overcome, or detour around, the barriers of indifference.

555

Obstacles to implementation vary among organizations. A reluctance to "rock the boat" by instituting changes in an apparently efficient operation is a common attitude. Sometimes there is a lack of appreciation for what newer management methods can accomplish. Or the reluctance is owed to frustations caused by experiments with the methods initiated without sufficient expertise. Experience is an unbiased teacher; it punishes the unprepared with no regard for excuses. Perhaps some harsh experiences should always be anticipated in new ventures, but discouragements are reduced by knowing what legitimately can be expected from the methods and how to earn those expectations.

Eager "management scientists" occasionally "hard sell" their services. Such tactics call attention to the subject but are seldom successful. Resorting to technical jargon and vague promises of hidden wealth can lead to uneasiness or outright rejection of proposals. Another approach, probably better but more difficult, is to involve potential users in a pilot project. The selling is done by a natural evaluation of the end product.

Common sense suggests that self-insurance should be built into a selling demonstration. The project selected should be large enough to be a recognized challenge but not too large to accomplish with the limited resources available. Realistic, even conservative, goals should be understood by all concerned. Current management expertise should be acknowledged and utilized. Since the avowed purpose of the implementation is to show the advantages of a systematic routine, a free and full flow of descriptive and procedural information is vital. The uninitiated are much more likely to become believers if they can watch the progress on their own, foresee conclusions, and evaluate success by their personal standards.

The accelerating development of management tools and techniques has created a vicious paradox. As newer tools are developed to treat more demanding problems, the tools are less easily understood by the personnel seeking solutions to those problems. Thus the emergence of better, more sophisticated managerial instruments has made their initial adoption more difficult and their efficient use more perplexing.

A related paradox is that the organizations most in need of an infusion of sophisticated managerial skills are often the ones least prepared to accept them. When such firms are desperate enough to undertake innovations, the immediacy of their needs tends to force change at a too rapid pace. Without supporting routines and procedures, otherwise well-formulated plans explode into chaotic, short-lived campaigns or wither into ineffectual forays.

If there is a summary answer to the paradoxes, it will be found in education—for both the innovators and the established. The prophets of change must learn to make haste slowly and to expect something less than complete acceptance at first. They must also moderate their critical outlooks with respect for achievements already made, without losing enthusiasm for improvements. The entrenched managers should elevate their improvement goals while subduing fear of change. They should train themselves to rely less on precedent and more on principles. Then they should seek more comprehensive knowledge of principles. The recent proliferation of management-training services designed to up-grade skills of established managers is a clue that such education is at work.

16-3 A PREVIEW In turning from an overview of implementation problems to a preview of future events, an easy first forecast is that system managers can expect more computerized assistance. Computer hardware will be more versatile and more widely available. Associated software routines will benefit from greater awareness of their potential and a larger body of trained technicians to utilize them effectively. On-line information and control systems are becoming more feasible. Automatic data processing will handle many routine decisions and accumulate data for more realistic models.

The permanent effects of electronic assistance are more difficult to anticipate than their interim developments. The triangular organizational hierarchy may become pinched in the middle. The bottom-heavy hourglass shape shown in Figure 16.2 could result from a garrote tightened around the traditional structure by bigger, faster, data-processing facilities and the managerial mastery required to harness the quickened data flow. The squeeze in the middle management section could take the form of programmed decisions—directives formulated auto-matically from structured-operating rules applied to incoming data. The bulge below the waistline accommodates a downward classification of some managers to the function of directing operations instead of planning them. At the top of the organiza-tional structure, the upper management group proportionately assumes enlarged functions for planning, coordinating, and innovating. The consequent challenges to maintaining morale,

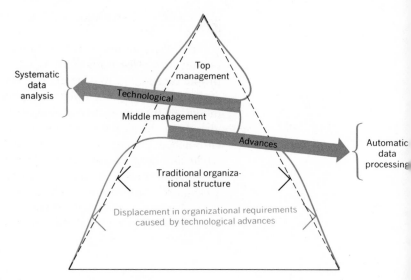

Figure 16.2 Distortion of traditional managerial hierarchy by advances in technology

evaluating personnel, developing "creators," coordinating actions, and controlling the "programmed structure" would be enormous.

The outgrowth of current research efforts should reveal better ways to use our electronic allies. We have barely tapped the surface of simulation possibilities; more complete and realistic simulations of real-world conditions will make better use of resources through pseudomanipulations of irreversible processes. Increased realism will also make simulated experiences more powerful teaching devices. Besides simulation, improved heuristic techniques for searching into ill-structured problems will reveal solutions to many managerial puzzles now considered outside the realm of quantitative analysis.

Future studies should provide assistance in solving the paramount problem of quantifying intangibles. Though this problem is in the nature of an irresistible force against an immovable object, at least better methods will be found to impose more objectivity on hitherto subjective evaluations.

More extensive application of management science techniques to sociologically rooted problems is a fascinating possibility. No one will deny the need for better analysis and control measures for social programs. This "society" system nicely fits within the broad framework we have erected for production systems; there are definite inputs, transformations, and outputs. Some production tools are already being applied and more are directly applicable. Management techniques developed for coordinating defense projects and industrial systems can be tailored to treat social projects. A return benefit from such effort will be an increased awareness of the sociological consequences of industry's applications of the same tools. A more worthwhile, exciting direction for system studies is difficult to visualize.

16-4 THE LAST VIEW The collection of system management tools we have surveyed provides a respectable repertoire for making production decisions. Experience will sharpen the tools. It will also reveal more areas for profitable study and the need to keep abreast of new developments. The history of production has been a parade of change. The future promises to be even more dynamic than the past. Few undertakings offer more important, challenging, or diversified opportunities than the planning, analysis, and control of production systems.

APPENDIX A

STATISTICAL TABLES*

Table A.1 Areas of a standard normal distribution

An entry in the table is the proportion under the entire curve which is between $z = 0$ and a positive value of z. Areas for negative values of z are obtained by symmetry.

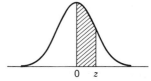

z	0.00	0.01	0.02	0.03	0.04	0.05	0.06	0.07	0.08	0.09
0.0	0.0000	0.0040	0.0080	0.0120	0.0160	0.0199	0.0239	0.0279	0.0319	0.0359
0.1	0.0398	0.0438	0.0478	0.0517	0.0557	0.0596	0.0636	0.0675	0.0714	0.0753
0.2	0.0793	0.0832	0.0871	0.0910	0.0948	0.0987	0.1026	0.1064	0.1103	0.1141
0.3	0.1179	0.1217	0.1255	0.1293	0.1331	0.1368	0.1406	0.1443	0.1480	0.1517
0.4	0.1554	0.1591	0.1628	0.1664	0.1700	0.1736	0.1772	0.1808	0.1844	0.1879
0.5	0.1915	0.1950	0.1985	0.2019	0.2054	0.2088	0.2123	0.2157	0.2190	0.2234
0.6	0.2257	0.2291	0.2324	0.2357	0.2389	0.2422	0.2454	0.2486	0.2517	0.2549
0.7	0.2580	0.2611	0.2642	0.2673	0.2703	0.2734	0.2764	0.2794	0.2823	0.2852
0.8	0.2881	0.2910	0.2939	0.2967	0.2995	0.3023	0.3051	0.3078	0.3106	0.3133
0.9	0.3159	0.3186	0.3212	0.3238	0.3264	0.3289	0.3315	0.3340	0.3365	0.3389
1.0	0.3413	0.3438	0.3461	0.3485	0.3508	0.3531	0.3554	0.3577	0.3599	0.3621
1.1	0.3643	0.3665	0.3686	0.3708	0.3729	0.3749	0.3770	0.3790	0.3810	0.3830
1.2	0.3849	0.3869	0.3888	0.3907	0.3925	0.3944	0.3962	0.3980	0.3997	0.4015
1.3	0.4032	0.4049	0.4066	0.4082	0.4099	0.4115	0.4131	0.4147	0.4162	0.4177
1.4	0.4192	0.4207	0.4222	0.4236	0.4251	0.4265	0.4279	0.4292	0.4306	0.4319
1.5	0.4332	0.4345	0.4357	0.4370	0.4382	0.4394	0.4406	0.4418	0.4429	0.4441
1.6	0.4452	0.4463	0.4474	0.4484	0.4495	0.4505	0.4515	0.4525	0.4535	0.4545
1.7	0.4554	0.4564	0.4573	0.4582	0.4591	0.4599	0.4608	0.4616	0.4625	0.4633
1.8	0.4641	0.4649	0.4656	0.4664	0.4671	0.4678	0.4686	0.4693	0.4699	0.4706
1.9	0.4713	0.4719	0.4726	0.4732	0.4738	0.4744	0.4750	0.4756	0.4761	0.4767
2.0	0.4772	0.4778	0.4783	0.4788	0.4793	0.4798	0.4803	0.4808	0.4812	0.4817
2.1	0.4821	0.4826	0.4830	0.4834	0.4838	0.4842	0.4846	0.4850	0.4854	0.4857
2.2	0.4861	0.4864	0.4868	0.4871	0.4875	0.4878	0.4881	0.4884	0.4887	0.4890
2.3	0.4893	0.4896	0.4898	0.4901	0.4904	0.4906	0.4909	0.4911	0.4913	0.4916
2.4	0.4918	0.4920	0.4922	0.4925	0.4927	0.4929	0.4931	0.4932	0.4934	0.4936
2.5	0.4938	0.4940	0.4941	0.4943	0.4945	0.4946	0.4948	0.4949	0.4951	0.4952
2.6	0.4953	0.4955	0.4956	0.4957	0.4959	0.4960	0.4961	0.4962	0.4963	0.4964
2.7	0.4965	0.4966	0.4967	0.4968	0.4969	0.4970	0.4971	0.4972	0.4973	0.4974
2.8	0.4974	0.4975	0.4976	0.4977	0.4977	0.4978	0.4979	0.4979	0.4980	0.4981
2.9	0.4981	0.4982	0.4982	0.4983	0.4984	0.4984	0.4985	0.4985	0.4986	0.4986
3.0	0.4987	0.4987	0.4987	0.4988	0.4988	0.4989	0.4989	0.4989	0.4990	0.4990

*The tables in this appendix were taken with permission from *Elementary Statistics* (2nd ed.), by Paul G. Hoel, John Wiley, New York, 1966.

Table A.2 Student's t distribution

The first column lists the number of degrees of freedom (v). The headings of the other columns give probabilities (P) for t to exceed numerically the entry value.

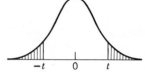

v	P 0.50	0.25	0.10	0.05	0.025	0.01	0.005
1	1.00000	2.4142	6.3138	12.706	25.452	63.657	127.32
2	0.81650	1.6036	2.9200	4.3027	6.2053	9.9248	14.089
3	0.76489	1.4226	2.3534	3.1825	4.1765	5.8409	7.4533
4	0.74070	1.3444	2.1318	2.7764	3.4954	4.6041	5.5976
5	0.72669	1.3009	2.0150	2.5706	3.1634	4.0321	4.7733
6	0.71756	1.2733	1.9432	2.4469	2.9687	3.7074	4.3168
7	0.71114	1.2543	1.8946	2.3646	2.8412	3.4995	4.0293
8	0.70639	1.2403	1.8595	2.3060	2.7515	3.3554	3.8325
9	0.70272	1.2297	1.8331	2.2622	2.6850	3.2498	3.6897
10	0.69981	1.2213	1.8125	2.2281	2.6338	3.1693	3.5814
11	0.69745	1.2145	1.7959	2.2010	2.5931	3.1058	3.4966
12	0.69548	1.2089	1.7823	2.1788	2.5600	3.0545	3.4284
13	0.69384	1.2041	1.7709	2.1604	2.5326	3.0123	3.3725
14	0.69242	1.2001	1.7613	2.1448	2.5096	2.9768	3.3257
15	0.69120	1.1967	1.7530	2.1315	2.4899	2.9467	3.2860
16	0.69013	1.1937	1.7459	2.1199	2.4729	2.9208	3.2520
17	0.68919	1.1910	1.7396	2.1098	2.4581	2.8982	3.2225
18	0.68837	1.1887	1.7341	2.1009	2.4450	2.8784	3.1966
19	0.68763	1.1866	1.7291	2.0930	2.4334	2.8609	3.1737
20	0.68696	1.1848	1.7247	2.0860	2.4231	2.8453	3.1534
21	0.68635	1.1831	1.7207	2.0796	2.4138	2.8314	3.1352
22	0.68580	1.1816	1.7171	2.0739	2.4055	2.8188	3.1188
23	0.68531	1.1802	1.7139	2.0687	2.3979	2.8073	3.1040
24	0.68485	1.1789	1.7109	2.0639	2.3910	2.7969	3.0905
25	0.68443	1.1777	1.7081	2.0595	2.3846	2.7874	3.0782
26	0.68405	1.1766	1.7056	2.0555	2.3788	2.7787	3.0669
27	0.68370	1.1757	1.7033	2.0518	2.3734	2.7707	3.0565
28	0.68335	1.1748	1.7011	2.0484	2.3685	2.7633	3.0469
29	0.68304	1.1739	1.6991	2.0452	2.3683	2.7564	3.0380
30	0.68276	1.1731	1.6973	2.0423	2.3596	2.7500	3.0298
40	0.68066	1.1673	1.6839	2.0211	2.3289	2.7045	2.9712
60	0.67862	1.1616	1.6707	2.0003	2.2991	2.6603	2.9146
120	0.67656	1.1559	1.6577	1.9799	2.2699	2.6174	2.8599
∞	0.67449	1.1503	1.6449	1.9600	2.2414	2.5758	2.8070

Table A.3 The χ^2 distribution

The first column lists the number of degrees of freedom (v). The headings of the other columns give probabilities (P) for χ^2 to exceed the entry value.

v \ P	0.995	0.975	0.050	0.025	0.010	0.005
1	0.0⁴3927	0.0³9821	3.84146	5.02389	6.63490	7.87944
2	0.010025	0.050636	5.99147	7.37776	9.21034	10.5966
3	0.071721	0.215795	7.81473	9.34840	11.3449	12.8381
4	0.206990	0.484419	9.48773	11.1433	13.2767	14.8602
5	0.411740	0.831211	11.0705	12.8325	15.0863	16.7496
6	0.675727	1.237347	12.5916	14.4494	16.8119	18.5476
7	0.989265	1.68987	14.0671	16.0128	18.4753	20.2777
8	1.344419	2.17973	15.5073	17.5346	20.0902	21.9550
9	1.734926	2.70039	16.9190	19.0228	21.6660	23.5893
10	2.15585	3.24697	18.3070	20.4831	23.2093	25.1882
11	2.60321	3.81575	19.6751	21.9200	24.7250	26.7569
12	3.07382	4.40379	21.0261	23.3367	26.2170	28.2995
13	3.56503	5.00874	22.3621	24.7356	27.6883	29.8194
14	4.07468	5.62872	23.6848	26.1190	29.1413	31.3193
15	4.60094	6.26214	24.9958	27.4884	30.5779	32.8013
16	5.14224	6.90766	26.2962	28.8454	31.9999	34.2672
17	5.69724	7.56418	27.5871	30.1910	33.4087	35.7185
18	6.26481	8.23075	28.8693	31.5264	34.8053	37.1564
19	6.84398	8.90655	30.1435	32.8523	36.1908	38.5822
20	7.43386	9.59083	31.4104	34.1696	37.5662	39.9968
21	8.03366	10.28293	32.6705	35.4789	38.9321	41.4010
22	8.64272	10.9823	33.9244	36.7807	40.2894	42.7956
23	9.26042	11.6885	35.1725	38.0757	41.6384	44.1813
24	9.88623	12.4001	36.4151	39.3641	42.9798	45.5585
25	10.5197	13.1197	37.6525	40.6465	44.3141	46.9278
26	11.1603	13.8439	38.8852	41.9232	45.6417	48.2899
27	11.8076	14.5733	40.1133	43.1944	46.9630	49.6449
28	12.4613	15.3079	41.3372	44.4607	48.2782	50.9933
29	13.1211	16.0471	42.5569	45.7222	49.5879	52.3356
30	13.7867	16.7908	43.7729	46.9792	50.8922	53.6720
40	20.7065	24.4331	55.7585	59.3417	63.6907	66.7659
50	27.9907	32.3574	67.5048	71.4202	76.1539	79.4900
60	35.5346	40.4817	79.0819	83.2976	88.3794	91.9517
70	43.2752	48.7576	90.5312	95.0231	100.425	104.215
80	51.1720	57.1532	101.879	106.629	112.329	116.321
90	59.1963	65.6466	113.145	118.136	124.116	128.299
100	67.3276	74.2219	124.342	129.561	135.807	140.169

Table A.4 F distribution (5% (Roman type) and 1% (boldface type) points for the distribution of F)

The degrees of freedom for the numerator and denominator (v_1 and v_2) are in the top row and first column, respectively. The values for α at 5% and 1% are in Roman type and boldface type, respectively.

Degrees of Freedom for Denominator (v_2)	Degrees of Freedom for Numerator (v_1)																							
	1	2	3	4	5	6	7	8	9	10	11	12	14	16	20	24	30	40	50	75	100	200	500	∞
1	161	200	216	225	230	234	237	239	241	242	243	244	245	246	248	249	250	251	252	253	253	254	254	254
	4052	**4999**	**5403**	**5625**	**5764**	**5859**	**5928**	**5981**	**6022**	**6056**	**6082**	**6106**	**6142**	**6169**	**6208**	**6234**	**6258**	**6286**	**6302**	**6323**	**6334**	**6352**	**6361**	**6366**
2	18.51	19.00	19.16	19.25	19.30	19.33	19.36	19.37	19.38	19.39	19.40	19.41	19.42	19.43	19.44	19.45	19.46	19.47	19.47	19.48	19.49	19.49	19.50	19.50
	98.49	**99.01**	**99.17**	**99.25**	**99.30**	**99.33**	**99.34**	**99.36**	**99.38**	**99.40**	**99.41**	**99.42**	**99.43**	**99.44**	**99.45**	**99.46**	**99.47**	**99.48**	**99.48**	**99.49**	**99.49**	**99.49**	**99.50**	**99.50**
3	10.13	9.55	9.28	9.12	9.01	8.94	8.88	8.84	8.81	8.78	8.76	8.74	8.71	8.69	8.66	8.64	8.62	8.60	8.58	8.57	8.56	8.54	8.54	8.53
	34.12	**30.81**	**29.46**	**28.71**	**28.24**	**27.91**	**27.67**	**27.49**	**27.34**	**27.23**	**27.13**	**27.05**	**26.92**	**26.83**	**26.69**	**26.60**	**26.50**	**26.41**	**26.30**	**26.27**	**26.23**	**26.18**	**26.14**	**26.12**
4	7.71	6.94	6.59	6.39	6.26	6.16	6.09	6.04	6.00	5.96	5.93	5.91	5.87	5.84	5.80	5.77	5.74	5.71	5.70	5.68	5.66	5.65	5.64	5.63
	21.20	**18.00**	**16.69**	**15.98**	**15.52**	**15.21**	**14.98**	**14.80**	**14.66**	**14.54**	**14.45**	**14.37**	**14.24**	**14.15**	**14.02**	**13.93**	**13.83**	**13.74**	**13.69**	**13.61**	**13.57**	**13.52**	**13.48**	**13.46**
5	6.61	5.79	5.41	5.19	5.05	4.95	4.88	4.82	4.78	4.74	4.70	4.68	4.64	4.60	4.56	4.53	4.50	4.46	4.44	4.42	4.40	4.38	4.37	4.36
	16.26	**13.27**	**12.06**	**11.39**	**10.97**	**10.67**	**10.45**	**10.27**	**10.15**	**10.05**	**9.96**	**9.89**	**9.77**	**9.68**	**9.55**	**9.47**	**9.38**	**9.29**	**9.24**	**9.17**	**9.13**	**9.07**	**9.04**	**9.02**
6	5.99	5.14	4.76	4.53	4.39	4.28	4.21	4.15	4.10	4.06	4.03	4.00	3.96	3.92	3.87	3.84	3.81	3.77	3.75	3.72	3.71	3.69	3.68	3.67
	13.74	**10.92**	**9.78**	**9.15**	**8.75**	**8.47**	**8.26**	**8.10**	**7.98**	**7.87**	**7.79**	**7.72**	**7.60**	**7.52**	**7.39**	**7.31**	**7.23**	**7.14**	**7.09**	**7.02**	**6.99**	**6.94**	**6.90**	**6.88**
7	5.59	4.74	4.35	4.12	3.97	3.87	3.79	3.73	3.68	3.63	3.60	3.57	3.52	3.49	3.44	3.41	3.38	3.34	3.32	3.29	3.28	3.25	3.24	3.23
	12.25	**9.55**	**8.45**	**7.85**	**7.46**	**7.19**	**7.00**	**6.84**	**6.71**	**6.62**	**6.54**	**6.47**	**6.35**	**6.27**	**6.15**	**6.07**	**5.98**	**5.90**	**5.85**	**5.78**	**5.75**	**5.70**	**5.67**	**5.65**
8	5.32	4.46	4.07	3.84	3.69	3.58	3.50	3.44	3.39	3.34	3.31	3.28	3.23	3.20	3.15	3.12	3.08	3.05	3.03	3.00	2.98	2.96	2.94	2.93
	11.26	**8.65**	**7.59**	**7.01**	**6.63**	**6.37**	**6.19**	**6.03**	**5.91**	**5.82**	**5.74**	**5.67**	**5.56**	**5.48**	**5.36**	**5.28**	**5.20**	**5.11**	**5.06**	**5.00**	**4.96**	**4.91**	**4.88**	**4.86**
9	5.12	4.26	3.86	3.63	3.48	3.37	3.29	3.23	3.18	3.13	3.10	3.07	3.02	2.98	2.93	2.90	2.86	2.82	2.80	2.77	2.76	2.73	2.72	2.71
	10.56	**8.02**	**6.99**	**6.42**	**6.06**	**5.80**	**5.62**	**5.47**	**5.35**	**5.26**	**5.18**	**5.11**	**5.00**	**4.92**	**4.80**	**4.73**	**4.64**	**4.56**	**4.51**	**4.45**	**4.41**	**4.36**	**4.33**	**4.31**
10	4.96	4.10	3.71	3.48	3.33	3.22	3.14	3.07	3.02	2.97	2.94	2.91	2.86	2.82	2.77	2.74	2.70	2.67	2.64	2.61	2.59	2.56	2.55	2.54
	10.04	**7.56**	**6.55**	**5.99**	**5.64**	**5.39**	**5.21**	**5.06**	**4.95**	**4.85**	**4.78**	**4.71**	**4.60**	**4.52**	**4.41**	**4.33**	**4.25**	**4.17**	**4.12**	**4.05**	**4.01**	**3.96**	**3.93**	**3.91**
11	4.84	3.98	3.59	3.36	3.20	3.09	3.01	2.95	2.90	2.86	2.82	2.79	2.74	2.70	2.65	2.61	2.57	2.53	2.50	2.47	2.45	2.42	2.41	2.40
	9.55	**7.20**	**6.22**	**5.67**	**5.32**	**5.07**	**4.88**	**4.74**	**4.63**	**4.54**	**4.46**	**4.40**	**4.29**	**4.21**	**4.10**	**4.02**	**3.94**	**3.86**	**3.80**	**3.74**	**3.70**	**3.66**	**3.62**	**3.60**
12	4.75	3.88	3.49	3.26	3.11	3.00	2.92	2.85	2.80	2.76	2.72	2.69	2.64	2.60	2.54	2.50	2.46	2.42	2.40	2.36	2.35	2.32	2.31	2.30
	9.33	**6.93**	**5.95**	**5.41**	**5.06**	**4.82**	**4.65**	**4.50**	**4.39**	**4.30**	**4.22**	**4.16**	**4.05**	**3.98**	**3.86**	**3.78**	**3.70**	**3.61**	**3.56**	**3.49**	**3.46**	**3.41**	**3.38**	**3.36**
13	4.67	3.80	3.41	3.18	3.02	2.92	2.84	2.77	2.72	2.67	2.63	2.60	2.55	2.51	2.46	2.42	2.38	2.34	2.32	2.28	2.26	2.24	2.22	2.21
	9.07	**6.70**	**5.74**	**5.20**	**4.86**	**4.62**	**4.44**	**4.30**	**4.19**	**4.10**	**4.02**	**3.96**	**3.85**	**3.78**	**3.67**	**3.59**	**3.51**	**3.42**	**3.37**	**3.30**	**3.27**	**3.21**	**3.18**	**3.16**

Table A.4 (continued)

Degrees of Freedom for Denominator (v_2)	\	Degrees of Freedom for Numerator (v_1)																						
	1	2	3	4	5	6	7	8	9	10	11	12	16	20	24	30	40	50	75	75	100	200	500	∞
14	4.60 / 8.86	3.74 / 6.51	3.34 / 5.56	3.11 / 5.03	2.96 / 4.69	2.85 / 4.46	2.77 / 4.28	2.70 / 4.14	2.65 / 4.03	2.60 / 3.94	2.56 / 3.86	2.53 / 3.80	2.48 / 3.70	2.44 / 3.62	2.39 / 3.51	2.35 / 3.43	2.31 / 3.34	2.27 / 3.26	2.24 / 3.21	2.21 / 3.14	2.19 / 3.11	2.16 / 3.06	2.14 / 3.02	2.13 / 3.00
15	4.54 / 8.68	3.68 / 6.36	3.29 / 5.42	3.06 / 4.89	2.90 / 4.56	2.79 / 4.32	2.70 / 4.14	2.64 / 4.00	2.59 / 3.89	2.55 / 3.80	2.51 / 3.73	2.48 / 3.67	2.43 / 3.56	2.39 / 3.48	2.33 / 3.36	2.29 / 3.29	2.25 / 3.20	2.21 / 3.12	2.18 / 3.07	2.15 / 3.00	2.12 / 2.97	2.10 / 2.92	2.08 / 2.89	2.07 / 2.87
16	4.49 / 8.53	3.63 / 6.23	3.24 / 5.29	3.01 / 4.77	2.85 / 4.44	2.74 / 4.20	2.66 / 4.03	2.59 / 3.89	2.54 / 3.78	2.49 / 3.69	2.45 / 3.61	2.42 / 3.55	2.37 / 3.45	2.33 / 3.37	2.28 / 3.25	2.24 / 3.18	2.20 / 3.10	2.16 / 3.01	2.13 / 2.96	2.09 / 2.89	2.07 / 2.86	2.04 / 2.80	2.02 / 2.77	2.01 / 2.75
17	4.45 / 8.40	3.59 / 6.11	3.20 / 5.18	2.96 / 4.67	2.81 / 4.34	2.70 / 4.10	2.62 / 3.93	2.55 / 3.79	2.50 / 3.68	2.45 / 3.59	2.41 / 3.52	2.38 / 3.45	2.33 / 3.35	2.29 / 3.27	2.23 / 3.16	2.19 / 3.08	2.15 / 3.00	2.11 / 2.92	2.08 / 2.86	2.04 / 2.79	2.02 / 2.76	1.99 / 2.70	1.97 / 2.67	1.96 / 2.65
18	4.41 / 8.28	3.55 / 6.01	3.16 / 5.09	2.93 / 4.58	2.77 / 4.25	2.66 / 4.01	2.58 / 3.85	2.51 / 3.71	2.46 / 3.60	2.41 / 3.51	2.37 / 3.44	2.34 / 3.37	2.29 / 3.27	2.25 / 3.19	2.19 / 3.07	2.15 / 3.00	2.11 / 2.91	2.07 / 2.83	2.04 / 2.78	2.00 / 2.71	1.98 / 2.68	1.95 / 2.62	1.93 / 2.59	1.92 / 2.57
19	4.38 / 8.18	3.52 / 5.93	3.13 / 5.01	2.90 / 4.50	2.74 / 4.17	2.63 / 3.94	2.55 / 3.77	2.48 / 3.63	2.43 / 3.52	2.38 / 3.43	2.34 / 3.36	2.31 / 3.30	2.26 / 3.19	2.21 / 3.12	2.15 / 3.00	2.11 / 2.92	2.07 / 2.84	2.02 / 2.76	2.00 / 2.70	1.96 / 2.63	1.94 / 2.60	1.91 / 2.54	1.90 / 2.51	1.88 / 2.49
20	4.35 / 8.10	3.49 / 5.85	3.10 / 4.94	2.87 / 4.43	2.71 / 4.10	2.60 / 3.87	2.52 / 3.71	2.45 / 3.56	2.40 / 3.45	2.35 / 3.37	2.31 / 3.30	2.28 / 3.23	2.23 / 3.13	2.18 / 3.05	2.12 / 2.94	2.08 / 2.86	2.04 / 2.77	1.99 / 2.69	1.96 / 2.63	1.92 / 2.56	1.90 / 2.53	1.87 / 2.47	1.85 / 2.44	1.84 / 2.42
21	4.32 / 8.02	3.47 / 5.78	3.07 / 4.87	2.84 / 4.37	2.68 / 4.04	2.57 / 3.81	2.49 / 3.65	2.42 / 3.51	2.37 / 3.40	2.32 / 3.31	2.28 / 3.24	2.25 / 3.17	2.20 / 3.07	2.15 / 2.99	2.09 / 2.88	2.05 / 2.80	2.00 / 2.72	1.96 / 2.63	1.93 / 2.58	1.89 / 2.51	1.87 / 2.47	1.84 / 2.42	1.82 / 2.38	1.81 / 2.36
22	4.30 / 7.94	3.44 / 5.72	3.05 / 4.82	2.82 / 4.31	2.66 / 3.99	2.55 / 3.76	2.47 / 3.59	2.40 / 3.45	2.35 / 3.35	2.30 / 3.26	2.26 / 3.18	2.23 / 3.12	2.18 / 3.02	2.13 / 2.94	2.07 / 2.83	2.03 / 2.75	1.98 / 2.67	1.93 / 2.58	1.91 / 2.53	1.87 / 2.46	1.84 / 2.42	1.81 / 2.37	1.80 / 2.33	1.78 / 2.31
23	4.28 / 7.88	3.42 / 5.66	3.03 / 4.76	2.80 / 4.26	2.64 / 3.94	2.53 / 3.71	2.45 / 3.54	2.38 / 3.41	2.32 / 3.30	2.28 / 3.21	2.24 / 3.14	2.20 / 3.07	2.14 / 2.97	2.10 / 2.89	2.04 / 2.78	2.00 / 2.70	1.96 / 2.62	1.91 / 2.53	1.88 / 2.48	1.84 / 2.41	1.82 / 2.37	1.79 / 2.32	1.77 / 2.28	1.76 / 2.26
24	4.26 / 7.82	3.40 / 5.61	3.01 / 4.72	2.78 / 4.22	2.62 / 3.90	2.51 / 3.67	2.43 / 3.50	2.36 / 3.36	2.30 / 3.25	2.26 / 3.17	2.22 / 3.09	2.18 / 3.03	2.13 / 2.93	2.09 / 2.85	2.02 / 2.74	1.98 / 2.66	1.94 / 2.58	1.89 / 2.49	1.86 / 2.44	1.82 / 2.36	1.80 / 2.33	1.76 / 2.27	1.74 / 2.23	1.73 / 2.21
25	4.24 / 7.77	3.38 / 5.57	2.99 / 4.68	2.76 / 4.18	2.60 / 3.86	2.49 / 3.63	2.41 / 3.46	2.34 / 3.32	2.28 / 3.21	2.24 / 3.13	2.20 / 3.05	2.16 / 2.99	2.11 / 2.89	2.06 / 2.81	2.00 / 2.70	1.96 / 2.62	1.92 / 2.54	1.87 / 2.45	1.84 / 2.40	1.80 / 2.32	1.77 / 2.29	1.74 / 2.23	1.72 / 2.19	1.71 / 2.17
26	4.22 / 7.72	3.37 / 5.53	2.98 / 4.64	2.74 / 4.14	2.59 / 3.82	2.47 / 3.59	2.39 / 3.42	2.32 / 3.29	2.27 / 3.17	2.22 / 3.09	2.18 / 3.02	2.15 / 2.96	2.10 / 2.86	2.05 / 2.77	1.99 / 2.66	1.95 / 2.58	1.90 / 2.50	1.85 / 2.41	1.82 / 2.36	1.78 / 2.28	1.76 / 2.25	1.72 / 2.19	1.70 / 2.15	1.69 / 2.13
27	4.21 / 7.68	3.35 / 5.49	2.96 / 4.60	2.73 / 4.11	2.57 / 3.79	2.46 / 3.56	2.37 / 3.39	2.30 / 3.26	2.25 / 3.14	2.20 / 3.06	2.16 / 2.98	2.13 / 2.93	2.08 / 2.83	2.03 / 2.74	1.97 / 2.63	1.93 / 2.55	1.88 / 2.47	1.84 / 2.38	1.80 / 2.33	1.76 / 2.25	1.74 / 2.21	1.71 / 2.16	1.68 / 2.12	1.67 / 2.10
28	4.20 / 7.64	3.34 / 5.45	2.95 / 4.57	2.71 / 4.07	2.56 / 3.76	2.44 / 3.53	2.36 / 3.36	2.29 / 3.23	2.24 / 3.11	2.19 / 3.03	2.15 / 2.95	2.12 / 2.90	2.06 / 2.80	2.02 / 2.71	1.96 / 2.60	1.91 / 2.52	1.87 / 2.44	1.81 / 2.35	1.78 / 2.30	1.75 / 2.22	1.72 / 2.18	1.69 / 2.13	1.67 / 2.09	1.65 / 2.06
29	4.18 / 7.60	3.33 / 5.42	2.93 / 4.54	2.70 / 4.04	2.54 / 3.73	2.43 / 3.50	2.35 / 3.33	2.28 / 3.20	2.22 / 3.08	2.18 / 3.00	2.14 / 2.92	2.10 / 2.87	2.05 / 2.77	2.00 / 2.68	1.94 / 2.57	1.90 / 2.49	1.85 / 2.41	1.80 / 2.32	1.77 / 2.27	1.73 / 2.19	1.71 / 2.15	1.68 / 2.10	1.65 / 2.06	1.64 / 2.03

Table A.4 (continued)

Degrees of Freedom for Denominator (v_2)		Degrees of Freedom for Numerator (v_1)

v_2	1	2	3	4	5	6	7	8	9	10	11	12	16	20	24	30	40	50	75	75	100	200	500	∞
30	4.17 **7.56**	3.32 **5.39**	2.92 **4.51**	2.69 **4.02**	2.53 **3.70**	2.42 **3.47**	2.34 **3.30**	2.27 **3.17**	2.21 **3.06**	2.16 **2.98**	2.12 **2.90**	2.09 **2.84**	2.04 **2.74**	1.99 **2.66**	1.93 **2.55**	1.89 **2.47**	1.84 **2.38**	1.79 **2.29**	1.76 **2.24**	1.72 **2.16**	1.69 **2.13**	1.66 **2.07**	1.64 **2.03**	1.62 **2.01**
32	4.15 **7.50**	3.30 **5.34**	2.90 **4.46**	2.67 **3.97**	2.51 **3.66**	2.40 **3.42**	2.32 **3.25**	2.25 **3.12**	2.19 **3.01**	2.14 **2.94**	2.10 **2.86**	2.07 **2.80**	2.02 **2.70**	1.97 **2.62**	1.91 **2.51**	1.86 **2.42**	1.82 **2.34**	1.76 **2.25**	1.74 **2.20**	1.69 **2.12**	1.67 **2.08**	1.64 **2.02**	1.61 **1.98**	1.59 **1.96**
34	4.13 **7.44**	3.28 **5.29**	2.88 **4.42**	2.65 **3.93**	2.49 **3.61**	2.38 **3.38**	2.30 **3.21**	2.23 **3.08**	2.17 **2.97**	2.12 **2.89**	2.08 **2.82**	2.05 **2.76**	2.00 **2.66**	1.95 **2.58**	1.89 **2.47**	1.84 **2.38**	1.80 **2.30**	1.74 **2.21**	1.71 **2.15**	1.67 **2.08**	1.64 **2.04**	1.61 **1.98**	1.59 **1.94**	1.57 **1.91**
36	4.11 **7.39**	3.26 **5.25**	2.86 **4.38**	2.63 **3.89**	2.48 **3.58**	2.36 **3.35**	2.28 **3.18**	2.21 **3.04**	2.15 **2.94**	2.10 **2.86**	2.06 **2.78**	2.03 **2.72**	1.98 **2.62**	1.93 **2.54**	1.87 **2.43**	1.82 **2.35**	1.78 **2.26**	1.72 **2.17**	1.69 **2.12**	1.65 **2.04**	1.62 **2.00**	1.59 **1.94**	1.56 **1.90**	1.55 **1.87**
38	4.10 **7.35**	3.25 **5.21**	2.85 **4.34**	2.62 **3.86**	2.46 **3.54**	2.35 **3.32**	2.26 **3.15**	2.19 **3.02**	2.14 **2.91**	2.09 **2.82**	2.05 **2.75**	2.02 **2.69**	1.96 **2.59**	1.92 **2.51**	1.85 **2.40**	1.80 **2.32**	1.76 **2.22**	1.71 **2.14**	1.67 **2.08**	1.63 **2.00**	1.60 **1.97**	1.57 **1.90**	1.54 **1.86**	1.53 **1.84**
40	4.08 **7.31**	3.23 **5.18**	2.84 **4.31**	2.61 **3.83**	2.45 **3.51**	2.34 **3.29**	2.25 **3.12**	2.18 **2.99**	2.12 **2.88**	2.07 **2.80**	2.04 **2.73**	2.00 **2.66**	1.95 **2.56**	1.90 **2.49**	1.84 **2.37**	1.79 **2.29**	1.74 **2.20**	1.69 **2.11**	1.66 **2.05**	1.61 **1.97**	1.59 **1.94**	1.55 **1.88**	1.53 **1.84**	1.51 **1.81**
42	4.07 **7.27**	3.22 **5.15**	2.83 **4.29**	2.59 **3.80**	2.44 **3.49**	2.32 **3.26**	2.24 **3.10**	2.17 **2.96**	2.11 **2.86**	2.06 **2.77**	2.02 **2.70**	1.99 **2.64**	1.94 **2.54**	1.89 **2.46**	1.82 **2.35**	1.78 **2.26**	1.73 **2.17**	1.68 **2.08**	1.64 **2.02**	1.60 **1.94**	1.57 **1.91**	1.54 **1.85**	1.51 **1.80**	1.49 **1.78**
44	4.06 **7.24**	3.21 **5.12**	2.82 **4.26**	2.58 **3.78**	2.43 **3.46**	2.31 **3.24**	2.23 **3.07**	2.16 **2.94**	2.10 **2.84**	2.05 **2.75**	2.01 **2.68**	1.98 **2.62**	1.92 **2.52**	1.88 **2.44**	1.81 **2.32**	1.76 **2.24**	1.72 **2.15**	1.66 **2.06**	1.63 **2.00**	1.58 **1.92**	1.56 **1.88**	1.52 **1.82**	1.50 **1.78**	1.48 **1.75**
46	4.05 **7.21**	3.20 **5.10**	2.81 **4.24**	2.57 **3.76**	2.42 **3.44**	2.30 **3.22**	2.22 **3.05**	2.14 **2.92**	2.09 **2.82**	2.04 **2.73**	2.00 **2.66**	1.97 **2.60**	1.91 **2.50**	1.87 **2.42**	1.80 **2.30**	1.75 **2.22**	1.71 **2.13**	1.65 **2.04**	1.62 **1.98**	1.57 **1.90**	1.54 **1.86**	1.51 **1.80**	1.48 **1.76**	1.46 **1.72**
48	4.04 **7.19**	3.19 **5.08**	2.80 **4.22**	2.56 **3.74**	2.41 **3.42**	2.30 **3.20**	2.21 **3.04**	2.14 **2.90**	2.08 **2.80**	2.03 **2.71**	1.99 **2.64**	1.96 **2.58**	1.90 **2.48**	1.86 **2.40**	1.79 **2.28**	1.74 **2.20**	1.70 **2.11**	1.64 **2.02**	1.61 **1.96**	1.56 **1.88**	1.53 **1.84**	1.50 **1.78**	1.47 **1.73**	1.45 **1.70**
50	4.03 **7.17**	3.18 **5.06**	2.79 **4.20**	2.56 **3.72**	2.40 **3.41**	2.29 **3.18**	2.20 **3.02**	2.13 **2.88**	2.07 **2.78**	2.02 **2.70**	1.98 **2.62**	1.95 **2.56**	1.90 **2.46**	1.85 **2.39**	1.78 **2.26**	1.74 **2.18**	1.69 **2.10**	1.63 **2.00**	1.60 **1.94**	1.55 **1.86**	1.52 **1.82**	1.48 **1.76**	1.46 **1.71**	1.44 **1.68**
55	4.02 **7.12**	3.17 **5.01**	2.78 **4.16**	2.54 **3.68**	2.38 **3.37**	2.27 **3.15**	2.18 **2.98**	2.11 **2.85**	2.05 **2.75**	2.00 **2.66**	1.97 **2.59**	1.93 **2.53**	1.88 **2.43**	1.83 **2.35**	1.76 **2.23**	1.72 **2.15**	1.67 **2.06**	1.61 **1.96**	1.58 **1.90**	1.52 **1.82**	1.50 **1.78**	1.46 **1.71**	1.43 **1.66**	1.41 **1.64**

Table A.4 (*continued*)

Degrees of Freedom for Numerator (v_1)

Degrees of Freedom for Denominator (v_2)	1	2	3	4	5	6	7	8	9	10	11	12	14	16	20	24	30	40	50	75	100	200	500	∞
60	4.00 **7.03**	3.15 **4.98**	2.76 **4.13**	2.52 **3.65**	2.37 **3.34**	2.25 **3.12**	2.17 **2.95**	2.10 **2.82**	2.04 **2.72**	1.99 **2.63**	1.95 **2.56**	1.92 **2.50**	1.86 **2.40**	1.81 **2.32**	1.75 **2.20**	1.70 **2.12**	1.65 **2.03**	1.59 **1.93**	1.56 **1.87**	1.50 **1.79**	1.48 **1.74**	1.44 **1.68**	1.41 **1.63**	1.39 **1.60**
65	3.99 **7.04**	3.14 **4.95**	2.75 **4.10**	2.51 **3.62**	2.36 **3.31**	2.24 **3.09**	2.15 **2.93**	2.08 **2.79**	2.02 **2.70**	1.98 **2.61**	1.94 **2.54**	1.90 **2.47**	1.85 **2.37**	1.80 **2.30**	1.73 **2.18**	1.68 **2.09**	1.63 **2.00**	1.57 **1.90**	1.54 **1.84**	1.49 **1.76**	1.46 **1.71**	1.42 **1.64**	1.39 **1.60**	1.37 **1.56**
70	3.98 **7.01**	3.13 **4.92**	2.74 **4.08**	2.50 **3.60**	2.35 **3.29**	2.23 **3.07**	2.14 **2.91**	2.07 **2.77**	2.01 **2.67**	1.97 **2.59**	1.93 **2.51**	1.89 **2.45**	1.84 **2.35**	1.79 **2.28**	1.72 **2.15**	1.67 **2.07**	1.62 **1.98**	1.56 **1.88**	1.53 **1.82**	1.47 **1.74**	1.45 **1.69**	1.40 **1.63**	1.37 **1.56**	1.35 **1.53**
80	3.90 **6.96**	3.11 **4.88**	2.72 **4.04**	2.48 **3.56**	2.33 **3.25**	2.21 **3.04**	2.12 **2.87**	2.05 **2.74**	1.99 **2.64**	1.95 **2.55**	1.91 **2.48**	1.88 **2.41**	1.82 **2.32**	1.77 **2.24**	1.70 **2.11**	1.65 **2.03**	1.60 **1.94**	1.54 **1.84**	1.51 **1.78**	1.45 **1.70**	1.42 **1.65**	1.38 **1.57**	1.35 **1.52**	1.32 **1.49**
100	3.94 **6.90**	3.09 **4.82**	2.70 **3.98**	2.46 **3.51**	2.30 **3.20**	2.19 **2.99**	2.10 **2.82**	2.03 **2.69**	1.97 **2.59**	1.92 **2.51**	1.88 **2.43**	1.85 **2.36**	1.79 **2.26**	1.75 **2.19**	1.68 **2.06**	1.63 **1.98**	1.57 **1.89**	1.51 **1.79**	1.48 **1.73**	1.42 **1.65**	1.39 **1.59**	1.34 **1.51**	1.30 **1.46**	1.28 **1.43**
125	3.92 **6.84**	3.07 **4.78**	2.68 **3.94**	2.44 **3.47**	2.29 **3.17**	2.17 **2.95**	2.08 **2.79**	2.01 **2.65**	1.95 **2.56**	1.90 **2.47**	1.86 **2.40**	1.83 **2.33**	1.77 **2.23**	1.72 **2.15**	1.65 **2.03**	1.60 **1.94**	1.55 **1.85**	1.49 **1.75**	1.45 **1.68**	1.39 **1.59**	1.36 **1.54**	1.31 **1.46**	1.27 **1.40**	1.25 **1.37**
150	3.91 **6.81**	3.06 **4.75**	2.67 **3.91**	2.43 **3.44**	2.27 **3.13**	2.16 **2.92**	2.07 **2.76**	2.00 **2.62**	1.94 **2.53**	1.89 **2.44**	1.85 **2.37**	1.82 **2.30**	1.76 **2.20**	1.71 **2.12**	1.64 **2.00**	1.59 **1.91**	1.54 **1.83**	1.47 **1.72**	1.44 **1.66**	1.37 **1.56**	1.34 **1.51**	1.29 **1.43**	1.25 **1.37**	1.22 **1.33**
200	3.89 **6.76**	3.04 **4.71**	2.65 **3.88**	2.41 **3.41**	2.26 **3.11**	2.14 **2.90**	2.05 **2.73**	1.98 **2.60**	1.92 **2.50**	1.87 **2.41**	1.83 **2.34**	1.80 **2.28**	1.74 **2.17**	1.69 **2.09**	1.62 **1.97**	1.57 **1.88**	1.52 **1.79**	1.45 **1.69**	1.42 **1.62**	1.35 **1.53**	1.32 **1.48**	1.26 **1.39**	1.22 **1.33**	1.19 **1.28**
400	3.86 **6.70**	3.02 **4.66**	2.62 **3.83**	2.39 **3.36**	2.23 **3.06**	2.12 **2.85**	2.03 **2.69**	1.96 **2.55**	1.90 **2.46**	1.85 **2.37**	1.81 **2.29**	1.78 **2.23**	1.72 **2.12**	1.67 **2.04**	1.60 **1.92**	1.54 **1.84**	1.49 **1.74**	1.42 **1.64**	1.38 **1.57**	1.32 **1.47**	1.28 **1.42**	1.22 **1.32**	1.16 **1.24**	1.13 **1.19**
1000	3.85 **6.66**	3.00 **4.62**	2.61 **3.80**	2.38 **3.34**	2.22 **3.04**	2.10 **2.82**	2.02 **2.66**	1.95 **2.53**	1.89 **2.43**	1.84 **2.34**	1.80 **2.26**	1.76 **2.20**	1.70 **2.09**	1.65 **2.01**	1.58 **1.89**	1.53 **1.81**	1.47 **1.71**	1.41 **1.61**	1.36 **1.54**	1.30 **1.44**	1.26 **1.38**	1.19 **1.28**	1.13 **1.19**	1.08 **1.11**
∞	3.84 **6.64**	2.99 **4.60**	2.60 **3.78**	2.37 **3.32**	2.21 **3.02**	2.09 **2.80**	2.01 **2.64**	1.94 **2.51**	1.88 **2.41**	1.83 **2.32**	1.79 **2.24**	1.75 **2.18**	1.69 **2.07**	1.65 **1.99**	1.57 **1.87**	1.52 **1.79**	1.46 **1.69**	1.40 **1.59**	1.35 **1.52**	1.28 **1.41**	1.24 **1.36**	1.17 **1.25**	1.11 **1.15**	1.00 **1.00**

APPENDIX B

INTEREST TABLES

½%

	To find F, given P:	To find P, given F:	To find A, given F:	To find A, given P:	To find F, given A:	To find P, given A:	
	$(1 + i)^n$	$\dfrac{1}{(1 + i)^n}$	$\dfrac{i}{(1 + i)^n - 1}$	$\dfrac{i(1 + i)^n}{(1 + i)^n - 1}$	$\dfrac{(1 + i)^n - 1}{i}$	$\dfrac{(1 + i)^n - 1}{i(1 + i)^n}$	
	CAF	PWF	SFF	CRF	SCAF	SPWF	
n	$(f/p)_n^{1/2}$	$(p/f)_n^{1/2}$	$(a/f)_n^{1/2}$	$(a/p)_n^{1/2}$	$(f/a)_n^{1/2}$	$(p/a)_n^{1/2}$	n
1	1.005	0.9950	1.00000	1.00500	1.000	0.995	1
2	1.010	0.9901	0.49875	0.50375	2.005	1.985	2
3	1.015	0.9851	0.33167	0.33667	3.015	2.970	3
4	1.020	0.9802	0.24183	0.25313	4.030	3.950	4
5	1.025	0.9754	0.19801	0.20301	5.050	4.926	5
6	1.030	0.9705	0.16460	0.16960	6.076	5.896	6
7	1.036	0.9657	0.14073	0.14573	7.106	6.862	7
8	1.041	0.9609	0.12283	0.12783	8.141	7.823	8
9	1.046	0.9561	0.10891	0.11391	9.182	8.779	9
10	1.051	0.9513	0.09777	0.10277	10.288	9.730	10
11	1.056	0.9466	0.08866	0.09366	11.279	10.677	11
12	1.062	0.9419	0.08107	0.08607	12.336	11.619	12
13	1.067	0.9372	0.07464	0.07964	13.397	12.556	13
14	1.072	0.9326	0.06914	0.07414	14.464	13.489	14
15	1.078	0.9279	0.06436	0.06936	15.537	14.417	15
16	1.083	0.9233	0.06019	0.06519	16.614	15.340	16
17	1.088	0.9187	0.05615	0.06151	17.697	16.259	17
18	1.094	0.9141	0.05323	0.05823	18.786	17.173	18
19	1.099	0.9096	0.05030	0.05530	19.880	18.082	19
20	1.105	0.9051	0.04767	0.05267	20.979	18.987	20
21	1.110	0.9006	0.04528	0.05028	22.084	19.888	21
22	1.116	0.8961	0.04311	0.04811	23.194	20.784	22
23	1.122	0.8916	0.04113	0.04613	24.310	21.676	23
24	1.127	0.8872	0.03932	0.04432	25.432	22.563	24
25	1.133	0.8828	0.03767	0.04265	26.559	23.446	25
26	1.138	0.8784	0.03611	0.04111	27.692	24.324	26
27	1.144	0.8740	0.03469	0.03969	28.830	25.198	27
28	1.150	0.8697	0.03336	0.03836	29.975	26.068	28
29	1.156	0.8653	0.03213	0.03713	31.124	26.933	29
30	1.161	0.8610	0.03098	0.03598	32.280	27.794	30
31	1.167	0.8567	0.02990	0.03490	33.441	28.651	31
32	1.173	0.8525	0.02889	0.03389	34.609	29.503	32
33	1.179	0.8482	0.02795	0.03295	35.782	30.352	33
34	1.185	0.8440	0.02706	0.03206	36.961	31.196	34
35	1.191	0.8398	0.02622	0.03122	38.145	32.035	35
40	1.221	0.8191	0.02265	0.02765	44.159	36.172	40
45	1.252	0.7990	0.01987	0.02487	50.324	40.207	45
50	1.283	0.7793	0.01765	0.02265	56.645	44.143	50
55	1.316	0.7601	0.01548	0.02084	63.126	47.981	55
60	1.349	0.7414	0.01433	0.01933	69.770	51.726	60
65	1.383	0.7231	0.01306	0.01806	76.582	55.377	65
70	1.418	0.7053	0.01197	0.01697	83.566	58.939	70
75	1.454	0.6879	0.01102	0.01602	90.727	62.414	75
80	1.490	0.6710	0.01020	0.01520	98.068	65.802	80
85	1.528	0.6545	0.00947	0.01447	105.594	69.108	85
90	1.567	0.6383	0.00883	0.01383	113.311	72.331	90
95	1.606	0.6226	0.00825	0.01325	121.222	75.476	95
100	1.647	0.6073	0.00773	0.01273	129.334	78.543	100

1%

	To find F, given P:	To find P, given F:	To find A, given F:	To find A, given P:	To find F, given A:	To find P, given A:	
	$(1 + i)^n$	$\dfrac{1}{(1 + i)^n}$	$\dfrac{i}{(1 + i)^n - 1}$	$\dfrac{i(1 + i)^n}{(1 + i)^n - 1}$	$\dfrac{(1 + i)^n - 1}{i}$	$\dfrac{(1 + i)^n - 1}{i(1 + i)^n}$	
n	$(f/p)_n^1$	$(p/f)_n^1$	$(a/f)_n^1$	$(a/p)_n^1$	$(f/a)_n^1$	$(p/a)_n^1$	n
1	1.010	0.9901	1.00000	1.01000	1.000	0.990	1
2	1.020	0.9803	0.49751	0.50751	2.010	1.970	2
3	1.030	0.9706	0.33002	0.34002	3.030	2.941	3
4	1.041	0.9610	0.24628	0.25628	4.060	3.902	4
5	1.051	0.9515	0.19604	0.20604	5.101	4.853	5
6	1.062	0.9420	0.16255	0.17255	6.152	5.795	6
7	1.072	0.9327	0.13863	0.14863	7.214	6.728	7
8	1.083	0.9235	0.12069	0.13069	8.286	7.652	8
9	1.094	0.9143	0.10674	0.11674	9.369	8.566	9
10	1.105	0.9053	0.09558	0.10558	10.462	9.471	10
11	1.116	0.8963	0.08645	0.09645	11.567	10.368	11
12	1.127	0.8874	0.07885	0.08885	12.683	11.255	12
13	1.138	0.8787	0.07241	0.08241	13.809	12.134	13
14	1.149	0.8700	0.06690	0.07690	14.947	13.004	14
15	1.161	0.8613	0.06212	0.07212	16.097	13.865	15
16	1.173	0.8528	0.05794	0.06794	17.258	14.718	16
17	1.184	0.8444	0.05426	0.06426	18.430	15.562	17
18	1.196	0.8360	0.05098	0.06098	19.615	16.398	18
19	1.208	0.8277	0.04805	0.05805	20.811	17.226	19
20	1.220	0.8195	0.04542	0.05542	22.019	18.046	20
21	1.232	0.8114	0.04303	0.05303	23.239	18.857	21
22	1.245	0.8034	0.04086	0.05086	24.472	19.660	22
23	1.257	0.7954	0.03889	0.04889	25.716	20.456	23
24	1.270	0.7876	0.03707	0.04707	26.973	21.243	24
25	1.282	0.7798	0.03541	0.04541	28.243	22.023	25
26	1.295	0.7720	0.03387	0.04387	29.526	22.795	26
27	1.308	0.7644	0.03245	0.04245	30.821	23.560	27
28	1.321	0.7568	0.03112	0.04112	32.129	24.316	28
29	1.335	0.7493	0.02990	0.03990	33.450	25.066	29
30	1.348	0.7419	0.02875	0.03875	34.785	25.808	30
31	1.361	0.7346	0.02768	0.03768	36.133	26.542	31
32	1.375	0.7273	0.02667	0.03667	37.494	27.270	32
33	1.391	0.7201	0.02573	0.03573	38.869	27.990	33
34	1.403	0.7130	0.02484	0.03484	40.258	28.703	34
35	1.417	0.7059	0.02400	0.03400	41.660	29.409	35
40	1.489	0.6717	0.02046	0.03046	48.886	32.835	40
45	1.565	0.6391	0.01771	0.02771	56.481	36.095	45
50	1.645	0.6080	0.01551	0.02551	64.463	39.196	50
55	1.729	0.5785	0.01373	0.02373	72.852	42.147	55
60	1.817	0.5504	0.01224	0.02224	81.670	44.955	60
65	1.909	0.5237	0.01100	0.02100	90.937	47.627	65
70	2.007	0.4983	0.00993	0.01993	100.676	50.169	70
75	2.109	0.4741	0.00902	0.01902	110.913	52.587	75
80	2.217	0.4511	0.00822	0.01822	121.672	54.888	80
85	2.330	0.4292	0.00752	0.01752	132.979	57.078	85
90	2.449	0.4084	0.00690	0.01690	144.863	59.161	90
95	2.574	0.3886	0.00636	0.01636	157.354	61.143	95
100	2.705	0.3697	0.00587	0.01587	170.481	63.029	100

1½%

n	To find F, given P: $(1 + i)^n$ $(f/p)_n^{1\ 1/2}$	To find P, given F: $\dfrac{1}{(1 + i)^n}$ $(p/f)_n^{1\ 1/2}$	To find A, given F: $\dfrac{i}{(1 + i)^n - 1}$ $(a/f)_n^{1\ 1/2}$	To find A, given P: $\dfrac{i(1 + i)^n}{(1 + i)^n - 1}$ $(a/p)_n^{1\ 1/2}$	To find F, given A: $\dfrac{(1 + i)^n - 1}{i}$ $(f/a)_n^{1\ 1/2}$	To find P, given A: $\dfrac{(1 + i)^n - 1}{i(1 + i)^n}$ $(p/a)_n^{1\ 1/2}$	n
1	1.015	0.9852	1.00000	1.01500	1.000	0.985	1
2	1.030	0.9707	0.49628	0.51128	2.015	1.956	2
3	1.046	0.9563	0.32838	0.34338	3.045	2.912	3
4	1.061	0.9422	0.24444	0.25944	4.091	3.854	4
5	1.077	0.9283	0.19409	0.20909	5.152	4.783	5
6	1.093	0.9145	0.16053	0.17553	6.230	5.697	6
7	1.110	0.9010	0.13656	0.15156	7.323	6.598	7
8	1.126	0.8877	0.11858	0.13358	8.433	7.486	8
9	1.143	0.8746	0.10461	0.11961	9.559	8.361	9
10	1.161	0.8617	0.09343	0.10843	10.703	9.222	10
11	1.178	0.8489	0.08429	0.09930	11.863	10.071	11
12	1.196	0.8364	0.07668	0.09168	13.041	10.908	12
13	1.214	0.8240	0.07024	0.08524	14.237	11.732	13
14	1.232	0.8118	0.06472	0.07972	15.450	12.543	14
15	1.250	0.7999	0.05994	0.07494	16.682	13.343	15
16	1.269	0.7880	0.05577	0.07077	17.932	14.131	16
17	1.288	0.7764	0.05208	0.06708	19.201	14.908	17
18	1.307	0.7649	0.04881	0.06381	20.489	15.673	18
19	1.327	0.7536	0.04588	0.06088	21.797	16.426	19
20	1.347	0.7425	0.04325	0.05825	23.124	17.169	20
21	1.367	0.7315	0.04087	0.05587	24.471	17.900	21
22	1.388	0.7207	0.03870	0.05370	25.838	18.621	22
23	1.408	0.7100	0.03673	0.05173	27.225	19.331	23
24	1.430	0.6995	0.03492	0.04992	28.634	20.030	24
25	1.451	0.6892	0.03325	0.04826	30.063	20.720	25
26	1.473	0.6790	0.03173	0.04673	31.514	21.399	26
27	1.495	0.6690	0.03032	0.04532	32.987	22.068	27
28	1.517	0.6591	0.02900	0.04400	34.481	22.727	28
29	1.540	0.6494	0.02778	0.04278	35.999	23.376	29
30	1.563	0.6398	0.02664	0.04164	37.539	24.016	30
31	1.587	0.6303	0.02557	0.04057	39.102	24.646	31
32	1.610	0.6210	0.02458	0.03958	40.688	25.267	32
33	1.634	0.6118	0.02364	0.03864	42.229	25.879	33
34	1.659	0.6028	0.02276	0.03776	43.933	26.482	34
35	1.684	0.5939	0.02193	0.03693	45.592	27.076	35
40	1.814	0.5513	0.01834	0.03343	54.268	29.916	40
45	1.954	0.5117	0.01572	0.03072	63.614	32.552	45
50	2.105	0.4750	0.01357	0.02857	73.683	35.000	50
55	2.268	0.4409	0.01183	0.02683	84.530	37.271	55
60	2.443	0.4093	0.01039	0.02539	96.215	39.380	60
65	2.632	0.3799	0.00919	0.02419	108.803	41.338	65
70	2.835	0.3527	0.00817	0.02317	122.364	43.155	70
75	3.055	0.3274	0.00730	0.02230	136.973	44.842	75
80	3.291	0.3039	0.00655	0.02155	152.711	46.407	80
85	3.545	0.2821	0.00589	0.02089	169.665	47.861	85
90	3.819	0.2619	0.00532	0.02032	187.930	49.210	90
95	4.114	0.2431	0.00482	0.01982	207.606	50.462	95
100	4.432	0.2256	0.00437	0.01937	228.803	51.625	100

2%

	To find F, given P: $(1 + i)^n$	To find P, given F: $\dfrac{1}{(1 + i)^n}$	To find A, given F: $\dfrac{i}{(1 + i)^n - 1}$	To find A, given P: $\dfrac{i(1 + i)^n}{(1 + i)^n - 1}$	To find F, given A: $\dfrac{(1 + i)^n - 1}{i}$	To find P, given A: $\dfrac{(1 + i)^n - 1}{i(1 + i)^n}$	
n	$(f/p)^2_n$	$(p/f)^2_n$	$(a/f)^2_n$	$(a/p)^2_n$	$(f/a)^2_n$	$(p/a)^2_n$	n
1	1.020	0.9804	1.00000	1.02000	1.000	0.980	1
2	1.040	0.9612	0.49505	0.51505	2.020	1.942	2
3	1.061	0.9423	0.32675	0.34675	3.060	2.884	3
4	1.082	0.9238	0.24262	0.26262	4.122	3.808	4
5	1.104	0.9057	0.19216	0.21216	5.204	4.713	5
6	1.126	0.8880	0.15853	0.17853	6.308	5.601	6
7	1.149	0.8706	0.13451	0.15451	7.434	6.472	7
8	1.172	0.8535	0.11651	0.13651	8.583	7.325	8
9	1.195	0.8368	0.10252	0.12252	9.755	8.162	9
10	1.219	0.8203	0.09133	0.11133	10.950	8.983	10
11	1.243	0.8043	0.08216	0.10218	12.169	9.787	11
12	1.268	0.7885	0.07456	0.09456	13.412	10.575	12
13	1.294	0.7730	0.06812	0.08812	14.680	11.348	13
14	1.319	0.7579	0.06260	0.08260	15.974	12.106	14
15	1.346	0.7430	0.05783	0.07783	17.293	12.849	15
16	1.373	0.7284	0.05365	0.07365	18.639	13.578	16
17	1.400	0.7142	0.04997	0.06997	20.012	14.292	17
18	1.428	0.7002	0.04670	0.06670	21.412	14.992	18
19	1.457	0.6864	0.04378	0.06378	22.841	15.678	19
20	1.486	0.6730	0.04116	0.06116	24.297	16.351	20
21	1.516	0.6598	0.03878	0.05878	25.783	17.011	21
22	1.546	0.6468	0.03663	0.05663	27.299	17.658	22
23	1.577	0.6342	0.03467	0.05467	28.845	18.292	23
24	1.608	0.6217	0.03287	0.05287	30.422	18.914	24
25	1.641	0.6095	0.03122	0.05122	32.030	19.523	25
26	1.673	0.5976	0.02970	0.04970	33.671	20.121	26
27	1.707	0.5859	0.02829	0.04829	35.344	20.707	27
28	1.741	0.5744	0.02699	0.04699	37.051	21.281	28
29	1.776	0.5631	0.02578	0.04578	38.792	21.844	29
30	1.811	0.5521	0.02465	0.04465	40.568	22.396	30
31	1.848	0.5412	0.02360	0.04360	42.379	22.938	31
32	1.885	0.5306	0.02261	0.04261	44.227	23.468	32
33	1.922	0.5202	0.02169	0.04169	46.112	23.989	33
34	1.961	0.5100	0.02082	0.04082	48.034	24.499	34
35	2.000	0.5000	0.02000	0.04000	49.994	24.999	35
40	2.208	0.4529	0.01656	0.03656	60.402	27.355	40
45	2.438	0.4102	0.01391	0.03391	71.893	29.490	45
50	2.692	0.3715	0.01182	0.03182	84.579	31.424	50
55	2.972	0.3365	0.01014	0.03014	98.587	33.175	55
60	3.281	0.3048	0.00877	0.02877	114.052	34.761	60
65	3.623	0.2761	0.00763	0.02763	131.126	36.197	65
70	4.000	0.2500	0.00667	0.02667	149.978	37.499	70
75	4.416	0.2265	0.00586	0.02586	170.792	38.677	75
80	4.875	0.2051	0.00516	0.02516	193.772	39.745	80
85	5.383	0.1858	0.00456	0.02456	219.144	40.711	85
90	5.943	0.1683	0.00405	0.02405	247.157	41.587	90
95	6.562	0.1524	0.00360	0.02360	278.085	42.380	95
100	7.245	0.1380	0.00320	0.02320	312.232	43.098	100

2½%

	To find F, given P: $(1 + i)^n$	To find P, given F: $\dfrac{1}{(1 + i)^n}$	To find A, given F: $\dfrac{i}{(1 + i)^n - 1}$	To find A, given P: $\dfrac{i(1 + i)^n}{(1 + i)^n - 1}$	To find F, given A: $\dfrac{(1 + i)^n - 1}{i}$	To find P, given A: $\dfrac{(1 + i)^n - 1}{i(1 + i)^n}$	
n	$(f/p)_n^{2\ 1/2}$	$(p/f)_n^{2\ 1/2}$	$(a/f)_n^{2\ 1/2}$	$(a/p)_n^{2\ 1/2}$	$(f/a)_n^{2\ 1/2}$	$(p/a)_n^{2\ 1/2}$	n
1	1.025	0.9756	1.00000	1.02500	1.000	0.976	1
2	1.051	0.9518	0.49383	0.51883	2.025	1.927	2
3	1.077	0.9386	0.32514	0.35014	3.076	2.856	3
4	1.104	0.9060	0.24082	0.26582	4.153	3.762	4
5	1.131	0.8839	0.19025	0.21525	5.256	4.646	5
6	1.160	0.8623	0.15655	0.18155	6.388	5.508	6
7	1.189	0.8413	0.13250	0.15750	7.547	6.349	7
8	1.218	0.8207	0.11447	0.13947	8.736	7.170	8
9	1.249	0.8007	0.10046	0.12546	9.955	7.971	9
10	1.280	0.7812	0.08926	0.11426	11.203	8.752	10
11	1.312	0.7621	0.08011	0.10511	12.483	9.514	11
12	1.345	0.7436	0.07249	0.09749	13.796	10.258	12
13	1.379	0.7254	0.06605	0.09105	15.140	10.983	13
14	1.413	0.7077	0.06054	0.08554	16.519	11.691	14
15	1.448	0.6905	0.05577	0.08077	17.932	12.381	15
16	1.485	0.6736	0.05160	0.07660	19.380	13.055	16
17	1.522	0.6572	0.04793	0.07293	20.865	13.712	17
18	1.560	0.6412	0.04467	0.06967	22.386	14.353	18
19	1.599	0.6255	0.04176	0.06676	23.946	14.979	19
20	1.639	0.6103	0.03915	0.06415	25.545	15.589	20
21	1.680	0.5954	0.03679	0.06179	27.183	16.185	21
22	1.722	0.5809	0.03465	0.05965	28.863	16.765	22
23	1.765	0.5667	0.03270	0.05770	30.584	17.332	23
24	1.809	0.5529	0.03091	0.05591	32.349	17.885	24
25	1.854	0.5394	0.02928	0.05428	34.158	18.424	25
26	1.900	0.5262	0.02777	0.05277	36.012	18.951	26
27	1.948	0.5134	0.02638	0.05138	37.912	19.464	27
28	1.996	0.5009	0.02509	0.05009	39.860	19.965	28
29	2.046	0.4887	0.02389	0.04889	41.856	20.454	29
30	2.098	0.4767	0.02278	0.04778	43.903	20.930	30
31	2.150	0.4651	0.02174	0.04674	46.000	21.395	31
32	2.204	0.4538	0.02077	0.04577	48.150	21.849	32
33	2.259	0.4427	0.01986	0.04486	50.354	22.292	33
34	2.315	0.4319	0.01901	0.04401	52.613	22.724	34
35	2.373	0.4214	0.01821	0.04321	54.928	23.145	35
40	2.685	0.3724	0.01484	0.03984	67.403	25.103	40
45	3.038	0.3292	0.01227	0.03727	81.516	26.833	45
50	3.437	0.2909	0.01026	0.03526	97.484	28.362	50
55	3.889	0.2572	0.00865	0.03365	115.551	29.714	55
60	4.400	0.2273	0.00735	0.03235	135.992	30.909	60
65	4.978	0.2009	0.00628	0.03128	159.118	31.965	65
70	5.632	0.1776	0.00540	0.03040	185.284	32.898	70
75	6.372	0.1569	0.00465	0.02965	214.888	33.723	75
80	7.210	0.1387	0.00403	0.02903	248.383	34.452	80
85	8.157	0.1226	0.00349	0.02849	286.279	35.096	85
90	9.229	0.1084	0.00304	0.02804	329.154	35.666	90
95	10.442	0.0958	0.00265	0.02765	377.664	36.169	95
100	11.814	0.0846	0.00231	0.02731	432.549	36.614	100

3%

	To find F, given P:	To find P, given F:	To find A, given F:	To find A, given P:	To find F, given A:	To find P, given A:	
	$(1+i)^n$	$\dfrac{1}{(1+i)^n}$	$\dfrac{i}{(1+i)^n-1}$	$\dfrac{i(1+i)^n}{(1+i)^n-1}$	$\dfrac{(1+i)^n-1}{i}$	$\dfrac{(1+i)^n-1}{i(1+i)^n}$	
n	$(f/p)_n^3$	$(p/f)_n^3$	$(a/f)_n^3$	$(a/p)_n^3$	$(f/a)_n^3$	$(p/a)_n^3$	n
1	1.030	0.9709	1.00000	1.03000	1.000	0.971	1
2	1.061	0.9426	0.49261	0.52261	2.030	1.913	2
3	1.093	0.9151	0.32353	0.35353	3.091	2.829	3
4	1.126	0.8885	0.23903	0.26903	4.184	3.717	4
5	1.159	0.8626	0.18835	0.21835	5.309	4.580	5
6	1.194	0.8375	0.15460	0.18460	6.468	5.417	6
7	1.230	0.8131	0.13051	0.16051	7.662	6.230	7
8	1.267	0.7894	0.11246	0.14246	8.892	7.020	8
9	1.305	0.7664	0.09843	0.12843	10.159	7.786	9
10	1.344	0.7441	0.08723	0.11723	11.464	8.530	10
11	1.384	0.7224	0.07808	0.10808	12.808	9.253	11
12	1.426	0.7014	0.07046	0.10046	14.192	9.954	12
13	1.469	0.6810	0.06403	0.09403	15.618	10.635	13
14	1.513	0.6611	0.05853	0.08853	17.086	11.296	14
15	1.558	0.6419	0.05377	0.08377	18.599	11.938	15
16	1.605	0.6232	0.04961	0.07961	20.157	12.561	16
17	1.653	0.6050	0.04595	0.07595	21.762	13.166	17
18	1.702	0.5874	0.04271	0.07271	23.414	13.754	18
19	1.754	0.5703	0.03981	0.06981	25.117	14.324	19
20	1.806	0.5537	0.03722	0.06722	26.870	14.877	20
21	1.860	0.5375	0.03487	0.06487	28.676	15.415	21
22	1.916	0.5219	0.03275	0.06275	30.537	15.937	22
23	1.974	0.5067	0.03081	0.06081	32.453	16.444	23
24	2.033	0.4919	0.02905	0.05905	34.426	16.936	24
25	2.094	0.4776	0.02743	0.05743	36.459	17.413	25
26	2.157	0.4637	0.02594	0.05594	38.553	17.877	26
27	2.221	0.4502	0.02456	0.05456	40.710	18.327	27
28	2.288	0.4371	0.02329	0.05329	42.931	18.764	28
29	2.357	0.4243	0.02211	0.05211	45.219	19.188	29
30	2.427	0.4120	0.02102	0.05102	47.575	19.600	30
31	2.500	0.4000	0.02000	0.05000	50.003	20.000	31
32	2.575	0.3883	0.01905	0.04905	52.503	20.389	32
33	2.652	0.3770	0.01816	0.04816	55.078	20.766	33
34	2.732	0.3660	0.01732	0.04732	57.730	21.132	34
35	2.814	0.3554	0.01654	0.04654	60.462	21.487	35
40	3.262	0.3066	0.01326	0.04326	75.401	23.115	40
45	3.782	0.2644	0.01079	0.04079	92.720	24.519	45
50	4.384	0.2281	0.00887	0.03887	112.797	25.730	50
55	5.082	0.1968	0.00735	0.03735	136.072	26.774	55
60	5.892	0.1697	0.00613	0.03613	163.053	27.676	60
65	6.830	0.1464	0.00515	0.03515	194.333	28.453	65
70	7.918	0.1263	0.00434	0.03434	230.594	29.123	70
75	9.179	0.1089	0.00367	0.03367	272.631	29.702	75
80	10.641	0.0940	0.00311	0.03311	321.363	30.201	80
85	12.336	0.0811	0.00265	0.03265	377.857	30.631	85
90	14.300	0.0699	0.00226	0.03226	443.349	31.002	90
95	16.578	0.0603	0.00193	0.03193	519.272	31.323	95
100	19.219	0.0520	0.00165	0.03165	607.288	31.599	100

4%

	To find F, given P: $(1 + i)^n$	To find P, given F: $\dfrac{1}{(1 + i)^n}$	To find A, given F: $\dfrac{i}{(1 + i)^n - 1}$	To find A, given P: $\dfrac{i(1 + i)^n}{(1 + i)^n - 1}$	To find F, given A: $\dfrac{(1 + i)^n - 1}{i}$	To find P, given A: $\dfrac{(1 + i)^n - 1}{i(1 + i)^n}$	
n	$(f/p)_n^4$	$(p/f)_n^4$	$(a/f)_n^4$	$(a/p)_n^4$	$(f/a)_n^4$	$(p/a)_n^4$	n
1	1.040	0.9615	1.00000	1.04000	1.000	0.962	1
2	1.082	0.9246	0.49020	0.53020	2.040	1.886	2
3	1.125	0.8890	0.32035	0.36035	3.122	2.775	3
4	1.170	0.8548	0.23549	0.27549	4.246	3.630	4
5	1.217	0.8219	0.18463	0.22463	5.416	4.452	5
6	1.265	0.7903	0.15076	0.19076	6.633	5.242	6
7	1.316	0.7599	0.12661	0.16661	7.898	6.002	7
8	1.369	0.7307	0.10853	0.14853	9.214	6.733	8
9	1.423	0.7026	0.09449	0.13449	10.583	7.435	9
10	1.480	0.6756	0.08329	0.12329	12.006	8.111	10
11	1.539	0.6496	0.07415	0.11415	13.486	8.760	11
12	1.601	0.6246	0.06655	0.10655	15.026	9.385	12
13	1.665	0.6006	0.06014	0.10014	16.627	9.986	13
14	1.732	0.5775	0.05467	0.09467	18.292	10.563	14
15	1.801	0.5553	0.04994	0.08994	20.024	11.118	15
16	1.873	0.5339	0.04582	0.08582	21.825	11.652	16
17	1.948	0.5134	0.04220	0.08220	23.698	12.166	17
18	2.026	0.4936	0.03899	0.07899	25.645	12.659	18
19	2.107	0.4746	0.03614	0.07614	27.671	13.134	19
20	2.191	0.4564	0.03358	0.07358	29.778	13.590	20
21	2.279	0.4388	0.03128	0.07128	31.969	14.029	21
22	2.370	0.4220	0.02920	0.06920	34.248	14.451	22
23	2.465	0.4057	0.02731	0.06731	36.618	14.857	23
24	2.563	0.3901	0.02559	0.06559	39.083	15.247	24
25	2.666	0.3751	0.02401	0.06401	41.646	15.622	25
26	2.772	0.3607	0.02257	0.06257	44.312	15.983	26
27	2.883	0.3468	0.02124	0.06124	47.084	16.330	27
28	2.999	0.3335	0.02001	0.06001	49.968	16.663	28
29	3.119	0.3207	0.01888	0.05888	52.966	16.984	29
30	3.243	0.3083	0.01783	0.05783	56.085	17.292	30
31	3.373	0.2965	0.01686	0.05686	59.328	17.588	31
32	3.508	0.2851	0.01595	0.05595	62.701	17.874	32
33	3.648	0.2741	0.01510	0.05510	66.210	18.148	33
34	3.794	0.2636	0.01431	0.05431	69.858	18.411	34
35	3.946	0.2534	0.01358	0.05358	73.652	18.665	35
40	4.801	0.2083	0.01052	0.05052	95.026	19.793	40
45	5.841	0.1712	0.00826	0.04826	121.029	20.720	45
50	7.107	0.1407	0.00655	0.04655	152.667	21.482	50
55	8.646	0.1157	0.00523	0.04523	191.159	22.109	55
60	10.520	0.0951	0.00420	0.04420	237.991	22.623	60
65	12.799	0.0781	0.00339	0.04339	294.968	23.047	65
70	15.572	0.0642	0.00275	0.04275	364.290	23.395	70
75	18.945	0.0528	0.00223	0.04223	448.631	23.680	75
80	23.050	0.0434	0.00181	0.04181	551.245	23.915	80
85	28.044	0.0357	0.00148	0.04148	676.090	24.109	85
90	34.119	0.0293	0.00121	0.04121	827.983	24.267	90
95	41.511	0.0241	0.00099	0.04099	1012.785	24.398	95
100	50.505	0.0198	0.00081	0.04081	1237.624	24.505	100

5%

	To find F, given P:	To find P, given F:	To find A, given F:	To find A, given P:	To find F, given A:	To find P, given A:	
	$(1+i)^n$	$\dfrac{1}{(1+i)^n}$	$\dfrac{i}{(1+i)^n-1}$	$\dfrac{i(1+i)^n}{(1+i)^n-1}$	$\dfrac{(1+i)^n-1}{i}$	$\dfrac{(1+i)^n-1}{i(1+i)^n}$	
n	$(f/p)_n^5$	$(p/f)_n^5$	$(a/f)_n^5$	$(a/p)_n^5$	$(f/a)_n^5$	$(p/a)_n^5$	n
1	1.050	0.9524	1.00000	1.05000	1.000	0.952	1
2	1.103	0.9070	0.48780	0.53780	2.050	1.859	2
3	1.158	0.8638	0.31721	0.36721	3.153	2.723	3
4	1.216	0.8227	0.23201	0.28201	4.310	3.546	4
5	1.276	0.7835	0.18097	0.23097	5.526	4.329	5
6	1.340	0.7462	0.14702	0.19702	6.802	5.076	6
7	1.407	0.7107	0.12282	0.17282	8.142	5.786	7
8	1.477	0.6768	0.10472	0.15472	9.549	6.463	8
9	1.551	0.6446	0.09069	0.14069	11.027	7.108	9
10	1.629	0.6139	0.07950	0.12950	12.578	7.722	10
11	1.710	0.5847	0.07039	0.12039	14.207	8.306	11
12	1.796	0.5568	0.06283	0.11283	15.917	8.863	12
13	1.886	0.5303	0.05646	0.10646	17.713	9.394	13
14	1.980	0.5051	0.05102	0.10102	19.599	9.899	14
15	2.079	0.4810	0.04634	0.09634	21.579	10.380	15
16	2.183	0.4581	0.04227	0.09227	23.657	10.838	16
17	2.292	0.4363	0.03870	0.08870	25.840	11.274	17
18	2.407	0.4155	0.03555	0.08555	28.132	11.690	18
19	2.527	0.3957	0.03275	0.08275	30.539	12.085	19
20	2.653	0.3769	0.03024	0.08024	33.066	12.462	20
21	2.786	0.3589	0.02800	0.07800	35.719	12.821	21
22	2.925	0.3418	0.02597	0.07597	38.505	13.163	22
23	3.072	0.3256	0.02414	0.07414	41.430	13.489	23
24	3.225	0.3101	0.02247	0.07247	44.502	13.799	24
25	3.386	0.2953	0.02095	0.07095	47.727	14.094	25
26	3.556	0.2812	0.01956	0.06956	51.113	14.375	26
27	3.733	0.2678	0.01829	0.06829	54.669	14.643	27
28	3.920	0.2551	0.01712	0.06712	58.403	14.898	28
29	4.116	0.2429	0.01605	0.06605	62.323	15.141	29
30	4.322	0.2314	0.01505	0.06505	66.439	15.372	30
31	4.538	0.2204	0.01413	0.06413	70.761	15.593	31
32	4.765	0.2099	0.01328	0.06328	75.299	15.803	32
33	5.003	0.1999	0.01249	0.06249	80.064	16.003	33
34	5.253	0.1904	0.01176	0.06176	85.067	16.193	34
35	5.516	0.1813	0.01107	0.06107	90.320	16.374	35
40	7.040	0.1420	0.00828	0.05828	120.800	17.159	40
45	8.985	0.1113	0.00626	0.05626	159.700	17.774	45
50	11.467	0.0872	0.00478	0.05478	209.348	18.256	50
55	14.636	0.0683	0.00367	0.05367	272.713	18.633	55
60	18.679	0.0535	0.00283	0.05283	353.584	18.929	60
65	23.840	0.0419	0.00219	0.05219	456.798	19.161	65
70	30.426	0.0329	0.00170	0.05170	588.529	19.343	70
75	38.833	0.0258	0.00132	0.05132	756.654	19.485	75
80	49.561	0.0202	0.00103	0.05103	971.229	19.596	80
85	63.254	0.0158	0.00080	0.05080	1245.087	19.684	85
90	80.730	0.0124	0.00063	0.05063	1594.607	19.752	90
95	103.035	0.0097	0.00049	0.05049	2040.694	19.806	95
100	131.501	0.0076	0.00038	0.05038	2610.025	19.848	100

6%

n	To find F, given P: $(1 + i)^n$ $(f/p)^6_n$	To find P, given F: $\dfrac{1}{(1 + i)^n}$ $(p/f)^6_n$	To find A, given F: $\dfrac{i}{(1 + i)^n - 1}$ $(a/f)^6_n$	To find A, given P: $\dfrac{i(1 + i)^n}{(1 + i)^n - 1}$ $(a/p)^6_n$	To find F, given A: $\dfrac{(1 + i)^n - 1}{i}$ $(f/a)^6_n$	To find P, given A: $\dfrac{(1 + i)^n - 1}{i(1 + i)^n}$ $(p/a)^6_n$	n
1	1.060	0.9434	1.00000	1.06000	1.000	0.943	1
2	1.124	0.8900	0.48544	0.54544	2.060	1.833	2
3	1.191	0.8396	0.31411	0.37411	3.184	2.673	3
4	1.262	0.7921	0.22859	0.28859	4.375	3.465	4
5	1.338	0.7473	0.17740	0.23740	5.637	4.212	5
6	1.419	0.7050	0.14336	0.20336	6.975	4.917	6
7	1.504	0.6651	0.11914	0.17914	8.394	5.582	7
8	1.594	0.6274	0.10104	0.16104	9.897	6.210	8
9	1.689	0.5919	0.08702	0.14702	11.491	6.802	9
10	1.791	0.5584	0.07587	0.13587	13.181	7.360	10
11	1.898	0.5268	0.06679	0.12679	14.972	7.887	11
12	2.012	0.4970	0.05928	0.11928	16.870	8.384	12
13	2.133	0.4688	0.05296	0.11296	18.882	8.853	13
14	2.261	0.4423	0.04758	0.10758	21.015	9.295	14
15	2.397	0.4173	0.04296	0.10296	23.276	9.712	15
16	2.540	0.3936	0.03895	0.09895	25.673	10.106	16
17	2.693	0.3714	0.03544	0.09544	28.213	10.477	17
18	2.854	0.3503	0.03236	0.09236	30.906	10.828	18
19	3.026	0.3305	0.02962	0.08962	33.760	11.158	19
20	3.207	0.3118	0.02718	0.08718	36.786	11.470	20
21	3.400	0.2942	0.02500	0.08500	39.993	11.764	21
22	3.604	0.2775	0.02305	0.08305	43.392	12.042	22
23	3.820	0.2618	0.02128	0.08128	46.996	12.303	23
24	4.049	0.2470	0.01968	0.07968	50.816	12.550	24
25	4.292	0.2330	0.01823	0.07823	54.865	12.783	25
26	4.549	0.2198	0.01690	0.07690	59.156	13.003	26
27	4.822	0.2074	0.01570	0.07570	63.706	13.211	27
28	5.112	0.1956	0.01459	0.07459	68.528	13.406	28
29	5.418	0.1846	0.01358	0.07358	73.640	13.591	29
30	5.743	0.1741	0.01265	0.07265	79.058	13.765	30
31	6.088	0.1643	0.01179	0.07179	84.802	13.929	31
32	6.453	0.1550	0.01100	0.07100	90.890	14.084	32
33	6.841	0.1462	0.01027	0.07027	97.343	14.230	33
34	7.251	0.1379	0.00960	0.06960	104.184	14.368	34
35	7.686	0.1301	0.00897	0.06897	111.435	14.498	35
40	10.286	0.0972	0.00646	0.06646	154.762	15.046	40
45	13.765	0.0727	0.00470	0.06470	212.744	15.456	45
50	18.420	0.0543	0.00344	0.06344	290.336	15.762	50
55	24.650	0.0406	0.00254	0.06254	394.172	15.991	55
60	32.988	0.0303	0.00188	0.06188	533.128	16.161	60
65	45.145	0.0227	0.00139	0.06139	719.083	16.289	65
70	59.076	0.0169	0.00103	0.06103	967.932	16.385	70
75	79.057	0.0126	0.00077	0.06077	1300.949	16.456	75
80	105.796	0.0095	0.00057	0.06057	1746.600	16.509	80
85	141.579	0.0071	0.00043	0.06043	2342.982	16.549	85
90	189.465	0.0053	0.00032	0.06032	3141.075	16.579	90
95	253.546	0.0039	0.00024	0.06024	4209.104	16.601	95
100	339.302	0.0029	0.00018	0.06018	5638.368	16.618	100

INTEREST TABLES

7%

	To find F, given P:	To find P, given F:	To find A, given F:	To find A, given P:	To find F, given A:	To find P, given A:	
	$(1 + i)^n$	$\dfrac{1}{(1 + i)^n}$	$\dfrac{i}{(1 + i)^n - 1}$	$\dfrac{i(1 + i)^n}{(1 + i)^n - 1}$	$\dfrac{(1 + i)^n - 1}{i}$	$\dfrac{(1 + i)^n - 1}{i(1 + i)^n}$	
n	$(f/p)^7_n$	$(p/f)^7_n$	$(a/f)^7_n$	$(a/p)^7_n$	$(f/a)^7_n$	$(p/a)^7_n$	n
1	1.070	0.9346	1.00000	1.07000	1.000	0.935	1
2	1.145	0.8734	0.48309	0.55309	2.070	1.808	2
3	1.225	0.8163	0.31105	0.38105	3.215	2.624	3
4	1.311	0.7629	0.22523	0.29523	4.440	3.387	4
5	1.403	0.7130	0.17389	0.24389	5.751	4.100	5
6	1.501	0.6663	0.13980	0.20980	7.153	4.767	6
7	1.606	0.6227	0.11555	0.18555	8.654	5.389	7
8	1.718	0.5820	0.09747	0.16747	10.260	5.971	8
9	1.838	0.5439	0.08349	0.15349	11.978	6.515	9
10	1.967	0.5083	0.07238	0.14238	13.816	7.024	10
11	2.105	0.4751	0.06336	0.13336	15.784	7.499	11
12	2.252	0.4440	0.05590	0.12590	17.888	7.943	12
13	2.410	0.4150	0.04965	0.11965	20.141	8.358	13
14	2.579	0.3878	0.04434	0.11434	22.550	8.745	14
15	2.759	0.3624	0.03979	0.10979	25.129	9.108	15
16	2.952	0.3387	0.03586	0.10586	27.888	9.447	16
17	3.159	0.3166	0.03243	0.10243	30.840	9.763	17
18	3.380	0.2959	0.02941	0.09941	33.999	10.059	18
19	3.617	0.2765	0.02675	0.09675	37.379	10.363	19
20	3.870	0.2584	0.02439	0.09439	40.995	10.594	20
21	4.141	0.2415	0.02229	0.09229	44.865	10.836	21
22	4.430	0.2257	0.02041	0.09041	49.006	11.061	22
23	4.741	0.2109	0.01871	0.08871	53.436	11.272	23
24	5.072	0.1971	0.01719	0.08719	58.177	11.469	24
25	5.427	0.1842	0.01581	0.08581	63.249	11.654	25
26	5.807	0.1722	0.01456	0.08456	68.676	11.826	26
27	6.214	0.1609	0.01343	0.08343	74.484	11.987	27
28	6.649	0.1504	0.01239	0.08239	80.698	12.137	28
29	7.114	0.1406	0.01145	0.08145	87.347	12.278	29
30	7.612	0.1314	0.01059	0.08059	94.461	12.409	30
31	8.145	0.1228	0.00980	0.07980	102.073	12.532	31
32	8.715	0.1147	0.00907	0.07907	110.218	12.647	32
33	9.325	0.1072	0.00841	0.07841	118.923	12.754	33
34	9.978	0.1002	0.00780	0.07780	128.259	12.854	34
35	10.677	0.0937	0.00723	0.07723	138.237	12.948	35
40	14.974	0.0668	0.00501	0.07501	199.635	13.332	40
45	21.002	0.0476	0.00350	0.07350	285.749	13.606	45
50	29.457	0.0339	0.00246	0.07246	406.529	13.801	50
55	41.315	0.0242	0.00174	0.07174	575.929	13.940	55
60	57.946	0.0173	0.00123	0.07123	813.520	14.039	60
65	81.273	0.0123	0.00087	0.07087	1146.755	14.110	65
70	113.989	0.0088	0.00062	0.07062	1614.134	14.160	70
75	159.876	0.0063	0.00044	0.07044	2269.657	14.196	75
80	224.234	0.0045	0.00031	0.07031	3189.063	14.222	80
85	314.500	0.0032	0.00022	0.07022	4478.576	14.240	85
90	441.103	0.0023	0.00016	0.07016	6287.185	14.253	90
95	618.670	0.0016	0.00011	0.07011	8823.854	14.263	95
100	867.716	0.0012	0.00008	0.07008	12381.662	14.269	100

8%

	To find F, given P:	To find P, given F:	To find A, given F:	To find A, given P:	To find F, given A:	To find P, given A:	
	$(1 + i)^n$	$\dfrac{1}{(1 + i)^n}$	$\dfrac{i}{(1 + i)^n - 1}$	$\dfrac{i(1 + i)^n}{(1 + i)^n - 1}$	$\dfrac{(1 + i)^n - 1}{i}$	$\dfrac{(1 + i)^n - 1}{i(1 + i)^n}$	
n	$(f/p)_n^a$	$(p/f)_n^a$	$(a/f)_n^a$	$(a/p)_n^a$	$(f/a)_n^a$	$(p/a)_n^a$	n
1	1.080	0.9259	1.00000	1.08000	1.000	0.926	1
2	1.166	0.8573	0.48077	0.56077	2.080	1.783	2
3	1.260	0.7938	0.30803	0.38803	3.246	2.577	3
4	1.360	0.7350	0.22192	0.30192	4.506	3.312	4
5	1.469	0.6806	0.17046	0.25046	5.867	3.933	5
6	1.587	0.6302	0.13632	0.21632	7.336	4.623	6
7	1.714	0.5835	0.11207	0.19207	8.923	5.206	7
8	1.851	0.5403	0.09401	0.17401	10.637	5.747	8
9	1.999	0.5002	0.08008	0.16008	12.488	6.247	9
10	2.159	0.4632	0.06903	0.14903	14.487	6.710	10
11	2.332	0.4289	0.06008	0.14008	16.645	7.139	11
12	2.518	0.3971	0.05270	0.13270	18.977	7.536	12
13	2.720	0.3677	0.04652	0.12652	21.495	7.904	13
14	2.937	0.3405	0.04130	0.12130	24.215	8.244	14
15	3.172	0.3152	0.03683	0.11683	27.152	8.559	15
16	3.426	0.2919	0.03298	0.11298	30.324	8.851	16
17	3.700	0.2703	0.02963	0.10963	33.750	9.122	17
18	3.996	0.2502	0.02670	0.10670	37.450	9.372	18
19	4.316	0.2317	0.02413	0.10413	41.446	9.604	19
20	4.661	0.2145	0.02185	0.10185	45.762	9.818	20
21	5.034	0.1987	0.01983	0.09983	50.423	10.017	21
22	5.437	0.1839	0.01803	0.09803	55.457	10.201	22
23	5.781	0.1703	0.01642	0.09642	60.893	10.371	23
24	6.341	0.1577	0.01498	0.09498	66.765	10.529	24
25	6.848	0.1460	0.01368	0.09368	73.106	10.675	25
26	7.396	0.1352	0.01251	0.09251	79.954	10.810	26
27	7.988	0.1252	0.01145	0.09145	87.351	10.935	27
28	8.627	0.1159	0.01049	0.09049	95.339	11.051	28
29	9.317	0.1073	0.00962	0.08962	103.966	11.158	29
30	10.063	0.0994	0.00883	0.08883	113.283	11.258	30
31	10.868	0.0920	0.00811	0.08811	123.346	11.350	31
32	11.737	0.0852	0.00745	0.08745	134.214	11.435	32
33	12.676	0.0789	0.00685	0.08685	145.951	11.514	33
34	13.690	0.0730	0.00630	0.08630	158.627	11.587	34
35	14.785	0.0676	0.00580	0.08580	172.317	11.655	35
40	21.725	0.0460	0.00386	0.08386	259.057	11.925	40
45	31.920	0.0313	0.00259	0.08259	386.506	12.108	45
50	46.902	0.0213	0.00174	0.08174	573.770	12.233	50
55	68.914	0.0145	0.00118	0.08118	848.923	12.319	55
60	101.257	0.0099	0.00080	0.08080	1253.213	12.377	60
65	148.780	0.0067	0.00054	0.08054	1847.248	12.416	65
70	218.606	0.0046	0.00037	0.08037	2720.080	12.443	70
75	321.205	0.0031	0.00025	0.08025	4002.557	12.461	75
80	471.955	0.0021	0.00017	0.08017	5886.935	12.474	80
85	693.456	0.0014	0.00012	0.08012	8655.706	12.482	85
90	1018.915	0.0010	0.00008	0.08008	12723.939	12.488	90
95	1497.121	0.0007	0.00005	0.08005	18701.507	12.492	95
100	2199.761	0.0005	0.00004	0.08004	27484.516	12.494	100

9%

n	To find F, given P: $(1 + i)^n$	To find P, given F: $\dfrac{1}{(1 + i)^n}$	To find A, given F: $\dfrac{i}{(1 + i)^n - 1}$	To find A, given P: $\dfrac{i(1 + i)^n}{(1 + i)^n - 1}$	To find F, given A: $\dfrac{(1 + i)^n - 1}{i}$	To find P, given A: $\dfrac{(1 + i)^n - 1}{i(1 + i)^n}$	n
	$(f/p)^9_n$	$(p/f)^9_n$	$(a/f)^9_n$	$(a/p)^9_n$	$(f/a)^9_n$	$(p/a)^9_n$	
1	1.090	0.9174	1.00000	1.09000	1.000	0.917	1
2	1.188	0.8417	0.47847	0.56847	2.090	1.759	2
3	1.295	0.7722	0.30505	0.39505	3.278	2.531	3
4	1.412	0.7084	0.21867	0.30867	4.573	3.240	4
5	1.539	0.6499	0.16709	0.25709	5.985	3.890	5
6	1.677	0.5963	0.13292	0.22292	7.523	4.486	6
7	1.828	0.5470	0.10869	0.19869	9.200	5.033	7
8	1.993	0.5019	0.09067	0.18067	11.028	5.535	8
9	2.172	0.4604	0.07680	0.16680	13.021	5.995	9
10	2.367	0.4224	0.06582	0.15582	15.193	6.418	10
11	2.580	0.3875	0.05695	0.14695	17.560	6.805	11
12	2.813	0.3555	0.04965	0.13965	20.141	7.161	12
13	3.066	0.3262	0.04357	0.13357	22.953	7.487	13
14	3.342	0.2992	0.03843	0.12843	26.019	7.786	14
15	3.642	0.2745	0.03406	0.12406	29.361	8.061	15
16	3.970	0.2519	0.03030	0.12030	33.003	8.313	16
17	4.328	0.2311	0.02705	0.11705	36.974	8.544	17
18	4.717	0.2120	0.02421	0.11421	41.301	8.756	18
19	5.142	0.1945	0.02173	0.11173	46.018	8.950	19
20	5.604	0.1784	0.01955	0.10955	51.160	9.129	20
21	6.109	0.1637	0.01762	0.10762	56.765	9.292	21
22	6.659	0.1502	0.01590	0.10590	62.873	9.442	22
23	7.258	0.1378	0.01438	0.10438	69.532	9.580	23
24	7.911	0.1264	0.01302	0.10302	76.790	9.707	24
25	8.623	0.1160	0.01180	0.10181	84.701	9.823	25
26	9.399	0.1064	0.01072	0.10072	93.324	9.929	26
27	10.245	0.0976	0.00973	0.09973	102.723	10.027	27
28	11.167	0.0895	0.00885	0.09885	112.968	10.116	28
29	12.172	0.0822	0.00806	0.09806	124.135	10.198	29
30	13.268	0.0754	0.00734	0.09734	136.308	10.274	30
31	14.462	0.0691	0.00669	0.09669	149.575	10.343	31
32	15.763	0.0634	0.00610	0.09610	164.037	10.406	32
33	17.182	0.0582	0.00556	0.09556	179.800	10.464	33
34	18.728	0.0534	0.00508	0.09508	196.982	10.518	34
35	20.414	0.0490	0.00464	0.09464	215.711	10.567	35
40	31.409	0.0318	0.00296	0.09296	337.882	10.757	40
45	48.327	0.0207	0.00190	0.09190	525.859	10.881	45
50	74.358	0.0134	0.00123	0.09123	815.084	10.962	50
55	114.408	0.0087	0.00079	0.09079	1260.092	11.014	55
60	176.031	0.0057	0.00051	0.09051	1944.792	11.048	60
65	270.864	0.0037	0.00033	0.09033	2998.288	11.070	65
70	416.730	0.0024	0.00022	0.09022	4619.223	11.084	70
75	641.191	0.0016	0.00014	0.09014	7113.232	11.094	75
80	986.552	0.0010	0.00009	0.09009	10950.556	11.100	80
85	1517.948	0.0007	0.00006	0.09006	16854.444	11.104	85
90	2335.501	0.0004	0.00004	0.09004	25939.000	11.106	90
95	3593.513	0.0003	0.00003	0.09003	39917.378	11.108	95
100	5529.089	0.0002	0.00002	0.09002	61422.544	11.109	100

10%

	To find F, given P:	To find P, given F:	To find A, given F:	To find A, given P:	To find F, given A:	To find P, given A:	
	$(1 + i)^n$	$\dfrac{1}{(1 + i)^n}$	$\dfrac{i}{(1 + i)^n - 1}$	$\dfrac{i(1 + i)^n}{(1 + i)^n - 1}$	$\dfrac{(1 + i)^n - 1}{i}$	$\dfrac{(1 + i)^n - 1}{i(1 + i)^n}$	
n	$(f/p)^{10}_n$	$(p/f)^{10}_n$	$(a/f)^{10}_n$	$(a/p)^{10}_n$	$(f/a)^{10}_n$	$(p/a)^{10}_n$	n
1	1.100	0.9091	1.00000	1.10000	1.000	0.909	1
2	1.210	0.8264	0.47619	0.57619	2.100	1.736	2
3	1.331	0.7513	0.30211	0.40211	3.310	2.487	3
4	1.464	0.6830	0.21547	0.31547	4.641	3.170	4
5	1.611	0.6209	0.16380	0.26380	6.105	3.791	5
6	1.772	0.5645	0.12961	0.22961	7.716	4.355	6
7	1.949	0.5132	0.10541	0.20541	9.487	4.868	7
8	2.144	0.4665	0.08744	0.18744	11.436	5.335	8
9	2.358	0.4241	0.07364	0.17364	13.579	5.759	9
10	2.594	0.3855	0.06275	0.16275	15.937	6.144	10
11	2.853	0.3505	0.05396	0.15396	18.531	6.495	11
12	3.138	0.3186	0.04676	0.14676	21.384	6.814	12
13	3.452	0.2897	0.04078	0.14078	24.523	7.103	13
14	3.797	0.2633	0.03575	0.13575	27.975	7.367	14
15	4.177	0.2394	0.03147	0.13147	31.772	7.606	15
16	4.595	0.2176	0.02782	0.12782	35.950	7.824	16
17	5.054	0.1978	0.02466	0.12466	40.545	8.022	17
18	5.560	0.1799	0.02193	0.12193	45.599	8.201	18
19	6.116	0.1635	0.01955	0.11955	51.159	8.363	19
20	6.727	0.1486	0.01746	0.11746	57.275	8.514	20
21	7.400	0.1351	0.01562	0.11562	64.002	8.649	21
22	8.140	0.1228	0.01401	0.11401	71.403	8.772	22
23	8.954	0.1117	0.01257	0.11257	79.543	8.883	23
24	9.850	0.1015	0.01130	0.11130	88.497	8.985	24
25	10.835	0.0923	0.01017	0.11017	98.347	9.077	25
26	11.918	0.0839	0.00916	0.10916	109.182	9.161	26
27	13.110	0.0763	0.00826	0.10826	121.100	9.237	27
28	14.421	0.0693	0.00745	0.10745	134.210	9.307	28
29	15.863	0.0630	0.00673	0.10673	148.631	9.370	29
30	17.449	0.0573	0.00608	0.10608	164.494	9.427	30
31	19.194	0.0521	0.00550	0.10550	181.943	9.479	31
32	21.114	0.0474	0.00497	0.10497	201.138	9.526	32
33	23.225	0.0431	0.00450	0.10450	222.252	9.569	33
34	25.548	0.0391	0.00407	0.10407	245.477	9.609	34
35	28.102	0.0356	0.00369	0.10369	271.024	9.644	35
40	45.259	0.0221	0.00226	0.10226	442.593	9.779	40
45	72.890	0.0137	0.00139	0.10139	718.905	9.863	45
50	117.391	0.0085	0.00086	0.10086	1163.909	9.915	50
55	189.059	0.0053	0.00053	0.10053	1880.591	9.947	55
60	304.482	0.0033	0.00033	0.10033	3034.816	9.967	60
65	490.371	0.0020	0.00020	0.10020	4893.707	9.980	65
70	789.747	0.0013	0.00013	0.10013	7887.470	9.987	70
75	1271.895	0.0008	0.00008	0.10008	12708.954	9.992	75
80	2048.400	0.0005	0.00005	0.10005	20474.002	9.995	80
85	3298.969	0.0003	0.00003	0.10003	32979.690	9.997	85
90	5313.023	0.0002	0.00002	0.10002	53120.226	9.998	90
95	8556.676	0.0001	0.00001	0.10001	85556.760	9.999	95
100	13780.612	0.0001	0.00001	0.10001	137796.123	9.999	100

12%

	To find F, given P:	To find P, given F:	To find A, given F:	To find A, given P:	To find F, given A:	To find P, given A:	
	$(1 + i)^n$	$\dfrac{1}{(1 + i)^n}$	$\dfrac{i}{(1 + i)^n - 1}$	$\dfrac{i(1 + i)^n}{(1 + i)^n - 1}$	$\dfrac{(1 + i)^n - 1}{i}$	$\dfrac{(1 + i)^n - 1}{i(1 + i)^n}$	
n	$(f/p)_n^{12}$	$(p/f)_n^{12}$	$(a/f)_n^{12}$	$(a/p)_n^{12}$	$(f/a)_n^{12}$	$(p/a)_n^{12}$	n
1	1.120	0.8929	1.00000	1.12000	1.000	0.893	1
2	1.254	0.7972	0.47170	0.59170	2.120	1.690	2
3	1.405	0.7118	0.29635	0.41635	3.374	2.402	3
4	1.574	0.6355	0.20923	0.32923	4.779	3.037	4
5	1.762	0.5674	0.15741	0.27741	6.353	3.605	5
6	1.974	0.5066	0.12323	0.24323	8.115	4.111	6
7	2.211	0.4523	0.09912	0.21912	10.089	4.564	7
8	2.476	0.4039	0.08130	0.20130	12.300	4.968	8
9	2.773	0.3606	0.06768	0.18768	14.776	5.328	9
10	3.106	0.3220	0.05698	0.17698	17.549	5.650	10
11	3.479	0.2875	0.04842	0.16842	20.655	5.938	11
12	3.896	0.2567	0.04144	0.16144	24.133	6.194	12
13	4.363	0.2292	0.03568	0.15568	28.029	6.424	13
14	4.887	0.2046	0.03087	0.15087	32.393	6.628	14
15	5.474	0.1827	0.02682	0.14682	37.280	6.811	15
16	6.130	0.1631	0.02339	0.14339	42.753	6.974	16
17	6.866	0.1456	0.02046	0.14046	48.884	7.120	17
18	7.690	0.1300	0.01794	0.13794	55.750	7.250	18
19	8.613	0.1161	0.01576	0.13576	63.440	7.366	19
20	9.646	0.1037	0.01388	0.13388	72.052	7.469	20
21	10.804	0.0926	0.01224	0.13224	81.699	7.562	21
22	12.100	0.0826	0.01081	0.13081	92.503	7.645	22
23	13.552	0.0738	0.00956	0.12956	104.603	7.718	23
24	15.179	0.0659	0.00846	0.12846	118.155	7.784	24
25	17.000	0.0588	0.00750	0.12750	133.334	7.843	25
26	19.040	0.0525	0.00665	0.12665	150.334	7.896	26
27	21.325	0.0469	0.00590	0.12590	169.374	7.943	27
28	23.884	0.0419	0.00524	0.12524	190.699	7.984	28
29	26.750	0.0374	0.00466	0.12466	214.582	8.022	29
30	29.960	0.0334	0.00414	0.12414	241.333	8.055	30
31	33.555	0.0298	0.00369	0.12369	271.292	8.085	31
32	37.582	0.0266	0.00328	0.12328	304.847	8.112	32
33	42.091	0.0238	0.00292	0.12292	342.429	8.135	33
34	47.142	0.0212	0.00260	0.12260	384.520	8.157	34
35	52.800	0.0189	0.00232	0.12232	431.663	8.176	35
40	93.051	0.0107	0.00130	0.12130	767.091	8.244	40
45	163.988	0.0061	0.00074	0.12074	1358.230	8.283	45
50	289.002	0.0035	0.00042	0.12042	2400.018	8.305	50

15%

	To find F, given P: $(1 + i)^n$	To find P, given F: $\dfrac{1}{(1 + i)^n}$	To find A, given F: $\dfrac{i}{(1 + i)^n - 1}$	To find A, given P: $\dfrac{i(1 + i)^n}{(1 + i)^n - 1}$	To find F, given A: $\dfrac{(1 + i)^n - 1}{i}$	To find P, given A: $\dfrac{(1 + i)^n - 1}{i(1 + i)^n}$	
n	$(f/p)_n^{15}$	$(p/f)_n^{15}$	$(a/f)_n^{15}$	$(a/p)_n^{15}$	$(f/a)_n^{15}$	$(p/a)_n^{15}$	n
1	1.150	0.8696	1.00000	1.15000	1.000	0.870	1
2	1.322	0.7561	0.46512	0.61512	2.150	1.626	2
3	1.521	0.6575	0.28798	0.43798	3.472	2.283	3
4	1.749	0.5718	0.20027	0.35027	4.993	2.855	4
5	2.011	0.4972	0.14832	0.29832	6.742	3.352	5
6	2.313	0.4323	0.11424	0.26424	8.754	3.784	6
7	2.660	0.3759	0.09036	0.24036	11.067	4.160	7
8	3.059	0.3269	0.07285	0.22285	13.727	4.487	8
9	3.518	0.2843	0.05957	0.20957	16.786	4.772	9
10	4.046	0.2472	0.04925	0.19925	20.304	5.019	10
11	4.652	0.2149	0.04107	0.19107	24.349	5.234	11
12	5.350	0.1869	0.03448	0.18448	29.002	5.421	12
13	6.153	0.1625	0.02911	0.17911	34.352	5.583	13
14	7.076	0.1413	0.02469	0.17469	40.505	5.724	14
15	8.137	0.1229	0.02102	0.17102	47.580	5.847	15
16	9.358	0.1069	0.01795	0.16795	55.717	5.954	16
17	10.761	0.0929	0.01537	0.16537	65.075	6.047	17
18	12.375	0.0808	0.01319	0.16319	75.836	6.128	18
19	14.232	0.0703	0.01134	0.16134	88.212	6.198	19
20	16.367	0.0611	0.00976	0.15976	102.444	6.259	20
21	18.821	0.0531	0.00842	0.15842	118.810	6.312	21
22	21.645	0.0462	0.00727	0.15727	137.631	6.359	22
23	24.891	0.0402	0.00628	0.15628	159.276	6.399	23
24	28.625	0.0349	0.00543	0.15543	184.168	6.434	24
25	32.919	0.0304	0.00470	0.15470	212.793	6.464	25
26	37.857	0.0264	0.00407	0.15407	245.711	6.491	26
27	43.535	0.0230	0.00353	0.15353	283.569	6.514	27
28	50.066	0.0200	0.00306	0.15306	327.104	6.534	28
29	57.575	0.0174	0.00265	0.15265	377.170	6.551	29
30	66.212	0.0151	0.00230	0.15230	434.745	6.566	30
31	76.143	0.0131	0.00200	0.15200	500.956	6.579	31
32	87.565	0.0114	0.00173	0.15173	577.099	6.591	32
33	100.700	0.0099	0.00150	0.15150	664.664	6.600	33
34	115.805	0.0086	0.00131	0.15131	765.364	6.609	34
35	133.176	0.0075	0.00113	0.15113	881.170	6.617	35
40	267.863	0.0037	0.00056	0.15056	1779.090	6.642	40
45	538.769	0.0019	0.00028	0.15028	3585.128	6.654	45
50	1083.657	0.0009	0.00014	0.15014	7217.716	6.661	50

20%

	To find F, given P: $(1 + i)^n$	To find P, given F: $\dfrac{1}{(1 + i)^n}$	To find A, given F: $\dfrac{i}{(1 + i)^n - 1}$	To find A, given P: $\dfrac{i(1 + i)^n}{(1 + i)^n - 1}$	To find F, given A: $\dfrac{(1 + i)^n - 1}{i}$	To find P, given A: $\dfrac{(1 + i)^n - 1}{i(1 + i)^n}$	
n	$(f/p)_n^{20}$	$(p/f)_n^{20}$	$(a/f)_n^{20}$	$(a/p)_n^{20}$	$(f/a)_n^{20}$	$(p/a)_n^{20}$	n
1	1.200	0.8333	1.00000	1.20000	1.000	0.833	1
2	1.440	0.6944	0.45455	0.65455	2.200	1.528	2
3	1.728	0.5787	0.27473	0.47473	3.640	2.106	3
4	2.074	0.4823	0.18629	0.38629	5.368	2.598	4
5	2.488	0.4019	0.13438	0.33438	7.442	2.991	5
6	2.986	0.3349	0.10071	0.30071	9.930	3.326	6
7	3.583	0.2791	0.07742	0.27742	12.916	3.605	7
8	4.300	0.2326	0.06061	0.26061	16.499	3.837	8
9	5.160	0.1938	0.04808	0.24808	20.799	4.031	9
10	6.192	0.1615	0.03852	0.23852	25.959	4.192	10
11	7.430	0.1346	0.03110	0.23110	32.150	4.327	11
12	8.916	0.1122	0.02526	0.22526	39.581	4.439	12
13	10.699	0.0935	0.02062	0.22062	48.497	4.533	13
14	12.839	0.0779	0.01689	0.21689	59.196	4.611	14
15	15.407	0.0649	0.01388	0.21388	72.035	4.675	15
16	18.488	0.0541	0.01144	0.21144	87.442	4.730	16
17	22.186	0.0451	0.00944	0.20944	105.931	4.775	17
18	26.623	0.0376	0.00781	0.20781	128.117	4.812	18
19	31.948	0.0313	0.00646	0.20646	154.740	4.843	19
20	38.338	0.0261	0.00536	0.20536	186.688	4.870	20
21	46.005	0.0217	0.00444	0.20444	225.025	4.891	21
22	55.206	0.0181	0.00369	0.20369	271.031	4.909	22
23	66.247	0.0151	0.00307	0.20307	326.237	4.925	23
24	79.497	0.0126	0.00255	0.20255	392.484	4.937	24
25	95.396	0.0105	0.00212	0.20212	471.981	4.948	25
26	114.475	0.0087	0.00176	0.20176	567.377	4.956	26
27	137.371	0.0073	0.00147	0.20147	681.853	4.964	27
28	164.845	0.0061	0.00122	0.20122	819.223	4.970	28
29	197.813	0.0051	0.00102	0.20102	984.068	4.975	29
30	237.376	0.0042	0.00085	0.20085	1181.881	4.979	30
31	284.851	0.0035	0.00070	0.20070	1419.257	4.982	31
32	341.822	0.0029	0.00059	0.20059	1704.108	4.985	32
33	410.186	0.0024	0.00049	0.20049	2045.930	4.988	33
34	492.223	0.0020	0.00041	0.20041	2456.116	4.990	34
35	590.668	0.0017	0.00034	0.20034	2948.339	4.992	35
40	1469.772	0.0007	0.00014	0.20014	7343.858	4.997	40
45	3657.258	0.0003	0.00005	0.20005	18281.331	4.999	45
50	9100.427	0.0001	0.00002	0.20002	45497.191	4.999	50

APPENDIX C

SIMPLEX METHOD

The simplex method is a procedure to solve linear programming problems of greater complexity than those we dealt with in Chapter 5. It is a collection of rules applied in a relatively mechanical manner to obtain sequentially improved solutions to a problem with linear relationships. The rules lend themselves nicely to computer programming, and the tediousness of iterative solution cycles makes the computer a most appreciated assistant.

We shall examine the rules and computational steps of the simplex method by applying them to the problem previously encountered in Section 5-3. The conditions of the problem are shown in the reprint below of Table 5.1:

	Hours per Unit		Hours
	Product A	Product B	Available
Machine center J	3	2	42
Machine center K	2	2	30
Machine center L	2	4	48
Contribution per unit	$12	$8	

The objective function in the simplex method is stated in the same form as the graphical solution—maximize the profit given by the equation

$$Z = 12A + 8B \qquad \text{where } A = \text{units produced of product } A$$
$$B = \text{units produced of product } B$$

Maximum profit is restrained by the limited amount of time available in each machine center. Instead of stating these machine constraints as inequations as was done in the graphical method, they are converted to restriction equations by inserting *slack variables* S1, S2, and S3, respectively, for machine centers J, K, and L:

$$3A + 2B + S1 = 42 \qquad \text{for machine center } J$$
$$2A + 2B + S2 = 30 \qquad \text{for machine center } K$$
$$2A + 4B + S3 = 48 \qquad \text{for machine center } L$$

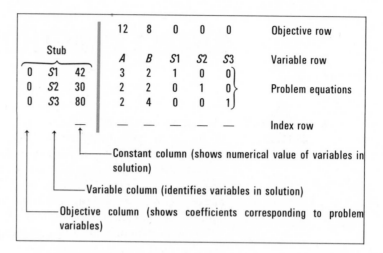

Figure C.1

When the entire capacity is used, the slack variables equal zero; otherwise they equal the unused capacity.

C-2 SIMPLEX TABLEAU The problem data are organized in the format shown in Figure C.1. The top two rows show the variables involved and the contribution of each to the objective function: profit. In the *stub* (entries to the left of the vertical line), the amount and contribution of the variables in successive solutions are recorded. In the initial tableau the objective column contains only zeros because the slack variables have zero coefficients in the objective equation. By considering the vertical line as an equal sign, the restriction equations are defined. For instance, the initial condition for machine center J (top line beginning with 42 in the "problem equations" portion of the tableau) is

$$42 = 3A + 2B + 1S1 + 0S2 + 0S3$$

which reduces to

$$42 = 3A + 2B + S1$$

as was given previously in the machine center J restriction.

The tableau is completed by calculating values for the index row to evaluate the initial feasible solution. The formula for each entry in the index row is

index number $= \Sigma\,[($number in its column$) + ($corresponding row number in objective column$)] - ($number in objective row heading its column$)$

The calculations required for all entries in the initial index row are shown below.

$$
\begin{array}{c|ccccc}
42 \times 0 & 3 \times 0 & 2 \times 0 & 1 \times 0 & 0 \times 0 & 0 \times 0 \\
+30 \times 0 & +2 \times 0 & +2 \times 0 & +0 \times 0 & +1 \times 0 & +0 \times 0 \\
+80 \times 0 & +2 \times 0 & +4 \times 0 & +0 \times 0 & +0 \times 0 & +1 \times 0 \\
-0 & -12 & -8 & -0 & -0 & -0 \\
\hline
0 & -12 & -8 & 0 & 0 & 0
\end{array}
$$

Constant column   Index row

Thus the initial index row is simply the objective row with each entry preceded by a minus sign. The trivial solution it represents gives zero profit from producing zero products; the variables are equal to the constants to yield $A = 0$, $B = 0$, $S1 = 42$, $S2 = 30$, $S3 = 80$, and, therefore,

$$Z = 0 = 12(0) + 8(0) + 0(42) + 0(30) + 0(80)$$

C-3 OPTIMALITY TEST   The initial feasible solution and each improved solution are tested for optimality by reference to the following criteria:

1. The solution is optimal if all entries in the index row are zero or positive.
2. An optimal solution with an infinitely large Z is indicated when all values in a column with a negative index number are zero or negative.
3. The solution can be improved when one or more values in a column with a negative index number are positive.

Our initial solution falls under criterion 3; there are positive values in both columns containing negative index numbers, -12 and -8. These negative index numbers serve almost the same mission as negative opportunity costs in the MODI and stepping-stone check for optimality in a transportation matrix.

C-4 REVISION OF A NONOPTIMAL SOLUTION   A *key column* is signified by the column containing the largest negative number in the index row of a nonoptimal solution. The column variable associated with the key column is introduced into a revised solution as a row variable. The row it replaces is the *key row* and is identified by dividing each number in the constant column by the corresponding nonzero, positive number in the key column. The *lowest* ratio obtained marks the key row. For

589

the example problem, the key column has -12 in the index row; the quotients formed by dividing the constant column values by the corresponding key column values are

$$\text{first row:} \frac{42}{3} = 14 \longleftarrow \text{key row}$$
$$\text{second row:} \frac{30}{2} = 15$$
$$\text{third row:} \frac{80}{2} = 40$$

which lead to the conditions shown in Figure C.2.

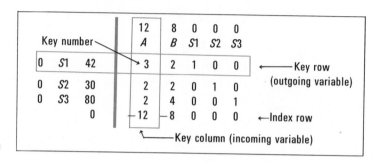

Figure C.2 First tableau

The intersection of the key row and column shows the *key number*. This key number is the dividend used to calculate all the new entries in the key row except those for the objective and variable columns. Thus the values for the key row of the second tableau are the quotients of existing entries divided by the key number as shown below:

Objective column	Variable column	Constant column		A	B	S1	S2	S3
12	A	$\frac{42}{3} = 14$		$\frac{3}{3} = 1$	$\frac{2}{3}$	$\frac{1}{3}$	$\frac{0}{3} = 0$	$\frac{0}{3} = 0$

Entries shown in the objective and variable columns are taken, respectively, from the key column values of the objective and variable rows, 12 and A.

The remaining values in the revised tableau, other than those in the objective and variable columns which are just repeated from the previous tableau, are calculated from the formula

$$\text{new value} = \text{old number} - \frac{\left(\begin{array}{c}\text{associated number}\\\text{in key row}\end{array}\right) \times \left(\begin{array}{c}\text{corresponding number}\\\text{in key column}\end{array}\right)}{\text{key number}}$$

For number 30 in the constant column,

$$\text{new value} = 30 - \frac{42 \times 2}{3} = 30 - 28 = 2$$

and for number 2 in the key column, A,

$$\text{new value} = 2 - \frac{3 \times 2}{3} = 2 - 2 = 0$$

(Both number 2's in the column have the same new value.) By continuing the new value calculations and determining the new index row numbers for the optimality check, the second tableau is completed (Figure C.3).

			12	8	0	0	0
			A	B	$S1$	$S2$	$S3$
12	A	14	1	$\frac{2}{3}$	$\frac{1}{3}$	0	0
0	$S1$	2	0	$\frac{2}{3}$	$-\frac{2}{3}$	1	0
0	$S2$	52	0	$\frac{8}{3}$	$-\frac{2}{3}$	0	1
		168	0	0	4	0	0

Figure C.3 Second tableau

C-5 OPTIMAL SOLUTION

The solution in the second tableau is optimal as defined by criterion 1 of the optimality test. The solution is shown in the stub. Variables entered in the variable column have the values shown in the constant column. In the given problem, there is only one variable, A, with a value of 14. The value of the objective function, 168, is shown in the index row of the constant column. When returning to the original objective function of the problem, the solution is written:

$$Z = 12A + 8B$$
$$168 = 12(14) + 8(0)$$

An optimal solution means no other solution will *better* satisfy the objective function, but other solutions may satisfy it equally well. This condition exists in our sample problem. The presence of equally optimum solutions is indicated whenever there is a zero in the index row in the column of a variable that is not in the variable column. In the example, the variable B does not occur in the variable column and there is a zero in the index row in column B.

C-6 DEGENERACY

A degenerate condition occurs when two or more rows tie for the smallest nonnegative quotient while the key row is being selected.

591

The tie affords the possibility of making the wrong choice for the key row. An incorrect selection could lead to problem cycling, a situation where the disappearance and reappearance of variables defy attaining an optimal solution.

A degenerate condition is resolved by dividing values in the tied rows by the key column number. Quotients obtained are compared in a left to right sequence among the columns of the slack variables first and then among the other columns. The key row is identified by the first column containing unequal ratios. The row with the lowest ratio marks the variable to replace.

C-7 SUMMARY AND EXTENSION OF SIMPLEX SOLUTION PROCEDURES

The procedure previously described and summarized below will satisfy the constraints of a linear problem and maximize the objective function.

1. Make a precise statement of the objective function and state all constraints as equalities through the use of slack variables.
2. Establish an initial feasible solution by placing only slack variables in the variable column.
3. Calculate index row values and test for optimality.
4. Identify the key column in a nonoptimal solution.
5. Find the key row and thereby establish the key number.
6. Calculate new entries in the key row.
7. Calculate new values for the remaining numbers in the revised tableau (those in the objective and variable columns remain unchanged).
8. Repeat Steps 3 through 7 until an optimal solution is obtained.

Additional rules are necessary to minimize an objective function. There are also rules available to convert the *primal* problem (original statement of the problem) to a *dual* problem. The conversion essentially amounts to reversing the rows and columns, and it thereby reduces the amount of calculations for problems with many rows and few columns. Such refinements are beyond the scope of this introductory presentation, but they are available in many books devoted primarily to LP.

More information than just the optimal solution is available in the final tableau. The index row shows *shadow prices*, the projected loss that would occur if variables not in the optimal solution were actually utilized. In the example problem, we already observed a zero cost for including product B, an alternate optimal solution. We can also observe that a $4 decrease in profit per unit would occur if the machine center represented by $S1$ (machine center J) is left out of the solution. Further familiarity with the simplex process allows analysts to evaluate the sensitivity of solutions to changes in the objective function and constraints. Such interpretations are extremely useful for the consideration of intangibles or other influencing factors that cannot be included formally in the simplex tableau.

TABLE OF RANDOM NUMBERS*

```
03 99 11 04 61    93 71 61 68 94    66 08 32 46 53    84 60 95 82 32    88 61 81 91 61
38 55 59 55 54    32 88 65 97 80    08 35 56 08 60    29 73 54 77 62    71 29 92 38 53
17 54 67 37 04    92 05 24 62 15    55 12 12 92 81    59 07 60 79 36    27 95 45 89 09
32 64 35 28 61    95 81 90 68 31    00 91 19 89 36    76 35 59 37 79    80 86 30 05 14
69 57 26 87 77    39 51 03 59 05    14 06 04 06 19    29 54 96 96 16    33 56 46 07 80

24 12 26 65 91    27 69 90 64 94    14 84 54 66 72    61 95 87 71 00    90 89 97 57 54
61 19 63 02 31    92 96 26 17 73    41 83 95 53 82    17 26 77 09 43    78 03 87 02 67
30 53 22 17 04    10 27 41 22 02    39 68 52 33 09    10 06 16 88 29    55 98 66 64 85
03 78 89 75 99    75 86 72 07 17    74 41 65 31 66    35 20 83 33 74    87 53 90 88 23
48 22 86 33 79    85 78 34 76 19    53 15 26 74 33    35 66 35 29 72    16 81 86 03 11

60 36 59 46 53    35 07 53 39 49    42 61 42 92 97    01 91 32 83 16    98 95 37 32 31
83 79 94 24 02    56 62 33 44 42    34 99 44 13 74    70 07 11 47 36    09 95 81 80 65
32 96 00 74 05    36 40 98 32 32    99 38 54 16 00    11 13 30 75 86    15 91 70 62 53
19 32 25 38 45    57 62 05 26 06    66 49 76 86 46    78 13 86 65 59    19 64 09 94 13
11 22 09 47 47    07 39 93 74 08    48 50 92 39 29    27 48 24 54 76    85 24 43 51 49

31 75 15 72 60    68 98 00 53 39    15 47 04 83 55    88 65 12 25 96    03 15 21 91 21
88 49 29 93 82    14 45 40 45 04    20 09 49 89 77    74 84 39 34 13    22 10 97 85 08
30 93 44 77 44    07 48 18 38 28    73 78 80 65 33    28 59 72 04 05    94 20 52 03 80
22 88 84 88 93    27 49 99 87 48    60 53 04 51 28    74 02 28 46 17    82 03 71 02 68
78 21 21 69 93    35 90 29 13 86    44 37 21 54 86    65 74 11 40 14    87 48 13 72 20

41 84 98 45 47    46 85 05 23 26    34 67 75 83 00    74 91 06 43 45    19 32 58 15 49
46 35 23 30 49    69 24 89 34 60    45 30 50 75 21    61 31 83 18 55    14 41 37 09 51
11 08 79 62 94    14 01 33 17 92    59 74 76 72 77    76 50 33 45 13    39 66 37 75 44
52 70 10 83 37    56 30 38 73 15    16 52 06 96 76    11 65 49 98 93    02 18 16 81 61
57 27 53 68 98    81 30 44 85 85    68 65 22 73 76    92 85 25 58 66    88 44 80 35 84

20 85 77 31 56    70 28 42 43 26    79 37 59 52 20    01 15 96 32 67    10 62 24 83 91
15 63 38 49 24    90 41 59 36 14    33 52 12 66 65    55 82 34 76 41    86 22 53 17 04
92 69 44 82 97    39 90 40 21 15    59 58 94 90 67    66 82 14 15 75    49 76 70 40 37
77 61 31 90 19    88 15 20 00 80    20 55 49 14 09    96 27 74 82 57    50 81 69 76 16
38 68 83 24 86    45 13 46 35 45    59 40 47 20 59    43 94 75 16 80    43 85 25 96 93

25 16 30 18 89    70 01 41 50 21    41 29 06 73 12    71 85 71 59 57    68 97 11 14 93
65 25 10 76 29    37 23 93 32 95    05 87 00 11 19    92 78 42 63 40    18 47 76 56 22
36 81 54 36 25    18 63 73 75 09    82 44 49 90 05    04 92 17 37 01    14 70 79 39 97
64 39 71 16 92    05 32 78 21 62    20 24 78 17 59    45 19 72 53 32    33 74 52 25 67
04 51 52 56 24    95 09 66 79 46    48 46 08 55 58    15 19 11 87 82    16 93 03 33 61

83 76 16 08 72    43 25 38 41 45    60 33 32 59 83    01 29 14 13 49    20 36 80 71 26
14 38 70 63 45    80 85 40 92 79    43 52 90 63 18    38 38 47 47 61    41 19 63 74 80
51 32 19 22 46    80 08 87 70 74    88 72 25 67 36    66 16 44 94 31    66 91 93 16 78
72 47 20 00 08    80 89 01 80 02    94 81 33 19 00    54 15 58 34 36    35 35 25 41 31
05 46 65 53 06    93 12 81 84 64    74 45 79 05 61    72 84 81 18 34    79 98 26 84 16

39 52 87 24 84    82 47 42 55 93    48 54 53 52 47    18 61 91 36 74    18 61 11 92 41
81 61 61 87 11    53 34 24 42 76    75 12 21 17 24    74 62 77 37 07    58 31 91 59 97
07 58 61 61 20    82 64 12 28 20    92 90 41 31 41    32 39 21 97 63    61 19 96 79 40
90 76 70 42 35    13 57 41 72 00    69 90 26 37 42    78 46 42 25 01    18 62 79 08 72
40 18 82 81 93    29 59 38 86 27    94 97 21 15 98    62 09 53 67 87    00 44 15 89 97

34 41 48 21 57    86 88 75 50 87    19 15 20 00 23    12 30 28 07 83    32 62 46 86 91
63 43 97 53 63    44 98 91 68 22    36 02 40 08 67    76 37 84 16 05    65 96 17 34 88
67 04 90 90 70    93 39 94 55 47    94 45 87 42 84    05 04 14 98 07    20 28 83 40 60
79 49 50 41 46    52 16 29 02 86    54 15 83 42 43    46 97 83 54 82    59 36 29 59 38
91 70 43 05 52    04 73 72 10 31    75 05 19 30 29    47 66 56 43 82    99 78 29 34 78
```

* The random numbers in this appendix were developed by the Rand Corporation.

APPENDIX E

TABLE OF LOGARITHMS

N	0	1	2	3	4	5	6	7	8	9
10	0000	0043	0086	0128	0170	0212	0253	0294	0334	0374
11	0414	0453	0492	0531	0569	0607	0645	0682	0719	0755
12	0792	0828	0864	0899	0934	0969	1004	1038	1072	1106
13	1139	1173	1206	1239	1271	1303	1335	1367	1399	1430
14	1461	1492	1523	1553	1584	1614	1644	1673	1703	1732
15	1761	1790	1818	1847	1875	1903	1931	1959	1987	2014
16	2041	2068	2095	2122	2148	2175	2201	2227	2253	2279
17	2304	2330	2355	2380	2405	2430	2455	2480	2504	2529
18	2553	2577	2601	2625	2648	2672	2695	2718	2742	2765
19	2788	2810	2833	2856	2878	2900	2923	2945	2967	2989
20	3010	3032	3054	3075	3096	3118	3139	3160	3181	3201
21	3222	3243	3263	3284	3304	3324	3345	3365	3385	3404
22	3424	3444	3464	3483	3502	3522	3541	3560	3579	3598
23	3617	3636	3655	3674	3692	3711	3729	3747	3766	3784
24	3802	3820	3838	3856	3874	3892	3909	3927	3945	3962
25	3979	3997	4014	4031	4048	4065	4082	4099	4116	4133
26	4150	4166	4183	4200	4216	4232	4249	4265	4281	4298
27	4314	4330	4346	4362	4378	4393	4409	4425	4440	4456
28	4472	4487	4502	4518	4533	4548	4564	4579	4594	4609
29	4624	4639	4654	4669	4683	4698	4713	4728	4742	4757
30	4771	4786	4800	4814	4829	4843	4857	4871	4886	4900
31	4914	4928	4942	4955	4969	4983	4997	5011	5024	5038
32	5051	5065	5079	5092	5105	5119	5132	5145	5159	5172
33	5185	5198	5211	5224	5237	5250	5263	5276	5289	5302
34	5315	5328	5340	5353	5366	5378	5391	5403	5416	5428
35	5441	5453	5465	5478	5490	5502	5514	5527	5539	5551
36	5563	5575	5587	5599	5611	5623	5635	5647	5658	5670
37	5682	5694	5705	5717	5729	5740	5752	5763	5775	5786
38	5798	5809	5821	5832	5843	5855	5866	5877	5888	5899
39	5911	5922	5933	5944	5955	5966	5977	5988	5999	6010
40	6021	6031	6042	6053	6064	6075	6085	6096	6107	6117
41	6128	6138	6149	6160	6170	6180	6191	6201	6212	6222
42	6232	6243	6253	6263	6274	6284	6294	6304	6314	6325
43	6335	6345	6355	6365	6375	6385	6395	6405	6415	6425
44	6435	6444	6454	6464	6474	6484	6493	6503	6513	6522
45	6532	6542	6551	6561	6571	6580	6590	6599	6609	6618
46	6628	6637	6646	6656	6665	6675	6684	6693	6702	6712
47	6721	6730	6739	6749	6758	6767	6776	6785	6794	6803
48	6812	6821	6830	6839	6848	6857	6866	6875	6884	6893
49	6902	6911	6920	6928	6937	6946	6955	6964	6972	6981
50	6990	6998	7007	7016	7024	7033	7042	7050	7059	7067
N	0	1	2	3	4	5	6	7	8	9

N	0	1	2	3	4	5	6	7	8	9
51	7076	7084	7093	7101	7110	7118	7126	7135	7143	7152
52	7160	7168	7177	7185	7193	7202	7210	7218	7226	7235
53	7243	7251	7259	7267	7275	7284	7292	7300	7308	7316
54	7324	7332	7340	7348	7356	7364	7372	7380	7388	7396
55	7404	7412	7419	7427	7435	7443	7451	7459	7466	7474
56	7482	7490	7497	7505	7513	7520	7528	7536	7543	7551
57	7559	7566	7574	7582	7589	7597	7604	7612	7619	7627
58	7634	7642	7649	7657	7664	7672	7679	7686	7694	7701
59	7709	7716	7723	7731	7738	7745	7752	7760	7767	7774
60	7782	7789	7796	7803	7810	7818	7825	7832	7839	7846
61	7853	7860	7868	7875	7882	7889	7896	7903	7910	7917
62	7924	7931	7938	7945	7952	7959	7966	7973	7980	7987
63	7993	8000	8007	8014	8021	8028	8035	8041	8048	8055
64	8062	8069	8075	8082	8089	8096	8102	8109	8116	8122
65	8129	8136	8142	8149	8156	8162	8169	8176	8182	8189
66	8195	8202	8209	8215	8222	8228	8235	8241	8248	8254
67	8261	8267	8274	8280	8287	8293	8299	8306	8312	8319
68	8325	8331	8338	8344	8351	8357	8363	8370	8376	8382
69	8388	8395	8401	8407	8414	8420	8426	8432	8439	8445
70	8451	8457	8463	8470	8476	8482	8488	8494	8500	8506
71	8513	8519	8525	8531	8537	8543	8549	8555	8561	8567
72	8573	8579	8585	8591	8597	8603	8609	8615	8621	8627
73	8633	8639	8645	8651	8657	8663	8669	8675	8681	8686
74	8692	8698	8704	8710	8716	8722	8727	8733	8739	8745
75	8751	8756	8762	8768	8774	8779	8785	8791	8797	8802
76	8808	8814	8820	8825	8831	8837	8842	8848	8854	8859
77	8865	8871	8876	8882	8887	8893	8899	8904	8910	8915
78	8921	8927	8932	8938	8943	8949	8954	8960	8965	8971
79	8976	8982	8987	8993	8998	9004	9009	9015	9020	9025
80	9031	9036	9042	9047	9053	9058	9063	9069	9074	9079
81	9085	9090	9096	9101	9106	9112	9117	9122	9128	9133
82	9138	9143	9149	9154	9159	9165	9170	9175	9180	9186
83	9191	9196	9201	9206	9212	9217	9222	9227	9232	9238
84	9243	9248	9253	9258	9263	9269	9274	9279	9284	9289
85	9294	9299	9304	9309	9315	9320	9325	9330	9335	9340
86	9345	9350	9355	9360	9365	9370	9375	9380	9385	9390
87	9395	9400	9405	9410	9415	9420	9425	9430	9435	9440
88	9445	9450	9455	9460	9465	9469	9474	9479	9484	9489
89	9494	9499	9504	9509	9513	9518	9523	9528	9533	9538
90	9542	9547	9552	9557	9562	9566	9571	9576	9581	9586
91	9590	9595	9600	9605	9609	9614	9619	9624	9628	9633
92	9638	9643	9647	9652	9657	9661	9666	9671	9675	9680
93	9685	9689	9694	9699	9703	9708	9713	9717	9722	9727
94	9731	9736	9741	9745	9750	9754	9759	9763	9768	9773
95	9777	9782	9786	9791	9795	9800	9805	9809	9814	9818
96	9823	9827	9832	9836	9841	9845	9850	9854	9859	9863
97	9868	9872	9877	9881	9886	9890	9894	9899	9903	9908
98	9912	9917	9921	9926	9930	9934	9939	9943	9948	9952
99	9956	9961	9965	9969	9974	9978	9983	9987	9991	9996
N	0	1	2	3	4	5	6	7	8	9

INDEX